^{THE} Panamericana

On the Road through Mexico
and Central America

<small>THE</small> Panamericana

On the Road through Mexico and Central America

by Simon Calder

with Emily Hatchwell and Andrew James

Published by Vacation Work, 9 Park End Street, Oxford
www.vacationwork.co.uk

THE PANAMERICANA
on the road through Mexico and Central America

by Simon Calder

with Emily Hatchwell and Andrew James

First Edition June 2000

Copyright Vacation Work 2000

ISBN 1-85458-234-8

Cover Design
Miller Craig and Cocking Design Partnership

Maps by Andrea Pullen

Cover photograph and picture editing by Charlotte Hindle

Colour photography by Charlotte Hindle, Andrew James and Simon Calder

Typeset by Worldview Publishing Services

Printed by William Clowes Ltd, Beccles, Suffolk, England

Contents

Headings *in italics* refer to boxes in the text

How to use this book

You are reading a new kind of travel book. *The Panamericana* is the story of a road, and a journey, that you can use on your own terms: from the comfort of an armchair at home, to the discomfort of a third-class bus bouncing over some of the worst roads in Nicaragua. Wherever you choose to read it, you will learn about the people of one of the world's most beautiful and exciting regions, and be taken to the best places along the road that serves as Main Street for Mexico and Central America. *The Panamericana* weaves tales of life on and around the Highway with the solid information you need to make the trip – or any part of it – yourself. The easy key to what you're reading is in the print.

Anything in this typeface is largely descriptive, revealing something of the places, people and history of Mexico and Central America. You can read nothing but these sections, and enjoy the journey without all the hard slog.

If you decide to take to the road, the sections in 'sans serif' type, like this, are the ones that count. The bulk of on-the-road research for this book took place in the last month of 1999, with a lot of additional work before and afterwards. But such is the pace of change in the region that no guide book can hope to be 100% reliable. In the course of your travels you will find errors or omissions; don't keep them to yourself. You can e-mail simoncalder@hotmail.com or write to me at Vacation Work Publications, 9 Park End Street, Oxford OX1 1HJ, UK.

No 'freebies'

The point of this book is to present an impartial and realistic view of Mexico and Central America. Accordingly, it has been written without the collaboration, knowledge or assistance of the authorities there. All travel was paid for in full. All research for this book was conducted anonymously and without requesting any special privileges. It follows that anyone seeking free facilities on the grounds of preparing the next edition is fibbing.

Prelude: highs and lows of the Panamericana

Shortly before dawn on New Year's Day 1988, my heart raced as I began a journey through a difficult, darkened land riven with divisions, in the company of weary, shadowy travellers. And that was just travelling from London out to the airport on the Gatwick Express.

By the time I reached Guatemala City, having paid a small fortune to Pan Am and Eastern Airlines (but not quite enough to prevent them both going out of business shortly afterwards), the year was nearly 24 hours old, and two questions were nagging. The immediate one: would the ugly civil strife tearing Central America's largest country apart manifest itself on the grubby streets of the capital? The longer term conundrum: could a region which appeared destined always to be linked with at least one of the terms 'much-maligned', 'misunderstood' and 'murderous' actually be any fun?

Luckily, the answers turned out to be 'no' and 'yes', in the right order. For three weeks I travelled up, down and around the *Carretera Panamericana*, the Pan-American Highway, which at the time was a thoroughfare through lowlife slicing through communities riven by collective madness. I eluded trouble and encountered a flawed version of heaven, meeting a sequence of people whose humanity transcended linguistic, cultural and ideological barriers.

Since then, I have been fortunate enough to return to Mexico and Central America many times, and on each occasion have been fascinated by the nature and symbolism of the Pan-American Highway as an artery for humanity across troubled lands. Often this long and winding road gets lost among the tangle of other highways, and I bet if you asked anyone in Mexico from the capital northwards what, and where, it was, they would have only the haziest notion. Elsewhere, notably snaking through the volcanos of Central America, it is the spine of life, with other roads reduced to stumpy ribs.

The region starts the 21st century with guarded optimism. Mexico, the mighty partner, found itself in the unusual position of having its fiscal probity endorsed by a US credit rating agency. In Central America, particularly in places like Nicaragua, El Salvador and Guatemala, the 20th century was especially cruel, with a dreadful range of natural and man-made disasters. People looked upon the new millennium as the chance to make a fresh start, with the region – for once – at peace.

This book is mainly inspired by a trip made in the last month of the 20th century, from the Tex-Mex border to Panama City and beyond, and the aim is to inspire you to make a similar journey – either in reality, or in your imagination. Either way, I hope you find what you need in these pages.

Simon Calder
London, May 2000

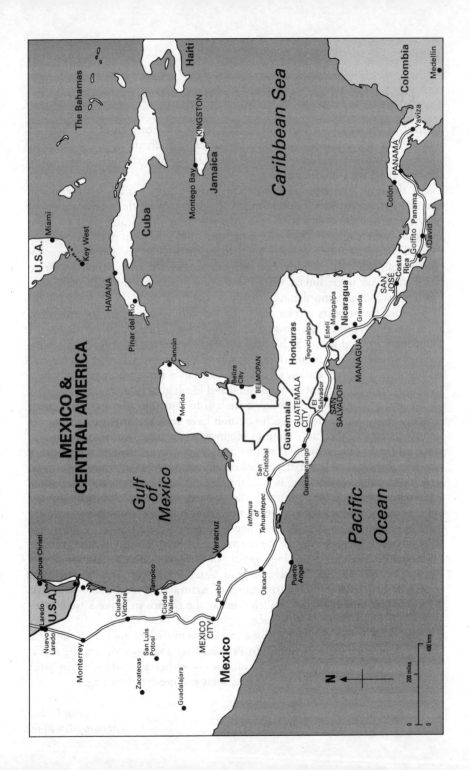

MEXICO & CENTRAL AMERICA

The Pan-American Highway –
the world's longest cul-de-sac

Somewhere outside Managua, the ugliest capital in the Americas, the Pan-American Highway loses its identity in a straggle of alternative routes. The world's longest road is well-used to this, since for most of its course it is anonymous – lost among the tangle of other highways, not credited on maps. Yet for most of its course through Central America it is the line around which societies and economies revolve.

This was part of the plan of the 21 nations who gathered in Buenos Aires in 1936, to ratify the construction of the Highway. 'Construction' is something of an exaggeration; most of it uses existing roads. But the Panamericana comprises a vivid symbol of unity in a part of the world riven by discord.

So: if it's the spine of the American continents, should it not be the ultimate in roadbuilding, a multi-lane freeway whisking buses, trucks and cars through the heart of the Americas? For parts of its route, such as the Interstate Highway through the USA and the stretches of autopista around Santiago de Chile, it fits this image perfectly. Be prepared, however, to set your sights a lot lower in most of Mexico and Central America.

From Fairbanks, Alaska, to the city of Ushuaia at the southern tip of Argentina, it covers a distance of around 24,000km (15,000 miles), though the point-to-point distance is a mere 14,000km (9,000 miles) as the crow or condor flies. It is easily the world's longest recognisable road, though pedants will correctly point out that the 160km (100-mile) Darien Gap breaks it into two distinct highways.

Along the way it adopts many other guises. The road begins life as the Alaska Highway, and continues with this name when it crosses into Canada. Through Whitehorse in the Yukon, the Highway heads southeast through the Rockies and across a corner of British Columbia. As the terrain subsides, the Pan-American Highway encounters its first big city: Edmonton, Alberta. The next stretch across the Prairie takes the road through Saskatoon to Winnipeg – the Manitoba state capital was once voted 'most boring city in the world'. Shortly afterwards, the road swerves due south, a course it holds across the US frontier at International Falls and through Minnesota, Iowa, Missouri, Kansas, Oklahoma and Texas as InterState and Defense Highway 35. At Laredo, it crosses the Rio Grande and becomes the Panamericana.

In northern Mexico, it masquerades as Highway 85, and retains a reasonable quality – though rarely more than two lanes. At Mexico City, the Pan-American turns sharp left to go east to Puebla and Oaxaca as Highway 190. Only beyond here does the term *Carretera Panamericana* (or *Interamericana*) start to be used with any enthusiasm.

From the Guatemalan frontier, it becomes Central America's main street, linking four or five capital cities (the uncertainty is because of the alternative routes through Nicaragua, only one of which passes through Managua) and hundreds of small towns and villages. In El Salvador the Panamericana runs through the middle of the main market in the capital, and makes several deviations around bridges destroyed by guerrillas; nevertheless it becomes a dual carriageway and even has a central reservation in places. The quality deteriorates gradually through Honduras and into Nicaragua where stretches of it are an axle-breaking series of pot-holes. In Costa Rica it miraculously improves to a smooth and fast two-lane highway, reaching a height of over 3,500m (12,000 feet) before descending into Panama. Here, there are stretches of fast dual-carriageway. After Panama City, the Pan-American Highway reverts to a condition similar to that found further north, before dissolving completely upon reaching the swamp and jungle known as the Darién Gap. The end of the road is a scruffy soccer field in the dilapidated township of Yaviza.

Happily, the Highway begins again on the Colombian side with a near-identical soccer pitch. The first few hundred kilometres are dismal in the extreme, through the Chocó region of Colombia, one of the wettest areas in the world. From there, the Pan-American picks up in stature to pass through many of South America's finest cities on the Pacific side of the Andes: Cali, Popayan, Quito (where it crosses the Equator) and Lima. Not far from the Peruvian capital, it cuts clean across the ancient and mystical Nazca Lines.

The Pan-American Highway dwindles somewhat through the deserts of northern Chile, before blossoming once more to become the main highway through Chile. South of Santiago, it crosses into Argentina, steers south through Patagonia to Rio Gallegos, finally switching back into Chile for the last few kilometres down to Punta Arenas on the Straits of Magellan.

No central body coordinates it; the obvious agency, the Organization of American States, shows little interest. Perhaps tourism can do for the Pan-American what it has done for the road that the Highway crosses at a lonely junction in Arizona: Route 66.

All roads are the same – they all end somewhere. But the Pan-American Highway goes further than the rest.

Mexico and Central America – Getting Going

Few parts of the world are as misrepresented as Mexico and Central America. The image that prevails is a picture of a permanent state of chaos: brutal governments vying with guerrillas in bloody ideological struggles, fought in an environment afflicted by every hazard from poverty and disease to earthquakes and hurricanes. That devastating acts of God and Man have affected and continue to affect the lives of many in the region is undeniable. Yet to write off the region as a battleground, or a desolate wasteland where civilised life has ground to a halt, is plain wrong. It is beautiful, fascinating and tremendous fun.

Funnelling into a narrow neck of land between the world's greatest oceans is a staggering variety of people and places, flora and fauna, culture and character. Central America and Mexico offer the chance to lie on deserted beaches with only the monkeys for company, hike among some of the world's finest volcanic landscapes, explore ancient Mayan ruins in tropical jungle, and enjoy music and cuisines ranging from Caribbean to Castillian.

Each of the countries is different. Mexico is by far the most developed, dwarfing the rest of the region economically and geographically – but it also has some of the finest vestiges of life before and after colonisation. Guatemala has the most perfect Mayan monuments and the most highly developed travellers' network. El Salvador has arguably the best beaches on the entire Pacific Ocean and a people whose tremendous spirit belies the years of civil war. Honduras is the forgotten country of Central America, and is the place to go to avoid the crowds; most travellers, though, will just race through the nation blighted by Hurricane Mitch.

Nicaragua is not reckoned to be a tourist's paradise either, as it sorts itself out after an heroic experiment in social reform conducted in the midst of war. Yet the frontiers between politics and art, and society and culture have broken down in Nicaragua, making it both a fascinating and startling place. In contrast, Costa Rica has long had a reputation for tranquility, vivid natural beauty and civilisation, and it is attracting increasing numbers of visitors. Neighbouring Panama, recovering from a bruising dictatorship and a foreign invasion, could hardly be more different. Superficially the least tempting nation in Central America, known only for its canal, hats and dictators, Panama is the most surprising destination, and a place to which many travellers wish to return.

Central America is not an easy region to travel in. The red tape involved in crossing half-a-dozen frontiers is immense; coming to terms with a multitude of currencies, conversion rates and con-men is tricky; and finding the best value in food, accommodation and travel needs clear recommendations. By following the advice in *The Panamericana*, you should enjoy the region to the full – or, instead, decide to stay at home and dream about it.

This chapter tells you everything you need to know for planning a journey along the Pan-American Highway, from choosing a starting place and buying an air ticket to getting the jabs you need. It also briefs you on how things work (or fail to work) in Mexico and Central America, from making an international telephone call to spotting an elusive quetzal.

Unique characters
If each country in the region were a celebrity, who would they be? That was the question posed in an informal survey carried out among travellers in Central America around Christmas 1999. These were the best suggestions:
Panama: Madonna
Costa Rica: Cliff Richard
Nicaragua: Ken Livingstone
Honduras: Peter Falk (Colombo)
El Salvador: Monica Lewinsky
Guatemala: David Hockney
Mexico: Frank Sinatra

Where to start – and end

As with driving in Latin America, so with choosing your trip along the Pan-American: there are no rules. You can start and finish where you wish, and deviate from the highway as much or as little as you like. But there are strong reasons for taking the central spine from Mexico City to Panama City – even if you choose to fly for some of the journey, e.g. from El Salvador to San José, avoiding Honduras and Nicaragua. If time and money permit, you can add the part from the Texas border to the Mexican capital, and/or the difficult journey east from Panama City into the Darién Gap. All the options are covered here; it's your call.

When to go

The Pan-American Highway through Mexico and Central America straddles nearly 20 degrees of latitude, from 27 degrees north of the equator at the Texas border at Laredo to 8 degrees north at the point where it melts into the Darién Gap of Panama. Between these extremes, Mexico City shares a latitude with Santiago de Cuba, Timbuktu (Mali) and Mumbai (formerly Bombay, India), while Managua is on the same latitude as Barbados, Banjul (Gambia), Bangalore (India) and Bangkok.

In northern Mexico, there are seasons that are properly discernable, but elsewhere in the region visitors from more temperate parts of the world must suspend old preconceptions of season. Southern Mexico and Central America have only two: the wet season from May to November, and the dry from December to April. The dry season is referred to as summer (*verano*), even though it is winter elsewhere in the northern hemisphere. And during the wet season (*invierno*, or winter) there may be just one downpour a day, often at a predictable time, and often in the afternoon or evening. However this is only a general rule – you can find yourself caught in downpours which last for several days. Thunderstorms are particularly common in July and August. However, August is also known for its dry spell which may last two or three weeks and is usually referred to as *el veranillo* or little summer. The months of May and November are often transitional months in which you should be prepared for anything. It is tempting to think that the rains will be tailing off by the end of the season, but many travellers find themselves being rained upon all day in November. The amount of rain varies unpredictably not only country to country, but also year to year. The locals say that a strong east wind denotes the change from the wet to the dry season.

There can also be tremendous variations in climate within one country, usually because of altitude. At 1,000m (3,300ft) or more, nights can even become chilly. You don't need to indulge in mountaineering to reach these heights, since many settlements and sights are at high altitude: the capitals of Mexico and Costa Rica are more than a kilometre high. So pack a jumper or sweatshirt.

The full range of climatic horrors sweeps across Central America periodically, from hurricanes devastating Belize and Nicaragua to severe flooding in Honduras. Advice on how to survive the weather is given in the section *Health and Hygiene*.

The period between November and January is the optimum time to visit most of the region. The terrain is lush after the 'winter' rains, the air is clear and humidity is low. Furthermore tourism has not built up to the levels encountered later on in the dry season, when the weather is as close to perfect as anyone has a right to expect. The temperatures hit a peak in March and April (earlier in the north and west, later in the south and east) after which the first rains begin and humidity increases. Those travelling at the end of the dry season will find much of the countryside parched, and water shortages are not uncommon. Visitor numbers decrease considerably after April, and hotels in tourist areas cut their rates.

The wet season is when you can expect to see few other foreigners yet plenty of wildlife. The main inconveniences are the regular downpours and the deterioration in roads, an important consideration if you plan to spend much time off the beaten track. In the case of Guatemala and popular parts of other countries, travelling out of season has many advantages.

Which way to go?

That depends on two things: the season, and your personal motivation. As mentioned above, the dry season starts and ends in the west and north earlier than in the south and east. So if you are seeking optimum weather, set off in December or January from Mexico, destination Panama.

The other variable is what drives your personal motivation. If you like life to get progressively wilder and less predictable, then stepping from stable, organised Mexico into a sequence of less developed countries will answer your desires (though you may see Costa Rica as something of a bland interlude between Nicaragua and Panama). The capital cities will answer your needs for a blast of modernity, while the buses get progressively less comfortable and predictable.

It may be, of course, that you rather like the idea that things can only get better, in which case you will enjoy the steady improvement in road surfaces, fast food restaurants and the amount your bus seat will recline.

Getting there ... and back

One of the many nonsenses of international air travel is that travellers from Europe, especially the UK, have access to better and more flexible fares than people in the USA and Canada.

From Britain: there are four basic options, of which the first is likely to give the most flexibility and best value

1: flying on a US airline, notably American Airlines or Continental Airlines, via New York, Miami, Dallas or Houston to a point in Texas, Mexico or elsewhere in the region, returning from any Central American capital with a so-called 'open jaw' arrangement. This was the kind of deal used for all except two of the research trips for this book; for the most recent round-trip, going from London Gatwick via Houston to Austin, then returning from Panama City via New York, the fare including all taxes was £430. You cannot get these deals direct from the airlines; the following specialist agents will be able to advise and offer many other options.

Journey Latin America, 12/13 Heathfield Terrace, London W4 4JE (tel 020-8747 3108; fax 020-8742 1312; sales@jla.co.uk). The company has a second office at 28-30 Barton Arcade, Deansgate, Manchester M3 2BH (0161-832 1441).

South American Experience, 47 Causton St, London SW1P 4AT (tel 020-7976 5511; fax 020-7976 6908; sax@mcmail.co.uk).

2: a direct scheduled flight from Europe to Mexico or Central America, for example on British Airways from London to Mexico City or KLM Royal Dutch Airlines via Amsterdam to Guatemala City. This may be much cheaper, thanks to avoiding the high taxes associated with US touchdowns, and the degree of competition among airlines that has halved fares to the Mexican capital in the past 10 years. In the Spring of 2000, British Airways (0845 773377) was selling its Mexico City flights for as little as £308 return, while Air France fares to the Mexican capital fell as low as £260 through discount agents.

The main problem is the need, in most cases, to return to the arrival point for the homeward flight. KLM no longer flies to Panama City, and British Airways abandoned its flights to San José in April 2000. Although Iberia appears to have a good network of flights to Mexico City, Guatemala City, San Salvador,

Managua, San José and Panama City, in fact all these cities are served by short-haul flights from and to Miami, with a further change of plane required in Madrid – so you get a long journey with no substantial cost saving.

To search out the possible options, consult the discount agents above, or the companies that advertise in the weekend travel sections of the quality press.

3: a charter flight to Mexico or Central America. There are plenty of charters year-round from Gatwick and Manchester to the Mexican airports of Cancún and Puerto Vallarta, with a few also serving Acapulco. Last-minute flights are often sold off at less than £200; a good source is the website teletext.co.uk, or its slower TV equivalent on ITV in the UK.

The main drawbacks of charter flights – apart from lack of on-board legroom – are that you are restricted to a fixed number of weeks (usually two), and that none of the gateways is close to the Pan-American Highway. If you are happy to pick up the road close to the Mexican-Guatemalan border, then the best bet is probably Cancún, from which you can travel down to San Cristóbal de las Casas by direct bus. You will need to travel back to Mexico to pick up the return leg, which could be expensive if you decide to fly.

Some people use cheap seat-only deals as a one-way ticket to Latin America, which is fine if you have no immediate plans to return home. But if and when you do investigate flights back, you are likely to find that the fare outbound from the region is vastly higher than the inbound one.

4: the Latin American option. A couple of airlines offer good deals if you wish to stop off elsewhere in the region. Colombia's leading airline, Avianca, offers good fares via its home base in Bogotá to Panama City and other Central American capitals. And if you want a stopover in Havana, then Cubana can offer combination tickets to a number of cities. Bear in mind, though, that Cuba's national carrier ended 1999 with two fatal accidents in five days, including a DC-10 that overshot the runway in Guatemala City. The Cuban airline began 2000 with easily the worst safety record in the world, and Avianca's is not especially good, either.

Air fares from London are usually so much lower than from other European cities that it is often a good idea to take a cheap flight to the English capital and travel onward from there. You can e-mail the companies recommended, or search for alternatives through the useful websites cheapflights.co.uk, e-bookers.co.uk or expedia.msn. Alternatively, the main gateways are Paris and Madrid for the services of Air France and Iberia respectively.

The leading departure points **from the USA** are Dallas, Houston, Los Angeles and Miami, though there are also flights from many other cities: Atlanta, Chicago, New York, Phoenix and San Francisco are good bets. A straightforward return from LA or Miami to Mexico City will cost around $300-$400, while an 'open-jaw', returning from Panama City, could be twice as expensive. The alternative is to fly to near the Texan-Mexican border (e.g. San Antonio or Laredo) and to cross by land.

How safe is your airline?

If it is the US carrier, Southwest Airlines, then the answer is spectacularly so. It has flown around nine million flights without causing a single passenger fatality. Many other airlines, from Virgin Atlantic to Airtours International, have equally clean records – they just haven't flown so many missions.

Airlines from Latin America – as well as parts of Africa and Asia – have alarming accident rates. To find out just how alarming, consult the website AirSafe.com, a privately-run source where accident rates since 1970 are tabulated according to airline and aircraft type. You will find Cubana anchored firmly to the foot of the table.

For more specific information, the US government publishes its opinion on safety standards at faa.gov/avr/iasa/index.htm. But bear in mind that even on the most dangerous airline, flying is still fantastically safe – especially when compared with driving along roads like the Pan-American Highway.

From **Canada** there is much less choice, though there are direct flights between the leading cities and Mexico City. Usually, it will work out cheaper to head south to the USA and get a flight from there – unless you can get a cheap charter to one of the Mexican resorts.

It will be a brave airline that starts the first direct flight between **Australasia** and Mexico, and an even more courageous one that begins flying from Melbourne to Managua. In the meantime, Los Angeles is the obvious choice for a flight from Auckland, Sydney or Melbourne. From here you can fly to San Antonio or Mexico City, or catch a bus direct to Tijuana, where buses or planes will take you more cheaply to the Mexican capital. The only flights crossing the South Pacific between South America and Australasia are on Aerolineas Argentinas (Buenos Aires-Auckland-Sydney) and Lan Chile (Santiago-Easter Island-Tahiti, with connections to Australia and New Zealand). The Australian airline Qantas code-shares on these routes, which means you can build South America into a round-the-world trip.

All the big airline alliances offer **round-the-world** options. If you want to work Mexico and Central America into the equation, then the best chances of globe-girdling are likely to be with the Star Alliance (the significant carriers being Mexicana and United) or the Wings partnership (Continental, Copa of Panama and KLM offer interesting possibilities). On **oneworld** (British Airways, American Airlines, etc), you may find you have to buy an extra sector to fit in with the airlines' network.

Not everyone relishes the thought of venturing unaided into unknown territory. Though this book attempts to demystify the region and empower the traveller, you may be more comfortable on a **tour**. No-one (yet) offers a trip that sticks to the Pan-American Highway, but Mexico and Central America are firmly on the tour operators' maps; Honduras, Nicaragua and Panama are lagging behind in the popularity stakes. The most common itineraries are those linking Guatemala with Mexico. The advantage of leaving the worrying to someone else must be set against the disadvantages of expense and inflexibility.

As well as JLA and SAX (details in previous pages), Trips Worldwide (9 Byron Place, Bristol BS8 1JT, 0117-987 2626, info@tripsworldwide.co.uk) has a wide range of options.

Red Tape

Passports

Every traveller needs one – except US and Canadian visitors to Mexico and Costa Rica, and US visitors to Panama; in these cases proof of citizenship, such as a driver's license or voter's registration card, is sufficient. Clearly, though, anyone who is serious about making a journey along a significant stretch of the Pan-American Highway will need a full passport. And what's more, you should make sure it is valid for six months beyond the duration of your visit – a number of countries are insisting upon this, which means that on a six-month trip through the region you need to ensure there is at least a month to run on your passport.

Tourists' passports are a popular target for the region's villains, so there is a risk that yours will be stolen. If this happens, first inform the police – not because there's any hope that they'll do anything about recovering it, but because you'll need an official report of the case to get a replacement. You may need to pay for the police report, which is inconvenient if you happen to have had all your money stolen too.

Getting a replacement passport from the consular department of your embassy will be much easier if you have a record of the passport number and its date and place of issue. You will also have to pay for the new passport, but at least you'll have the prestige of possessing one issued in Managua or San Salvador.

Crossing borders

Approach every frontier in Mexico and Central America expecting to have a long and difficult time. Crossing some borders in the region can feel rather like walking through a Wild West town which has gone quiet in anticipation of a duel. At some, there are still bunkers, sandbag barricades and barbed wire as a reminder of the turmoil of the 20th century.

There is also certain to be a large floating population of not entirely savoury characters whose precise role is not clear. Many of them will offer their services as 'helpers' or unofficial bureaux de change, while others are out to fleece visitors by various illicit means. Keep smiling, and keep an eye on your possessions. Try not to let anyone but an official handle your passport.

The procedures are likely to involve a great deal more time, effort and cash than you are used to. You will be pleasantly surprised if it turns out to be speedier and less hassle than predicted. The more you look like a regular traveller, the less trouble you will have. The officials expect all *gringos* to be carrying around a motley collection of unwashed socks, well-thumbed novels, etc. More importantly, they expect you to be carrying a ticket out of their country, or at least reserves of cash or travellers cheques sufficient to sustain the most profligate visitor.

Each of the seven countries in the region implements its own frontier policies. As a result, the traveller can become bemused by details of visa requirements, onward tickets, frontier opening times, etc. Few subjects are as hard to grasp and as quick to change as the entry requirements for Central American countries. Check the latest visa position with the appropriate embassy, though don't be surprised if it turns out to be entirely at variance from what you find on the ground. Remain courteous, even when they turn you away and you have to retrace your steps for 200km. You'll have a great story to tell afterwards.

While your case is being considered, you may have to wait for immigration officials to leaf through a book or dial up a computer which lists undesirable aliens. On entering the country you will be asked to fill in a badly printed form asking innocuous questions, and the official will decide the length of stay permitted. When saying how long you plan to stay, you tread a tightrope between asking for too little – in which case you might have to endure the Kafka-esque procedures involved in extending your stay – and seeking too much, thereby triggering awkward questions from the official such as proof of your extensive financial resources. If you are called upon to prove your economic well-being, make full use of credit cards to extol your financial status.

Assuming you are let in, check carefully what is stamped in your passport, as mistakes or misunderstandings on entering cause problems when you try to leave.

It comes as a shock to some Westerners to discover that an international frontier can **close down at night**, but those in Central America do. An agreement signed between the Central American nations in 1990 laid down provisions for borders to stay open for 24 hours a day, but in the ensuing decade nothing much happened. At present most borders are open at some time between 6am and 8am and close at 4pm, 5pm or 6pm; some also close in the middle of the day, and you may have to pay extra to be let across during the lunch break. An excellent rule to adopt is to get to the border as early as you can in the day – not only does this maximise the chance that you can get across before closing time, it will also be quicker: traffic builds up steadily during the day.

When discussing **bribes and taxes**, it is hard to say where one begins and the other ends. Entry and exit fees are payable when crossing almost any frontier in Mexico and Central America. These seemingly arbitrary fees may constitute your single biggest expense, and it is easy to believe that the only people to benefit are the frontier officials who collect them. Charges vary – largely at the whim of the official – but are usually between $1 and $10. It is not a politically good move to quibble over the 'fee', however unlikely you think it is that the money is going to the government.

Jeux avec frontières

By getting a posting to a border crossing, the bureaucrat achieves Nirvana. Suddenly, he (and officials almost always are male) is endowed with precepts, protocols and powers about which lesser functionaries can only dream. And he promptly sets about using and, often, abusing them.

In Latin America, combining a position of authority with scope for some freelance earnings has been raised to an art form. Even if you know what the rules are, you may find that government regulations do not necessarily coincide with the views of individual frontier officials. Practice fails to conform with theory in Honduras, where some British travellers – who officially do not need a visa – have been turned away for not having one. Until recently, Guatemala's consulate in London advised British travellers arriving at that country's land frontiers to obtain a visa, even though technically none was needed. At many desolate Central American border posts, your immediate future lies in the hands of a frontier official whose understanding of the rules may be very different to yours.

If you go the distance through Mexico and Central America, you will get all too used to a sinking feeling when you approach a frontier. After the last big town on the Highway before a border post, traffic dwindles significantly and the road surface gets even shoddier. Then, perhaps a kilometre or two before the frontier, the Highway begins to broaden, finally bulging like a blister into a messy assemblage of truck parks, official buildings and free enterprise – all the side industries from insurance bureaux and liquor stores to currency touts and soft-drink vendors.

Amid this shifting (and shifty) collection of humankind, your immediate future rests in the hands of half a dozen key people. The guard who allows you to approach the frontier; the immigration official and his colleague from customs who allow you to check out of the 'departure' country; and the counterparts on the 'arrival' side. Bear in mind that their professional lives are not as satifying, intellectually and financially, as they might be. They are not necessarily focussing on issues such as the potential benefits of tourism to their nation, nor the heightening of international understanding that travel provides. They are quite possibly bored and greedy. They are also a long way from the capital, and endowed with a generous amount of autonomy. And they would, if asked, actually say that they are the moral and economic guardians of the state.

Which explains why they will give you a good going-over. First, they will look you up and down to assess how likely your dress or attitude is to outrage public decency. This is a very good occasion on which to look presentable: as anywhere in the world, your image conveys a lot of potentially misleading information. While the people of Mexico and Central America are now used to the idea of backpacking, there is still not too much tradition of alternative lifestyles. In other words, the less you look like a 'hippie', the better.

Next, your passport may be minutely examined. One reason is that it's a heck of a lot more interesting than most of the ones that they see: from a distant land, filled with exotic stamps and with the added bonus of your ridiculous passport photograph. Also, each frontier official has a mental list of 'unfriendly' countries; if you happen to have been to several of these, they may take against you.

Finally, they want to make sure you will not become a burden on the already overstrained economy. The two main instruments for this are the evidence of ample funds and a ticket out of the country. Both are problematic for modern travellers: you can happily rely on Automatic Teller Machines (cashpoints) for finance all the way down the Highway, so there is little practical point carrying excess cash. And if you are heading to the end of the Highway, you will have a ticket out of Panama City – not Guatemala City, Tegucigalpa or San José. The best way to address the question is to avoid it being asked, which goes back to looking the part. 'If you don't turn up at a border with straw in your hair, you'll stand much more chance of getting across without a problem', says one specialist agent.

Perhaps one reason British citizens get particularly badly treated by officialdom in Latin America is the lasting memory of a diplomatic incident perpetrated by the late Lord George-Brown at a reception in the Peruvian capital. After enjoying plenty of the local speciality, the pisco sour, the then Foreign Secretary heard the band strike up. Keen to share his conviviality with some lucky lady, he approached a figure clad elegantly in red and asked for a dance.

'I won't dance with you for three reasons', came the reply. 'First, you're drunk. Next, they're playing the Peruvian national anthem. Third, I'm the Archbishop of Lima.'

Extended stays

For a stay of a month or more – for example, to learn Spanish – you will need to obtain a visa in advance, or apply for a visa extension and possibly an exit visa once in the country. These are obtainable from each country's Immigration Department, but only after a process which requires heroic stamina; it is normally easier to leave the country temporarily and re-enter. Better still, begin the procedures early by applying for a visa before you arrive in Mexico and Central America.

Customs

Unlike immigration procedures – where every step of the process must be followed slavishly – there is something of an optional quality to customs checks at many Central American frontiers. Customs officials, if and when they happen to be awake, are generally more interested in the contents of vehicles than backpacks. But it helps to know the rules for the occasion when they decide to give you a complete going-over. Officials may claim the power to make a charge for baggage checks, so you end up paying a couple of dollars for their entertainment.

Embassies in the UK and USA

Costa Rica: Flat 1, 14 Lancaster Gate, London W2 3LH (020 7706 8844); 2114 S Street, NW Washington DC 20008 (202 328 6628, costarica.com/embassy).

El Salvador: Tennyson House, 159 Great Portland Street, London WIN 5FD (020 7436 8282; for visa enquiries dial 0891 444 580); 2308 California Street, NW Washington DC 20008 (202 265 9671).

Guatemala: 13 Fawcett Street, London SW10 9HN (020 7351 3042); 2220 R Street, NW Washington DC 20008 (202 745 4952).

Honduras: 115 Gloucester Place, London WIH 3PJ (020 7486 4880); 3007 Tilden Street 4M, NW Washington DC 20008 (202 966 7702, hondurasemb.org)

Mexico: 42 Hertford Street, London WIY 7TF (020 7499 8586); 2827 16th St, NW Washington DC 20006 (202 736 1000)

Nicaragua: no embassy in the UK; the nearest is in Brussels, at 55 avenue de Wolvendael (+32 2 375 6500); 1627 New Hampshire Avenue, NW Washington DC 20009 (202 939 6570, embanic_prensa@andyne.net).

Panama: 48 Park Street, London WIY 3PD (020 7493 4646); 2862 McGill Terrace, NW Washington DC 20008 (202 483 1407).

Personal effects in reasonable quantities can be imported free of duty. A certain amount of liquor and tobacco is allowed, but this is worth doing only if you crave a particular brand of cigarettes or malt whisky; prices for both vices are low throughout the region. Meat, animal products and fruit may be confiscated (and will probably be eaten by officials when you have gone).

Books of any kind are likely to attract attention. In Central America the authorities are curiously paranoid about communism, so avoid carrying left-wing literature. This is not usually a problem in Mexico, except when entering the troubled province of Chiapas from Guatemala

Note that customs checks are just as likely to happen on the way out of countries as well as on the way in. If you are really unlucky, you may be searched twice by the authorities in each country: first by customs officials looking for contraband, and again by army officers seeking weapons or literature.

Illegal **narcotics** comprise an integral part of the economy in Mexico and Central America, and a big problem for the authorities. One consequence is that you can expect a lot of attention to be paid to any medicines in your luggage. Keep them in their original containers, and bring along copies of the relevant prescriptions. Be warned that any opiate derivatives – such as kaolin and morphine – are strictly prohibited, even though they are sold openly in the UK. It goes without saying that anyone caught importing marijuana or other illegal drugs can expect to be locked up for a long time.

Numerous traders in Mexico and Central America will try to sell you products made from **endangered species**. These include tortoiseshell, black coral, various butterflies and items made from reptile skins. Quite apart from moral considerations, you may offend the Convention on International Trade in Endangered Species (CITES), an international agreement covering all animals at risk.

In Mexico and Guatemala, and to a lesser extent El Salvador and Honduras, the looting of pre-Columbian sites is big business and artifacts are sold for huge sums on the black market. Do not get involved in this illegal and destructive trade, not least because the export of archaeological objects is forbidden.

Meet the locals

Most people in Mexico and Central America are *mestizo*, of mixed Spanish and Indian blood. Yet through the region's chequered history the ethnic mix has become disparate, with elements from Asia and Africa adding to the mix.

The largest group of indigenous people is in the Chiapas region of Mexico and in neighbouring Guatemala, where the Indians are in the majority and their culture is commensurately strong. In the other countries and the remainder of Mexico, more-or-less pure-blooded indigenous people comprise one-20th or less of the population, and traditional customs and languages are disappearing.

At the time of the Spanish Conquest, Indian settlements were large and well-established throughout the region. In Mexico and Guatemala the communities were highly organised, so the *conquistadores* took them over as they were, and used the inhabitants as an instant labour force. To the south and east, the indigenous groups were often nomadic, isolated and less easy to control. Many were massacred, or died after contracting foreign diseases. But while many Indian men were murdered, the women were often spared and intermarrying subsequently took place.

Given the amount of mixing which has taken place to produce the mestizo majority, it is surprising that so many pure-blooded whites of Hispanic descent have survived. These people are often referred to as creoles. The greatest concentrations are found in Costa Rica and Panama – in Costa Rica there was little intermarriage between the Spanish and Indians since so few indigenous people survived the Conquest; the number of white people in Panama stems more from an influx during the 19th century. In Mexico and most Central American countries, people of European descent make up the ruling elites.

Black people form a less numerous group, but one of greater cultural importance. All of the countries in this book except Mexico and El Salvador have a significant number of blacks, whose communities are concentrated along the Atlantic coasts. They are descended from African and West Indian blacks who were brought in as slaves following the Conquest. Others were shipped in during the 19th century to work on the railways and plantations.

What they believe

Most Mexicans and Central Americans are nominally Catholic. Many of them do not practice, however, and the large number of people turning up for

The Black Caribs

The Garifuna, as the 'Black Caribs' are locally known, comprise an important element of the black community. It is thought that they are descended from an accidental encounter between Carib Indians from South America and African slaves. In the late 16th century a ship transporting slaves to the colonies appears to have sunk off the Antillean island of St Vincent. This island had earlier been settled by a group of Carib Indians, warlike marauders who had moved up through Latin America causing general mayhem. The Carib Indians on the island killed the male survivors of the shipwreck and took the women as wives. When the British took over St Vincent, the Garifuna worked for them, reluctantly, but in the late 18th century they rebelled and were exiled to the Bay Islands off Honduras. From here they spread to the mainland and settled in Guatemala, Honduras and Nicaragua – mostly on the Caribbean coast, but with increasingly many moving to the capital cities.

The Garifuna, also known as Garinagu, combine Caribbean and Indian elements but African features are predominant; they retain many African songs, dances and traditions. They speak their own Garifuna language among themselves, though most speak Spanish and English too. The most obvious elements of Caribbean culture seen in everyday life are dependence on the sea, the communal organisation of labour, and a strong sense of community. They are famous for their festivals, and for reggae music.

religious festivals can be misleading; a cynic might say it demonstrates that they enjoy a good gathering more than they do a church service. Nevertheless, Mass is celebrated most evenings in the majority of towns, and the churches are seldom empty. Going to church is a relaxed business: doors are left open and people drift in and out.

In El Salvador and Nicaragua there has been a swing towards various Protestant denominations, many of them evangelical. Some attribute this to a right-wing reaction against the liberation theology preached by some members of the Catholic church. Among the indigenous people pre-Columbian animist beliefs have survived, especially in Guatemala – one of the more unusual cults is that of a 'smoking and drinking' saint known as Maximón, believed to be a thinly disguised Judas Iscariot. Among the nominally Christian, Garifuna shamen continue to invoke their magic to cure the sick, and at night people lock their doors to keep out the evil spirits.

Making friends

Travellers from overseas, especially those of fair skins, stick out a mile. You will be instantly identified as a person of uncertain morals, imperfect language and almost infinite wealth. These categorisations are made not through xenophobia but through experience, and it does not automatically mean that you will be ripped off, treated rudely, etc. On the contrary, the majority of Mexicans and Central Americans are friendly and welcoming, and even those who seem shy at first usually respond warmly to your overtures.

You are certain to meet people who show you kindness and hospitality. Whilst you need not feel compelled to reciprocate, most Westerners are keen to offer small presents as a way of showing gratitude. The kinds of gifts which go down well are, in short, anything Western: chewing gum, pens, clothes (particularly brash T-shirts or baseball caps), postcards and badges, rock music cassettes, whisky, perfume and toiletries.

Giving needs to be carried out thoughtfully. You must be careful to avoid appearing arrogant, dishing out Western trinkets as if they were beads being offered to grateful natives. Give modestly, not least to preclude an escalation of the gift-giving process.

What they speak

Spanish is the lingua franca even among Indian groups, although the most isolated communities of indigenous people may have some difficulty with Spanish, and may not speak it at all, preferring to speak their own dialect. Do not assume that people outside the hard-core tourist traps can speak English. Travellers without at least a modicum of Spanish will find life in Mexico and Central America difficult, although this situation is improving now that English is regarded as the key to success in life among the locals. Nevertheless, the ability to make friends – or argue your case – in Spanish is invaluable.

The best plan is to learn Spanish in Mexico or Central America. In particular, Oaxaca, San Cristóbal and Antigua, Guatemala, have developed the teaching of Spanish into a major industry, and courses are also run in Nicaragua. If you have neither the time nor the devotion to attend a regular evening class, then try to learn some Spanish at home. The BBC produces an excellent *Get By In Latin Spanish* course, which costs £4.99 for the book (optional audio extra).

Latin Americans **pronounce** Spanish very differently from the pure Castillian mostly taught in England. In particular, the soft 'th' sound corresponding to the letters ce, ci or z is rendered as 's'; the use of the 'th' will cause great amusement and lead the locals to assume that you have a lisp.

Unless an accent indicates otherwise, Spanish words which end in a vowel or *n* or *s* are always stressed on the last-but-one syllable: so, for example, Guate*ma*la and Hon*du*ras. Words ending in any other consonant are always stressed on the last syllable, e.g. Da*vid*. If a word is to be stressed on any other syllable, an acute accent is written over the vowel which needs to be stressed: San Cristóbal. Unlike some languages (e.g. French), an acute accent on a letter does not affect the sound of that letter; it merely indicates where the stress should fall on a multi-syllable word if it does not comply with the rules outlined above.

The letter *h* is never pronounced, i.e. hola is pronounced ola. *J* is pronounced as an aspirated *h*, as is *g* when followed by *e* or *i*; so José should be spoken as Ho-*say*. The conjunction ll is pronounced y, as in allá – aya. The letter v is almost indistinguishable from the letter b, so veinte (20) sounds like beinte. The wave above an n (ñ), known as a tilde, changes the letter n to ny. Thus mañana is pronounced man-yana. Accents other than the tilde are rarely used on capital letters, and are not used in this book. The letter x, found mainly in Guatemala, is pronounced sh. The letter *s* at the ends of words may be missed out. Thus *buenos* is spoken as 'bueno', and *dos* as 'do'. At the end of words *n* is pronounced more like 'ng', though this is merely hinted at.

In dictionaries, indexes and telephone directories, listings beginning ch (pronounced as in chair) are listed after c; ll follows l, and ñ follows n.

Useful Words and Phrases

hello	*hola*	I am hungry	*tengo apetito*
goodbye	*adiós, hasta luego, ciao*	I am thirsty	*tengo sed*
yes	*sí*	a little	*un poquito*
no	*no*	more	*más*
please	*por favor*	less	*menos*
thank you	*gracias*	to go	*ir*
excuse me	*perdón, permiso*	help me	*ayúdeme*
how much	*cuánto*	quickly	*rapidamente*
where is	*dónde está*	slowly	*despacio*

good	*bueno*	stop	*párese*
bad	*malo*	here	*aquí*
good morning	*buenas diás* (or *hola*)	there	*allí*
good afternoon	*buenas tardes*	is there any ...?	*hay ...?*
good evening	*buenas tardes*	no, there isn't	*no hay*
goodnight	*buenas noches*	school	*escuela*
don't mention it	*de nada*	garden	*jardín*
how are you?	*qué tal?*	house	*casa*
pleased (to meet you)	*mucho gusto, encantado, a*	town	*ciudad*
I don't understand	*no entiendo*	village	*pueblo*
I don't speak Spanish	*no hablo español (castellano)*	big	*grande*
do you speak English?	*habla usted inglés?*	small	*pequeño*
my name is ...	*me llamo ...*	hot	*caliente*
what is your name?	*como se llama?*	cold	*frió*
can I photograph you?	*puedo tomar su fotografiá?*	queue	*cola*
I am ... years old	*tengo ... años*	don't touch	*no tocar*
I would like ...	*quisiero ...*	no smoking	*no fumar*
I need ...	*necesito ...*	no entry	*no pase*
I am well	*estoy bien*		

Weather

rain	*lluvia*	storm	*temporal*
sun	*sol*	hurricane	*huracán*
it's hot	*hace calor*	shower	*chubasco*
it's cold	*hace frió*		

Time

what time is it?	*qué hora es?*	Sunday	*domingo*
one o'clock	*la una*	Monday	*lunes*
two o'clock	*las dos*	Tuesday	*martes*
minute	*minuto*	Wednesday	*miércoles*
hour	*hora*	Thursday	*jueves*
day	*diá*	Friday	*viernes*
week	*semana*	Saturday	*sábado*
month	*mes*	January	*enero*
year	*año*	February	*febrero*
yesterday	*ayer*	March	*marzo*
today	*hoy*	April	*abril*
tomorrow	*mañana*	May	*mayo*

morning	*mañana*	June	*junio*
afternoon	*tarde*	July	*julio*
evening	*tarde*	August	*agosto*
(early); *noche* (late)		September	*septiembre*
now	*ahora*	October	*octubre*
never	*jamás*	November	*noviembre*
precisely	*punto*	December	*diciembre*

Numbers

1	*uno* or *una*	23	*veintitrés*
2	*dos*	24	*veinticuatro*
3	*tres*	25	*veinticinco*
4	*cuatro*	26	*veintiséis*
5	*cinco*	27	*veintisiete*
6	*seis*	28	*veintiocho*
7	*siete*	29	*veintinueve*
8	*ocho*	30	*treinta*
9	*nueve*	31	*treinta y uno*
10	*diez*	32	*treinta y dos*
11	*once*	40	*cuarenta*
12	*doce*	50	*cincuenta*
13	*trece*	60	*sesenta*
14	*catorce*	70	*setenta*
15	*quince*	80	*ochenta*
16	*dieciséis*	90	*noventa*
17	*diecisiete*	100	*cien* (before nouns) or *ciento*
18	*dieciocho*	200	*doscientos* or *doscientas* (before feminine nouns)
19	*diecinueve*	500	*quinientos* or *quinientas*
20	*veinte*	1000	*mil*
21	*veintiuno*	10,000	*diez mil*
22	*veintidós*	1,000,000	*un millón*

Nationality and Status

Cuban	*cubano, a*	married	*casado, a*
English	*inglés*	single	*soltero, a*
England	*Inglaterra*	widowed	*viudo, a*
Scotland	*Escocia*	mother	*madre*
Wales	*País de Gales*	father	*padre*
Great Britain	*Gran Bretaña*	sister	*hermana*
Ireland	*Irlanda*	brother	*hermano*
Germany	*Alemania*	wife, woman	*esposa, mujer*
Netherlands	*Paises Bajos*	husband	*esposo, marido*
Canada	*Canadá*	boy/girlfriend	*novio, a*
Australia	*Australia*	daughter	*hija*
New Zealand	*Nueva Zelanda*	son	*hijo*
United States	*Estados Unidos (EEUU)*	man	*hombre*
US citizen	*norteamericano, a*	children	*niños, hijos*

What they spend

Of the seven currencies used in the countries covered in this book, only one really counts: the Panamanian Balboa. That's because Panama's currency is actually the US dollar. The world's most popular money says much more about you than Costa Rican cordobas or Honduran lempiras ever can.

The US dollar is the only universal accepted foreign currency in Mexico and Central America. You should be able to change other Western currencies at hotels catering for foreigners, but don't bother trying to pay the bill at an out-of-the-way restaurant in sterling or Irish punts.

Technology has come to the aid of the traveller in Mexico and Central America, in the shape of Automatic Teller Machines (ATMs) which can be found in larger towns and cities. Your bank card from home will enable you to withdraw the local currency, assuming you have enough money in your account. Trying to guess exactly how many pesos or quetzales you might need is

The informal market – are you a hotshot foreign exchange dealer?

The Central American equivalent of the Bureau de Change is a much more flexible affair than dealing with banks. Large men in dark glasses, clutching wads of notes and waving pocket calculators, are to be found in every large city and at all border crossings and international airports. They deal in currency quite openly. Usually they give better rates than the banks, because they have few overheads apart from the capital investment of a pocket calculator. As well as this modest bonus, the advantages of black market dealings are the convenience (much longer hours than banks) and speed (no form-filling).

Because of the level of competition, you are likely to get a good deal from these gents, and there are relatively few stories of rip-offs. If you're suspicious, ask to count the cash before handing over your dollars, a practice which any honest dealer will agree to.

Some black marketeers at borders (the location when you are most likely to use their services) offer less than the bank rate, hoping to cash in on new arrivals unaware of what the rates are. Ask other travellers or border officials for the current rate of exchange against the dollar. Sometimes, e.g. on entry to Nicaragua, the officials themselves will offer you a deal. As well as dealing in cash dollars, some traders accept travellers cheques at a slightly worse rate. They also handle other Central American currencies, so if you leave Honduras with no plans to return, you can exchange Honduran lempiras for Guatemalan quetzales.

Sometimes you can actually turn a profit from trading in currencies. Dealers occasionally find themselves with an excess of a particular currency, and may be keen to offload córdobas at bargain rates. If you are planning to visit these countries as part of your trip, you stand to benefit.

a tricky business, but thankfully there are plenty of informal opportunities to change money, particularly at borders, so that you need not accumulate a pocketful of odds and ends of dodgy currencies that no-one else wants.

Take low denominations of **cash dollars** ($1, $2, $5 and $10) to avoid the recurring problem of a shortage of change.

The safest way to carry money is in **travellers cheques**, and the only sensible currency is the US dollar. If your travellers cheques are stolen, the issuing company should provide replacements, although this may be difficult if you have no record of the serial numbers.

Visa, Mastercard, Amex and Diners Club **credit and charge cards** are accepted widely in Mexico, less so in Central America. The further south and east you go, the fewer enterprises that accept them, and those that do tend to be expensive hotels and shops; most places levy a surcharge of 5 or 10% on customers using credit cards. A credit card (or preferably two) is worth taking, though, since it can help in the event of an emergency e.g. when you need to buy an air ticket in a hurry. The most widely accepted brand is Visa; Diners Club is accepted in few places. In addition, certain banks (especially branches in the capital cities), give cash advances on a credit card even if you cannot remember or do not have a PIN number to use it in an ATM. Take as many pieces of plastic as you can, because a particular card may be refused for all sorts of reasons.

Spend, spend, spend

abierto	open
centro comercial	shopping centre
cerrado	closed
cigarillo	cigarette
comprar	to buy
discoteca	record shop
librería	bookshop
mercado	market
película	film (camera)
pilas	batteries
tienda	shop

Anything worth buying?

Wandering around any Mexican or Central American market, where stalls are piled high with weird and wonderful products, is always an entertaining experience. As a general rule, in Mexico you can rely on buying almost anything, and indeed I once flew in with no possessions apart from credit card, dollars and passport. But if you are thinking of buying an extra large rucksack just so that you have lots of spare room in which to put all the crafts and souvenirs you're going to buy, think again. Unless you visit Guatemala, you are unlikely to find much to spend your money on. A country's craft scene, like its music and dance, depends critically on the size of its indigenous population, and in Mexico and the other six Central American nations the Indian communities are struggling to keep their traditions alive.

The Indians of Guatemala make up for the lack of tempting goods elsewhere – they produce some of the best crafts found anywhere in the world, and are particularly famous for their brightly-coloured weavings. A certain amount of weaving goes on in the rest of Central America but in a limited way; some of the most interesting textiles outside Guatemala are those made by the Kuna Indians who live on the islands off the north coast of Panama.

The rest of the region is not devoid of artisans, however, and each country has villages where the local people still make pots, weave baskets or carve wood, etc. Be warned that some of the better shops rely, more sensibly, on imported crafts (principally from Guatemala) which they sell at vastly inflated prices.

Basket-weaving is a common skill and although baskets are not convenient to pack, hats are good buys, particularly in Mexico and Panama. Hammocks, which can be bought in much of the region, are also excellent presents. Wherever possible go direct to the craftsman rather than just to a dealer.

An eye for a bargain

Haggling over prices is hard for most Westerners to master. In Mexico and Central America you need to start bargaining from the moment you get a taxi from the airport and continue for most of the trip. First, you should establish where haggling is inappropriate: prices in restaurants and from street food stalls are usually fixed, as are fares for public transport. Almost everything else is worth arguing about, even down to the amount a frontier official wants to charge you for inspecting your luggage.

It is understood that as a Westerner you are far wealthier than the average local resident could ever hope to be. It is seen as entirely reasonable that traders should try to separate you from as much of your money as possible. Therefore you can never expect to get as good a deal as a local, but by conducting negotiations sensibly and pleasantly you can cut costs and have some fun. Bargaining is a game, and played enthusiastically it can be most enjoyable. After asking the price and being quoted an outrageous figure, offer about one-third – the exact amount becomes easier once you have found your feet in a country and you get accustomed to the going rates. Eventually you will probably settle at between one half and two thirds of the initial asking price. Do not hesitate to walk away, and never allow the negotiations to get heated; some travellers and traders have become deeply antagonistic over a trifling sum. Enjoy the sport, and maintain a certain levity.

Emergency Cash

Many are the travellers who end up hanging around waiting anxiously for bank transfers from home. Having money sent to you in Central America can be a harrowing business. The best way is to arrange for the money to be transferred by telex through an international bank or travel agent, such as American Express or Lloyds. Alternatively, this can be done from your own bank to a nominated branch of a local Central American bank (preferably to one of the major city branches). Whichever method you decide to use, ask the sender to get written confirmation from your bank that the remittance has been made and to send you a copy.

If you have neither resources nor friends who can bail you out, then the absolute last resort is to persuade the British Embassy to repatriate you. This they will do, though you can expect a large bill when you return home.

Weights and Measures

The countries of Mexico and Central America use the metric system. Distances are measured in millimetres (25.4mm = 1 inch), metres (0.3m = 1 foot) and kilmetres (1.6km = 1 mile). Volume uses the millilitre (550ml = 1 Imperial pint) and the litre (4.5l = 1 Imperial gallon). Weights are given in grams (27g = 1 ounce) and kilograms (0.45kg = 1 lb). One weight you will sometimes encounter in shops is the livre, in fact a hangover from the days when the pound was the unit of weight. These days, one livre is half a kilogram.

The old Spanish system of weights and measures is widely used. The one you are most likely to encounter is the vara, a unit of length just over one yard and under one metre. The others are unlikely to concern you unless you are trading in real estate or buying in bulk. For the record they are the *manzana* (1.75 acres), the *caballería* (112 acres), the *arroba* (25lb) and the *quintal* (101lb).

On the Highway

The first thing to appreciate is the challenge of distance – starting with the sheer size of Mexico. From Tijuana in the extreme northwest to Cancún at the tip of the Yucatán Peninsula is an east-west distance of 3,200km (2,000 miles), straddling three time zones. The Pan-American Highway covers around 1,800km (1,150 miles) through the country, just about the same as in the whole of Central America. And despite the relatively small size of Central America, moving around the isthmus can take considerably longer than you might think.

Travelling is usually fun, but not if you are in a hurry nor if you try to impose Western notions of comfort, speed and predictability. The quality of roads, including the Pan-American Highway, varies from adequate to abysmal. The further south and east you get, the more you will find that travel is severely restricted during the wet season; landslides, rockfalls and flooding are not uncommon. Alternatives to road travel are few: the region's rail network has been erased from the map, so the best option is to fly over some of the less rivetting bits.

Any chance of a good map?

Yes – so long as you buy it in advance. The AA in Britain publishes an excellent map of Mexico, which actually covers a good proportion of Central America. An option is the Hallwag map of Central America (published in Germany), which includes the whole of Mexico, part of Brazil and even New York City. The map produced by Kummerley & Frey covers exactly the same area. The International Travel Map – Central America goes only from the south of Mexico to Panama; for general route planning, the cheap Rand McNally map of Mexico and Central America is adequate. Basic road maps of Central America are published by Esso and Texaco, and are distributed through their service stations in the area. Maps of individual countries range from excellent (Mexico, Costa Rica, Guatemala) to sketchy (Honduras) to downright misleading (Nicaragua). Area maps, of use to hikers, are not widely available in the way that Ordnance Survey maps are in the UK: most governments regard them as threats to security, and for some you have to apply through the Defence Ministry. It makes sense, therefore, to obtain whatever maps you ahead of time.

Map and travel guide specialists

In the past few years the options have expanded considerably. The *Stanfords* selection of wild, wonderful and mostly accurate maps from Latin America and elsewhere remains first-rate, but there are other options around the UK:

Blackwell's Map and Travel Shop, 53 Broad St, Oxford OX1 3BQ; tel 01865 792792, bookshop.blackwell.co.uk
Daunt Books, 83 Marylebone High Street, London W1M 4DE; tel 020 7224 2295.

Heffers Map Shop, in Heffers at 19 Sidney St, Cambridge CB2 3HL; tel 01223 568467, heffers.co.uk.

Newcastle Map Centre, part of Traveller, 55 Grey St, Newcastle upon Tyne NE1 6EF; tel 0191 261 5622, newtraveller.com.

Stanfords, 12-14 Long Acre, London WC2E 9LP; tel 020 7836 1321, stanfords.co.uk; there are also branches at 156 Regent St, London W1R 5TA (as part of the British Airways Travel Shop) and 29 Corn St, Bristol BS1 1HT; tel 0117 929 9966.

Spanish in motion

aeropuerto	airport
barco	boat
barrio, colonia	suburb or district
bus extraurbano	long-distance bus
camión	lorry, truck
camioneta	any bus, from a converted truck to a pullman
cruce de escolares	schoolchildren crossing
cruce de peatones	pedestrians crossing
cuadra	block
boleto	ticket
equipajes	luggage
estación	railway station
horario	timetable
ida	one-way
ida y vuelta	round-trip
llegada	arrival
parada de buses	bus stop
paradero	layby
paso a nivel	level crossing
rincón	corner
rumbo	(bus) route
salida	departure
taquilla	ticket office
terminal	bus station
tren	train
norte	north
sur	south
este	east
oeste	west
izquierda	left
derecha	right
recto	straight on

The Map Shop, 30a Belvoir St, Leicester LEI 6QH; tel 0116 247 1400.
The Map Shop, 15 High Street, Upton-upon-Severn, Worcestershire WR8 0HJ; tel
01684 593146, themapshop.co.uk.
The Travel Bookshop, 13 Blenheim Crescent, London WII 2EE; tel 020 7229
5260, thetravelbookshop.co.uk.

On the buses

The air-conditioning was just a touch on the cool side, so when the smartly
dressed young hostess brought the drink to my seat I asked her to turn it down.
For the rest of the journey, I stretched out and dozed happily inside the double-
glazed cocoon of a *de lujo* Mexican express. Can there be a more comfortable
bus anywhere in the world?

Not in Nicaragua, nor Honduras, nor the rest of Central America. Before
you get too comfortable and used to the high standards on the best buses in
Mexico, you should be aware that travelling across rough terrain on a second-
class bus resembles a ride on an out-of-control mechanical bull. The standard
conveyance in Central America is a secondhand American school bus; many are
still in the original yellow, with notices reading 'Rules for Riders'. They have
hard, narrow seats and woefully little leg-room. Most are packed to capacity
with short, slim and patient locals; therefore tall, plump or intolerant visitors
are likely to be at a disadvantage.

You will be assailed by other passengers' sweat, noise from the driver's
heavily distorted radio and a platoon of vendors selling sickly soft drinks or
snacks which are impossible to eat tidily. Management of this heaving, lurching
mass is the responsibility of one or more conductors. They pack on the
passengers, load luggage onto the roof, collect the fares and orchestrate the
whole lumbering affair.

Actually boarding a bus in the first place can be quite a performance. You
will soon wise up to the manner in which an apparently orderly group of
people at a bus stop disintegrates into complete mayhem when a bus arrives.
Typically two or three times as many people as the bus can comfortably carry
will force their way on board. Men often give up their seats to women, and
foreigners are particularly well looked after. You are advised to accept gratefully
– standing up for hours is agonising for tourists who are neither designed nor
used to the prospect. In addition, owing to the design of the buses it is
virtually impossible for standees to see anything but the verge through the
windows. To lessen the cramped conditions in which you will have to sit or
stand, take as small a pack as possible, and take it on the bus with you. If you
have to wait to have it put on the luggage rack you will lose any chance there
might be to travel in comfort.

On some particularly busy routes, the local men join the luggage on the
roof; although it may sound tempting to have some leg-room and enjoy the
fresh air, during the hottest part of the day you'll be burnt alive. On the other
hand, those inside will have to get used to record-breaking numbers sharing one
seat (if you are lucky enough to sit down in the first place), being unable to

move (you may lose vital inches of space if you do), and feeling broken springs poking into your bottom. Sleep is impossible. The speed that bus drivers like to maintain sometimes gives cause for concern, but accidents are rare, largely due to the lack of traffic on the roads; perhaps the array of paintings of the Virgin Mary and the multitude of other religious trinkets with which many drivers surround themselves has some use after all. Buses are often called *camionetas* ('little trucks'), and in rural areas the bus service is indeed operated by a converted truck.

To stop the bus, whether the going has got too tough, or whether you have simply arrived at your destination, shout *parada* ('stop'), or whistle loudly. Whenever possible make it known – either to a fellow passenger or to the conductor – where you want to get off.

While buses along the Pan-American Highway and main roads are comparatively frequent, services diminish dramatically once you head into rural areas. Small or remote towns may only have one or two buses a day and minor villages only a couple a week. Many services start early, e.g. at 4am or 5am; they also finish early and there are few departures after 4pm. Pack an alarm clock. Timetables exist on some routes in theory, but are not necessarily paid much heed to; buses can leave 30 minutes early or an hour late if it suits the driver. Approximate journey timings for bus routes are given in this book, but these take no account of stops for refuelling, for the driver to be booked by police, punctures, army checks, etc.

International buses are just as prone to delay, but they are generally comfortable – and along with your ticket you are paying for someone else to

Timescale

Every country in the region except Panama and the far west of Mexico maintains Central Standard Time throughout the year, i.e. GMT -6. In winter, therefore, noon in Central America corresponds with 6pm in London, 1pm in New York, noon in Chicago, 11am in Denver, 10am in Los Angeles and 4am – the following day – in Sydney. When much of the northern hemisphere adopts daylight saving time from March to September, Central America is only 5 hours behind London and on the same time as New York and the eastern USA.

Panama runs at GMT -5 all year, so noon in Panama City in winter is 5pm in London and noon in New York, while in summer noon in Panama is 4pm in London and 1pm in New York. The southern part of the Baja Peninsula in Mexico – a very long way from the Pan-American Highway – is at GMT -7, while the northern portion is GMT -8, to match the time north of the border in California.

Times in Mexico and Central America, and in this book, are quoted as am or pm; the 24-hour clock is rarely used.

worry about the border bureaucracy. The main line is Ticabus, based in San José, Costa Rica, but there is plenty of competition on routes from Mexico City through every Central American capital to Panama City

The buses most likely to try to keep to some sort of schedule are the big, fast first-class services. Local services are likely to depend more on when the bus fills up. If a driver or conductor tells you he is leaving *ahorita* ('right now'), take it with a large pinch of salt; they will say almost anything to get you on the bus (and your fare).

Collective taxis

Colectivos are common in Central America (but rare in Mexico). They offer the speed, convenience and relative comfort of a taxi at a price not much higher than the bus fare. Colectivos tend to depart from around the bus station; any local should be able to point out exactly where. Alternatively, they may find you – e.g. at the Mexican-Guatemalan border, or the frontier between Nicaragua and Costa Rica, where there is a long 'no-man's-land' on which they comprise the only public transport.

When a taxi is full it sets off, but note that it may take a long time to fill. While some taxis follow an established route, others go wherever the individual passengers wish – the driver will drop you off in the most convenient order. Taxi drivers who pick up foreigners tend to be reluctant to take other passengers so that he can charge you an inflated fare. You are advised to hail only those which already contain other passengers. Either way be prepared to negotiate; there are no meters.

If the frustrations of trying to get around by public and semi-public transport grow too strong, you could hire a taxi and driver for long journeys; it is occasionally comforting to know there is an alternative to fall back on if a bus or colectivo fails to turn up. As a very rough rule of thumb, expect to pay about $20 for every 50km (30 miles) in most countries, more in Mexico, Costa Rica and Panama.

Most towns have a number of taxi ranks for urban journeys, often including one in the main square. In Nicaragua, taxis are often horse-drawn carts.

Top tip: don't
Do not tip a taxi driver unless you hire him (or, very rarely, her) for the day. The only circumstances in which you should ever need to **tip** in Central America is in a posh hotel or restaurant. Add 10% to the bill, unless a service charge is already included, in which case just leave small change. In Mexico, life is a bit trickier: near the US border and in the big tourist destinations, taxi drivers, waiters and almost anyone else involved in providing services has been conditioned to expect 15%.

Finding your way

Streets in most Mexican and Central American towns are laid out on a grid pattern, with *avenidas* (avenues) running perpendicular to *calles* (streets). All streets should have names or numbers, but few locals use them. In Central America (but not so much in Mexico), locals use buildings or other landmarks as points of reference. They are seldom able to tell you the name of the street you are in, and often unable to direct you. Ask the advice of several local residents before moving too far in any one direction. When arriving in a town for the first time, ask for the *Parque Central* (main square, known in Mexico as the *Zócalo*). This is the focus of every community, and is a good place to get your bearings.

Cycle the Highway?

Bicycles are becoming more popular in Mexico and Central America, with cycling a trendy habit among the middle classes. There are lots of shiny new mountain bikes. These are excellent for the mountainous terrain in the region, and relatively easy to rent in places like San Cristóbal in southeast Mexico and tourist spots in Guatemala and Costa Rica.

Serious cyclists can bring their own bikes. Most airlines allow you to take your bike free of charge, and in Mexico and Central America you should be able to load your bike on to a bus or an aircraft whenever you feel like a rest. If you belong to the idle fraternity of cyclists, the region has plenty of scope for taking your bike on a bus to the top of a hill or mountain, and freewheeling back down.

The problem is: the Pan-American Highway through Mexico and Central America is extremely tough on bicycles: road surfaces are bad enough for cars, and you should be wary of puddles which may conceal a drop of several feet. Take a good supply of tools and spares. Note that the prevailing wind is from the northeast, so you can plan a route to maximise the benefit; east to west is marginally best. At frontier crossings you can expect to pay an extra fee for your bicycle.

For more specific advice, join the Cyclists' Touring Club (69 Meadrow, Godalming, Surrey GU7 3HS; tel 01483 417217; fax 01483 426994). The CTC can provide members with a useful information sheet on Mexico and Central America, plus a fascinating account of crossing the Darién Gap from Panama to Colombia by bicycle – not an endeavour to be tried at present.

Driving

The ultimate motoring dream, surely – taking a car south across the Mexican border and through Central America to Panama. But it could easily turn into a nightmare.

At the most basic level, driving is not a polite business in Mexico and Central America. Do not expect the niceties typically exchanged between motorists in the West, e.g. indicating or giving way. When coping with other drivers (as well as with animals, children, etc.) the key is the use of the horn. Drive defensively and be particularly wary after dark since the few rules and regulations that exist are completely disregarded at night. Motorists in the region take a liberal approach to traffic lights at any time of the day, however, and it is common practice to turn right on a red light.

The trouble with topes

Signs such as *Respete el limit de velocidad* (*'respect the speed limit'*, or *Disminuya su velocidad* (*'reduce your speed'*) are widely posted and comprehensively ignored. About the only language that the average motorist understand is the *tope*, or *vibrador*, or speed bump.

The sign for speed bumps looks like the silhouette of a pair of breasts. But there is nothing benign about the devices intended to slow motorists. These humps range in size from mere corrugations to barricades, and appear all the way along the Highway, to reduce the speeds of vehicles passing through towns and villages, or to persuade them to stop for official checks. Whether you are a driver or passenger, you will have to become inured to the familiar slowing down followed by a couple of upward jolts and bumps as you come back down to earth. In general, the worse the condition of the road the higher the frequency of *topes*; a small town may have a dozen sets. Bus drivers know where they are, and the maximum speed at which they can be tackled; first-time motorists do not enjoy this privilege.

Traffic nominally travels on the right throughout Mexico and Central America, but all too often this rule is transgressed – with tragic consequences. In December 1999, I saw seven separate accidents along the Highway, from an overturned pick-up truck in Monterrey to a rush-hour shunt in Panama City. Not only was I shocked at the total (one every four days, compared with perhaps one every couple of years on the roads of Britain); the attitude of the local people was also startling. On a bus, everyone stands to try to get a better view of a particularly nasty accident.

The frequency of accidents is evident in the battered state of the majority of cars on the road – if vehicles were as rigorously inspected for roadworthiness as in the West, there would be virtually no traffic on the Pan-American Highway. Breakdowns are frequent, and the standard warning sign for other motorists is a few leafy branches strewn in the road a short distance before the vehicle.

Evidence of catastrophic driving standards is available from almost any tabloid newspaper in the region, which routinely shows the grisly aftermath of fatal accidents. There is no shortage of material: each year, 13,000 people die on the highways of Mexico, and several thousand more on the roads of the Central American countries. This represents an accident rate twice as bad as Britain, but because of much lower vehicle use it is actually much worse than that. Drivers have an exagerrated idea of their skills, and underestimate the considerable highway hazards.

Whose fault? Yours

Those who are determined to drive in Mexico and Central America may be interested to read the following extract from a US State Department official warning about Nicaragua:

'Traditionally, vehicles involved in accidents in Nicaragua are not moved (even to clear traffic) until authorized by a police officer. Drivers who violate this norm may be held legally liable for the accident. Any driver who is party to an accident where injuries are sustained will be taken into custody, even if the driver is insured and appears not to have been at fault. The detention lasts until a judicial decision is reached (often weeks or months), or until the injured party signs a waiver relieving the driver of further liability (usually as the result of a cash settlement).'

If you are serious about driving, the easiest way to do it is by **renting a car** locally. While you can normally negotiate a one-way rental within Mexico, it is a lot tougher in the countries of Central America and you are rarely permitted to take a hired car out of the country in which you rent it. Everywhere in the region – with the exception of the main cities in Mexico – hiring a car is an expensive business, with a day's rental costing an average of around $50 plus tax, insurance, etc. In addition, rental vehicles are tempting targets for villains. Nevertheless, unless you are willing to do a lot of hiking or hitching, renting your own vehicle may be the only way to reach some places off the highway. Since many of the roads not served by public transport are exceedingly rough, it is often necessary to hire a four-wheel drive jeep which might cost 50% more than a standard car.

Your national licence will suffice when renting a car. Optional insurance premiums are heavy (around $10 on top of a day's rental), but worthwhile. Because of the high accident rates and crime in Latin America, it is also worth paying for collision damage waiver; otherwise, the car rental company will insist that you must pay the first $200 or so of loss or damage. The minimum age for those renting a vehicle is usually 23 or 25.

The rental boys

The multi-national car hire companies have good representation in the big cities of Mexico and Central America. If you prefer to book one in advance, you can call the big rental companies in the UK before you go.

Autos Abroad 020 7409 1900	Dollar 01895 233300
Avis 0990 900500	Hertz 0990 996699
Budget 0541 565656	Holiday Autos 0990 300400

The first and last on that list are likely to offer rentals in Mexico only, while the remainder should be able to book you a car at any of their locations in Mexico or Central America.

Owing to the complex and expensive **documentation** involved in driving through Mexico and Central America, it is worth consulting the motoring organisations in your home country, such as the AA, RAC or AAA. As well as issuing the necessary forms, they can offer advice about driving abroad. Unfortunately, useful information related specifically to driving through the region is limited. Motoring organisations can issue International Driving Permits (IDP) which are not strictly necessary for Mexico and Central America, but may be useful since they are printed in a number of foreign languages, including Spanish. An IDP is valid for one year.

When you **cross borders** with a car within Mexico and Central America allow plenty of time and have lots of money ready. At most frontiers, cars must be fumigated on entry, for which a charge is made, and there are countless other sundry fees to pay and forms to fill in. If all the paperwork is not completed by the time the border closes, you may well have to park up and go back the next morning.

Vehicular vocabulary

alquilar	to hire
alto	stop
autopista	motorway/freeway
camino cerrado	road closed
carretera	highway
ceda el paso	give way
carro	car
cuidado	take care
cuota	toll
curva peligrosa	dangerous bend
desviación	diversion, detour
desvío	turn-off
dirección única	one way
doble tracción	four-wheel drive
escape	exhaust
gasolina	petrol
gasolinera	petrol station
no adelantar	no overtaking
no estacionarse	no parking
no hay paso	road closed
peaje	toll
peatones	pedestrians
preferencia	priority
reduzca velocidad	reduce speed
silenciador	silencer
topes	sleeping policemen, bumpy road
velocidad permitida	speed limit
zona de derrumbes	landslide zone

The availability of fuel is not usually a problem along the Highway, though there are long stretches in Mexico and Costa Rica where there may not be any filling stations. So keep your tank topped up, especially if you head away from the Highway. Unleaded petrol (gasoline) is now obtainable almost everywhere, as is diesel. Fuel is sold by the US gallon (80% of the UK equivalent), and oil by the US quart (32 fluid ounces or just under one litre). The price of fuel has risen sharply along with the rising cost of crude oil. As a general rule, it is more expensive than in the USA but cheaper than in the UK.

Never leave anything in the car if it is **parked**, particularly in the capital cities. There are guarded car parks and you are strongly advised to use them. For a short period during the day, you may be able to pay a local boy to keep his eye on it for you. Alternatively a group of youths may offer to 'look after' your vehicle; you have little choice but to pay up.

Motorcycling

It would be splendid to report that Westerners on motorbikes have a much easier time than ordinary motorists. Unfortunately, it is not the case. Not only is the bureaucracy just as awful for bikers as for drivers, but the possible dangers are much increased – both in terms of personal danger, and theft. Do you really think the chains on your Harley or Honda are going to deter the professionals?

Hitch-hiking

El ride (pronounced 'ree-day') or *el lift* ('leeft'), is an extremely useful supplement to the public transport services in Mexico and Central America, particularly when you stray off the Highway. Even if you have never hitched you will find that it is an accepted and necessary way to get around. A degree of discretion is required, however. While taking lifts in the rural areas is recommended, do not hitch in the vicinity of the capital cities. At best, every taxi driver in the capital will demand to know why you are not paying him for a ride; at worst, local hoodlums will pick you and then rob you.

Hitching is often more comfortable than travelling by bus; you will almost always end up with a seat in a car, or find yourself in the back of a truck with plenty of room to stretch out, a welcome breeze and a fine view. You will also be exposed to the elements. Even if you are huddled in the back of a cement truck in a tropical rainstorm it is the most entertaining way to travel.

On roads served by comparatively few buses there is a custom of communal hitching. This involves a group of people – gathered by the side of the road, sometimes waiting for a bus – hailing any passing truck. If an empty pick-up truck is going in the right direction, everyone piles on. You can get off wherever you like. The driver expects the equivalent of the bus fare for his trouble, though this is often waived for foreigners. Indeed, you should always offer money to any driver who picks you up, though it will usually be refused. While conventional hitching is not recommended for women on their own, communal hitching is usually safe for women travellers.

End of the line for the railways

Mexico and Central America owe a great debt to the men who built the railways through the region. Every single one, from the Trans-Isthmian line through Panama, via the coast-to-coast connection across Costa Rica and the lowland lines through Nicaragua to the awesome engineering achievements in Mexico, helped build the economy and cement the society.

By the 1990s, those lines that still functioned were ponderous, much more suited to Sunday outings for admiring the scenery or enjoying the company of the locals than as means of rapid transit. As entertainment, however, they were ideal. Trains were generally open-sided, breezy, and provided good, if shaky, vantage points from which to take photographs. In addition, train fares are often half what you would have to pay for a bus ticket to cover the same journey.

A decade later, they had virtually all closed. There were rumours of one or two agricultural lines in Panama still running, and the main tourist line from Chihuahua down to the Pacific in Mexico was still running, but elsewhere lines were being torn up and stations closed down. The great unifying force of the 19th century did not make it to the end of the 20th. Strangely, the railway will still have some effect on your journey. Even though there are barely two rails to rub together, the tradition of stopping before crossing railway lines persists in Mexico and Central America.

The flyover option

If time is limited, flying is the best way to get around Mexico and Central America quickly. Planes are typically ten times faster than travelling by land, and costs about ten times as much as the corresponding bus fare. Standards of security, safety and service in flight are not what you might be used to. Meals are virtually unknown; instead, the airlines tend to ply their passengers with free liquor.

The names of airlines in Mexico and Central America look like bad hands at Scrabble – besides the two big players, Aeromexico and Mexicana, there is Tan-Sahsa, Lacsa, Taca, and Sansa. Many of the Central American airlines are now owned, or at least managed, by the well-regarded Taca consortium of Central America.

Within Mexico, fares are good – particularly if you buy tickets in advance through a specialist agent. On domestic services within the other Central America nations, they start falling to silly levels: in Panama, the maximum is $55 for the flight between the capital and David, and less than $10 for some short hops.

Your problems start when you decide to fly internationally. Reflecting the rigours of overland transport and the minimal competition between airlines, fares are high. For the 40-minute hop between San Salvador and Tegucigalpa, you can expect to pay close on $100, once miscellaneous taxes are applied. You may be able to find some cheaper flights, e.g. on Mexicana between Guatemala City and San José, or avoid some of the tax by buying outside the region. If you intend to do this, then you can consider getting full value out of the high fares by organising a Mexico City – Oaxaca – Guatemala City – San Salvador – Managua – San José – Panama City trip for around $300 one-way, the same as the non-stop flight between the Mexican and Panamanian capitals. This is for a fully flexible ticket, valid for up to a year. The problem is the departure taxes at each individual airport could add close to $100 to the total.

Nada es fácil – **nothing is easy**
However carefully you plan, you will soon find that Mexico and Central America confounds all known plans. Airlines depart when they, not you, are good and ready, while buses and officialdom take as long as they need. One consequence is that even if you meticulously plan your journey so that you arrive in big cities in broad daylight, it is certain not to work on every occasion. Arriving in Guatemala City or San Salvador after dark is a challenging experience. Get accustomed to the idea of responding flexibly to events, and to the notion of taking taxis, or go travelling somewhere else.

Keeping in touch
At my job at *The Independent* I am happy to receive all matter of calls, letters and e-mails from readers, and to give advice where possible. But I was slightly lost for words when the mother of a young woman traveller called to ask if I knew how to get in touch with her daughter. All I could do was assure her that, from Latin America, no news generally meant good news and her child was probably having the time of her life. And so it proved – the daughter kindly called me on her return to say all was well. But on the basis that your mum and/or other near and dear people may want to hear from you, rather than me, you should seriously consider getting on line.

A message
People in Mexico and Central America have taken to the **internet** just as enthusiastically as have geeks in California and publishers in Oxford. The cheapest and easiest way to stay in touch with friends, family and fellow travellers is on the world wide web, using one of the web-based e-mail services such as Microsoft's hotmail. All the internet cafés along the Highway offer easy access to these services, subject to the vagaries of the local telecommunications operator. Usually, they work well in Mexico, Costa Rica and Panama (where prices are also highest, at up to $5 per hour), malfunction in Nicaragua, and everywhere else in between is in between.

A stamp
Letters from Mexico and Central America take between five days and three weeks to reach Britain. Postal services from Mexico, Panama and Costa Rica are

the fastest, Nicaragua the slowest. The chances that your postcard will arrive quickly will be greatly enhanced if you post letters in the capital city or big towns. Collections from rural offices (few countries have mail boxes) may be only once or twice a week.

Any of your friends, relations or bank manager who are not yet online can write to you care of the *lista de correos* (poste restante) at a nominated post office in Mexico or Central America. While in theory letters could be sent to any post office in the region, you are advised to use only the central office in the capital city, where they are used to handling the poste restante service.

Good connections

apartado de correos	post office box
buzón	mail box
centro telefónico	telephone exchange
correo	post
correo central	main post office
larga distancia	long distance
lista de correos	poste restante
llamada por cobrar	collect (reverse-charge) call
oficina de correos	post office
paquete	parcel
periódico	newspaper
por avión	air mail
recogida	(postal) collection
sello, estampilla	stamp
sobre	envelope
tarifa	rate
teléfono	telephone
telegrama	telegram

Some offices, such as Managua, will ask you to prove your identity when you collect mail; others, like that in Panama City, will even let you take away letters for a friend. Similarly, while some offices return mail to the sender's address after a month, the majority throw out letters that have been hanging around gathering dust. If you are expecting a letter that doesn't appear to have arrived, check under your first name too in case your letter has been filed wrongly. It is sometimes necessary to pay a few cents to pick up mail. Never have anything of value, or anything that looks as if it could be valuable, sent to you.

Alternatively, you can ask people to write to a particular hotel. They should mark the envelope *esperar* ('to wait the arrival of') followed by your name.

A call

Telephone systems in Mexico and Central America vary from highly efficient (in Mexico) to chaotic (Nicaragua). They all, however, use the same system of tones as the rest of the Caribbean and North America, i.e. a constant buzz or tone before you begin to dial, long rings with even longer pauses when you connect, or short, frequent beeps if the line is engaged. You will also hear the continuous 'number unobtainable' tone more often than you might care to.

In the 21st century, you can dial numbers in the region direct from the UK and North America. Country codes start with 51 for Mexico, then continue through the isthmus in the same order as the chapters in this book: Guatemala 502; El Salvador 503; Honduras 504; Nicaragua 505; Costa Rica 506; Panama 507. (If you misdial, the prefix 500 routes your call to the Falkland Islands.)

To dial a number in Central America, use the international access code (00 from the UK), the country code, the area code if any (without the initial zero) and the number. Thus to call the British Embassy in Panama City from the UK, dial 00 507 69-0866. Note that a significant proportion of attempts fail, and that if you get a ringing tone it doesn't actually mean that a telephone is ringing somewhere in Central America. After you've held on for a while, try again.

If you are **calling abroad** from Mexico and Central America, it is usually easiest to find a telephone office. Every town of any size has a *centro telefónico*. A typical one looks like a waiting room, with a number of poorly insulated booths where calls are made. You can make long-distance and international calls with relative ease. The operators rarely speak English, but this is not usually a problem since all you need to do is to write down the number and wait. You will find it helps if you add the country code (1 for the USA and Canada, 44 for the UK). The dial-out code for all countries is 00. You must usually pay for the estimated cost of a three-minute call in advance, and this will be refunded in full if no connection is made.

Charges are high: typically $12 for three minutes to the USA, $20 to Europe – which could buy you a whole day on the internet. Person-to-person calls cost about one-third more than ordinary station-to-station rates. Collect (reverse-charge) calls may be made from most countries, but whoever you ring will be appalled when they get the bill for the call.

Reading, listening, watching

Mexican and Central American newspapers suffer from a preponderance of gory photographs and reliance on wire services, rather than original journalism, for their news stories. Nevertheless, since you are travelling in a region where turmoil and disaster is not unheard of, it is wise to keep abreast of the situation by reading the paper everyday. The most common English-language newspapers are *USA Today* and the international edition of the *Miami Herald*. The British newspaper you are most likely to find is the *Financial Times*.

The biggest choice of decent **radio** stations can be found near the Texan border. Elsewhere, the British forces radio network BFBS can be picked up in parts of eastern Mexico and Guatemala thanks to its transmitter in Belize, while its US counterpart AFN is still easy to receive in Panama. The best source of news is the BBC World Service. It is broadcast to Central America on various short wave frequencies, but there is also a Caribbean relay station on medium wave (940kHz AM) which means you may be able to pick it up on an ordinary receiver. BBC Radio domestic programmes are available in real time on the internet at bbc.co.uk.

Most Mexican and Central American **television** is so crass that the material picked up from US satellite stations looks good by comparison. Increasingly many hotels offer satellite TV, which often includes BBC World.

A room

Accommodation in Mexico and Central America ranges from the luxurious to the uncomfortable and positively insanitary, but fortunately there are plenty of places which fall somewhere in between. With the rise in visitor numbers, some unscrupulous proprietors have opened unsavoury hotels to exploit the expanding tourism market. Always insist upon inspecting the room offered, checking in particular for protection against mosquitoes, and security against thieves. Don't hesitate to look under the covers for interesting wildlife. As a rule, the smaller the town the more basic the accommodation will be.

Payment in advance is generally expected. Hotels require passport details, which they either enter in a book, or ask you to fill out on a form. Others will demand your passport – try to avoid leaving it with them, since the police may

Room with a vocabulary

agua caliente	hot water
aire condicionado	air-conditioning
cucurcha	cockroach
cama	bed
con baño	with bathroom
desayuno	breakfast
doble	double
habitación	room
hamaca	hammock
huésped	guest
jabon	soap
lavandería	laundry
mosquitero	mosquito net
piso	floor (storey)
planta baja	ground floor
pulga	flea
rata	rat
saco de dormir	sleeping bag
servicios	toilet
sencillo	single (room)
tienda (de campaña)	tent
toalla	towel
ventilador	fan

demand to see it if they stop you while you are out and about. The one thing you can rely upon in Mexico and Central America is excellent value for money compared with costs in Europe and the USA.

What do you expect for 40 pence?

This question was never asked, because it did not need to be. The fact that there were four walls, a roof and an electric light included in the price of four quetzales (then $0.65 or 40 pence) meant there could be no arguments about the value of the converted stables in Escuintla, southern Guatemala. For goodness' sake, there was even a bed, though the springs had seen a fatal amount of action and the mattress comprised a biological experiment that was threatening to get out of hand.

No windows, though this turned out to be an advantage: the raucous engines and foul exhaust fumes of the trucks and buses passing within a few centimetres of the outer wall were slightly muted by the time they reached the interior. The ill-fitting door on the facing wall creaked open upon an informal urban farmyard, where scraggy chickens ran around the domestic wreckage doing a pretty good impression of headlessness.

They refused to acknowledge the onset of darkness, keeping up a high-frequency chorus of discontent all night long. Similarly, the temperature and humidity refused to decline with the sun, turning the room into a putrid, airless cell. I didn't wake at dawn, because I hadn't slept. As the first light inspired fowl *fortissimo*, I fled the Hostal Familiar, leapt aboard the first bus out of Escuintla and vowed to move to unfamiliar upmarket accommodation. That night, the Hotel Colonial in Guatemala was worth every one of the ten dollars I paid.

Hotels are at the top of the scale. Most hotels provide a fan or even air-conditioning, towels and soap, and toilet paper. The availability of hot water should never be taken for granted, unless you are staying in an upmarket establishment. During the low season don't hesitate to ask for a discount.

Hospedajes and **pensiones** are at the lower end of the scale but are often indistinguishable from cheap hotels. They may consist of just a few rooms forming part of a private home – often quite basic, but generally clean. Private washing facilities are rare. In some places you must pay extra for hot water; don't expect a discount if the electricity is cut off.

Mexico and Costa Rica have networks of **youth hostels** which are affiliated to the International Youth Hostels Federation. Most of these are in isolated areas and are worth considering. Youth hostels are unlikely to catch on in the region because of the low cost of ordinary accommodation.

Preaching to the convertor

You may wish to take a radio with you, and even a travel iron or hair dryer. Before you pack, make sure that they will work correctly on the local electricity supply. This is the same as elsewhere in the Americas, i.e. 110 volts at 60 Hz, compared to the European supply of around 240 volts at 50 Hz. Some equipment is switchable between these voltages and frequencies, but other items will not work correctly at the lower voltage, and those with motors will run too fast. You can buy a convertor, but for most cheap bits of kit you might as well just buy new.

Power cuts, voltage drops and frequency fluctuations are regular occurences, so think twice before plugging in sensitive equipment such as a portable computer. Most electrical sockets in the region accept plugs with two flat or round pins. Travel adaptors sold abroad should be able to cope with the sockets. Note that there is rarely an earth pin, and that the state of most electrical fittings is dreadful; an alarming number of hotel rooms have bare live wires showing, even in the shower.

Camping

If you plan to go off the beaten track, or deep into Panama, you can expect to have to use your initiative when it comes to finding somewhere to sleep. In some places you may be able to stay with one of the locals if there is no formal accommodation. This cannot always be relied upon, so you are likely to end up **camping**. If you don't bring a tent from home, invest in a hammock; although quite bulky they are not heavy to carry. You should be able to buy one in most good Mexican and Central American markets; a decent one might cost $40. If you plan to camp or sleep out you should also buy a mosquito net and plaster on plenty of insect repellent. A sleeping bag is unnecessary unless you plan to do a lot of high-altitude camping.

Smelling of lavandería

Having your clothes washed is one of the modest luxuries of travel in Central America. Most cheap hotels will organise it for you, or there are plenty of laundries (*lavanderías*) in towns. A rucksackful of unsavoury clothes might cost $2 to be thoroughly cleansed. The washing is usually so good that you'll find it hard to believe the launderer hasn't gone out and bought brand-new replicas of all your clothes.

A meal

If you don't like the food, stay out of the region. Those for whom eating is an essential part of the travel experience will find Mexico and Central America to be a kind of economy-class heaven, where most things are good, fresh and nutritious. Though you can't expect everything (or, perhaps, anything) to be served with the kind of panache you would find in the USA or Europe, it will usually be cooked with kind heart and a low price.

Many of the staple dishes found throughout the region would be described by Europeans and North Americans simply as 'Mexican'. The cuisine is maize-

Eat your way through Mexico and Central America

arroz	rice
asado	roast
autoservicio	self-service
azúcar	sugar
boca	tapa, snack
cantina	bar
carne	meat
cocido	cooked
comedor	simple restaurant, dining room
cuchara	spoon
cuchillo	knife
cuenta	bill
desayuno	breakfast
emparedado	sandwich
frijoles	beans
huevo	egg
jamón	ham
naranja	orange
pan	bread
panaderiá	bakery
pasteleriá	cake shop
pescado	fish
a la plancha	grilled
plátano	plantain (like a banana)
pollo	chicken
tenedor	fork

based: this is found extensively in the flour used in the various kinds of pancakes (sometimes soft, sometimes crisp), which feature in most meals. These include:

tortillas – soft and served as an accompaniment to whatever else you order.

enchiladas – tortillas rolled up and stuffed with meat, cheese or vegetables.

tacos – the same, except the tortilla is fried and therefore crispy.

quesadillas – tortillas made with cheese, sometimes served stuffed.

tamales – made of a thick corn dough rolled and stuffed and baked in banana leaves; they look delicious, but in fact they take the definition of the word stodgy to new extremes.

empanados – deep-fried meat-filled pasties, often sold on the streets.

Despite the number of avocados grown in the region, *guacamole* (mashed avocado with tomato, coriander, etc.) is often hard to find. It is most common in Guatemala.

Do not expect to find 'Mexican-style' food in every restaurant; in small towns you are unlikely to find it anywhere. It can therefore be as much of a treat as it is back home. Red kidney beans or *frijoles* (often cooked into a pulp) and rice are as vital a part of the local diet as tortillas, and are served up far more frequently than the Mexican delights described above. *Gallo pinto* (or simply *pinto*) is the common term to describe an amalgam of rice and beans; at its most basic it may be just that, but it can also include peppers, chilli and tomatoes, and is very tasty. Throughout much of Mexico and Central America most meals revolve around gallo pinto. It will arrive with a number of accompaniments, such as a lump of meat or a stew of some kind, a fried egg, fried plantain (fried bananas), tortillas, and so on. This is commonly known as *plato típico*, or sometimes *comida típica* or *comida corriente* – dish of the day is a loose translation. Sometimes it is delicious, at others cold and unappetising; either way you will undoubtedly end up eating a lot of it, not least for breakfast. In most places, however, you can usually order eggs, either fried (*frito*) or scrambled (*revueltos*) for your morning meal. Only in places accustomed to travellers' tastes will you find fruit salads, pancakes and toast.

One of the best dishes in Central America is the *pupusa*, a stuffed tortilla native to El Salvador. Salvadorean refugees have set up pupuserías all over the region, and these are often lively places to eat. One pupusa makes a nice snack, three or four make an ample meal.

Chicken and beef are the only meats worth eating in Central America. Pork, goat and lamb are sometimes available, but are not recommended. For a more interesting meal try iguana (*garrobo*), found particularly in Nicaragua and El Salvador, although it features on few restaurant menus. Tripe (*mondongo*) is also fairly popular; it is usually served in a soup (*sopa*), but is very much an acquired taste. Of more immediate appeal is cassava (*yuca*) which serves as a vegetable. It is common in Panama and Nicaragua and is a flavoursome alternative to potato.

Central America has an extensive coastline in proportion to its size and there is a fine supply of fish and seafood. When the monotony of gallo pinto gets too much, the Atlantic coast can supply lobster, shrimps and other pleasures which are likely to be among the tastiest things you can eat in the region. The preparation of seafood is particularly interesting in the Garifuna communities which use coconut in much of their cooking. Be careful where you eat shellfish since it is a common source of disease.

One of the fishy delights of Mexico and Central America which luckily is not found only along the coasts is *ceviche*. This is raw fish marinated in lime juice that is chopped up with tomatoes, onion, chilli and coriander. (Don't worry unduly about eating raw fish – the lime juice kills off most known germs.) It is usually served with a few crackers and is the perfect snack, usually costing 50c-$1. So obsessed do some travellers become with ceviche that they have to track down a cevichería in every town; surprisingly, these exist in even some of the more remote villages – they are often popular meeting places for the locals.

Foreign cuisine can be found principally in the capital cities, although Chinese restaurants turn up in an astonishing number of places. The most obvious influence is from the USA. It is easy to get the impression that Central America is one enormous fast food emporium – if you get a sudden craving for McDonalds, Kentucky Fried Chicken or Dunkin' Donuts, you can satisfy it in any Central American city.

The exotic fruit is one of the joys of travelling in the tropics. Everything from bananas and pineapple to papaya and coconut is available in the markets, and people set themselves up as purveyors of fruit snacks – they peel pineapples, oranges, etc. ready to eat on the spot, and costing just a few cents. Street traders sell all manner of things, and itinerant ice cream vendors walk the streets jingling a bell to attract attention. Unfortunately, it is inadvisable to eat the ice cream – the stuff is often prepared in insanitary conditions, made from questionable local water and possibly re-frozen a number of times.

Restaurants in the traditional sense are few and far between in most towns and villages since they are too expensive for the local people. Instead they eat in simple places known as *comedores* which may be a simple shack or a table and bench in the market – join them there.

A drink

The beers and rums of Mexico and Central America are described in each country section. Beer tends to be characterless, standard fizzy lager. The cheapest spirit is *aguardiente*, a rough distillation made from sugar cane. Rum is smoother and more expensive. Prices for imported liquor are high: wine costs around $5 for the worst sort of plonk, while a bottle of good whisky may be $50.

For a region so well-endowed with tropical fruits, there is a distressing tendency towards sweet and fizzy drinks rather than natural fruit juices. In a typical city street there may be dozens of vendors selling Coke and Fanta, but none offering fresh fruit juice. Local concoctions in bottles are usually hideously sweet. Bottled mineral water is sold only rarely by soft drink sellers.

Drink your way through Mexico and Central America

agua mineral, soda	bottled mineral water
botella	bottle
cerveza	beer
jugo	juice
hielo	ice
hora feliz	happy hour
leche	milk
licuado	liquidised fruit drink
refresco	soft drink (both fizzy and otherwise)
ron	rum
trago	shot
vino	wine

Stick to the fruit juices if you want to quench your thirst or save money. They can range from tamarind to coconut milk and are often sold in plastic bags at bus stops – just bite a hole in one corner and suck. Fruit juice sold in shops is seldom pure, so seek out stalls where juice is served out of a big tub or where you can watch the oranges being squeezed; whole young coconuts, whose milk you suck through a straw, are also popular.

Licuados are liquidised fruit drinks which can be made either with water (*con agua*) or with milk (*con leche*), and nearly always with sugar unless you ask for it to be left out. They are almost invariably delicious but are not as common as the usual fruit juices – they are found most commonly in those places used to a large number of travellers passing through. One final soft drink worth trying is *horchata*, made of rice water and flavoured with cinnamon; the quality varies a lot but it can be delicious and is very thirst-quenching.

The experience

If you want the very finest examples of **archaeological sites** along the Highway, there are three specific targets: Teoutihuacán, just north of Mexico City, Monte Albán just outside Oaxaca in southern Mexico, and the San Andrés/Joya de Cerén complex of El Salvador. This omits, of course, the great Mayan sites in Guatemala and Honduras. The ruins in these countries are the most developed for tourists, but they are usually a long way from the Pan-American Highway.

Mayan methods

If you decide to visit places like Palenque in Mexico, Tikal in Guatemala and Copán in Honduras, you should be aware of the common features of these and other Mayan sites. The basic design of a ceremonial centre consists of a central plaza, surrounded by several lesser ones, each with temples, acropoli and other buildings such as palaces:

acropolis: a Greek word, used to describe a raised platform on top of which stand a number of temples.

ball court: with a wall on either side, the court was used for a game called pelota played between two teams (with religious significance perhaps, or just for entertainment).

pyramid: usually built facing each other across a plaza. A staircase leads to a small temple at the top. Notables were buried in tombs beneath the pyramid.

stela (plural *stelae*): a carved stone slab usually used as a monument or gravestone, often inscribed with pictures or glyphs recording dates, names of rulers, important events, etc.

Mexico has several superb **museums**; Central America has fewer, but they are almost all worth making a diversion for. This may not always be because of the exhibits themselves so much as the buildings in which they are housed – often in some of the loveliest old colonial palaces.

In Mexico, the museums of Monterrey, Oaxaca and the capital are the best. In Central America, the vast majority of museums are in the capital cities, and this is also where you'll find the best collections: from the one in San José's jade museum or the pre-Columbian ceramics in the Popol Vuh in Guatemala City to Museos de la Revolución in Nicaragua (if there are any left by the time you get there). The provincial museums can be equally informative and frequently more entertaining, whether they contain a dusty array of colonial relics or a room full of mannequins dressed up in the local costume.

Labelling is almost entirely in Spanish, except in certain museums in Mexico and Guatemala. There is normally a small admission fee.

A night out

Few people go to Central America expecting to find much in the way of formal entertainment. This is just as well, since contemporary culture in most of the region consists of pool halls and cinemas showing Rambo-style movies.

Films shown in Mexico and Central America are almost all violent, macho and sexist, in that order. Many films come from the US, in the original language but with Spanish subtitles. Regular outings to the **theatre** are unlikely to feature in your schedule unless you spend a good deal of time in the capital cities. Each has its own 'national theatres', but the staging of shows is a somewhat erratic business. Programmes may be published in the newspapers, but you would do better to go direct to the theatre box office, preferably in the evening since they are often closed during the day.

The closest some travellers come to live **music** in Mexico and Central America is a trio of ageing guitarists doing the rounds of the local restaurants, or a couple of kids banging out a rhythm on an old box. Indeed those who do not devote some time and effort seeking out the local venues or finding out about forthcoming events, may well come away disappointed. The amount of music and **dance** performed is proportionate to the size of the indigenous population, although both arts show an interesting blend of pre-Columbian and Hispanic influences. Percussion and wind instruments were popular before the Conquest, but stringed instruments, brought by the Spanish in the 16th century, have also become an integral part of Mexico and Central American folk music traditions. Other forms of music were introduced, and many native rhythms and dances were adapted to European musical patterns.

The *marimba*, which some believe originated in Africa, is the most commonly played instrument in the region. It is rather like a xylophone and is made up of strips of wood beneath which are sound-boxes; these were originally gourds, but are now man-made. Marimbas vary in size and can be so large that up to seven players are required. Although your only chance to see a marimba band may be in one of the upmarket hotels where the players are paid to entertain package tourists, there are roving bands all over the region which give spontaneous performances in the local markets or bars. Marimba bands are most common in Guatemala where many towns have their own resident mini-orchestra. Panama, to the south of Costa Rica, has only a marginally bigger indigenous population, and yet it has the most flourishing music and dance scene after Guatemala. While most Central American countries have been influenced by Mexico, Panama's influence comes from the Caribbean and countries in the north of South America, particularly Colombia.

Many dances originated in Spain and have been coloured by local influences. The most famous is the Danza de la Conquista, which is based on the so-called Moors and Christians dance of the Spanish. It is a strange sight to watch the local people re-enact the Conquest, since the Spanish invariably win. The significance of the dance is of no great importance, however, and everyone simply has a good time and gets roaring drunk.

A game

The late Bill Shankly, former manager of Liverpool FC, once said 'football isn't a matter of life and death – it's much more important than that'. Never underestimate the average Central American's interest in **soccer**. Even in remote corners of the region, British visitors have been closely questioned on Arsenal's prospects for the coming season or the chances of Manchester United coming a cropper in the next decade or two. Mexico has historically under-achieved – it has staged two World Cups, but never reached the final – and none of the nations of Central America has a sufficient population base or depth of skill to succeed at a global level.

Nevertheless, every town and village has its own soccer pitch, and in some places it forms the main square of a village. Soccer is played everywhere and with great enthusiasm – watch a game on weekday evenings or at weekends, or join a kick-around. The official season runs from March to November or December.

It is not surprising that **baseball** is so popular in an area which has been so heavily influenced by the USA. Ironically its greatest following is in Nicaragua, where the game is even more popular than soccer. Most large towns have a general-purpose sports stadium, which is used predominantly to stage baseball games. Watching a game is an excellent pastime at weekends or on midweek evenings. Any young local should be able to tell you when the next game is.

Basketball and **American football** also have a significant following, particularly in Mexico.

A swim

Guatemala undoubtedly has the worst collection of **beaches** in the region. Mexico and the other Central American countries battle over the prize for who has the best – most of them can boast sandy, palm-fringed beaches along at least part of their coast. Mexico would win easily, except that many of the best beaches are a long way from then Pan-American Highway. The most accessible good resort is Zipolite, which you can reach from Oaxaca.

Many beaches throughout the region remain unspoilt; this is a problem if you're keen on beachside bars and other side industries (don't expect a roaring nightlife), but blissful if you want to escape crowds and commercialism. Those who opt for the most remote beaches will probably have to depend on a hammock, a tent or on the hospitality of one of the locals when it comes to finding somewhere to sleep.

Costa Rica has plenty of fine beaches along the Pacific shore; and although some of these have been developed for the American tourist market, it is not difficult to find quieter, and more secluded places. There is a good alternative route to the Pan-American Highway that takes you along the Costa Rican coast to many of these. The same applies in El Salvador.

Safe swimming

The strongest currents occur along the Pacific coast, and certain beaches are infamous for the height or power of the waves. While this may attract surfers or strong swimmers, it can also be dangerous. Lifeguards and red warning flags are rare. At unattended stretches of beach, you need to be able to identify potential problems – notably the rip current.

Rip currents are typically formed by a body of water approaching the shore; the water level is built up and the water is then sucked rapidly back out to sea. Such currents are usually associated with wave action: the larger the waves, the more powerful the rip.

Before entering the water, have a look at the wave patterns. Rip currents can usually be identified by a large streak of discoloured water extending from the shore beyond the surf line. This is easy in otherwise crystal- clear waters, less so in the brown windsor soup on some British beaches. Other signs to look for include waves breaking further out from the beach, at the edges of the track of water forming the rip; debris such as weed stretching out from the shore in a parallel tract; or a similar tract of foam extending beyond the surf line.

Sometimes a rip can occur with little or no warning. If you get caught in one, don't panic. A swimmer of limited ability should ride with the current and swim parallel to the beach for 30 or 40 metres, then swim to shore on a perpendicular course. Strong swimmers should swim at a 45-degree angle across the rip, and in the same direction as the prevailing side current.

Breaking waves are potentially lethal. Plunging waves, known as dumpers, break with tremendous force and can throw an adult straight to the shallow bottom. When large plunging waves are seen at the edge of the beach even experienced swimmers should take care.

Surging waves, which never break as they approach a beach, contain an enormous amount of energy. They can carry swimmers out into deeper waters, and are especially dangerous around rocks. Turn sideways to reduce the wave's impact, or dive beneath it and keep as flat to the sand as you can before surfacing.

– Dr Steve Ray, former RNLI lifeboatman, and currently Senior Lecturer in Clinical Physiology at Oxford Brookes University

Nicaragua's Pacific beaches are not as impressive as the sweeping sandy shores of El Salvador, but the island of Omotepe in Lake Nicaragua is a good alternative for people wanting to escape from the rat-race on the Highway. Panama's most accessible beaches are on the Pacific coast west of the capital, and the Pan-American Highway almost touches the sea at several points, though they are highly developed. The best option is probably to nip across to the Atlantic coast and head for Isla Grande.

The outdoors: how great?
There is plenty of good scenery along the Pan-American Highway through Mexico and Central America, though in places you may forget this – near the Texan border, through the Isthmus of Tehuantepec and in Panama east of the capital, for example. The region has some wonderful wilderness, but tramping through the highlands of Mexico and Central America is not as easy as it sounds. There are no trails geared for recreational purposes except in the national parks, most of which are in Mexico and Costa Rica. Nevertheless, since in rural areas many people get around on foot there are tracks linking small villages; many of these are old Indian mule trails. Of course these paths won't necessarily take you along a circular route as you may be used to in the west, but you can usually piece together walks yourself. Ask the local people for suggestions, or for directions en route; but remember that the locals rarely go walking for pleasure, so expect most of them to think you mad.

Take local advice at all times. Wherever you decide to hike you would be ill-advised to go alone, since robbery in isolated areas is not unheard of. Try to obtain topographical maps of any area you wish to explore. These are produced by the Instituto Geográfico Nacional (or its equivalent) in each country. Unfortunately they are not on general release since most Central American governments like to keep tabs on who buys them. Permission from the Defence Ministry may be necessary before you can get hold of them.

The **flora and fauna** of Central America (but not so much Mexico) provide a greater natural wealth of flowers, birds and wildlife than almost anywhere else in the world. Even the most uninterested visitor is likely to be thrilled by a

---

Elusive, but not yet extinct: the quetzal
One creature you'll be very fortunate to see is the quetzal. It is a magnificently coloured bird, sadly faced with extinction. Quetzals exist in appreciable numbers only in remote parts of Central America, and your best chance of seeing one is in Guatemala (where it is the national bird) or Costa Rica. The male bird is a stunning sight, a mass of brilliant green, red, black and silver plumage; one traveller describes them as 'bonsai peacocks'. The feathers are extremely sought-after, and hunters and egg-collectors have nearly made the quetzal extinct, especially after swathes of its previous habitat were destoyed when the jungle was cleared.

particularly colourful butterfly or orchid, or charmed by monkeys swinging inquisitively down from the trees. By the end of your visit you may be adept at spotting a three-toed sloth high in a tree, or even a crocodile lurking on the river bank.

One of the more common species of bird is the cattle egret, a small white heron seen in fields and marshes feeding off the insects disturbed by the feet of cattle. Less pleasant are the hundreds of vultures which scavenge for food on rubbish tips and are often seen circling around in the sky. More comical are the brown pelicans which are seen all over the region along the coast. The best time to go birdwatching is in the early morning or late afternoon.

Animal life is more elusive, although few travellers who have gone hiking through the jungle come away without seeing monkeys, usually the black howler which is named after its piercing cry. Another species to look out for is the peccary or wild pig – not the world's most beautiful creatures, but one of the least shy in Central America.

How to stay alive. And well

Mexico and Central America enjoy a higher proportion of delightful vistas, and exotic flora and fauna than anywhere else in the world, but they probably also have a greater concentration of threats to health than most places you're used to. The problems of staying healthy in the tropics, where sanitation is poor and disease is widespread, are exacerbated by the range of disasters waiting to befall you: from a stomach upset to malaria, and from sunburn to hurricanes. Even so, few travellers encounter anything more serious than a bout of diarrhoea as their system adjusts to alien food. The following advice, coupled with sensible precautions and medical assistance, should ensure that distress, disease and disaster do not spoil your trip.

Get tough on the causes of death, injury or illness. The list of threats against you is so long that it would be ridiculous not to minimise at least the known enemies, notably preventable diseases. Once you know where you are going, seek advice about what precautions are necessary. Your GP may know something about tropical diseases, but you are strongly advised to go to a specialised centre where doctors are experienced in dealing with travellers. MASTA (Medical Advisory Services for Travellers Abroad) runs an excellent database, which you can access by calling 09068 224 100, a premium-rate service costing £1 per minute. You give details of where you are going and what you intend to do, and a personalised health brief is despatched. In conjunction with MASTA, British Airways has set up clinics to cater specifically for travellers, administering immunisations and malaria tablets as well as giving out more general advice. These British Airways Travel Clinics can be found all over the UK, from Purley to Manchester; call 020 7831 5333 to find out the number of the one nearest you.

Read *Travellers' Health: How to Stay Healthy Abroad* by Richard Dawood (Oxford University Press) which is a comprehensive, up-to-date and readable guide for anyone concerned about their health. Dr Dawood is one of very few British people to have crossed the Darién Gap by land, so he knows both the theory and practice of tropical medicine.

The Tropical Traveller by John Hatt (Pan) provides invaluable practical information on travelling in hot countries and an entertaining introduction to the physiological and psychological surprises which await you. Lonely Planet's *Healthy Travel* series has a volume devoted to Central and South America. A good source of online help is the US Center for Disease Control and Prevention (cdc.gov).

Do not assume that you will be able to obtain the **medicines** you might need, and any that you do find are likely to be expensive. Take supplies of any medication you require, together with a copy of the prescription: this should avoid problems at Customs.

Women are unlikely to find **tampons** (*tampones*) anywhere in Central America, although sanitary towels are sometimes available. The only widely available contraceptives are condoms, and the quality of these is dubious, so take any contraception with you.

Mountain high

Much of Mexico and Central America is higher than the tallest mountain in Britain (1,219m/4,024 feet). Altitude sickness affects different people at different heights, but most are unlikely to feel the affects of the thinness of the air until they have reached about 2,400m (8,000 feet). Taking a climb in stages means your body will be able to adapt to the reduced level of oxygen. If you experience symptoms ranging from headaches and breathlessness to nausea and palpitations, you should rest and continue at a slower pace. Should there be no improvement, the best and safest treatment is descent; those attempting to go any higher risk, in severe cases, contracting pulmonary or cerebral oedema. Diamox, which you take before you reach high altitudes and continue to do so until you descend, seems to help acclimatisation but is not a cure. It also has some alarming side effects such as making your fingertips tingle and making soft drinks taste odd.

Other altitude problems include dehydration, sunburn and fluid retention. Hiking up mountains and volcanoes can also be cold, particularly if you need to sleep out. A sleeping bag is essential as are numerous layers of clothing or jumpers. It is tempting to drink copious amounts of alcohol to warm yourself up, but this is not recommended at altitude. High altitudes can affect menstrual cycles too: periods may last for two or three weeks and then return after a few days, and cramps may be worse than usual.

Restless earth

Earthquakes and volcanic eruptions occur with worrying frequency in Mexico and Central America. Earthquakes have left many towns permanently scarred, particularly in central Mexico, Guatemala, Nicaragua and Costa Rica. There are fairly frequent minor quakes, but these are rarely alarming unless warnings of more serious activity to follow have been broadcast. If you are in a building during a strong quake stand in a doorway or shelter under a strong piece of furniture.

The volcanic chain which runs through Mexico and Central America contains a number of active volcanoes. Many of these have erupted in the past, burying towns and villages in the process, but the only evidence of seismic activity you are likely to see nowadays is a string of smoke coming out of the odd crater. However, a few also spit out molten rock and strong sulphurous fumes, and you should not attempt to climb them.

Some handy information about natural disaster preparedness is available via the internet from the US Federal Emergency Management Agency (FEMA) at fema.gov

Angry skies

Hurricane Mitch tore through Central America in 1998, wreaking especial devastation on Nicaragua and Honduras. The Caribbean areas of these countries were most severely affected, but there are chunks of the Pan-American Highway in Honduras that were washed away by the ensuing floods. If you are caught in a hurricane try to find a ditch to lie in and keep well away from anything which might be blown on top of you.

Getting warmer

If you are not accustomed to the heat of the tropics, allow time to adjust. To avoid collapsing from heat exhaustion in the first week, wear suitable clothing and a hat to keep as much of the sun off as possible. Drink plenty of non-alcoholic fluids, and avoid over-exertion until you acclimatise. If you experience headaches, lethargy or giddiness after a long day outside, you probably have a mild case of heat exhaustion caused by a water deficiency; drink plenty of water and sit in the shade until the symptoms subside. Your body's requirements of salt also rise dramatically in the heat so compensate for this by adding salt to your meals.

Heatstroke is the failure of your body's heat control mechanisms. This causes headaches and delirium, and must be treated immediately; remove all your clothes, cover yourself with a wet sheet (or similar) to stop the body temperature from rising further, and seek medical help. Heatstroke must be taken seriously since if the body temperature continues to rise the effects can be fatal. This same condition is often described as sunstroke, but this is misleading since it can occur when you haven't been in direct sunlight.

Prickly heat is the most common heat-related skin problem. It can usually be prevented by following your mother's advice: having frequent showers, keeping your skin clean and dry, and by wearing loose, non-synthetic clothes. The best treatment is calamine lotion. Since the condition is caused by the blockage of sweat ducts avoid any exertion which would induce excessive sweating.

Glaring errors

It is tempting for those escaping a cold European winter (or summer) to ignore their better judgement and spend a whole day on the beach as soon as they arrive. You should, however, expose yourself to the sun as gradually as you do to the heat. If you are unfortunate enough to be sunburnt, apply calamine lotion or cold cream liberally, or soak a towel in cold water and place it over the most tender areas. For burns use a mild antiseptic and keep the skin clean and dry.

Deadly drink?

The local water supply is usually safe in most of Mexico, Costa Rica, Panama and in the bigger towns and cities elsewhere. But a waterborne bug – be it a disease or parasite – could wreck your trip, so you may prefer to buy bottled water (not available everywhere) or to take some method of water-purification. The most effective method is liquid iodine which kills both bacteria and amoebic cysts; chlorine-based purifiers do not. Allow six drops per litre of water and wait at least 20 minutes. Since the tincture comes in glass bottles that can break easily, you are advised to transfer it to a non-breakable container before you leave. Using iodine continuously for more than six months is considered unsafe, so if you are going on a long trip you may decide to opt for chlorine-based tablets. Of those currently on the market the most palatable are Puritabs, which take effect in just ten minutes.

You won't be able to purify an entire lake, so avoid swimming in obviously dirty water where parasites and diseases can be picked up this way. Lake Atitlán in Guatemala, for example, is said to be heavily contaminated.

Ticking off those leeches

Lots of creatures just can't wait to get their teeth into you. As far as getting rid of a tick is concerned, applying a cigarette does not work, and nail polish remover is not the most useful thing to carry around Central America; take tweezers instead – these are generally the best thing for easing the head of the tick away from the skin.

Leeches are a nuisance, but they do not carry disease. If you don't wish to wait for the leech to drink its fill of blood, you can remove it by sprinkling it with salt or alcohol. Applying a hot cigerette is likely just to smell horrid and make a mess.

Snakes and scorpions

These threats increase the further south and east you go. The most common poisonous snake found in the Central American jungle is the fer de lance (terciopelo). Since snakes hunt mainly at night, you would have to be extremely unlucky to come face to face with one. If you do, don't panic, remember that the snake will be more frightened of you than you are of it, and move away (without treading on any of his pals). If you are bitten try to kill the snake to make identification easier; alternatively, remember what it looks like. Seek medical advice immediately.

Only a small number of travellers encounter scorpions. Although they can be dangerously venomous, their bite is rarely fatal. If you are unfortunate enough to have one in your room you should tell the management who will probably be better prepared to do battle with it; a heavy saucepan is a suitable weapon whereas a paperback book is not. If you are stung, rest, drink lots of water and call a doctor.

The world's nastiest creature

The mosquito kills at least one million people each year by infecting them with malaria or other fatal diseases, and causes suffering among millions of others – including a good number of travellers. Avoiding their bites is of prime importance. They bite primarily at dusk and dawn, so this is when you must be at your most vigilant. Those that spread dengue fever – a gruesome but not usually fatal illness – confuse matters by biting during the day. At nightfall cover your limbs and apply insect repellent to exposed parts. Sleeping in a room with screened windows is not always possible in budget hotels, so if you do not have your own net, smother yourself in repellent and sleep with (a) your clothes and (b) the fan on. If you plan to spend much time in jungle or rural areas, take your own mosquito net.

Of the insect repellents that you can buy in the West the most effective are those containing high concentrations of DEET. Use it liberally to avoid contracting one of the following nasty diseases.

Malaria is the most serious health hazard facing travellers to Mexico and, especially, Central America. Every *day*, six Britons contract malaria somewhere in the world, and there is an average of one death each month. Fatal cases are relatively rare, but it is a thoroughly unpleasant disease, as well as being recurrent. Anti-malaria tablets cannot guarantee protection, but they reduce the severity of the illness and decrease the risk of fatal complications.

Jaws too

Sharks are found off certain stretches of the coasts of Central America. The most common species you are likely to come across is the nurse shark, never more than two metres (six feet) long, which is unlikely to leave you in need of something rather more heavy-duty than a puncture repair kit.

Bob Brannan, of the US dive company Aquatic Encounters (001 303 494 8384), says the most dangerous area for attacks by Great White Sharks (the Jaws species) is the so-called 'Golden Triangle' off the coast of San Francisco, southern Australia and South Africa. The next most serious threat, from the Tiger Shark, is around Hawaii and coast of Japan

'Most sharks are real cautious of what they attack', he says. If you have a close encounter of the shark kind, don't wield anything that our toothy pal could interpret as a weapon. 'Head in the opposite direction, and get to the surface as soon as you can', says Mr Brannan. Swim away calmly and smoothly. Sharks may interpret a human flailing and splashing around as a large, wounded fish, and regard it as a meal. If you get involved in a face-to-face confrontation, says Mr Brannan, 'Hit it on the nose – that will disorient it because that is where its sonar is located.'

Your doctor will advise you on what to take; most recommend a combination of chloroquine and proguanil (brand name: Paludrine), which can be bought over the counter at any pharmacy. Lariam, which has a reputation for side effects in some users, is generally more effective in parts of Central America such as Panama where immunity against the other drugs has built up. In my travels in Latin America in 1999, I took part in trials for a new drug, Malarone, which has fewer side effects and will, with luck, be licenced for prevention soon.

Whatever regime you follow, you must begin the course one week before your departure and continue for four to six weeks after your return. The biggest mistake you can make is to stop taking the tablets when you get back since the parasite left by the mosquito can spend 28 days incubating in the liver. Most victims show symptoms of malaria once they are at home.

Dengue Fever is a viral infection, also known as 'haemorrhagic fever' or – more vividly – 'breakbone fever', which is found in many tropical regions and spreading rapidly through Mexico and Central America. It is most prevalent during the wet season and often occurs in urban areas. Transmission is by daytime-biting mosquitoes, and it has an incubation period of five to eight days. Symptoms include a high fever, headaches, photophobia (shrinking from light), loss of appetite and severe muscle pains; haemorrages occur only in very severe cases. There is no specific treatment for dengue fever. Do all you can to avoid being bitten in the first place.

Yellow Fever is an unpleasant tropical disease endemic among monkeys and transmitted to humans by daytime-biting mosquitoes. In many cases the infection is only mild but in others it can be fatal: about one in 20 sufferers dies. Typical symptoms are fever, headaches, abdominal pain, vomiting, etc. In serious cases, kidney or liver failure can follow. No drug exists to combat the disease but there is a vaccination which is highly effective and lasts for years.

You will be issued with an International Certificate of Vaccination which becomes valid ten days after the vaccination has been administered. Some countries will ask to see this flimsy piece of paper if you are coming from a Yellow Fever zone (or if you have been to one in the previous ten days), so when you leave Central America hang on to it.

Biting the bosses

The cause of malaria was discovered in Panama during the building of the canal; previously it was believed to be 'bad air' – mal aire. The process of deduction involved one of relatively few triumphs of the working man over his bosses. Labourers on the canal slept in huts with only nets across the windows, while the managers' houses had glass windows which were frequently left open, and the bosses were heavily bitten. After much of the management perished from malaria, correct conclusions were drawn about the cause.

And the rest

The most common ailment among travellers is a stomach upset from eating contaminated food. **Gastric problems** do not necessarily stem from eating street food – indeed, places where you can see the food being freshly cooked in front of you are often safer than smart restaurants. Avoid eating salads that you have not washed yourself, as well as food that appears to have been lying around in a fly-infested environment. Be particularly careful about seafood, and particularly shellfish which are a common cause of illness. You are less likely to have problems if you stick to a vegetarian diet. Fruits such as papaya and pineapple are good to eat since they contain protein-digesting enzymes which help digestion and protect against infection from intestinal worms.

Diarrhoea is likely to be the first clue that you have eaten something you shouldn't have. If left to its own devices it should clear up in two or three days. Rather than take drugs you should drink as much water as possible to avoid dehydration and take an oral rehydration solution; in extremis, Coca-Cola can work. Immodium alleviates the effects of the diarrhoea (and will block you up if you are going on a long bus journey) but does nothing about the cause. Antibiotics can have a detrimental effect and are best avoided unless fever or serious infection is suspected. In this case you should seek medical advice since it could be that you have amoebic dysentery. Some travellers like to include antibiotics in their medical kit; flagyl or tinidazole are recommended for both dysentery and intestinal parasites such as **giardia**.

Hepatitis is a viral infection of the liver and comes in various types. The one which is most likely to affect travellers is Hepatitis A, found where there are poor standards of hygiene. Incubation takes two to six weeks and symptoms include general malaise, loss of appetite, lethargy, fever, pains in the abdomen, followed by nausea and vomiting. The whites of the eye and the skin turn yellow (though this can be difficult to see if you have a suntan), urine turns deep orange and stools become white. Serious infection can lead to liver failure, coma and death. If you think you are infected you must rest and seek medical advice immediately. Do not smoke or drink alcohol, and keep to a fat-free diet. Some people are lucky enough to be only mildly affected, but hepatitis can sometimes take six months to clear up, so you are strongly advised to go straight home and recover in comfort. Hepatitis A is easy to catch from contaminated food and water. The best protection is a vaccine called Havrix, but this is much more expensive than the old gamma globulin protection.

Mexico and the countries of Central America have not been hit by **Aids** nearly as badly as South America has. Of the seven countries covered in this book Honduras has had the largest number of reported cases, Nicaragua the smallest. For visitors who take sensible precautions against contracting Aids through sexual contact or intravenous drug abuse there is very little risk. However, infection through contaminated blood is less easy to control due to the state of medical treatment in Mexico and, especially, Central America: facilities are poor, hypodermic syringes are reused, and blood used for transfusions may be infected; donations are rarely screened effectively. If you are in an accident a blood tranfusion may be essential in which case try to get in touch with the nearest UK or US Embassy where they will know the nearest source of 'clean' blood. If a transfusion is not a matter of life and death, you must decide whether there is more risk involved in having a blood transfusion or going without one. Whether or not you are in a possession of an Aids pack may help you to make this decision. Aids packs are a standard feature of many a traveller's backpack nowadays. A kit should contain hypodermic needles, suture material (for stitches), intravenous drip needles and alcohol swabs; it is also a good idea to label your pack with your blood group. Doctors can make up kits for you, or you can buy them pre-packed, from MASTA (09068 224100) for example. You should ask whoever gives it to you to supply a letter explaining that the kit is for medical use only – this will save you potential hassle at Customs, especially if you are entering a country where there are strict anti-drugs laws.

Rabies is an exceedingly dangerous viral infection and is transmitted by mammals: notably dogs, monkeys or bats. Although the disease is rare among travellers, anyone who plans to spend extended periods in rural areas is strongly advised to get inoculated. The vaccine gives good protection, but does not make you immune; it slows the spread of the disease to your brain (at which point it becomes invariably fatal) and means that any treatment you receive if you are bitten is likely to work more effectively than it would otherwise. The rabies vaccine is expensive. It is administered in two or three doses, usually one month apart.

The other standard inoculations are for typhoid, tetanus and polio – the World Health Organisation no longer recommends jabs against cholera. **Cholera** and **typhoid** are both diseases which are caught by consuming contaminated food or water. The typhoid vaccination is administered in two doses. The first should be about six weeks before you depart, with the second just before you leave. The injections can leave you with a sore arm and make you feel lousy for 24 hours. Travellers who have already had a course need only a booster injection.

Meningococcal **meningitis** is a bacterial infection of the brain and spinal cord that can occur anywhere in the world. It is spread by 'droplet' infection. Although Mexico and Central America is not a specific risk area, since it can occur in areas of crowding you may consider being immunised, which will give you good protection for three years.

A suitable place for treatment?

In Mexico City, Monterrey (Mexico) and Panama City, medical facilities are among the best in the world. Elsewhere along the Highway, the standard of medical treatment is not what most travellers are used to. Hospitals are poorly equipped and are often a health risk in themselves. Furthermore, in many countries, particularly in rural areas, bad communications and poor roads hamper emergency services. If you fall seriously ill, call your consulate and find out which clinic the expatriate staff use. This will probably be an expensive

A suitable lexicon for treatment

analgésico	painkiller
brazo	arm
caballeros	gents
consultario	surgery
culebra	snake
damas	ladies
estómago	stomach
estoy enfermo	I am ill
dolor	pain
farmacia (de turno)	pharmacy (on duty)
fiebre	fever
insolación	sunstroke
inyección	injection
llame a un médico	call a doctor
paño higiénico	sanitary towel
picadura	sting, bite
pierna	leg
píldora	pill
radiografiá	X-ray
sangre	blood
socorro	help

private clinic, but as long as you have an adequate insurance policy this should not be a problem. The alternative is to return home or to fly to Miami or another North American city.

The best policy

Given the range of calamities which might befall you in Central America, it is essential to have adequate **insurance**. In rural areas you may receive free medical treatment, but it will be only of the most basic kind, and probably carried out in insanitary conditions. A good insurance policy will pay for transportation to somewhere with medical facilities of the highest standards.

Furthermore, insurance covers you against a range of risks from theft to flight delay compensation. The cover provided by most policies is fairly standard: delay and cancellation insurance of up to £2,000; £2,000,000 or more for medical expenses; the same amount for personal liability; £20,000 for permanent disability; and lost or stolen baggage up to about £1,000 (sometimes valuable single items are excluded). Most now also offer an emergency repatriation service. Every enterprise in the travel business is delighted to sell you insurance because of the high commission earned on it. Shopping around can save you money or get better cover for the same premium. Check the advertisements in the travel pages of the quality press and compare this with prices for a similar policy issued by your travel agent.

If you are unfortunate enough to have to claim on your insurance, the golden rule is to amass as much documentation as possible to support your application. In particular, compensation is unlikely to be paid for lost baggage or cash unless your claim is accompanied by a police report of the loss. Thefts from tourists are sufficiently commonplace that the police usually issue a copy of the report to the victim as a matter of routine.

A word of warning

'Belizeans had predicted the Guatemalans would mug me, Guatemalans that the Salvadoreans would murder me, Salvadoreans that the Hondurans would rob me, and Hondurans that the Nicaraguans would forcibly turn me into a communist'. P.J. O'Rourke's words go some way to expose the web of rumour and misinformation that is spread about Central America and Mexico. The image created by the Western media is one of a region teetering permanently on the brink of total anarchy, from which you will be lucky to escape with your life. This is not a picture that travellers returning from Mexico and Central America would recognise. Nevertheless, to maximise the chances of a pleasant trip you must take all the necessary precautions to ensure safety.

The constant political conflict that has characterised the region for so long is calmer now than it has been for some time, but it is always worth checking the latest position with the online authorities in Washington (the Bureau of Consular Affairs home page at travel.state.gov) or London (the Foreign Office travel advice at fco.gov.uk/travel). The Americans are way ahead in providing good, reliable advice, though sometimes they are a bit too alarmist.

Given the appalling poverty in much of Mexico and Central America, it is hardly surprising that some of the locals turn to **crime**. As in most countries of the world, this is most prevalent in the cities. All the capitals have a bad reputation for street crime, as do Colón in Panama and Antigua in Guatemala. Western visitors make ideal targets for villains, since they are easily identifiable. Furthermore the fact that you are rich enough to travel to the region is taken to be evidence that you have money to spare. To avoid becoming easy prey do not carry around expensive cameras, shoulder bags, etc. This book warns of places to avoid and where you should take extra care, but, wherever you are, be especially vigilant when out on the streets after dark. While it is normally safe enough in the streets where there are people and cars, avoid dark and quiet alleys. Most cities in the region have poor levels of street-lighting, particularly Managua.

Although muggings are worryingly frequent in some cities in the region, it is rare for violence to be used; as long as you comply with the robber's instructions, you are unlikely to get hurt. Typical robbers work in pairs. One standard *modus operandum* is for one of them to grab your arms while the other goes through your pockets. Other popular techniques include slashing bags, and pockets. Also be particularly careful on crowded city buses which are the favourite domain of pickpockets.

If you are robbed, the police should be fairly efficient and co-operative. To reclaim losses from your insurers, you will need to provide evidence of the incident: the police should issue a duplicate statement (in Spanish), although they may try to palm you off with just a record of the case number. If you lose air tickets, e-mail your travel agent or contact the airline direct. Lost passports should be reported to your consulate. Some travellers prefer to photocopy all the pages in their passport and carry those around, leaving the real thing in their hotel room. The military or police are empowered to check papers at any time, and a photocopy is normally acceptable. If all your money is stolen, the consul can also arrange for funds to be sent from your home country or, as a last resort, repatriate you.

Don't get overly **drunk** in public places. While over-indulgence is tolerated in most hotel bars, if you wander drunk around the streets you run the risk of being arrested and locked up until you sleep it off. If you are robbed while drunk, expect little sympathy from the police.

Mexico and Central America produce some of the best **marijuana** in the world, and is on the cocaine-smuggling route from South America. Illegal drugs are easily obtainable, but the penalty paid for possession is severe. Officials do not turn a blind eye where tourists are concerned, and may well make an example of you even for possession of small quantities.

Foreigners are subject to a whole series of rules and regulations as regards what they may and may not **photograph**. You can safely assume that it is forbidden to take photographs of military installations or anything with military connnections; this includes airports, sea ports, radio stations, bridges, factories and research institutes. It is probably wise to ask permission if you are in any doubt whatsoever, as it is not unheard of for the militia to wrench a camera off a tourist and confiscate the film. The authorities are also sensitive about photographs that can be seen to be harmful or embarrassing to the state, e.g those of strikes, drunkenness or brawls.

Many locals are extremely photogenic, but individuals do not always take kindly to having their picture taken. In any case it is good manners to ask your subject if he or she is happy to be photographed. In tourist areas the cute kids who make you reach instinctively for your camera make a good living.

Mexico and Central America comprise a heavily militarised region. With the exception of Costa Rica (which abolished its army in 1949), every country in the region has a highly visible military presence which can be unsettling at first – after a month you become used to the sight of teenaged soldiers dressed in US uniforms and carrying rifles or sub-machine guns.

The most likely place you will come face to face with soldiers is at military checkpoints. These are a part of everyday life in El Salvador, Honduras and Guatemala, and occur now and again in Mexico, Nicaragua and Panama. At most checkpoints buses or cars are waved through, but occasionally everyone is asked to get out so that documents can be checked; and the bus may be searched. The first time this happens can be an unnerving experience, particularly in El Salvador and Guatemala where the armies have a bad reputation. Foreigners are of little concern to the military, however, who are keener on finding left-wing activists and other subversives than weather-beaten travellers. Nevertheless, you should line up with everyone else; be meek and mild, since some of these teenagers can be a little over-zealous.

Such infringements of your privacy may be aggravating, but to ensure a peaceful and happy trip, be polite and cooperative whenever you are approached.

A word of advice

If you get into difficulties, whether caused by theft, ill-health, running out of cash or involvement with crime, your first point of contact should be your Embassy (or the Embassy of the country which represents you). The staff have a thorough understanding of the way things work – or fail to work – in Mexico and Central America, and have better lines of communication with home countries than you are likely to be able to organise. In a real emergency, the Consul and other staff will do their utmost to help you out.

Any **women** who have travelled in Spain, Italy or Greece will be well prepared for travel in Mexico and Central America, and the macho tendencies of the Latin male. Female travellers undoubtedly attract attention, and not all of it wanted, but compared to the European Latins most of the local men seem fairly innocuous. This is particularly true in those countries where there is only a small tourist trade – here the people show great curiosity in foreign travellers,

---

The language of law – and outlaws

arma	gun
asalto	mugging
bandido	bandit
carcél, prisión	prison
cartera	wallet
contrabandista	smuggler
drogas	drugs
ejército	army
golpe de estado	coup d'état
guerra	war
herido, a	injured
ladrón	thief
multa	fine
policía	police
prohibido entrar	no entry
propiedad privado	private property
(punta de) control	checkpoint
seguridad	security, safety
testimonio	witness
toque de queda	curfew

but there is also a certain shyness. Seeing a mixed couple tramping around together is unusual enough, but the sight of two women or, in particular, a woman on her own, gives rise to even greater wonderment. The attention of the men usually ranges from silent, curious stares to whistles or audible but incomprehensible comments. Neither need be threatening, and outside the bigger towns you are unlikely to be pestered by such overt demonstrations of machismo. To keep the attention down to a minimum, avoid wearing skimpy shorts and T-shirts.

Some single women like to carry a photograph of a partner, real or imaginary, but on the whole you will not have to rely on these props to discourage unwelcome approaches. You should rely instead on your wholesome, confidently independent and (if necessary) aloof manner to dodgy-looking strangers. As long as you don't allow yourself to be paranoid about the attentions you will inevitably receive, there is no reason why you shouldn't have as rewarding a time or an even better time than male travellers. In fact travelling alone can be a real bonus since the sight of a lone female traveller tends to bring out the protective instinct in the local people, particularly the women. You are likely to find yourself invited into their homes more often than those travelling in groups and more than single men.

If planning to travel while pregnant, check carefully the effects of any vaccinations you might require. It is advisable not to be inoculated with a live vaccine such as polio or yellow fever, especially during the first three months of pregnancy. Malaria tablets present no problem as long as you are prescribed a folate, or vitamin tablet.

Most parts of Mexico and Central America are far from ideal for **small children**. Not only is the journey to the region arduous, but once you get there, there is a host a hazards likely to make life uncomfortable, from the extremes of temperature to the large number of diseases to which young children are particularly susceptible. Another difficulty is the shortage of supplies of essentials such as disposable nappies and baby food. On the plus side, the locals can be incredibly kind and considerate towards Western children. Those with blond hair are likely to become the subject of adoration among doting middle-aged women.

Travellers with disabilities will find Mexico tough going, and Central America very tricky. Few concessions are made to those with mobility difficulties, and the average urban street presents a tough enough challenge even for the able-bodied. **Blind** and partially sighted people will find the region particularly hard going. The help of an able-bodied companion is, unfortunately, essential.

Travel can be extremely problematic for known **HIV carriers and Aids sufferers**: some countries either bar entry if they know you are a carrier, or will advise you to leave. The other great problem for those who have been diagnosed as HIV positive is that obtaining travel insurance becomes a virtual impossibility: most policies have an exclusion clause relating to sexually transmitted diseases.

Read all about it

Specific reading recommendations for individual countries are given in the appropriate sections – these are books that cover a number of nations.

Through the Volcanoes: A Central American Journey by Jeremy Paxman (Paladin, 1987). Yes, it is the *Newsnight* and *Start the week* presenter. Travelling through the seven countries of Central America, Paxman uses the incidents that befall him to focus upon the political turmoil within the region.

So Far From God by Patrick Marnham (Penguin, 1985) recounts a journey through Central America, with particular emphasis on Guatemala and El Salvador. You may not agree with Marnham's political stance – right of centre – but it is a good read nonetheless.

Holidays in Hell by P. J. O'Rourke (Picador, 1989). Do not be discouraged that the author of this book singles out four Central American countries – El Salvador, Nicaragua, Costa Rica and Panama – to sit alongside the Lebanon and Northern Ireland. The chapters give a brief but vivid image of each place in the recent bad old days.

The Old Patagonian Express by Paul Theroux (Pengiun, 1980). The tale of a journey from Boston to the tip of Chile by rail, taking in much of Mexico and Central America. Mr Theroux does not demonstrate great affection for the region covered by this book.

Incidents of Travel in Central America, Chiapás and Yucatán by John Lloyd Stephens (Century) is an entertaining tale of a Victorian archaeologist who tramped through the jungle in the 1840s.

And we sold the rain: Contemporary fiction from Central America, edited by Rosario Santos (Ryan Publishing, 1989) is a collection of stories, the majority of which give an invaluable insight into the life led by the ordinary people of Central America.

Of the wealth of literature on the Maya, the most readable account is probably *Time Among the Maya* by Ronald Wright (Bodley Head, 1989) which deals with Mayan history and with the indigenous people's contemporary struggle. *The Maya* by Michael D. Coe (Thames and Hudson, 1987) is more of a reference book, but is ideal for the uninitiated. It is well-illustrated, and covers all aspects of the ancient civilisation. A more definitive, and also more expensive, study of the Maya is *The Ancient Maya* by Morley, Brainerd and Sharer (Stanford University Press).

Those living in London or other capital cities have plenty of choice of **bookshops** – elsewhere, websites such as amazon.com and bol.co.uk offer a good selection.

Daunt Books (83 Marylebone High Street, London W1M 4DE; tel 020 7224 2295; fax 020 7224 6893) has taken the concept of a travel bookshop to its logical conclusion; as well as a good collection of guide books, literature on a country or region is included: from novels to biographies, and from cookery to art.

The *Travel Bookshop*, 13 Blenheim Crescent, London W11 2EE (tel 020 7229 5260, thetravelbookshop.co.uk) was the model for the bookshop where Hugh Grant's character worked in the film *Notting Hill*. It adopts a similar approach to Daunt Books. Secondhand guides and literature are also available.

Another specialised travel bookshop is *Stanfords* at 12-14 Long Acre, London WC2E 9LP (tel 020 7836 1321). It has some of the more obscure titles published in Central America, as well as US publications, and the best selection of overseas maps in the capital.

One of the best sources of books in the USA is *TravelBooks* (113 Corporation Road, Hyannis, MA 02601-2204; tel: 508-771-3535), which produces a detailed catalogue of titles available by mail order. Another good bookshop is the *Travellers Bookstore* (Rockefeller Center, New York, NY); the Doubledays chain also has a large section devoted to travel books.

Click all about it

The following websites are useful wherever you are in the world

netcafeguide.com – a fairly comprehensive listing of cybercafes all around the world. It can be laborious homing in on the small Central American town you are heading from, only to find that there is no listing.

huracan.net – tells you when the next hurricane is likely to strike.

thetrip.com – useful for making all kinds of travel arrangements, including complicated flight routings.

tripprep.com – this is the place to check out any health-related information, including the types of vaccinations you need for a given destination, local health hazards and the state of the drinking water.

worldclimate.com – this gives the average annual temperatures for the city of your choice.

travel-guides.com – choose a country and select information from a drop-down list; this includes history, getting around, and so on.

In addition, there are two specific sites for locations in Central America: monteverdeinfo.com (dealing with the Costa Rican wilderness of that name) and xelapages.com (from the Guatemalan city of Quezaltenango) which have excellent links to all manner of sites that can help travellers in the region.

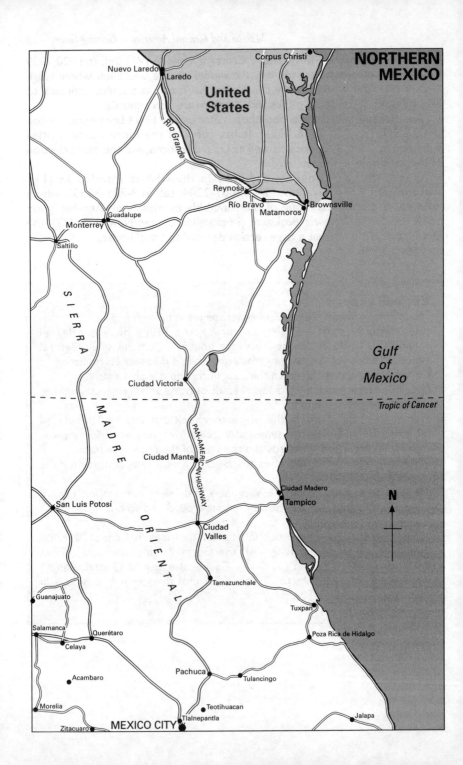

Into Mexico

TEXAS - GUATEMALAN FRONTIER

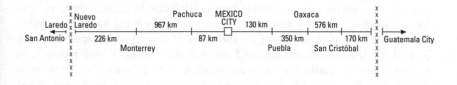

South of the Borderplex

Start off in the right place, and you can walk to Latin America. The right place is at the end of the line in Laredo. The Texas city, together with its unidentical twin of Nuevo Laredo, together make up the 'Laredo Borderplex', but they are as unlike as East and West Berlin at the height of the Cold War. A brisk five-minute stroll will take you from the suburban indulgences of south Texan life, right across the frontline of the battleground between rich and poor, North and South.

It looks like a war zone. A sunny version of Checkpoint Charlie has concreted and barred itself all over the four-lane sweep of Interstate 35 as it crashes against the natural barrier of the Río Grande. Never mind the North American Free Trade Agreement, the economic union intended to remove barriers between Mexico, the United States and Canada: this far-from-mighty river separates the richest country in the world from thousands of miles of Third Worldliness.

Once across the border, you enter the joyful, frenetic bewilderment that is Latin America. Between here and Tierra del Fuego, at the southern tip of Chile, you can find everything you might possibly want from a journey. But you may well conclude that there is no need to look further than Mexico. This great and crazy nation has somehow managed to preserve the remains of ancient civilisations of amazing complexity, conserve the vestiges of the Spanish colonialism that destroyed Mayan and Aztec life, and keep alive the fiery revolutionary spirit that helped carve out a national identity in defiance of the giant north of the border.

The tourism invasion is already well under way. Some of the finest historical sites and best beaches on the Caribbean and Pacific coasts are well-colonised by tourists, particularly the *Norteamericanos* from above the line. But such is the mighty scale of Mexico – eight times the size of Britain, three times as big as Texas, and with at least 100 million souls at the last, flawed count – that much of Mexico remains culturally unsullied.

Travelling through Mexico involves blazing a trail between the ultra-modern and the endearingly traditional. The average off-the-beaten-track village is a picture of indolence, ranged raggedly around a Plaza Mayor where only the church seems to peek above shoulder height. At the other extreme, the high-altitude, high-octane capital is rapidly acquiring high-rises. The grinding poverty that surrounds the glitter inevitably leads to crime, while natural hazards from earthquakes to tropical storms routinely bring havoc to a nation that, at the best of times, seems on the brink of imminent collapse. But look beyond the breezeblock facades, and you will see a country, and a people, as refined as any on earth. For every reason there is to be wary, there is an even greater incentive to go. The biggest risk is that once you have been south of the borderplex, you may never want to cross back.

'Nosotros llegamos in Laredo'

By the time I reached Laredo, the driver of the Greyhound from San Antonio didn't bother to make his announcements in anything other than Spanish. He had nursed the bus through the South Texas Plains to 'The epitome of cultural variety and historic adventure'. Actually, what Laredo's tourism authorities say about the place is wide of the mark, but there is more to it than some of the other border towns along the Rio Grande.

The story of Los Dos Laredos, 'the two Laredos', tells you a lot about the shifting frontiers and allegiances in this part of the world. It was founded as a single Laredo, on the now-Texan side of the border, in 1755. As part of the northward and westward push by Spanish adventurers, an army officer named Tomás Sánchez led a settlement by three families to develop the livestock potential of the region. On 15 May that year, they named it Villa San Agustín de Laredo. The last part of the name, like so many in the Americas, was borrowed from a location in Spain which has precious little in common with northern Mexico. The small town of Laredo clings to the north coast of Spain, on the rugged shoreline between Bilbao and Santander.

You will not be in Laredo, Texas for long before one of the 170,000 inhabitants reminds you that it is the only place in Texas to have lived under seven flags. You could, if you wish, ask them to name all seven. Check that they can remember each of Spain, Nuevo Santander, Mexico, Texas, the Republic of the Rio Grande, the Confederacy and the USA. Of these, the most curious is the Rio Grande. Laredo's historical equivalent of 15 minutes of fame began on 17 January 1840, when the states of Tamaulipas, Coahuila and Nuevo León joined forces to break away from the centralists controlling all of Mexico from the capital. This buffer state formed its own army and issued its own currency, but the wayward nation was not to Mexico's liking, and it was brought back into line after 10 months. The town slumped back into its undemanding role as a border backwater until the early 1880s, when two competing railway companies converged on Laredo: the Missouri-Pacific line from San Antonio and the Midwest, and the Tex-Mex from Corpus Christi and Houston.

The arrival of the railway put Laredo on the map, and injected both life and cash. The first International Bridge was finished in 1889 – before that the Flores Avenue ferry was the only way across to Mexico. The heyday of Laredo was the next four decades, when the finest buildings in town were constructed. After the 1910 Mexican revolution, there was a surge in immigration from the south. Since then, Laredo has faded while the southern partner of Nuevo Laredo has been ascendant: at holiday weekends, it can seem as though the entire population of Texas is being funnelled across the river to shop, eat and drink till they drop.

For a town that seems to be afflicted by perpetual slumber, Laredo is surprisingly easy to reach. There is an 'international' **airport** 8km (five miles) northeast of the town centre, but there are relatively few flights and they tend to be expensive. The 'proper' international airports at San Antonio, Austin, Houston and Dallas tend to offer cheaper flights, and have good Greyhound bus connections to Laredo. **Buses** arrive at the main Greyhound station close to the town centre at the corner of San Bernardo and Matamoros Streets. For schedules and fares, click on greyhound.com or call 723 3402. There is a second station, called Greyhound Latinos, on the corner of Santa Maria and Houston Streets, which is where southbound services originate. On Matamoros St and San Bernadino Avenue, Autobuses Americanos (726 8942) functions mostly as a pitstop for international buses between the USA and Mexico. From Autobuses Americanos you can buy cheap northbound tickets – $15 to San Antonio and $99 to Chicago.

You can board a bus from Laredo straight through to Monterrey, but any southbound journey is much cheaper and easier if you pick up the bus in Nuevo Laredo. First, the traffic and bureaucracy delays are likely to be far longer in a bus than on foot. Next, you may be hustled through Immigration without being allowed the time to get the visitor permit you need. Third, it adds $6 to the price of the ticket to the same destination when bought across the border.

For **getting around** Laredo, there is a bus service of sorts, though as with urban transport elsewhere in the USA, it is operated more as a social service than anything else. As a result, fares are nominal and departures infrequent. Most places of interest are all within walking distance, but if you prefer there is a Heritage Trolley Tour which takes you anywhere even vaguely interesting. It begins from the Museum of the Republic of the Rio Grande/La Posada (see below), at 9am on Tuesdays and Thursdays, and Saturdays at 10am. Bookings at least 24 hours in advance are recommended, through Webb County Heritage Foundation (727 0977). The price in 2000 is $8.

The main supply of **places to stay** is strung along the northern approaches on I-35, but for anyone without transport these motels are not much use. Downtown, a single night at Laredo's loveliest **hotel** would undoubtedly be a highlight of your trip – but the price you will pay could keep you in accommodation in Mexico for a month. **La Posada** Hotel and Suites is a lavish reconstruction of a hacienda on a site that was originally the Old Laredo High School. Rooms are ranged around a quiet courtyard containing a swimming pool, and cost from $99 to $425 per night, plus taxes that add around 10 per cent to the total. The address is 1000 Zaragoza St, Laredo 78040, tel 722 1701, or toll-free 1 800 444 2099.

More economically, a good prospect may be the handsome Art Deco **Hamilton Hotel** at 815 Salinas just north of Jarvis Plaza. At the start of 2000, its Twenties interior was being refurbished; when the work finishes, it will be the best choice. The current 'budget' alternative (i.e. $70 double) is the entertainingly archaic **Rio Grande Plaza**, a circular monstrosity straight out of the Seventies. It protrudes above the skyline at 1, South Main Avenue (722 2411), close to the river towards the western end of town. The hotel is part of the Howard Johnson chain. If cash is a consideration, it is a much better plan to head across the Río Grande and find somewhere to stay there. The two best options are the **Sabina** (two blocks south of International Bridge number 1 and diagonally across Plaza Juárez) and the **Alameda** (on the south side of Plaza Hidalgo, seven blocks south of the bridge). You will pay much less and get more south of the border.

Ditto, as far as **eating and drinking** is concerned: the choice is much wider, and prices much lower, across the river. But to set yourself up with a good breakfast there is nowhere better than **Danny's**, on the northwest corner of Jarvis Plaza. And if you happen to be staying at La Posada, the adjacent **Tack Room Bar & Grill** is one of the better breed of American bar. From 1889, it served as the first international telephone exchange, with 100 lines between the two Laredos.

Besides the border itself, best seen from International Bridge number 1, there are three areas that deserve attention when you go **exploring**. The first is the **San Agustin Historic District**, around the plaza and church of that name. The church of **San Agustin de Laredo** is wholly unexceptional in European, or even Mexican, terms, but it is historical on the Texan scale. The early settlers built a church on the site, and Tomás Sánchez is reputed to be buried somewhere on the plaza. The first church was replaced by a sturdier stone version in 1778. The present French Gothic Revival model, a crisp, white version, dates from 1872. The nave is guarded by a couple of stucco angels. In 1886, it witnessed a shoot-out in the plaza between two groups of what would now be regarded as paramilitaries: the *botas* ('boots') and *guaraches* ('sandals') left almost 30 dead between them.

The main sight is at 1005 Zaragoza Street, on the south side of San Agustin Plaza. A diminutive building that looks a bit like an elongated lean-to shed turns out to have been the **Capitol of the Republic of the Rio Grande**. It was originally the home of an early rancher. Inside you can learn more about the US city that has lived under more flags than any other (and all seven are hanging outside over the doors), and see a series of recreated rooms with 19th century furniture, saddles and, inevitably, guns. It won't take you too long to look around, but you'll probably end up chatting to whoever's on duty. The museum opens 9am-4pm Tuesday to Saturday, 1-4pm on Sundays, admission $2.

On the next six blocks north along **Flores Avenue**, notice that the streets are named alternately for US and Mexican heroes: Grant, Iturbide, Lincoln, Hidalgo. You will see in succession the former Laredo National Bank, the former City Hall (now El Mercado) and the Arte Moderne Plaza Theater on Hidalgo. Go west along Farragut and you reach the modern centre of town at **Jarvis Plaza**, with the courthouse and post office on the north side. A couple of blocks west, you enter the **St Peter's Historic District**, bounded by Santa Maria, Victoria, Santa Rita and Hidalgo Streets. Compared with the colonial wonders south of the border, this is a relative youngster, but there are some handsome mansions – and, on the northwest corner of Victoria and Main, the splendid **Marvelizing Laundry** is a piece of 20th-century kitsch.

The main railway line between the USA and Mexico gets in the way of anyone continuing west to **Fort McIntosh**. A bridge on Washington St or a level-crossing on Zaragoza St will take you to a promontory with views across the river valley, where the fort was established in 1849, immediately after the Mexican-American War, and remained in active service until 1946. Even though a community college has taken it over, there is still plenty of evidence of its military role. Wandering around the former barracks is an amusing way to spend an hour, seeing how the US Army – or at least the officer class – carved out a comfortable life for itself. There is also an old railroad engine on display.

Laredo's place in aviation history

From Enola Gay – which dropped the first atom bomb on Japan in 1945 – via the Boeing B52 to the Stealth Bomber, the US Air Force has long been the most powerful on the planet. But military aviation began at Fort McIntosh.

After the Mexican Revolution began in 1910, the USA was alarmed at developments south of the border, but did not wish to intervene militarily. The need to find out about troop movements led to the US Army borrowing a Wright-B biplane from a co-operative wealthy newspaper proprietor. He had bought it to use for the first-ever aerial photographs, which James H Hare took in February 1911. On 3 March 1911, Lieutenant Benjamin D Foulois and Phil Parmalee – a Wright Brothers pilot – took off to fly west along the Rio Grande to observe manoeuvres.

The flight lasted 2 hours 10 minutes, an American record. After refuelling at Eagle Pass, they set off for the return flight and promptly crashed. Both pilots survived, but Phil Parmalee died the following year in another crash. On the basis of the first, successful flight, the US Army ordered several aircraft. The world was never the same again.

Crossing the Line

The busiest crossing point on the whole of the US-Mexico border – legal or otherwise – is the one on the Pan-American Highway. The twin towns of Laredo in Texas and Nuevo Laredo in the Mexican state of Tamaulipas see a frenetic amount of trade in people and goods between them. About 20 million people traverse International Bridges 1 and 2 in the course of a year, which works out at one every 1.5 *seconds*.

The ditch that acts as geographic, cultural and economic barrier is called, by the Americans at least, the Rio Grande, while Mexico insists it is the Río Bravo del Norte. Technically, the northern portion is called the former, while the southern half is known as the other. The river, which at most times of year resembles an inconsequential stream at the foot of a broad chasm, forms the frontier between the two countries for most of its length.

A rail bridge rumbles to constant freight trains, while two big road bridges struggle to cope with the vehicle traffic. International Bridge number 1 is the only one you can walk across; International Bridge 2 is the continuation of Interstate 35, and is not designed for, nor open to, pedestrians.

To walk across, you pay a pedestrian fee of 35 cents heading southbound. Technically, you are not allowed to take photographs from the bridge, but it would seem a shame to miss the opportunity. The officials on the Mexican side are likely to be more accommodating – security guards on the US side actively prevent anyone taking pictures of the border. The last thing you see as you leave America behind is a sign reading 'Illegal to carry firearms/ammunition into Mexico. PENALTY – PRISON by Mexican law'. So don't carry that Colt .45 over by mistake.

Red tape

If all you want is a quick hop across the border from the USA, then you need hardly bother even waving your passport at the dozing frontier official. Tourists can stay for up to three days in the frontier area without formality. When you step ashore in Mexico from Puente Internacional I (as it has become), it will be assumed that you are one of the millions who arrive in Mexico from the USA purely to eat, drink or shop in the Nuevo Laredo area. Pedestrians who intend to travel beyond there have to undergo formalities at the Migración office. All frontier formalities for pedestrians take place on the right once you cross the bridge (i.e. on the west side heading south into Mexico, on the east side heading north back into the USA). In theory, you will be asked to present proof of citizenship and photo identification for entry into Mexico. If you are a US citizen, this does not need to be a passport; a certified copy of a US birth certificate, a Naturalization Certificate or a Certificate of Citizenship are acceptable.

On the southbound track to Mexico, your first problem is to find someone prepared to take you seriously as a traveller. Officials will automatically assume that you are merely a daytripper or weekender, intending to get souvenirs, get

Check-out is easy, check-in is hard

The US Immigration and Naturalization Service (INS) has a tough job, so they don't even bother looking at who's leaving the country. This can lead to all kinds of problems. If you are a US citizen, then you will be able to enter Mexico with ID as flimsy as a driver's permit or a voter registration card. But, says the State Department, *They will not be recognised for readmission to the USA.*

For foreign visitors, the complications are worse. When you entered the USA, a piece of card will have been attached to a page in your passport. This is known as the I-94 (if white) or I-94W (if green), and is the 'counterfoil' that needs to be re-united with the form you filled in upon entry. The trouble is, if you leave by a land frontier then no one will collect it from you. As far as the INS is aware, you are still in the USA – and soon to be outstaying your welcome. You will be blissfully unaware of this until next time you travel to the USA, when your case will pop up on the computer screen as an 'overstayer'. Try as you might to explain your story, the immigration officer may well turn you away.

The solution is to seek out an INS official, on the inbound side of the crossing, and hand him or her the counterfoil. Don't bother with this if you plan to return to the USA before the expiry date – keeping the I-94 will save you having to fill in more forms on re-entry.

drunk and get back across the border. Every traveller who is staying for more than 72 hours, and/or travelling beyond the US-Mexico border zone, must have a tourist card. Officially, this is called a *Forma Migratoria de Turista*, but everyone refers to it as a *tarjeta de turista*. It takes time and effort to pay the $17 necessary to buy one. So why bother? If you don't, you'll find out about 20km down the road when your passport is checked at one of a series of inspections. You will probably be sent back to the border and told to sort all the bureaucracy. If you manage to elude it, then you risk being found out as an irregular visitor. You'll face some tough questioning and heavy fines, not all of them legitimate. Being a paragon of virtue is not regarded as an essential qualification for every Mexican official. So get it all sorted out at the first opportunity.

Flying into Mexico

If you are arriving by air, the airline will probably supply the necessary form. You fill it in, and the immigration official at the airport of arrival will assign a length of stay (up to 180 days) and stamp the form in return for the $17.

Customs – not *more* bureaucracy?

Luckily, no. No 'green channel' for Mexican customs; they prefer something a little more random. You press a button on a device like a traffic signal. If the green bulb, marked *pasa*, illuminates, you go clean through. If red lights up, your baggage is subject to a *previsión* – thorough inspection – unless, that is, you look as though you have spent the past 12 hours being ground through the mill of economy air or bus travel. Mexico being a friendly, flexible country, you will probably be waved straight through.

Bringing in a car

In a private car or pick-up truck, you are likely to be waved through with a cursory inspection, on the assumption that you are, like most of the other automobiles, going to remain in the immediate vicinity of the frontier – the border strip runs 20km (12 miles) inland. The Mexican tourist authorities publish a guide called *Traveling to Mexico by Car*, which begins with the following words: 'IMPORTANT NOTICE – If you are traveling only within the border region, there is no need to follow any of the procedures contained in this guide'. If you are going further south, then pay attention: take either bridge (there is some talk of making each bridge one-way only if the volume of cars and trucks increases much further). Whichever bridge you cross, you should turn sharp right as soon as you have obtained your tourist card and are over the river. This will lead you along the south bank of the river to a big road junction. From here, follow the signs around the west side of town to the **Módulo de Control Vehícular de la Aduana en la Frontera**, where you can set about the considerable red tape in being allowed to import a vehicle into Mexico.

Here you will need to immigrate personally, which means handing over $17, your passport and a completed tourist card form. Next, show your vehicle title (log book), receipt for its current registration, and your driver's license. You will need to fill in a Temporary Application for Vehicle Import and a Promise to Return a Vehicle. This is to stop you selling the vehicle within Mexico. The authorities do not rely entirely upon your word: they will also demand a deposit. You must lodge, with the adjacent Banjército (Army Bank), a bond of several hundred dollars. The precise amount depends on the age of your vehicle (the older, the cheaper): 1999 and 2000 vehicles pay $800, 1994-1998 $600, and anything earlier than 1993 $400. On top of this, you pay a non-refundable transaction fee of $17.25. You are strongly advised to pay by credit card, even though you have to pay commission on this transaction; it will make claiming a refund when you leave much easier. Otherwise, you could find yourself at a lonely Mexican-Guatemalan border post arguing with an unco-operative bank official (who, by the way, will be on duty 8.30am-3.30pm only, Monday to Friday) that he should hand over a wad of cash equivalent to his annual salary.

If you are likely to enter Mexico more than once in a six-month period, keep hold of your permits – they allow multiple entry, which means that you could get from Mexico, into Guatemala and beyond, and come back without additional bureaucracy. But, whatever you do, make sure you keep your vehicle paperwork absolutely safe. There are no refunds if you lose the documents, and you will also have a lot of explaining to do when you come to leave Mexico. The worst case of all is if the vehicle gets stolen with the paperwork in it. Reporting a theft is tough enough if you have all the documents in perfect order; but when you have nothing at all to prove your entitlement, then the police officers are likely to take their responsibilities even less seriously than usual. Should something more minor happen, like a total write-off of your car, then (assuming you are still alive and conscious), you will need to go through an improbable amount of bureaucracy to reclaim your bond.

Bypassing bureaucracy

In March 2000, David Orkin found a handy way to beat the border bureaucrats on the Tex-Mex divide:

'Visitors to West Texas's magnificent Big Bend National Park can simply park their cars (in a designated area between the Park's Castolon Ranger Station and Cottonwood Campground) and walk for less than five minutes to the banks of the Rio Grande. The river marks the frontier between the two countries, but there are no border posts on either side. A boatman will be waiting to row you across the river for $2 round trip – and no taxes payable. Three minutes' walk up the hill is the sleepy authentic Mexican village of Santa Elena, population about 40. There are two churches, a school (with a museum which may or may not be open – you are in Mexico), some simple craft shops. The backdrop of the nearby mountains and the views back across the river are stunning. Lunch at one of the four restaurants (El Cañón by the Plaza is recommended) costs $5 (dollars are preferred so no need to change money) and a beer is $1.50. Look out at the adobe buildings, the slightly run-down plaza, and moustachioed men in stetsons driving by in battered pick-up trucks. Then it's back downhill to cross the river back to a different world.'

When do we get to Mexico?

What attracts you south of the river is the intriguing collusion of cultures and magnificent landscapes in Mexico. What attracts most of the people who are joining you on the journey south is the prospect of cheap booze and lax laws. This helps to explain why a pair of less identical twins is hard to imagine. While Laredo is a study in drowsiness, its Mexican counterpart *Nuevo Laredo* is a frenzy of activity. Of course, the two phenomena are related. Because every indulgence is much cheaper on the Mexican side, the town is full of bars, restaurants and the inevitable tacky souvenir shops. As an introduction to Mexico, it is as unsuitable as Calais is to France or New York is to the USA.

Nuevo Laredo was founded in 1775 when disillusioned Mexicans moved south across the river from Laredo. They wanted to reside in their home country rather than part of the USA; perhaps their descendants are wishing they had stayed put, given the much higher standards of living north of the border. But Nuevo Laredo has a population twice as large as that of the original Laredo, 340,000, swollen by arrivals from elsewhere in Mexico seeking better pay and prospects.

Puente Internacional 1, as it has become, continues southward to become the main drag of Nuevo Laredo, Avenida Guerrero. The first sign that you are, in fact, in a country that could be Mexico appears on the left after two blocks. Plaza Juárez is an ordinary sort of square, but at least it has a church on the opposite side, a hotel – the Sabina, which is the obvious place to stay if you are using Nuevo Laredo as a cheap place to stay while you visit Laredo – and lots of elderly men busy doing nothing in particular.

Five blocks down from the bridge, you pass the Mercado Juárez on the right, and two blocks after that you find yourself on Plaza Hidalgo. This is the closest you will get to real Mexican life while in Nuevo Laredo, but it still isn't very close. You will probably want to get going pretty soon.

Besides the **Hotel Sabina**, you could try the **Hotel Alameda** on the south side of Plaza Hidalgo, which corresponds to Calle González. If you have your own transport and you want to get well south of the town, the Campo Real Motel is 6km (four miles) out of the city on the *autopista* to Monterrey. The main drawback (unless you are hitch-hiking) is the huge truckstop adjacent.

Eating and drinking anything vaguely authentic is tricky on the main drag. A typical example is Señor Frog's, a 'restaurant' whose main task is serving vast amounts of alcohol and Americanised food to people with unsophisticated palates but lots of cash. There are plenty of places selling good, cheap food around the bus station.

The most expensive **taxis** in any town along the whole Pan-American Highway through Mexico and Central America operate around Nuevo Laredo. You can expect to pay a flat fare of $5/50 pesos per vehicle, which will cover the 4km journey out from the city centre to the bus terminal. An alternative is to find a local bus heading in that direction, but the route system is confusing.

At the **bus station**, you will find one of the better organised terminals. The main operators are Frontera, Oñibús de México and Transportes Nacional del Norte. You can get a bus every half-hour or so to Monterrey, and there are less frequent departures to other big cities in northern Mexico – and several buses a day all the way to Mexico City.

The flyover option

There are regional flights from the small airport at Nuevo Laredo airport, 14km (eight miles) south, on the road to Monterrey. You can expect to pay a minimum of $10 (100 pesos) for a taxi from town; rather than fly to the main destination, Monterrey (about $50 one way), you may as well take a first-class bus past the airport – which will cost no more than $12 to go all the way.

That was then – the roots of Mexico

The first visitors

Before the Spanish Conquest the region was peopled by numerous indigenous groups; they are erroneously but universally called Indians because of Columbus' mistaken belief that he had discovered Asia at the end of his first transatlantic voyage in 1492. Like the natives of North America, the Indians of Mexico and Central America crossed the Bering Strait from northeast Asia, and are estimated to have reached the region 12,000 years ago. The tribe that was to dominate the region was the Maya. They settled in Mesoamerica (a term used by archaeologists to encompass the area from the Valley of Mexico southwards through Guatemala to Honduras and El Salvador) and constituted the greatest civilisation to occupy the region – perhaps even of the New World.

The earliest traces of nomadic life date back as far as 7000BC. Slowly, simple farming was introduced; gradually their lifestyle developed, weaving and pottery became important pursuits, and village life flourished. Some of these small communities developed into powerful, often militaristic, empires, whose legacy is still evident today at locations on the Pan-American Highway: the ruins of Teotihuacán (north of Mexico City) and Monte Albán, near Oaxaca, were once the headquarters of powerful tribes. But despite the huge achievements of some of these civilisations, they were isolated from the rest of the world, and their development was restricted. Empires such as those of the Toltecs or the Olmecs often disappeared as rapidly as they had gained power, in a pattern that was repeated across the whole Latin American continent.

At the point when the Spanish first began their exploration of the New World, the Aztecs were the dominant force in the Valley of Mexico, where they had succeeded in conquering various neighbouring tribes from the base they had built at Tenochtitlán – now Mexico City.

The Conquest

The first incursions into what is now Mexican territory were made by Velázquez de Cuéllar, who explored the Yucatán coastline. But it was Hernán Cortés who first penetrated into the interior. By 1521, through a combination of high courage, low cunning and sheer good fortune, he had defeated the Aztecs and taken control of their valley.

The motivating force behind the Spanish exploration of the New World was economic, and the *conquistadores* quickly found wealth in great quantities in northern Mexico's rich seams of silver. The first discovery was in Taxco in 1522; from there they set off northwards in search of more. The province of Zacatecas proved even more fruitful, and during the 1840s, the town of La Bufa became an important centre for both mining and further exploration of the region. The richest seams were found to the north, in the provinces of Durango, Chihuahua and Sonora, close to what later became the border with the United States.

Once they had established a base for themselves, the conquerors set about imposing a harsh, alien society on the existing population. Missionaries, brought over from Europe, attempted to convert the native Indians to Christianity. The indigenous people were to be protected by the Spanish Crown, as long as they agreed to be instructed in the ways of the Catholicism. When everyone in a particular area had agreed to conform, the missionaries moved on, leaving behind them a church and the community that had grown up around it. At first, the process proved successful; but converting the natives to Christianity proved more difficult as the Europeans moved further north.

As the power and wealth of the Catholic church increased, the status of the native Indian population diminished even further. They had few land rights, and were oppressed, second-class citizens (very much, some would say, as the indigenous people throughout the Americas today). By the end of the 18th century, even the King of Spain was worried about the amount of money and power being amassed by the church, and ordered that the clergy should hand over its money to the crown. The consequences were catastrophic. The clergy became disenchanted with the monarchy and began to plan a revolt. They shifted their gold out of the country, the economy went into sharp decline, and the mass of the local Mexican population became disaffected with its distant rulers. Support for change began to grow.

Independence

The first effective call for rebellion was issued in September 1810 in Guanajuato, under the leadership of Vicente Guerrero. Various towns were quickly captured – Zacatecas, Valladolid and the silver mining town of San Luis Potosí were soon in the hands of the rebels – but over a decade of struggle ensued before something approaching independence for the citizens of Mexico could finally be declared. Guerrero joined forces with a former royalist commander, Agustín de Iturbide, and together they formulated the Plan de Iguala, a treaty to which the Spanish finally agreed. The Plan guaranteed an independent constitutional monarch, a single religion – Catholicism – and equal rights for the native population; Spanish troops were to remain, alongside rebel fighters, to protect the country.

Iturbide became president, and then, in the absence of a Bourbon prince ready to accept the crown, he was proclaimed emperor as Agustín I. He was overthrown in 1824 in a coup whose organisers included an ambitious young soldier, Antonio López de Santa Anna. A new constitution established a federal republic. The southern boundary has remained the same ever since, but the northern frontier was soon to shrink.

The struggle with Spain continued; its troops were finally expelled in 1829, after a Spanish army had tried to land in Tampico in an attempt to restore colonial rule. In 1833, Santa Anna seized power and threw out the existing constitution. Mexican society was strongly divided between the powerful conservatives, with their loyalty to the Spanish crown and the Catholic church, and the liberals, with their federalist, anti-clerical attitudes, who looked

Lone Star state of independence

Prior to 1836, Mexico's borders extended far to the north into what is now the USA. A line from the Pacific coast extending north of Salt Lake City, and following parts of the Arkansas and Red Rivers, before running south to the Gulf of Mexico, marked the division between the two countries. It included most of Texas, but settlers were increasingly from the infant United States and Anglo-Saxon rather than Hispanic in origin. In 1835, the Texas war of independence began.

The Texan insurgents took San Antonio, and fortified themselves inside the Alamo. In January 1836, Santa Anna's forces spent two weeks breaking down the rebels' resistance with an attack of bloody attrition, in which almost all the defenders died. Within three months, General Sam Houston had harnessed Texan vengeance and defeated Santa Anna at the battle of San Jacinto River. Texas was now a self-proclaimed republic.

The Río Grande was the natural southern frontier, but a series of border disputes ensued that embroiled Mexico, the USA and the Republic of Texas. In the middle of all this, in 1840, unilateral independence was declared by the self-styled Republic of the Río Grande. It was based in Laredo, comprising the three most northeasterly Mexican provinces. The pocket-sized breakaway nation did not last for long before Mexico brought it back into line, and within five years the whole of the present state of Texas had been annexed by the USA. By 1848, most of the rest of Mexico's possessions had been handed over to the United States. The Río Grande has marked the Tex-Mex border since then. The river represents for Mexico a permanent reminder of the loss of its empire.

towards the USA as a model for the future governance of their country. Rebellion was rife throughout the country. An uprising in Zacatecas was quashed, quickly followed by more serious problems in Texas, which ultimately saw the loss of much of Mexico's northern territories and the beginnings of a national sense of inferiority.

The Mexican-American War began in 1845, largely as a result of the annexation of Texas. It proved a comprehensive disaster for Mexico. The American army crossed into Mexico and fought their way to Mexico City, which fell to the USA in September 1847. A peace treaty was finally signed in the following year. More than half of Mexico's existing territory was given up, and New Mexico, Arizona, Nevada, Colorado and California all became part of the United States.

As if things could get any worse for Santa Anna, he still had to face sporadic uprisings amongst groups of native Indians around the country. Money he received from the United States as part of the peace settlement helped to rebuild his shattered army, who brought the rebellions under control. Santa Anna's final humiliation took place in 1853 when dire economic circumstances forced his government to sell southern Arizona and part of New Mexico to the Americans, in order to raise a badly-needed $10 million, a transaction known as the Gadsden Purchase. In 1855, Santa Anna was overthrown by the reformer Benito Juárez, whose name is celebrated in plazas and streets all over Mexico.

When the dire financial situation forced Juárez to default on his international debt repayments, the French launched an invasion of Veracruz. They moved inland, fought a battle at Puebla, and continued on to Mexico City where they took control. The Habsburg Archduke, Maximilian, was put in as emperor, but this turned out to be a temporary posting: the French were soon forced to withdraw, Maximilian was executed and Benito Juárez returned to power.

Juárez was replaced in 1872 by Porfirio Díaz, who ruled, on and off, for the next 30 years, in a period known as the *Porfiriato*. During this time, although the country underwent several modernisations, political freedoms were crushed, and life became harder and harder, particularly for the workers. The gap between rich and poor widened, and this led to a series of nationwide strikes, organised by a popular opposition movement. Díaz called an election in 1910 in which he was opposed by Francisco Madero. Had opinion polls existed in those days, Madero would have been way ahead in them. On the day of the election, Díaz imprisoned him, thus guaranteeing his own election.

When Madero was released he took refuge in Texas, from where he began to plot against Díaz. Revolution began, and after a slow start, Madero joined forces with the rebel leaders Pancho Villa and Emiliano Zapata; together they gained control of Sonora and Chihuahua. Díaz resigned in 1911, new elections were held, and Madero became president. But demands for reform increased, and the factions that had supported him became fragmented. Two right-wingers organised a bloody counter-revolution which became one of the blackest episodes in Mexican history. In the *decena trágica* ('ten tragic days'), thousands died. Madero was deposed and executed in 1913.

Several years of instability followed. A provisional government led by Pancho Villa – Mexico's Che Guevara – was set up in Guanajuato in north central Mexico. This was in opposition to the power base set up in Veracruz by the army commander, Venustiano Carranza who, supported by American troops, eventually became president. Among other measures, the constitution he introduced separated church from state, and established that land originally belonging to the peasants should be returned to them.

The presidents who followed him introduced various reforms, and in 1929, under Plutarco Elías Calles, the Partido Nacional Revolucionario was established. This is the precursor to the Partido Revolucionario Institucional, the political party which maintained a tight grip on the nation – and, say some, the ballot boxes – for the rest of the century. During this period, economic development in the north of the country received a boost when the United States introduced prohibition; Americans headed across the border to buy the alcohol that they could no longer buy at home. The frontier towns flourished, as casinos and brothels were set up south of the border.

Some of the most important reforms of the 20th century took place after Lázaro Cárdenas became president in 1934. He introduced land reforms, and set up a national oil company, driving out many foreign investors. Mexico was always one of the world's major oil-producing countries during the 20th century, but as reserves were running out in the early 1970s huge new oilfields were found – just in time to benefit from the price-hikes choreographed by OPEC. But as the price of oil slowly fell, the economy slumped. Inflation and unemployment accelerated, and the chances of Mexico repaying its huge foreign debts vanished. The bankrupt nation was saved, on more than one occasion, by the USA and the world financial community, but with increasingly tight conditions attached.

The *annus horribilis* for Mexico, or at least the ruling PRI, was 1994. The North American Free Trade Agreement (NAFTA), establishing a 'common market' between the USA, Canada and Mexico, had been widely welcomed as opening up two of the world's richest nations to Mexican exports. The precarious political situation, and considerable human rights concerns, were brought to the world's attention on the day the agreement came into effect, 1 January 1994. A guerrilla organisation called the Ejército Zapatista de Liberación Nacional seized control of several parts of Chiapas state. The *Zapatistas* made headlines worldwide for their campaign for a just society, land reform and the elimination of corruption.

As the government was forced into negotiations with the rebels, attention swerved to the other corner of the country: in March 1994, the PRI's candidate for the impending presidential elections was assassinated in Tijuana. The replacement candidate, Ernesto Zedillo, won the contest, but by December the decision – in the face of economic necessity – to allow the peso to float on the international foreign exchange markets had plunged Mexico into yet another financial crisis.

Mexico has somehow emerged from years of turmoil and austerity with its economy in fair shape, to the extent that in 2000 its credit rating was upgraded by Moody's to investment-grade status. Much of the economic dynamism comes from the north of the country: maquiladoras – tax-efficient manufacturing facilities in border areas, run by US companies – and Monterrey, Mexico's version of Wall Street.

On the Highway

Don't get too used to the first few kilometres of Mexican highway 85, as the Panamericana is known on this stretch. The wide, smooth dual-carriageway is the exception to the rule that the Pan-American Highway has been bashed about something rotten by man and nature. But do get used to the idea that the rules of the road have all changed, and that most of the time you won't have the faintest idea what they are.

On the buses: class warfare

The backbone of the transport system from here southwards is the **bus**. In Mexico, this term covers a multitude of conveyances: from battered cages-on-wheels fitted with the least user-friendly seats ever devised, to supremely comfortable air-conditioned coaches complete with on-board meal service. Much of the time you will have a choice between different buses on the same route. Don't assume that the flashier and more expensive buses are necessarily better. A second-class bus connects you much more effectively with local life than does the artificial cocoon of an air-conditioned executive version. It is an organic entity, with lots going on – and the added bonus that it will stop anywhere on demand. If you're on a 300km ride, this can get a bit tedious – and adds typically 50 or 100 per cent to the journey time compared with a first-class, limited-stop bus. If you are planning to do any overnight trips, you might not appreciate the company of colourful characters so much. They are also older and less well-maintained (indeed, on some, it is difficult to detect any sign of maintenance at all).

On some first-class buses, particularly the premium *de lujo* kind, there is often a **stewardess**, who may give a short speech at the beginning of the journey, outlining the expected journey time, intermediate stops and facilities on board. A drawback of the first-class buses is the **on-board video**. Gratuitously violent, poorly acted and badly dubbed films play constantly at an ear-cripplingly high volume. Ear-plugs and eye-shades are advisable to avoid such 'Entertainment'.

First-class buses almost always have **toilets** on board. Second-class buses, particularly those which were once first-class buses, may have toilets but these will usually be sealed closed. On some, the toilet may have been removed to make room for squeezing in an extra couple of seats. On the best buses, cleaners get on at intermediate stops for a tidy-up. On the worst buses, cleaners could not get on even if they wanted to (which they almost certainly wouldn't). And while first-class buses usually sell no more tickets than they have seats, on second-class ones there are no explicit capacity limits. A bus built for 40 can easily carry 60 or 70. (On second thoughts, the word 'easily' is not appropriate in that sentence.)

Another factor that will affect your decision is **luggage**. On first-class buses between towns with proper depots, your bags are likely to be consigned to the luggage compartment beneath the passenger cabin. You will be given a tag, and at the destination will be allowed to claim it only upon handing over the tag. On second-class buses there is no such system, and you have to try to be first off the bus to stop local villains (or other passengers) pinching your pack from the luggage compartment. Further south and east, as the buses degenerate, the space is likely to be on the roof, and there will not be any bureaucracy – the lads who load it will keep an eye on it, and return it to you.

If you want a first-class bus and/or a decent seat, **advance reservation** is advisable. On routes where there are relatively few buses (e.g. Puebla to Oaxaca or San Cristóbal to the Mexican border), it is always worth booking in advance. Elsewhere, you may not be able to book at all – and even if you are, then you might not want to commit yourself to a particular departure. Reservations are harder to move than they are to procure in the first place. The other problem occurs if you want to catch a bus from a midway point on its itinerary. Most of the hops recommended in this book allow you to catch a bus at the start of its journey, but for some there is no choice but to wait for a *de paso* service – a bus from A to C that is prepared to pick you up at B. A couple of potential problems here: the first is that you may not get on. Few reservations systems are sophisticated enough to allow for people hopping on and off, and if there is no room, that is tough. The other danger is that it may be dismally late, leaving you standing by the side of the Highway for an hour or more. So before you get off a bus on a whim in the middle of nowhere, consider how you will move on.

Most of the Pan-American Highway from Mexico City to Panama has a southerly or easterly trajectory, which is relevant when **choosing your seat**. The sun can be a hazard for much of the day if you are in a right-hand seat, while on the left only the morning sun poses a problem, and then only on the southbound sectors. You'll spend a lot of time **looking out of the window**. First, be aware that if there is glass in the way, it is likely to be tinted to a peculiar tone, or filthy, or both, giving a strange effect to your perceptions. Next, consider opting for seats 3 and 4. Normally these are the two right-hand seats at the front, and sometimes there is a clear view out of the front. If you are unlucky, though, you will find that there is a partition with glass, a curtain and minimal legroom.

Your next problem is finding the place the bus leaves from. In small towns, and in mid-sized Mexican cities, life is relatively easy. There is usually one **bus station**, where you can get information on the whole range of services. In some cases, especially big cities, it is a long way from the city centre. Local people have an ingrained knowledge of where buses go from, though in the biggest cities there may be a complexity of departure points – from Mexico City and Puebla, for example, there are three possible bus stations.

Don't expect the actual departure time to bear much resemblance to anything written on your ticket. Even if a bus company official says the bus is leaving *ahorita*, right now, assume the opposite. That 'immediate departure' could take place anything up to two hours from now. **Timekeeping** is not a significant factor in the average bus driver's lifestyle. The luggage may be all stowed, the engine may roar into life at the appointed second ... and then nothing much may happen for half an hour. More likely though, at around the time the bus is supposed to depart, a whole bunch of people will melt out of the shadows and materialise in the general vicinity of the bus. Some of them will wander off to buy tickets, while others will start to explore the possibilities of stowing luggage. None of this is carried out with the remotest sense of urgency, because the principal players know that the bus will not go without them. There is no imperative to depart, or arrive on time. And if you think

The last train to Ciudad Valles
In March 2000, the *Thomas Cook Overseas Timetable* had the sad duty to report almost the final demise of passenger railways in Mexico, with the exception of the Chihuahua-Al Pacífico – the so-called Copper Canyon railway.

Once upon a time, there was a beautifully engineered railway network through Mexico and Central America, carving spectacular routes through the mountains. But, as with every train operator in the Latin American world, the system has collapsed.

Officially services are only 'temporarily suspended', but it seems unlikely that there will ever be any revival: the survivor owes its stay of execution to the impossibility of cutting a road through the terrain, and to its popularity as a tourist trip. Elsewhere, the competition from road transport is just too strong. The only likely entrant to the market would be if a luxury tourist train could be introduced on routes that are still used by freight. But don't hold your breath.

there is, you must be an uptight Westerner. Of 19 buses I took to cross the country in December 1999, only one departed within five minutes of the appointed time: a second-class bus from Mexico City to Cholula. All the rest were anything up to two hours behind schedule, with one being cancelled entirely for no apparent reason. Think British Rail at its worst – and remember that there's a fat lot that you, or anyone else, can do about it. The driver will go when he's good and ready, and stop wherever he wishes. He is the *jefe* (chief), and you are not. So build the expectation of delays into your planning, and chill out.

Occasionally, a driver may show some interest in making up time. He will come up against the national **speed limit** for buses of 95km/h (57mph). On the newer models of bus, a red light illuminates if the driver goes too fast – look for the *alarma exceso de velocidad*. Don't expect it to be working, and if it is don't expect the driver to take the blindest bit of notice.

Hitch-hiking

'US citizens should not hitchhike nor accept rides from or offer rides to strangers anywhere in Mexico.' That's what the State Department says. Who am I to argue? Well, a long-in-the-tooth hitch-hiker who finds short- and medium-range hitching works extremely well in Mexico. You probably wouldn't want to hitch from Mexico City to Oaxaca, not least because of the difficulties of (a) finding anywhere sensible to hitch on the outskirts of the capital and of (b) persuading a driver that there are good reasons why you have chosen not to take the bus. One case when the latter should be easy is around holiday time, at Christmas or Easter, when many long-distance buses are fully booked; another is on stretches of the Highway where buses are thin on the ground, such as across the Isthmus of Tehuantepec between Oaxaca and Chiapas states.

In rural areas off the beaten track, hitching is often necessary and usually easy – though women should not hitch-hike alone. A gringo's raised thumb is correctly interpreted everywhere in the country as a request for a ride, and normally any vehicle with space will stop. You should offer approximately the bus fare. The likelihood of this being accepted is in inverse proportion to the quality of the vehicle – the driver of a new, air-conditioned 4x4 will probably reject the cash (and you may decide it is inappropriate to offer), while a poor *campesino* whose pick-up is even older than he is may be inclined to take the money.

Driving

Where to begin? Perhaps with the 13,000 deaths on the roads of Mexico every year. That is one fatality every 40 minutes of every day, on average – about three times the rate in Britain, and in a country with far fewer vehicles. Or how about the current advice from the US State Department: 'Criminal assaults occur on highways throughout Mexico. Kidnapping, including the kidnapping of non-Mexicans, is increasing. So-called express kidnappings have reportedly taken place on well-traveled highways such as the Toluca Highway leading out of Mexico City. The US Embassy advises its personnel to exercise extreme caution for safety reasons when traveling on any highways after dark.'

Most of the time, of course, the local hoodlums will wait for you to get out of the car. As soon as you turn up in any town in a nice-ish car, every villain for miles around will get you in their sights. Everything on and in the vehicle will be removed. Yes, a car gives you greater flexibility, but trying to find yet another replacement set of windscreen wipers when you're in a village in the Chiapan highlands is the kind of stress you can do without.

If you are still happy to drive, good luck. Prepare to dig deep to pay for everything from replacement bumpers (if vaguely removable, a favourite target for petty thieves) to bribes for police. And another thing: some stretches of the Pan-

Walking into trouble

The slogan I saw in one small northern Mexican village, that *'En Matlapa el peatón es primero'* is a complete joke. The pedestrian comes last in Matlapa and everywhere else in the region. One newspaper report I saw alleged that bus drivers were instructed that it was much better to kill a pedestrian outright than merely to maim him or her – the legal consequences of a fatality were easier and cheaper to deal with than the possibility of a claim for compensation from an injured pedestrian. So: not only do you have no rights or recognition, some people are actually out to kill you.

American Highway in Mexico are on **toll roads** described as *autopistas* (freeways, motorways), and charge a toll – *cuota*. Typically you will pay 0.50 pesos per kilometre, which adds up quickly. On the 230km stretch between the Texas border and Monterrey, for example, the standard toll for a driver is 133 pesos.

An alternative to battling with the bureaucracy of bringing a vehicle in is to **rent a car**. All the big multinationals are represented in Mexico, though be warned that the chances of a reasonably priced one-way rental are low, and there is no prospect of being able to take a hired car across the border into Guatemala and beyond.

The flyover option

Good idea. Distances are so vast, and Mexican airlines so good, that you could sensibly hop from Monterrey to Mexico City or from Oaxaca to San Cristóbal. Mexico is the one country in the world where flying is still a pleasure. On Aeroméxico, Mexicana and AeroCalifornia, flights are punctual and fun: inflight refreshments often offer an endearingly straightforward approach: Johnny Walker Red Label, or water, or both. Each flight around the vast country can cost as little as £50, flying on a Mexican air pass.

You will need to book this in advance from a specialist agent such as Journey Latin America (020 8747 3108, sales@journeylatinamerica.com) or South American Experience (020 7976 5511, sax@msmail.com). Otherwise you will end up paying the full economy fare, plus miscellaneous taxes, totalling perhaps $150 for a longish flight.

What's different about Mexico?

In short: it's very big, very diverse, and very beautiful. Starting with size, Mexico is eight times as big as Britain. Much of it lies above 1,300m (4,200), the height of the highest mountain in the UK. The Pan-American Highway stays close to the Sierra Madre Oriental that stretches down the eastern part of the country, and spends much of its time a mile or more (1,600m plus) above sea level.

Climate

It may seem silly to generalise about the weather in a country the size of Mexico, but there are distinct patterns that are fairly simple. In most parts of the country, including the area through which the Pan-American Highway passes, there are broadly two seasons: May to October, when it is hot and wet, and November to April, cooler and dryer. An important influence, though, is altitude. Mexico City and Oaxaca, both high up, are relatively cool and dry throughout the year. If you venture up one of the volcanoes, as Andrew James did for this book, you will need to be kitted out in cold-weather gear.

Is Mexico a good place to start or finish a trip along the Pan-American Highway?

Yes; the question is, where is the best place to start or finish? The real pearls are strung out from Mexico City through Puebla and Oaxaca to the state of Chiapas. So, if time is tight, start in the capital and head east. If you can afford the time to indulge yourself, spend a week or two heading south from Texas on the Panamericana, enjoying the blissful absence of other tourists all the way from Monterrey to Pachuca. Or, approach Mexico City from a different direction entirely, for example south along the Pacific coast then inland via Guadalajara.

Who are the Mexicans?

The 100 million or so people are a tremendous mix from pure-blooded descendants of the indigenous Maya to inbred Hispanic, but most are a mestizo blend of these and other influences. They are mostly friendly, and deeply moral – though many Mexicans also take a relaxed view of the dominant religion, Catholicism. As elsewhere in the Spanish-speaking world, the influence of the Church has declined significantly in recent years.

Given the growth of tourism – from Britain alone, numbers have risen five-fold in five years – the nature of the relationship between the visitor and the host is changing. But the vast majority of people will be hospitable and helpful, and can usually be counted upon to rescue you from most scrapes in which you find yourself.

What they eat

From *desayuno* (breakfast) to *cena* (dinner), you can expect to eat some of the best food of your life in Mexico. As everywhere, habits are changing as multinational fast food encroaches. But from wonderfully fresh street snacks to elaborate dining, you are likely to have a splendid time tucking in to Mexico.

The basic element of Mexican food is the *tortilla* – a flat, unleavened pancake – made with either wheat (when filled, becoming a *burrito*) or cornflour (a *taco* when filled). *Frijoles* (beans) are usually served refried – boiled, mashed, fried and fried again.

Breakfast in a hotel or a café usually comprises eggs of some description – often *huevos mexicanos*, where eggs are scrambled with green chilis, tomatoes and garlic to match the green, red and white of the Mexican flag. They will be served with a pile of tortillas. The main meal of the day is lunch (*comida*), begun at around 2pm and continuing through much of the afternoon if at all possible. Dinner (*cena*) starts at around 8 or 9pm, though in a reasonably sized town you can always find somewhere to eat at midnight or beyond – there are a lot of 24-hour places that serve remarkably good food.

These are the highlights of any culinary journey through Mexico: ceviche, a seafood starter marinated in lime juice; **guacamole**, mashed avocadoes, tomatoes and garlic; **enchiladas**, tortillas filled with chicken and served with a **mole** (sauce) made from vegetables, chilis and even chocolate. The lowlights are likely to be **dried grasshopper** (sold by the sackful in places like Oaxaca's markets) and poor imitations of American fast food. For more details of the breadth and depth of Mexican food, see the Lonely Planet's *World Food Guide to Mexico* (£6.99).

What they drink

Beer, and lots of it. The standard drink in Mexico is *cerveza*, always served ice-cold and usually with a glass. If you shun the glass and insist on a segment of lime being wedged in the neck, *à la* trendy bars in the 1990s, you may well be thrown out. You may have to work hard to get drunk: the domestic drink, as opposed to that exported to British bars, is usually well below 5 per cent alcohol.

With **tequila**, on the other hand, staying sober can be a problem. The drink is mainly made in the town of the same name and is distilled from the hearts of agave plants. The 'gold' version is the same as the clear or 'silver' variety but with colouring (and cost) added. In bars, tequila is usually served with a lime segment and salt. The theory is that you sprinkle salt on the back of your wrist, suck the lime, swallow the tequila, lick the salt and repeat *ad nauseam*. Some local people will be keen to encourage you. A much better bet is Mexican **wine** (*vino*), the finest of which now matches those of California. Be warned that red wine is often served inappropriately chilled.

Choose your drinking venue with care. In the typically rough *cantina*, women may feel uncomfortable or positively vulnerable. In addition, many Mexicans, especially habitués of dodgy bars, are gregarious in the extreme and welcoming towards visitors. If you do not wish to become embroiled in a hard-drinking session, decline offers of drinks politely.

A simple black **coffee** is known as either a *café Americano* or a *café negro*. Many cafés have espresso machines (*café espresso*), served without milk unless you ask for it. A *café con leche* differs from a *café con crema* because the former is served with hot milk mixed in, while the latter arrives with a separate small jug of room-temperature cream (or, more likely these days, a small plastic container that splashes ultra-heat-treated-non-dairy-whitener all over you). If you need **tea** (*té*), either give Mexico a miss, or bring your own tea bags and prepare to cause much merriment as you demand hot water and start brewing.

What they read, watch and listen to

El Día, Excelsior, Novedades and *Uno más Uno* are the main newspapers nationally, and mostly quite sensible. *La Prensa*, a mass-market tabloid, is not. Two English-language newspapers are published in Mexico City and widely available: *The News* and the *Mexico City Times*. Most Mexican newspapers are available online, as, of course, are British publications such as independent.co.uk.

Almost any hotel beyond the $20-a-night mark will offer satellite television. A selection of US television networks are available, as is BBC World TV in many locations.

Mexico City seems to be aiming for the world record of radio stations for a single location, with every space on the FM waveband used up. They are almost all terrible. For some decent audio, find an internet café with audio available, and visit one of the live networks available at bbc.co.uk.

How they enjoy themselves

The main social activity in any Mexican town is the evening promenade around the main square at the end of each day: language is no barrier when you join the swirl of humanity.

For more structured entertainment, the most accessible is the **cinema** – you can find one in even the smallest of towns. The problems are that most English-language films (and television programmes) are dubbed, often clumsily, and that gory violence is the standard cinematic fare in many cinemas. The most likely place to find foreign films in the original language is at art-house cinemas in the larger cities. You are unlikely to find good **theatre** outside the biggest cities. Mexico has many fine auditoria, but these days there is a paucity of interesting drama. A good alternative is **dance**: the Ballet Folklórico, based in Mexico City, where traditional Indian dance is fused with modern techniques.

In terms of **music**, you will not travel far before mariachi bands begin to encroach. This is normally a happy experience, with singers, guitarists and brass players circulating around city squares and popular restaurants. In the clubs, there is a constant clash between American/British dance music and Latin influences, especially salsa from Cuba.

Mexico is the only country to have hosted soccer's World Cup twice since World War II, in 1970 and 1986, which says much about the nation's obsession with *fútbol*. The best teams are in Mexico City and Guadalajara, but almost every street in every town has an impromptu pitch. Most foreign visitors find a game of soccer more palatable than the other great national sport, bullfighting.

Festivals and holidays

New Year's Day	Jan 1
Epiphany	Jan 6
Holy Thursday	
Good Friday	
Labour Day	May 1
Ascension Day	
Corpus Cristi	
Saints Peter and Paul	Jun 29
Independence Day	Jul 20
Assumption	Aug 15
Columbus Day	Oct 12
All Saints' Day	Nov 1
Independence of Cartagena	Nov 11
Immaculate Conception	Dec 8
Christmas Day	Dec 25

What they spend

'Peso' means weight, but for much of its troubled life the Mexican currency has been a complete lightweight. After a nasty dose of hyperinflation in the 1980s, several zeroes were knocked off the old peso to create a new one, known as the nuevo peso. It took another hit in 1994, but has calmed down since then, and has maintained its dignity along with an exchange rate of 10 to the US dollar (16 to the pound).

Almost everything in Mexico is attractively inexpensive. As a new arrival, you would be forgiven, though, for thinking the opposite. The symbol used for the peso is $ – exactly the same as for the US dollar, and only occasionally qualified by the initials MN, for *moneda nacional* ('national currency'). In border areas, where many prices are shown in American currency for the benefit of daytrippers (or the benefit of sharp traders wishing to fleece them), it will not always be clear which is intended.

You can change money easily almost anywhere except in banks, where a staggering amount of bureaucracy surrounds the simplest transaction. You could die of excessive air conditioning in the time it takes to change a traveller's cheque. So instead find a bureau de change. These are usually easy to spot. Some places spell out *Casa de Cambio* ('house of change'), others simply *Cambio*, while some just put a sign with a number like 9.85 on it – this means you will get that many pesos to your dollar.

The figure always refers to cash; if the enterprise accepts travellers' cheques at all, it will probably be at a worse rate. You will certainly find it difficult to change other currencies away from the big cities and resort areas – Canadian dollars, sterling and Deutschmarks are the most widely recognized, but usually the rate will be dreadful.

Every sizeable town has a range of automatic teller machines, called a *caja permanente* or *cajero automático*. Most British cash cards seem to work in these.

Easy money

Every Mexican knows the approximate prevailing peso-dollar rate. The median rate (the average of buying and selling rates) appears on the front page of newspapers, and in big cities dealers compete to offer the closest rate they can to this figure. Anyone offering you more for your dollar than the median rate is almost certain to be a crook. With no significant controls on currency transactions, there is no rational basis for the kind of black market that flourishes elsewhere.

So what sort of 'special deals' does that chap with the flashy calculator and flashier smile have in mind? The easiest trick is obsolete currency; the peso has gone through high inflation and revaluation in the past decade, and some villains pass off old notes and coins to unsuspecting tourists. Next, there is the risk that you are about to participate in an elaborate and carefully orchestrated charade involving an accomplice who pretends to see, or to be, a policeman. In the confusion, your cash is certain to disappear along with the villains, leaving you with a pittance of pesos.

The worst outcome is likely to take place at night. The transaction is carried out to your satisfaction, and you gleefully walk away knowing that you have got over 1,000 pesos for your $100. The buzz lasts for as long as it takes for you to find yourself isolated and cornered. A couple of accomplices will set about retrieving the pesos. Since they also know where you keep your stash of cash, you can expect the rest of that to disappear, too.

Anything worth buying?

Textiles produced by people of Indian origin are colourful, easy to find, and good value – until you get to Guatemala, and find the same on sale for half the price. If your benchmark is prices in the USA, then you will find shoes, jackets, belts and handbags are usually much lower than north of the border.

Every town has a regular market, always a colourful occasion. Prices for items that are clearly aimed at tourists are usually open to negotiation, but otherwise the price you see is the price you pay. Markets tend to open at dawn, and close down early. Most ordinary stores open from 8 or 9am to noon or 1pm, and again from 4pm to 7 or 8pm, daily except Sunday.

Keeping in touch

Telephone

Mexico is emerging from the telephonic stone age in which it has been locked for the 20th century – but only slowly. Anyone who recalls the sad old Soviet car known as the Lada will be dismayed to see that the name is used for the long-distance phone number, being a contraction (vaguely) of *Larga Distancia* – long distance.

Local calls can be made from any phone, including the coin-operated ones dating from the Jurassic age. If you want to make any kind of long-distance or international call, buy a phone card (*tarjeta telefónica*), find a payphone which is (a) working, and (b) not on a terminally noisy street corner, and hope for the best. With a 100-peso card, you can usually talk to Britain for about three minutes.

Mail

The postal service in Mexico is neither cheap nor cheerful. If you can, save your postcards for elsewhere in Central America, where the service may not be any

---

Away in a mailbag

If you were expecting a Christmas card from me in 1999, my apologies. All of them were posted in early December, from the handsome central post office in Monterrey – chosen deliberately because of its location in Mexico's most go-ahead city. The first arrived around 10 January 2000, and most of the remainder trickled through letterboxes over the following two months. Some of them simply disappeared altogether. Honest.

swifter but at least you will not end up paying the earth for it. In Mexico, not only is the cost of the stamp high (6 pesos for a postcard to Britain), it is also slow and unreliable.

Internet

There are more internet cafés in a single street in San Cristóbal than in the whole of Monterrey. By now that may be an exaggeration, but it remains the case that internet cafés are 'backpacker-driven'. Where there is a significant population of travellers, there will probably also be several cyber cafés, with rates squeezed down to as little as $2 per hour. Elsewhere, the best chances are at educational institutes, where surplus computer power is often rented out on an ad-hoc basis. Rates are likely to be much higher where there is no competition. For a patchy list of internet cafés, consult amcc.org.mx – but remember that only the cafés that could be bothered to join the Asociación Mexicana de Cyber Cafés are listed.

A handy site for pre-planning or checking out while on the road is mexicanwave.com, which was launched in April 2000. It contains up-to-date information on everything from food to football, and you can also sign up for an e-mail newsletter.

The outdoors – how great?

You might not think so when stuck in the middle of the capital, but Mexico is thinly populated: the UK is four times more crowded. So there is plenty of wilderness; the problem lies in exploring it. Little interest is shown among the local people in exploring the outdoors, so in many places it is difficult to get a decent map of the terrain and there are no signposted trails. A day's hike often involves a high degree of guesswork and requires an adventurous nature. With a few precautions, however, there is nothing to stop you enjoying the largely unspoilt natural beauty of Mexico and its flora and fauna. Take local advice, a hat and sunscreen, and make sure you carry enough water.

The most attractive area to explore is the Chiapas highlands, but there have been a series of attacks on backpackers in this area. You are most likely to avoid problems if you sign up for a tour – which may involve hiking, cycling or horseriding – with a reputable company in San Cristóbal.

Staying safe

A bunch of thugs who will stop at nothing to relieve the unwary victim of cash and valuables. And that's just the Mexican police. They have been discovered to have been involved in perpetrating numerous crimes, which is perhaps why they show so little interest in solving other misdeeds. Given the dreadful reputation and hopeless amateurism of the local constabulary, it is a miracle – and a tribute to the moral rectitude of the population – that crime is not worse.

Bag-snatching and pick-pocketing are a danger mainly in Mexico City (and the unsavoury border towns of Ciudad Juárez and Tijuana), but are not unheard of elsewhere. The logic is simple. As a foreigner, you are probably carrying a lot of cash, perhaps US$100, which for the average Mexican represents wages for a month or more. Therefore theft of a wallet or purse presents understandable temptation, particularly to poor young urban dwellers.

Western visitors displaying ostentatious wealth in darkened backstreets are asking for trouble – as is anyone who leaves their worldly goods on a beach while going for a swim. Leave as much money as possible in your hotel, and carry what you take with you in a moneybelt beneath your clothes or a pocket that can be buttoned or zipped shut. Do not carry around shoulder bags that can be easily swiped. Cameras symbolise gringo wealth and can be a big temptation too.

If you fall victim to a crime, the police are unlikely to show any interest in registering the event, let alone solving it. To reclaim losses from your insurers, you will need to provide evidence of the theft, and the police may make a charge for this 'service'. Make sure that the statement or *denuncia* is stamped.

For lost or stolen air tickets, contact your agent back home (most easily done by e-mail) or talk to the airline direct. Lost passports should be reported to your consulate. As well as obtaining new documents you will need to visit the immigration office to get a new tourist card: this is a formality as long as you have the police report of the robbery, and your new passport. If all your money is stolen, the consul can also arrange for funds to be sent from your home country or, as a last resort, repatriate you. Should the worst happen and you lose everything shortly before departure, ways and means can usually be found to get you home bereft of tickets and passport.

Mexico is awash with illegal **drugs.** The country is on the established route between the cocaine and marijuana producers of South America and the world's biggest narcotics market, the USA. There is also a prodigious amount of local production of marijuana, which is used by many young Mexicans. The penalties for possessing illegal drugs are severe, and will at the very least involve deportation. Penalties for dealing are harsher still, with long prison sentences.

From Texas to Monterrey

There are several points along the Pan-American Highway at which you are likely to get that sinking feeling and wonder if you haven't made a terrible mistake. Heading south from Nuevo Laredo, you are likely to lurch into despondency as soon as you hit the road. A dusty dual-carriageway ploughs through a drab landscape punctuated by auto repair shops and corpses of the vehicles that proved to be beyond help. The poor state of the road means that travelling at anything approaching the 60km/h limit will rattle every tooth in your mouth and render sensible conversation impossible.

To make matters worse, the dismal film 'That thing you do' has been dubbed into loud and lousy Spanish and is assailing three senses: your eyes, ears, and taste. At least, you think as you settle back into the unsavoury stickiness on your seat created by years of humanity sweating against the PVC covering, the trip only lasts three hours. Then, out of the blank horizon, looms the Instituto Nacional de Migración, and alongside it the Aduana de Nuevo Laredo. What, you may wonder, are the officials who normally control frontiers doing so far inland?

The answer is that the first 25km (15 miles) of Mexico comprise nothing but a buffer zone, the no-man's territory between the promised land and the country that is the third-class citizen of North America. The border here is not so arbitrary as the 49th parallel (49 degrees north) that divides the USA from Canada, but there are a lot more people trying to cross it without the knowledge of the authorities. So, a short way north and south of the Rio Grande, a secondary line of defence is established. All traffic is channelled through the control point, and the whole stretch is a mass of speed bumps resembling a bad case of Tarmac acne. Officials whose expressions are as opaque as their sunglasses climb aboard and inspect credentials with a kind of 'they should have done this at the border, but I suppose I'll have to cover for them again' sigh, and slowly, after some mutterings with the driver on a subject that appears to have a lot more to do with sex and alcohol than illegal immigration, swagger off to do battle with the bus that left town an hour after you did.

A few stumpy trees appear on either side of Highway 85, and after 20km a few more start rising through mountains on a road hacked through the rock. Misty range upon misty range stacks into the distance, while in the foreground tame palms and wild horses frolic. Already, this is a different world from the one you left an hour – or was it two? – ago.

The Panamericana takes advantage of the flat terrain to hold an arrow-straight course. The highest point on the 226km (143 miles) journey from Nuevo Laredo to Monterrey is towards the end, when the road climbs imperceptibly to the summit of the Mamulique Pass – altitude 700 metres (2,300 feet). Monterrey itself spreads across the plain beneath the foothills of the beautiful Sierra Madre Oriental, the southbound continuation of the Rocky Mountains.

Border skirmish

Anyone seeking solid evidence that the US is contemptuous of life south of the border could do worse than consult the official Texas Department of Transport road map. The Nuevo Laredo side of the border is shown as plain grey, apart from a single highway heading south which is described as 'Paved Route to Mexico City', as though this is something of an achievement.

In fact, the road that allowed the Pan-American Highway to link Nuevo Laredo with Monterrey arrived in 1935.

Monterrey

Nowhere on the Pan-American Highway in Mexico or Central America compares with the sprawling, hard-working city of Monterrey. A permanent settlement was established here in 1596, but the motive was little more than territorial expansionism: the location had few natural advantages. Until the Mexico City-Laredo railway arrived in 1888, Monterrey was little but an overgrown market town. But the train changed all that: pride of place in the city's remarkable museum goes to a locomotive, celebrating the municipal industrial revolution that took place over the next century.

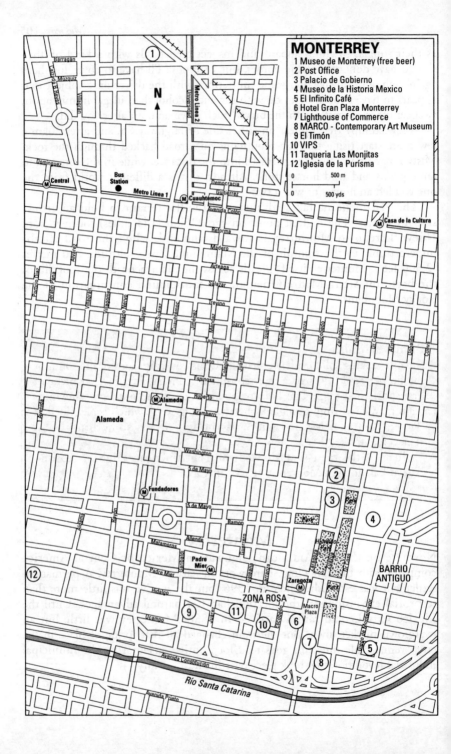

MONTERREY

1 Museo de Monterrey (free beer)
2 Post Office
3 Palacio de Gobierno
4 Museo de la Historia Mexico
5 El Infinito Café
6 Hotel Gran Plaza Monterrey
7 Lighthouse of Commerce
8 MARCO - Contemporary Art Museum
9 El Timón
10 VIPS
11 Taqueria Las Monjitas
12 Iglesia de la Purísma

0   500 m
0   500 yds

N

Barragán
Tapia de Mexquiz
Villarón
Dominguez
Central
Bus Station
Metro Linea 1
Metro Linea 2
Universidad
Democracia
Gutierrez
Cuauhtémoc
Avenida Colón
Casa de la Cultura
Reforma
Madero
Arteaga
Salazar
Treviño
Sarza
Alvarez
Jardín Fina
Porfirio Díaz
Villagrán
Amado Nervo
Bravo
Juan Suárez
Cuauhtémoc
Galeana
Garibaldi
Naranjo
Juárez
Guerrero
Rayón
Terán
Zaragoza
Aramberri
Escobedo
Dr. Cross
Alofa
Universidad
Tapia
Llano
Espinosa
Ruperto
Alameda
Alameda
Aramberri
Arreola
Washington
5 de Mayo
Fundadores
5 de Mayo
Ramon
2
3
Park
4
Park
Hidalgo Park
BARRIO ANTIGUO
Allende
Matamoros
Degollado
Padre Mier
Hidalgo
Padre Mier
12
Zaragoza
ZONA ROSA
9
11
10
6
Macro Plaza
Park
Ucampo
Escobedo
Juan de Montemayor
7
5
8
Avenida Constitución
Río Santa Catarina
Avenida Prieto

The raw statistics of modern Monterrey are unappealing for the tourist: it leads the nation in the production of everything from steel to soap. Most of Monterrey's two million people are busy turning the economic dynamo that powers much of Mexico, north and south. You approach on an ungainly highway that has been driven ruthlessly through shabby suburbs. These crowd around the colonial core so effectively that it can be difficult to find the real heart of the city. And then, when you do, you discover the strangest plaza in Mexico, a confection formed from reckless civic ambition.

City essentials

Getting your bearings

The Highway from Nuevo Laredo approaches from the north parallel to the railway line. At the point when it encounters the university, about seven kilometres/four miles north of the centre, the motorist can elect to avoid the city altogether, by taking the ring road that acts as an ineffective barrier to traffic. If you are heading on for the south, take the left-hand (eastbound) side of this circle.

Much better, though, to plough on (as the bus will) to the Avenida Colón, which marks the northern boundary of the city centre. This is the venue for the huge **bus terminal**, and also the **cheap hotel** and **red light district** (as everywhere in Mexico, inexpensive accommodation and the sex trade are never far apart).

The street layout gets much denser, with the city crammed into a grid system which seems inadequate to deal with so much humanity. The **centre** is south and east of here, bounded by the extraordinary **Macro Plaza**, a ten-block deep, one-block wide strip between the main post office and the southern ring road, the Avenida Constitución. Just east of here, there is a corner of colonialism, the **Barrio Antiguo**, that somehow has evaded the bulldozers.

Arrival and departure

The **bus station** must have won the longest-terminal-in-Mexico competition at some stage. It runs for about 500m along Avenida Colón. Given the complexity of the place, you should allow plenty of time to locate and catch your bus (not that there's much chance of it leaving on time). You can travel direct from here to many points in north and central Mexico, to Brownsville in Texas and even to Chicago on Autobuses Americanos.

The main bus companies are Frontera, Oñibús de México and Transportes Nacional del Norte, all of which compete on the Pan-American Highway routes north to Nuevo Laredo and south to Ciudad Victoria. Those on the luxury services to Mexico City may take advantage of the Sala VIP in the centre, while people who are merely stopping off for the afternoon can use the left-luggage office to the west of it (on the left as you look at the buses). Finally, if all you want to do is write some postcards in between buses, there is a post office at the western end of the upper floor.

Getting around

Metrorrey is the name of the modest **underground/overground railway** that makes getting around the city straightforward – so long as you confine your travels to the skewed cross-shape formed by lines 1 (yellow) and 2 (green). The latter is underground, short and stumpy, running north-south with a dog-leg to the east at the bottom end. The entire journey takes seven minutes from end to end. Line 1 is longer, elevated and stretches out to the northwest suburbs and a long way east. The two lines meet just east of the bus station. Free connections between the lines can be made for the flat fare of 2.80 pesos, or less if you buy multiple tickets from the machines or staff at station entrances. The system runs from 5am to midnight daily, with trains at least every 10 minutes.

If this is your first experience with a big Mexican city, heighten your tolerance threshold to deal with the constant clamour of **buses**. Should you be a veteran of municipal Mexico, you might think that the usual city commotion of overcrowded and undermaintained buses might be muted by the presence of the Metrorrey, but no such luck. Neither is there any chance of a map that reveals where they might be heading. The standard advice is to hop on anything going in the right direction, and hop off when it veers away from your intended course. With fares of just two or three pesos, there is not much to lose with this method.

A room

There are a number of comfortable, civilised hotels in the city centre, of which the best value is the elegant turn-of-the-20th-century **Gran Plaza Monterrey**, a Howard Johnson property on the edge of the Macro Plaza (tel: 380 6000, toll-free within Mexico 01 800 832 4000, toll-free in the USA 1 800 432 9605). The nightly rate is around $80 single, $100 double, not including breakfast in the coffee shop on the ground floor. If your sights are set lower, then there is little option but to head for the dodgy area around the bus station. The streets directly south of the terminal are full of places that cost around $10 single/$15 double per night, and it is usually easy to work out which ones rent rooms by the hour to hookers and their clients.

A meal

At **breakfast**, choose from a couple of extremes – the market is the first real chance south of the border to get good, cheap street food and coffee with a kick. Alternatively, the branch of VIPS at Hidalgo 401 is always reliable for good breakfasts and clean loos. To pose at **lunch**, head for El Infinito on the corner of Calles Jardo and Diego de Montemayor, which promises 'libros, cafe, arte'. For an **appetiser**, there is nowhere better than El Timón, which electrifies the centre of town, with dazzlingly bright fluorescent lighting and vivid blue marine décor. It also serves excellent ceviche, the marinated raw fish that you can enjoy all the way between here and Panama City. But it doesn't get much better than this. At **dinner**, the speciality at the Taquería Las Monjitas is the Monjita, a slab of beef with bacon, onion and peppers. Alternatively, the Sabanita is an exquisitely thin layer of beef. But the good food is not what will get your attention; much more significant is that the waiting staff are all dressed as nuns, gliding between the lavishly tiled walls bearing plates of burgers.

An exploration

Plan your sightseeing as a series of broad-brush strokes, taking in the main attractions. You'll need a fair amount of energy to cover the ground, but the reward is to feel the pulse of a city that is racing ahead of the rest of Mexico.

Nowhere is this better illustrated than at the **Macro Plaza**, a public open space the size and shape of an airport runway decked in a haphazard but mighty collection of modern architecture, whose glass and steel reflects the bare hills that surround Monterrey. In the 1980s, when the conurbation was enjoying an economic boom, the city fathers had a problem: how to distinguish Monterrey from its two main rivals, Mexico City and Guadalajara? Both are much bigger, and richer historically, than the northern contender. The solution was to celebrate the new-found wealth with a bit of *nouveau-riche* flash. A ten-by-one-block strip of land was flattened, flanked by steel and glass monoliths straight out of Houston, and bedecked with public displays of affectation, in the form of grandiose modern sculpture.

Start at the northern end, where the post office and the Palacio de Gobierno are the sole survivors from the 19th century. The first sector is the Esplanada de los Héroes, a barren area save for the sculptures of all the usual revolutionary suspects from Pablo González to Benito Juárez. You move south into the Bosque Hundido, a shadier garden area with a striking, gaunt statue of a mother and two children. The area is framed by two hunky structures, the Palace of Justice to the west and the City Library to the east. At 800 Zaragoza Sur – the name of the street on the western side – the Infonavit conglomerate has its brash headquarters.

Inconveniently, a couple of roads stripe across the Plaza, bringing the pedestrian back down to the brutal reality of life at the bottom of the transport chain. On the south side of the busy Calle Padre Mier, structures commemorate the Fountain of Life, the Workers of Nuevo León and the Fountain of Commerce, the trinity that keeps the city ticking. The greatest of these assets is celebrated by the enormous Lighthouse of Commerce, an uncompromising slab that dominates proceedings – and humbles the cathedral just southeast of it. The Municipal Palace hovers uncomfortably at the foot of the Plaza, failing to provide a dazzling finale.

No matter. Thread your way between the cathedral and MARCO – the Contemporary Art Museum – into the **Barrio Antiguo**, the closest Monterrey gets to dilapidated colonialism. Turn left onto Diego de Montemayor, and meander north for seven blocks. You will find yourself at the new and excellent **Museo de la Historia México**, a highly stylised and high-tech repository for the nation's history, with lots of audio-visual effects. There are some pre-Classical ceramics, though many of the exhibits are replicas of artefacts on display elsewhere in Mexico. One notable exception is the 55-ton locomotive, a lone survivor from the Mexico City-Laredo line which opened in 1888. The carriage attached shows revolutionary films. Assuming you are heading south to the capital, the museum provides an excellent preview of Mexico City, including the original Aztec plan, and there are examples of pre-Columbian arithmetic which used a base of 20, rather than 10. The Museo de Historia México (345 9898) is open Tuesday-Thursday from 11am to 7pm; Friday-Sunday from 11am to 8pm; it is closed on Mondays. Admission is 10 pesos, except on Sundays (5 pesos).

Your next mission will take you way across town. Cut down diagonally to the **Zona Rosa**, the pedestrianised shopping and dining centre; unless you want to buy or eat something, there is no need to pause. Locate Hidalgo, and head west across a couple of viciously pumping traffic arteries. Four blocks on, in an anonymous inner suburb, you reach the bizarre and beautiful **Iglesia de la Purísima**. This church looks like a prototype for the Sydney Opera House – which, in a way, it was. Enrique de la Mora based his plans for the church on an arrangement of parabolic shells, a design which combines strength with a certain grace. The bolt-on shed at the back detracts from the overall effect, as do the undisguised air-conditioning units. But waiting inside is a tiny, and officially miraculous, figure.

Chiquita was supposed to be perched on the altar. The Virgin Chiquita was created in the 18th century, and has resided in a church on the site ever since. Her moment of glory was in 1756, when she turned the tide away from the city in the Great Flood. The Catholic church has since recognised this as a miracle. It was a minor miracle to track her down, but I finally found her sitting in a cupboard, her crown bestowing sainthood on her delicately carved 25cm-high figure.

She was, explained the verger, being kept safe because of construction work in the church. I suspect that the real reason was to shield her from the Virgin of Guadalupe cult, which outside on the streets was reaching a crescendo. Mexico's national virgin has a much higher profile than Chiquita. A manifestation of Mary, she appeared to an Indian in what is now Mexico City a few years after the Conquest and helped to accelerate the rate of spiritual conversion. To celebrate her impending festival, on 9 December, the Transportes Sultana organisation deafened the city of Monterrey when their entire fleet drove along the main streets with a cacophony of air horns underpinned by the rumbling chorus of unhealthy diesel engines. It was enough to turn you to drink.

On the trail of free beer

The **Museo de Monterrey** is a hilarious enterprise built on (and amid) the site of one of Mexico's leading breweries. Part of the original plant has been adapted as a beautiful and characterful museum, where 19th century red brick mingles with huge copper vats and merges with 21st century glasswork to create a singular art space.

That doesn't mean, of course, that the paintings hanging on these handsome walls are any good. Apart from the huge angelic sculpture made of (full) beer bottles, most of the artistic contents are a lot less inspiring than the surroundings. But, to compensate, there is a series of intriguing extras. The Cine Elizondo shows art films; and a café, in a glassed-in-courtyard, where you can sip coffee and pose.

Why bother with that, though, when outside in the grounds someone is prepared to give you **free beer**? The exterior is described as 'interactive experimental gardens', which is an elaborate name for what might strike you as a few trees, bushes and patches of grass. But these are the Planta Monterrey gardens, open 9am-5pm from Monday to Friday, and 9am-2pm on Saturday. The most significant component is the kiosk. 'As a courtesy', reads the sign on it, 'Cuahtémoc Brewery offers a Carta Blanca beer to our visitors'. The idea, of course, is that you will be tempted to continue drinking the company's products elsewhere in Mexico and, indeed, when you return home. But attempts to over-indulge in free beer are likely to be quashed by the serving staff. So, instead, aim for the adjacent baseball hall of fame. The Salón de la Fama del Beisbol Profesional de México opens 9.30am-5.30pm from Tuesday to Friday and 10.30am-6pm on Tuesdays, and comprises ranks of athletic statues of men you will never have heard of.

Fast track to Mexico City?

The route taken by most of the direct buses runs east of the Pan-American Highway. Highway 40 heads east from Monterrey through the mountains for about 40km, before linking up with Highway 57 coming in from the north. This runs due south for about 350km (218 miles) to the silver-mining city of San Luis Potosí, so named by the Spanish in the hope that it would prove as productive as the Bolivian city of Potosí. Here, Highway 57 become a fast road all the way into Mexico City, 400km (250 miles) further on. But the Pan-American Highway offers better scenery and more interesting places to stop off.

Skirting the Sierra

When you start to move further on down the Highway, try to get a seat on the left – at least for the first segment of the journey. Highway 85, the local title of the Panamericana, heads south past Tecnológico, where a couple of vast shiny cubes have fallen to earth, mimicking the rugged terrain that surrounds the city. You can opt to make do with the view from your vehicle (on the left as you leave the city), or if you are travelling on a bus belonging to the Senda group (Sendor or Transpaís) you can board at the sub-office very close to the site. Keep a look out, too, for the big orange globe on the eastern outskirts of town which is a children's museum.

A fast dual-carriageway speeds southeast to Linares, 121km (74 miles) distant. Beyond here, the Pan-American Highway crosses into Tamaulipas state and settles down to the form it continues to have for the vast majority of its journey through Mexico and Central America: a two-lane highway with shoulders broad enough for vehicles to seek refuge on when two trucks decide to race each other to Panama. It is fast and twisting, with over-confident and under-competent drivers, for the 153km (95 miles) to Ciudad Victoria. Letting someone do the driving for you will cost you the bus fare of $13.

Ciudad Victoria

By now, you are exactly 500km (300 miles) south of the US border, and probably in need of a break. Ciudad Victoria is where the alternative route from Texas (the Brownsville-Corpus Christi-Houston axis) joins the headlong rush towards the capital. Ciudad Victoria is a good place to reassure yourself that there is more to Mexican life than tarmac and traffic; like, for example, tacos and tequila.

The **bus station** is on the northeast side of town, about 2km from the main square. There are plenty of minibuses that charge 3 pesos to take you to the centre – 6, 8, 14 and 25 are the numbers to look for. Some of them take a route along the north bank of the San Marcos **river**, actually a dried-up trough for most of the year. The main street is Hidalgo, which runs southwest-northeast across the centre of town.

Compared with many of the options in northern Mexico, Ciudad Victoria is handsomely endowed with characterful **hotels**. If you want somewhere handy for the bus station, the Blanquita and the Savi are adjacent to it; the former is better. In town, the best choice is around Plaza Hidalgo. The Sierra Gorda is much the better of the two on the south side of the main square, charging 355 pesos single/400 pesos double. A couple of doors along, the Los Monteros is much cheaper and tattier at $20 single/$26 double. A few blocks away, on Calle 13 between Hidalgo and Juárez, the Hotel Scala is modern but a bit scruffy, and charges $10 single/$13 double.

It is difficult to walk for more than 10m in any direction in the centre of town without finding somewhere to **eat**, but for the optimum meal you need to head out through the dusty suburbs to the northern ring road. At the unprepossessing address of Avenida Berriozábal 1748 (on the south side, between Calles 5 and 7), Gorditas Estilo Doña Tota serves up superb gorditas – thick tortillas, a bit like pitta bread, stuffed with beef and cactus. Order two or three to start, and see if you can resist the temptation to have more. A real institution.

When you start **exploring**, Ciudad Victoria will amuse you, but not amaze you. After a gentle walk along the riverbank, switch sharp right along the broad avenue of Calle 17. At the junction with Hidalgo, the architecture is as grand as it gets for a smallish market town.

When **moving on** there are frequent buses to the obvious places – Matamoros (for the Texan border at Brownsville), Monterrey, Tampico (on the coast), San Luis Potosí and Mexico City. The capital lies due south, but you may wish to stop along the way.

On the Panamericana, Highway 85 south, the terrain starts to get more interesting after Ciudad Victoria towards Ciudad Mante. Mesas begin to appear on the horizon like giant bookends, while the landscape becomes increasingly lunar. The first truly stirring scenery of the trip is 40km (25km) south, with the shells of ancient volcanoes studding the plateau. At about this moment, you cross into the tropics by passing the **Tropic of Cancer**. The line is defined, of course, by being the latitude at which the sun is directly overhead at noon on the summer solstice.

The only reason you might mind yourself stopping off at **Ciudad Mante** is to change buses for Tampico, on the Gulf coast. An adequate place to stay is the Casa de Huéspedes Chona, adjacent to the bus station. **Ciudad Valles** is another dot where two lines meet on the map. The bus station, on the south side of town, has so many hotels and restaurants dotted around it that you wonder who on earth can support them all. The Hotel Melania does not suffer too much from bus noise and charges $10/$14 single/double.

There is something poignant about an anonymous night in an anonymous town like this. The grumpy hotel manager who wheezes up the stairs to show you a five-dollar room in all its indistinction. The bright-eyed girl whose teeth flash with the fluorescence of the tubes on the ceiling, who serves you hot chicken and cold beer even though every other customer has wandered off into the overheated midnight. The awkward dawn departee stumbles down uneven stairs after a troubled night, waking the old man whose mood has not improved with a few hours' sleep. Slipping across the uneven, unlit plaza, with the sole purpose is to get out of here as quickly as possible. Life, in all its semi-consciousness, will continue forever like this in Ciudad Valles, occasionally enriched by a few dollars by another gringo who stayed just long enough to get to know the people, but didn't.

Vencedor is an unashamedly budget operator, which charges 42 pesos for the run down from Ciudad Valles to **Tamazunchale**. The bus was defiantly second-class, loaded with market produce. Dawn was rising slowly in the east, but every so often the effect was interrupted. There would be a huge shuddering and all the lights would come ablaze to see who had stowed their worldly goods so badly that they had shifted to alter the whole balance of the bus. The sun rose to reveal a vast blank emptiness, populated only by the Rio Coy, while the Sierra Madre Occidental took shape with an extra degree of daylight to the right.

If you whizz through Tamazunchale without stopping (apart from the traffic jams that plague the main drag day and night), the place may strike you as a one-street town. This is grossly unfair: it is a two-street town. The one that forms part of the Pan-American Highway is Avenida 20 de Noviembre, and is a mass of hotels, street stalls, and buses. The parallel Calle Morelos is identical, but with fewer buses and more street stalls.

All the **bus** companies in Tamazunchale have offices on Avenida 20 de Noviembre. The leading southbound company is Flecha Roja, nearly opposite the Hotel Virrey and adjacent to the Hotel González. There are frequent second-class departures to Ixmiquilpan for 69 pesos, which is where you will need to change for the recommended slight deviation to Pachuca. You can reach Mexico City direct for 127 pesos. Note that most services are *de paso*, so finding a seat can be tricky on some first-class departures. Heading north, Vencedor has departures every 15 minutes to Ciudad Valles, which is a 42 peso ride.

Quantity, rather than quality, is the characteristic of the local **hotels**. The best of the bunch is the three-star Hotel Tamazunchale at the eastern end of Avenida 20 de Noviembre, which charges $30 single/$48 double. At the other end of the scale, the Casa de Huéspedes El Triunfo on Calle Morelos (opposite the BBV bank) is $5/$7 respectively. The remainder on the Pan-American Highway are somewhere in between, but you may regret taking a room that faces out on to the main road.

For street **food**, the stalls on Calle Morelos cover every option. For a 'proper' meal, try La Baura de Tampico fish restaurant on the south side of the Pan-American Highway.

The main reason to stop in Tamazunchale is to prepare yourself for the best stretch of road so far. After the entire harvest of tangerines had been loaded into the hold, we set off to climb into the mountains. The next stage of the journey is wonderfully dramatic, but you should sit on the right to make the most of it.

After 30km (18 miles) you leave Veracruz behind – having sampled no more than 60km of the state – and cross into the large and powerful state of Hidalgo. Soon you enter a vast canyon, running north-south, and the bus claws its way up the eastern side. The hills fade into the mist as you pass Puerto Obscuro.

Jacala is a jolly market town, and sufficiently big to have its own truckstop. **Minas Viejas**, in the same municipality, indicates that mineral territory is beginning. The clumsy chunks carved out of the hillsides, and the dusty nothingness that constitutes the town these days, suggest that the mining business is not what it once was. At the same time, the terrain becomes more arid and some cacti begin to appear, their spiky limbs looking as though they have frozen mid-flail.

As the ravaged hills begin to dwindle, you finally rumble down into the truckstop known as Ixmiquilpan. Here, you can already begin to sense the proximity of Mexico City, even though it is another 162km away: the pace of life and the density of traffic has stepped up a couple of gears. You will have no problem finding a bus onward to Actopan, though the road is dreary, dusty and riddled with *topes* to slow down the traffic. Don't bother going off the Highway to investigate the town of Actopan; all the through buses stick to the main road, which soon becomes a fast dual carriageway through cactus-strewn wilderness. But before you surrender yourself to the all-consuming capital, pause for some provincial fun.

Pachuca is entertaining for many reasons. For a start, the bus station is the only one in Mexico with a chapel in the middle of the main concourse. Passengers in a hurry can find themselves tripping over worshippers, while those with time to spare can experience a Mass before mass transit. Outside the bus station – which sits on the southern edge of town, close to the freeway to Mexico City, local buses depart every few seconds to the centre of Pachuca – venue for more pastie shops than Penzance.

Cornish miners were brought over in the 19th century to work the silver mines. They brought over their traditional underground meal, a savoury mix of meat and veg wrapped up in thick pastry. The concept of the pastie was of an easy-to-eat, filling and vaguely nutritious parcel, the ideal subterranean snack. The Cornish community has waned to nothing (though look closely in the Plaza de la Independencia and you may see the odd streak of red hair or flash of blue eye. The main square is unusually handsome, a result of well-proportioned buildings clustered around it and the impressive Reloj Monumental – a clock perched atop an illustrious tower.

If you need a **place to stay**, take your pick from the Hotel Emily on the south side of the plaza, or Ciro's on the north face. On the east side is the amusing neo-classical Bancomer, and just south of there is Pastes Kiko's. This **pastie shop** is the best in town (I checked), and is decorated with a mural of a cartoon miner in a mine shaft hacking away at a pastie.

There is much to be said for spending a morning or afternoon here. The city rambles up into the hills, and is decorated with a dozen churches, ancient and modern. The oldest is the monastery of San Francisco, half a dozen blocks east of the main square. (Just next to it, by the way, on Calle Arista, is Pachuqueños pastie shop.)

The lavish church of San Francisco leans out across a small, tranquil square. Amid the dripping décor you will find a casket containing – it is said – the remains of Santa Columba, who died in 273AD. Adjacent, the National Museum of Photography is well worth a visit; it opens 10am-6pm, from Tuesday to Saturday. The history of the art from Niepce's first efforts is explained in Spanish, while exhibits such as a walk-though darkroom remind you of life before the Polaroid and 60-minute express developers. There are some lovely old cameras, and expositions on the use of photography in 19th-century archaeology, but best of all are the images. The pioneering American photographer shot his way around Mexico in the 19th century, while in the 20th century Nacho López has a hilarious sequence involving a campesino carrying a naked female mannequin around town, into cafés and onto buses.

Teotihuacán – the most historic place in the Americas?
Ambitious users of the bus system will want to visit Teotihuacán direct from Pachuca, which is possible with a couple of changes. But most of us are content with making it a day trip from the capital.

The greatest architectural site within reach of the Pan-American Highway is 50km (30 miles) northeast of the capital. As you struggle free of the shanty settlements, there is no hint that you are about to encounter 'the place where men become gods'. The first Mesoamerican civilisation planned that this transition should take place in suitably heavenly surroundings. So 21 centuries ago, the Avenue of the Dead was laid out. The approach is encumbered by souvenir vendors, but once free of them you can walk through a petrified city of awesome proportions. Much of the fabric of this once-noble place lies ruined on either side of the thoroughfare, whose name is appropriate. Teotihuacán had expired by the eighth century, abandoned in favour of the lower altitude and better water supplies on the present site of Mexico City. But time has had only the most superficial effect so far on the miraculous Pyramid of the Sun and its smaller, younger sibling, the Pyramid of the Moon.

That was then

Built in a fertile valley 50kms (33 miles) to the northeast of present-day Mexico City, Teotihuacán was the first urban civilisation in Mexico. It remained the most important city for several centuries before the Spanish conquest. Once the centre of a flourishing civilisation, Teotihuacán was at the height of its powers at the end of the sixth century, when it covered an area of around 20 square kilometres (eight square miles) and was home to more than 150,000 people.

Construction of the city is thought to have begun at around the same time as the beginning of the Christian Era, although there is evidence that people may have been living in the area several hundred years before that. The long Avenida de los Muertos, (Avenue of the Dead), forms the main north-south axis of the site. There is sure to have been some astrological significance in the choice of its position, but no-one seems entirely sure what. This avenue was crossed at right angles by another main street, and together these formed the basis of the grid system on which the rest of the city was constructed.

The buildings along the Avenue of the Dead were mainly ceremonial, although the wider community of Teotihuacán would have contained many artisans and peasants as well as an élite ruling class. At the northern end of the avenue is the Pyramid of the Moon; this is truncated at the top to allow for the building of a temple, and surrounded by smaller pyramids. The avenue is dominated by the Pyramid of the Sun to the east, the largest structure in the city. This is built in several tiers, and is also truncated at the top to allow space for a temple. A grand staircase rises up on one side of the pyramid, facing the Avenue of the Dead. To the south, the Ciudadela, or citadel, is a sunken courtyard surrounded by temples built on their own platforms. In the centre of this structure is the Temple to the Aztec god Quetzalcóatl.

It was originally believed that the buildings in between these main structures were tombs, but they are now believed to have been palaces. The common people would have been relegated to far less luxurious living quarters on the edge of the city.

The influence of Teotihuacán was felt throughout the region through trading and cultural links, and artefacts, particularly pottery copied from the Teotihuacanos, continue to be found in excavations throughout central America. After flourishing for several centuries, Teotihuacán was finally invaded by the Toltec, whose own capital was at nearby Tula, during the sixth century AD.

Although some of the links between the different cultural groups of this part of Latin America are unexplained, it is thought that the Teotihuacanos might have been ancestors of the Aztecs, although expert opinion is divided on this. Their city became a place of pilgrimage for the Aztec rulers, in whose language, Nahuatl, the name Teotihuacán means the City of the Gods.

A complete investigation of the ruins will take about five hours. Thus, this could make a pleasant day trip. Alternatively, it is possible to stay the night before. Either way, arrive early to avoid the swarms of buzzing school kids and if you get there before 10am, the only beings to disturb your correspondence with the ancients will be the extended families of stray dogs that have taken up residence there.

The ruins are open 8am-6pm daily. Entrance is $2.50, with a $1 surcharge for video cameras. The site is free on Sundays and public holidays (when large crowds are usual). The famous 'Sol y Luna' light show has been abandoned. Visitors unprepared for the weather can be seen to leave the ruins lobster pink or a goose-pimpled blue. Suncream, thick jumper and a hat are recommended; alternatively, a rolled umbrella, bowler hat and suit will leave you prepared whatever the weather. Hawkers are numerous, but they do not go for the hard sell: a simple 'no gracias' and a smile will suffice.

Three kilometres (two miles) from the ruins is San Juan Teotihuacán which has a splendid 16th century church, and a few hotels and restaurants. In February, 2000, a cybercafé should have been installed at Plaza Juárez 8; e-mail amtze@hotmail.com for more information.

San Juan and the archaeological site are served by buses from gate 8 (on the far left as you enter) of the Autobús del Norte terminal in Mexico City (reachable on the Metro line 5 to Autobús del Norte). Buses cost $1.50 each way, and depart every 20 minutes. San Juan buses stop in the central plaza before going on to the ruins. Buses going direct to the ruins stop outside gate 1. The last one leaves the ruins at 11pm. Buses leave Mexico City from 7am to 6pm.

In San Juan itself there are two **hotels**: the Posado Silverio, just off main square, with four rooms at a flat $7 single/double, which is pretty grotty (plastic undersheets for bed-wetters). Much better is the clean and quiet Hotel Pirámides Plaza on Calle Guerrero 12 (01 595 601 67), which costs $10 single/double with bathroom. One kilometre from San Juan and 2 km from the ruins is Posado Sol y Luna, (01 595 623 68/71), which is $20 single, $24 double, $35 with jacuzzi. It is a good, cheap alternative to Villas Arqueológicas (01-595-60909), whose main advantage is that it overlooks the ruins – oh, and that there are tennis courts and a swimming pool.

In San Juan, the place to **eat** is Los Pinos, where the food and prices are straightforward and the owner Luis Díaz is extremely chatty (in Spanish). At the ruins, the smart restaurant at gate 1 ($10 per head) is open 11am-5pm. Five minutes away from gate 5 is La Gruta ('the grotto') which is literally in a cave, and is remarkably lively for a place so close to a pile of old stones. Call 01 595 60104 or visit lagruta.com.mx for more details. It opens 11.30am to 7pm, and costs about $12 per head. On Saturdays and Sundays, a free dance show with live music is put on for diners between 3.30 and 5.30pm.

One kilometre from gate 2 on the road to San Juan outside Los Jardines de Cactoses is a hut served by two jolly, plump sisters. Full breakfast or lunch costs about $2.

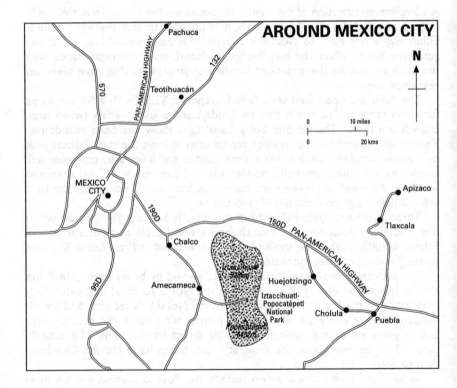

Mexico DF: the place that puts the 'city' in 'terminal velocity'

Before you come down to earth, take a deep breath. Mexico City hides in a volcanic hollow, normally nestling beneath a blanket of smog – hence the smouldering glow that greets incoming planes. Humanity can become too intense. Since 1970, the number of people living in Mexico has more than doubled – to 100 million. From your experience of the *Distrito Federal* (capital area), you would be forgiven for thinking that the increase has taken place entirely within the ambiguous city limits.

To decide whether or not you will enjoy Mexico City, try this simple test. Someone has plonked an international airport well within the boundaries of the world's biggest capital. Your reaction is either (a) yikes! – the final horror in a gallery of urban squalor; or (b) gosh, how convenient, and what a spectacular introduction to the city – particularly at dusk, when a smouldering blood-orange glow drapes over the whole vast arena. If you choose the latter, and happen to turn up at said airport, or indeed any of the city's bus stations, your person and possessions will soon be packed tightly into a taxi that defies most known principles of mechanics. The driver will pick the right beat to join the complex choreography that constitutes traffic here. Imagine large lumps of steel being hurled at high speed in seemingly random directions on a surface better suited to tanks than to clapped-out Volkswagen Beetles, then remember you are enclosed in one of them. Welcome to Mexico City.

At the point when a tram, a truck and Tristar are about to converge on your taxi, you could start to feel breathless from both fear and the high altitude. But hold on tight, and your anxieties will evaporate. The world's biggest city is also one of the wildest, yet simultaneously a place of immense grace and civility. Mexico City turns out to possess a serene soul, which rewards those with the modicum of courage required to seek it out. Graceful colonial architecture, ground down by time and tectonics, has been amplified by handsome flourishes by 19th-century architects and the odd eruption of Mexico moderno brashness.

The archaic street layout reflects the fact that the Spanish imposed their capital upon an ancient Aztec site, and furthermore one which straddles a geological fault line. In 1985 the earth shrugged a little, and at least 8,000 citizens died. Perhaps this was a final murmur of revenge from Moctezuma, whose palace lies buried beneath the present Palacio Nacional. Traces of the original have been eradicated by an edifice that shows up all the eccentricities inherent in Mexico.

Today, Mexico City has perhaps 20 million citizens. Tomorrow, 3,000 more citizens will join them, as the capital hurtles towards the demographic equivalent of terminal velocity. Get there soon, before the city reaches its inevitable conclusion.

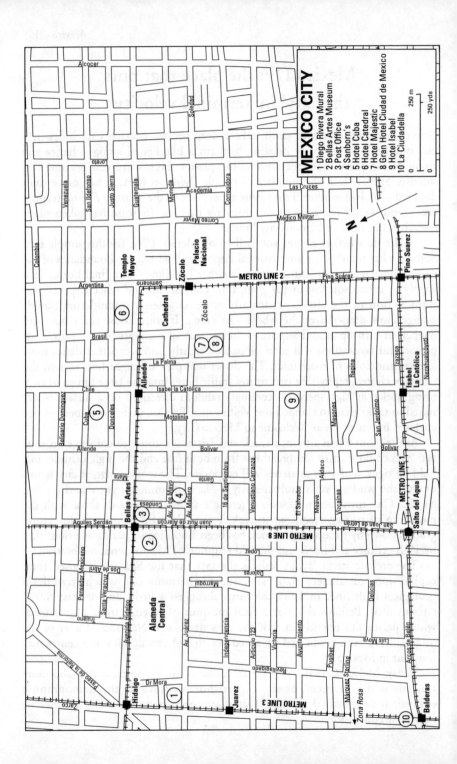

That was then

The Aztecs, a tribe of hunter-gatherers from northern Mexico, began migrating southwards during the 12th century. The sun god Huitzilopochtli had, they believed, predicted they would see a sign to indicate where they would settle, and they lived a nomadic existence until they found it. Eventually some of the tribal elders saw an eagle sitting on a cactus, attacking a serpent with its beak. After a brief, intense discussion, they concluded that this spot, on an island in the middle of Lake Texcoco, was where they should set up their base. Despite these less-than-ideal surroundings, this was that place that they adopted as their capital. A temple was built, land was reclaimed, and the world's greatest megalopolis was born.

This unlikely geographical location conferred serious problems upon the Aztecs. The inhospitable terrain made building tricky; *chinampas*, or floating platforms, were anchored into the lake, and buildings put up on top of them. Eventually the lake was filled in, but this fragile subsoil continues to cause difficulties for city planners, in an area that is also afflicted by seismic activity. The site had one big advantage, too: no one else was willing to venture into such territory, which had become a kind of no man's land between three opposing tribes.

The Aztecs were also known as the Tenochca, so the city they founded became known as Tenochtitlán. They used the base for incursions into enemy territory, conquering the neighbouring tribes and eventually building up the beginnings of a powerful empire, unrivalled throughout Latin America by anyone except, perhaps, the Incas. Tenochtitlán reached the height of its power and influence under the 'god-king' Montezuma II, who built up a vast political and military bureaucracy at the beginning of the 16th century. But by this time the days of the empire were numbered. Hernán Cortés had been exploring the Mexican coastline since 1517. When he penetrated the interior, he found a flourishing city of more than 400,000 people; eventually he laid siege to Tenochtitlán, and despite the spirited defence put up by the Aztecs, succeeded in destroying it. Montezuma was captured by Cortés, and later died in custody.

The Spanish conquistadores took over the city, and turned it into the centre of their operations in northern Latin America. Like many of the towns and cities they conquered, they imposed upon it a rigid development plan. The ceremonial centre of the old Aztec city was turned into their main square, the Plaza de la Constitución, known to everyone as the Zócalo. This was where all their public buildings were located: on one side, the Metropolitan Cathedral where the main Aztec temple once stood, on another, the National Palace replaced the vast palace occupied by King Montezuma.

Rapid expansion followed, although always on a rather haphazard basis. Spanish rule continued in Mexico for nearly 300 years, with very little resistance. As a result of the War of the Spanish Succession, between 1701 and 1713, the Bourbons became the new ruling family, and various administrative reforms were instituted.

As everywhere in Latin America, the 19th century was when the people found a voice and their nations won independence. In September 1821, Agustín de Iturbide and his followers entered the capital, independence from Spain was declared, and Iturbide was installed as president. He was deposed by Antonio López de Santa Anna, who declared a Republic three years later. The country adopted a federal constitution, which aimed to centralise government in Mexico City, and the Federal District was established.

Santa Anna's misguided adventurism during the Mexican-American War in the 1840s cost Mexico much of its territory and saw the capital captured by American troops. The country's geographical boundaries were severely limited by the Treaty of Guadalupe of 1848, under which considerable amounts of territory were given up to the United States.

Despite the losses, Mexico City flourished as the 19th century progressed. The Habsburg archduke, Maximilian, arrived from Trieste to become Emperor in 1864. He set about expanding the city limits, and built the Paseo del Emperador to connect his palace with the castle at Chapultepec. The Paseo is still one of the city's main thoroughfares, although it is now known by its modern name, the Paseo de la Reforma. Rapid modernisation took place in the city during the last quarter of the 19th century; the changes introduced were similar to those made in Paris under Haussmann. The architectural influence at this time was predominantly French, and buildings from this period include the Post Office and the Palace of Fine Arts. A drainage system was completed, and street lighting was installed. All in all, the city must have looked an awful lot smarter than it does today.

During the Revolution of 1910-1917, the city became a battlefield, and people poured into the capital from the countryside. A badly-needed modernisation took place in 1924, when another main thoroughfare, the Avenida Insurgentes, was constructed; modern buildings replaced many of those that had been influenced by French design. Until 1930, expansion continued but on a very haphazard basis. Then a series of planning commissions were set up, which resulted in the reorganisation of the city, and the destruction of many of its oldest districts.

The first skyscrapers were built in the 1930s, and the influence of modern architects continues to be felt throughout the city. But the city's marshy subsoil has always been a problem for the planners, a fact underlined by the serious earthquake that hit Mexico City in 1985, destroying many buildings.

The Olympic Games, held in Mexico City in 1968, led to the building of a new district on the southern outskirts of the city. One of the landmarks of this area is the headquarters of UNAM, the Universidad Nacional Autónoma de México, with its well-known, mural-bedecked tower blocks. The Games also marked a low point in the city's history, when hundreds of protesting students were killed during a demonstration. The next three decades were as rocky in Mexico City as in the rest of the country, but the capital began the 21st century with something approaching enthusiasm.

City essentials

Getting your bearings

Of course Mexico City looks bewildering and ungainly to the new arrival. Whether you arrive by air or road, you find yourself caught up in a tide of humanity, most of it swirling – or stuttering – around town in beaten-up vehicles. But so long as you base yourself in the ancient Aztec core of the city, you will find it surprisingly manageable.

Since long before Cortés arrived, the centre of the capital, and of Mexico, has been the huge **Zócalo** (square). During the day, a Mexican flag the size of a tennis court flies over the square. Just west is the old commercial centre, the **Centro Histórico**, the area where you can happily spend most of your time. There are some great places to eat, and many of the main attractions are within easy reach. The western boundary of this area is marked by the huge Palacio de Bellas Artes, and beyond that the Alameda Central, the green(-ish) heart of the capital.

The next most popular area with foreign visitors is the **Zona Rosa** ('pink zone'), a couple of miles south west. These are not especially pleasant miles to walk, taking you through some rough areas where tourists have been attacked in the past. But, perhaps surprisingly, almost all the remaining places in which you could find yourself are pretty safe – so long as you take the usual precautions to make sure you are not an easy target.

To the north of the centre is the **Terminal Norte**, a bus station that occupies an area the size of a small country. To the east stands a similar-sized bus station known as **TAPO** (for destinations in the east of Mexico), and a short way beyond that the city's **airport**. To the south, there are some attractive suburbs, such as **Coyoacán**, together with the **Terminal Sur**. Over in the west, the wide and beautiful Bosque de Chapultepec contains the country's best museum, devoted to anthropology. And in between you will encounter many millions of people.

Arrival

New arrivals on the Pan-American Highway from Pachuca or further north will turn up at the Terminal Norte. If it is daylight and you do not have too much money, you may be happy to take the Metro from the adjacent station, Autobuses del Norte. Otherwise, join the locals on the hard shoulder of the main road into the city and try to flag down a taxi. On the meter fare, this should take you to the centre for no more than $5.

The world's favourite airport?

You may elect to begin your Panamericana experience at Mexico City, in which case you have the exciting prospect of arriving by air. If coming in to land in the early evening – as flights from Europe tend to do – be sure to take a window seat on the right-hand side. As one old hippie observed, this will allow you to 'Watch the coal-fires of the Western horizon smoulder on the setting day, and feel your heart glow for adventures that lie ahead'. Alternatively, sit on the left to avoid the hippies. At the airport, formalities can be overwhelmed if several big planes arrive at once. Get off the aircraft as quickly as possible to try to avoid the considerable queues at customs. Smugglers should beware that all luggage is X-rayed.

Aeropuerto International Benito Juárez is about 10km (six miles) east of the city centre. It is divided into six zones: A-D are for domestic arrivals and departures. E and F are for international arrivals and departures respectively. Bureau de changes and ATMs are liberally spread throughout the airport. Rates vary little. A post office is in zone A, keeping normal office hours. A helpful tourist information booth can be found in zones A and E, with staff who speak some English. The office is open 9am-8pm. Note that it is run by Century XXI, a private company and so advice is not entirely independent. The company offers tours in and around the city and a limousine service from the airport if required.

If you don't require a limousine, take an official taxi (white with a yellow strip). Pay around $7 for a ticket to the city centre, at the booth in zone E. No further payments whatsoever should be made before, during or after the journey. Do not let the driver have his part of the pre-paid ticket until reaching the hotel or he will swindle you. Make sure you have a reservation at the hotel you are heading for – the taxi fare does not include ferrying you to alternatives. If the taxi-driver warns you at the airport that your chosen hotel is 'closed' he is probably trying to divert you to the one owned by his brother-in-law. Come back a few minutes later and use another driver.

The other option is the Metro. Avoid rush hour or come out like a hot rolled taco. Pick-pockets are said to be numerous on the Metro. The airport has its own station (called Terminal Aérea, not the stop named Boulevard Puerto Aéreo), but it will take a minimum of two trains to get you to the centre of town. Buses are available but involve a changeover in the city outskirts and are therefore not recommended.

Getting around

The civilised way to travel around is the **Metro**, where a flat fare of a couple of pesos will take you anywhere. Buy a token at the kiosk – or invest in ten to cover your future trips – and drop it in the entrance gate. Trains arrive frequently and efficiently. Rush-hour services tend to be full to bursting, but during the rest of the day you should get a seat.

The Metro is supplemented by about a million **buses**, or at least that is what you will think when trying to cross a busy road. Take care out there. After six visits, I am still not entirely confident that any bus will go where I think it is supposed to, or where the driver says he is heading. It may also get woefully stuck in traffic, partly because of the one billion or so **taxis.** The standard conveyance is a Volkswagen Beetle with the front passenger seat taken out to allow easier access, and space for your luggage. They mostly have working meters, but the driver may be unwilling to use it. If he does not, then you are likely to pay several times the going rate.

As a **pedestrian**, you are an endangered species. Even in the rare pedestrian-only precinct, you run a risk of being knocked over. When crossing a busy main road, adopt the 'safety in numbers' technique used by local people.

A room

The finest places in town, in terms of both location and style, are undoubtedly the **Gran Hotel Ciudad de México**, a marvellous 20th-century Art Nouveau extravaganza just off the main square (street address Calle 16 de Setiembre number 82, tel: 510 4040), and the handsome **Hotel Majestic**, overlooking the square itself (street address Avenida Madero 73, tel: 521 8600). Double room rates for either are around $140. So do what I did and have a good look around both places – and a drink on the rooftop bar at the Majestic – then slink off to somewhere cheaper. There are plenty of options nearby, starting with the authors' favourite cheapie: the **Hotel Isabel** (Isabel la Católica 63, tel: 518 1213 to 17, fax: 521 12 33). It has large, old-fashioned rooms and lobby; the friendly reception staff are offset by the grumpy waiters (though the restaurant and bar are reasonably priced). Free local calls can be made from rooms, and all this for a rate of $10/$12 for a single/double, about $16/$19 if you want a bathroom. Note the portrait of Isabel la Católica (the Queen of Spain when Latin America was discovered) in the lobby.

Nearby, and charging the same rates, is the **Hotel Rioja** (Cinco de Mayo 45, tel: 521 8333 or 73 or 52), but it is noisier and less friendly. Moving slowly upmarket, the **Hotel Cuba** at República de Cuba 69 (tel: 518 1380) is a perfectly good option if the first two are full, and many of the $12/$14 rooms have TVs. This is not an area of especial moral rectitude, as the Cinema Río at number 85 reveals with its all-day porn movies.

The **Hotel Canadá** (Cinco de Mayo 47, tel: 518 2106 to 13, fax: 512 9310) is a step up, and the prices for comfortable rooms with clean bathrooms and lots of hot water are $24/$26 single/double. The **Hotel Gillow** (17 Isabel la Católica 17, tel: 518 1440 to 46, fax: 510 2636) is a friendly, family-owned hotel with a decent restaurant and bar for $27/$31.

The best middle-market option is the modern **Hotel Catedral**, so-called because it stands two blocks behind the cathedral at Donceles 95 (tel: 518 5232 or 521 6183, fax: 512 4344, hotelcatedral.com.mx), which runs at $40/$50. Finally, the Holiday Inn, neatly positioned on the corner of Cinco de Mayo and the Zócalo (tel: 521 2121, fax: 521 2122), is just like any other **Holiday Inn**, down to the room rate of a flat $100, single or double.

A meal

Assuming you are staying in the Centro Histórico, then you will be awash with good places to eat and drink. But there is somewhere that will meet all your requirements for breakfast, lunch and dinner, not to mention elevenses, afternoon tea, a midnight feast or a takeaway at 3am. The **Café El Popular**, on Avenida Cinco de Mayo 10 – between Filomeno Mata and Eje Central – has been, as it boasts, a tradition since 1948. It serves good, fresh food 24 hours a day, with a constantly changing clientele and improbably cheerful staff. The *pan* *de dulce* (literally sweet bread) is the house speciality, but anything else from pizza to salad is possible.

The branch of **Sanborn's** – the quasi-American restaurant chain – at Avenida Madera 4 (the end away from the Zócalo) is the best in the nation, occupying the extravagant, tile-clad Casa de los Azulejos. For lunch, vendors of grilled and copiously salted corncobs will find you before you find them. If you prefer to wind back a century or two, the **Café La Ópera** at Cinco de Mayo 10, is a sturdy Baroque gem with a good line in lunch.

The name of the most intriguing restaurant I found is also its address: **Bolivar** 12. Stylish and fun, it serves excellent food and 130 varieties of tequila; in my experience one brand is more than enough. In the immediate vicinity there are numerous other options. In keeping with its upmarket name, the **Mercedes** at Calle Cinco de Mayo 57 serves good, upmarket Mexican food for $30 per head. If you are feeling particularly hungry (or poor), at **Bonko**, Isabel la Católica 33, you can eat as much buffet as you can for $8.

An exploration

There is so ridiculously much to see in Mexico City that in this book, you will get only the definite highlights. You could spend all day perambulating around the **Zócalo** (main square), possibly the greatest public square in the world. The Plaza Mayor, as it is officially known, has been the city's main meeting-place for a millennium or more. Start gently just off the southwest corner with a wander around the atrium of the **Gran Hotel** de la Ciudad de México, a century-old palace to Art Nouveau and one of the capital's most stylish locations. Occupying the north side of the square, the **Catedral Metropolitana** is a bewildering mix of architectural styles and building work: a repair programme called the *Correción Geométrica* is trying to straighten out seismic distortions. Mimicking the desecration of the Aztec palace, the cathedral was built above the site of the temple. (Or rather, the sites. The ancient calendar was based on a cycle of 52 years, and at the end of each cycle a new temple was built.) Adjacent, the **Templo Mayor** was the centre of the Aztec world, and the walk around its uncovered ruins gives a strong sense of the pre-Columbian life.

The **Palacio Nacional**, another monumental edifice, takes up the eastern face of the Zócalo. New arrivals can brush up on Mexican history with Diego Rivera's dramatic mural on the development of the nation. Tourists are allowed to delve into the heart of Mexico, and tour the Palacio Nacional for free. It resembles a promising but not perfect hand at poker: a scarlet-tinged frontage of solid Baroque, topped by Twenties triumphalism that belongs to a quite different suit. Inside, you are instantly diminished by the size and power of Diego Rivera's murals. Mexico's history, from civilisation through subjugation to revolution, wraps itself tortuously around a grand staircase.

Some of the architecture of conquest was borrowed from the vanquished civilisation – for example the pyramidical references in the cathedral – but mostly they set about constructing a city in the image of Europe. That they succeeded is most evident along the Paseo de la Reforma. The broadest and grandest of avenues slices arrogantly across the city, depositing elegant edifices along the way. It unravels in the **Bosque** (forest) **de Chapultepec**, a flourish of green that marks the western extent of the city centre. And here you find the finest museum in all of Latin America.

The people's republics

The **Anthropological Museum** celebrates the extraordinary achievements of the pre-Columbian peoples of Mexico, from the art of the Mayans to the science of the Aztecs. Three historical strands are entwined here. The first is that the indigenous cultures of Mexico were not wholly eradicated by the *conquistadores*. Descendants of the survivors can be found in communities scattered around the country; soon their numbers will exceed pre-Conquest levels. The second is that the boundaries of modern Mexico comprise an arbitrary geographical creation of the Spanish colonialists: citizens of Tijuana have much more in common with Californians just across the state line than with the Mayan people of Chiapas. The third is that the Sixties saw an assertion of *Mexicanidad*, as the country clawed its way into the polite society of established nations. The double climaxes were the Olympics of 1968 and the World Cup of 1970, but the most lasting token is the extraordinary Anthropological Museum.

Forget the Internet; Mexico invented a network for exploring cultural cross-references 30 years ago, and housed it in (still) dramatic halls that sprout out of the parkland. Everything that could be salvaged from the Conquest has been assembled here, from the tablets used to calculate the Aztec calendar to the dazzling images of the Mayans. The descriptions are almost exclusively in Spanish, but English-speaking guides are on hand to help explain the repository of national heritage. More than just a collection of geological relics, this is a reconstruction of how people actually lived. Displays of tribal costumes are placed alongside reconstructions of fishing boats, and ancient cooking utensils. In the grounds outside are reconstructions of the buildings that each of the native peoples would have occupied.

'Heritage' seems too dismissive a word to describe the collection. Its main effect is to make you want to leave town straight away and see some of the original sites. Fortunately, the most striking of all is close to Mexico City (and getting nearer all the time, as the suburbs advance): if you did not visit the pyramids of Teotihuacán on your way here, you should make your way out there for a day. Or two.

Trail of the unexpected: Line 3

Mexico City's Metro system seems ever-expanding – the latest new underground line arrived at Estación Buenavista in December 1999, connecting the city's main railway station to the Metro for the first time. Unfortunately, earlier that year train services ended. But the Metro can get you almost everywhere in the city, and if you stick to Linea 3 all day you will see a slice of the capital that eludes most tourists.

For my trail along Line 3, I arrived at the northern end by bus. This was deliberate, because although some maps show this station by its old name of Guadalupe, it is actually quite a hike from the superb Basílica de Guadalupe. Or make that basilica*s*. The first was built around 1700, at the foot of the hill where a Mexican Indian named Juan Diego witnessed the Virgin Mary. The manifestation is now revered in the 1970s dome next door, where thousands of pilgrims can pay tribute to the patron saint of Mexico. Every morning at dawn they turn up from some part of the country, everyone dressed up to the nines and bearing elaborate floral arrangements, many of them like gigantic horseshoes of flowers, dedicated to Nuestra Señora de Guadalupe. The scenes outside are a hoot: the more devout among the worshippers follow tradition and approach on their knees, with groups around them shuffling into every possible permutation for the mandatory photographs. Tourists are welcome to join in.

Take time to study the elaborate **astronomical clock**, a modern structure that keeps time according to the Aztec calendar. To escape the crowds, climb the hill for a superb view of the entire Valley of Mexico, smog willing. The Capilla del Cerro is said to be built on the site where Juan Diego saw the apparition, but few of the pilgrims make it through the gardens – which are strewn with other, lesser chapels, and up the stairway for a panorama with the stone angels who are keeping an eye on the city.

Good luck finding the station known as **Indios Verdes**. Head due west – away from the sun, assuming you can see it through the haze and did, indeed, start at dawn. The top of Line 3 is buried beyond half a dozen main roads. From here, head four stops south (the only possible direction) and hop off at **Tlatelolco**. The terrain has changed completely, from rambling outer suburbs to the fierce Sixties regimentation of apartment blocks, arranged artlessly with wide concrete voids between. Go east for almost a kilometre, and you will find the biggest void of all – the **Plaza de las Tres Culturas** – perhaps the saddest places in Mexico. The three cultures 'celebrated' here are the original Indians, the Spanish who subjugated them in a crushing battle on the site in 1521, and the people that rose from the subsequent loveless union. A plaque records the conflict as 'neither victory nor defeat . . . it was the sad birth of the *mestizo* people which is Mexico today'. Another tragedy struck the square in October 1968, when hundreds of demonstrators were killed by the security forces just as the Olympics were to begin in the capital. A new memorial pays tribute to those who came that day to change the world and ended up leaving it.

As well as unhappiness, the plaza contains some fine **ruins** of the original Aztec market square. Unlike the Templo Mayor in the centre of the capital, these are open to the public (and the elements) 24 hours a day. The claim to fame of the fine church of Santiago that presides over the plaza is the baptismal font of Juan Diego, he of the Guadalupe apparition.

You possibly won't want to trail back to the Metro, so instead you could hop onto a bus marked Hidalgo – your destination is the Metro station of this name. Close by is the **Museo Mural Diego Rivera**, home to one of the finest pieces of art in the Americas. In an unassuming modern building, the artist's heroic *Dream of Sunday Afternoon at the Alameda* depicts important figures from the Conquest onward. There is English-language information showing who is who in this marvellous ensemble of *Mexicanidad*, from Cortés to Rivera himself, but the easy option is to tag on to an English-speaking tour. An intriguing adjunct to the startling 15 x 4 metre mural tells, in contemporary photographs, the story of how it came to be located here. The original site for the piece was the Hotel del Prado, then the greatest place to stay in Mexico City. The 1985 earthquake mortally wounded the hotel, and a massive rescue operation was mounted to preserve Rivera's masterpiece. The museum opens 10am-6pm daily except Mondays, and admission is $2. Diego Rivera will pop up later in this tour.

From here, you could dream your way into a Sunday afternoon at the adjacent Alameda – or continue the trail by walking not one but two stations south, past Juárez to Balderas. Just before you reach the latter station, you will pass on the right a grand old barracks called **La Ciudadela**, which featured heavily in the Mexican revolution and is now the premier library in Mexico. As it is a public building, you are at liberty to wander through the cool, shady courtyards.

At Balderas, hop on for three stops to **Centro Médico**, where Lines 3 and 9 meet. Hop off to inspect the fabulous murals that decorate the ticket hall – you should be able to do this without passing through the barrier, so you need not use another token.

The longest stretch of the journey takes you five stops to **Coyoacán** station, which is actually some way from the suburb of that name. So too is the big attraction here, the superb **Museo Casa de León Trotsky**, at Avenida Río Churubusco 410 (tel: 658 8732, fax: 554 0687, open daily except Mondays 10am-5pm, admission $1).

Trotsky's first home in Mexico was a handy three blocks southwest at Londres 247 (streets in this part of Coyoacán celebrate European capitals), at the 'Blue House' then occupied by Diego Rivera and Frida Kahlo. Her home is now a museum to her life and art. From the front door onwards the place is a flourish of bold colours. But however bright the **Museo Frida Kahlo** (open 10am-5pm, daily except Monday) appears, it conceals a dark story, of a woman tortured by (a) childhood polio, (b) a road accident aged 18 and (c) her cruel and philandering husband.

From here, walk due south down Allende into the pretty (in Mexico City terms, at any rate) village-like suburb of Coyoacán. First you pass the local market, which boasts an excellent seafood restaurant, then you arrive in the elegant Plaza Hidalgo, which is the closest the capital gets to a 'normal' town square.

If you want, you can cop out here and grab a cab for the $2 ride to the Ciudad Universitaria, or wander back to the Metro and take the train to the

Break the ice at communist parties

That's what you'll be able to do, by revealing the secrets of the revolutionary's home. Trostky was one of the key figures in the 1917 October Revolution that brought the Bolsheviks to power in the world's largest country and saw Russia expanding to control a massive empire. After falling out with Stalin – never a politic move – following the struggle for succession after the death of Lenin – Trotsky went into exile in Mexico.

He lived for a time with the man who had negotiated the deal with the Mexican authorities, Diego Rivera, and the artist's wife Frida Kahlo (see below). After a tiff, Leon and his wife, Natalia, moved to a handsome villa at Calle Viena 45 (the museum's official address refers to the adjacent street). After a failed assassination attempt, the house was fortified; you can see the watchtowers and heavy steel gates. A Stalinist agent infiltrated with the infamous ice axe in 1940, and murdered Trotsky at his desk. It is chilling to see the site of the assassination of one of the 20th century's most significant figures exactly as it was when he died, with texts by Hitler and Lenin on the desk along with the shattered spectacles. His tomb, topped by a defiant hammer and sickle, takes pride of place in the shady garden. On my first visit, I was shown around by a Leon-lookalike, who even wore the same round glasses, but now it has become much more of a tourist attraction. Nothing wrong with that – there is now a proper exhibition centre where the story of his life and death is told in photographs and newspaper extracts. You will find it amusing to see how rural this neighbourhood was 60 years ago, and intriguing to see the revolutionary's enthusiasm for gardening and keeping rabbits.

last stop. The Universidad Nacional Autónoma de México is always contracted to **UNAM**, and always an entertaining sight for the first-time visitor. To see an ambitious colection of political murals that students at British universities in 1968 could only aspire to, walk around the baffling scattering of functional concrete blocks which were put up in a hurry half a century ago. They have been camouflaged as a tribute to the soul of the Aztec, the working man and Che Guevara – the latest addition, completed in January 2000 occupies the wall of a lecture theatre. The spirit of '68 was particularly poignant at UNAM, because in the build up to the Olympics in the stadium across the road, several hundred students were killed during the Tlatelolco protest.

While you wander across the campus, marvelling at the heroic reliefs on the library and administration building, remember that until 1965 this single university had more students than the entire British higher education system. At the start of 2000, though, the quarter-million students were conspicuous by their total absence, the result of a highly organised nine-month strike.

> **I don't like Mondays**
> As in much of the world, the worst day to attempt some diligent museum visiting is Monday. Almost every official 'sight' in the capital closes all day. Plan to spend it travelling instead.

Strike off campus towards Coplico station (*not* Universidad), and enjoy yet more strident murals while waiting for the train home.

A night out
The 43rd floor of the Torre Latinoamericana presides over the city. In return for paying three times the going rate for a beer (i.e. London prices), you can enjoy smogset over Mexico City. The sun declines through the pollution, bestowing a dull orange glow upon the capital shortly before it disappears behind the mountains ringing the city. As artificial lighting takes over, you can speculate about the stresses in being an air-traffic controller at Mexico City airport, where a phenomenal amount of traffic seeks to use a single runway.

A shopping expedition
There are flashy shops in the Zona Rosa, dowdy ones in the Centro Histórico, suburban malls dotted all around the city – and markets almost everywhere. But to witness the demographic conclusion of Mexico's history, go back to the centre and explore the frantic commerce around the Mercado de la Merced, for which the term 'bustling street market' seems woefully inadequate.

Keeping in touch
Cybercafés are just getting going, with many of the present generation being in the city's many language schools (including the one in the courtyard directly opposite the Hotel Catedral, Donceles 95). The best 'real' one in the Centro Histórico is Express-Net on the second floor at República del Salvador 12 (tel: 512 4001), where you get free coffee in return for spending $4 per hour on a slow terminal.

A word of advice
Or, rather 300 words of warning. The US State Department is more vitriolic about Mexico City than any other capital. These are just some of the extracts from the current Consular Advice to travellers:

'In Mexico City, the most frequently reported crimes involving tourists are taxi robberies, armed robbery, pickpocketing and purse snatching. In several cases, tourists have reported that men in uniforms perpetrated the crime, stopping vehicles and seeking money, or assaulting and robbing tourists walking late at night. The area behind the US Embassy and the Zona Rosa are frequent sites of street crime against foreigners. Caution should be exercised when walking in these areas.

'Tourists and residents alike should avoid driving alone at night anywhere in Mexico City. In a new tactic, thieves stop lone drivers at night, force them to ingest large quantities of alcohol and then rob them of ATM and credit cards. A US citizen was killed in such an assault in 1998. Mexican authorities subsequently arrested police officers for this murder. US citizens are advised to exercise good judgment when ordering beverages in nightclubs and bars, especially at night. Some establishments may contaminate or drug the drinks to gain control over the patron. Victims, who are almost always unaccompanied, have been robbed of personal property, abducted and then held while their credit cards were used at various businesses and ATM locations around the city.

'Robbery and assaults on passengers in taxis are frequent and violent, with passengers subjected to beatings, shootings and sexual assault. Avoid taking any taxi not summoned by telephone or contacted in advance at the airport. In December 1997, a US citizen was murdered in a taxi robbery.'

A Mexican wave of phonecard fraud

On the scale of scams worldwide, this one is actually quite fun and harmless. You're walking through the centre of Mexico City, chatting to a fellow traveller. Suddenly an American voice behind you calls out, 'Gee, I haven't heard English spoken for a while'. You get talking, and it turns out that the guy's from Nevada and about to fly home. Trouble is, he's not quite got the $15 he needs for departure tax – nor the five dollars for the cab to the airport. But he's certainly not asking for cash, no sirree. He's got a Mexican phone card that cost him $10 but he hasn't yet used it. So maybe you'd like to take it off his hands. You'll be able to phone your mum to wish her Happy New Year, won't that be nice?

Except when the deal is done, and you find a payphone, you discover the card's credit has all been used up. Then you look around the ground and notice that there are expired phone cards everywhere, just waiting to be picked up and sold by people with plausible stories.

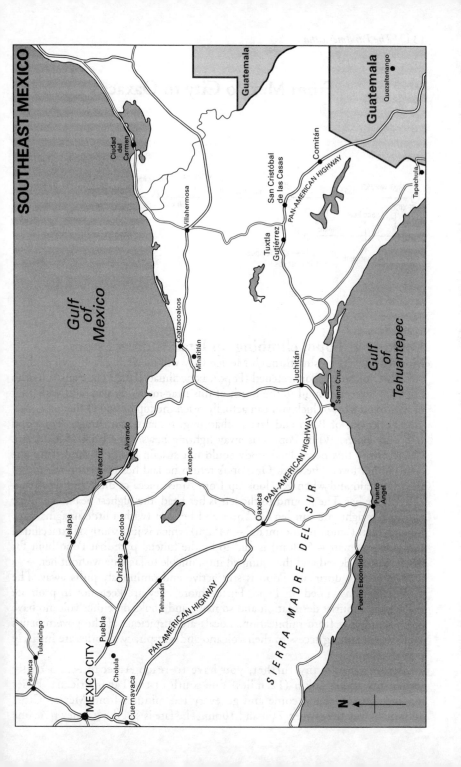

From Mexico City to Oaxaca

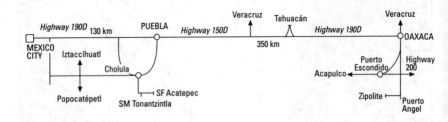

Looking at Popo, climbing up Izta: Andrew's story

Mountain-lovers passing through Mexico City will inevitably be drawn to these awesome volcanoes. Popocatépetl (Popo), Ixtaccíhuatl (Izta). The Pan-American Highway sweeps around to the north of this near-matching pair, and with a lot of effort and a bit of luck you can actually reach the top of one of them.

The legend of Popo and Izta is charming, romantic and tragic. Popo and Izta were lovers. While Popo was away fighting news came back of his death. On receiving this news, Izta's body could not sustain the grief she felt for the death of her lover. She died. On Popo's return he laid her to rest on the top of the mountain and when you look up from Amecameca at dusk and dawn you can still see her. The mound to the left is her head, the highest peak, her breast and to the right you can see her knees and her feet (with a little imagination). Popocatépetl ('smoking mountain' – 5452m) which is just south of Ixtaccíhuatl ('smoking woman' – 5286m) is said to be the funeral pyre that Popo built for his deceased beloved and then jumped into, unable to face life without her.

Izta is now dormant. Popo is still active and ominously puffs away. The government has closed off Popo. Furthermore, they are keen not to promote the area as a tourist destination and so maps and books on either volcano have been withdrawn from publication. Locals are suspicious of the government's motives in banning access to their volcano and conspiracy theories are furtively passed about.

Before you go any further, you have to reach **Amecameca**, a chilly settlement about 20km (12 miles) due south of the Panamericana. Buses marked 'Los Volcanes' come and go every ten minutes from Mexico City's Terminal Oriente between 7am and 10pm. The fare is $2, the journey time one hour. When you come to move on, there are direct buses to Oaxaca (duration eight hours, fare $14).

The cold air sweeps down from the over-shadowing Ixtaccíhuatl, but the locals are warm enough and a day or two can be happily passed while arranging any mountain treks. There is even an internet café on the Plaza.

There are three possible **places to stay**. *El Marques* is five minutes out of town, on 20 de Noviembre at the corner of Guadalupe Victoria (tel 01 597 8 11 92, fax 6 02 97). It has large, spotless motel-type rooms. The per-person charge is $12. *San Carlos*, in the Plaza (tel 01 597 8 07 46), is clean but basic, as you would guess from the single/double rates of $5/$8. The *Bonampak*, Reforma 8 (tel 01 597 807 58) is new, and slightly better than San Carlos. Rates without TV are single $6, double $10; with TV these increase to $10 and $15.

The place to begin **exploring** is just above the town at the exquisitely beautiful church of El Señor de Sacromonte. The church is built where one of the conquistadors lived in the 16th century. His statue now stands proudly watching over his chosen neighbourhood. To arrive at the start of the path, go out of the main square via the arc ('el arco'). After two blocks, turn right. Leading up to the church are 13 stations each of which will ask you to consider this place to be like that from a scene in the New Testament. After each, there then follows a prayer. For example, 'Consider, Spirit, this sixth station is like the place where the woman Veronica came to Jesus so exhausted, and her face darkened with sweat, dust, spittle and the insults she had suffered and He took out a cloth with which he cleaned her – consider... '

There are picnic tables along the path, where you can stop under the shade of the trees and enjoy the view of Amecameca and the volcanoes. The path continues past the first chapel up to a second at the top of the hill. This latter building is less well-kept but brings this brief biblical voyage to a suitable end in the surrounding graveyard where some tame cattle, sheep and a donkey graze among the tumbling headstones.

For a journey to the top, you will need a **mountain guide**. To find one, contact Luís Soriaro Escobar, Progreso 57, tel 01 597 8 03 71. Go out of the main square via the arc, and he can be found in his repair shop, 100m down on the right. Everyone knows him simply as 'Luís'. While no longer guiding himself, he has equipment to rent and is in charge of the mountain rescue and should therefore be informed of your intended route and return time. He can arrange for a local guide for around $25 per person per day.

Luís is a friend of the moustachioed ex-special services soldier Patrick, who lives at Cornel Silvestre Lopez 5 (tel 01 597 8 05 17 or 8 03 03). He knows the volcanoes better than anyone, and loves to tell everyone about them. If taking you on a tour or just because he likes you, an invite to stay at his house may well follow. Patrick charges $20-30 per day according to group size.

Getting to the top

The weather is normally best for climbing between October and March. Only the most popular route up Izta is listed here. To research this book, I made the climb alone. At the time I was very fit but not acclimatised to the altitude nor experienced in crossing glaciers. It is from this perspective that the above advice and details are derived.

There are other routes, some involving a two- or three- day trip. More details are available from the guides. Popo is officially closed to climbers but some guides, including Patrick, have special permission to take groups up.

Day-trippers beware: weather conditions can change rapidly and altitude sickness is a real danger. Izta is a fiery woman and she can play rough. Inexperienced climbers should not climb alone. If you intend to go without a guide, inform several people, including Luís Escobar, of the route and return time intended. The absolute **essentials** are crampons, boots, pickaxe, jacket, gloves, lots of water, torch, food, sun block and fitness. The **time** for the round trip will be 10 hours (for the extremely fit) to 15 hours (still pretty fit).

Arrange for a **taxi** to La Joya to arrive pre-dawn. Cost of the set-down and pick-up is about $40. The car will pass through Paso de Cortés between Izta and Popo, which affords some fantastic views. Note in particular the supremely majestic white top of Pico de Orizaba (5760m) rising above the clouds to the east. To the west, a blue hue may be noticeable in the distant valleys. This is the infamous smog of Mexico City. There is an **albergue** at Paso de Cortés, and a television mast, which is passed 3km before the end of the road at La Joya. The path to the top should be easy to follow, but the following instructions will help the directionally challenged. They are based on a 10-hour trip. If there appears to be no path ahead a wrong turn has probably been taken.

From the La Joya car park the path rises to the right. The first pass is reached in 40 minutes. Note here the blue plastic box chained to the cliff on the left. It contains a book dedicated to Stacey Levitt, an American who died here in August 1995. A second book is enclosed for those who wish to leave a message. The path then crosses into the shadow on the west side of the main ridge and traces gently upwards with the rock-face on the right-hand side. There are a few places to pitch a tent under the cliff face. The second pass is reached in 1 hour 40 minutes after departure. The path crosses over to the east side of the north-south ridge. The path turns upwards and towards Amecameca. The third pass is reached in 2 hours 10 minutes. Now turn to the right and follow the ridge northwards and then downwards to meet **El Refugio de Repúblico Chile** (2.30). This contains 12 wooden beds and nothing else: if sleeping here a reasonably early arrival (say 3pm) is advised. The easy part is over.

Follow the path up the scree above the refugio (3.30). Now some simple rock-climbing is required to pass to the left of the crucifix. A plaque for Roberto Basua Estabil (died October 1995), another fatal victim of Izta, is also passed. At four hours the defunct refugio of **Ayoloco** is reached at a minor peak (4680m). Put your crampons on (4.15). Follow the path along the ridges and over the glaciers and you should reach the breast of Izta (5286m) at 6.45mins. Take a deep breath (or ten), let your head stop spinning, try not to vomit, pat yourself on the back, turn round and re-trace the path back to La Joya at a fast pace (10 hours in total).

That's the theory; this is how it was for me. The first couple of hours of the ascent seemed relatively easy apart from losing the path once. Even the altitude did not seem too burdensome, but after El Refugio de Repúblico Chile things became very much worse. It took an hour to scramble up the small but sheer face of loose volcanic scree and for every five metres that I climbed I would slip down three. Only by planting the pickaxe and using it as a miniature pole vault was it possible to climb this part at all. After the wall of scree, the terrain became better but steeper and then the breathlessness began. It is humiliating and agonising to find oneself crawling and floundering like a baby and still gasping for air.

Crampons were a whole new experience. The way that they stick into the ice and their generally cumbersome nature makes it easy to fall. This would not have been a problem in itself but for the fact that vanity insisted that I use my camera's self-timer to prove that I really was on my way to the top of the world. Gingerly, I lined up the shot with the camera laid on the ice, trotted into position, spun round and went flying backwards off an ice ridge and landed six metres below in a puddle of near-freezing water, rocks and mud. That is the sort of silly mistake that you cannot afford to make on the mountain. Fortunately, the only damage was the ripped seat of my trousers, a gash from a crampon spike slicing through my calf and a deep sense of foolishness. Unfortunately, the photograph did show me on the top of the World but falling head first towards the bottom.

Crossing the flat part of the small glaciers was not technically difficult. However, every now and then the ice seemed to moan and creek ready to swallow me up into a hidden crevasse. Looking down, the ice was sometimes a clear blue and the distinct sense was of walking across a sea in an alien landscape, petrified and forgotten. The ice ridges up to the top would have made simple climbing but now my limbs were weary and the air very thin. The tropical sun was hot but the wind was dry and icy cold. At every stop my heart pounded and my head throbbed to its rhythm. Without proper sunblock or gloves, I could feel my exposed skin and lips being frayed by the elements and screaming for shelter.

Finally, the summit came. I forced myself to drink, took some pictures and admired the view. Now it was obvious that I had mild altitude sickness and a rapid decent was imperative. Furthermore, some clouds began to rush in from the north. But God, what a view. All of Mexico and beyond and for that moment it was mine and I was the *conquistador*, alone and majestic for just a few minutes. Out of necessity, I hurtled down extremely fast, taking just one wrong turn and delighted in telling those going upwards that it got worse and worse.

Ten hours after departure I returned to La Joya. I thought the climb would take nine hours but Juan, my faithful taxi driver, representative of all friendly Mexicans, had waited patiently for an extra hour. Indeed, he was as happy to see me as I him. I am sure the $5 tip was ample reward for the wait but it seemed as much a gift to him that I was alive. Despite this all this, Juan still did his best to kill us on the darkened, winding road back to Amecameca. I was not reassured by the fact that his break-neck speed was only interrupted by him removing his hands from the wheel (but not stopping), bowing his head and crossing himself.

Anyway, the headache of altitude sickness subsided to be replaced by the pains of my fall and the sting of sunburn and chapped lips. But I did not care, I had done it and my heart glowed, my mind boggled and my body ached in appreciation of such a fantastic experience. Travel writers love to scaremonger – thieves in the cities, rockfalls in the mountains and undercurrents at the beach. Climbing Izta can be a precarious business and, as is clear, people have died on her unforgiving slopes. But this was one of the most exhilarating trips I experienced in Central America.

And if that doesn't appeal, there's always Cholula

You can go climbing here, too, so long as the pyramid is open to the public. While Andrew was mountaineering, I continued through to a warmer, lower challenge. This is the home of something quite remarkable, though it doesn't look like it. The tallest pyramid in the world is hidden in this small and sleepy town.

How do you hide a pyramid that big, then? With considerable ease, it turns out. Something that would overawe even the Temple of the Sun at Teotihuacán has itself been humbled by the years. Vegetation has clambered all over it, and a small (and crumbling) church has been dropped on the top. Given the monumental mountains in this vicinity, it looks like a modest outcrop from the natural world, rather than one of man's greatest-ever achievements. And at the moment you can't even climb right to the top, because the church is in a dangerous state.

To prove this all to your satisfaction is an awful lot easier than climbing Itza. First, get a **bus** (second class) from Terminal Oriente in Mexico City for the two or three hour run to Cholula. The final stop is on the corner of 12 Poniente and 5 de Mayo. Go south to the **Zócalo**, which is one of Mexico's finer squares – thanks to the bandstand, the trio of churches on the east side and the colonnade on the west flank. If you need **food**, turn right at the end of the square and find Taco Robert on Hidalgo between 1 Norte and 3 Norte, which serves the finest kebabs in Mexico. For a **room**, there is little choice but the San Juan suites (tel 470378), just south of Hidalgo on 7 Sur, where a giant room will cost $25, whether there is one or four of you.

The **Great Pyramid** towers, a touch ineffectively, over Calzada San Andrés – the continuation of Moreles, which runs east from the Zócalo. The best you can say about it is that you get a good view of the surrounding countryside. As you gaze down, you may reflect on the futility of man, and in particular the number of man-millennia that were devoted to building something that the casual visitor would not even recognise as a work of artifice. If the **archaelogical zone** is open (it wasn't in December 1999), then you can take a trip into some of the tunnels that disappear into the pyramid – these are closed off unless the zone is open.

Cheer yourself up with an easy trip down to a pair of the most impressive churches in Mexico. Five kilometres (three miles) south of Cholula, accessible in a shared taxi for $0.25, you reach **Santa María Tonantzintla**, which has a village church guarded by a squadron of angelic figurines, made of stucco. Inside, you are overwhelmed by the ornate ceiling and amazed by the intensity of the carved décor, depicting all manner of figures – animal, human, supernatural.

A 20-minute walk or another shared cab takes you to **Acatepec**, where you find other fine – and completely unrelated – example where art has taken over a church just as surely as the grass has claimed Cholula's pyramid. The **Templo de San Francisco** is striking because of the facade, where the tiles create a dazzling mosaic, and the similarity of the design to something by Borromini.

Puebla

Shattered city of the angels

Whether or not you have deviated to climb a volcano or a pyramid, you have to make contact with Puebla to get back on track. This is splendid news, because it is one of the most beautiful colonial cities of the Americas, a study in gracefully declining magnificence. But you will encounter sadness, too, over the last tectonic rattle of the 20th century.

In 1999, Puebla was close to the epicentre of a dreadful earthquake. It rumbled along the fault line that created such a beautifully flawed landscape. The towers of the **Cathedral**, Mexico's tallest, shook mightily, and remain under repair. Some lesser structures were destroyed altogether, though the skills of the colonial builders mean that modern edifices were worst affected. The process of recuperation has been so swift that you may not be especially aware of the earthquake, but it served to remind the people of Puebla de los Angeles that the fragile works of man are all too easily shattered.

Getting your bearings

The original highway from Mexico City to Oaxaca used to run right through the middle of Puebla, but the Panamericana now takes the toll road to the north. The **bus station** is a big, difficult-to-deal-with place about 3km (two miles) north of the centre. There are frequent departures to Mexico City, and buses every couple of hours to Oaxaca.

From the bus station, plenty of **local buses** run to the main square. If you have come from Cholula by minibus, it will drop you by the railway station, at Calle 15 Norte and Avenida 6 Poniente. The last train ran some years ago, but the site is now an impressive **railway museum**. Three blocks south of here you reach the main road, the Avenida Reforma (which, confusingly, changes its name beyond the Zócalo to Avenida Avila Camacho). The main perpendicular street is Avenida Cinco de Mayo – all the other streets parallel to this are Calles.

A room
Most of the options are clustered close to the main square. Optimum position and style goes to the **Hotel Colonial** (Calle 4 Sur number 105, a block east of the Zócalo; tel 246 4292, colonial@gig.com), which charges $32 single/$39 double for considerable comfort in a quiet location. Much cheaper is the **Hotel Catedral**, a couple of blocks west of the main square at Avenida 3 Poniente 310, which costs $11 single/$13 double.

A meal
Plenty of good options, from some of the tastiest street food in Mexico to the height of colonial indulgence. For the latter, the best choice is the **Villa Rosa**, on Avenida 5 Oriente between Calles 2 and 4 Sur. Almost opposite is the best deal of all, the unlimited Sunday buffet at the **Barra Vegetariana La Zanahoria** at Avenida 5 Oriente number 208.

The main attraction
For many people it will simply be the ambience of a fine colonial city, and indeed a few days ambling and absorbing the atmosphere could be just the recuperation you need after time on the Highway. But if you go to see just one sight, make it the excellent **Museo Amparo**. A couple of colonial places have been knocked together, with various walls removed to create a venue which feels entirely different from the average museum. The expertly created spaces are used to chronicle the cultural conflict between the indigenous people and the invaders. It opens 10am-6pm except Mondays and Tuesdays, and costs $2.

Keeping in touch
Puebla may not be so much of a backpackers' haunt, but it has a couple of good cybercafés. The most comfortable (and expensive) is the **Cyberbyte** at Calle 2 Sur number 505B, while Internet Sandoval Vallarta is on Avenida 5 Oriente between Calles 2 and 4 Norte.

Moving on
There is a handy APO **bus office** in the city centre at the corner of Avenida Avila Camacho and Calle 6 Norte, where you can book in advance for departures to Oaxaca, saving the long slog out to the bus station.

The journey onwards to Oaxaca is fast and smooth, a revolutionary ride compared with just a few years ago. The Highway remains as route 150D for about 100km (60 miles) east of Puebla, until this road continues to Veracruz on the coast and 190D takes over as the Panamericana. One of the trickiest stretches of terrain in the whole country has been overcome with liberal use of dynamite. Back in 1524, Hernán Cortés complained to Charles V of Spain that 'This land is so mountainous that it cannot be crossed, even on foot.' The new road has halved the time compared with the wiggly old 190 – the 350km (218 miles) take just four or five hours. It is a beautiful, if desolate, journey, with little sign of human habitation until you are almost upon Oaxaca.

Oaxaca: locked in by the land

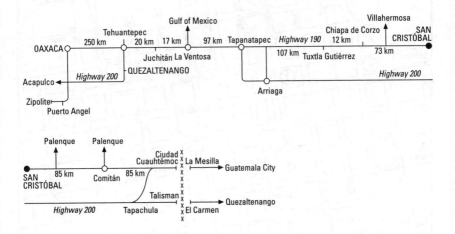

Look at a map, and you see that the body of Mexico is a bit of an old slouch: the country leans back casually into the Pacific, propped up by the arm of Baja California, with feet (in the shape of the Yucatán peninsula) comfortably up. So much for the body – the soul is in much better shape, and resides in the fine city of Oaxaca. Here, in the fresh, mile-high air, Unesco has had the good sense to declare the colonial centre a Cultural Heritage Site, with another for good measure above the city at the strange and wonderful location of Monte Albán. Oaxaca was not so landlocked that it remained off-limits for long, but the Mixtecs and Zapotecs put up some spirited resistance to the *conquistadores*. Cortés was smitten with the place, and the King conferred upon him the title Marquess of the Valley of Oaxaca. The city was founded in 1521.

The valley proved good farming land, for raising sheep and growing crops, and Oaxaca prospered despite a tectonic tremble or two. Both its generous colonial

proportions and its indulgent cuisine are a result of this wealth. The city survived the turbulent 19th and 20th centuries remarkably intact – and later changed its name to Oaxaca de Juárez to commemorate the Mexican national hero. Teenagers still flirt among the the ornate colonnades where their ancestors courted.

One quarter of a million residents are compressed into a compact, lively mountain city. Their numbers have been amplified, in the past, by notables such as John Lennon and D H Lawrence.

Getting your bearings.

The main part of Oaxaca is decanted into a sloping valley, while the mountains almost surround it. The **bus station** is, for once, handily located fairly close to the centre at Calzada Niños Héroes de Chapultepec (the main northern bypass) and Emiliano Carranza. From here, Oaxaca rolls gently downhill to the Río Atoyac, with the colonial core clustered around the fine Zócalo, a main square fringed by cafés and steeped in history – with a fancy 1901 bandstand in the middle.

Arrival and departure

There are plenty of **buses** from all the obvious places – Mexico City, Puebla, San Cristóbal – mostly on Cristóbal Colón, but such is demand that you should book to leave as soon as you arrive. Alternatively, the local **airport** has plenty of **regional flights** – the best way to or from is in a $5 cab. The city has the usual array of raucous old buses and battered 'combi' minibuses, but Oaxaca is one place which is compact enough to walk everywhere.

A room

Oaxaca has more choice than anywhere else outside the Mexican capital. These suggestions start with the cheapest.

Hostal San Pedro, Avenida Juarez No 200 (corner with Morelos), $5 per bed with 10% discount for students. Use of kitchen, dining table, laundry TV. Rarely full, highly recommended.

Posado Del Rosario, 20 de Noviembre 508 (tel 6 41 12); the refurbished rooms are quiet and spotless – recommended at around $7 single, $10 double.

Hotel Suites del Centro, Avenida Hidalgo 306 (tel 6 82 82). If you do not mind the risk of falling off, there are some very nice (and cheap, around $7) single rooms on the roof, from where the lights of the surrounding hills can be seen to twinkle with the night sky. Use of loungers and tables on the roof-top terrace is also yours. Recommended.

Hotel Posada Yagul, Avenida Juarez No 106 (tel 4 36 94). Arranged around a pretty courtyard with fountain. Quiet with spacious rooms. The chambermaid leaves an apple on the bed. Rates around $10 single, $15 double.

Parador San Andrés, Avenida Hidalgo No 405. Small, very clean with a pretty courtyard and terrace. Recommended. 'The receptionist is an effeminate young gentleman who may give discounts to handsome travellers', comments one recent (male) guest, who earned a reduction on the normal $15 single/$20 double rates

Casa de Sierra Azul, Hidalgo No 1002 (corner with Fiallo), tel 4 71 71. Small but wonderfully elegant. Quadrangle with fountain. Black umbrellas are available at reception for guests' use. Highly recommended, if you can afford the $50/$60 room rates.

A meal

It is hard to go wrong in a city that boasts some of the most imaginative cooking in Mexico, and where the local mole has more than 30 ingredients. The options are best around **Zócalo**, where a dozen cafés and restaurants compete for custom and mariachi musicians tout for tips. The key word there is 'compete' – prices even at the most elegant outdoor places are reasonable. If you want to move further upmarket, you could try the **Café Candela** (Calle Allende 211), for drinks, food or music, or any combination of these, in a colonial setting, but it tends to be expensive and quite empty. The **Restaurant del Vitral** (Calle Guerrero 201), for a range of local dishes – including the grasshoppers that are sold by the thousand in the local markets – served in sumptuous surroundings; expensive but worthwhile. The markets themselves offer wonderfully fresh food (grashoppers excepted) for, predictably, a fraction of the normal fare. For non-meat-eaters, **Restaurant Flor de Loto del Sureste** (Calle Portfiro Díaz 217) is a reliable vegetarian place with reasonable prices and not a grasshopper in sight.

A drink

While most Oaxacans tend to go to bed at 11pm, the young and free head for the zone just north of the bus terminal. Here there are several lively discos and bars. Those recommended are the Maria Bar, Sabino disco and Snob. This is generally gringo-free territory but the atmosphere is relaxed and this is a great place to meet locals and practice speaking Spanish or even the international language of love.

An exploration

Get an overview of the city by climbing the stairs along Calle Mier y Talán, adjacent to the **Basilica de La Soledad**, or – more ambitiously – clambering to the top of the **Escalera del Fortín** (from Calle Crespo in the north west of the city) to Cerro de Fortín, a hill topped by a giant cross. (You may not want to venture up here alone near dawn or dusk; there have been reports of robberies.)

When you come back down to ground level, the two dominant buildings on the **Zócalo** – the **Palacio de Gobierno** and **Cathedral** – are worth investigating, but most people simply relax and take in the street life. Oaxaca has much more than its fair share of beguiling colonial buildings dotted around quiet cobbled streets – and, accordingly, more than its fair share of tourists. They tend to congregate at the top of the town, the **Iglesia de Santo Domingo**, which owes its survival in the face of two massive earthquakes to heavy stone walls. These have helped preserve the most impressive colonial church in the city. Behind it, you find quiet gardens and a lively cultural centre. Prior to a visit to Monte Albán (see below), you can learn about the Mixtecs and Zapotecs at the **Museo Regional de Oaxaca**, adjacent to Santo Domingo. In the same area, you can visit the home of Benito Juárez, now the **Museo Casa de Juárez**. Four times President of Mexico, Juárez steered the country through the turmoil of the mid-19th century. There isn't much of huge interest to see in the house, but then there isn't much to stop you just poking your head in to the shady courtyard and taking in the ambience, without going the whole hog and buying a $3 ticket.

Marketing – theory and practice

Oaxaca is justly celebrated for its pre-Columbian and colonial heritage. But what's really good about the city is the collection of markets. There are a couple of fine examples just two blocks south of the Zócalo, where humanity and commerce mingle with great exuberance. D H Lawrence was in Oaxaca when he observed that 'men have invented two excuses in order to share freely in crowds without arousing any suspicion: religion, and the market'. He possibly had in mind the breathtaking **Central de Abastos**, which spread for a five-by-three-block area between the (old) railway line and the river. This mixes fresh produce, cheap clothes and obsolete electronics (being sold off at a deep discount south of the US border) – and several million grasshoppers.

An excursion

It is unthinkable that the dedicated *panamericanista* could visit Oaxaca without seeing Monte Albán. Zapotec culture is less celebrated than Mayan and Aztec civilisations, but this site – a short way west of Oaxaca – reveals an extraordinarily sophisticated pre-Columbian city. Get there early in the day – it officially opens at 8am, but I arrived at 7.30am and reached 'an understanding' with the security guard. To have this magnificent old ruin, with temples ranged around the market place on a flattened mountaintop, to yourself is splendid.

Monte Albán means 'white mountain', but 'plateau' is more like it. The first settlers, who arrived around BC200, levelled the mountain as a precursor to establishing some sort of ceremonial or governmental base for the central valleys in which Oaxaca stands. The Zapotec people started to develop the site in about 500AD, and over the next two centuries developed most of the structures and monuments that you will see.

The site is clearly laid out on the maps that are dotted around. The central feature is the main plaza, which served as a market place. Creating a largely flat 200m-square space at the top of a mountain is no mean feat. Notable structures include the ball court, the palace and 'tomb seven', but the most intriguing figures are the *danzantes* ('dancers'), tablets carved with human figures in grotesquely contorted shapes – a large one on the south side of the group has clearly been disembowelled.

The site officially opens from 8am to 5pm, though this can often be stretched at either end of the day. A taxi is the simplest way of reaching the site – a $10 fare for the 9km/6 mile ride is reasonable, because of the tricky uphill route. There are organised bus trips from the Hotel Mesón del Angel at Mina 518, but these do not offer sufficient saving for the amount of hassle involved – you are alloted a specific return time.

Admission to the site is $3, which includes the small (and not hugely rivetting) museum. After your visit, you can walk back down as far as the local bus terminus – a superb hike, with a shack of a café at the end where you can recuperate while waiting for the bus.

Moving on

A free treat awaits you at the start of the long journey to San Cristóbal – about 30km along the Pan-American Highway, a massive tree appears on the left. The driver or his mate may well point it out and claim, correctly, that it is the oldest in the world, at 2,000 years. Well, certainly the oldest living tree. The specimen of ahuehuete cypress looks in fine fettle, spreading over a diameter of 58m (190 feet) – it's hard to miss, even in a crowded bus.

And, in terms of interest, that's about it for a while. The Pan-American Highway rolls through the low, hot and sweaty Isthmus of Tehuantepec. If you have to stop overnight, try to make it in the jolly town of Juchitán, where the hotels are a shortish walk from the bus station, the town centre is only a little further on, and the locals are friendly.

Detour to lotus-land

So far you will have seen nothing of the sea. There is a diversion that can change all that. If you go due south from Oaxaca, you collide with the Pacific at a point where there is nothing much to do but indulge yourself. From there, you can continue along the coast towards the Guatemalan border, not adding a great deal to the overall journey time. A day or a night's bus ride will take you to Pochutla (and then on the Puerto Angel) and to Puerto Escondido.

These leave early in the morning or late in the evening. Journey time is 8-10 hours, price $10 on Oaxaca Pacifico but $5 more for the rather better quality on Cristóbal Colón. Tickets and further information are available from one of the numerous travel agencies in the town centre.

Pochutla is little more than a town defined by the crossroads on which it lies. There are a couple of cheap restaurants and hotels and the small but bustling bus terminal. There is also a prison. This can be visited in normal working hours and is only 10 minutes walk from the bus terminal. The guards will show you in and as long as you left that herbal package in Zipolite, out again. It is expected that you will buy some of the handicrafts (good value) of the guests. Until it became an endangered species, beautiful jewellery of black coral used to be made there. Ironically, the prisoners now bide their time producing decorated paraphernalia for cannabis smoking; this may be a second reason for visiting before Zipolite.

Collective taxis and a bus run from 6.30am to 7pm to and from Puerto Angel, Zipolite and Mazunte ($0.50). At other times an individual taxi will cost $5. Regular collective taxis and a bus run to Puerto Escondido: one hour and $3 or $2 respectively. The taxis are probably more fun and, with six people per cab, a conversation is near obligatory. This is a good way to practice Spanish. Many long distance services are available. Oaxaca-Pacifico tends to be slightly down-market but cheaper than Cristóbal Colón. Those going south tend to be starting at Puerto Escondido and are often full when they reach Pochutla. See Puerto Escondido for more information on southbound buses.

Puerto Escondido

Forget the implication of the name, that this is the 'forgotten port' – Puerto Escondido is a well-developed holiday resort. Its character has been strongly influenced by the Zicatela beach that is one of the best surfing beaches in the world. This does not mean that you need to be a rad dude to enjoy the place. Indeed, the crowd is eclectic, with a substantial proportion being Mexican holidaymakers. Having a good time is easy. Having an amazing time can be a bit hit and miss; depending on you finding a group of friends to hang out with. For this reason some stay for a couple of days and others a couple of months: whichever, little harm can come from enjoying the beaches by day and partying by night. High season is from November to April.

The town is divided into two main areas. The main and quieter part of town is located uphill of the main crossroads with the coast road. Half a mile down from the crossroad Avenida Peréz Gasga turns to the East to run parallel with the town's beach (Bahía Principal). It is along Avenida Peréz Gasga that most of the shops, hotels and nightlife is located.

PUERTO ESCONDIDO ENVIRONS
1 Acuario Hotel
2 Banamex Bank
3 Buses to Cristóbal Colón
4 Buses to Estrella Blanca
5 Hotel Castillo del Rey
6 Tourist Information
7 Pool
8 Pony Man
9 Un Tigre @ Zul

A good time was had by all?

While researching the book, Andrew James met Parker, a heavily tattooed and way-out surf boy from California with the attitude to match. He recounted his Escondido experience:

'Ya man, we (him and Eezel) just been boardin' this las win'er and came out to catch some waves like in the sea, man – right? Ya, anyway we met these re-uul cuul guys who taught us how ta surf. Excellent, they were genuine surf rats, man.'

'So you can stand up?'

'You don't understand. Stand up, lie down, it's all about being out there with the sea. You gotta find yourself and loose yourself. Know what I mean?'

'Sure... I'll, er, take that as a 'No' then'

'Oh, dude, that's just so not it, man'

'So, you've had a good time, anyway. How about the nightlife?'

(Now he becomes really animated)

'We were in Bar Fly last night, man, just chillin' out, checkin' the scene. Eezel went home, as he must have eaten some of that chilly shit or summin'. And I'm sittin' there and there's this chick start's givin' me the eye. I start talkin' to her and stuff. Yuh, bought this babe loadsa tequilas and margarita and that mezcal shit. Anyway, off in the corner there's this mad Alaskan old muther and he's re-ul gone, man. He starts going like all crazy and shit and buyin' everyone drinks. I didn' even spend five bucks. All the while there's another old dude goin' on all the time 'bout long boardin' and how the Beatles were better than the Stones. Yuh, uh, where was I, oh yeah. This babe she starts french kissing me man, like, says she's trying to get Chucho the waiter jealous. Anyway there was, like salsa dancin' and stuff and I woke up in this Helen babe's cabaña. Don't even know if I got lucky, man. Crazy.'

'A good night then?'

'You said it, man.'

Indeed, but the same cannot be promised for everyone.

There are two **bus stations**: the Estrella Blanca (tel 582 0457) just by the main crossroads, and the Cristóbal Colón (tel 582 2050) several blocks uphill from there. The Cristóbal Colón buses tend to be a few dollars more expensive but marginally more comfortable. Direct services are available for the following destinations, mostly from both stations: Tehuantepec, Mexico City, Salina Cruz, Tapachula and Acapulco. To and from Pochutla, there are buses every hour and collective taxis frequently from dawn to dusk, going from the main cross-roads and the Cristóbal Colón bus station; they cost $3 and $2, respectively, for the 75-minute journey. The *colectivos* are cramped but more fun and you are bound to have a Spanish conversation with fellow passengers.

A **tourist booth**, at the bottom of the hill on Avenida Peréz Gasga, is open 9am-noon and 2pm-7pm. The three cyber cafés are: a shop just below the Banamex bank on Peréz Gasga; Tigre @zul in the centre of Avenida Peréz Gasga; and one in the Acuarios hotel on Zicatela beach. Tigre @zul is the cheapest and most comfortable ($3 per hour).

A room

Escondido is packed full of **hotels**. These are just a few of the more recommended ones. On Zicatela beach is **Acuario** with rooms and bungalows (tel 958 21027): what more could you want than a vegetarian restaurant, internet café, weights room, casa de cambio, pool, some rooms with balconies, hammocks and fridges? Single/double: $20/$25 in the low season; $30/$35 in the high season.

Hotel Rincon del Pacifico, Avenida Peréz Gasga No 900, right on Bahia Principal. Single $25, double $27.

Hotel Casa Blanca, Avenida Peréz Gasga No 905 (tel 958 20168): Large rooms, some with a balcony, some with a fridge, clean, speak English, swimming pool, and centre of the action. Single $18, double $26. Recommended.

Hotel Rocamar, Peréz Gasga, opposite tourist office booth: the private balconies are a bit noisy because of all the surrounding nightlife, but it is very popular with backpackers and recommended. Single, double: $12, $14.

Hotel las Palmas, Avenida Peréz Gasga: Clean. Recommended for low season. Single, double: $11, $13 low season; $25, $30 high season.

Hotel Loren, Peréz Gasga No 507: Peaceful, pool, rooms not spotless. Single, double: both $25 low season, $30 in high season.

Castillo del Rey, Av Peréz Gasga, five minutes downhill from crossroads with main coastal road: Manager friendly, watchman not, spotlessly clean, big rooms, shared balcony, hot water. Highly recommended. Single, double: $10, $12.

A meal and a drink

Most of the restaurants serve very good fish dishes. The restaurant opposite the Castillo del Rey hotel sells excellent cold snacks for a beach picnic and very good beef stew (*estofado del res*) during the daytime. Good cocktails are available in Escondido's three main watering holes: Bar Fly, the Wipe Out Bar and La Sol y Rumba. The latter normally plays salsa.

A swim, a surf

Bahía Principal is the bay on which the main town lies. Swimming is relatively safe and there is a fresh water lagoon shared by the crowds. **Zicatela** is 1km east of Bahía Principal. It is one of the best surf beaches in the world. Ponies are available to ride ($3 per hour). Surf equipment can be hired from the Acuarios hotel behind the centre of the beach for $3-5 per hour. Boogie-boarding can be enjoyed by nearly anyone and the Malibu (serious) boarders will not get annoyed as long as you do not catch the same wave as them and get in the way.

Puerto Angelito is a pretty beach 1km west of Bahía Principal, perfect for a dip. **Carrizilillo** is another 1km west of Angelito and is both good for swimming and snorkelling. Puerto Angelito and Carrizilillo are accessible by walking along the main coastal road and then turning off or by catching a taxi, for $2 each way, which will leave you still with a short walk down to the beach. Further west, Playa Bacocha has big waves.

A shopping expedition

Some excellent indigenous and highly professional jewellery and painted furniture can be found along Avenida Peréz Gasga. The exotic furniture of Brenda at La Maraposa Monarca, opposite Banamex, is recommended for purchasers and window-shoppers alike.

An excursion

Some terrific tours including canoeing, horseback riding, trips to lagoons and Indian villages are arranged by Ana's Ecotours, in Un Tigre @zul, Avenida Peréz Gasga, tel 582 1871, anasecotours.com. Scuba diving and snorkelling trips are available at Aventura Submarina, Peréz Gasga 601 (tel 582 2353). To gain a certificate costs $320 for a five-day course. Once certified the cost per dive is $35. The snorkelling trip costs $20 for three hours. They also run sport fishing trips, costing $25 per hour for four people.

A night out

Nightlife can be lively in Escondido. As well as the bars mentioned under 'A meal and a drink' there is also a disco and pool table at El Tubo. Lone women should beware of reports that Chucho and Pepe of Bar Fly are dangerously charming.

Puerto Angel

This place will appeal to people looking for beach life in a place relatively unaffected by tourism, but with a few more amenities than are available in Zipolite. The high season for tourism is July to November. Between Puerto Angel and Zipolite is the **Universidad del Mar**. Its students can sometimes be seen, borne by the boats of fisherman, ready to take samples and analyze the mysteries of the deep blue. If you are interested in marine biology, they are also a great source of knowledge.

Collective taxis and buses run from 6.30am to 7pm and pass by the beachfront to and from Pochutla, Zipolite and Mazunte ($0.50). At other times an individual taxi will cost $5. Playa Panteón is possibly the most tranquil part of the village. It has three places to stay: **La Cabaña** (hot water, clean, fan, peaceful, recommended), costing $15 single, $17 double; **Posada Cañon de Vata** (a bit dark but good restaurant, popular with travellers, $8 single, $10 double). **Restaurant Quetita** may have a double cabaña available: $12 with bathroom.

A swim

There is some lovely swimming and snorkelling around but with two caveats: some of the beaches have strong tides; and for up to three weeks after heavy downpours, the water can become darkened and polluted on all the beaches leading to a risk of conjunctivitis and upset stomach. In both cases ask the locals. Playa Panteón: good for swimming; follow the stone pathway west, which starts at the bridge in the centre of the village (five minutes). Estacahuite: 20 minutes walk east, clean, clear and good for snorkelling. Scuba diving ('el buzeo') is available for the certified at $40 for one dive from the fisherman at west end of Playa Panteón.

Zipolite

This used to be the hippy hang-out *par excellence*, but now it has developed, and is best considered as a long and pretty beach where you can chill out. There are plenty of big waves, but swimming is usually safe as long as you remain within your depth, and take the advice of the locals. There have been fatalities, but mostly among those who swim under the influence of alcohol or other substances.

At the western end of the beach you will find 'Cosmico' ('cosmic') and 'La Fogata de Shambhala' ('the campfire refuge'). The clients of this congregation of cabañas and rooms tend to be older and more peaceful than on the rest of the beach. There have been attacks on tourists in the past, but the vigilance of locals with a vested interest has meant that this end of the beach should now be safe to wander around at any time. Incidentally, this is really the only area of the beach which remains resolutely nudist. As might be expected, *meals* served are vegetarian and nothing stronger than beer is given out. Those of artistic talent are permitted to try their hand putting up some murals. Bucko is a sixties throw-back who has been threatening to leave Shambhala for India for the last 15 years but never quite managed the walk to the end of the beach. He still holds the Shambhala fort, resplendent in embroided waist-coat, long hair and little else. He has an interesting habit of bursting into soprano song in the middle of convesation. Still, well worth a visit.

Collective taxis and buses link the main paved road with Puerto Angel, Pochutla and Mazunte from 6.30am to 7pm, fare $0.50. At other times an individual taxi will cost $5. The **cabañas** vary little along the length of the beach in price or quality – single $8, double $10 without bathroom – save two exceptions: they are slightly better at Roja Blanca and at Cosmicos and Shambhala. Neat and balconied rooms are available at Paraíso and Brisa Marina for around $20. Hammocks with use of a bathroom and luggage store are widely available for a mere $3. Most beach huts serve food and drink. Recommended is the pizza and red snapper ('huachinango') of Roja Blanca: do not worry about the drunk waiter; he is perfectly harmless. Mopeds can be hired from the shop just opposite La Puesta disco on the street behind the beach.

One kilometre along the road behind the beach, in the opposite direction to Puerto Angel, is Mariposario Zipolite (open daily except Sunday 9am-4pm, children $0.50, students $1, normal people $1.50). Seven hectares have been put aside as a mini-biological park, in which Luz gives tours in English. Things to see include many butterflies, iguanas and frogs. Highly recommended for those interested in ecology. If he is there, ask to speak to Luz's father, Balin, who describes himself as a 'little hippy'. Amongst other things, he earns money guiding wealthy European fisherman on his 30,000 hectares Patagonian estate.

San Agustín is 40mins walk along the main road, west of Zipolite. Swimming is good and you can be sure that few others will be sharing the beach. Cabañas are available for $5 double, $3 single.

After another 20 minutes you can find Mazunte beach, which is calm and beautiful with good snorkelling on the left-hand side. Camping and cabañas are available. Mazunte may be considered the Zipolite of 20 years ago or, as one local said, 'full of lots of long-haired people.'

Into Chiapas

The coastal route (Highway 200) and the Panamericana (Highway 190) converge to pass through the narrow Isthmus of Tehuantepec, meeting at the town of Tehuantepec, whose name is officially prefixed Santo Domingo. After a further 134km, the two routes split again at San Pedro Tapanatepec (usually known simply as Tapanatepec). Only those desperate to reach Guatemala should be tempted by the fast Highway 200, even though it is shown on some maps as being the official Carretera Panamerica; this road roars along the flat, dull coast to the frontier at Tapachula.

Turn left at the fork, and within 15km you move from the state of Oaxaca into Chiapas. Life – or at least the roadside scenery – takes a definite turn for the better. The Highway climbs through the Sierra Madre de Chiapas for 107km (66 miles), then swoops down to the city of **Tuxtla Gutiérrez**. The closest approximation to a bustling metropolis in southeast Mexico is a blot on an attractive part of the map. If you are in your own transport, you might care to zip straight past on the southern bypass.

Many travellers have no choice but to change **buses** here, and if this is the case you might as well sample the few modest attractions. An ADO bus will drop you inconveniently far west of the centre, at 9 Poniente Sur and 5 Sur Poniente; Cristóbal Colón is handily placed two blocks west of the Zócalo; Autotransportes Tuxtla Gutiérrez is a few blocks southeast. For onward travel, you are advised not to visit any of these, but to use one of the minibuses that departs from the corner of 2 Oriente Sur and 3 Sur – these will take you to Chiapa de Corzo, the recommended next town along.

If you are obliged to **stay the night** in Tuxtla Gutiérrez rather than in Chiapa or San Cristóbal, the best options are grouped together on the north side of the Zócalo, on or around 3 Norte Oriente. The Casablanca (corner of 1 Oriente Norte) is highly recommended at $6 single, $10 double. Almost next door, the Posada del Rey (tel 22755, fax 22924) is $16 single/$25 double and rather more posh. **Internet** access is available a block north of here. Of the many **food** options, Charly's steak house (on Boulevard Albino Corzo, the continuation of Avenida Central Oriente, at 14 Oriente Sur) is the most fun.

Seeing the **sights** is not likely to take you long. The elegant white **Cathedral** is a good place to retreat from the noise and bustle of the Zócalo outside, but a better place to find some peace and quiet is at one of Mexico's best **zoos**. A $2 taxi ride will take you into the hills south of the city, to Zoomat – a slighty run-down showcase for the ample fauna of the Chiapas region. Some of the larger mammals, like jaguar and puma, are kept in unhappy conditions, but most visitors feel the park is a worthwhile outing to get an early feel for the country – and creatures – of Chiapas. It opens 9am-5pm daily, and admission is around $1. The helpful staff will look after your bags while you look around, if you are only passing through.

The best you can say about the bus to **Chiapa de Corzo** is that it is mercifully quick, taking just 15 minutes to drop you on the edge of the town for a fare of $0.25. From here there are frequent collective taxis, charging the same for the short hop to the Zócalo. The modest attractions of Chiapa de Corzo are arrayed around the main square, which is notable for the fine octagonal fountain. The square is ringed by vendors, shops selling hats and less useful items, and a few cafés. A dusty old hotel occupies the southeast corner: the Los Anbgeles (tel 60048, $9 single, $11 double); while a block south from here is the Santo Domingo church, a fine colonial relic. A path leading from here takes you down to the main reason for visiting Chiapa de Corzo: the Grijalva river. Before you even reach the quayside, touts will be soliciting for your business – to sell drinks and souvenirs, look after your luggage or arrange a boat trip through the Sumidero Canyon.

This is one of the best excursions on the whole Pan-American Highway, or rather *under* the Highway. Get there as early as you can in the day, to maximise your chances of paying a reasonable amount, and not being fried by the midday sun. A co-operative of boat owners charges about $80 in total for each launch with a dozen or so people on board – meaning about $7 or $8 each if you are part of a full boat load. Later in the day, there may not be a quorum of tourists, so you will be left with having to bid high, or postpone your trip to the following day. Whenever your go, you should be equipped to deal with cool temperatures as well as excess sun.

Once you get on board, you speed along the artificially swollen Río Grijalva, which passes under the Pan-American Highway a short way north of the quay. Beyond here, you enter the extraordinary Cañon del Sumidero, a sheer-sided slash through the Sierra with walls that sometimes rise to 1,000m (3,300 feet). The extremes of the microclimate, and the absence of widespread attentions of man, attract a wide range of birdlife, which the guides will be pleased to point out. The reservoir at the far end – the Presa Chicoasén – is a bit of an anticlimax, but the dam is interesting enough, and you will probably have no choice but to stop for a meal at one of the lakeside restaurants.

When the boat returns, the best way to travel on to the spiritual hub of Chiapas, San Cristóbal de las Casas, is on one of the local **minibuses** that depart frequently from the edge of town, and charge $2 for the 73km (46 mile) ride. The chances are that you will find yourself travelling in a vehicle driven, and largely occupied, by some of the region's indigenous people. The tail-end of Mexico is, in many ways, its most intriguing state. The people are much more closely connected to the pre-Columbian past than in any other part of the nation, and they retain their traditions much more visibly than elsewhere.

Nowhere is the separateness of Chiapas more evident than in San Cristóbal de las Casas, the capital of the state and the spiritual home of the Zapatista movement, who are fighting for the rights that have eluded them for the past five centuries. This manifested itself on 1 January 1994, the day the free-trade agreement with the USA and Canada came into effect. The rebels took over the city, and much of the surroundings, in a surprise attack that captured headlines around the world. Since then, the Mexican authorities have been engaged in a low-level war of attrition against the Zapatistas, interspersed with sluggish talks with the rebels. Despite their best endeavours, the national authorities have failed to supress the rebels' cause from the eyes of the world.

Tourism and politics: do they mix?

Not according to the Mexican government. Many foreign activists are sympathetic to the Zapatista cause, and concerned about the way that the rebels are being confronted by the Mexican government. But anyone participating in the political process could be deported.

Mexican immigration law prohibits foreigners from engaging in political activity, and a number of people who entered the country as tourists have been detained, expelled or deported for violating their status. To stay on the right side of the law, tourists are warned to avoid demonstrations and other activities that could conceivably be deemed as interference in domestic politics by the Mexican authorities.

San Cristóbal de las Casas

From Chiapas, the road to San Cristóbal appears to go onwards and upwards forever, but in fact within an hour you can peer down though the mists into a grand valley, and see the tops of buildings juggling for space with the clouds. San Cristóbal is isolated not just geographically, but culturally too. The bus driver and his passengers were speaking a dialect that had nothing to do with Spanish – nor with many of the other languages spoken in the highlands of Chiapas. What binds them together, besides centuries of oppression, is the city where they gather to buy, sell and meet.

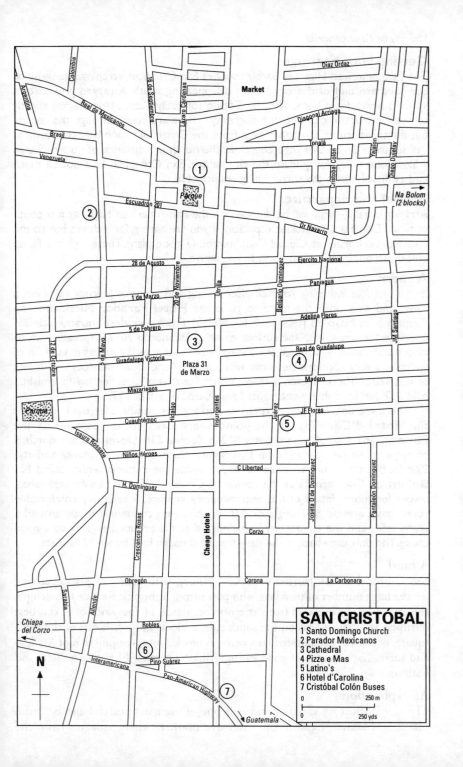

SAN CRISTÓBAL

1 Santo Domingo Church
2 Parador Mexicanos
3 Cathedral
4 Pizze e Mas
5 Latino's
6 Hotel d'Carolina
7 Cristóbal Colón Buses

0   250 m

0   250 yds

Getting your bearings

The Pan-American Highway barely touches San Cristóbal, scraping a tangent on the southern end of the city before disappearing south. A ragged grid pattern spreads north from here, with the Zócalo (officially Plaza 31 de Marzo) slightly to the west of the city's 'centre of gravity'. There are buses through the centre, but distances are so short that even from the Cristóbal Colón **bus terminal** at the south to Santo Domingo church at the north is a distance of no more than 1.5km (one mile). Away from the city centre, San Cristóbal does not so much end as dissolve into the surrounding countryside.

Arrival and departure

Arriving is easy – you will be dumped on the Pan-American Highway just south of town. Departing is trickier, especially if you are aiming for a direct bus to the Guatemalan border at Ciudad Cuauhtémoc (a good plan). These services fill up quickly, so book to leave as soon as you arrive.

A room

If you feel like indulging yourself after a long and arduous journey (or even a short and easy one), the place to go is the **Hotel Parador Mexicanos** on Avenida 5 de Mayo 38 (tel 81515, fax 80055). From a modest entrance (almost opposite the street with the curious name of Escaudrón 201), it spreads back to incorporate an airy, atmospheric dining room and a series of **cabinas**, each of which is a very comfortable room with cable TV and clean bathroom, with lots of hot water. There is even a tennis court for clients' use. For my first night I paid $32, but for subsequent nights I negotiated a rate of $27.

There are dozens of less expensive options. The handiest for the Highway is the **Hotel d'Carolina**, at the point where Crescencio Rosas meets the Panamericana. A single room costs $12, a double $16. Down another notch, a straggle of *hospedajes* runs up Insurgentes between the Highway and the Zócalo. But the optimum place to stay is inside the cultural centre called **Na Bolom**, on Guerrero 33 at the corner of Chiapa de Corzo; see *An exploration*, below, for more details of this extraordinary venture. A relatively comfortable room costs around $30 single or $40 double, with communal meals around a grand table and the comforting knowledge that the profits are going to a good cause. The only drawback is the daily traipse through by a bunch of tourists.

A meal

San Cristóbal is real 'banana pancake' territory, with plenty of places catering for the large number of travellers who pass through the city. Real de Guadelupe, the street extending east from the northern side of the Zócalo, is the best territory: try Pizze e Mas on the south side, a block-and-a-half east of the main square, or the Creperia directly opposite. A block south, the junction of Madero and Juárez has a couple of good eating/drinking venues, El Huarache Real and Latino's.

An exploration

The city is short on specifics, but it is one of the most peaceful and beautiful places in Mexico. Explore the extensive **market**, where villagers from the surrounding highlands come in to sell their produce and buy domestic wares. Of the many and various churches, the **cathedral** sits primly in the middle of town like a large, sculpted Cheshire cheese. To the north is the expansively decorated church of **Santo Domingo**, which turns from pink to a rich golden brown in the evening sun. But mostly just walk, admire and enjoy what seems on the surface to be a cool, civilised and relaxing town.

To find out more about the tensions that lie beneath the skin of this fine cities, visit **Na Bolom**, a cultural centre set in a fine colonial home at Guerrero 33 on the corner of Chiapa de Corzo. A Danish archaeologist and Swiss anthropologist, Frans Blom and his wife Gertrude, established the house as a basis for their explorations of the Mayan sites and societies in Chiapas. Tours take place every afternoon at 4.30pm prompt, in both English and Spanish. In return for $2, you are taken through a home that has been turned into a museum, and into the acres of gardens behind it. At the end of the tour, you get to see a film (not entirely fascinating) about the couple and their work.

Before you venture deeper into the **highlands** of Chiapas, be warned that the encounter may not be beneficial to you – because there have been a number of reports of attacks on visitors – or to the people of the highlands, who object to becoming little more than adornments for tourists' photographs. An excellent way to tread sensitively, while receiving an insight into the complex cultures of Chiapas – and getting some exercise – is to sign up for a **bike trip** with Penguin Tours, a bicycle company based on Avenida 5 de Mayo (near the junction with 5 de Febrero) that takes tourists on sensitive trips around a sensitive area. The guides are, quite rightly, strict about the use of cameras. On a tour of three or four hours, costing around $15, you will be amazed at how quickly you can get away from the city into areas that the 20th century appeared to pass by entirely.

Keeping in touch
You can barely walk a block in San Cristóbal without tripping over an internet café. The highest concentration is on Real de Guadelupe and Madero, a couple of blocks east of the square. Some are shockingly slow – ask other travellers for advice on the current best and worst.

Moving on
From San Cristóbal to the Guatemalan border, the Pan-American Highway is not going to be a highlight. The most significant point on the road as it descends from San Cristóbal to **Comitán** is the turning 12km (seven miles) out of town for **Palenque**. This Mayan site, one of the finest in Mexico, is 200km (125 miles) northeast of San Cristóbal, a long and slow bus ride away. If you decide to make the trip, you could impress your pals by continuing into Guatemala by **river**, ending up at the glorious Mayan ruins of **Tikal**. But it would involve straying a very long way from the Pan-American Highway.

Back in the humdrum world of the Highway, Comitán is a dusty and ugly town, where the smartest building is the **bus terminal** on the western side of town. If you are changing buses here, you will be disappointed by the almost complete lack of any charm, and decent food and drink. Comitán is not the sort of place you ought to be staying. Either have longer in San Cristóbal, or stay over in much cheaper and more cheerful Guatemala. Comitán is bland and best left behind on the first bus out.

The approach to the Guatemalan border is not over-exciting, and you may be surprised to be abandoned at Ciudad Cuauhtémoc – a place that looks much like any other Mexican town rather than a border crossing. One reason is that the road merely brushes against Guatemala here, with much traffic continuing south to the real last city, and southernmost point in Mexico, at Tapachula. But don't be tempted to go there – you need to cross the border into a very different world.

Guatemala

MEXICAN FRONTIER - GUATEMALA CITY

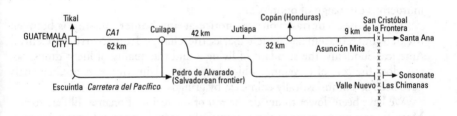

'Eternal spring' is the spurious and completely unsupportable claim the Guatemalan tourism authorities make about their country. Anyone crossing the overcooked border post from Tapachula on the coast will grumble about the heat, humidity and bad feeling that prevails near sea level. In the Highlands, you can spend all day trudging or trundling miserably through endless drizzle, known chirpily (and irritatingly) as *chipi chipi*. Cheer up: things, and your mood, can only get better.

The Panamericana follows a tortuous course through a country about the size of Ireland or the state of Louisiana, slicing across the south and west of a nation of staggering diversity. Nine million people live in a country shaped like a piece of jigsaw puzzle. But few of them occupy the vast areas of flat land in the north and east. Most reside in settlements scattered among the volcanic chain which runs across the southwest of the country – the line followed by the Pan-American Highway. One in five live in the crowded, noisy capital, Guatemala City, through which the Highway claws its messy way.

This is the country where, if time allows, you are most likely to stray from the not-very-straight but often narrow Pan-American Highway. If coming to grips with a Third World capital does not appeal, you can escape to the graceful and gently crumbling former capital of Antigua Guatemala, or to Lake Atitlán in its near-perfect setting amid the volcanoes. Such attractions have not gone unnoticed by travellers. The reputation of Guatemala as the closest place to paradise in the western hemisphere has been passed by word of mouth to a growing band of devotees. The graceful and gentle indigenous Indian population infuses depth and colour into the country's culture. The colour stems from the vivid fabrics used to make their costumes. These are woven and worn by the majority of Indians and can be bought in even the remotest of villages. Sadly, the increase in tourism has led to a profusion of decidedly unauthentic crafts: some of the lively markets, which feature so strongly in Guatemalan life, are now aimed at wealthy visitors. Even so, it is difficult not to marvel at the beauty and richness of the colours.

That Guatemala is not yet overflowing with tourists is due partly to the perceived instability of the country. The civil war that claimed tens of thousands of lives is still a dreadful memory for many Guatemalans, particularly Indians in isolated regions where security forces and paramilitaries conducted a murderous campaign of oppression.

The sharpest contrast you will notice at any border crossing is between Mexico and Guatemala, which marks the change from North to Central America. Suddenly, the standard of living – and the quality of life – drops. So, too, does the cost of travelling, which helps to explain why parts of Guatemala have been so enthusiastically colonised by gringos.

We have been slower to invade the rest of the region. Bonanza, El Paraíso and More Tomorrow are some of the optimistically named towns in Central America. None is remotely attractive, and each is of interest only because of the strange characters and odd creatures which inhabit any town in the region. Most visitors to the area are attracted not only by curious little towns, and the exquisite cultural wealth, but also by the concentration of astonishing natural beauty.

'Isthmus' is defined as a narrow neck of land connecting two larger portions: a constriction. Central America, the link between the great continents of North and South America, is constricted by a landscape thoroughly crumpled by seismic activity. Volcanoes, some still smouldering, punctuate the terrain of the isthmus. In few places in El Salvador, for example, are you out of sight of a volcano. A crooked spine of mostly dormant peaks runs through Central America from the Mexican frontier to the highlands of Panama. Other ranges splay across the region, such as the central highlands of Nicaragua. Flat land is at a premium; it is found mainly on the Caribbean coastal plain. This sea – warm, welcoming and rarely wild – is mild in comparison with the rough Pacific and its rugged coast. All in all, the Highway beyond Mexico becomes even more intriguing.

But first you have to get in.

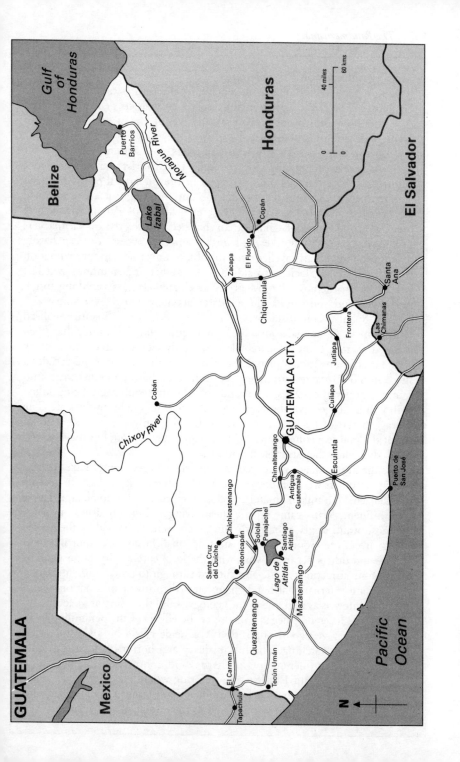

Making a dream out of a crisis

When, in 1990, the Ramada Inn opened at the former capital of Antigua Guatemala, the rate of attrition suffered by indigenous people in Central America's most drawn-out human tragedy was at last in decline. The two events were not, of course, related – or were they?

Tourism takes a bad rap in many quarters. Just within Guatemala, for example, there is a strong case to argue that tourists have degraded a culture than can trace its origins to well before the arrival of the Spanish. The market at Chichicastenengo has become nothing but a circus aimed at, and despoiled by, tourists. The serene village of Panajachel, sitting prettily on the shores of Lake Atitlán, has been desecrated by backpackers demanding banana pancakes and instant internet access. You can hardly blame the individual traveller who stumbles upon this fair approximation to lotus-land and decides to stay as long as his or her money will last (which, given the absurdly low prices in Guatemala, is a very long time). And, I contend, tourism has done Guatemala more than a few favours.

The Spanish conquistadores introduced widespread, institutionalised repression to Guatemala, and since then quasi-judicial murder has been elevated to an art form. Guatemala is the only Central American country where indigenous Indian people are in the majority, but over the decades a succession of brutal governments have done their best to butcher them into a minority. By the 1970s, thousands of Mayan people were being killed each year as alleged 'collaborators' with the guerrillas fighting the state. The average batch of backpackers may begin with only the haziest of ideas about the political complexities of a particular destination, but they know a good idyll when they stumble upon one.

As the death squads rampaged through the villages around Lake Atitlán, the first travellers were winding down and lighting up at the Last Resort cafe in Panajachel – a mile high and the closest approximation to Shangri-La on the continent. Many came for the cheap living and quality drugs in one of the most beautiful places on earth, but others were enchanted by the people and their culture. Some stayed to start up small businesses exporting local fabrics, and others began to work with the local community. Soon news of the sublime attractions of the area filtered through to other, more upmarket visitors, and international hotel chains started to invest in a nation whose infrastructure was as unstable as the geology – and the fabric of society.

Soon the foreigners began to hamper the efforts of the paramilitaries to snuff out every vestige of opposition. Genocide gets a bit awkward when the tourists are watching. The full intricacy and horror of the catastrophe that befell the indigenous people is beyond comprehension, let alone simplistic analysis. But I believe the suffering would have been even more intense were it not for the theology of liberation preached by travellers who found their personal dreams in a nation in the middle of a nightmare.

At the frontier

The bus arriving along the Panamericana will drop you off at the unprepossessing 'city' of Ciudad Cuauhtémoc, which comprises a couple of shacks and Mexican border formalities. Being first off the bus is a good move, to dodge the long queues. No man's land here is very wide, so you have to get a collective taxi (a big American saloon, fare $0.50 per person) to haul you across the border to La Mesilla, location for Guatemala's frontier control. Before jumping in, it is *essential* to check out of Mexico first – if not, the Guatemalans will send you straight back.

Admission to Guatemala is straightforward these days. Once across, there are frequent buses from La Mesilla to Huehuetenango, and El Condor buses run direct to Guatemala City.

If you are coming direct from Mexico City, the crossing at Talismán is the least interesting of those into Guatemala from Mexico, but it is also the busiest, most obvious, and the easiest to negotiate. A bus from Mexico City takes 22 hours, changing at Oaxaca; Omnibus Cristóbal Colón runs these services. From Tapachula there are buses covering the 8km (five miles) to the border which is open 24 hours a day. The bus service is not particularly efficient, however, so some people hitch or share a taxi. There are moneychangers on both sides of the border offering bank rates. From Talismán, on the Guatemalan side, there are regular buses along the coastal highway to Quetzaltenango and Guatemala City. From various points along this road you can make onward connections up to the Pan-American Highway and the Western Highlands. For a more scenic route, take a truck, bus or taxi along the rough road due east to San Marcos, from where you can make onward connections.

Red tape

The following information represents the official line at the time of going to press, but you should be prepared for considerable variations. In particular, some Guatemalan frontier guards do not miss a chance to benefit from the country's popularity among travellers. Visitors arriving or leaving by land are often required to pay more than the official amount of a couple of dollars to cross the border.

Officially British visitors, in common with US and Canadian citizens, do not need a visa; a tourist card can be obtained upon arrival. However, such is the inconsistency among frontier officials, that you could benefit from getting one in advance. Those who do not need a visa must pay $5 for a **tourist card** at immigration. It permits a maximum stay of 30 days, and allows one side trip to be made from Guatemala during its validity. Officials will ask you how long you plan to stay and will stamp your passport accordingly. Tourist cards may also be extended to a maximum total stay of 90 days. Each **visa** is valid only for a single journey. The usual maximum stay allowed is 30 days, though those planning to study Spanish can get 60 days if an official letter from the college is supplied. The application form asks, among other things, for your parents' full names and the colour of your skin. At consulates, particularly in Mexico and Central America, you can expect to pay anything between $2 and $10 for a visa. You may also be asked to show a credit card and state how much money you have. Addresses of Guatemalan consulates in the UK and USA, and across the border in Honduras and Mexico, are as follows:

UK: 13 Fawcett St, London SW10 9HN (tel: 020-7351 3042). Open 11am-2pm, Monday to Friday.

USA: 2220 R St, NW Washington DC 20008 (tel: 202-745-4952); plus consulates in Chicago, Coral Gables, Houston, Los Angeles, New Orleans and San Francisco.

Mexico: Avenida Explanada number 1025, Lomas de Chapultepec 11000, Mexico 4 DF (tel: 520 2794); Alvarado Obregón 342, Chetumal (tel: 0983-21365); Avenida Central Norte number 12, Ciudad Hidalgo (tel: 80193); 1 Calle Sur Poniente number 42, Comitán; Tapachula: 2 Calle Oriente number 33 (tel: 0962-61252).

Honduras: 8 Avenida 5-6, Avenida Noroeste 38, San Pedro Sula; 1 Avenida Suroeste 4-04, Nueva Ocotepeque; corner 2 Avenida and 2 Calle, Puerto Cortés.

For people planning to stay long enough to learn Spanish: a visa can be **extended** beyond the original 30 days permitted. To do this go to the Immigration office (Migración) at the corner of 8 Avenida and 12 Calle, Zona 1 in Guatemala City, and ask for a *prórroga* (extension). For those with a tourist card this should not present a problem: you require a photograph and can collect your newly-stamped passport the next day. For those with visas it can be a lengthy and costly business: unless you have plenty of cash and travellers' cheques, you need a Guatemalan guarantor, bank statements from him to prove he can support you and legal documents signed by a lawyer. Often the easiest thing to do is to leave the country for three days and get another visa, from one of the consulates mentioned above, or a tourist card at the border. Visitors who stay for more than 30 days are required to obtain an exit visa, which can also be done at the Immigration office.

Bringing in a car
The initial entry permit for cars is valid for 30 days. To extend it to a maximum of six months, you must approach the customs office (Aduana) on 10 Calle between 13 and 14 Avenidas (Zona 1) in Guatemala City.

Any chance of a decent map?
That depends on how long you've got. The government-run Instituto Geográfico Militar in Guatemala City produces topographical maps which are essential for anyone planning adventurous trips into out-of-the-way places. Maps can be consulted or bought at the institute, which is at Avenida Las Américas 5-76 in Zona 13. You must get permission, in the form of a letter from the Ministry of Defence, to buy those to a scale of 1:50,000 or 1:250,000; this can be done in the same building. Otherwise, you may just consult them and try to memorise the details. The small-scale maps cost $2, the large country maps (for which no permit is needed) cost $3-$5.

That was then

The first visitors

Guatemala has the greatest number of pre-Columbian sites in Central America, most of them Mayan. The largest concentration is in the province of Petén, where ancient cities such as Sayaxché, Uaxactún and – most splendid of all – Tikal, are found. During the Pre-Classic period there were important centres in the Pacific area, including Kaminaljuyú, which is the site of the modern capital, but the eruption of Ilopango volcano in around AD250 destroyed much of them and triggered the Classic period (AD250-900) which was to become the Golden Age of the Maya. The Petén was the heartland of the Maya during this period. During the Early Classic period Tikal became the most powerful centre, but a period of war or revolt known as the Middle Classic Hiatus, marked the start of Tikal's decline. This coincided with the rise in importance of previously less significant centres such as Quiriguá. Nevertheless, by the ninth century, many of these too had been abandoned, for reasons that are still a topic for discussion.

When the centres in the Petén declined, many of the Indians moved their commercial and cultural centre east to the Yucatán. Others moved south into the highlands and it was during the Post Classic period that the Maya culture as we know it developed. The Indians did not form a homogenous group and migrations, principally from Mexico, added other aboriginal strains. The greatest group was the Quiché who dominated the central highlands; the Tzutuhiles occupied the land south of Lake Atitlán; the Pokomchís had territory in the present-day area of Verapaz; while the capital of the Cakchiquel state was Iximché, close to Tecpán.

These Indians continued to live a subsistence lifestyle in the jungle, and smaller communities survived the initial attentions of the Spanish invaders. Only at the very end of the 17th century did the last Mayan city, Tayasal (on Lake Petén Itzá and the present site of Flores), surrender to the Spanish.

The Conquest

Pedro de Alvarado, the first conquistador, arrived in 1523. Using the same techniques employed elsewhere in the region for subjugating the native people, his men initially made rapid progress. They forged short-lived alliances with some groups and attacked others with superior arms; foreign diseases also helped to lay low much of the opposition. The main battle with the Quiché Indians was fought near where Quetzaltenango now stands, where the Quiché king, Tecún Umán, was killed by Alvarado himself. The king is commemorated in the name of a nearby town on the Mexican border. Alvarado had enlisted the support of the Cakchiquel Indians for the battle; after it he established the first Spanish capital near Iximché, which was the heart of the Cakchiquel nation. He called it Santiago de los Caballeros de Guatemala (St James of the Men of Guatemala).

The Maya

Playboys of the ancient western world?

Arguing about which was the greatest civilisation of the ancient world is about as tricky as a debate about whether the pre-Munich Manchester United squad of '58 was better than the team that won the Premiership in 2000. Just as Bobby Charlton and David Beckham are not directly comparable, neither can you play the Late Classic Maya off against the height of the Inca civilisation several centuries later. Both cultures were remarkably sophisticated, creating economies strong enough to generate surpluses that could be used for great ceremony or simple entertainment. The Maya's great strengths were understanding the fundamentals of astronomy, and the fact that they had writing – a skill that completely eluded the Inca people in their mountain-locked society.

Evidence recently unearthed at Cuello in Belize shows that the Maya existed as early as 2500BC. The crystallisation of their civilisation occurred during the Late Pre-Classic period (250BC-AD250), which saw the rise of the great Mayan dynasties and city states including Tikal, El Mirador and Kaminaljuyú in Guatemala. By AD300 Maya centres stretched from northern Guatemala, Belize and the Yucatán Peninsula down into western Honduras and El Salvador.

The cities of the Maya were dominated by great ceremonial complexes focussed around temples. Supernatural power was attributed to the Maya gods, but more earthly authority lay in the hands of the aristocratic and almost deific rulers. These high priests-cum-kings were warlike, and there was constant fighting between the cities. Battles are known to have taken place between Tikal and El Mirador, and recent discoveries have shown that Caracol in Belize successfully challenged Tikal on more than one occasion. Oppression was part of everyday life; in a parallel with several Central American countries today, the high priests lived in great luxury at the expense of the lowest echelons of Maya society who were treated as slaves.

Despite sporadic wars, it was during the Classic period (AD250-900) that the Maya established the greatest civilisation in the region. Tikal was almost certainly the most powerful centre in the Early Classic Period, but it declined during the so-called Middle Classic Hiatus which is thought to have resulted from a war or revolt of some kind. Tikal's diminished role, coupled with the destruction by fire of the powerful Mexican city of Teotihuacán in the 8th century, gave an impetus to other, smaller centres. Some of these, such as Copán in Honduras, had been established as colonies of Tikal, and for them the Late Classic period (AD500-900) was particularly productive. Despite expansion and development, however, the Maya never formed a single cohesive empire.

The Classic Maya were great traders by both sea and land. Their contacts stretched from Mexico to Panama and encompassed the Caribbean islands, while at home considerable intellectual advances were being made. The mathematicians were remarkably sophisticated, and were the first to make use of the concept of zero. A new understanding of astronomy led the Maya to calculate the motion of the planets. Elaborating on observations made by the Olmec in Mexico, they developed a calendar system which measured the length of a year with astonishing precision. The Maya also created America's most refined writing system. It took the form of glyphs, each a symbol representing a word or idea. The code was cracked in the 1950s, and almost two-thirds of the glyphs have been deciphered. The art of the Maya is easier to appreciate. Maya craftsmen were skilled carvers in stone, wood and jade, and were also accomplished potters. Though highly cultured in some ways, in others the Maya were decidedly primitive; they used no iron tools, no wheels and no beasts of burden, making their architectural achievements all the more remarkable.

The last century of the Late Classic period saw the gradual decline of the Maya civilisation. The reasons remain a mystery; theories put forward include social unrest, foreign invasion, famine and disease. Many of the survivors moved to the Yucatán. At the end of the first millenium they were attacked by the Toltecs from Tula in Mexico. The Toltecs conquered the Maya in the Yucatán and Guatemala, and took over their cities; the two groups absorbed aspects of each other's culture. The Toltecs were conquered by the Aztecs (also from Mexico) some time around 1300, but by then many of the sites had already been abandoned.

The Indian groups of today developed in the period building up to the Spanish Conquest. After the decline of the principal Maya centres, many people moved southwards and established scattered settlements in the highlands of Guatemala and beyond. These groups mixed with migrants from Mexico and other indigenous peoples; although Indians of pure Mayan descent are rare today, many of them have some Mayan blood. Foremost among today's Indians are the Quiché of Guatemala who are said to be the most direct descendants of the Maya. Other indigenous groups were scattered throughout Central America and were for the most part nomadic. As a result, their history is hard to trace, although the majority of them appear to have filtered down from Mexico. The larger groups which descended independently of the Maya were the Pipil (Guatemala and El Salvador) and the Lenca (Honduras and El Salvador). The Miskito and Sumo (Nicaragua) and the Kuna (Panama), on the other hand, are descended from South American Indians. These isolated groups were antagonistic to each other, and in no position to fight off the Spanish onslaught. Indeed, some allied with the Spanish to fight their traditional enemies, only to be turned upon later by the conquistadores.

Through a combination of treachery and political intrigue, Alvarado attained power over the other Indian groups. Only the Kekchí Indians, in what is now Alta Verapaz, proved a match for the Spanish militarily, but they eventually obliged the cause of colonialism by submitting to conversion to Christianity.

The capital of the new nation moved several times in its early years, through a combination of Indian and seismic activity. The second Santiago de los Caballeros de Guatemala was at the present site of Ciudad Vieja, and the third – and greatest – at Antigua Guatemala. This city, as capital of the Kingdom of Guatemala, was to control much of Central America for over two centuries: at its most extensive, the kingdom stretched from the (now Mexican) province of Chiapas to the western frontier of Panama.

Antigua flourished; new colonists from Spain settled around the city, in the south and west of Guatemala, where the climate and terrain most closely matched those in Spain. Agriculture and industry developed, based upon the needs of the mother country and its merchants. A succession of earthquakes, however, wrecked the capital. Although a surprising amount of Antigua's colonial beauty has survived, the rulers were sufficiently shaken by a severe earthquake in 1773 to relocate the capital to somewhere presumed (erroneously) to be safer – the present Guatemala City.

Independence

The colonisers, rather than the Indians, grew to resent Spanish control. The role of what is now Guatemala in the movement to liberate Central America was crucial, and independence for the whole region was declared in Guatemala City in 1821. It served initially as the capital of the 'province' of Central America during its temporary annexation by Emperor Agustín de Iturbide of Mexico, then as adminstrative seat for the Central American Federation. After the Federation fell apart in 1833, Guatemala was left isolated. The Liberals, representing the intellectual élite and original 'freedom-fighters', attempted to fill the power vacuum. They promised social and constitutional reform, but were unable to deliver due to a combination of insufficient funds and disease; cholera debilitated many of the people, weakening the economy still further. Rafael Carrera took power in an almost bloodless coup in 1838. He was unusual in Guatemalan politics, being both a strong Conservative and an illiterate Indian. The Conservatives ruled for over 30 years, taking retribution against Liberal factions and presiding over economic decline, as Guatemala – with poor infrastructure and growing competition – fell behind the rest of the region. Carrera's most radical attempt to solve the problem of communications involved signing away the province of Belize to the British in return for a promise of a road to the Caribbean. It has not yet been built, and only in 1990 did Guatemala relinquish its claim to the territory.

Public disquiet over the economy led to the Liberals seizing power under Miguel García Granados and his immediate successor, Justo Rufino Barrios. A Perón-like figure, Barrios was a populist who did much to modernise the country and reduce the power of the Catholic church. The greatest beneficiary of economic development was big business, however, rather than the poor. The wealth his government earned was squandered on a pointless military operation to impose a new Central American Federation upon the neighbouring countries. Barrios was killed in battle in El Salvador in 1885.

The Twentieth Century

Liberals succeeded Barrios until the turn of the century, when a strongman in the finest Central American tradition – Manuel Estrada Cabrera – took over. He was dangerous, greedy (à la Ferdinand Marcos of the Philippines) and mad. His successors, from 1920 onwards, were ineffectual, but established a kind of democracy which allowed Jorge Ubico to come peacefully to power in 1931. He, too, was disturbed (though less dangerous), and was forced to resign following a general strike in 1944. Students, professionals and even some military officers demanded democracy, and feelings ran so high that this period became known as the 1944 revolution. Elections followed, and a 'spiritual socialist', **Juan José Arevalo**, became president. He set about instigating a far-reaching programme of reforms, but his political doctrine proved unpalatable to business interests; they were behind the coup which returned power to the Conservatives in 1954.

The next thirty years were traumatic for the country, particularly the political opposition. A succession of hard-line leaders cracked down on dissidence and let the economy steadily collapse. Corruption encouraged the steady increase in the gulf between the rich minority and the poor.

Recent History

The region's most savage civil war, which began in the early 1960s, has been responsible for the deaths of over 100,000 people. It was at least in part instigated by the CIA, under pressure from foreign enterprises in Guatemala, whose privileged tax position was being threatened by new measures under consideration by the government. The CIA orchestrated a military coup and installed a military junta. Political opponents, largely drawn from the Indian community, began a guerrilla campaign.

Successive military leaders proved unable either to win the war or to revive the economy, and the political scene was characterised by rigged elections and coups. Violence and repression increased steadily during the 1970s. The early 1980s saw one of the worst phases of the war when whole villages in the Western Highlands were bombed and thousands of people killed. In 1986 Guatemala was on the brink of total anarchy when a civilian government took over. Its leader was Marco Vinicio Cerezo, a hard-drinking, smooth-talking and womanising Christian Democrat. He promised an end to repression and endeavoured to create the image of a leader intent on peace and security for his country. He achieved a certain stature among world opinion, most recently for organising the 1990 general election; he was only the third elected president in Guatemala to complete his term this century.

Under his régime, however, killings of the government's political opponents by the unofficial Civil Defence Patrols (PACs) continued. Human rights activists in Guatemala, who have themselves been frequent targets, maintained that the army was responsible for most political murders. It has been estimated that there were over 7,000 paid assassins in Guatemala, many of them organised into death squads every bit as vile as those in El Salvador. Cerezo himself was quoted as saying: 'We are not going to be able to investigate the past – we would have to put the entire army in jail.' It seems that governments can retain power in Guatemala only by appeasing the military and foreign business. US aid continued to flow into Guatemala, much of it used to finance the army's campaign against the guerrillas.

By the end of 1990 the strength of the rebel forces was believed to have been reduced to just 1,500, but they proved to be highly resilient. Their campaign was geared to forcing the government to negotiate by crippling the country economically. Unfortunately the rebel groups made some serious blunders: blowing up bridges vital for the transport of local produce to markets turned many local people against them.

Complex political wranglings followed the 1990 election in Guatemala. The only serious contenders for the elections were right-wing candidates. Jorge Carpio, leader of centre-right Unión del Centro Nacional (UCN) narrowly won the first ballot, but Jorge Serrano, leader of the Movimiento de Acción Solidaria (MAS) and an evangelical Protestant, won the second ballot in January 1991. Most candidates made a show of saying they would curb the power of the military, but cynics maintained that anyone who tried it would not be left in government long enough to do so. Certainly, the power of the military was widely blamed for the lack of progress in curbing human rights abuses, and there was harsh criticism of Serrano's government from both the United States and the European Union. In 1993, Serrano dismissed Congress and placed various senior figures, including the human rights ombudsman, under house arrest. Amid international condemnation, vital aid programmes were suspended, the military took control, and new elections were held.

Ramiro de León became president, to considerable public optimism, which quickly dissipated as he failed to address the two main domestic problems, poverty and corruption. Although a human rights agreement was signed, there was little evidence of improvement, and little progress was made in negotiations with the Guatemalan National Revolutionary Union (UNRG), representing the four main guerrilla groups.

There were real signs of progress following the election of Alvaro Enrique Arzú as President in 1995; an accord was adopted recognising Guatemala as a multi-cultural, multi-ethnic country, and acknowledging the rights of the indigenous population. Shortly afterwards, the guerrillas announced a ceasefire, leading to an agreement, in December 1996, which ended the civil war. The URNG demobilised, and became a political party. Steps were taken to create a new police force, and to reduce the size of the military.

But again, the momentum for change flagged. There was a sharp rise in the level of crime, and land disputes increased. Plans announced by the government to increase spending on education and health were dropped.

This is now

In April 1998, a bishop, who had just delivered a report on human rights abuses, was assassinated in Guatemala City; his killers were widely suspected to be members of the military forces, to whom his report had directed its criticism. In February 1999, the report of a Commission set up to examine human rights in Guatemala during the civil war, concluded that 200,000 people had been killed or disappeared between 1962 and 1996, and that in 90% of those cases, state terrorism could be held to blame. Now that the civil war is over, a crucial task for any government is to ensure that the power of the military is curbed, so that the country's citizens no longer need to fear the forces of law and order. The man who is charged with this task is Alfonso Portillo, of the right-wing Guatemalan Republican Front (FRG), who was elected President five days before the end of 1999.

On the Highway

Many of the roads are diabolical, and impassable during the rainy season, but luckily the worst are over towards the Caribbean side of the country. Around the Highway you can expect decent surfaces and a reasonably good, if erratic, bus service.

Travelling by bus

The all-American Bluebird yellow school bus is the normal mode of transport in Guatemala. So popular is it that there is now a Bluebird assembly plant in the capital. The supply of buses, however, fails to meet the demand, and going on a long journey can easily become a test of endurance. Following some tragic accidents in which dozens died in overcrowded buses, stricter rules about the numbers allowed on were introduced; there has been no obvious reduction in overcrowding, and the only consequence has been that all the standing passengers have to crouch down when a police patrol is spotted. First-class buses do not exceed their design capacity so frequently, but on these you should avoid the back seat; it is used to soak up excess demand, so is often occupied by ten, rather than five, passengers. Furthermore you are only inches from the engine, so it is guaranteed to be hot, smelly and noisy.

The combination of overcrowding and chronic shortages is particularly galling when you are hoping to board a bus en route, since often they will sail straight past. In addition, travel along dirt roads is difficult, and often impossible in mountainous areas during the wet season. The imponderables of travel are made still less certain by the enigmatic approach to scheduling adopted by bus crews in Guatemala. Times given in this chapter are the most accurate available, but can vary by an hour or more.

The first-class buses should be used whenever possible. They leave less frequently than second class buses, but are much faster and more comfortable. For reaching destinations off the Pan-American Highway, it is often best to take any first class bus as far as the required turn-off and then pick up a local bus. These first class services usually require advance booking and rarely pick up passengers en route.

Note that the destination boards on buses usually show an abbreviated destination (e.g Guate for the capital, Huehue for Huehuetenango), and that intermediate destinations are rarely given.

Driving

In theory, you are always required to carry your passport, driver's licence and vehicle registration documents at all times. In practice, rules and regulations are fairly relaxed and the speed limits (60km/h in towns, 90km/h outside) are rarely enforced. Motorists frequently run red lights in the riskier parts of the capital. The main impediment to motorists is the sleeping policemen near every military establishment. These are not always well signposted, and can cause serious damage to axles, backs, heads, etc, if hit at speed. Drunken drivers are another hazard, although you are probably more likely to run into drunken pedestrians; the latter are out in force at festival time.

Much of the hassle of driving in Guatemala is removed by **hiring** a car. This can only be done reliably in the capital. Most of the big multi-national companies are represented in the international airport, and may also have agents in the top-class hotels, such as the Sheraton or Camino Real. To rent a car costs about $40 per day with unlimited mileage, or $220 per week, plus insurance and tax.

Hitch-hiking

The only serious hitching I have done so far in Guatemala was along the Coastal Highway, when buses were in short supply, and on cross-country journeys close to the Salvadoran border. Lifts were easy to come by, but it would be harder to justify on the Pan-American Highway except at holiday time when all the buses are full and everybody knows it. While you should offer the equivalent of the bus fare to your driver, nine times out of ten it will be declined.

The flyover option

The only real short-cut to the Pan-American Highway in Guatemala is between Quezaltenango and the capital, which means missing the country's highlights. You may, though, want to consider flying from Guatemala City to San Salvador

Last train to Puerto Barrios – thank goodness
When the late and unlamented Ferrocarriles de Guatemala (FEGUA) was still running trains, the coast-to-coast service took two-and-a-half days, including two overnight stops in Guatemala City – the schedules did not mesh well. That was assuming the trains ran to time, which was highly unlikely. No wonder the network shut down a few years ago.

airport (which is nowhere near the Salvadoran capital, but is close to some superb coast), or even onward to Managua or San José. This will save you a fairly unrewarding slog across eastern Guatemala, but could cost close to $100, including all taxes, for the short 30-minute flight.

Is Guatemala a good place to start or finish a trip along the Pan-American Highway?

Yes, both practically and intellectually. Guatemala City is a starting point for many travellers to Central America. It has direct services from Mexico City and Cancún on the Yucatán; numerous flights from US cities, most frequently from Miami, Houston and Los Angeles, but also to New York and Washington DC; links with Amsterdam and Madrid in Europe; and good services from cities in Central America.

Guatemala's national airline is Aviateca, whose main selling point is not its safety record or its modern aircraft, but the fact that it serves free champagne, whisky, and cognac on its flights. Two other carriers – Aeroquetzal and Aerovías – are expanding international air services; the Aerovías service between Belize City and Flores (for Tikal) is particularly useful for travellers. Another valuable route is the daily service on the Panamanian carrier Copa which links Guatemala City with San Salvador, Managua, San José and Panama City. The country's main airport is close to the centre of the capital.

Who are the Guatemalans?

Guatemala has a much higher proportion of indigenous people than do other countries in Central America – Indians make up more than half of the population. Most of them are descended from the ancient Maya, but owing to migration from Mexico and elsewhere following the Classic period, few are now pure Maya. They are a very traditional and overwhelmingly gentle and meek people – beaten, by colonisers and more modern governments, into a state of simply wanting to be left alone.

Maya influence is everywhere in Guatemala, giving it a far stronger sense of character than the other countries of Central America. Its uniqueness is shown in everything from the bold, colourful weavings to the extraordinary folk religions: these ancient rituals bear a thin veneer of Catholicism and may involve anything from animal sacrifice to flagellation, and, always, ample amounts of alcohol. One of the most curious cults, found in a few villages in the Western Highlands, is that of Maximón, a 'saint' whose favourite offerings are cigarettes and rum.

Even the stunning costumes show the heavy hand of the Spanish colonisers. Although some traditional Mayan designs survive, the current ones reflect the laws imposed by the Spanish which made towns and villages develop a different dress so that they knew where people came from – rather like a school uniform.

The next largest group is described variously as mestizo or ladino, words which have slightly different meanings. The term mestizo, used in Mexico and elsewhere in Central America, usually means of mixed Indian and Hispanic race. In Guatemala, however, the term ladino is more accurate, since it also encompasses Indians who have adopted Western traits, Spanish-speaking blacks, and so on. It literally means one who has been Latinised, i.e. who has adopted European dress and customs, even though he may be pure-blood Indian. (A female is described as ladina.)

The ladinos, who live mainly in the towns, rank above the Maya in terms of wealth and power. The ruling classes are drawn mainly from this ladino population, and include the tiny group of whites of mostly Hispanic descent. However, there are also many ladinos who are as poor as the Indians (and who may indeed be Indian). Income and social class decides status more than the relative proportions of Indian and Spanish blood.

The whites number less than 150,000, about the same as the blacks, some of whom are concentrated around the isolated Caribbean port of Livingston. Most blacks are Garífuna, or Black Caribs, found also in Belize and Honduras. Many have moved to the capital, where they encounter a considerable amount of racism. Those that have remained in the Caribbean region have maintained their traditional lifestyle more easily. Their distinctive dances and music are best witnessed at festival times.

Guatemala receives more tourists than the other Central American countries, and the locals' attitudes towards foreigners have been shaped by this large number of visitors. There is some resentment towards *norteamericanos* because of the perceived manipulation of Guatemalan affairs by the USA. The sheer number of backpackers, and the not-always-benign influence that foreigners have had upon traditional communities, has led to an uncharacteristic cynicism among some Guatemalans.

Nevertheless the majority of the people, especially the Indians in the more rural parts of the country, are friendly and hospitable, and perhaps more chatty and animated than people elsewhere in Central America.

What they speak

There are even more Guatemalans learning English than there are foreigners learning Spanish in Guatemala, but you should not assume that you will find English speakers wherever you go. The highest proportion of English-speakers, predictably enough, is in the capital, and at the prime tourist sites of Antigua, Panajachel and Tikal. There are some native English speakers among the black community on the Atlantic coast. Many of the Indian people speak Spanish exclusively, but some communities – especially the more isolated ones – continue to use indigenous dialects. Indeed you may meet Indians who have just as many problems with Spanish as you do. This is particularly true of the indigenous women who hold on to their traditions more than the men do.

Your life in Guatemala will be made much easier if you know that *x*, which crops up in many town names, is pronounced *sh*. Therefore Ixil becomes Isheel, Iximché becomes Ishimchay.

What they eat

Sharing a long common border with Mexico, it is not surprising that Guatemala has been heavily influenced by its northern neighbour. This applies particularly to its cuisine. You can eat some excellent Mexican food in Guatemala, though the best tends to be in the more expensive restaurants. There is little to distinguish the dishes of the Maya from those found across the frontier in Mexico, except that the Guatemalans put even more emphasis upon corn.

As in other Central American countries, **comida típica** is sold mainly at roadside shacks or comedores and involves the usual array of frijoles, rice, tortillas, meat, fried plantain, etc. Also popular are stalls selling piping hot tortillas wrapped around meat to form an enchilada. With luck there will be plenty of **guacamole** (mashed avocado) to accompany it. In an interesting encounter between American-style fast food and more traditional cuisine, street vendors in Guatemala City sell hot dogs garnished with guacamole. **Ceviche** (marinated raw fish) is another favourite, and even small towns up in the mountains will have a cevichería where the locals go to have a beer and a snack in the evenings.

Most restaurants put the emphasis on less traditional dishes, such as the bistec, hamburguesas and pork chuletas. More recently there has been an increase in the number of places catering specifically for travellers, selling the kind of goodies found in Asian shangri-las such as Bali and Koh Samui: exotic fruit salads, milk-shakes, pancakes and toasted sliced white bread. This type of food predominates in Panajachel and Antigua.

Eating out, like most things in Guatemala, is extremely cheap, and a simple meal at a local comedor seldom sets you back more than 50c. Prices are higher in the capital. In Guatemala City, and to a lesser extent Antigua, there is a good selection of foreign restaurants. More upmarket places will levy IVA tax of 7% on the bill, and you are expected to tip another 10%. In cheaper comedores, there is no need to tip.

What they drink

Short answer: as little as possible of the local tap water. Even if it is safe, it is never pleasant, since it is heavily chlorinated. The distribution system is hard-pressed to cope with the demands placed upon it by the vastly increased population, so cuts in the supply occur frequently. Bottled water is widely available.

Bottles of cheap and sweet red or white wine are sold in the villages, along with the national spirit, distilled from sugar cane and known as **aguardiente**; the best-known brand is Quezalteca. A 25cl bottle costs less than $1, and has created a severe alcoholism problem among Guatemalan males, particularly the indigenous people. Those who prefer to drink for pleasure, rather than to numb the senses, stick mainly to the **beer**. The two leading brands are Gallo (which means rooster) and Monte Carlo, which is slightly stronger and more expensive. The dark, treacly version of Gallo is sometimes available, and is strikingly similar to the British brew Mackeson. **Rum** is the main alternative to beer, Ron

Botrán being the local brew. There are various local concoctions e.g. Caldo de Frutas, a sangría-style drink from Salcajá near Quetzaltenango.

What they read, watch and listen to

Most of the Spanish-language **press** is typical of that elsewhere in Central America: right-wing, and with a propensity to publish gory pictures of victims of accidents and murder. *El Gráfico* has, if nothing else, a cultural page which lists museums, galleries, etc. (but also advertisements for massage parlours and other places of dubious repute). US newspapers are available in the capital and Antigua. Up-to-date copies of the international edition of the *Miami Herald* are easy to find.

If you want to be a disc jockey, Guatemala is the place to look for work. The capital alone has over 40 **radio** stations, with another 60 serving the rest of the country. The only one likely to be of interest to those with a taste for western rock music is 95FM in Guatemala City, which transmits an interesting mixture of ancient and modern, ranging from Nirvana to Nenah Cherry.

Guatemala City has a good claim to be the satellite capital of the world. Half the homes seem to have a satellite dish peering into space, with which Mexican and US **television** can be picked up; big American sporting events are particularly popular. Hotels and bars in tourist areas advertise the fact that US stations (especially CNN) can be watched. Terrestrial television is less popular, because of the poor quality of the programming and the difficulty in transmitting a decent signal in mountainous terrain.

What might you want to read

One of the best travelogues is *Bird of Life, Bird of Death*, by Jonathan Evan Maslow (Penguin, 1987). It is subtitled *A Naturalist's Journey Through a Land of Political Turmoil*; although it describes the author's search for the elusive quetzal, the book is far more than just an ornithologist's diary. Also worth a read is *Beyond the Mexique Bay* by Aldous Huxley; published in 1934, it describes a very different Guatemala. A more recent addition to the Guatemalan reading list is *Sweet Waist of America – Journeys around Guatemala* by Anthony Daniels (Hutchinson, 1990).

Guatemala's greatest novelist is Miguel Angel Asturias, who died in 1974. His most famous novel is *Hombres de Maíz* which is a complex book describing the relationship between the Indians and mestizos; it has been translated into English and is available as *Men of Maize* (Verso). *El Señor Presidente*, which presents a gruesome but all too realistic picture of dictatorship at its worst, and *El Papa Verde*, which investigates the United Fruit Company, are available only in Spanish but make good reading. For another insight into the history and politics of the country read *Guatemala in Rebellion* (Grove Press), which contains a fascinating collection of eye-witness accounts of events spanning the Spanish Conquest to the 1980s. It gives an excellent and accurate account of the civil war and the overthrowing of the socialist government in the 1960s.

How they enjoy themselves

Most of Guatemala's museums are in the capital and in Antigua, and include some of the finest collections in Central America. The shortage of interesting museums and art galleries elsewhere in the country is more than compensated for by the remarkable Mayan sites. The greatest concentration of ruins, and the most spectacular ones, are to be found in the jungle-covered Petén region in the north, but there are others scattered elsewhere. Many of the ancient centres are hard to reach and you will sometimes need to hire a guide to reach them.

The Popol Vuh Museum in Guatemala City organises lectures on archaeology and is a good source of books. Here and in other good bookshops you can usually pick up a bi-monthly paper called *Cultura Maya*, which carries articles which deal with the history of the Maya, and each issue usually highlights a specific site. If you want to read up or ask more detailed questions about a particular site the best place to go is the Centro de Investigaciones Regionales de Mesoamérica in Antigua, whose library has a good selection of books on archaeological and ethnographical subjects.

Everyday life on an average day proceeds fairly quietly, but on fiesta days Guatemala becomes one of the most exciting places to be in the world. During festivals the culture of the indigenous people comes alive, and you are guaranteed to hear music and see traditional dancing. There are variations from village to village, and between the ladino, Indian and black communities, but the music is almost always dominated by the *marimba*, the wooden xylophone played in other parts of Central America.

Each community chooses its own fiesta day, a date often linked to its patron saint, and there is a festival in at least one community every day of the year; you would have to be extremely unlucky if your visit didn't coincide with one somewhere. If your projected itinerary appears to deny you the chance, it is well worth making a detour. At certain times there are celebrations in all corners of Guatemala, principally during Holy Week, and on All Saints' Day (1 November). Among the towns particularly famous for their festivals are Antigua, Todos Santos, Joyabaj and Santiago Atitlán.

Activities on patron saints' days may be both religious and secular events, but the atmosphere is almost always one of madness and chaos. Entertainments range from beauty contests to horse racing, but the dancing, music and the drinking of large amounts of alcohol are constant features. If you join in the latter, stick to the brews you know rather than the local concoctions.

There are a few **theatres** and **concert halls** in Guatemala outside the capital, and the repertoire is mainstream. In terms of formal entertainment, your best bet is the cinema; every town has one, or at least a sala de video, where English-language films are shown with Spanish subtitles. Admission costs 50c-$2, depending on the newness of the film and the comfort of the venue.

Nightlife is confined mostly to some extremely dodgy clubs in Guatemala City, which attract a clientele that looks to be comprised mainly of mercenaries and prostitutes. Travellers looking for a relaxing evening are best off in a local bar with a chum and a few bottles of beer.

The national **game** is soccer, which is played everywhere in Guatemala with great enthusiasm. The best team is Municipal of Guatemala City. The season runs from February to early December. Baseball is also followed with interest, and there always seems to be a game on television. Basketball and American football are also popular.

Festivals and holidays

January 1	New Year
March/April	Holy Thursday
March/April	Good Friday
May 1	Labour Day
June 30	Anniversary of the Revolution
August 15	Ascension Day (holiday only in Guatemala City)
September 15	Independence Day
October 20	Revolution Day
November 1	All Saints' Day
December 24	Christmas Eve (public holiday from noon)
December 25	Christmas Day
December 31	New Year's Eve (public holiday from noon)

What they spend

The Quetzal, a lovely name for a mediocre and often mucky currency. But who cares that the average Q1 note has been through the pockets of most of the nine million Guatemalans, when it is worth so little but goes so far?

The Q1 note might originally have been green, but most of them have long since muddied to the same nondescript shade as the Q5 (originally mauve), Q10 (red), Q20 (blue) and Q50. The Q100 comes closest to preserving its brick red, but you should try to avoid this denomination since few traders seem to have change. The 25c coin is called a *choca*.

Travellers' cheques can be exchanged only at banks, and not every bank accepts them; a good supply of US dollars in cash is therefore essential. **Banks** open at 8am, 8.30am or 9am and close at 2pm or 3pm, Monday to Friday. They remain closed on an annoying number of days: as well as the full repertoire of public holidays, banks close on the Wednesday of Holy Week, 1 July (Bank Employees' Day) and 3 December.

The **parallel market** is active in Guatemala City and at border crossings. Traders in out-of-the-way places will change money (cash only) outside banking hours but at an unfavourable rate. ATMs can be found widely in Guatemala City and in big towns outside the capital. If your credit card fails to work in a cash machine, and you manage to retrieve it, then call in at Credomatic in Guatemala City. Travellers with a credit card can usually draw cash on it in a few minutes from the office in the basement of Plaza 6-26 (everyone knows it as *seis-veinte-seis*) on 7 Avenida. It opens 8am-8pm from Monday to Friday, and 9am-1pm on Saturdays. A passport is required for identification.

Guatemala has the most sophisticated (i.e. irritating) indirect taxation system in Central America. Virtually every transaction is subject to IVA (value-added tax) of 7%. An additional **tax** of 10% is levied on a number of tourist-related activities, including air tickets and accommodation.

Anything worth buying?

Yes. People who have travelled the length of Central America are usually staggered by the richness of the crafts scene in Guatemala. This is solely due to the size of the Indian population. Crafts range from the silverware made in Cobán to the ceramics made in Totonicapán, but the art of weaving, handed down by the ancient Maya, reigns supreme. Guatemala's markets are worth visiting not so much to make purchases, but rather to marvel at the colours.

The bold simplicity of Guatemalan fabrics is well known, and almost every visitor comes away with a weaving of some sort. Each community in Guatemala has a distinctive weave, rather like the distinctive tartans of Scottish clans. The colours and pattern are a village's fingerprint, each of them unique. One of the most popular garments is the *huipil,* the simple yet elegant blouse worn by Indian women. This is made of up to three pieces of colourful woven cotton, and can be bought virtually everywhere in Guatemala. Other traditional Indian clothes include the *corte* (wrap-around skirt), *perruje* (shawl) and *pantalones* (men's trousers). Unfortunately, much of the material sold in the towns firmly on the tourist trail, such as Antigua and Panajachel, is mass-produced and often geared for the undiscriminating tourist. In addition, prices are at a premium when coachloads of rich package tourists are disgorged into the crowds. You are advised to stick around until they have all gone.

You should buy in the remoter communities. The best quality and the best prices are to be found in isolated parts of western Guatemala, notably the villages of Todos Santos, Nebaj and Chajul. Markets in the small villages are generally dominated by stalls selling food and household goods, and you may have to wait for the weavers to approach you in the street or at your pensión in order to make purchases. Otherwise, you must go yourself in search of the private houses where the weaving is done. Many towns and villages have a daily market, but one or two days a week more traders than usual gather to do business – this is 'proper' market day, and the best time to buy weavings.

Keeping in touch

Telephone

Following the regional trend, Guatemala has simplified its immensely complex phone system so that there are no area codes, just seven figure numbers. Antigua is prefixed 832, Panajachel 762 and Quezaltenango 761.

The network is run by Guatel, which has an office in every town. Three offices in Guatemala City open 24 hours, while outside the capital normal hours are 7am-midnight daily. These offices are primarily of use for international calls. They are surprisingly efficient, and having given your number you need only wait a few minutes before you are called to a booth; the wait may be longer in the evenings. The cost to the UK of a three-minute call is very high, around $30, and to the USA $15.

Given the uncertainties of the Guatemalan telephone system, it is not surprising that many locals prefer to use **telegrams** for long-distance communication within the country. At any post office you fill in a form and pay a small fee of around 3c per word. International telegrams, though, have to be sent from Guatel offices and are much more expensive. Guatel has the monopoly on publicly available **fax** machines, and it costs a fortune to send one; there is a charge of 40c to receive each sheet.

Mail

The difficult terrain and inadequate road network mean that Guatemala's mail system is one of the least efficient in Central America. Letters posted from one side of the country to the other are rumoured to be consigned to the railway, and so might take a week to arrive. Air mail cards and letters to addresses in Europe and North America take about a week when posted in Guatemala City and its environs, but this can be doubled if you post from an obscure, out-of-the-way village.

To make up for the slightly erratic service, rates are cheap. Postcards and letters to the USA cost around $0.25, to Europe $0.40. An aerogramme costs $0.40, but you must buy one at a stationer's. Post offices open 8am-4.30pm from Monday to Friday. Mailboxes are yellow.

The most reliable places from which to send parcels back home are Antigua and Panajachel, where there are companies specialising in air freight. Most people would prefer to carry their purchases with them owing to the high cost, however. To send a parcel weighing 3kg by sea mail, expect to pay about $40 to the UK and $30 to the USA. Air mail for the same weight costs $80 and $65 respectively. These places seem to be used mainly by semi-professional entrepreneurs sending cheap Guatemalan crafts to shops in North America and Europe.

Internet

In some places popular with backpackers – Antigua, Quetzaltenango, Panajachel – you can barely move without tripping over a traveller hunching over a terminal and wanting, digitally at least, to be home. With so much competition, rates are the cheapest in Central America.

The outdoors – how great?

Most visitors find themselves at some point **hiking** through the country's stunning scenery, or scaling volcanoes. As yet the development of national parks has been very limited, so there are few places with organised trails. One of the most popular wildlife reserves is the quetzal sanctuary near Cobán, which is a private concern. The government has shown some interest in getting involved in the 'debt for nature' programme, which has been adopted by Costa Rica, for example, so it is to be hoped that other areas of the country may one day be protected.

In most country areas there are trails used by the local people which are often good for walks. In some instances, particularly when climbing volcanoes, it is necessary to hire a guide. While in Antigua this is quite an organised business, for trips up volcanoes in less touristy areas you will have to make your own arrangements. This usually involves going to the village nearest to the start of the path up the volcano, and asking around among the locals. If there is a hospedaje in the village, it is likely to be a good source of information.

The best river for **rafting** is the Cahabón which flows from the Alta Verapaz region in the centre down to the Caribbean – a long way from the capital, and the Highway. But of all the countries in Central America, Guatemala has the worst selection of beaches. The country's seashores are mostly dirty or rocky or both. Of the Pacific beaches the one at Champerico is probably the best, but the swimming is not brilliant. The diminutive beach at Panajachel on Lake Atitlán is popular, if chilly, and the lake is also becoming a scuba diving venue.

Staying safe
The tap water in Guatemala City is usually safe but never pleasant, since it is heavily chlorinated. The distribution system is hard-pressed to cope with the demands placed upon it by the vastly increased population, so cuts in the supply occur frequently.

Apart from the usual hazards of unhygienic food, inhospitable insects, and dangerous drivers, the altitude of much of Guatemala can be a problem. The capital and many places of interest are a mile high or more, and the thinness of the air takes some getting used to. In particular, you may tire more easily, and alcohol has more of an effect at high altitude

Medical treatment is adequate in the capital and the bigger towns, but primitive elsewhere. It has been estimated that two million people have no access to proper medical care. These are primarily Indians living in rural areas, who have a life expectancy of more than ten years less than ladinos. Try to avoid falling ill in rural areas. At public hospitals you can be examined for a nominal fee, but drugs are expensive. Ambulances are run by the Cruz Roja, and one can be summoned by dialling 125.

Pick-pocketing, bagsnatching and violent crime are increasing. This is especially true in Guatemala City, but robbery is also rising in other places popular with tourists, notably Antigua, Panajachel and around Tikal. **Bus searches** by the military can be unnerving. Men are usually lined up alongside the bus, leaning against it with their arms uplifted. Tourists are exempt as a rule, but it's better to do like the rest and then be told to get back on the bus, rather than assume they don't want to search you.

The whole point of a visit to Guatemala, for some people, is the easy availability of **drugs**. One consequence of the way in which the local economies in parts of Guatemala have evolved to meet the needs of western travellers is the wide availability of soft drugs. Marijuana is easy to obtain in Guatemala City, Antigua and (especially) Panajachel, and cocaine is also widespread. The minimum penalty for possession in Guatemala is five years, and it appears that dealers are sometimes in cahoots with the police, a cosy relationship in which the police improve their figures for convictions and the dealers protect their businesses. An embellishment on this is that the police may offer the chance of 'bail', at a figure calculated to be the absolute maximum that you could afford; $5,000 is not unknown. The idea is that you rustle up the cash, hand it over, and scarper. Since the alternative is a mandatory jail term, most people pay up.

Guatemala has recently taken over from Mexico in seventh place on the world list of opium poppy production. Most is grown in the north of the country, and the industry attracts a large number of unpleasant characters.

Long-distance information

The state tourist board is the Instituto Guatemalteco de Turismo – Inguat. Its head office is on the ground floor of the huge office block at 7 Avenida 1-17, Centro Cívico, Zona 4, Guatemala City (tel: 331-1333). Inguat has branch offices in Antigua, Panajachel and Quetzaltenango and at Guatemala City's airport. There are also several private 'tourist information centres'. The quotes are used advisedly, since these places are usually run by interested parties: tour operators selling only their own products, booking agencies taking commission on hotel reservations, etc. Understandably you are unlikely to get impartial advice, and can expect to be steered towards whatever it is that the office is trying to sell. Therefore it is best to rely upon other travellers for advice and opinion, or to call Inguat toll-free on 1 801 464 8281.

For advice abroad, you could send a large stamped addressed envelope to the Embassy of Guatemala at 13 Fawcett St, London SW10 9HN, and in return you will be sent a supply of Inguat brochures. They may not be highly informative but they include lots of pretty pictures.

From the frontier to the capital

Huehuetenango

This is one of the largest towns in western Guatemala, and is capital of the Huehuetenango department. Travellers arriving from Mexico via La Mesilla may decide to spend their first night here. Huehue, as everybody calls it, was quite an important mining town during the colonial era, although nowadays agriculture is a more important source of income. Huehue has a large population of ladinos, and lacks the colour and life so typical of Quiché department. However Indians dominate the market in the eastern district of the town and this area is more reminiscent of the rest of the highlands. There is little to do in Huehue itself but it gives access to one of the most rugged and fascinating parts of the country.

Lying on the Pan-American Highway, Huehue is easy to reach. It is just a couple of hours from the Mexican border at La Mesilla, and about six from Guatemala City. First class buses to the capital are run by Transportes Los Halcones and Rápidos Zaculeu from 9 Calle 11-42, Zona 1 (3 Avenida 5-25 in Huehue). Second class buses leave more frequently from the bus station south of the town centre to go to the Zona 4 terminal.

There are also buses from Quezaltenango, a journey taking about three hours. Those approaching from points further east should change at Cuatro Caminos rather than going right into Quezaltenango to change buses. If you are approaching from the Ixil Triangle or other points east of Huehue, there are buses from Sacapulas via Aguacatán. Most buses serving the surrounding area, and second-class buses to towns further afield, leave from 1 Avenida between 2 and 3 Calles.

The **best place to stay** is Hotel Central (5 Avenida 1-33; tel 764 1202), a charmingly run-down colonial-style building, north of the square in the nicest area of town. Other recommended places are Hotel Mary (2 Calle, 3-52; tel: 764 1618), and Hotel Zaculeu (5 Avenida 1-14; tel: 764 1086. It is also possible to camp at Zaculeu. For the most authentic and cheap **food** try the comedores on the west side of the Plaza.

Five kilometres northwest of Huehue are the ruins of **Zaculeu**. This is the site of the former capital of the Mam tribe, one of the main tribes to inhabit the area in pre-Columbian times. Zaculeu dates from the Post-Classic period and was abandoned soon after the Conquest. As at Utatlán near Santa Cruz del Quiché the setting is the best thing about Zaculeu; but here there is the aggravation resulting from seeing an ancient ruin appallingly restored (at the hands of the United Fruit Company). Ask the guards to show you the underground escape passages. Buses to Zaculeu leave from the Maya Hotel (3 Avenida); since the journey there is uphill, if you are going to walk, it's best to do so on the way back.

The Cuchumatanes mountains north of Huehue are higher and more awesome than further east. They are dotted with Indian villages, left largely untouched by the Spanish who were not keen to tackle this mountainous area; folk Catholicism and other traditions remain strong as a result. There have been clashes here between guerrillas and the army throughout the last twenty years – forcing many Guatemalans to flee to Mexico – and this turbulent period partly explains why travellers have not ventured far into the area. As long as you seek local advice and don't travel alone, exploring in this remote and dramatic region should be a unique rather than an alarming experience.

At Paquix, about 19km (11 miles) north of Huehue, a road heads northwest through fantastic country west to **Todos Santos**. It lies almost 3,500m above sea level in a dramatic river valley, and is one of the most interesting villages in Guatemala. The village is extremely isolated, and the Todos Santeros, who are Mam Indians, have changed little over the centuries. The weaving done in Todos Santos is among the best and most colourful to be found anywhere in the country. The men's costume, which is thought to have been copied from what Spanish noblemen wore in the 16th century, is the most striking; their boater-style hats give them a decidedly dapper air.

There is a wonderful Saturday market, but you will probably find that the best place to buy weavings is the local cooperative. Near the village are a number of small Mayan sites, including Tecumanchum, and Tojcunanchén, where pagan rites are still practised. During the fiesta celebrating All Saints Day on 1 November, the village goes mad, and there is riotous drinking and dancing which lasts several days. One of the highlights of the celebrations is a horse race around the town, in which the male inhabitants – for the most part exceedingly drunk – participate. The other main event is the Dance of the Conquest which is performed, in an equally drunken haze, around the main square.

Like San Mateo Ixtatán, Todos Santos is quiet most of the time, but the surrounding countryside is beautiful and good for walking. One of the nicest

Talismán to Quezaltenango: into the Third World

On the journey from Talismán to Malacatán, it soon becomes obvious that you have entered the Third World proper. Along the side of the road you can see men sweating in the fields, campesinos riding horse-back, the odd overturned truck, and small girls carrying water.

When the bus arrives in Malacatán, watch as a procession of women and children enters, selling essential refreshments for surviving the journey. These are usually followed by a disabled person in need of alms, and then the would-be door-to-door, smooth-talking salesperson with an ointment that will cure acne, fungus, baldness, headaches and even gullibility. Now look around and see how for every adult there numbers a child. Take a deep breath and smell the toil of a people working to heave themselves out of the social and economic depths into which the country had sunk. This is Guatemala; vibrant, colourful and honest.

From Malacatán the road climbs through the lush growth of the lower mountain slopes. After an hour or so the dense vegetation gives way to a sparse mix of coniferous and deciduous trees. In parts, the woodland has been cleared away to make space for the odd smallholding surrounded by paddocks of grazing cattle. Shortly before reaching the town of San Marcos, high on a plateau, the road passes through swathes of maize fields. In the scattering of shacks the maize is dried, then cooked and milled ready for your tortillas.

In San Marcos the buses normally pass down a bumpy track to the right of which lies the graveyard where every tomb is adorned by a colorful painted shrine. The bus then strains to reach the pass within two-and-a-half hours of leaving Talismán before dipping down to Quezaltenango, at 2,335m (7,500 feet) above sea level.

walks takes you over ridges and through forests west to **San Juan Atitlán** – a hike of four or five hours, following the fairly worn main track. The men's costume in San Juan is as impressive as that in Todos Santos. At San Juan there are various options open to you. You can return the same way, but this makes for a very long day. It is better to camp out (or ask around for a bed) and start back the following morning. Alternatively, you can walk three or four hours south to the Pan-American Highway and get a bus back to Huehue; the road from San Juan forks south of the village: take the left fork which joins the highway at San Sebastián. If you plan to do this hike, leave the bulk of your luggage in Huehue beforehand so as to avoid having to return to Todos Santos or carrying a heavy pack while walking. A shorter day trip from Todos Santos involves walking for about three hours west to San Martín. This is a predominantly ladino village, but the market on Friday is distinctly Indian.

Buses to Todos Santos from Huehue leave at 4am and around 1pm, and take a couple of hours. Avoid going on Friday if possible because the bus is packed with people going to Todos Santos for the market. Buses back leave at a similar hour. There are a couple of hospedajes.

Quezaltenango – Xela by any other name
The name Quezaltenango means 'the place of the quetzals'. Inexplicably the official name of the town has lost the central T, though both spellings are used widely. Furthermore the alternative name Xela – pronounced 'shela' – is used even more widely; it is short for Xelaju, an ancient Quiché Indian capital. Xelaju means 'under the ten' which probably refers to the ten mountains and volcanoes which encircle the town. One of these volcanoes, El Santiaguito, was responsible for destroying the city in 1902.

Whatever you call it, the town is Guatemala's second largest, with a population of 75,000. Although it may not hold the attractions of Antigua or Atitlán, Xela has its own interesting features and also provides an excellent base from which to explore the area. It also has the best community website in Latin America, xelapages.com/trans.htm.

Arrival and departure
Xela is the transport hub of the Western Highlands, and there is a constant stream of buses in and out of the city. You can also fly in and out.

Air: to and from Guatemala City there is one flight in the morning (around 8am) and one in the afternoon (around 2pm). In Guatemala City, contact Inter de Grupo Taca, Guatemala (tel 361 2144) or Guatemala City airport (tel 331-8222). In Xela contact Bonifaz Hotel or Xela Sin Limites Travel Agency (owner speaks English) (tel 763-0692). Flights cost around $50, but fares are cheaper at weekends.

Bus: Atitrans offers expensive tourist shuttle services in mini-vans regularly to **Guatemala**, **Antigua**, **Panajachel** and **Chichi** – ask at the tourist office or a travel agent. Three companies offer a first-class service to **Guatemala City**

($5, 4 hours): Galgos, Calle Rodolfo Robles 14-43 (tel 761 2248): 4am, 5am, 8.30am, 10am, 2.30pm, 3pm, 4.30pm. Linea America, from Av 7, 3-33: 5.15am, 9.45am, 1.15pm, 8pm. Alamo (4 Calle 14-04, Zona, tel 761-2964), from Av 14, 3-60: 4.30am, 8am, 10.15am, 2.30pm. There are fairly regular second class buses from the Minerva bus terminal.

Direct first-class buses to **Panajachel** ($2, two hours 30 minutes) are run by Transportes Morales at 5am, 6am, 8am, 10am, noon and 3pm. There are also second-class buses running to Los Encuentros and Panajachel ($1, three hours, change for Panajachel at Los Encuentros if the direct bus does not turn up) at a quarter to the hour from 10am to midnight from the Minerva bus terminal. It is recommended that departures are made in daylight.

There are regular direct buses to **Chichicastenango** ($2, three hours), run by Transportes Veloz, but the last one leaves at 3.30pm. Buses for **Zunil** depart every 20 minutes from the road behind the tourist office ($0.50, 30mins). The last one returns at 6pm.

A room

The following are recommended, in descending order of cost: **Pension Bonifaz**, 4 Calle, north east corner of Parque Central (tel 761 4241): clean, quiet, some rooms with a balcony, cable TV. Single $55, double $75. **Villa Real Plaza**, 4 Calle, northwest corner of Parque Central (tel 761 6780): Simple, restaurant, bar, cable TV. Single/double: $35/$40. **Kiktem-Ja**, Avenida 13, 7-18 (tel 761 4304): nice rooms, pretty terrace, hot water, can light a fire in room for $2 of firewood for the night. Single/double: $12/$14. **Casa Kaehler**, Avenida 13, 3-33 (tel 761 2091): pretty terrace, clean, shared bathroom, basic, run by a friendly brother and sister, she has a family and he acts at the local theatre and does tours of the volcanoes. Single/double: $9/$11. **Hotel Altense**, 9 Calle, 8-48: restaurant, clean, hot water, private bathrooms, TV room. Single/double: $6/$10. **Pension Horiana**, 14 Calle, 0-7: restaurant, hot water, clean. Single/double: $5/$7. **Casa Argentina**, by the Mercado del Flores, Diagonal 12, 8-13 (tricky to find), Zone 1 (tel 761 2470): Rooms okay/basic, shared bathroom. Dormitory bed, single, double: $3, $4, $7. The main gringo ghetto surrounds and includes the Casa Argentina hotel where there are a number of Spanish schools. The hotel also organises excursions, the profits of which go toward helping street children.

A meal

The best and most expensive restaurant is in the **Pension Bonifaz** hotel. **Utz-Hay** ('pretty place'), on the corner of Avenida 12 and Calle 3, is a slight cut above the other Guatemalan restaurants. **Video Café Bar Colores** on Avenida 15, 7-30, is open to 11pm and serves sandwiches. It has a bar, internet service, free video showings every night and salsa classes. **Ricca Burger** on Avenida 14, 4 is a branch of the Guatemalan fast food chain but serves well-priced and perfectly good breakfasts, salads and two-course menus including either burgers or chicken. There is a **McDonalds** near the Terminal Minerva on the far north of town. **El Kopetin**, Av 14, 3-41 serves international dishes. **Café Berna**, Swiss bakery and café at Avenida 12, 0-36 and Avenida 16, 3-25. Italian dishes including Pizza on Av 14, 3-25. **Maxims** specialises in Chinese, at Avenida 20, 2-68.

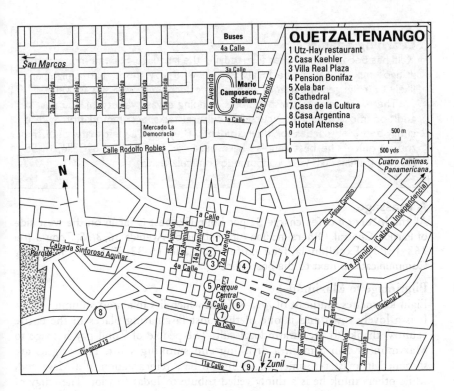

QUETZALTENANGO

1 Utz-Hay restaurant
2 Casa Kaehler
3 Villa Real Plaza
4 Pension Bonifaz
5 Xela bar
6 Cathedral
7 Casa de la Cultura
8 Casa Argentina
9 Hotel Altense

A drink

The most popular places to go boozing change rapidly, and it is worth asking foreign students for recommendations. To start with, the **Xela** bar is good and has a starlit sky. This is one block down from Tecún, on the Parque Central, which always has a reasonable crowd in spite of recently losing its music licence. The latter also likes to employ blonde *gringettas* if you are looking for work (or blonde *gringettas*).

An exploration

The main square is a monument to neoclassical architecture and the buildings which line the square are striking, if a little sombre. Only the crumbling 17th-century facade remains of the old cathedral, the building behind it being modern, but it is currently under restoration. On the south side is the Casa de la Cultura which contains a number of museums, the best of which traces the history of marimba music; other exhibits range from Mayan artifacts to old photographs and documents. By the entrance is a map of the local area. Open 8-noon and 2pm-5pm.

Mercado La Democracía is in Zona 3, about ten blocks west of the Parque Central; the market sells food and household goods, and is a good example of a local, untouristy market. In the same zone but quite a way further west is the Minerva Temple, another neoclassical oddity; nearby are the bus terminal and market.

Learning Spanish

Xela has become a hot spot for studying the language. For the moment the gringos mix well with the locals. People who stay more than a night are likely to make genuine friends among the eclectic mix who stay in Xela.

There are many Spanish schools, running a vast variety of courses. In addition, most organise excursions, cultural talks, accommodation with a family and even parties for their students. They have all left material in the tourist office. The best reports have been for Celas Maya, 6 Calle, 14-55 Zone 1 (tel/fax 761 4342, todomundo.com/celasmaya).

A message

All the **internet cafes** charge $2 per hour. The best is Tacún on the west side of Parque Central. Others include Alternativas on Avenida 16, 3/35, Zone 3 (tel 763 1383); Excellencia, free coffee, at Calle 15-33, Zone 1; Marketing Communications next to the post office.

Pilgrimage to Maximón

Eight kilometres southeast of Xela is **Zunil** which lies in a most stunning valley. It is a lovely town and is one of the most fascinating places in the entire country, thanks to the bizarre local cult. The people of Zunil pay homage to Maximón or San Simón, a drinking and smoking saint. His origins are shrouded in mystery: some believe him to be a reincarnation of a Maya god, while others think he is a thinly veiled tribute to Judas Iscariot. The effigy of Maximón is more like a dapper Guy Fawkes, dressed in a smart suit with a hat and gloves, and propped up in a rocking chair. Locals light cigarettes for him and bring alcohol which they pour down his throat. Maximón apparently works miracles and there is a constant flow of people who come to ask favours – there are minders who perform the rituals and recite weird and wonderful prayers.

Maximón is moved around each year since the locals take it in turns to look after him; ask anyone and they will tell you where to find the current shrine. Take cigarettes or Quezalteca (the local liquor) and if you wish to take photographs you must pay $2. Anyone taken by the cult of Maximón should visit Santiago Atitlán or San Andrés Iztapa, where he is also worshipped; the effigies and rituals in all three places are different.

Up in the hills above Zunil are **Las Aguas Georginas**, thermal baths created out of the largest geysers in Guatemala. The setting is beautiful and you can languidly soak, Roman-style, for hours; there is a café which serves hot meals. You can walk to the baths in a couple of hours along an easy road that climbs gently.

Santa María volcano dominates the valley at a height of 3,772m, and there are magnificent views from the top. The climb takes about five hours but is tough so only attempt it if you are fit. The starting point for the climb is Llanos del Pinal (buses leave from close to Pensión Altense), and start early. Arrows give you a helping hand at the start, but the climb becomes steadily more difficult. Shortly after leaving the saddle take the path striking left from the good track; if you remain on the good path you'll get hopelessly lost since this isn't the way to the summit.

Guides may be hired for trips up to the surrounding volcanoes. As good and inexpensive as any are Patrick and William at the Salon Tecún or the manager at the Casa Kaehler.

Moving on

A short way west of Tecpán, the Pan-American Highway comes to a junction at Los Encuentros. Turning north takes you to Chichicastenango. To the south, off the highway, lie Sololá, Panajachel and Lake Atitlán. This sequence begins with **Chichicastenango**.

More commonly and easily known as **Chichi**, this town is in the department of El Quiché, which occupies the heart of the Western Highlands. The local Quiché Indians are the purest descendants of the Maya, and were the most important of the Indian tribes to inhabit what is now Guatemala in pre-Columbian times. Chichi's typically colonial cobbled streets and whitewashed houses belie the influence of the Indians.

Unfortunately the overriding influence nowadays is summed up by the sign proclaiming Chichi to be *La Meca del Turismo* which greets you as you enter the town. The reason for its fame is the combined attraction of the market and the folk Catholic religious practices of the local Indians. The market is the most popular for tourists in all Guatemala, and Indians flock here from all over the mountains to sell their wares. The traders tend to be a little over-zealous and not everyone finds the atmosphere conducive to buying. It is hard not to be drawn to Chichi, however, but be prepared to contend with busloads of package tourists. To get a taste of what the place is really like, don't come just on market day (Thursday and Sunday) when the majority of visitors come; during the rest of the week Chichi is positively quiet.

There are buses direct to Chichi from both Guatemala City and Panajachel. Alternatively, get any bus along the highway to Los Encuentros, from where you can catch local buses to Chichi or hop on to any long-distance one that passes. The journey is dramatic, takes 40 minutes and costs 70c. Be prepared to push and shove to board on market day. Trying to pick up buses bound for Chichi at other points along the highway is not always successful since buses don't necessarily stop; you are therefore advised to aim first for Los Encuentros.

Buses from Chichi to Guatemala City run until 6pm, otherwise wait by the arch (Arco Gucumatz) north of the square where you can pick up buses on their way to the capital from Santa Cruz del Quiché.

There is a fairly small selection of **places to stay**, and rooms fill quickly on market days. The best deal in town is Hospedaje Salvador (Calle 10, Avenida 5) a couple of blocks south of the square. It resembles a huge and gaudy rabbit warren, but there is a good atmosphere, and wonderful views from upstairs. The other two main options are Pensión Chugüilá on 5 Avenida near the arch, and Hospedaje Girón on 6 Calle off 5 Avenida. Stalls in the market sell delicious tortillas, eggs, beans and coffee, and other stalls sell similar fare in the street at night. For western food the best restaurant is El Torito above Hospedaje Girón, although Restaurant Tapena opposite Pensión Chugüilá is also popular in the evening. A pleasant place for a drink is Café Icokij in the main square.

The **market** envelops the centre of the town on Thursdays and Sundays, and the sea of stalls is overwhelming. In the main square, however, the churches of Santo Tomás and El Calvario at either end rise above the melée, and this is the best place to sit and contemplate the huge colourful spectacle. Women in their multi-coloured costumes gather on the steps too, where they sell flowers or sit chatting apparently oblivious to the constant flow of tourists (unlike the serious traders with stalls). The best time to see the Indians en masse is the night before market day since preparations begin on the afternoon of the previous day; if you are tempted to buy anything you should do so then, when prices are usually lower. When the scene gets too much on market day you should escape to the quiet back streets, where life appears to carry on with some normality.

Sunday is the busiest day in Chichi since this is when the Indians flock to church. Religious activity centres around the 16th-century church of Santo Tomás which was built on the site of a Maya pyramid. The folk Catholicism practised in Chichi is one of the best examples of the amazing mix of pre-Hispanic and Christian ritual found among the Indian communities in Guatemala. The Spanish had difficulty in subduing the Maya people in this region, so after building their churches, they allowed the Indians to practise their ancient rituals alongside those of the Catholic church. Mass is held on Saturday and Sunday in the morning and afternoon. It is conducted in the Quiché language (Spanish is also used on Sundays), and a marimba usually accompanies the choir. While the religious images inside the church are firmly rooted in the 16th century, the atmosphere is positively pagan – there is not the slightest pretence that the rites are based on Christian tradition. Worshippers cover the altars with offerings such as rose petals and pine needles, light candles and offer prayers. Meanwhile, on the steps of the church, people burn incense – this is a particularly beautiful sight in the half-light of dawn or sunset. Some travellers have been offered a swig from a bottle of raw alchohol which is seen as an aid to extra-sensory perception and therefore enlightenment. While taking photographs on the steps is all right, you should refrain from doing so inside the church. (Children demand a dollar every time you raise your camera at them.) Indian women have set themselves up as guides; they give only a cursory outline for which they expect a tip. Nowadays there often seem to be more tourists than Indians inside the church. Similar rituals are practised in the church of El Calvario but on a smaller scale.

Next door to the church of Santo Tomás is a former Dominican monastery where the manuscript of the Mayan sacred text called the *Popul Vuh* (People's Book), was discovered in 1690 by Francisco Ximénez. The book describes the origin of the universe and the history of the early Quiché Indians. It was transcribed, and Ximénez translated it into Spanish in the early 18th century. The original Spanish manuscript is in Chicago. The cloisters are surprisingly peaceful given their proximity to the square and are a serene place to sit and collect your thoughts. Also in the square is the rather dusty Museo Regional, which contains pre-Columbian artifacts, including ceramics and some fine jade jewellery; open 8am-1pm.

The cemetery, down the hill behind El Calvario, is a peaceful haven and offers lovely views; the graves are strewn with gladioli and saplings, and people burn incense. For another insight into pre-Christian worship go to the shrine of Pascual Abaj (or Turkaj), a Maya god, on a hill south of the town. It's just a 30-minute walk, but the route is circuitous and you should take the local boys up on their offers to take you there, not least because the path has a reputation for armed robbers. Sadly, the rituals, which may include the sacrifice of chickens and flagellation, are in danger of becoming a tourist show. Do not take photographs.

Chichi's local festival is 13-21 December.

Sololá

This is a lovely village with a colourful market where both the men and women wear traditional costume. Food is the main commodity, but look out for the earthenware pots. Sololá has a couple of modest hotels if you wish to avoid staying in Panajachel: La Posada del Viajero, on the main square, and the Hotel Isoloj-ya just around the corner on the road to the lake.

The walk downhill to Panajachel is pleasant save for the tourist coaches and hire cars tearing up and down the road. Two miles down from Sololá is the first mirador (viewpoint), giving a breathtaking panorama of the lake. At the next one, a mile further on, it is possible to reach the Brujos Caves where Indian *chuchkajaus* (witch doctors) come to make offerings to the gods. From the mirador, go 20 metres towards Panajachel then take a track to the right. A couple of hundred metres further on is a white hut on the right, in fact a shop whose owner will look after your bags; this is necessary because you climb down a steep track opposite the hut. It winds down to the caves, about ten minutes' walk (or slide). In the wet season it is impassable except to those who know it very well. Less strenuously, you could enjoy the waterfall which is a few hundred metres down the road from the mirador.

The end of the road, for now: Lake Atitlán and Panajachel

Atitlán is one of the most beautiful places on earth – a deep green lake in the middle of a landscape which looks too perfect to be real; three volcanoes complete an almost aggressively lovely scene. Native Indians still live in idyllic and colourful villages on the lakeshore, supporting genuine crafts and traditional markets. A mile above sea level, Atitlán's climate is as benign as the views, cooler and more comfortable than the capital, yet warm enough to spend the day sunbathing in January. In short, Atitlán is preposterously pleasant.

Sadly for the cognoscenti among travellers, and for Atitlán itself, the secret has been out for long enough for real damage to have been done. While most of the lakeside settlements have escaped extensive development **Panajachel**, Atitlán's main town, is overrun by tourists and is dedicated to providing for them. Leaving aside the ecological considerations about how an isolated lakeside settlement can cope with thousands of visitors without environmental injury, Panajachel is already taking a beating. Visitors include an array of wealthy Guatemalans, rich foreign tourists, and backpackers. The latter are in the majority in Panajachel, on Atitlán's shore. The town has even gained the nickname *Gringotenango*.

For most, Panajachel has everything. Its elevation is ideal, bringing warm days with little humidity and coolish nights. Its appeal to travellers stems not only from the beauty of the place, but also from its laid-back atmosphere, the bars, cheap and varied food, book exchanges and the abundance of clothes and weavings to buy. Avenida Santander, the main street, is flanked by stalls, and stretches for about half a mile all the way to the lakeside. The market here is geared almost solely to western tastes, and while you can buy hats and waistcoats that will be all the rage back home, it is increasingly hard to buy traditional clothes. For good quality weavings you would do better to head for the remoter villages or even to Chichicastenango.

While some travellers feel there is a pleasant balance between the gringo and local flavour, others believe that it has already gone too far. Many simply pass through Panajachel and head for one of the smaller and much less developed villages dotted around the lake. Few, however, can resist altogether the overriding temptation of Atitlán.

If you are approaching from east or west, get any bus along the Pan-American Highway, ideally one of the first-class buses which run between Guatemala City and Quezaltenango – you can ask to be dropped off. Los Encuentros is a windswept place with little appeal – a crossroads with a petrol station, a few comedores, and a worrying large number of people waiting for buses. The locals will assume you are bound for Panajachel and bundle you aboard the right bus. There is a fairly constant stream of minibuses which go to Sololá, where there should be another bus loading up for the dramatic descent into Panajachel. Sololá lies in a breathtaking spot overlooking the lake, and some prefer to stay here rather than in Panajachel.

There are a few direct buses linking Panajachel with Chichicastenango and Quezaltenango (Xela), but it is usually more convenient to head for Los Encuentros, from where buses run frequently along the Pan-American Highway. When leaving Panajachel, most buses begin near the food market, but also stop near the tourist office. This notably helpful office opens 8am-noon and 2-5pm daily, but closes on public holidays. When closed, a list of bus and ferry schedules is shown.

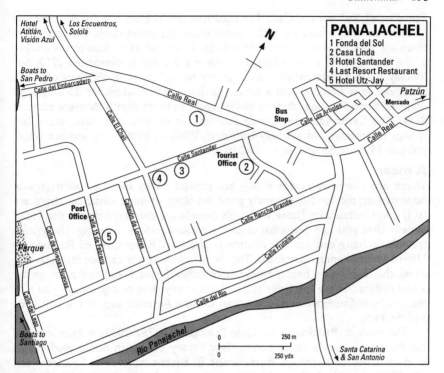

PANAJACHEL

1 Fonda del Sol
2 Casa Linda
3 Hotel Santander
4 Last Resort Restaurant
5 Hotel Utz-Jay

A room

Panajachel has more **places to stay** per hectare than anywhere else in Central America. They fall into three broad categories: luxury hotels with a lake view, cable TV and high rates; mid-range places which are comfortable and clean; and low-budget hospedajes. The luxurious **Hotel Atitlán** is a long way west of town, and overpriced at $100 a night, though the antique 78rpm gramophone behind the reception is worth seeing. The **Visión Azul**, nearby, is half the price but equally inconvenient. The private beach and pool opposite are open to the public for a small fee. Of the more expensive hotels, the **del Lago** is the most aesthetically alarming but the best value. It is in Panajachel proper, although in a fairly quiet part, and costs $50 for a double room. The nearby **Monterrey** is rather like an upmarket Butlin's, but costs only $18.

A new place called **Hotel Utz-Jay** (which means 'pretty place'), two blocks from the lake at Calle 15 de Febrero (tel 762 1358, atitlan.com/utz-jay.htm, e-mail utzjay@atitlan.com) comprises cabins made in a naturalistic but comfortable style, very peaceful, TV room, shared kitchen, sweet dog called Corta, multilingual owner, and a herbal sauna (extra charges) which is highly recommended. Single or double, a cabin costs $14. The management runs treks and tours to volcanoes and local villages; $50 a day for two people and $10 more for each extra person.

Among mid-range places, the **Santa Isabel** has the most beautiful garden in town. The hotel is quiet and comfortable, and costs $10 for a double room. The

Fonda del Sol, on the Calle Principal just down from the tourist office, is further from the beach, but better value; it accepts credit cards. The rooms are clean and have bathrooms, but cost only $6. **Las Casitas** is close to the market in the 'real' part of town, adjacent to the market, and is overpriced ($10) but friendly. **Casa Linda** (which means 'pretty house'), is in an alley just off Calle Santander. It is friendly, with a pretty garden and hot water, for $5 single, $8 double. **Montufar**, next door, is similar apart from its slightly different rates of $6/$7. The **Santander**, on Avenida Santander, is friendly, with clean rooms, but spongy mattresses and a smelly bathroom. Without bathrooms and hot water you pay $4 single/$6 double, or $9/$10 with.

A meal

There are numerous cafés which are geared solely for the tourist trade; nevertheless, the food is generally good. All along Avenida Santander there are fairly good restaurants. Those with grills outside are the best bet with the added benefit that you can see what is being cooked before entering. The gringo travellers' hang-out par excellence is the Last Resort, or **El Recuerdo Ultimo**, off Avenida Santander. This is probably the most popular place in Panajachel. It serves a hearty breakfast of coffee, beans, bread, and porridge for a few dollars. There is a lively atmosphere at any time of day, though you may feel you're in San Francisco rather than Central America, such is the ambience and the music.

The pizza at **Pulcinella** on Calle Principal (tel 762 2032) is excellent and can be enjoyed while reading from their library of English books available to read, rent, buy or exchange. **Restaurant El Bistro** on Avenida Santander (tel 762 0508), two blocks from the lake is a very good Italian serving. The freshly-made pasta and the thick steaks (*un bistec gordissimo*) is recommended. Excellent coffee and sandwiches are available at the shop opposite the tourist office.

The greatest congregation of **bars** (of all kinds) is found around the intersection of Calle Principal with Avenida Santander. If you're missing the cinema, The Turquoise Bull is basically a big TV screen. The Chapiteau discoteque is found on the intersection of Calle Principal with Avenida Santander. Entrance $2.

An exploration

For many visitors, life in Panajachel is an endless round of sun, snacks and sipping cocktails. It is an ideal place for idleness, perhaps interrupted by the occasional stroll. There are numerous surprises to encounter, such as the industrious men quarrying gravel from the lakeside, and the pace of the small food market to the northeast of the village. For a taste of rural life, explore the back yards of Panajachel. Go north on the road past the market, beyond the 120km marker. A few hundred yards further on the right is the Tienda La Manzanilla. Immediately before it is an alleyway. Follow this as it crosses a high wall, and twists and turns on the way to the riverbank. The locals are most welcoming.

The beach might not be up to seaside standards, but a swim is fresh and lovely in the morning. If you are more inclined to watch the sun go down than to swim, it is a good place to sit with a beer and gaze out over the lake. During the day you can hire a canoe at the public beach for about $3 per hour. A stroll along the lakefront, heading east, takes you to some modest hot springs. Keep heading west until the beach finally ends; about 50 metres further on, amid the rocks, are a couple of warm pools. The locals do their washing here.

A visit to Nima'ya de Atitlán next to Hotel Atitlán is a must if you are into nature. In this mini-nature reserve you find waterfalls, hanging bridges, monkeys, a butterfly reserve and bird observation point. Entrance costs $3, open 8am-5pm.

You can even **scuba dive**, if you contact Jonathan who runs scuba diving for the shop opposite the tourist office, tel 762 2646. The main office is in the La Iguana Perdida Hotel in Santa Cruz, santacruz@guate.net or utidivers.com. The things to see are volcanic geological features such as lava walls, thermal springs and submerged vegetation. The cost is $25 per dive if certified, $160 for the four-day course to become certified, and $125 for the advanced course. NB: you are diving at altitude and it recommended that you do not leave the town for 24 hours after a dive.

Around Lake Atitlán

Most of the lakeside villages can be reached by boat, and some by minibus, foot or bicycle. Boats leave from the public beach in Panajachel and there are also boats connecting individual villages. The first boats depart from Panajachel around 6am (but check at the tourist office as they are unpredictable until 8am) and the last boat back from Santa Pedro is at 5pm. Boats go both ways every half-hour. A boat to Santa Cruz and Tzununa takes about 30 minutes, and the boat back from San Pedro takes about 75 minutes. Bike hire is around $5 per day and available at many places. Take provisions such as sunscreen, swimming costume, and a toothbrush in case you decide to stay away for the night. The standard ferry fare is $2 return, with a bit more if you bring a bike. If you plan to climb volcanoes, note that during the rainy season the summits are nearly always enveloped in cloud.

San Pedro La Laguna lies on the western shores of the lake, and is popular among travellers. In fact it is probably the least attractive place by the lake. The local people do not wear the brightly-coloured costumes worn elsewhere around Atitlán, and evangelical Protestantism is strong. It is a more relaxing place to stay, however, than some of the other lakeside villages.

San Pedro is the starting point for a climb up Volcán San Pedro (3,020m/9,920 feet). This is the smallest of the three lakeside volcanoes, and is the only one which can be climbed in a day. The ascent takes about five hours (a guide is necessary) and you should aim to reach the summit before noon when the clouds close in. There is also a lot of vegetation which can spoil the view a bit.

Santiago Atitlán was once capital of the Tzutuhil Indian nation, and is a most beautiful village. It is ironic that what later became an important missionary centre during the colonial period should also be the home of

Guatemala's idiosyncratic smoking and drinking saint, Maximón. Santiago sees a steady flow of tourists (especially on Sunday) but it is not as crowded as Panajachel. The main street leading up from the lake is lined with stalls aimed at the tourist trade but most of the locals pay little heed to visitors. The market is a sea of colour and the headdresses, sometimes known as 'halos', worn by some of the women are particularly striking. Among other produce are the amazingly beautiful and colourful wooden sculptures unique to this village. To be able to get a feel for the place you should stay overnight; there is a hospedaje on the left at the start of the main street which charges about $5.

From Santiago it is possible to climb the **Tolimán** and **Atitlán** volcanoes, 3,158m/10,360 feet and 3,535m/11,604 feet respectively: both involve camping out overnight. There are no longer guerillas in the region, but you should still hire a guide since it is rumoured that they left land mines and above all, it is all

Self-propelled

This is a more interesting and adventurous day-trip than the normal 'semi-packaged' boat tours. It allows a full appreciation of the lake and its surroundings, and can be made as follows:

1. Hire a bike if you want (best arranged the day before).
2. If biking take a boat to Tzununa as the path from Santa Cruz to Tzununa is not suitable for biking.
3. Take a boat to Santa Cruz. In this quiet and picturesque spot you will find a weaving collective and several pretty and expensive hotels.
4. On the way to Tzununa, stop and go for a dip at Jaibalito beach. One of the most perfect places for a swim.
5. Continue along the path to Tzununa. Very quiet, this is a genuine indigenous village where locals can be seen going about their normal business, unaffected by tourism.
6. San Marcos La Laguna is next. This village now holds a new age refuge well worth a visit. The small Piramides del Ka have been built in such a way as to trap the spiritual energy of the sun. Apparently solar panels do not work. There is a hotel and meditation temple and a medical garden where volunteers have committed themselves to providing massage, yoga sessions, 'channelling sessions every full moon' and whatever else is needed to discover your inner self.
7. San Pablo follows; another unspoilt village which affords the best views of the volcanes.
8. Past San Pablo and it is time for another refreshing swim, this time at Las Cristalinas beach under the dominant visage of the volcanoes.
9. Get your skates on and pass through San Juan to reach San Pedro which has various hotels, hot springs and horse-back riding.
10. Ferry home as the sun sets on this magnificent landscape.

too easy to take the wrong path and get lost/stuck. References for guides, especially cheap ones, should be obtained from the tourist office as it has been known that the cheapest guides then arrange the robbery of their charges ('When the cheap becomes expensive,' as a tourism official explained drily). The volcanoes can also be approached from San Lucas Tolimán.

The people living in the two villages of **Santa Catarina Palopo** and **San Antonio Palopo**, which lie east of Panajachel, tend to be cool towards outsiders and many people feel slightly uneasy there. They are both good places to buy weaving, however, although you should beware in San Antonio of people who try to sell cheaper machine-woven fabric. (If you buy from the Textiles Co-operative this will prevent a purchase at the wrong price or of machine-woven rather than hand-woven materials.) Santa Catarina is just a couple of miles and a lovely walk east of Panajachel. It has an attractive church and both the men and women wear vivid purples and pinks, the men's trousers matching the colour of the women's huipiles. An hour's walk further on is San Antonio Palopo, where the predominant colour of dress is red. The church is one of the oldest in Guatemala and there is a great view over the lake from the main door. There is one hotel, and the locals also put people up.

Antigua awakes

The town most downtrodden beneath the relentless march of tourism is the old Spanish capital, Antigua. It was the first place in the Americas to be laid out on a grid pattern, thus setting the style for cities from New York to Santiago de Chile. But soon the careful mesh was disrupted by an earthquake. And another, and another. Antigua was abandoned as capital in the 17th century as too earthquake-prone, and subsided into backwaterdom until the foreigners started to arrive – and report back to their friends at home.

The first capital of Guatemala, founded in 1543, is the perfect antidote to its successor. Set in a lush valley surrounded by volcanoes, Antigua is a colonial gem enhanced by Indian tradition. Until two devastating earthquakes in 1773 reduced the city to ruins, Antigua was the heart of Central America – it was the seat of the colonial Spanish administration for the region, the so-called Audiencia. The ruins which give the city an awesome sense of history date from this era, when the number of grand mansions and churches was commensurate with Antigua's position and influence. Antigua remains the country's cultural capital.

After the earthquakes, a new site was chosen in the erroneous belief that Guatemala City (as it is now) would be less susceptible to seismic activity. Antigua was more or less abandoned by the colonisers, and the Indians moved in. Only recently have they been followed by tourists in their thousands, and travellers who come to learn Spanish in one of the many language schools. Tourism has brought substantial changes – the streets are kept cleaner than in any other Guatemalan town, and the colourful blankets and clothing sold by local Indians in the main square are aimed purely at foreign visitors. It is perhaps surprising that Antigua manages to retain the relaxed, provincial atmosphere that it does. This is largely due to minimal modernisation and careful restoration work. An earthquake in 1976 further damaged the city, but the town's scarred facade has considerable charm.

Getting your bearings

The first grid had names, not numbers, and there were no distinctions between Calles and Avenidas. Subsequently it was decided that these sophistications were useful adjuncts to a grid system, so east-west streets were numbered Calle 1 to Calle 9 and north-south ones became Avenidas 2 to 8. Their direction from the Parque Central was determined by a suffix – Calles were either East (Oriente) or West (Poniente) of the main square, while Avenidas were North (Norte) or South (Sur). Unfortunately, in the last few years there has been a move back to the old colonial street names, with predictable confusion. In this book the numbers are used, with the suffix O, P, N or S as appropriate.

Arrival and Departure

Antigua lies just 28 miles (45km) west of the capital. To reach Antigua from Panajachel, Chichicastenango and points west, first travel to Chimaltenango and wait for a local bus to Antigua. There are also direct minibuses at 'gringo' prices.

The bus terminus in Antigua is behind the market at the western end of 4 Calle P. Buses onward to Guatemala City leave every 15 minutes (or when they are full) to the terminus at the corner of 15 Calle and Avenidas 3 and 4 (Zona 1). Services run between 7am and 8pm; the fare is $1 for the one-hour journey. The dual carriageway is the best road in Guatemala and offers breathtaking views of the capital. Travellers can easily avoid Guatemala City if arriving or leaving by air. Buses Inter Hotel y Turismo or BIT (tel: 32-0011/015) operate several minibus services each day between the airport and Antigua and although the fare is steep ($10), it enables visitors to get a more pleasing first view of Guatemala. Departures from the airport are at 7.15am, 11.15am and 5.15pm. For the return journey buses do the rounds of the smart hotels; the best place to pick it up is Doña Luisa's café on 4 Calle O at 4.55am, 9.15am and 3.15pm.

For the Pacific coast, take a bus to Escuintla from where there are easy connections: the journey takes two hours and costs $2.

Cheap seats

Flights can be booked for the rest of Central America in Antigua. Prices may be dramatically cheaper for those holding a student card, which are available from Sin Fronteras, 3 Calle Poniente, No 12, tel 832 1226, fax 832 2672, e-mail, sinfront@infovia.com.gt. Up to 36 hours may be needed to obtain the card ($10), as it is collected from OTEC, Turismo Joven, Avenida Reforma, 12-01, Zona 10, Guatemala City (tel 331 9474).

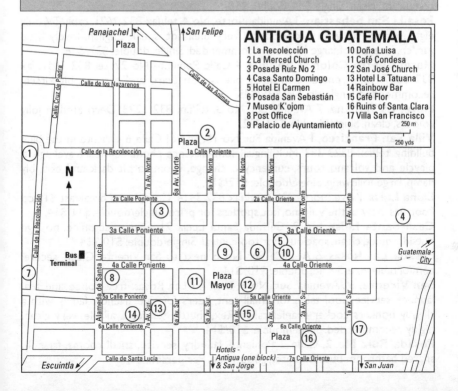

ANTIGUA GUATEMALA

1 La Recolección
2 La Merced Church
3 Posada Ruíz No 2
4 Casa Santo Domingo
5 Hotel El Carmen
6 Posada San Sebastián
7 Museo K'ojom
8 Post Office
9 Palacio de Ayuntamiento
10 Doña Luisa
11 Café Condesa
12 San José Church
13 Hotel La Tatuana
14 Rainbow Bar
15 Café Flor
16 Ruins of Santa Clara
17 Villa San Francisco

A room

Antigua has dozens of options. Hotels fill quickly, however, so if you arrive in the afternoon be prepared to scout around for a vacancy. This selection is in descending order of price:

Casa Santo Domingo, 3 Calle Oriente No 28 is five or ten minutes walk from the centre, tel 832 2628, fax 361 1784, casasantodomingo.com.gt, domingo@quetzal.net. This is the poshest in the pueblo, with swimming pool, tennis courts, room service, good restaurant, a good museum with prehispanic finds plus antiques in some rooms, cable TV. Prices vary within the range $50-$350.

Hotel Antigua, 8 Calle Poniente No 1, three blocks from the centre, tel 832 2801, fax 832 0807, hainfo@hotelant.com.gt. It boasts cable TV, access to internet, transport to and from airport, restaurant and a big pool. Some rooms have balconies. The place is well polished but not tacky, with a big garden, comfortable, good parking, fires in rooms, recommended. Single $100, double $120.

Hotel San Jorge, Calle Del Conquistador, 4 Avenida Sur No 13, Tel/fax 832 3132. It is quiet and has a pretty garden. Single/double with breakfast costs $37/$43.

Hotel El Carmen, 3 Av Norte, No 9, tel 832 3850/3132, hotelcarmen@ conexion.com.gt. Opposite Posada San Sebastian, modern, restaurant, cable TV, restaurant, clean. Single $44, double $50.

Posada San Sebastian, 3 Avenida Norte, No 4, tel/fax 832 2621, cable TV, only eight rooms, six with proper bath, very pleasant, speak English, lovely little garden, free use of large kitchen, recommended. Single, double: $37, $46.

Hotel Centro Colonial Antigua, 4 Calle Poniente No 22, tel 832 1641, fax 832 0657: very central, extremely pretty courtyard and terrace, bit kitsch, recommended. Single/double: $35/$45.

Hotel La Tatuana, 7 Avenida Sur, No 3, tel/fax 832 1223, Decorated in jolly colours, clean. Single/double: $13/$22.

Villa San Francisco, 1 Avenida Sur No 15, End of Calle 6 Oriente in the blue building. tel/fax 8323 383: Multilingual, long-distance phone service, travel agent, bicycle and volcano tours, currency exchange, rooms a bit dark and possibly damp, large following. Single/double: $12/$14.

Doña Luisa, 7 Ave Norte, No 4. tel/fax 832 3414. Continental breakfast $1, top floor has view of the volcano, not spotless for price. Single/double: $11/$14.

Casa Santa Luisa No 2, Calzada Santa Lucia 21, near post office, no sign outside: quiet, clean, spacious, not too central. Single/double: $10/$14.

Posada Las Rosas, 6 Avenida Sur No 8, next to San Vicente: Clean, secure, comfortable, fine. Single, double: $10, $14.

San Vicente, 6ª, Avenida Sur, No 6, next to Las Rosas: free coffee and tea, laundry service, pool table for small rent, beers for sale, friendly family with a slightly bonkers cocker spaniel called Rex, shuttle service available, very clean, highly recommended. Single/double: $10/$14.

Posada Ruiz No 2, Calle 2 Poniente, laundry service, small rooms, friendly, shared bathroom but hot water, good value. Per person: $3.

A meal

There is a large number of restaurants and cafés to choose from, most of which are aimed squarely at the gringo clientele. The most popular place is **Doña Luisa's** on 4 Calle O. It costs considerably more than the average Guatemalan restaurant, but visitors seem happy to pay for the comforting ambience which resembles that of a Tea Room at a British seaside resort. Doña Luisa's also has good food, and a comprehensive noticeboard with details of everything from Spanish courses to treks in the hills.

The best **Japanese and Thai** food in Central America is available at a reasonable price at the restaurant on 6 Avenida between Calles 4 and 5. **Travel Menu**, 6 Calle Poniente No 14, one block south of the Parque Central has a limited menu (normally stir fry or curry) but gives big helpings at a low price. There is a good steak house, **La Casa Escobar**, and next to it a restaurant specialising in typical Guatemalan barbecued food – **Madre Tierra** – at 6 Avenida Norte No 3 (tel 832 2858) and No 5, respectively. On the north side of the Parque Central, **Café Condesa** serves excellent coffee and cinnamon rolls. Pizza to eat in or take away at **Express Piccadilly**, 4 Calle Poniente with 7 Av Sur, tel 832 0392.

There is a cluster of places on 5 Avenida N the best of which are **Café Sueños del Quetzal** (vegetarian and health food) with a nice balcony, and **Fonda de la Calle Real** (Mexican food, barbecued meat, soups). Also popular is the **Zen Restaurant** on 3 Avenida between 4 and 5 Calles, which has a lovely courtyard and good music. More expensive but recommended is **Café Flor** on 4 Avenida Sur, which serves Mexican food ($2 for an average dish).

To mingle with the locals go to the comedores around the market or on 4 Calle P and Alameda de Santa Lucía. Recommended is **Tacos** on Alameda de Santa Lucía Norte. Nearby (at number 34-36) and popular among the wealthier locals is **El Peroleto** which serves a good breakfast, ceviche and the best licuados in Antigua.

A drink

The two most popular venues for evening drinking (frequented exclusively by gringos) are **La Boheme**, where there is occasional live music, and the **Picasso Bar**, which would look more at home in Covent Garden; both are on 3 Calle P and 7 Avenida Norte. The **Rainbow bar**, 7 Avenida Sur No 8, also has a travel agent, library, and (mainly vegetarian) restaurant. It is a great place to have a quiet one, grab a bite to eat, read a novel and study Spanish all at the same time. A surprisingly unpretentious place is the **Café Jardín** in the Plaza Mayor – outside are street vendors selling delicious crispy corn pancakes with guacamole.

For something approaching a disco, **El Afro** 6, Calle Poniente between 5 and 6 Ave Sur actually plays salsa most of the time but is very lively and popular with gringos. The other major gringo honeypot is **El Chimenea**, 7 Ave Norte with 2 Calle Poniente. Both are fun and have good bars.

An exploration

If you started in one corner of the city and set out to explore every inch of every street, you would find the experience richly rewarding. The crumbling churches

Close encounters

Most foreigners are in Antigua to learn Spanish. It follows that social life tends to revolve around the class to which you belong. Apart from language students, there are also some foreigners working in tourism-related jobs and some just hanging out soaking up the ambience. To those who are just passing through it may appear that the cliques have already set solid and there is little chance of breaking the ice. The exact opposite is true and it is easy to fall in with a friendly bunch of Guatemalans or gringos. Though patronisingly obvious, the following suggestions may help:

1. Join a Spanish class even if only for a few days especially as many of the schools arrange social events.

2. Stay with a Guatemalan family as this will give you insight into their culture as well as providing cheap board and lodging – this option is open to those studying Spanish or not – ask at the tourist office.

3. Go on one of the many excursions from Antigua, such as mountain biking, horse-back riding or climbing a volcano.

4. Learn to dance salsa by taking lessons at El Afro on Tuesday, Thursday or Saturday nights or at Escuela de Danza, 5 Avenida Norte 25.

5. Go to either El Afro or Bar Chimenea, get absolutely off your head and stumble around hugging people and saying 'Youz me bez fren ever' or 'Tu eres mi mejor amigo/a'

you encounter just walking around provide the most lasting memories. In addition, there are a number of museums and buildings open to the public. Opening hours vary but are generally between 9am and 4pm, some closing noon-2pm. You must pay a nominal sum to get into each of the ruins, so take a good supply of small change.

The buildings in the **Plaza Mayor** were badly damaged in the 1976 earthquake, but have all been restored. On the east side of the square are the ruins of the cathedral, originally built in 1545, which was once one of the largest in Central America. The earthquake of 1773 left it with just two chapels standing, which were later incorporated into the church of San José. Entering by the main door in the huge facade you expect to be confronted with a huge interior but instead you come face to face with a wall. Behind this hotchpotch of a church are the crumbling remains of the original cathedral which you can walk around; Pedro de Alvarado was buried here but the location of his tomb is unknown.

On the north side of the square is the **Palacio de Ayuntamiento**, the 18th-century City Hall which contains a couple of museums. The Museo de Santiago (part of which is housed in the old prison) contains a motley collection of objects from the colonial era – among these are Pedro de Alvarado's sword, and an 18th-century marimba. Next door is the **Museo del**

Libro Antiguo which is dedicated to the history of printing. It contains only a replica of Guatemala's first printing press, copies of old documents and a miscellaneous assortment of books, most of which were actually printed in Spain; it is worth a visit nonetheless.

On the opposite side of the square is the 18th-century **Palacio de los Capitanes-Generales**, one of the finest examples of colonial architecture in Guatemala. It was the headquarters of the Kingdom of Guatemala government, and the home of Pedro de Alvarado for a time.

A couple of blocks north of the main square is the arch of **Santa Catalina** which was once used by nuns belonging to the adjacent convent. Around the corner on 1 Calle P is the 16th-century church of **La Merced**. It has one of the finest facades in the city, showing a strong Indian influence. While the ornate facade miraculously survived the 1976 earthquake, the convent didn't – the entrance to the ruins is to the left of the church. Further west, beyond the ruins of San Jerónimo school is the church and monastery of **La Recolección**. Although it was destroyed in 1773 the jumbled ruins are so dramatic that it is as if the quake had happened just a few days ago. (The ruins are open Wednesday to Sunday only.) By heading south past the football pitch you pass the **Museo K'ojom**, which is devoted to Maya culture and music. Beyond is the cemetery which is quiet and fascinating; the building near the entrance used to be a leper hospital.

Heading east along 5 Calle and past the cathedral, you come to the **Universidad de San Carlos de Borromeo** which houses the Museo Colonial (closed on Monday). The fine Moorish-style building is stunning and more interesting than most of the displays of art and sculpture. Further east, near the corner of 1 Avenida N, is Casa Popenoe. This is a beautifully restored 17th-century house which gives an unrivalled insight into domestic life during the colonial period. It is one of the highlights of Antigua (a bargain at 20c) and there is a magnificent view from the terrace. It is open only 2pm-4pm Monday to Saturday.

At the southern end of 1 Avenida N is the church of **San Francisco** which is dedicated to El Hermano Pedro, a monk who lived there in the 17th century. Prior to his conversion he was a notorious womaniser and the museum at the back of the church (closed on Monday) contains the whip which he used upon himself as penance, and a skull with which he contemplated death – doubtless used as an antidote to carnal desire. In 1990 his remains were removed from a wooden chest (in the museum) to the grand tomb in the north transept. Next to the church are the extensive ruins of the monastery, from where there are good views; this is a quiet spot where you can sit, read and escape the crowds.

Heading back towards the centre along 2 Avenida N you pass the ruined church and convent of **Santa Clara** which contain the most beautiful cloisters in the city. Notice the old washing place in front of the church.

When you've overdosed on colonial heritage you can seek solace in the **market** where the local people from villages nearby come to sell vegetables and weavings. Get there early in the morning, not least to avoid the video-wielding American tourists who are bussed in from 10am onwards. Antigua has a tremendous variety of fabrics on offer, but prices are high (and increase after the first busloads of tourists arrive).

Language Schools

So many foreigners come to Antigua to learn Spanish that a fair amount of dedication is necessary to finish the course with a decent knowledge of the language. A typical language school charges about $100 a week for food, accommodation (usually with a family) and four hours of classes per day. If you have to find your own accommodation, look on the notice boards in Doña Luisa's or the Casa Andinista where rooms rented by the month are sometimes advertised.

The tourist office gives good and unbiased advice about choosing a school. Among the best are: Instituto Antigueño (1 Calle P 33), Alianza Lingüística (7 Avenida N 98), Tecún Umán (6 Calle P 34) and Atabal (1 Avenida N 6).

Antigua Essentials

Casa Andinista on 4 Calle O 5, opposite Doña Luisa's, is the best bookshop in town, with books on every aspect of Guatemala and its people, both new and old. **Hamlin y White**, 4 Calle Oriente No 12, next to Doña Luisa's, is another option.

Viajes Tivoli on the west side of the main square has a good selection of books and postcards but is quite expensive. If you are interested in doing serious research on the Maya, etc. go to the Centro de Investigaciones Regionales de Mesoamerica (**CIRMA**) on 5 Calle O which has a library.

The **Tourist Office** in the Palacio de los Capitanes-Generales in the main square, opens 9am-noon and 2-5pm Monday to Saturday.

Post Office Alameda Santa Lucía at 4 Calle P, open 9am-5.30pm, Monday to Saturday.

Banco del Agro on the north side of the square is open on Saturday mornings (9am-1pm) and has an exchange counter which is open out of office hours (3pm-5pm Monday to Friday and 1pm-3pm on Saturday).

Mobicar, 7 Calle P 11, rents bicycles and motorbikes, and is open 8am-8pm. $10 per day for a motorbike, $4 per bike, plus $500 and $100 deposit respectively. For **mountain-biking**, ask at Villa San Francisco.

Horse-back riding, either European or Western style, can be arranged at Hotel San Jorge or directly by contacting the Ravenscroft Riding Stables, 2 Avenida Sur No 3, San Juan del Obispo, Antigua, tel 832 62289.

Travel agents: shop around as prices vary but good reports have come from the following: Sin Fronteras, 3 Calle Poniente, No 12, tel 832 1226, fax 832 2672, e-mail sinfront@infovia.com.gt; and Antonio Ramos, 4 Calle Oriente No 10, tel 832 1370, fax 832 5690, e-mail antigua@tivoli.com.gt.

Internet venues have little difference between them. There are three shops on 6 Avenida between 3 and 5 Calle Poniente. There is one on 5 Calle Oriente between Avenidas 3 and 4 and another just one block north of this. The one with the longest hours (7am-9pm every day) and a competitively priced long-distance telephone service is beside El Afro on 6 Calle Poniente between 5 and 6 Avenida Sur. All charge around $2 per hour.

Around Antigua

Each of the nearby villages gives a more accurate picture of life in Guatemala than Antigua. Buses to them leave from behind the central market.

A 30-minute bus ride south from Antigua takes you to **Santa María de Jesús**, the highest village in the area. It is a short distance east of the less picturesque village of Ciudad Vieja – from 1527 until a catastrophic mudslide destroyed it in 1541 this was the site of the capital of Central America. Santa María is a pleasant village where some of the men still wear traditional costume. The small market is devoted to food and is a pleasant change from the rather overwhelming one in Antigua. The local festival is on 2 January.

Santa María is the starting point for the climb up **Agua volcano** (3,760m/12,350 feet), the easiest volcano to climb in the area. The climb allegedly takes five hours but most people do it in eight; take good shoes. Have no illusions that you are going completely off the beaten track – the path is well-trodden and there is a football field in the crater. If you want to see the dawn you must camp; there is a hut just below the lip of the crater which serves soup and tortillas, but there's no accommodation. There have in the past been reports of rapes and murders while climbing in the Antigua area, but a conspiracy theory circulating among travellers maintains that some of these have come from the tourism authorities in a bid to support the local tour companies. Ask at your hotel or other locals about the present situation.

Buses leave Antigua every 30 minutes for Santa María, between about 6am and 5pm. The last buses back leave at 6pm. By getting the first bus and walking at a brisk pace you could do the trip in a day; otherwise stay in one of the hospedajes in the village.

Acatenango Volcano southwest of Antigua is 3,975m/13,040 feet high. The climb is tough, takes a good eight hours and is best done over two days. There are places where you can camp on the way up and a hut at the top; it's very cold so take a sleeping bag. The views of the smoking Volcán Fuego nearby are magnificent (this volcano is active and dangerous to climb). The best place to start from is La Soledad. There are occasional buses but otherwise either get a taxi from Antigua, or take a bus to San Miguel Dueñas from where it's a two-hour walk. Guides from Antigua (see Doña Luisa's noticeboard) take groups for $10 per person.

San Andrés Itzapa lies off the Antigua-Chimaltenango road and is one of the few places in Guatemala where Maximón, the smoking and drinking saint, is worshipped. The shrine in San Andrés is more touristy than those in Santiago Atitlán and Zunil. Catch a bus to the turn-off and pick up a bus from Chimaltenango.

Guatemala City

The worst capital in the world?

First-time travellers to Guatemala who arrive at the capital may be forgiven for thinking they have made a terrible mistake – how could a country with such a reputation for beauty possess so brutal a capital? Guatemala City is the largest of the Central American capitals, and takes their characteristics to extremes – it is dreadfully noisy, overpopulated, and frustrating. It has been flattened periodically by earthquakes to the extent that little of historic beauty remains; there is nothing aesthetically pleasing about its physical appearance nor its social structure. The capital is mostly owned, operated and occupied by the ladino population of Guatemala, among them some extremely wealthy families. It is shared with an increasing number of poor Indian migrants from the country; every morning buses from all over Guatemala disgorge people in the capital; many indígenas come simply to sell their wares, but some arrive intending to stay. The capital also has a horde of street children, most of whom are treated cruelly by the authorities. The accumulation of so many people has created a population of approaching two million.

In addition to its physical brutishness, Guatemala City attracts an unpleasant collection of those who seek to make a fortune from conflict; little has changed since the early 1980s when, according to the late Bernard Falk, you could hire a hit-man for $25 a day (plus ammunition). Mercenaries and arms dealers are still habitués of the city's ritzier bars.

Few people recommend a visit to 'Guate', as the city is known. Yet it contains the site of Kaminaljuyu, a great Maya centre from pre-classic times, some of the best museums in Central America, and a good selection of places to eat and sleep. Most travellers pass through it almost grudgingly en route to the breathtaking places outside the capital. Guatemala City is never going to win any prizes for beauty, sophistication or flair, but beneath the grime it is a pleasant enough place, full of characters and full of character.

Getting your bearings

Guatemala City's only possible similarity with Paris is that it, like the French capital, is divided into a large number of districts. These zonas are critical, since everyone in the city refers to them. The city centre occupies Zona 1 where most of the budget hotels are. Most of the expensive hotels are in Zonas 9 and 10, as are the majority of diplomatic missions; others are in Zona 4. Most commercial offices are found in the strip going south from the centre along Avenida 7 towards the airport at La Aurora, taking in Zonas 1, 4 and 9. Most bus terminals are also in Zonas 1 or 4, so few travellers would wish to go to many of the other Zonas.

The next layer of orientation is the grid system of numbered Avenidas, which run north-south, and Calles going east-west. Unfortunately the terrain means that there are substantial distortions to this system, and some streets are termed Diagonal if their course is sufficently obtuse. In addition, some streets have names as well as or instead of numbers: Diagonal 3 is also known as Avenida del Ferrocarril, and Avenida La Reforma is where you would expect 8 Avenida to be. Also, some streets and avenues have a short parallel neighbour, which is suffixed A. To confuse matters the numbered streets in the centre have recently been given names. These have yet to catch on (not least because some of the locals object to living on streets named Purgatory or Torment) but are given below to help you find your way; the name plates have replaced numbers on most streets. Avenidas 1 to 12 are straightforward enough, but Calles 8 to 18 are more problematic because on some the name changes at Avenida 5. The conversion is as follows

Avenida becomes	Calle:	Avenida becomes	Calle:
1	Hospital	7	Asamblea
2	Niñado	8	Carmen
3	Olvido	9	Universidad
4	Oratorio	10	Belén
5	San Augustín	11	Teatro
6	Real	12	Santo Domingo

Calle east of Av 5	becomes:	Calle west of Av 5	becomes:
8	Mercadores	8	Santuario
9	Beatas Indias	9	Pierson
10	Capuchinas	10	Capuchinas
11	Libertad	11	Libertad
12	Fortuna	12	Belasco
13	Santa Clara	13	Tortuga
14	Tormenta	14	Tormenta
15	Beatas	15	Laguna
16	Purgatorio	16	Peligro
17	Joroba	17	Ladrillera
18	Habana	18	Perú

The street address conventions appear confusing at first sight, but in fact are quite straightforward. The Salvadoran Embassy, for example, is at 12 Calle 5-43, Zona 9. The number before the hyphen defines the location on 12th street, being the lower of the two cross-streets, i.e. 5 Avenida; therefore it is between 5 and 6 Avenida. The number after the hyphen indicates the approximate position between the avenues, according to the idea that 01 is at the corner of Avenida 5 and 99 at the junction with Avenida 6. A further sophistication is that on avenidas, the odd numbers are on the east side of the street.

The last part of the address establishes the area of town. You need to know the Zona to find an address – taxi drivers are literally lost without them.

The **map** sold by the tourist office (50c) includes a map of Guatemala City. A free map of the city (which shows clearly the zonal boundaries) is also available from Budget Rent-a-Car at Avenida La Reforma 15:00, Zona 9.

Arrival and departure

La Aurora **airport** is in the suburbs south of the city centre. The local bus service to the centre is route 5 which can be picked up easily outside the airport – cross the road, go down the steps and across the concrete plaza, and find the bus shelter off to the left. From the city centre, bus 5 runs from the south side of the Plaza Mayor along Avenida 10 to calle 16, along Avenida 8 to Calle 20, then along Avenida 6, then veers off on an imaginative route, taking a good half-hour to reach the airport. Not all number 5 buses go right to the airport, however, so check with the driver before getting on.

If you want to take a taxi, the official tariff to city centre hotels is pasted up in the airport. At the time of going to press the rate was $5, but most taxi drivers will try to charge at least $8.

The airport closes between 12.30am and 4.30am, so you can't sleep there if you are booked on an early morning flight. The airport itself is a gloomy 1960s structure, which gets horribly overcrowded when several flights arrive simultaneously. In the early morning passengers converge for services to Flores and to US and Central American destinations, choking the check-in area. If you buy any duty-free goods, they will be delivered to the aircraft door. There are more souvenir shops in the departure lounge than anywhere else in Guatemala, with prices about three times higher than outside. If your flight is delayed, as well as going shopping you can admire the diminutive museum between gates 4 and 6.

Arriving passengers can change money at the bank in the arrivals hall; in departures, the bank is open 7.30am to 6.30pm from Monday to Friday, 8am-11am and 3pm-6pm at weekends. Car rental offices are immediately outside the arrivals hall.

The prospect of catching a **bus** from Guatemala City is daunting, simply because there are so many terminals. First-class buses leave from individual companies' terminals, which are centred around 8 and 9 Avenida and 18 Calle (though there is also a cluster on Avenida 1 and 2). The second-class bus terminal is an overwhelming affair, occupying a large slice of Zona 4. Second-class services to nearby destinations depart from a random selection of street corners at the southwest corner of Zona 1; most locals are clued up enough to help.

Several companies operate direct services between Guatemala City and San Salvador. All charge around $15. Several of them are based near the Zona 4 bus station. The most reliable service is operated by Transportes Melva y Pezzarossi (4 Avenida 1-20, Zona 4) which runs buses almost hourly between 5.30am and 3pm. Nearby is Taca, with buses at 8.30am and 1pm, and El Condor with services at 5.30am, 8am and 1.30pm. More convenient is Transportes Centro América (9 Avenida 15-06, Zona 1) which runs one daily service at 5.30pm and will pick you up from your hotel on request. The journey takes about six hours. Book tickets in advance.

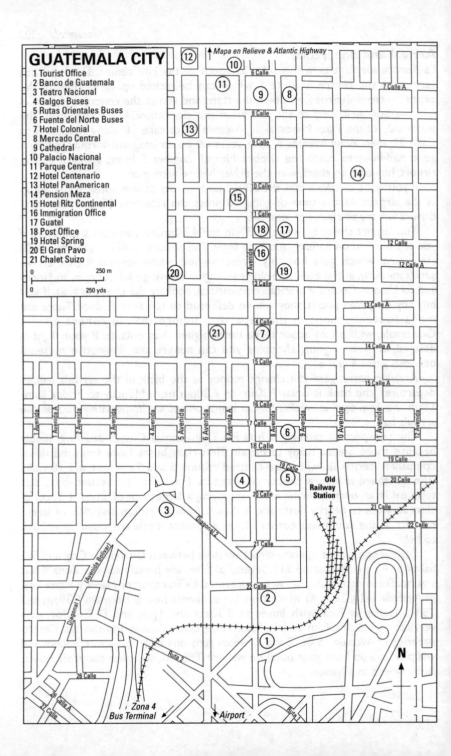

GUATEMALA CITY

1 Tourist Office
2 Banco de Guatemala
3 Teatro Nacional
4 Galgos Buses
5 Rutas Orientales Buses
6 Fuente del Norte Buses
7 Hotel Colonial
8 Mercado Central
9 Cathedral
10 Palacio Nacional
11 Parque Central
12 Hotel Centenario
13 Hotel PanAmerican
14 Pension Meza
15 Hotel Ritz Continental
16 Immigration Office
17 Guatel
18 Post Office
19 Hotel Spring
20 El Gran Pavo
21 Chalet Suizo

0   250 m

0   250 yds

Mapa en Relieve & Atlantic Highway

6 Calle
7 Calle A
8 Calle
9 Calle
10 Calle
11 Calle
12 Calle
12 Calle A
13 Calle
13 Calle A
14 Calle
14 Calle A
15 Calle
15 Calle A
16 Calle
17 Calle
18 Calle
19 Calle
19 Calle
20 Calle
21 Calle
22 Calle
21 Calle
22 Calle
26 Calle
26 Calle A
27 Calle

1 Avenida
1 Avenida A
2 Avenida
3 Avenida
4 Avenida
5 Avenida
6 Avenida
6 Avenida A
7 Avenida
8 Avenida
9 Avenida
10 Avenida
11 Avenida
12 Avenida

(Avenida Bolívar)
Diagonal 2
Diagonal 1

Old Railway Station

Ruta 2

Zona 4 Bus Terminal

Airport

Ruta

N

Getting around

Bus scheduling seems to be non-existent, but there is a constant stream of buses along the main thoroughfares. The buses are easy to use, not too crowded out of peak hours, and are essential for getting around this huge city. Your best chance of getting on a bus in the right direction is to simply ask the driver which Zona he's headed for; the route number and ultimate destination is also written on the windscreen. Fares are low – 25c covers most journeys – and must be paid on entry. One of the most useful bus routes is 2 which runs from the centre south along Avenida 6 and then Avenida La Reforma, and is useful for getting to the museums. Another is route 5, which takes an extraordinarily convoluted route around the city, during the course of which it passes most places of interest. Buses to the Zona 4 bus terminal are conveniently marked 'Terminal'.

Regular city buses are supplemented by minibuses, some of which duplicate the routes of real buses and others which serve the suburbs. Fares are about twice the ordinary bus fare.

The capital's **taxi** drivers know a thing or two about ripping off visitors. They seem to have established a cartel, whereby a gringo is required to pay a minimum of $3 for any journey within Zona 1, increasing rapidly to $8 or more for trips to or from the airport.

A room

Prices are much higher in the capital than elsewhere. New arrivals are advised to stay centrally, not least because the sort of business which travellers need to transact in Guatemala City is most easily carried out in the centre. There is no shortage of choice, but places tend to fill up early. Many of the budget hotels are clustered in Zona 1, in a block between 10 and 15 calles and 5 and 11 Avenidas. In this area are there are a good supply of restaurants, barbers, travel agents, etc.

The **Pensión Meza** is a backpackers' favourite, and has a 'Che room' where Guevara once stayed (or so it is claimed). It has a garden and a faded colonial feel. The management is helpful, and there is an international telephone and a useful noticeboard. A dormitory bed costs $6 per night, a single without bath $12; there are free hot showers. The Meza also has an adjoining café which is good for breakfast and evening beers.

One of the most recommended places is **Hotel Spring** which is housed in a beautiful colonial building and has huge rooms for $14 with bath. A couple of blocks to the south is **Hotel Colonial**. This is by no means the cheapest place in this area, but it is one of the most pleasant and represents good value. The rooms are spacious and airy, and it has a cool and quiet courtyard. The staff are friendly and will look after excess luggage while you travel around the country. A double room costs around $18. One block west is **Chalet Suizo**, which charges $18 a double, but being popular it is likely to be full if you arrive late in the day.

Anyone looking for an upmarket hotel in this area will have to choose from the **Pan-American**, **El Centro** or the **Ritz Continental**; the latter occasionally offers substantial discounts. If you would like to be in the main square the **Hotel Centenario** on the north side has double rooms for $50 – you pay for the position rather than the quality of the room.

All of these are in Zona 1:

Centenario, 6 Calle 5-33 (Parque Central), tel 238 0381
El Centro, 13 Calle 4-55, tel 253 3970
Chalet Suizo, 14 Calle 6-82, tel 251 3786
Colonial, 7 Avenida 14-19, tel 232 6722
Meza, 10 Calle 10-17, tel 232 3177
Pan American, 9 Calle 5-63, tel 232 6807
Ritz Continental, 6 Avenida 10-13, tel 238 1671
Spring, 8 Avenida 12-65, tel 230 2858

A meal

Guatemala City has a good selection of restaurants, at least in Central American terms. One of the best places in Zona 1 is the **Mesón de Don Quijote** on 11 Calle between 5 and 6 Avenidas. It is a lively place with Spanish music (sometimes live). The ceviche is excellent and you get free tapas. Around the corner on 5 Avenida between 12 and 13 Calles is a Spanish restaurant called **Altuna**, opulent and expensive. **El Gran Pavo** is a popular Mexican place on 13 Calle between 4 and 5 Avenidas. A recommended Chinese restaurant is the **Kin Ha**; as well as serving cheap food it also has a bar. There is a lively atmosphere, and this is a good place to meet locals.

The **Picadilly** (corner of 6 Avenida and 11 Calle, with another branch at the Plazuela España) is uninspiring and unexceptional, but its breakfasts are recommended for sheer quantity. A tastier breakfast can be found at **Delicadezas Hamburg** on the south side of the square on Calle 15 between Avenidas 5 and 6. It is extremely popular with the locals, and you may have to wait for a seat on busy mornings. Nearby on 15 Calle between 6 and 7 Avenidas is Antojitos, a good place for Mexican food, with a lousy marimba band; sit well away from it. **Antojitos** does the best guacamole in town, and accepts almost any credit card known to man.

Much further south, nearer the museums, is **Bar El Establo**, on Avenida La Reforma between 13 and 14 Calles. This is a good place for a meal during the day, or for a coffee and a quiet read of the paper. It is a café-cum-book exchange and serves sandwiches, soup, etc. It opens noon-7pm Monday to Saturday. To push the boat out, stay in this part of town and visit the Zona Viva which loosely refers to the area between 10 and 16 Calles and Avenidas 1 and 4 and Reforma in Zona 10. Some of the most sophisticated and expensive places are here. **Siriacos**, on 1 Avenida between 12 and 13 Calles, is the most elegant, serving French and Italian cuisine in a beautiful setting. **Gauchos**, on the corner of 1 Avenida and 13 Calle, is also worth considering.

Zonas 9 and 10 are best for **late-night food**, mainly of the burger/pizza variety.

A drink

Most of the bars are not the sort of places your mother would like to see you in – the hotel bars are generally more savoury than those on the streets.

Out of doors, people set themselves up on street corners and sell huge glassfuls of delicious orange juice. You may not wish to emulate the locals' habit of mixing in two raw eggs. One of the best selections of fresh fruit juices and licuados is sold at the stalls by the park on 5 Avenida between 14 and 15 Calles.

An exploration

The linear nature of the city (or at least the interesting parts of it) means that you can see most places of interest by progressing south from the main square. The following survey of sights runs in that order.

Parque Central: all the locals call the main square **Parque Central** although it is technically two squares: Parque del Centenario on the west side, and Plaza de Armas on the east. The old colonial buildings, including the Palace of the Captains-General where independence was declared in 1821, were all destroyed in the 1917 earthquake. The square has been spruced up recently but it still lacks the ambience of most Central American parques centrales; the best time to see it is at night when the streetlights add some atmosphere that is absent during the day.

The most imposing structure is the **Palacio Nacional** on the north side. On the orders of President Jorge Ubico it was built, largely of reinforced concrete, between 1939 and 1943. You are allowed inside from 8am-4.30pm, Monday to Friday, but since the president and other bigwigs work here, security is tight. On the east side is the 19th-century cathedral. The heavy baroque style, designed (in vain) to resist earthquakes, creates a rather dark interior. Nevertheless it is one of Central America's most handsome houses of worship, if only for its scale. Behind the cathedral is the Mercado Central

Teatro Nacional: the worst thing about the **National Theatre** is reaching it; close to the chaotic Plaza Bolívar, west of 5 Avenida, off Diagonal 2 and near 21 Calle. It is part of the Centro Cultural which was built on top of a fortress and the old battlements were incorporated into the design. It is a futuristic place which would be more at home in an episode of Star Trek. The theatre is worth a visit if only for the excellent views. Visitors are not usually allowed into the building unaccompanied – if you go to the hut on the right in the car park the attendant will call for a guide to take you around; no fee is charged but you are expected to tip. You may be able to sneak in on your own; if not, go to a performance: see *Nightlife*.

Museo Popol Vuh: buried on the east side of town, on 6a Calle east of Diagonal 6, this miraculous **archaeological museum** boasts a fine collection of Mayan artifacts and should not be missed. Exhibits include enormous funerary urns from the Quiché region, and an excellent model of Tikal. A room devoted to post-Columbian exhibits includes models of Pedro de Alvarado, Tecún Umán and Maximón and some fine colonial silver. The museum is extremely well laid out, although the labelling is a little inconsistent. For $1 you can buy a small guide to the exhibits in the shop; ask here for information on lectures. Open 9am-5.30pm Monday to Saturday, admission $2.

Adjacent is the **Museo Ixchel**, which contains an outstanding collection dedicated to Indian costume and weaving. Every year the displays are changed and they follow a particular theme, usually concentrating on one specific area.

Both the layout and labelling are excellent and detailed explanations of weaving techniques and of the evolution of styles are given in Spanish and English; this is a good place to get to know the names of traditional garments before you begin your travels around the country. The museum opens 8.30am-5.30pm Monday to Friday, 9am-1pm on Saturday. Not too far away, at the northern end of Zona 9, a miniature **Eiffel Tower** is perched over 7 Avenida at 2 Calle.

Museo Nacional de Arqueología y Etnología: Maya enthusiasts who did not have their fill at the Popol Vuh, should also visit this museum which boasts its own fine collection of archaeological relics. It's worth going just to see the strong room full of jade, and there are some impressive stelae too. There is also an excellent model of Tikal. The museum is in Parque Aurora, Zona 13 (near the airport), and is open 9am-4.30pm daily except Monday; there is a break for lunch noon-2pm at the weekend. Catch bus 5 or 6 along 10 Avenida in Zona 1. There are various other museums in Parque Aurora.

Mapa en Relieve: about the only sight north of the Parque Central is this **relief map** of the whole country in Parque Minerva. It was made in 1905 and gives a good overview of Guatemala (plus Belize), although the scale isn't quite right so that the volcanoes appear much higher than they are in reality. Looking down from the viewing platform it looks most impressive. It opens daily 8am-5pm. To get there take bus 1, 45 or 46 from the west side of Parque Centenario. From the top of Avenida Cañas walk through the gates and the map's on the right.

Kaminaljuyú: these ruins on the western outskirts of Guatemala City in Zona 7 mark the site of what was once a huge **Mayan city**. The excavated walls amongst the earthworks are protected by a corrugated iron roof. Kaminaljuyú is quite a trek from the centre, and it's often only the real Maya devotees who make the effort. As a result foreigners attract a lot of attention, but the locals are friendly. The site is supposedly open 9am-4pm, but some people have found the gates locked; this may be because it isn't deemed necessary to open up – the perimeter fence is so full of holes that it is easy to get in that way. Catch bus 17 (marked Kaminaljuyú) from 4 Avenida in Zona 1.

A night out

Guatemala City has around 30 cinemas, many of which are clustered along 6 Avenida in Zona 1, and they show a surprisingly up-to-date selection of films. The National Theatre (see above) actually consists of three theatres. Big performances are put on in the Gran Teatro. The Teatro de Cámara is used mainly for chamber music and smaller events. Performances, usually of traditional music, take place every Tuesday and admission is free. The third theatre is open-air. There are shows on most evenings; look in the papers or ask the attendant in the car park for the programme. Tickets cost about $2.

For something a little more exciting, join the rich and reckless in the Zona Viva, in the overpriced discos and nightclubs of a dubious nature. Free, and probably more fun, is an open-air performance by mime artists or jugglers at the corner of Avenida 5 and Calle 15 in Zona 1.

A shopping expedition

The term 'bric-a-brac' covers a multitude of objects, and most of them are sold at the sprawling **street market** adjacent to the capital's main bus station in Zona 4. Although you may not find much with which to impress friends and relations, you can get a fascinating insight into what people will buy and sell – half-smoked cigarettes, sunglasses without lenses, etc.

The **Mercado Central** is a two-storey affair under the car park behind the cathedral. The upper level is devoted almost entirely to weavings and crafts, but little business seems to go on. Nevertheless, this is probably the best place to come if you have last-minute presents to buy, although prices are higher than outside Guatemala City. In contrast to the second floor, the lower level, where food is the main commodity, is full of bustle, although even here the atmosphere associated with markets is lacking. It opens daily from 9am to 6pm (Sundays to noon only). At the opposite end of the social spectrum, go to Zona 10. On 1 Avenida between Calles 11 and 12 is the **Géminis** International Mall.

Among **bookshops**, the museum bookshops are the best in Guatemala City. The one in the Popol Vuh has a big selection of books covering most aspects of Guatemalan culture. Its books on Tikal are cheaper here than elsewhere, and crafts and prints are also on sale. The books in the Museo Ixchel are primarily about weaving and costume. One of the best shops in Zona 1 for books on Guatemala is the Piedra Santa bookshop on 11 Calle between 6 and 7 Avenidas. It stocks a good selection of books on Guatemala, including all those published by the Piedra Santa publishing house. Librería Bremen in Pasaje Rubio (which cuts through from 6 Avenida to 9 Calle) is a tiny shop with books in German and other languages, and old editions of *National Geographic*. For secondhand novels and guide books, go to Café El Establo, on Avenida La Reforma between 13 and 14 Calles.

A word of advice

The **tourist office** is at 7 Avenida 1-17, Zona 4 (tel: 331-1333). Open 8am-4.30pm Monday to Friday, 8am-1pm on Saturday and Sunday. The staff sell maps, give out sheets with information on buses, museums, etc. and try to answer all your questions.

Keeping in touch

The main **post office** is the garish pink building on 7 Avenida between 11 and 12 Calle, Zona 1. Open 8am-4.30pm Monday to Friday. For *poste restante* go to Room 110. Although you need to show your passport when picking up mail, you are allowed to pick up other people's; you may not wish to be sent anything of value, therefore. Each piece of mail you collect costs a few cents. **Internet** cafés are thin on the ground, though the Pension Meza is likely to get connected soon.

Moving on to El Salvador – or the Coast

It has to be said that the journey from Guatemala City to the Salvadoran border is not the highlight of a Pan-American trip. It is worth considering a detour to

Copán in Honduras, a journey fairly easily made from Guatemala City, with an onward connection to Tegucigalpa and Nicaragua. It is much easier to start from Guatemala than from points in El Salvador, or even Honduras itself.

Alternatively, you could try the **Coastal Highway**. Following a winding course roughly parallel to the Pan-American Highway, the Coastal Highway forms a link between the Mexican and Salvadoran borders. Few of the towns along this road – particularly those along its more westerly stretches – are worth visiting. The scenery is uninspiring, save for the occasional volcano on the horizon. Nevertheless, the coastal highway is a fast road well-served by buses, and is the best road for those intent on getting from Guatemala City to the Mexican border as quickly as possible; this is why it is so heavily used by trucks hurtling back and forth.

Unlike its counterpart in El Salvador, the Guatemalan coastal highway does not give access to numerous beautiful beaches. The resorts that exist are down-at-heel, and cheap accommodation is hard to find. Furthermore, the climate in the coastal areas is humid, and can be unbearably hot. The main towns dotted along this road are, for the most part, busy commercial centres, though now by-passed by the Coastal Highway. Numerous roads branch to the north, connecting with the Pan-American Highway, and south to the Pacific coast.

Coatepeque is the first town as you approach from Mexico, but there is little to encourage you to stick around. Retalhuleu, usually referred to simply as Reu, is further east and marginally more pleasant. To the south is the lifeless port town of Champerico. People arrive at weekends to take advantage of the beaches, but the current is strong and the black sand beach not overly inviting. There are buses from both Reu, and Quezaltenango, and there are a couple of hotels should you decide to stay over.

At Cuyotenango, a road turns south to El Tulate, which is the best of a bad lot of beaches along this stretch of coast, and has plenty of cheap hotels. Buses run there from Reu and from Mazatenango, a few miles east of Cuyotenango.

Continuing eastwards, **Cocales** is one place you may decide to get off the bus. This is not because this dowdy crossroads itself holds any interest at all, but because a road branches north from here to Lake Atitlán. For those approaching from Mexico who wish to head straight for Atitlán, this is a possible alternative to following the Pan-American Highway. Buses run from Cocales to San Lucas Tolimán and Panajachel, taking about three hours to reach the latter along a beautiful route. Note that Cocales is not shown on the standard Inguat road map of Guatemala; it is the road junction three miles (5km) southwest of Patulul.

Eight kilometres (five miles) east of Cocales, the bridge carrying the highway over a river has been blown up by guerrillas, and traffic is still diverted onto two adjacent Bailey bridges. Some 16km further on is **Santa Lucía Cotzumalguapa**, perhaps the most intriguing site on the highway. The town is unattractive and the pensiones basic though cheap: the Reforma, half a block northeast of the Parque Central on Avenida 4, costs $2 for two. If you have a couple of hours in hand you could walk to Bilbao, an ancient archaeological site about a mile north of Santa Lucía. Most of the **stelae** found here now sit in museums abroad (plus a few in the town's Parque Central), but a few have been left behind, scattered randomly in a cornfield. They date from the Late Classic Period, and were the work of the Pipil Indians. Those fresh from Tikal are unlikely to be impressed, but the quality of the carving is good, and the improbability of these objects is part of their charm.

These remains are not easy to find, but the following directions should help. Go north along Avenida 4 from the Parque Central in as straight a line as possible. The road degenerates into a track; keep aiming for the volcano in the distance. The park takes you into a cornfield, and after a few minutes you encounter a stream on the right where the locals bathe and wash. Shortly after you first join it, there is a distinctive Y-shaped tree on the far side of the stream. Having established your location, walk back down the path for ten metres. On your right is a track leading into field, and 20 metres along it there is a large half-submerged stela. Go back to the main track, then 50 metres further up beyond the tree is another turning to the left; go 30 metres along here for an even larger slab. Retrace your steps, go back down the main path, past the stream, and look for a more substantial path to the right. About 200 metres along here, close to the path and on the right, is a more modest stela. A little further on, turn left onto another track; if you still have your bearings, you should now be heading back to the town. A short way along here on the right is the biggest and best stela of all.

Continue along the path back to town, and climb through the hole in the fence opposite a green-painted house; the locals will not be surprised to see you. A short way along on the left is Calle de los Leones, a street which winds back down to Avenida 4, where your walk began.

At Siquinalá, further east, a road heads off south to the coast. While a trip to the beach at Sipacate is hardly worth thinking about, you should consider visiting **La Democracía**, eight kilometres (five miles) south of Siquinalá. This town is famous for some unusual Pre-Classic Maya statues and artifacts discovered at Monte Alto nearby, and a number of other fincas in the area. Some of the best carvings have been moved from Monte Alto to the town's main square; others can be seen in the museum. The crude figures outside are the most interesting with their small, fat bodies and massive heads. The origin of the statues is the object of debate, but some archaeologists believe they share more similarities with Olmec art than with that of the ancient Maya. The actual site at Monte Alto is not open to the public. The museum in the square is badly laid out, and rather a mess, but it is worth a quick look around. It is open 9am-noon and 2pm-5pm daily except Monday. Catch any Sipicate-bound bus to get to La Democracía, or hitch south.

Escuintla is the most important town along the coastal highway – roads meet here from all directions – but it is hot, humid, and has little to recommend it. Nevertheless, there is a certain bustle to the place, particularly in the market and the main square.

Because of the town's position on a major road junction, there are plenty of hotels and cheap places to eat; look for both along 4 Avenida and the market. On this street you'll be confronted by a bizarre turreted barracks, painted bright turquoise.

The main bus terminal is on the southern side of town, from where buses leave for the Salvadoran border, the coast, and – once a day – Antigua. Buses to Guatemala City leave frequently from the western edge of town, two blocks west of the main square at the corner of 9 Calle and 1 Avenida.

Some 50km (30 miles) south of Escuintla is San José. Once Guatemala's main shipping port, San José has now been superseded by Puerto Quetzal to the east, and seems to depend on tourism as its source of income these days: drunken weekenders from the capital have replaced drunken sailors of yesteryear. It is a hot, dusty and ramshackle place that has changed little over the last few decades. If only for this reason, San José is an interesting place to visit. The beach is uninviting, and the accommodation grimy; but there are plenty of places serving good seafood.

Between the main town and the beach is the Canal de Chiquimulilla, which runs close to the coast from west of San José almost to the Salvadoran border. The more interesting stretches of the canal can be explored further east, from Iztapa or Monterrico. Most of the hourly buses from Guatemala City (4 Avenida and 1 Calle, near Zona 4 terminal) to San José continue east to Iztapa.

Iztapa is the country's oldest port, and the only one that has succeeded in retaining a certain amount of charm. Iztapa gets fairly busy at the weekends, but is little more than a ghost town at other times. Ferries take people across the Chiquimulilla canal to the beach, but the beach at Puerto Quetzal is marginally better and less crowded; you can get there by boat or on foot. There are a couple of affordable hotels in Iztapa.

Monterrico has the nicest stretch of coast in Guatemala. The black sand beach is more pleasant than most, and the surf is better and the atmosphere more relaxed than elsewhere. It is worth coming just to go to the nature reserve, which consists of dense mangrove swamps that are home to fish and birds, and an unusual selection of mammals, including anteaters and raccoons; sea turtles also lay their eggs along the shore. You will be lucky to see anything but birds, but the swamp is fascinating enough in its own right to warrant the trip. To explore the reserve, you can hire a *cayuco* (dugout) in the village.

To get to Monterrico from Iztapa, take the ferry to Pueblo Viejo, from where buses run an erratic service to Monterrico. The approach from Taxisco on the coastal highway east of Escuintla is likely to involve less waiting around; there are buses to La Avellana, from where regular ferries take people across the canal to Monterrico. Monterrico gets quite busy at the weekends, when accommodation is in short supply. Monterrico is the last place of interest in the Pacific coastal area before entering El Salvador at Pedro de Alvarado. If you have time in hand, head south to Las Lisas, which is a remarkably pleasant beach not far from the Salvadoran border. Inland, Taxisco – the 'city of cheese' – is a modest market town. If you are obliged to stay overnight, e.g. en route to or from El Salvador, then the Hotel Jeresol is surprisingly smart; it even has a pool.

Guatemala City to El Salvador

Both visually and ethnically, the region east of Guatemala City is uninteresting, and there is little to delay those heading east to El Salvador. You can choose between two possible border crossings – San Cristóbal (on the Pan-American Highway) and Valle Nuevo (further south). Both give access to Santa Ana in western El Salvador, but the latter is the faster route, used by buses from Guatemala City. The road to Valle Nuevo branches off the Pan-American Highway at the El Molino junction, just beyond the dismal town of **Cuilapa**. This route takes you through one of the pleasantest stretches of countryside in the eastern highlands.

If time is not important, take the longer route along the Pan-American Highway. The main town in this area is Jutiapa, which is a good place for making bus connections (from Esquipulas, Chiquimula, etc.), and a possible overnight stop if you are running late; there are cheap hotels near the bus station. There are a couple of pensiones at San Cristóbal, but you would do better to stay at Asunción Mita, about 30 minutes from the border.

East to El Salvador.

There are four road crossings into Guatemala from El Salvador. Most traffic uses the Pan-American Highway crossing at San Cristóbal, for several good reasons: formalities are usually brisk, it can be relied upon to be open between 6am and 8pm. Start early from Guatemala City if you want to reach San Salvador by dusk. Direct buses do the journey in half a day. Melva y Pezzarossi runs the best and most frequent bus service direct from Guatemala City to El Salvador.

El Salvador

GUATEMALAN FRONTIER - HONDURAN FRONTIER

Into the darkness

When night descends in Central America, it plunges everything into a shadowy, formless world where little is what it seems and strangers become sinister. The effect is to move you on to the set of one of those dark, gloomy films of which Hollywood was so fond in the 1980s: location, somewhere in Latin America; time, the present; story, well-meaning gringo gets mixed up in horrific political violence involving a government that represses everything except the death squads, and does not live to tell the gory tale.

So when a shadowy figure insists in heavily accented American English that you 'get in the car', under the watchful eye of a cigarette-smoking, gratuitously sunglass-wearing policeman, you comply, but with a certain anxiety.

Luckily, the civil war in El Salvador has been over for nearly a decade, and the gentleman with the beaten-up Buick was genuinely trying to help me find the Hotel Sahara in Santa Ana, a city which is several hundred volts short of a street lighting system. He circled the city centre a few times before people's directions stopped conflicting, and dropped me off at the front door. And no, he wouldn't take any money, though he left a few colones' worth of burning rubber on the hotel forecourt as he roared off into the night.

As soon as you cross into El Salvador, whether from Guatemala or Honduras, you may feel that you have stumbled into some weird mutation of suburban USA. Partly, this is because it is by far the most 'Americanised' of the Central American republics, with seemingly everyone having relatives in the USA. El

Salvador feels a far more dynamic place than either of its neighbours – which is partly the effect of it being far more crowded, with six million people crammed into a nation the size of Wales or the state of Vermont. Indeed, the nation has the highest population density in the western hemisphere. And it feels a far scarier place, too, because of the memories of a recent history which, even by the brutal standards of Central America, is starkly savage. Oliver Stone's film *Salvador* depicts the shocking violence that afflicted this tiny country during the 1980s and 90s. The civil war that El Salvador's military government waged against left-wing guerrillas is the one fact most foreigners know about the country.

An image takes longer to shake off than to acquire, and as a result most foreigners give El Salvador a wide berth. They are doing themselves, and the nation, a disservice. The country at the heart of Central America features on few travellers' itineraries. Yet El Salvador has one of the finest volcanic landscapes in the world. Magnificent volcanoes form a rough chain through the centre of the country, dotted either side of the Pan-American Highway. Most are extinct, although San Miguel, Santa Ana and Izalco are considered to be merely dormant. These tectonic imperfections have provided great wealth since coffee – the main cash crop – thrives on volcanic soil. Scattered along the Panamericana are some notable Mayan sites, and at the heart of the country is the most dynamic city this side of the Mexican capital.

The Highway carves a fascinating slice through the country, but it is one that offers more in the way of scenery than serenity. Yet by stepping off CA1 (and its parallel coastal counterpart, CA8), the pace of life subsides. El Salvador is the only Central American country without an Atlantic coastline, but its Pacific shore more than compensates. The southern coast stretches for 320km (200 miles) and has some of the world's finest surfing beaches. It is dotted with bays and lagoons which, together with the marshy areas inland, are home to a rich birdlife.

El Salvador is known locally as the *pulgarcito* or 'little thumb' of the Americas. Three-quarters of the land is given over to agriculture: farming is so intensive that large areas of forest have been replaced by crops. Every precious patch of flat land is occupied – people crowd the streets, they fill the fields, and they pack into buses like sardines. The scars of the killing decade will take years to heal, but a nation that has suffered so much is now bursting with humanity.

At the frontier

Border procedures in El Salvador seem to take a tenth of the time of those in Guatemala and Honduras, and you may feel that you're almost back in the developed world. That, at least, is the state of play at the start of 2000. All the road frontiers function well during their hours of opening, which are 6am to 8pm. As elsewhere in Central America, you are not advised to test the rigidity of the closing time – do not arrive much after 6pm and hope to get across.

If you happen to arrive by air at El Salvador's International Airport, you will not need to worry about opening times. But you may be dismayed to find yourself a long way from both San Salvador and the Pan-American Highway.

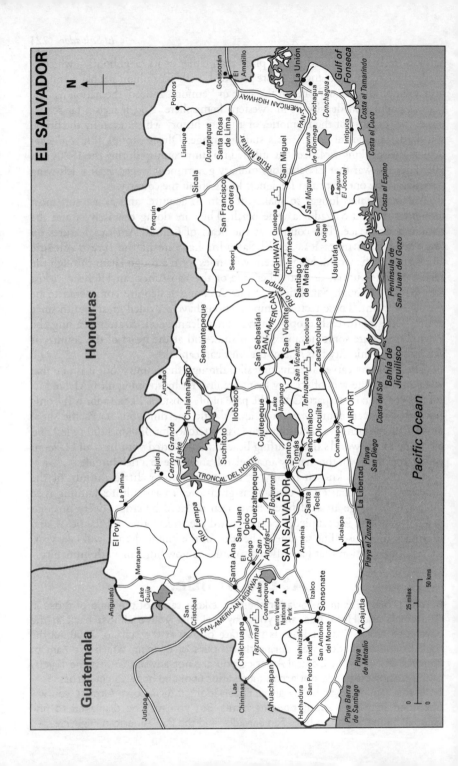

Red tape

British passport holders do not need visas, and neither do citizens of other EU countries or the USA or Canada, for visits of up to 30 days. Any longer than that, and it is wise to apply in advance for a visa through the Salvadoran Embassy (in London at Tennyson House, 159 Great Portland Street, WIN 5FD, 020 7436 8282; the nearest tube station is Great Portland Street, and the opening hours 9.30am-5pm, Monday to Friday, In the USA, the Consulate General of El Salvador is at 1010 16th Street NW, third floor, Washington, DC 20036 (202-331-4032), and there are Salvadoran consulates in Chicago, Houston, Los Angeles, Miami, New Orleans, New York and San Francisco.

Extending your stay beyond that allowed upon entry requires you to attend the Immigration Department of the Ministry of the Interior in the Centro de Gobierno in San Salvador, which opens Monday to Friday, 8am to 4pm. The attitude of officials here, as at the border, depends upon your personal circumstances (you must be able to show you have sufficient funds to support yourself) and the current political situation. You are unlikely to get an extension of more than 30 days. All in all, given the small size of El Salvador, it is far easier to go to the nearest border, cross into Guatemala or Honduras, and come back in.

If political tensions are running high, the immigration officials may take especial interest in evidence in your passport of a visit to Cuba (El Salvador and neighbouring Honduras are the only Central American countries with no air link to the communist island). If your interest in Fidel Castro's homeland is raised, stress that Cuba is a very popular destination for holidaymakers these days. Even though the former left-wing insurgents, the FMNL, now comprise a respectable political party, there is an ingrained suspicion of radical politics among the authorities.

Unlike most other Central American countries, El Salvador does not require you to have an onward or return ticket when you enter the country by air, but however you arrive you may have to demonstrate 'adequate finances' for the intended duration of your stay. Immigration policy is not always interpreted to the letter by every frontier official, and for a time in the 1990s a number of visitors found visas were demanded. At the time of research there was no indication that this was still the practice.

Should you have the misfortune to get your luggage searched, it may help to know that the customs officials won't show much interest in your smoking habit (600 cigarettes are allowed) but may question why you need more than one camera and six rolls of film (the official limit). Again, it helps to have a good story ready. If the officials should discover overtly left-wing literature, it is likely to be confiscated and you may be closely questioned.

Frontier fees

Expect to pay between C10 and C20 for each entry or exit. Officials are flexible about whether you pay in Salvadoran currency or US dollars, but will probably direct you to the nearest currency spiv rather than accept Guatemalan quetzales or Honduran lempiras. Officials have the power to make charges for baggage checks, but this is rarely put into practice. Before you decide to leave by air, note that a 10% tax is payable on international air tickets bought in El Salvador, plus an airport tax of around $10 and migration fee of $5.

Bringing in a car

The cost multiplies if you bring in a vehicle. On entry into El Salvador, motorists must show their driver's licence and proof of the vehicle's ownership. A permit for 15 or 30 days will be issued, for a fee of around C100. This can be extended by another 30 or 60 days (90 is the maximum), at the Dirección General de la Renta Aduanas near the Terminal de Oriente in the capital.

When you leave El Salvador, you will have to pay a further C20 or so. While you are in the country, local insurance cover is not obligatory, but you are strongly advised to arrange it in addition to the existing policy covering the vehicle.

Any chance of a decent map?

Surprisingly, yes: on your way into the country, you can ask for a free tourist office handout, which has as good a map of the country and the capital as it is reasonable to expect on either side of a piece of A4-sized paper. For something more elaborate, most fuel stations along the Pan-American Highway sell clear and generally reliable road maps for around C20. For more detail, you could try the Instituto Geográfico Nacional (Avenida Juan Bertís 59, San Salvador).

That was then

The first visitors

The Olmecs, originally from Mexico, settled in El Salvador some time between 2000BC and 1000BC. There is some evidence that Tazumal, in western El Salvador, was occupied as early as 5000BC. Remains from the Classic Maya period (AD250-900) are more abundant, and the two fascinating sites of San Andrés and Joya de Cerén date from this time.

Various groups of Indians settled in El Salvador during this period, including the Lencas and the Chortís. The Lencas were influenced by the Maya and were renowned for their beautiful pottery. They settled mainly in eastern El Salvador, notably in Usulután, San Miguel and La Unión, but also spread as far north as Chalatenango.

In the 11th century came another influx from Mexico, this time Pipil Indians who settled principally in the western and central areas. The Pipiles were also influenced by the Maya; the most creative of the Indian groups, their weavers, potters and carpenters showing great artistic flair. They were considerable builders too – the main pyramid at Tazumal, the country's principal archaeological site, was built by the Pipiles. A number of the large towns in modern El Salvador, such as Sonsonate and Ahuachapán (both southwest of the Highway, close to the Guatemalan border), began as Pipil trading centres.

The Conquest

The Pipil and Maya city states had fallen apart or were in decline by the time the Spanish arrived. The first expedition, led by Andrés Niño, arrived in the

Gulf of Fonseca in 1522, but more than two years elapsed before Pedro de Alvarado began his conquest of El Salvador. Alvarado, a lieutenant of Hernán Cortés and one of Spain's cruellest conquistadores, crossed into El Salvador from Guatemala across the Río Paz. In the bitter war that ensued much Spanish and Indian blood was spilt. Alvarado was initially defeated and, having been wounded, he abandoned the fight and commissioned his brother Gonzalo and cousin Diego to continue in his stead. They defeated the Indians, and the first settlement, San Salvador, was founded in 1525. The new territory of El Salvador was absorbed into the Kingdom of Guatemala.

Spaniards arrived in dribs and drabs to settle in the new colony – in view of the paltry mineral deposits there was no rush. The country had been called Cuscatlán ('land of precious things') by the Indians, but not because El Salvador was overflowing with gold and silver. Some money-making crops were developed – indigo was an important source of income – but even by the mid-19th century there were only a few hundred thousand inhabitants. It was long after independence that El Salvador developed economically.

Independence

In 1821 the country signed the Declaration of Independence with the rest of Central America; the date of the signing, September 15, is still commemorated as Independence Day in El Salvador. Along with its neighbours, El Salvador was swallowed up into the newly-created Mexican empire. When this disintegrated within a couple of years, El Salvador joined the doomed United Provinces of Central America. Despite the unhappy ending of this attempt at federation, much is still made of the part El Salvador played in the region's campaign for independence. José Matías Delgado, the priest who led the first uprising against the Spanish in 1811, is the national hero.

The next change in the fortunes of El Salvador was heralded by the introduction of coffee in the late 19th century. Coffee thrived on the volcanic soil, profits poured in, and the population increased dramatically. But the wealth brought by coffee and other crops including cotton, sugar cane, fruit, and cereals, remained in the hands of the landowners. The poor emigrated in large numbers to other Central American countries, many going to work in the mines and plantations of Honduras. Conflict with the northerly neighbour still persists, exacerbated by the long-held Honduran suspicion that El Salvador has territorial ambitions, notably for access to the Atlantic coast. (Tension between the two countries surfaced most violently in the 'soccer war' of 1969 – see the end of this chapter.)

The Twentieth Century

El Salvador's perennial problem is that all-too-familiar Latin litany of a vast rift between rich and poor, powerful and powerless. The sore caused by the unequal allocation of land and power continued to fester for the next century. In 1932, a peasant rebellion was murderously subdued. The following 40 years were characterised by a succession of coups and brutal military regimes.

By the 1970s there was a mounting tide of protest as a result of blatant electoral fraud, and against the steadily increasing power of the military. Opposition became organised, with trade unions taking a leading role in the co-ordination of left-wing groups. In October 1979 a military coup overthrew the right-wing General Carlos Humberto Romero, and installed a reformist civilian-military junta. One of the prime aims of this regime was to push through badly needed land reforms, and to raise the minimum agricultural wage. The landowners took fright, as did the military who regretted backing the junta they had helped to power. A coup in 1980 heralded the start of the bitter civil war that was responsible for the deaths of 75,000 people, most of them civilians.

The deadly decade

During the 1980s the Pan-American Highway rumbled under the weight of military convoys, armed to the teeth by the USA. Washington in the Reagan years was under the dangerous misapprehension that left-wing guerrillas from Nicaragua, El Salvador and Guatemala were queuing up to invade across the Rio Grande. Little thought was given to the intervening bulk of Mexico, and plenty of thought was given to the implausible notion of a pincer movement involving an attack on the Panama Canal Zone. It was during this period that the infamous *esquadrones de muerte* (death squads) became a feature of life in El Salvador. The military ran campaigns in which thousands were persecuted, tortured and assassinated. The death squads killed an estimated 40,000 Salvadorans during the height of their campaign from 1979-85.

The death squads consisted largely of low-ranking policemen and a motley collection of thugs, but it is generally believed that the military gave the orders. Despite evidence of army involvement, no officer was ever brought to trial. Various civilian right-wingers were also behind the death squads. The most well-known figure was Roberto D'Aubuisson, a notorious fanatic known as Blowtorch Bob after his favourite instrument of torture. He is thought to have been behind the murder, in March 1980, of Archbishop Oscar Romero who championed the cause of the poor. Many priests and church workers were murdered during the 1970s, when a favourite slogan was 'Be a patriot – kill a priest'. This campaign culminated in the assassination of the Archbishop as he conducted a service in San Salvador's cathedral.

By 1980 the right-wingers in the military who had helped the officers to power in 1979 could tolerate the progressive policies no longer and, under pressure from the landowners, staged another coup. José Napoleón Duarte, a civilian and leader of the Christian Democrats, became president. Exasperated left-wingers took to the hills, and thus began the guerrilla warfare which has continued ever since. The Farabundo Martí National Liberation Front (FMLN) was founded in 1980, bringing together five left-wing groups demanding political, economic and judicial changes. Together with Cuban-style nationalisation, land reform was one of the most important issues; poor farmers have always formed the backbone of FMLN support. In 1981, the standing of the FMLN was enhanced by the formation of a military-political alliance with the Frente Democrático Revolucionario (FDR). Meanwhile, at the other end of the political scale the Nationalist Republican Alliance – the Arena party – was founded as a 'political-military organisation to fight international communism'; D'Aubuisson was a founding member.

The Christian Democrats remained in power for most of the 1980s, during which time a new constitution was adopted providing for an elected presidency and a National Assembly of 60 members. Real power remained firmly in the hands of the military, however, and the government condoned or encouraged the persecution of human rights campaigners, trade unionists, church workers and anyone else considered subversive. Thousands of innocent Salvadorans suffered, often as a direct result of the army's campaign against the guerrillas; many have died or been forced to flee as the army burned their homes and crops.

The guerrillas proved stronger than expected. Government troops were pushed out of many rural areas and a number of towns, with the result that the FMLN gained control of a large chunk of the northeast. The government appealed to Washington for military assistance. President Reagan, haunted by what he saw as the build up of a 'Soviet Empire' in his backyard, was happy to come to the aid of the Salvadoran government. Millions of dollars were poured into the military campaign as tanks, military advisors and CIA officials headed for El Salvador. The American attitude did not encourage efforts towards finding a solution; during the whole of the 1980s the only real chance for peace came in 1987, with the signing of the Arias Peace Plan. Despite this Nobel prize-winning initiative, a workable peace process in El Salvador was to take several more years.

In June 1989 there was some semblance of democracy in the midst of savage internal strife. In elections which were boycotted by the FDR-FMLN, President Duarte was voted out of power. He had lacked the political skill to heal the split in his own party and to control the military and right-wing extremists. Indeed Duarte was regarded as little more than a puppet in the hands of the army and the USA. He had made no progress in negotiating a solution to the war – his attempts at peace talks were dubbed 'dialogues of the deaf'. Duarte, a devout Catholic who believed God was on his side, died of cancer in February 1990, exhausted and disillusioned.

In the 1989 elections the right-wing Arena party played down its association with death squads and claimed readiness to negotiate an end to the war. Arena won under the leadership of Alfredo Cristiani, though it is widely believed that real power was wielded by Roberto D'Aubuisson. After the elections the FMLN seized the political initiative by proposing a ceasefire and an eventual end to their campaign, in return for participation in the political life of the country and an end to US support for the right.

The Arena party and the army made it clear they did not wish to discuss anything but terms for the rebels' surrender. Frustration at the intransigence of the government led to the heaviest fighting in ten years of civil war. In November 1989 the FMLN launched its biggest offensive. San Salvador itself was the principal target as some 1,500 guerrillas occupied large areas of the capital. An estimated 2,000 people were killed – many of them civilians caught in the crossfire – as government troops and rebels fought in the streets. The FMLN was finally beaten back by relentless air attacks. They had hoped for some kind of popular uprising in support of their campaign. This did not materialise, and the immediate result was the resurgence of the ultra right-wing hardliners. The Government vowed to wipe out the insurgents, and a new law was passed curbing still further an individual's right to criticise those in power. These moves, together with the reappearance on the streets of the armoured trucks used by the death squads, raised fears of even more vigorous campaigns of persecution and assassination.

An event which took place during the FMLN offensive changed attitudes in the outside world, especially in the USA. On 16 November 1989, six Jesuit priests, together with their housekeeper and her daughter, were savagely murdered in San Salvador. The priests were all professors at the University of Central America, leading leftist intellectuals who had been calling for a negotiated settlement to the civil war. The right wing had voiced its hatred of the Jesuits for years, accusing them of using the pulpit to persuade the campesinos to side with the FMLN.

An investigation into the murder of the Jesuit priests was conducted as a result of international pressure. The involvement of the armed forces in the killing was strongly denied initially, but Colonel Benavides, head of the Military Academy, and seven officers, were eventually arrested, amid accusations of a cover-up of senior members of the government.

The FMLN had talks with the government in Geneva in April 1990, which resulted in a human rights agreement, and later that year published a manifesto calling for, among other things, total demilitarisation (as in Costa Rica) and a new political party encompassing all anti-Cristiani camps from social democrats to liberation theologists. Little progress had been made by November, however, and the FMLN endeavoured to strengthen its hand by launching another offensive. It targeted key provincial capitals in the north and east, and penetrated the outskirts of the capital; Ilopango airport was attacked and the rebels launched smaller guerrilla attacks on several banks in San Salvador in response to Cristiani's plans to privatise banking.

The long and bitter stalemate was finally brought to a messy kind of conclusion at the start of 1992, with a peace agreement that legitimised the FMLN. At the same time, the rebels were demobilised, and several especially nasty units of the armed forces disbanded. Since then, the armoured trucks with smoked windows that were the hallmark of the death squads have disappeared from the streets of the capital, and the substantial patches of the country that were off-limits in the hands of guerrillas have been assimilated back into the fabric of a nation. A new civilian police force has been established; but the number of violent deaths in El Salvador is higher now than it was during the civil war.

Even though the FMLN has become a mainstream party, Arena's right wingers have maintained their grip on power. Elections since the war ended have been characterised by disenchantment and consequent low turnout. There is still a vast amount of resentment about the way the security forces were granted an amnesty for atrocities committed during the civil war, and this has led to a lack of confidence in the political process. In the 1999 presidential elections, 60% of the population failed to turn out to vote.

Discontent spread during the 1990s, as the government failed to honour the peace agreement. Retired soldiers, who had not received the financial benefits they had been promised, occupied the Parliament building; prisoners around the country staged a hunger strike; and the Metropolitan Cathedral in San Salvador was occupied in protest at redundancies in the public sector. In parliamentary elections in 1997, Arena lost many seats to the FMLN, resulting in a centre-left majority, but, contrary to expectations, the FMLN was still too divided to win the 1999 election, when Arena's Francisco Flores became President. None of this is of great interest to most of the population, which is more concerned about unemployment, grinding poverty, and the high levels of crime which now afflict the country.

This is now

One in five Salvadorans was displaced by the war and forced to live in resettlement camps within El Salvador or in refugee camps abroad. Since the war ended, the economy has not been kind to the poor. In some areas, unemployment is running at 50 per cent, and many of those who have jobs are paid less than the legal minimum wage. As a result of increasing poverty, more children are suffering from malnutrition. Much of this poverty is concealed, or at least far less visible than the conspicuous consumption of the country's rich; the Zona Rosa in San Salvador is an area of chic shops and ritzy restaurants which would not look out of place in California. Indeed some visitors come away from El Salvador thinking that the country is more prosperous than its neighbours; but the deceptive wealth of a small group obscures the poverty of the majority.

All of which is impossible to reconcile with the gregarious good humour of almost everyone you meet in El Salvador. The spirit of the Salvadorans is inspiring. Even during the worst of the war, they were talkative and vivacious; buses ran (most of the time), circuses still toured, and festivals were celebrated with the usual verve. Nowadays, everyday life, for the foreigner at least, appears to be calm and normal. One lingering social effect of the war is a reluctance to venture into the streets at night. Otherwise, there is precious little evidence of the decade of civil war, though beneath the surface there are deep scars that will take generations to heal.

On the Highway

El Salvador was the first country in Central America to complete its section of the Pan-American Highway. It stretches 300km (185 miles), right through the middle of the country. Official literature boasts that El Salvador has the best highways in Central America, and more paved roads per square mile than the USA. This may be the case on paper, but the reality is that a decade of civil war reduced most roads to a sorry state. Some roads in former zones of conflict are fit only for buses and stout trucks. These are slowly being repaired, a process which itself slows traffic considerably. To top it all, road bridges were popular targets for guerrillas during the war, and as a result many rivers are still crossed by temporary Bailey bridges or fords.

At first, though, you may think you're back in Mexico, or Panama, such is the quality of parts of the Pan-American Highway, notably from Santa Ana to San Salvador and around the capital. The locals refer to these fast four-lane highways as *autopistas*; unhappily, there is usually no central divide. Away from these fast and dangerous stretches, most of the road system is slow and dangerous.

Like the population, the traffic density is higher in El Salvador than elsewhere in Central America, which makes driving even more challenging than usual. 'Mini-bus, bus and taxi drivers who provide private transportation generally do not adhere to traffic rules and regulations', says the US State Department. Nevertheless, though, the local buses are fun to travel on. Uniquely for a Central American country, every bus in El Salvador has a number to identify its routes. Mind you, it can be difficult to identify the digits among all the decorations: the buses in El Salvador are locked in battle with those of Panama for the title of the flashiest in Central America. Every bus has an elaborately inscribed name on the side, many of them Anglo-American – Eric Elvis is one to look out for.

However colourful the exterior, the inside is even more of a sensual experience, because of overcrowding on a scale to match Nicaragua – indeed, the national specialist subject seems to be how many people can be crammed on a bus. The long-suffering passengers are a stoical bunch, and you will be greeted good-humouredly and probably be offered a seat. Note that there are very few options to 'upgrade' to a classier kind of bus; with the exception of a few buses between San Salvador and San Miguel, and the international services running through to Guatemala and Honduras, there are no comfortable express buses running in the country.

Services along the Pan-American Highway (CA1) are frequent (but still crowded), while the Coastal Highway (*Carretera Litoral*, CA8) is quite well served by buses. Services on the northern highway to the Honduran border are more spasmodic. When travelling on minor roads be prepared for erratic schedules, since bus drivers are reluctant to leave unless the bus is full.

Even by the standards of Central America, buses can be shockingly dangerous. In October 1999, a bus crashed in Apopa, 15km south of San

Salvador, killing 43 passengers. If you are not deterred by the carnage on the roads – or you believe you could do better than the average Salvadoran bus driver – then Hertz, Avis and Budget will rent you a vehicle at the country's international airport, and in San Salvador. Information on traffic and road conditions is available from Automóvil Club de El Salvador (tel 221 0557).

The flyover options

The Salvadoran airline, Taca, operates flights connecting San Salvador with various other Central American capitals. Flights leave from the international airport, Comalapa, in La Paz, 40km (25 miles) south of San Salvador. For schedules, fares and reservations, call Taca at Comalapa on 267 8222 or 339 9155, or on 001 800 535 8780. Buses (number 138) into the city leave from a bus station about 1km from the airport terminal

What's different about El Salvador?

Climate

Of all the Central American countries, El Salvador comes closest to having a reliably temperate climate. Between the volcanoes and mountain ranges much of the country consists of a high, hilly plateau about 600m (2,000 feet) above sea level, so it rarely gets unbearably hot. The average temperature is 28C/78F; naturally it gets hotter and more humid in the coastal and lowland areas, though the breezes blowing in off the Pacific often help keep it cool. Except in the highlands at night, you are unlikely to need warm clothing. Usual Central American seasons apply: wet from May to November, dry from December to April.

Is El Salvador a good place to start or finish a trip along the Pan-American Highway?

In terms of access, most definitely. Air links to all the leading Central American cities are good. One very good reason for this is the extremely successful Salvadoran national airline Taca – an acronym for Transportes Aereas Centro América. It is easily the best in the region (there is a certain flair to an airline whose in-flight refreshments consist solely of Coca-Cola and Johnny Walker Black Label whisky), and even during the civil war was remarkably well managed. As a result, the Grupo Taca has taken over much of the running of other Central American airlines.

From North America, the main gateways are Miami, New York, New Orleans, Houston, San Francisco and Los Angeles. From Europe, you have to fly via a US city or transfer in Bogotá. A 10% tax is payable on international air tickets bought in El Salvador, plus an airport tax of around $10 and migration fee of $5.

Who are the Salvadorans?

Nine in every ten Salvadorans are mestizo, of mixed Spanish and Indian descent. After the Spanish arrived in El Salvador, they interbred with the Indians to such an extent that by the mid-17th century over half the population was mestizo. Only one in twenty Salvadorans is pure Indian. The Indians live mostly in the western areas, particularly around Sonsonate, although the odd village has survived elsewhere. The main Indian group is the Pipil, whose ancestors came to El Salvador from Mexico in the 11th century. Their language is Nahua, which is related to the language of the Aztecs. It is still spoken in certain Indian villages, such as Panchimalco, south of San Salvador, but it is in danger of dying out among the younger generations along with the traditional crafts of the Pipiles.

The same proportion of the population – one in twenty – is white, chiefly of Spanish colonial origin. It is mainly from this group that the fourteen families who own much of El Salvador are drawn.

What they eat

The national dish of El Salvador is the *pupusa*, and you are likely to end up eating a lot of these, because they are cheap, and delicious once you acquire a taste for them. A pupusa is a stuffed corn tortilla which comes with a variety of fillings, but usually cheese or frijoles. They are cooked on a griddle and are best when eaten piping hot. There is often a huge jar of semi-pickled cabbage from which you are expected to take a dollop to slam on top of your pupusa. You may also brave the *loroco* (chilli sauce) which is found on most restaurant tables. Although chili is popular, Salvadoran food is not particularly hot and spicy.

Pupusas vary from place to place, so if you don't enjoy the first one, try another venue. There are pupuserías everywhere, and they come in all guises – from a make-shift stall on the pavement, to a proper bar with tables and chairs. Pupusas are often sold at bus stops, but these are rarely fresh; since a tepid or cold pupusa is one of the least appetising things you could wish to eat, you would do well to avoid buying them there.

Cattle-breeding is a big industry in El Salvador, and the beef is often both tender and tasty. Chicken, as in the rest of Central America, is the other most common meat. One of the more unusual animals eaten in El Salvador is iguana (*garrobo*), which tastes uncannily like chicken. *Sopa de garrobo* is a speciality in the San Miguel area, where the locals are known as *garroberos*, the 'iguana eaters'.

On the Pacific coast there are plenty of opportunities to eat seafood. A couple of specialities worth looking out for are *cazuela de mariscada* (a rich, creamy seafood soup, rather like chowder) and *sinfonía de mar* (fish oysters, crabs and lobsters in a soup). Most seaside towns – such as La Libertad – have cheap stalls as well as the more expensive seafood restaurants.

What they drink

Lots of beer. Lager is brewed locally and is cheap and easy to find. Suprema and Pilsener are the main brands; Suprema is the stronger and tastier one and is 50c more expensive. Coca Cola and other fizzy drinks are sold everywhere for a couple of colones. Fruit juices are also available, and are often sold in plastic bags for 50c-70c at bus stops. Coffee, a leading export, is sold everywhere.

Unfortunately the stuff consumed locally is rather disappointing, and there is no incentive to take a huge stock home.

What they read, watch and listen to

The two main daily newspapers in San Salvador, *La Prensa Gráfica* and *Diario de Hoy*, are unerringly right-wing. Each is sold in a kind of wrapper, with the outer pages carrying only cartoons. There are also a couple of afternoon papers, *El Mundo* and *Diario Latino*. For a slightly more human response to world affairs look out for the weekly magazine called *Semana*.

Of the main television networks two are state 'information' channels and the others are commercial. Cable and satellite is widespread, with a dizzying number of US and Latin American stations on offer.

There is one national radio station and about 40 commercial radio stations. Radio Cuscatlán is controlled by the army and the rebels have their own clandestine radio station, called Radio Venceremos. If all you want is western music, one of the capital's dozen stations should oblige.

How they enjoy themselves

Soccer is the most popular sport in El Salvador, and all the large towns have their own stadium. The most important venue is the Flor Blanca National Stadium in San Salvador. The other well-supported sport is motor racing. The main El Jabalí Formula 1 racetrack is 32km (20 miles) west of San Salvador – although Grand Prix events are not staged here. Other popular games include baseball and basketball, but you will have to go to San Salvador to see the best matches.

Watersports are the main sports in which travellers can take part. Some of the Pacific beaches are renowned for their surf, which attracts significant numbers of Californians. The coast is dotted with lagoons, the most interesting being those around Costa del Sol and the Bahía de Jiquilisco, where you can hire canoes to go exploring.

What they spend

The local currency is the Salvadoran colón, sometimes called the peso. It somehow managed to maintain its strength as one of the more stable currencies in the region even during the civil war. US dollars (notes only) are accepted in many places, but not necessarily at a decent rate. Change will be given in colones. Make sure you know which currency is being referred to when you are quoted a price.

Those crossing a land border will have to deal with any moneychangers who happen to be hanging around, since there are no other exchange facilities (see *Unofficial Dealers*, below). For those arriving by air the first opportunity to obtain colones is at the bank inside the airport; the exchange rate offered is good. As a rule, banks charge a flat fee of $1 for an exchange transaction, as do the more expensive hotels which exchange foreign currency. Travellers cheques are acceptable in banks and hotels, but few shops are accustomed to taking travellers

Festivals and holidays

Every Salvadoran town has an annual fair which usually entails a mixture of music, dancing and religious ritual. Since these festivals provide one of the few occasions when you can witness local traditions, you are strongly advised to time your visit to coincide with one. Those held in predominantly Indian villages are often the most interesting. There are many festivals in August, including in the capital where the Fiesta del Salvador takes place in the first week.

The national public holidays are as follows:

December 31/January 1	New Year
March/April	Easter
May 1	Labour Day
June 15	Corpus Christi
June (end)	Bank Holidays
September 15	Independence Day
October 12	Columbus Day
November 2	All Soul's Day
November 5	First Call for Independence (half day)
December 24	Christmas Eve (half day)
December 25	Christmas Day

cheques as payment. Some banks show an unusual unwillingness to cash travellers cheques if you do not have the printed form listing the serial numbers (which you get when you buy the cheques). This piece of paper is of little significance, but some Salvadoran cashiers appear to have been instructed otherwise.

Colones are nigh-impossible to exchange outside El Salvador, so spend all your money before departure or reconvert what you have not spent; given the plentiful supply of dollars in circulation, it is a good way to recharge your supply of US currency.

Banking Hours

In San Salvador banks open 9am-1pm and 1.45pm-3.30pm, Monday to Friday. Some branches stay open until 7pm. Outside the capital there is no hard and fast rule, but opening hours tend to be 8.30am-noon and 2.30pm-5pm. All banks are closed for balancing for a couple of days at the end of June and December. Automatic teller machines are widespread in the capital, with some also in La Libertad, Santa Ana, San Miguel and San Vicente.

Unofficial dealers

The only places where you are likely to find moneychangers are at the land borders and in the Centro de Gobierno (around the main post office) in San Salvador. You should be able to get a small premium on the official rate. Travellers cheques are readily acceptable among the hordes of men toting pocket calculators and wads of notes outside the post office in the capital; moneychangers at the border are less likely to accept them.

Travelling budget

The price of a decent double room in a basic hotel can cost anything from $10-$30. A room for two in an average hotel costs $25-$50, more in the capital. You can keep costs down by camping (most easily achieved on the coast), or by staying in a Turicentro – a cross between a tourist complex and a park. These centres are set up by the tourism institute and offer a variety of recreational activities. The thought of such a place might not appeal, but most turicentros are in or near picturesque spots such as the Cerro Verde volcano, and they sometimes offer the only accommodation in the vicinity. As well as cabañas (cabins), most have camping facilities or places where you can sling a hammock. You must pay an admission fee, but this is nominal. The drawback is that these turicentros tend to be crowded at weekends.

Anything worth buying?

Crafts are the main thing to spend your spare colones on in El Salvador. Baskets, hammocks, ceramics and textiles are better buys than the rather tacky souvenirs. Certain towns are famous for a particular craft; San Sebastián for its hammocks and quilts, Ilobasco for its ceramic figures and Quezaltepeque for its pottery. Even if you don't visit the towns in question, you should be able to buy the products in shops or markets around the country, particularly at the Mercado Cuartel in San Salvador. While every Salvadoran male sports a hat, it is surprisingly difficult to track down any hat shops. Your best chance is to look for a hat stall in a market. You can buy a straw hat for about $5, while a traditional Panama hat will set you back $20-30. Perhaps the best present to take home is an El Salvador T-shirt; these can usually be found in one of the many street stalls in the capital; pay no more than a few dollars.

Shop opening hours vary but are generally 8am-noon and 2pm-6pm, Monday to Friday, 8am-noon on Saturday. Some shops open all day Saturday and on Sunday morning also.

Keeping in touch

Internet access

The provision of internet facilities in developing countries is usually in direct proportion to the number of backpackers passing through. Because El Salvador is mostly regarded as a necessary evil between Guatemala and the rest of Central America, there is low demand for walk-in facilities. For example, in the second city of Santa Ana the only known publicly available terminal is at a hotel. Your best bet is to ask the nerdiest-looking person you can find on the street and get their local knowledge.

Mail

Post offices generally open 8.30am-4pm, Monday to Friday. Air mail letters and postcards take at least a week, and sometimes a month, to reach Europe. During the civil war, mail boxes were removed from just about everywhere, because of the rebels' tendency to plant bombs in them. They have yet to make a complete comeback, so if the post office is closed, you may have to be content with shoving your letter under the door and hoping for the best. Rates for sending postcards abroad are $0.50 to Europe, $0.35 to the USA.

For poste restante, the main post office in San Salvador (tel: 271 0301) is in the Centro de Gobierno, and is open 7.30am-5pm Monday to Friday, 8am-noon on Saturday. Letters from Europe take about a fortnight, those from the USA 7-10 days. There is no charge made for collecting mail, but the staff are careful to check that you are the addressee.

Telephone

ANTEL, the state telecommunications company, has lost its monopoly and found its way to improving the catastrophic phone system. (The communications network was a prime target of the FMLN guerrillas; when they ran short of ideas, the rebels attacked another telephone exchange.) In competition with other operators, ANTEL now runs an excellent network with reasonable prices. Calls within the country use a six-digit number (no area codes). International Direct Dialling is feasible from any payphone, private line, or hotel, though the latter is likely to be expensive.

Public telephones mostly accept prepaid telephone cards. Rates for calls to North America are around C50 for three minutes, and are cheaper at night. Calls to Europe cost around C100 for three minutes at any time of the day. Directory enquiries are answered (in Spanish only) on 114. For long-distance calls via the operator dial 110. For local time in Spanish, dial 117.

The general number for emergencies is 123; see San Salvador for the numbers of specific services.

The outdoors – how great?

El Salvador is so heavily populated and so extensively cultivated that few big areas of land are protected as national parks. The destruction of forests to make way for crops has meant that many mammals native to the highlands have diminished greatly in number, or have disappeared altogether. Jaguars and crested eagles, for example, have long since died out, and even hummingbirds are an endangered species. Not all animal life is immediately threatened, however; deer and jungle cats continue to roam the hills, and birds and monkeys fill the trees in a few areas.

Despite the need to create reserves, only a handful of national parks exist. There was also enormous ecological damage as a direct result of the fighting. Monte Cristo Park is the most prestigious reserve, but its position west of El Poy in northern El Salvador is remote and potentially unsafe.

Permits are required for certain reserves, although they are not necessary for the more accessible ones such as Cerro Verde (west of San Salvador) and El Jocotal Lagoon near Usulután. Check at the National Parks office at Calle Rubén Darío 619 in San Salvador.

Staying safe

You should avoid, more than in any other Central American country, arousing the suspicion of the authorities by taking photographs of military or politically sensitive subjects. The Salvadoran constitution prohibits foreigners from taking an active part in domestic politics, e.g. joining a demonstration. Don't get into political discussions with strangers.

Go to bed early. Most towns in El Salvador close down after 9pm, and few people venture out after this time. It is effectively an unofficial curfew, and anyone on the streets later than that is regarded either as a predator or a target.

Theft is common in the capital, particularly on crowded buses, even during the daytime in San Salvador. One final thing: El Salvador is not an ideal place to go hiking. One of the main hazards are the land mines which are scattered throughout the north of the country.

The strongest government health warning
This bulletin was issued in March 2000:
'The US Embassy warns its personnel to drive with their doors locked and windows raised; to avoid travel after dark; and to avoid travel on unpaved roads at all times because of random banditry, carjackings, criminal assaults and lack of police and road service facilities. Most fatal accidents or robberies and assaults occur during the evening or early morning hours. Travellers with conspicuous amounts of luggage, late-model (new) cars and foreign licence plates are particularly vulnerable, even in the capital.

Many Salvadorans are armed and shootouts are not uncommon. Foreigners, however, may not carry guns, even for their own protection or for use on the road from the United States, without first procuring from Salvadoran officials a firearms licence. Failure to do so will result in detention and confiscation of the firearm, even if it is licensed in the United States.

Mine removal efforts ceased several years ago, but land mines and unexploded ammunition in back-country regions still pose a threat to off-road tourists, backpackers and campers.

Visitors should avoid carrying valuables in public places. Armed assaults and carjackings take place both in San Salvador and in the interior of the country, but are especially frequent on roads outside the capital where police patrols are scarce. Criminals have been known to follow travelers from the international airport to private residences or secluded stretches of road where they carry out assaults and robberies. Criminals often become violent quickly, especially when victims fail to cooperate immediately in surrendering valuables. Frequently, victims who argue with assailants or refuse to give up their valuables are shot.

From the frontier to the capital

The word 'scruffy' seems always to attach itself to any Central American border post, and the point where the Pan-American Highway crosses from Guatemala to El Salvador is no exception. But when you have struggled through the bureaucracy, you can congratulate yourself on traversing an invisible boundary: the 90-degree-west line of longitude. El Amatillo, the frontier point is, like Memphis and New Orleans, exactly one-quarter of the way around the world from Greenwich.

As you make your way along the unravelling highway to El Salvador's second city, Santa Ana, you will feel that you have jumped into another world compared with the slumber of western Guatemala. By the time you reach **Santa Ana**, 63km (40 miles) northwest of San Salvador, you may start to miss the rural tranquility. Santa Ana has a quarter of a million people and enough to sustain your interest for an afternoon, including the late Gothic cathedral and El Calvario church.

Bus 201 leaves the Terminal del Occidente in San Salvador regularly for Santa Ana, and takes about 90 minutes to get there. The city is a route centre and is well served by buses from Sonsonate, Ahuachapán and San Cristóbal (Guatemalan border) among others.

The choice of **hotels** is wide, with a number of hospedajes to be found on or close to Avenida Sur. The best of these, and probably the best value in town, is the Hospedaje Livingston (441 1801) at number 10 – the rooms are clean and the owners are helpful. A double room costs C100. Of a similar standard and price is Hotel Colonial, at 8 Avenida Norte 2. The most expensive place is Hotel La Libertad near the cathedral. Most of the hotels serve reasonable meals, but the other restaurants in town tend to be dear and not terribly good. There are plenty of *comedores*, though, and the market in front of the cathedral has a few food stalls.

Midway between San Andrés and Santa Ana, a road branches off to the left to **Lake Coatepeque**. This crater lake was born out of a series of volcanic eruptions, and is in an implausibly beautiful setting. The water, fed by hot mineral springs, is warm and good for swimming. The exact depth of the lake has yet to be established, but parts of it have been measured at more than 350m (1,200 feet). Being just 45 minutes drive from San Salvador, Coatepeque is a popular resort at weekends and holidays. At other times, however, it is a pleasant place, and probably the closest thing El Salvador has to the 'traveller's paradise' of Lake Atitlán in Guatemala; certainly the water is cleaner. *Guapote*, a fish caught in the lake, is considered a delicacy.

Lake Coatepeque is 13km (eight miles) south of Santa Ana. Get off bus 201 to San Salvador near El Congo, which lies between the new and the old highway. There are also direct buses (number 220) which leave Santa Ana every hour, and go via El Congo; the route terminates at Hotel del Lago. Buses between Santa Ana and Cerro Verde (see below) also pass by the lake, the route between the lake and Cerro Verde being particularly beautiful.

It is quite possible to go on a day trip to Lake Coatepeque, but there are a number of hotels, including Hotel del Lago and Hotel Torremolinos. You can rent a cottage if you want to stay for a while, but the cheapest option is to sleep on beds in cabins at the Balneario Los Obreros, literally 'workers' resort.

A volcanic trilogy

South of Lake Coatepeque is **Cerro Verde National Park**, which contains the volcanoes of Cerro Verde, Izalco and Santa Ana. The volcano after which the park was named is long extinct, two craters on the northern side being the only remaining evidence that it was ever active. The park contains areas of cloud forest where rainfall is high and a damp mist hangs among the trees. The vegetation is lush, and orchids and ferns abound. South of the volcanoes, green plain stretches to the coast; this is a beautiful and tremendously fertile area where coffee thrives on the rich volcanic soil. Those not wishing to climb the volcanoes can enjoy walking in the forest where there are good trails, and the plants are well labelled; there are magnificent views from many different spots in the park.

Cerro Verde is 72km (45 miles) west of San Salvador, reached by the road which connects the Pan-American Highway and the Santa Tecla-Sonsonate road, passing to the east of both Lake Coatepeque and the park. The southern approach road branches off about midway between Santa Tecla and Sonsonate, 22km (14 miles) east of Sonsonate. No buses direct to Cerro Verde run along this route, so you must catch any bus along the main road; bus 205 operates between San Salvador and Sonsonate and passes the junction. You can hitch from the turn-off; there is usually quite a steady flow of traffic. The last stretch of road to Cerro Verde is unpaved but good.

The approach is easier from the north, via El Congo where the road branches off the Pan-American Highway. Bus 248 runs to Cerro Verde from Santa Ana twice a day. Alternatively, catch any bus going along the highway and get off at El Congo, from where there are more frequent buses, or hitch.

Hotel de la Montaña Cerro Verde (usually known as the Hotel de Montaña) has a fine view over Izalco and Santa Ana. The hotel was built on this spot to give visitors a bird's eye view of Izalco's crater and its fiery activity; sadly for the developer the volcano has been dormant since 1957, the year the hotel was completed.

Until the late 18th century, **Izalco** volcano did not exist. It now reaches a height of 1,910m (6,269 feet). In 1770 a hole appeared at the foot of Cerro Verde; then a cone developed around this hole, and in a matter of weeks became 1,300m high. The volcano was so active, spitting out smoke, rock and flame, that it could be seen by sailors off the coast and earned the nickname

Faro del Pacífico – Lighthouse of the Pacific. The volcano, with its slopes streaked black by lava, and smoke wafting from the top, is harder to climb than it looks. The slopes are bare of vegetation and partially covered in loose lava, making the ascent at times tough and demoralising as you fall back a step for every two you take. The descent is equally daunting, but much quicker as you slide down the scree. The path is signposted and starts below the car park on Cerro Verde; allow a couple of hours to climb Izalco, an hour or so for the descent. Some say you can appreciate Izalco more from Cerro Verde, but few things are as thrilling as peering into the depths of a volcanic crater from the rim. The views of the area from the top are magnificent too.

Across the plateau from Cerro Verde is **Santa Ana** volcano, also known as Lamatepec, which means 'Father Hill'. This is a fitting title since at 2,365km (7,759 feet) it is the highest peak in El Salvador. It is much older than Izalco; the lava on its slopes is probably that left by the eruption of 1524 which was described by Pedro de Alvarado as '*una de las bocas del infierno*' (one of the mouths of Hell).

The climb up Santa Ana, in contrast to that up Izalco, is something of a Sunday afternoon stroll. Rather than scree, Santa Ana's slopes are covered by trees, thickly in places. Vegetation thins out considerably towards the top, however, providing a number of approaches to the crater rim. The sulphurous fumes become increasingly pungent as you near the summit, especially if there is a strong wind. Reaching the top is dramatic as you look over the edge and behold the small, tranquil lake, turned emerald green by the sulphur content. There is no trail down to the lake, but you can walk around the rim in about 90 minutes and enjoy good views of the other volcanoes, and of the landscapes north towards Santa Ana and south towards the coast.

There are several starting points for the walk, including Finca Santa Ana and Finca Las Naranjas. The shortest route, which takes less than half an hour, is from Cerro Verde car park. A nicer walk is that from Finca San Blas, down a track that branches off the road before you reach Cerro Verde. Allow 60-90 minutes for this route.

The Mayan Miracle

Where were you for the last winter solstice of the 20th century? Unless you are an American with a propensity for communing with nature, you are unlikely to have been at the most accessible Mayan site in Central America.

San Andrés is an easy five-minute walk from the highway – the driver of any 201 bus will drop you off at the right spot if you ask for *las ruinas*. San Andrés was an Indian ceremonial centre, thought to date back to 900BC, although the visible structures were built during the Late Classic period. The pyramids and other remains were excavated and partially restored only recently; the main concentration is near the confluence of the Sucio and Agua Caliente rivers. It is not the greatest Mayan site in the meso-American world, but the location is superb – amid languid meadows, with every horizon pierced by a volcano.

At noon on 21 December 1999, no one was looking at the horizon. A group of 30 Americans, decked out in white, were sitting in a circle close to the stumpy foot of a pyramid. I didn't hear them humming with the electromagnetic force which so often seems to be detected in places like this by people like these. But there was plenty of chanting as the sun reached its highest point on the shortest day of the last year of the Millennium. To reach an emptier archaeological site, you may have to hitch.

I thought *I'd* had a long and difficult journey but the number plates on the four-wheel drive pick-up that lurched off the highway and on to the hard shoulder showed that its home was in the Canadian province of Ontario. The owner, Carlos, and his family had packed into the 4x4 in Toronto, 3,000 miles away, and driven furiously through the Canadian and Midwestern midwinter to feel the warmth of the Texan, Mexican, Guatemalan sun – and the welcome from their family.

It would have been (a) not funny and (b) plain rude to ask Carlos if he worried that the vehicle might live up to his name, but loss of cars is a serious problem in El Salvador. Indeed, many things are a serious problem in El Salvador, but that does not stop tens of thousands of Salvadoran expatriates returning, all steel and chrome and dollars, to escape the misery of the northern winter and visit relations. In the north, they tend to live on the fringes, driving taxis, pumping gas or making pupusas for the Salvadoran community. In the south, their relative wealth makes them central to the community – and the economy. El Salvador would not have rebuilt so fast were it not for the dollars being pumped in from expatriates in the USA and Canada.

For Carlos' children, who had grown up speaking barely accented Canadian English, the journey 'home' was a traumatic one. Not simply for the four gruelling days on the road and the three tough border crossings – but because of the inevitable tension between those who have remained behind, to maintain the vestiges of traditional El Salvadoran life, and those who have settled in a land of rather more opportunity than this.

Not that they were letting this cultural clash impinge upon their enjoyment of El Salvador's most notable piece of human history. Joya de Cerén, a short distance east of San Andrés and south of San Juan Opico, was discovered in 1976. It is a Mayan town preserved by the layer of ash that resulted from an eruption of the nearby Laguna Caldera volcano in AD600. Beneath the swirling layers of volcanic dust, which buried them six metres (20ft) deep, the ancient adobe houses seem to have melted into position. Their gently curved walls seem waxen, with only the stern angles of the occasional doorframe suggesting the presence of man.

The site was uncovered by labourers preparing the ground to build silos for the national agricultural organisation. They chanced upon some remains of a Mayan town. Work was halted while the excavation was made. Most of it has been covered by a succession of big tin sheds. The silos, by the way, were built anyway adjacent to the site. In the tin shed which serves as a museum, some of the minutiae of daily life is on display. Fossilised maize, carbonised chilis and petrified beans show that the basic meso-American cuisine remains the same. Inside some storage jars, ancient pests – including ants and rats – were discovered. Other objects found include pots, kitchen utensils and agricultural tools.

Like Pompeii, a moment of antiquity has been frozen in time by volcanic ash. Unlike Pompeii, you cannot wander around quite in the footsteps of citizens from more than a millennium ago. But also unlike Pompeii, there are no crowds, unless Carlos and his family can be so described.

There is one more detour on the journey to the capital. **El Boquerón** (the big hole) is the common name for San Salvador volcano (1,943m/6,375 feet). Whatever you call it, the peak offers spectacular views and has an awesome crater, which is about 1,500 feet (450m) deep. Trees grow on the inner slopes; at the bottom, there is another much smaller black crater.

Having made the steep, mile-long climb from the road to the edge of the main crater you should walk the two-mile circumference of the rim, which takes a couple of hours. Walking in a clockwise direction the path gets steadily rougher but is not difficult. For more excitement – but without the magnificent views – you can go down into the crater itself.

El Boquerón is 11km (seven miles) along a rough road which heads north from the centre of Santa Tecla, also known as Nueva San Salvador. Bus 103 leaves from the town every hour for the volcano; try to visit as early as possible since the last bus back leaves at 3pm. Alternatively, if you come down El Boquerón feeling hot, sweaty and tired, continue six kilometres (four miles) along the road west of Santa Tecla by bus or hitching to **Los Chorros**, a beautiful gorge where a series of waterfalls forms pools where you can swim. There are also trails in the surrounding forest and gardens. Los Chorros is a Turicentro (with camping facilities), so avoid the weekends. From here there are direct buses to the Occidente terminal in San Salvador, taking about 30 minutes.

San Salvador: a city in need of salvation

Arriving at San Salvador causes a nerve-tingling excitement, only part of which is due to terror at arriving in one of Central America's more dangerous capitals, and the alarm of plunging into the soup of smog that fills the basin in which the city is located. When you can properly see it, San Salvador is one of the most stunning cities anywhere, draped over breathtaking volcanic terrain where churches and monuments vie for space with the slums and mansions of the city's one million inhabitants.

San Salvador has had a disturbed history. It was founded in April 1525 when Pedro de Alvarado, who played a leading role in the Spanish conquest of El Salvador, commissioned his cousin Diego to establish a settlement. The city was built near the city of Suchitoto, just south of the Cerrón Grande Lake. The soil in this area proved to be of poor quality, however, and in 1540 San Salvador was moved to the banks of the Río Acelhuate in the shadow of San Salvador volcano. This move was ill-advised, since the valley proved to be a centre of seismic activity. The worst earthquake to hit San Salvador occurred in 1854, when the city was completely destroyed. The capital was rebuilt on a new site nearby which was itself devastated by another earthquake in 1986.

The centre of San Salvador, like that of Managua, still bears the scars of this last earthquake. Most of the once-fine squares, boulevards and colonial buildings are little more than a memory, and there are still thousands of people living in temporary housing. As you approach the capital you pass row upon row of prefabricated huts perched precariously and incongruously in ravines. As a result, it is hard to appreciate fully San Salvador's setting, surrounded on every side by mountains and volcanoes. The city's altitude 680m (2,240 feet) above sea level means temperatures are high during the day but pleasantly low at night.

Ten years of civil war, abetted by earthquakes and pollution, helped reduce San Salvador to a run-down, chaotic and overcrowded city. Many of the capital's finest buildings suffer from neglect, and you are sure to encounter some dwellings that are nothing but empty shells. If you head up the hill into the western districts, however, it is hard to believe that you are in the same city. A juxtaposition of wealth and poverty is the hallmark of most capital cities, but it is particularly pronounced in San Salvador. The western zone is taken up largely by residential areas where huge villas lurk behind unfriendly iron gates, and the clean, shady streets are virtually devoid of people.

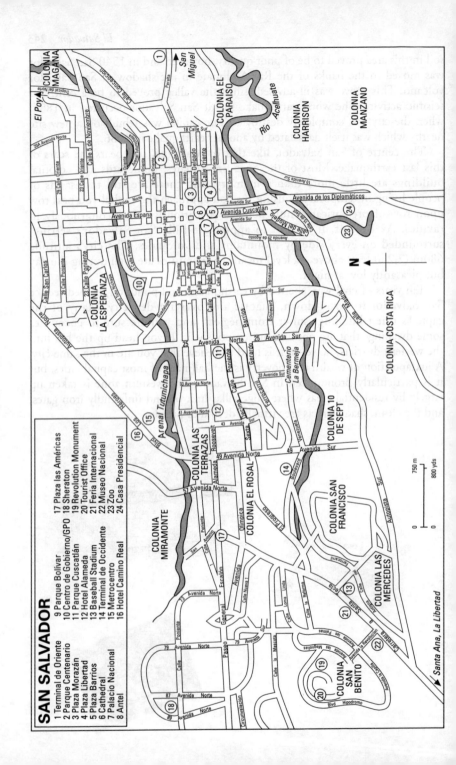

City essentials

Getting your bearings

A map of San Salvador presents a daunting prospect. It looks as though the usual grid pattern has been first stretched east-west, then contorted. There is, however, a logical system behind the layout which works well as far as the grid network lasts. Avenidas run north to south and calles east to west, with four main thoroughfares meeting at the centre, just north of Plaza Barrios. These are Calle Delgado which runs west into Calle Arce, and Avenida Cuscatlán which runs north into Avenida España. Even-numbered avenidas are east of the main Cuscatlán-España axis, odd-numbered ones are west. They are referred to as Norte or Sur, according to their position north or south of Calles Delgado and Arce. Similarly, even-numbered calles are found south of the Calles Delgado and Arce, and odd-numbered are north. Calles west of the central avenidas are called Poniente, and those east Oriente. Thus 17 Avenida Sur is west of Avenida Cuscatlán and south of Calle Arce, while 23 Calle Oriente is east of Avenida España and north of Calle Delgado.

The Pan-American Highway goes right through the middle of San Salvador, under a variety of names as it progresses west to east. The Highway approaches from the southwest as Carretera a Santa Tecla (the town immediately west of the capital), through rich residential areas. Anyone wanting to avoid the city centre can follow directions east along Autopista Sur or Boulevard Venezuela, both of which loop around the south of the city.

The Highway continues until it joins the main west-east axis at the Plaza las Américas. It continues as Avenida F D Roosevelt through the downtrodden city centre, where at Avenida Gustavo Guerrero it heads two blocks north then east along Alameda Juan Pablo II, which eventually turns into the Boulevard del Ejército Nacional. The continuation of Avenida Roosevelt, which is indisputably San Salvador's main street, turns into Calle Rubén Darío (named after Nicaragua's national poet).

As in other Central American cities, suburbs or districts are referred to as colonias. There is little need to know the names of individual districts, although certain colonias have a definite identity. For example, colonias Mejicanos and Zacamil – in northern San Salvador – are some of the worst slum areas. In contrast, El Escalón and San Benito, on the slopes of San Salvador volcano west of Plaza Las Américas, are the most exclusive residential areas in the capital, with mansions, embassies and armed guards.

The most useful free map of San Salvador is on the reverse of the map produced by the tourist office, although it covers only the central area and is poorly printed. The Esso map of Central America, sometimes available from the tourist office, includes a plan of the whole city and can help you to get your bearings.

Arrival and departure

Two bus stations co-ordinate transport to and from destinations around El Salvador. These are the Terminal de Oriente on Boulevard del Ejército Nacional, at the end of Avenida Peralta; and Terminal de Occidente, off Boulevard

Venezuela. It is usually clear which station you will need to go to, but the logic behind the system sometimes fails. The correct terminal for a particular destination is indicated in the text; check before setting off if you are in any doubt. Those wishing to take an international bus to Guatemala City should go to the Terminal de Occidente (224 4083; 223 2784) from where a variety of companies operate. Melva y Pezzarossi buses (the most efficient) leave San Salvador at 5.30am, 7.30am, 8.30am, 10am, 11am, noon and 2pm daily.

Both bus stations are well served by city buses: numbers 4, 27 and 34 for Occidente, and 4 and 29 for Oriente (you do not need to be a genius to work out that bus 4 connects them both). Once at the station you should have no difficulty finding the right bus, since boys dispatched by drivers in search of passengers make bee-lines for foreigners and will probably offer to carry you and your baggage to make sure you get on their bus. Except on international services there is no need to buy tickets in advance, and both stations are so crowded that you would do well to delay your arrival until just before the departure time of the selected service (the only danger being that you may not get a seat).

Getting around

Away from the downtown area, make the most of the excellent city buses. These are not usually too crowded, simply because there are so many of them. There is a constant stream of buses running the length of the main thoroughfares, and getting the hang of them makes San Salvador much less daunting. Destinations are written up on the windscreen and fares within the city are 20c-40c.

Some of the most useful bus routes (and the locations of the most central bus stop on each) are as follows:

Terminal de Oriente: 4, 29 (11 Avenida Norte and 3 Calle Poniente).

Metrocentro, Paseo Escalón: 29 (Alameda Juan Pablo II and 17 Avenida Norte).

Terminal de Occidente: 27, 34 (7 Avenida Sur and 4 Calle Poniente).

Feria Internacional – Museo Nacional: 34 (7 Avenida Sur and 4 Calle Poniente).

The other main bus routes are:

2: Avenida Cuscatlán – Calle del Modelo – Zoo
5: Estadio Cuscatlán
30: Hotel Camino Real – Metrocentro
42: Plaza las Américas – Terminal de Oriente
101: Plaza las Américas – Avenida de la Revolución – Santa Tecla

As with anywhere, a shortcut is to find a friendly local and place your problem in their hands. Parque Centenario, the square on 10 Avenida Norte and Alameda Juan Pablo II, is a major stopping place for many city buses, and a good place to begin whatever your final destination.

Taxis are yellow and in plentiful supply. Meters are not used so you should negotiate the fare before embarking. Within the city centre you shouldn't pay more than C10, unless you are travelling at night, in which case it may be double that.

A room

The main problem in San Salvador is finding somewhere you can afford which feels safe. At the bottom of this scale is **La Hacienda** (Alameda Roosevelt 2937, tel 245 2463, fax 245 2464), which charges C100/C150 for a single/double. Alameda Roosevelt has seen more prosperous days, but it is a relatively safe area to stay in, and there is a good choice of restaurants within walking distance of the hotel. **Hotel Alameda** (43 Avenida Sur and Alameda Roosevelt, tel 260 0299, fax 260 3011, hotelalameda.com) in western San Salvador is more expensive and is priced in dollars, but offers good value with single/double rooms for $65/$70 with a vast breakfast. The rooms are comfortable and have a private bathroom, air-conditioning and hot water. There is also a swimming pool and bar.

The top international class hotel is the **Sheraton** (89 Avenida Norte) which hit the headlines in 1989 when some Americans were held hostage here by the FMLN. More friendly is the **Camino Real** on Boulevard de los Héroes, frequented by foreign journalists and business executives. Also in this area, former rebels have set up guest houses complete with Che and Castro memorabilia.

Some cheaper hotels are grouped on and around Calle de Concepción, northeast of Plaza Barrios; the area does have a reputation for being rough, however, so be wary about venturing out after dark. **Hotel San Carlos** (Calle de Concepción 121, tel 222 8975) is a pleasant place in an unpleasant location, and has rooms from C80-C160. A rather more salubrious area is that northwest of the centre, although the streets are often eerily empty. The **Hotel American Guest House** (17 Avenida Norte 119; tel 271 0224, fax 271 3667) is friendly and has good facilities, including a laundry, library, restaurant and left luggage. The rooms – with private bathroom – cost C150 (single), C160 (double) and C200 (triple). The **Hotel Family Guest House** (1 Calle Poniente and 17 Avenida Norte, tel 221 2349, fax 222 9252,) is clean and also recommended.

A meal

Looking for breakfast downtown tends to involve a search for somewhere which is open but is not a fast food joint. Your best bet is to go down the smaller back streets where you will find simple restaurants serving pupusas, tamales, scrambled eggs, etc.

For lunch and dinner it is well worth going a little upmarket, since San Salvador has some restaurants which provide excellent value; cheaper places tend to be plain grotty. The biggest choice is at the huge Metrocentro shopping complex northwest of the city centre. **Rancho Alegre** is an open-air 'food bazaar', where you select your dishes from numerous competing counters. Most of the city's middle class seems to eat here. Nearby are some conventional restaurants, ranging from hamburgers to Chinese. The most upmarket eateries are in San Benito and along Paseo Escalón (El Escalón's main street). More convenient, however, are the less pretentious bars and restaurants on Alameda Roosevelt.

The last cathedral of the 20th century

Earthquakes and war have curtailed any man-made beauty that San Salvador might have achieved, but the Plaza Barrios – the central square on the eastern side of Avenida Cuscatlán – is the place where the city begins to reclaim some sense of civic pride, even though it is often buried beneath an indignity of pigeons.

The plaza is named after General Gerardo Barrios, a former president of the Republic who died in 1909; a statue of him stands in the centre of the square. On the west side is the Palacio Nacional, built during the first decade of the 20th century, and housing a number of government offices. To the north, and dominating Plaza Barrios, is the huge Catedral Metropolitana. The original mother church for El Salvador was built in the 1880s, but suffered considerable damage from fire, earthquakes and the occasional trigger-happy soldier.

For the past decade or more, it has been difficult for the passer-by to determine whether the cathedral is in the process of construction or destruction. Finally, in July 1999, the place was completed – and the effect on the square, and the city, has been immense.

The Metropolitan Cathedral is best visited in early afternoon, when the sun strikes the simple-yet-eloquent facade. Mosaics of Mayan motifs run around the entrance arch, framed by two tall towers each topped in indigo and gold. Awesomely airy and cool, the interior consists of a simple rectangular – almost square – floor plan, a couple of side chapels the size of barns and a semicircle surrounding the altar to the north. On this hemisphere, two tiers of six huge frames depict biblical events. But outer ones – four in all – have been left empty.

As the traffic howls by outside, people queue quietly for confession, or simply wonder at the spiritual calm induced by the last cathedral to be consecrated in the second millennium. The floor is of polished grey marble with a maroon compass at the centre. There is just one stained-glass window, above the main entrance. Much more visual interest is focussed on the halo of angels hovering over the silver and marble altar. At the centre, a *trompe l'oeil* depicting a fantastical ascent to heaven from what looks like a Salvadoran village, boasts a lion, an elephant and some African people.

It's not Italy, but it is impressive. Only the already shabby garden chairs in place of pews spoil the effect.

Exploration

Until the cathedral was completed, perhaps the most impressive building – and certainly the best preserved – was the neoclassical **National Theatre**, built in 1917, east of Plaza Barrios on Calle Delgado. It contains a main auditorium and four smaller halls; the lavish marble, velvet and crystal of the interior recall better days.

Beyond the cathedral and theatre, the quality of the tourist experience in San Salvador deteriorates rapidly. **Plaza Libertad**, on 4 Avenida Sur and 2 Calle Oriente, is something of a shrine to José Matías Delgado, a leader of the Central American independence movement. At the centre stands a monument to liberty, facing the church of El Rosario on the eastern side. Delgado's tomb is housed in this most unusual church, whose interior is a bizarre mixture of modern and traditional styles. To Delgado and to the other men who led the 1811 rebellion, is dedicated the Monumento a los Próceres de 1811, next door to the Palacio Municipal, on the south side of Plaza Libertad. Nearby, on 10 Avenida Sur and Calle Modelo, is the church of La Merced. Its bell (still in position) was rung by Delgado on 5 November 1811 to call for independence.

On the Avenida de la Revolución, a broad, tree-lined boulevard off the Carretera a Santa Tecla, you reach the **Museo Nacional David J. Guzman**, named after the naturalist who was its first director. The museum is small but worthwhile. Its main collection is devoted to archaeology and includes some fine pre-Columbian artifacts from all over the country. Among them are *metates* (grinding stones), stelae, and the Xipe Totec ('Our Lord of the Flayed Hide') found near Tazumal. Xipe Totec was the Maya/Toltec god of fertility and penitential torture, and is represented by a life-size figure of a priest wearing the skin of a human killed in sacrifice. Dating from the 12th or 13th century, the figure has been spoilt by bad restoration. There is also an interesting collection of objects dating from the colonial and post-independence era. These include portraits of important figures of the independence movement, and the bell from La Merced church (see Plaza Libertad). The museum is open 9am-noon and 2pm-5pm, Tuesday to Sunday, admission free.

Continuing north up Avenida de la Revolución from the Museo Nacional, you reach the smart residential area of **Colonia San Benito**. At the top of the hill is the Monument to the Revolution, a huge Soviet-style structure depicting an heroic athlete; from the grassy area just opposite there is a fine view of the city and a close-up of some of the city's worst shanty towns. Back down the hill, the first road you reach is Boulevard del Hipódromo. Heading left takes you to the so-called Zona Rosa. This is a supposedly fashionable area of boutiques, street cafés, restaurants and nightclubs, patronised by the wealthy; it is without character and lacks appeal.

A night out

While in San Salvador, don't stay out drinking until the early hours. Unless your hotel is within easy reach of a local bar or you can afford to travel everywhere by taxi, you would do well not to go wandering around at night looking for some cosy spot in which to drink or dance the night away. There are some pleasant bars at the western end of Alameda Roosevelt which are among the few places that stay open beyond 9pm. They are often crowded, lively and friendly. For more upmarket entertainment head up to the Zona Rosa in San Benito, where there are bistros with live music and a few clubs;

most of the clubs admit guests only with members. In the dodgier parts of town, 'juke-box' dance halls are the norm.

For alternative entertainment consult the daily newspapers which list films showing locally. A lot of American films are shown, with Spanish subtitles, but most of them are macho movies of the kind you see incessantly on Mexican buses. More cultured amusements may be found at the Teatro Nacional on Plaza Barrios, though the schedule of plays, recitals and ballets is erratic. The National Symphony Orchestra performs a season of concerts here between July and December. Ask at the tourist office for programmes. If you're confined to your hotel room, listen to some of the stations on the FM dial; San Salvador has the best selection in Central America. Salsa is on 89.0 and 96.2; Latin slush on 94.6 and 105.0; Western pop oldies on 91.3 and 93.0; more modern rock on 92.2 and 97.0; and jazz on 93.8.

A game

You can hear **soccer** commentaries in Spanish on 106.6FM. The main venue for football matches is the Estadio Nacional Flor Blanca which is south of Alameda Roosevelt between 45 and 49 Avenida Sur. Fixtures are listed in the daily newspapers; most matches are held on Wednesdays and Sundays in the afternoon. The other football stadium is the Estadio Cuscatlán, east of the University of Central America in southwest San Salvador. **Baseball** enthusiasts can see matches at the stadium on Calle Las Mercedes, opposite the Feria Internacional on the Santa Tecla road. Basketball is popular, and both national and international games are held in the Gimnasio Nacional just east of the Flor Blanca stadium. A little further east is the Parque Cuscatlán, which is a lovely park and the best place to recuperate between forays into the congested streets of the centre.

A shopping expedition

Besides the street stalls that fill many of the streets in central San Salvador, there are two main markets – the Mercado Cuartel, and the Mercado Central. The **Mercado Cuartel** lies a few blocks east of Plaza Barrios, on Calle Delgado and 8 Avenida Norte. The market is huge and the majority of the stalls sell crafts, including woven hammocks, leather goods, textiles, pottery, etc. from all over the country. Even if you don't want to buy anything, you should come here to browse. This is the place to buy an FMNL T-shirt with which to impress your friends.

The **Central Market** is off Calle Gerardo Barrios, near 5 Avenida Sur and 6 Calle Poniente. It is a two-storey concrete building resembling a massive garage. This is the best place to go to see the locals bargain, since food is the main commodity on sale here. Inside is a maze of stalls with carcasses strung up all around. Traders spill over on to the streets, and shoppers laden with bags block the pavements.

The **Mercado Nacional de Artesanías**, where craftsmen from all over the country gather, may be a better place to buy handicrafts if you are concerned about quality; you should, of course, expect to pay a slightly higher price. The market is in the Feria Internacional on the right off the Carretera a Santa Tecla, virtually opposite the baseball stadium.

The largest shopping complex in San Salvador is the **Metrocentro**, along Boulevard de los Héroes, opposite the Hotel Camino Real. It is claimed to be the biggest shopping centre in Central America. Shops here and in other complexes are open 8am-noon and 2pm-6pm, closed Sunday.

A word of advice

The least helpful tourist office in Central America is right on the main street at Calle Rubén Darío 619 (tel: 222-8000/2220960). Unfortunately it no longer welcomes tourists, and instead you will be despatched to an office miles away in the suburbs: the Corporación Salvadoreña de Turismo is at Boulevard del Hipódromo 508, in Colonia San Benito (tel: 243-7835).

Embassies and Consulates. *US*: Final Boulevard Santa Elena Sur, Antiguo Cuscatlán (tel: 278 4444).

UK: Edificio Inter Inversión, Paseo General Escalón 4828, Colonia Escalón (tel: 263-6520/263-6527/263-6529). Open Monday to Friday, 8am-1pm and 2pm-4.30pm; consular matters are only dealt with in the morning. The embassy is a long way up Paseo General Escalón (catch bus 52) and lies on the corner of 83 Avenida Norte.

Costa Rica: Calle Cuzcatlán 4415, Colonia Escalón (tel: 264-3863).

Guatemala: 15 Avenida Norte 135 and Calle Arce (tel: 222 2903).

Honduras: 89 Avenida Norte, between 7 and 9 Calle Poniente 561, Colonia Escalón (tel: 263-2808).

Nicaragua: 71 Avenida Norte 164, Colonia Escalón (tel: 224-1223).

Panama: 55 Avenida Norte, Alameda Roosevelt 2838 (tel: 260-5453).

Keeping in touch

A message

Reflecting the relatively small number of travellers to El Salvador, the capital – like the country – is short of internet cafés. There is one in the Metrocentro, and much talk of others springing up in San Benito and around the University.

A stamp

The main post office is at the Centro de Gobierno. Open 8am-5pm Monday to Friday, 8am-noon on Saturday. Stamps sold at windows 4-11, poste restante at window 19. Black market moneychangers outside, Banco Cuscatlán inside.

A call

The biggest telephone bureau is the crumbling office block on Calle Rubén Darío at 5 Avenida Sur. It opens 5am-10pm for international telephone calls, but most people just come here to pay their domestic phone bills. There is another office in the Centro de Gobierno, but these days most long-distance and overseas telephone calls are made from payphones using pre-paid cards.

An emergency
Police – 243 0387. American Express: Carretera Santa Tecla, km 4.5, corner Condominio La Mascota, local I (tel: 279-3844).

A day out – three options

Because of the compactness of El Salvador, you could easily base yourself in the capital and make a succession of excursions into the surrounding countryside. These three ideas will take you into the hills, to an Indian village and to a crater lake. Besides these ideas, you could also consider an outing to La Libertad or the Costa del Sol – see the Coastal Highway section.

Parque Balboa and La Puerta del Diablo

Going south from the city centre along Avenida Cuscatlán and Avenida los Diplomáticos, you pass close by both the Presidential Palace and the **zoo**. The latter, on Calle Modelo, claims to be the most modern in Central America and is open Wednesday to Sunday, 9.30am-5pm.

South of the zoo, the road heads uphill into an area known as Planes de Renderos, a shady residential area with some fine houses. Twelve kilometres (seven miles) from San Salvador is **Parque Balboa**, 1,200m (3,900 feet) above sea level. This beautiful park is not too spoilt by the fact that it is a Turicentro, although it is busy at the weekends. There are paths through the gardens and woods, and you can get a wonderful view of San Salvador and Lake Ilopango from the north-facing observation point called El Gran Mirador.

Beyond Parque Balboa the road continues a short distance to the summit of **Cerro Chulo**, and the rock formation known as the Puerta del Diablo or Devil's Door. It consists of two craggy rocks which form a giant gateway framing a fine view of the valley. You can climb further up for more extensive views, taking in San Vicente volcano to the east, Izalco and Santa Ana volcanoes to the west, and the Pacific to the south. At the base of the mountain is the Indian village of Panchimalco (see below). People are warned not to go up to the Puerta del Diablo on their own since muggings are common.

There are regular buses from San Salvador. Bus 12 (destination Mil Cumbres) goes to both Parque Balboa and La Puerta del Diablo and leaves from the east side of the Mercado Central (Avenida 29 de Agosto and 12 Calle Poniente). A cab will take you there for around C40.

Panchimalco

This old Indian village is 14km (nine miles) south of San Salvador, and is one of the most interesting excursions. The inhabitants of the village are Pancho Indians who are directly descended from the Pipiles. Nearby, at the base of Cerro Chulo, are some enormous boulders which, according to the locals, were rolled down the hill by Indians to stop the advance of the Spanish conquistadores. It is more likely, however, that the boulders were brought down by streams flowing down the mountainsides.

Thank goodness it's not like that anymore

Emily Hatchwell first visited El Salvador in 1990, when large areas of the country were in the hands of the guerrillas, and life proved extremely difficult for the traveller:

'The typical Salvadoran soldier is described by the locals as a *chafarote* – a combination of words meaning falseness and filth. The army has a poor reputation as undisciplined and vicious, with a penchant for using loaded guns to threaten innocent citizens.

'As a rule, in the areas where the guerrillas are strong, the army controls the main towns while the FMLN has a firm grip of the country. Whether you travel by bus, hired car, or hitching, be prepared for roadblocks set up by the army. For example, while along the Troncal del Norte (which traverses the disputed department of Chalatenango) the military stop all vehicles and searches are taken seriously. Along the coastal highway, checks tend to be cursory and spasmodic. The number and intensity of roadblocks is in proportion to the level of conflict in the area at any given time.

'As in Belfast or Colombia, the locals are wearily accustomed to the procedures. Bus passengers are required to get off the bus, and men and women line up in separate rows by the side of the road, documents in hand. If there has been a spate of serious attacks in the area, there may be body searches, although foreigners are often spared this indignity. Mixed foreign couples are usually allowed to stand together (in the men's line). Old women and young children are sometimes allowed to stay on the bus. Luggage is left on board, and soldiers get on to the bus to peruse it; watch them carefully since they are notoriously dishonest.

'The checkpoints also give the military the opportunity to recruit Salvadoran men into the army by force and to apprehend anyone they don't like the look of. Foreign travellers have little to fear as long as they have their passports. Many soldiers are teenagers sporting Rambo-style headbands who go around posing in the back of lorries, armed to the hilt. It is not always easy to remain calm at the prospect of a gun-toting teenager with your fate in his hands.

'The FMLN guerrillas have sporadic campaigns of warning traffic to avoid certain roads or risk attack. This tactic, like the sabotage attacks on the communications and power networks, is aimed at paralysing the country. The FMLN gives ample warning before these campaigns, by announcing the ban a few days in advance on Radio Venceremos, the rebel radio station. The locals are sure to warn you about the existence of a traffic ban, but the fact that the buses are not running is a sure enough sign that you shouldn't venture on to the selected road. Check carefully if you aren't sure; since the transport companies are private, the odd one continues to operate despite the warnings, simply because they can't afford not to.'

Panchimalco's proximity to the capital means that visitors are commonplace, but they have not destroyed the charm of the village. The people live in adobe houses which line the irregular cobbled streets. Some of the Indians, particularly the older women, continue to dress traditionally in brightly-coloured skirts and blouses and locally made headscarves (pañuelas). In the main square is a 15th-century church which shows an interesting blend of Spanish and Indian styles. Notice the fine woodcarvings inside and the bell's inscription commemorating the Holy Roman Emperor Charles V. Beneath the huge ceiba tree is a small market with stalls displaying cloth woven locally. In May, Panchimalco celebrates its so-called Palm Festival.

Bus 17 from the Mercado Central (Avenida 29 de Agosto and 12 Calle Poniente) in San Salvador leaves for Panchimalco about once an hour, taking 45 minutes. If you are in your own car, you can reach Panchimalco by turning off the road between Puerta del Diablo and Balboa Park.

Lake Ilopango

Fourteen kilometres (nine miles) east of San Salvador is **Lake Ilopango**, the largest crater lake in the country, measuring 72 square kilometres (28 square miles). The water level has risen and fallen dramatically in the past as a result of seismic activity, but the lake seems calm nowadays. The Indians of the pre-colonial era believed the area to be inhabited by gods, and it is said that every year four virgins were sacrificed in the hope that it would bring a good harvest. Virgins these days can come to the lake without fear of being drowned by Indian priests, but everyone would be advised to avoid the weekends when Salvadorans flood here from the capital and surrounding area. The lake manages to retain something of its ethereal atmosphere during the week, however, especially in the early morning or late afternoon.

The beaches are pleasant for lazing around but the water is dirty. It is possible to arrange waterskiing and other watersports, but the best and cheapest pastime is to go out on the lake in a dugout; boats can be hired by the hour.

From 2 Avenida Norte and Plaza Morazán in San Salvador catch bus 15 which is marked Apulo and goes via Ilopango airport. Visits to Lake Ilopango are best done as day trips, although there are hotels around the lake, and the Turicentro Apulo has camping facilities. By the shore are lots of restaurants, most of which serve fish caught from the lake; try the excellent crab soup.

A worthwhile diversion: the San Salvador bypass

A detour to superb Pacific beaches and characterful fishing ports

If those appeal more than the frenetic capital and rugged interior, then the answer is the coastal highway. The *Carretera Litoral* stretches from the western end of El Salvador to the east. It runs right from the Guatemalan border via Acajutla, La Libertad and Usulután to La Unión in the east. The road follows the shoreline for part of the way – principally west of La Libertad where the coast is rockier and more dramatic than further east. The coastal highway runs roughly parallel to the Pan-American, and since numerous roads connect the two it is easy to hop between them.

La Costa del Balsamo

This is the name given to the section of coast between the port of Acajutla and La Libertad. The balsam trees after which the coast is named are not as abundant as in the past, but continue to be used in the manufacture of medical drugs and cosmetics. Balsam resin was erroneously called balsam of Peru when it was first shipped to Europe after the Spanish conquest. At that time El Salvador was just a small territory within Guatemala and was unknown in Europe. Europeans were more familiar with Peru and somehow the misunderstanding that balsam originated there grew up. In those days it was used as a base for perfume and soap, as well as a medicine. It became a prize export, in demand not only among the Spanish and other Europeans, but also by battle-worn pirates who welcomed its pain-relieving properties.

The port of **Acajutla** is eight kilometres (five miles) south of the coastal highway and 53 miles (85km) west of San Salvador; it is accessible by bus 207 from Occidente terminal. It is an industrial town and is not particularly pleasant, but there are a number of beaches nearby. Playa Barra de Santiago, El Salvador's westernmost beach, about 24km (15 miles) west of Acajutla, is probably the best in the area although it is very busy during holiday time. Playa Metalio, nearer the town, is also good. Both beaches are popular among surfers.

Midway between Acajutla and La Libertad, the highway begins to twist and turn along the foot of the mountains which reach almost to the sea. Fine views of rocky promontories and cliffs, enchanting coves and the ocean make this the finest stretch of the entire coastal road. About 55km (35 miles) east of Acajutla, a road to the left (opposite Playa Shalpa) leads to the village of **Jicalapa**. There is a pleasant church, but the village is most famous for its festival in honour of St Ursula, held on 2-4 November.

Shortly after this turn-off, you reach the attractive Playa El Zonte. Stay on the coastal highway, though, to reach El Salvador's version of The Beach. **Playa El Zunzal** is eight kilometres (five miles) west of La Libertad, and has excellent surf; it is considered to be one of the best surfing beaches along the Pacific coast. The existence of a colony of semi-resident Americans here supports this claim.

Once a thriving port, **La Libertad** has been superseded by Acajutla to the west. The town has seen better days (borne out by several large, abandoned hotels) but a good deal of fishing still goes on and La Libertad has become a popular seaside resort. North Americans who sail up and down the Pacific Coast have begun to settle in the area, building themselves huge and luxurious villas. Their tranquillity was disturbed by FMLN incursions in the November 1990 offensive, but life has now returned to drowsy near-normality.

Puerto La Libertad, as it is officially but rarely known, is not an ordinary resort. Instead it is more like California with character, where you can watch real fishermen mending real nets on the waterfront, and where cows roam on the beach alongside the locals who are searching for crabs. Away from the bustle of the seafood restaurants overlooking the Pacific, La Libertad resembles any inland town, with its Parque Central and pupusa stalls. There is even a corn exchange, where the local men gather to discuss the latest prices.

Don't miss the fishermen bringing in their catches. Since there is no actual harbour, boats must dock at the pier where a winch is used to haul the boats out of the water. This involves a remarkable piece of timing on the part of the fishermen who, when a wave carries them high enough, must attach the winch's hook to the boat. Once safely landed, the boats are pushed into positions down each side of the pier where the locals arrive in hordes to bargain for the best fish. (Auctions sometimes take place on Sundays.) At any time of day rows of fish are draped over the sides of the boat or are piled up – in a rather unappetising fashion – in huge buckets. The whole chaotic scenario is a marvellous piece of theatre.

La Libertad is 31km (19 miles) south of San Salvador, 45 minutes by bus along Highway CA4. Bus 102 goes direct from the capital to La Libertad; don't be persuaded to take bus 166 which operates on a longer route via Comalapa. Bus 185 runs a direct service from Comalapa and Zacatecoluca. Those arriving at the international airport can take a pick-up to the main road from where it is possible to catch any La Libertad-bound bus. Buses also run direct from Sonsonate (taking four hours) and Santa Tecla.

There are a couple of hotels at the western end of the seafront in La Libertad (try Apartamentos Familias), but the cheaper places are in town. There is also a Turicentro. Seafood restaurants line the waterfront in La Libertad. These range from smart places housed in restored old port buildings, to the cheaper bars near the pier and at the eastern end of the town. Oysters are very popular, and you can also eat octopus and shark. The Nueva Altamar, near the west end of the beach, serves the best seafood in town. Wherever you eat, be prepared to encounter roving troubadours and El Salvador's closest approximation to beach hawkers – in the form of local lads trying to sell bootleg cassettes of abysmal quality, and T-shirts.

The beaches in this area are black volcanic sand and tend to be rather dirty. This is particularly true of Playa del Obispo in La Libertad itself, but if you feel tempted, there are beach huts near the eastern end of the waterfront which you can hire for a few dollars a day. There are better beaches within easy access of La Libertad, some of which have excellent surf. Beware of strong undercurrents, and be warned that sharks make an appearance now and again.

Beaches and Boeings: from La Libertad to Usulután

Playa San Diego is a pleasant beach six miles east of La Libertad. There are bungalows and restaurants here, and numerous private homes belonging to San Salvadorans who escape from the capital at the weekend. Nevertheless, the beach is often deserted during the week. You can walk to a couple of nearby waterfalls – Salto San Antonio and Salto Los Mangos; ask the locals for directions. Buses run to Playa San Diego every 30 minutes from town, although

Mexican hats

The Clock Tower,
Pachuca, Mexico

CHARLOTTE HINDLE

Street directions, Mexico

CHARLOTTE HINDLE

The Aztec Calendar Clock, Mexico City, Mexico

CHARLOTTE HINDLE

Time for a new mural at U.N.A.M, Mexico City, Mexico

SIMON CALDER

The Gran Plaza, Monte Albán, Mexico

Embarkation point for the Sumidero Canyon, Mexico

Fried grasshoppers are a popular snack in Oaxaca, Mexico

Statue in Museo Amparo, Puebla, Mexico

On guard at the Palacio Nacional,
Guatemala City, Guatemala

From Quezaltenango to Panajachel on a crowded 'chicken bus', Guatemala

Metropolitan Cathedral,
San Salvador, El Salvador

The paperboy, San Miguel, El Salvador

San Andrés archaeological site, El Salvador

Coconut seller on Pan-American Highway

Joya de Cerén archaeological site, El Salvador

One-horse petrol station, Rivas, Nicaragua

ANDREW JAMES

Mural in the Parque Central, Estelí, Nicaragua

CHARLOTTE HINDLE

Travelling Pan-American style, Nicaragua

SIMON CALDER

Riding the rapids to Fortuna, Costa Rica

White-faced Capuchin, Manuel Antonio
National Park, Costa Rica

Esquinas Rainforest Lodge, La Gamba, Costa Rica

In the Rainforest, La Gamba, Costa Rica

A billboard heralding the return of the canal, Panama

A brightly painted city bus, Panama City, Panama

A brightly painted city street, Colón, Panama

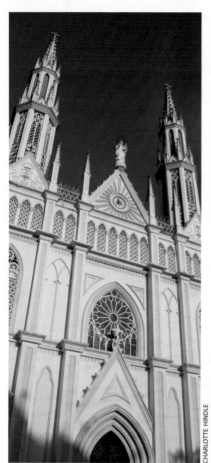

Iglesia del Carmen, Panama City, Panama

La Campāna, San Felipe, Panama City, Panama

Miraflores Locks, near Panama City, Panama

King's Bridge, Panama Vieja, Panama

you can catch any bus heading for Comalapa. Do not get off at the signposted turn (reading San Diego 7km), but ask to be dropped off at the Hacienda San Diego, from where there is an easy track to the beach.

El Salvador's international **airport** is extremely handy for the southern beaches, but not much use if your destination is San Salvador (technically the airport's name), which is 40km (25 miles) away – a vast distance in tiny El Salvador. It is near Comalapa, just south of the coastal highway. It has replaced the old airport at Ilopango, east of San Salvador, which is now used only for domestic and military flights. The airport is well laid-out and even has an observation deck from where you can watch the modest number of arrivals and departures. It has exchange facilities, a next-to-useless tourist desk, agents for Avis, Hertz and Budget car rental, and a post office. There is no left-luggage office, but you may be able to sweet-talk one of the security guards into keeping an eye on your bags if you wish to go off for a while. There are no buses direct from the airport to San Salvador. A taxi to San Salvador costs about C100, C200 after dark. More cheaply, pick-up trucks run a regular service to and from Comalapa. From here you can make onward connections. If you wish to travel east or west along the coastal highway, get dropped off at one of the junctions on this highway.

Thirty-five kilometres (22 miles) east of La Libertad, just beyond El Rosario, a road branches off the main coastal highway and heads south to the so-called **Costa del Sol**; the road takes you past countless cotton plantations. Three beaches – San Marcelino, Costa del Sol and Los Blancos – make up the spit of land known as the Costa del Sol. It overlooks the Pacific on one side, while on the other it faces the Jaltepeque Estuary, where there is a fascinating collection of lagoons, mangrove swamps, and canals. Birdlife and fish thrive here, and it is possible to hire canoes to explore. The hotels organise trips with guides, but it is cheaper and more fun to arrange something directly with the local fishermen who live in stilted houses dotted along the banks. Deep-sea fishing is another popular pastime, but this is expensive.

This part of the Salvadoran coast boasts upmarket accommodation of a standard found nowhere else along the coast. Do not rule out coming here on the grounds of over-commercialism, however. The white-sand beaches are, without doubt, among the finest in the country and this is an interesting section of coast to explore. It is not necessary to stay in the comparatively expensive private cottages and resort hotels since the Costa Del Sol Turicentro has cabañas and poles for hammocks, as well as camping facilities.

Bus 495 runs direct to the Costa del Sol from the Occidente Terminal in San Salvador. If you are already travelling along the coastal highway, get off at the turn-off and hitch or catch another bus. The road goes to La Herradura (where boats can be hired), and the side road to the Costa del Sol leads off to the west some eight kilometres (five miles) to the north of this village.

Continuing east along the coastal highway, you pass through **Zacatecoluca**. It is the capital of La Paz Department and has a population of about 82,000. There is little worth stopping for except lunch – the town has some good pupusa places. Twenty kilometres (12 miles) east of Zacatecoluca, you cross the magnificent Río Lempa. The road now crosses the Puente San Marcos, the old and impressive suspension bridge having been destroyed in the war. Just beyond the bridge a road heads south to the **Península de San Juan del Gozo**, a distance of 22km (14 miles). This is a good alternative to the Costa Del Sol since as well as some impressive beaches, the Bahía de Jiquilisco offers much greater scope for exploration. The lagoon is dotted with islands and mangrove swamps, and is the home of an abundance of fish.

Usulután is the principal town of the department that bears its name, and is the former capital of the ancient Lenca nation of Indians; this busy and dusty town has a population of some 70,000. It is 45km (28 miles) southwest of San Miguel and a similar distance east of Zacatecoluca. Bus 302 runs from San Salvador to Usulután; there are also buses to and from San Miguel that take about 75 minutes. Usulután has a couple of churches worth poking your nose into, and there is an interesting cemetery full of most ornate graves just west of the town on the Zacatecoluca road. Sadly no sign of the Lenca Indian culture remains. There is not much reason to stay overnight, although there are a number of hotels. The best beach within reach of Usulután is Playa El Espino, 22km (14 miles) down a road which branches off the highway 12km (7 miles) east of the town.

If you are heading to La Unión or any of the beaches south of San Miguel, and can't get a bus going direct, get any San Miguel-bound bus and get off at El Delirio, the turn-off where the San Miguel road meets the coastal highway.

Laguna El Jocotal lies just south of the coastal highway about 20km (12 miles) east of Usulután. It is in a beautiful spot, with San Miguel volcano to the north and Cerro el Mono and the coastal hills to the south. A wide variety of birds is found here, resident species including herons, grebes, and various types of duck. The lake is a protected area, but local fishermen are allowed to continue working as long as they do not disturb the birdlife. There is a track around the lake and the warden should be able to arrange for you to hire a canoe. If you catch any bus travelling along this stretch of the coastal highway, ask the conductor to drop you off at the turn-off for El Jocotal, around the 132km mark. The lake is a mile or so down a lava road south of the highway; much of this area was made barren by lava from San Miguel volcano.

Some people consider **Playa El Cuco** to be the finest beach in the country. The broad, sandy beach stretches for six miles and rivals the best in California. The sea is generally clean, and has good waves which make swimming fun. In addition, there has been comparatively little development, and during the week you could well have the whole beach to yourself. Facilities are basic but adequate. On the beach there are simple beach huts made from palm leaves which you can rent. There is also an array of stalls selling freshly cooked seafood and the road down to the beach is lined with seafood restaurants too. In fact you'll be hard pushed to find anything *but* seafood, although there is usually someone cooking pupusas.

The tranquility is disturbed at the weekends, not so much by the busloads and truckloads of people from San Miguel and neighbouring villages, but by the cars which roar recklessly up and down the beach. Watching them zig-zag between the bathers is an alarming experience. Since visitors to El Cuco are day-trippers most of the year, you should not have any problem finding a room in one of the pensiones in the village. Playa El Cuco lies eight kilometres (five miles) south of the coastal highway, at the end of a road which branches off to the right 12km (seven miles) south of the junction with the San Miguel road.

Playa El Tamarindo is a beach in the same class as El Cuco, but is less developed. El Tamarindo is a delightful fishing village on the Gulf of Fonseca, 32km (20 miles) east of El Cuco and 15km (nine miles) south of the coastal highway. The bay of El Tamarindo, with its fine white-sand beach, is one of the most sheltered along the coast. The sea is excellent for swimming if you enjoy calm waters. You should be able to arrange boat trips around the Gulf of Fonseca too. Accommodation is limited, but there are huts where you can hang a hammock. Other pleasant beaches between El Cuco and El Tamarindo are El Icayal 6km (4 miles) south of Intipuca and Las Tunas 5km (3 miles) south of the highway about 10km (6 miles) east of Intipuca.

Transport along this stretch of coastal highway between El Cuco and El Tamarindo is a little more erratic than elsewhere. Some of the buses running this route include the 375 between San Miguel and El Tamarindo via Intipuca and Las Tunas, the 339 between Intipuca and La Unión, and the 383 between La Unión and El Tamarindo. A good deal of communal hitching goes on among the locals and there are plenty of empty trucks around ready to oblige.

After the goldrush

Intipuca was for decades an unremarkable village on the coastal highway, but it is now the richest settlement in El Salvador. In 1970, an Intipuqueño whose marriage had failed went to the USA. He settled in Washington DC, and soon became rich. Encouraged by his example, other townspeople became economic migrants. Nowadays about three-quarters of the population works in the US capital, and they send back remittances which have turned Intipuca into the most affluent place in the country.

East to Honduras

A torrent of traffic ushers you out of the capital, grazing just to the north of Lake Ilopango. On the slopes of a hill known as Cerro Las Pavas, 34km (20 miles) from the capital, is **Cojutepeque** (population 30,000), capital of the Cuscatlán Department. Cojutepeque is dusty and noisy, and has suffered from its location directly on the Highway. From the road the town appears to be nothing but a chaotic bus stop, but its colourful market is one of the best in the region. The daily market spreads out around the church and along the main street. Fresh produce makes up a large part of what is on sale; also look out for the smoked sausages and tongue for which Cojutepeque is famous. Quacks come from around the region to sell all kinds of exotic remedies. Other stalls sell straw hats, pottery and hammocks – the best time to buy handicrafts is during the town's annual fair on 29 August.

To escape the heat of the market, follow the road up Cerro Las Pavas (also known as Cerro de la Virgen) from where there are fine views of the surrounding valleys and mountains. You may be joined by pilgrims who go up the hill to visit the shrine of the Virgin of Fátima, particularly on her feast day, 13 May. The shrine is housed in a cave, and inside are plaques recording the miracles worked by the virgin; outside, tasteless religious trinkets are on sale. Bus 113 for Cojutepeque leaves from San Salvador's Oriente terminal (or catch any bus going along the Highway).

The road improves dramatically beyond El Carmen, east of Cojutepeque. Ten kilometres (six miles) east of Cojutepeque, at San Domingo, a road turns north off the Pan-American Highway and heads three miles north to **San Sebastián**. This delightful town was the scene of serious fighting on occasion during the 1980s, but life has been calm more recently. San Sebastián is famous for its weaving, which is not dissimilar to some Guatemalan textiles. You can watch the locals at work on the looms. Many of the brightly-coloured hammocks and textiles in the markets in San Salvador are made here – and you can buy them without paying extra for the added bonus of some high-pressure sales techniques.

Sixty kilometres (37 miles) east of San Salvador is the town of **San Vicente**. Its setting on the banks of the Río Alcahuapa is one of the best in the country – the view of the valley and San Vicente church as you approach down the hill from the Pan-American Highway is superb. San Vicente is dominated by Chinchontepec volcano (also known as San Vicente) which, at 2,182m, is one of the highest in the country. The town was founded by Spanish settlers in 1635. They had originally set up homes in the surrounding countryside (where they cultivated indigo), but they rode roughshod over the local Indians who in the end forced them to settle elsewhere, in this case San Vicente.

The Parque Central is dominated by a fine 18th-century church, known as El Pilar, which became famous during the Indian rebellion of 1833 when the Indian chief, Anastasio Aquino, used the crown of San José (still in the church) to crown himself King of the Nonualcos here. At the centre of the square is a clock tower which offers an excellent view of the town. For this reason, if you climb further than half way up the first flight of stairs, you will have a soldier armed with a machine gun to contend with. On the western side of the square is a monument recalling the foundation of San Vicente in 1635. This is celebrated in the town's annual festival, which is held on All Saints' Day (1 November).

Bus 116 leaves regularly from Oriente Terminal for San Vicente. The journey takes two hours. If you don't catch a bus going right to San Vicente, get a San Miguel bus or any other eastbound bus and get off at the junction 55km (35 miles) from San Salvador. You should get a lift into town with no trouble, although the views are so good that walking down the hill is also recommended. To continue eastwards, take any bus (or other vehicle) out of San Vicente and catch a San Miguel bus from the bus stop at the top. The last bus to San Miguel or San Salvador passes between 6pm and 6.30pm. There are a few cheap hospedajes along the back streets, but the best place to stay is the Hotel Central Park on the main square.

Northeast of San Vicente, on the other side of the Highway, is **Laguna de Apastepeque**. The small lake lies a short distance along a dirt road which leads north off the Highway east of Apastepeque town. It is a pleasant spot and you can go swimming; there is a Turicentro here, so unless you enjoy crowds avoid the weekend. Eight kilometres (five miles) south of San Vicente, along the road to Tecoluca and beyond to the coastal highway, are the Mayan ruins of Tehuacán.

The journey east of San Vicente towards San Miguel is interesting, especially where the Pan-American Highway crosses the great Río Lempa. There is a fine view of the remains of Cuscatlán suspension bridge, attacked by guerrillas in 1983; the dam at the San Lorenzo power station served as a bridge until the new one was built. Midway between San Vicente and San Miguel a road turns south to Berlín. This is a charming place and is one of the highest villages in El Salvador.

A worthwhile excursion – or a possible diversion for travellers between San Vicente and San Miguel – is to **Chinameca**, a village two miles south of a turn-off from the highway, ten miles west of San Miguel. It is a beautifully quiet place with an enchanting church, gardens and fountains.   If you don't want to return to San Miguel or intend to bypass it altogether, continue south from Chinameca to the coastal highway via San Jorge. This journey takes you through beautiful hilly country dotted with coffee plantations, and gives excellent views of San Miguel volcano. There are buses from San Jorge to Usulután.

Eight kilometres (five miles) before San Miguel, and a short distance along a dirt road north of the highway is **Quelapa**, the site of some archaeological ruins. Quelapa ('stone jaguar' in Lenca) is not outstanding architecturally, consisting of just a few mounds and terraces. Most objects found on the site are now in private collections, although there is a small village museum. The archaeological site stretches from the village of Moncagua (two miles west of Quelapa) to El Obrajuelo, a mile east of Quelapa.

San Miguel

El Salvador's third city (population 170,000) is 85 km (53 miles) east of San Vicente. It is a hot, dusty and rather sprawling place, with little of the charm of San Vicente. San Miguel lies near the foot of Chaparrastique volcano, often referred to as San Miguel volcano. Despite its height of 2,130m, its magnificence is hard to appreciate from the city; only once you head south can you grasp the splendour of one of the country's mightiest volcanoes. Chaparrastique last erupted as recently as 1976.

Founded in 1530, San Miguel contains few great architectural treasures, although the 18th-century cathedral survives. The Parque Central and surrounding streets are alive with stalls during the day. It is a great commercial centre; during the civil war, people came down from the rebel province of Morazán to trade in arms and ammunition.

It is difficult to avoid passing through San Miguel at some stage in your trip through El Salvador. All roads in the east seem to meet here, and buses go in every direction. A good road leads south to the coast, and there are a couple of trips worth doing around San Miguel too. Autumn visitors can join in the festival of the Virgen de la Paz, held from 17-21 November.

Bus 301 leaves frequently from the Oriente Terminal in San Salvador and takes about four hours. Bus 330 from the Honduran border and Santa Rosa runs regularly too. Other services include bus 328 from San Francisco Gotera, 324 from La Unión, 373 from Usulután, 320 from Playa El Cuco, and 345 from El Tamarindo. Last buses generally leave at about 4pm. When catching a bus from San Miguel, if you wish to leave immediately, avoid the terminal and go one block towards the cathedral where most buses pause to fill up with passengers before leaving town. Otherwise you can expect to drive around the block at least once and often twice.

Most of the cheap places to stay are between the Parque Central and the bus station. There is little choice of restaurants in San Miguel, and if you look for food after 9pm you would be lucky to find anywhere open at all. There are a couple of burger joints near the Parque Central, but for a heartier meal try El Gran Tejano. The décor is a little wanting in taste, but the food and atmosphere is good. Expect to pay around C20 for a good feed and a beer.

Moving on from San Miguel

There are three choices. The worst is to head straight along the Highway to El Amatillo, the border with Honduras. Another is to head down to the coast to see the sleepy port of La Unión – that jaunt is described as part of the Coastal Highway section that precedes this. Next, is to take the shorter and more beautiful journey northwest from San Miguel on the Ruta Militar, an old colonial road. This will take you to the lovely town of **Santa Rosa de Lima**, an excellent place to get your last (or first) taste of El Salvador.

Santa Rosa lies 34km (21 miles) northeast of San Miguel and 22km (14 miles) from the Honduran border. Set in the hills, with Ocotepeque volcano to the north, it is an enchanting and relaxed town. In the shady Parque Central with its beautiful colonial church, there are the usual bars where locals while away the hours, gossiping with friends and eyeing up any new arrivals. Santa Rosa is much friendlier and more attractive than San Miguel.

The population of almost 30,000 is joined regularly by Hondurans who come across the border to shop. Santa Rosa is a good place for shopping, since the Parque Central is packed with stalls, one of which has the best choice of hats in this part of El Salvador. The street behind the bus terminal is covered by mountains of luscious fruit.

Buses to Santa Rosa de Lima from San Miguel take about 75 minutes. There is a fair amount of accommodation choice for a town this size, but the best is Hotel Recreo which has spacious and clean rooms, and if you get up early you can get a great view of the sunrise from the roof. The hotel is opposite the ANTEL office a couple of blocks from the Parque Central. Hotelito El Tejano has a decent enough restaurant if you fancy a proper meal, but by far the best eatery in town is a makeshift pupusería called El Hispano. It is a constant hive of activity, with children running about and people arriving in a steady stream to place take-away orders.

La Unión and the islands

One of the most worthwhile detours is to the port of La Unión on the Gulf of Fonseca, 42km (26 miles) southeast of San Miguel. It is a delight to visit in its own right, being a somnolent old fishing port with superb sea views and a laid-back pace – like California, but without the Californians.

It is also worth visiting **Conchagua**, five kilometres (three miles) south of the town, in the shadow of the volcano which gave the town its name. It is the home of one of the few surviving colonial churches in this part of the country. Those willing to cope with a steep climb can also enjoy the magnificent views over the gulf from the top of Conchagua volcano. There is a regular bus service from La Unión, or you can grab a cab for a couple of dollars.

To visit any of the gulf islands – such as Zacatillo, Meanguera and Conchagüita – you must catch a boat from La Unión, but there appears to be no predetermined schedule. Some of the islands have good beaches but beware of sharks. Facilities are almost nil, so take food and a hammock.

Bus 324 runs from San Miguel to La Unión (fare C3). From La Unión, bus 346 to Santa Rosa will take you close to the Honduras border; get off at San Carlos to continue along the Pan-American Highway to the border at the Goascorán river.

The border town, El Amatillo, is 208km (130 miles) from San Salvador. Buses depart for the frontier from Santa Rosa de Lima and San Miguel regularly until 6pm. Minibuses also run the 30-minute ride from Santa Rosa, but these are more expensive. There is a hospedaje at the frontier, but a better place to stay is Santa Rosa de Lima.

The soccer war

As you wait in line to cross the bridge over the River Goascorán, you can at least be grateful that people are not actually shooting at each other.

The so-called soccer war began after a World Cup qualifying match in 1969. Honduras beat El Salvador in Tegucigalpa with a last-minute goal, causing a teenage Salvadoreña so much anguish that she killed herself. She was given a lavish funeral attended by the president and the football squad, and the return leg in San Salvador was played in an atmosphere of pent-up aggression. After El Salvador won that match 2-0, Honduran and Salvadoran troops clashed and air strikes were launched. El Salvador had the edge in the fighting, which lasted for a hundred hours and cost 6,000 lives.

Deep antagonism remains between the two neighbours. Diplomatic ties were restored in 1980, but trade and cultural contact is still limited. The clash did little to stem the flow of Salvadorans to Honduras and other countries – even now, you can meet Salvadorans in every other Central American nation, often hawking the delicious *pupusas* that constitute the national dish.

Honduras

SALVADOREAN FRONTIER - NICARAGUAN FRONTIER

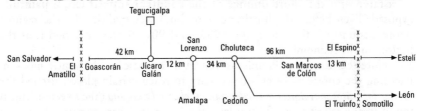

The unlucky country

The northern half of Central America resembles a chicken leg. If you look at the map to verify that it does, you will also see that the route of the Pan-American Highway through Honduras is the nasty, sinewy bit along the shin that no-one ever wants to eat. Honduras is the least-visited country in the region. Most of the people who spend any time here are heading to the great Mayan city of Copán (accessible on an easy day-trip from eastern Guatemala) or for the Bay Islands off the north coast for some diving. These, though, are a long way from the Pan-American Highway.

Honduras, slightly smaller than England and about the size of Pennsylvania, is the second-largest Central American republic after Nicaragua. The country is roughly triangular, its Caribbean coastline stretching 640km (400 miles) while the Pacific shore around the Gulf of Fonseca extends just 64km (40 miles). The Pan-American Highway runs close to the Gulf, then in the latter stages rising into the mountains that dominate much of the country. The mountainous areas are largely forested, an attribute which the Honduran tourism authority has feebly tried to promote as 'the little Switzerland of Central America'. Among other Central Americans, however, Honduras is more commonly – and unfairly – known as the ugliest country in the region. It is certainly the one where faithful adherents to the Highway will spend the least time.

The Panamericana takes the route of (almost) least resistance through Honduras, from a hot and dusty shambles at the frontier with El Salvador to a cool and beautiful highland border crossing into Nicaragua. Along the short journey, you should meet some good people and enjoy a few modest sights, but for a deeper look at Honduras you will need to stray far from the Highway. And the further you stray, the more tragedy you will encounter. There are not too many jokes in this chapter.

Sandwiched between Guatemala to the west, El Salvador to the south and Nicaragua to the east, Honduras has more foreign borders than any other Central American country. Once the political turmoil in each of these neighbours eased, Honduras was poised to profit from its central position on the tourist trail. But it was dealt a brutal blow by Hurricane Mitch in 1998, with at least seven thousand people dying, large amounts of agricultural land devastated and the shortcomings of the country's infrastructure painfully exposed. Even before the hurricane, Honduras was traditionally the region's poorest country – though in the 1980s and 90s Nicaragua joined it at the bottom of the economic heap.

Before the hurricane, Honduras' tourist literature could be gently mocked. Excusing the considerable effort necessary to reach certain places, it cited the saying *los frutos más dulces se encuentran en el árbol más alto* ('the sweetest fruit is found in the tallest tree'). These days, the Honduran harvest seems harder to reach than ever. The country is a long way from being a significant stop on the backpackers' trail, and further still from being slapped all over the pages of tour operators' brochures. But – as the scars heal – the Mayan and colonial heritage, stately mountain ranges and resilient good nature of the people make a case for diverting from the Pan-American Highway.

The storm that wasted a generation

Hurricane Mitch – the fourth-strongest hurricane to hit the region this century – left a trail of devastation throughout Central America at the end of October 1998. Heavy rainfall caused serious flood damage in the Cayman Islands on 25 October; from there the storm veered manically around the Caribbean, increasing in intensity as it did so, to Jamaica, Panama, Cuba and across Central America.

By the time it reached Honduras, Hurricane Mitch had been classified as category 5, one of the strongest ever known; winds blew through the country at 290km/h (180mph), but occasionally gusted to 320km/h (200mph).

First to be hit was the remote northeastern coastal region of Mosquitia, a sparsely-populated area mainly inhabited by Miskito Indians. This area is isolated from the rest of the country by a mountain barrier. Even before the hurricane hit, there were no roads linking Mosquitia with southern Honduras, and transport within the area was almost all by water. Communication was possible only by radio, with no telephones or electricity in the region, and all these factors made the relief operation particularly difficult. The flat terrain provided no natural windbreaks, and so nothing was able to slow the hurricane as it blew along the Mosquito Coast and west towards the Bay Islands. The battering continued for two days, until little was left standing.

Gradually Mitch was downgraded to a tropical storm, but it still had the power to wreak enormous harm. It turned towards the mountains and into central Honduras. This part of the country had already been badly damaged earlier in the year by forest fires. At least 50 Honduran rivers were flooded, one of the worst affected areas being the northern Sula valley, around the country's second city of San Pedro Sula, devastating the banana plantations. In a matter of a few days, over a metre of rain fell on the mountains, and entire villages were flattened by mudslides. The huge problems facing the population were made worse because the hurricane hit during harvest, and almost three-quarters of that year's crop was destroyed. This not only devastated the food supply to the region, but also removed any source of income for the people on the coast.

A state of emergency was declared on 30 October by the country's president, Carlos Flores, who described his country as 'mortally wounded' when he appealed for help from the international community. Other countries in the region – Nicaragua, El Salvador, Belize, Mexico and Costa Rica – were also affected, but Honduras bore the brunt of the devastation. Mitch finally blew itself out over Florida.

In total, more than 17,000 people were reported dead or missing in Honduras alone; throughout the region as a whole, half a million people were either left homeless, or unable to return to their homes until the damage had been repaired. One in five of the population of Honduras was homeless.

The whole of Honduras was declared a disaster area. An international relief operation was put together with money and manpower from around the world, but this was severely hampered because so much infrastructure had been destroyed by Mitch. Bridges were washed away; parts of all the major highways were swept away and blocked by fallen trees; landing strips, where they had existed, became unusable. Heavy flooding eradicated some communities, including parts of the capital, in their entirety.

Looting became a serious problem, exacerbated by the lack of any meaningful police presence in the cities. A curfew was imposed, together with fuel rationing. A cautious estimate of the cost of the damage put the bill for repairing the infrastructure alone at $2 billion; the UN World Food Programme estimated that development in the region would be set back by 20 years as a result of Hurricane Mitch.

At the frontier

This is where you realise just how far Central America is from achieving the goal of a Common Market. What should be a beautiful vista, with a broad river carving through gentle hills against a backdrop of rugged mountains, is shattered by one of the slowest and ugliest frontiers on the planet. The bridge across the Río Goascorán at the border at El Amatillo perches between frontier posts staffed by some of Latin America's more belligerent and inefficient bureaucrats. Consequently, huge delays can be expected by anyone in a private vehicle or a truck, and even long-distance bus services are likely to be slowed down by a few hours.

The local people are wise to this, of course, which is why a neat and informal piece of public transport operates on the El Salvador side of the border. The local buses from Santa Rosa and San Miguel pull up at the end of the queue, wherever that happens to be, and passengers transfer to a small pick-up truck for a C2 ($25c) ride to the border post. It can weave in and out of the mostly stationary traffic to beat the queues. Given the time-saving, the fare is a bargain. But you should still allow plenty of time to get through the formalities, particularly on the Honduran side. If it seems unlikely that you will reach the border in time to complete all the formalities before it closes at 6pm, stay the night in El Salvador, in Santa Rosa de Lima (about 30 minutes from the frontier at El Amatillo) or La Unión (one hour).

Red tape

First, find the concealed window on the Salvadoran side of the river marked *Salida a Honduras*, where you should not have to pay to leave the country – nor, unless you are very unlucky/provocative, should you get your bags searched.

Walking over the bridge across the river should be a pleasure, with the river valley snaking up into the hills to the north, and sliding down into the coastal plain to the south. But it isn't, because you will find yourself squeezed by a procession of trailer trucks (articulated lorries) that are likely to be motionless, but with their engines running.

The walk is the easy bit. On the far side, you will find yourself in a scrum of vehicle owners, bus couriers and pedestrians all trying to get into the tiny office that serves as Migración. Just when you think you are getting to the front, someone will push through ahead of you claiming some pressing need for priority (if you're under time pressure, you could try this trick, too; let me know how you get on.)

When you finally get to the front of the queue, good luck. Many of those crossing the border here are Hondurans on shopping sprees who attract little attention, but travellers can expect a thorough grilling by officials. For a poor country in great need of foreign exchange and hence tourists, Honduras takes a surprisingly aggressive stance towards visitors; you could well have more difficulty entering Honduras than any other Central American country. It is not uncommon for travellers to be turned away because of a stamp in their passport, or because they do not have an onward or return ticket. So take every step possible to avoid problems at the border. If your passport carries evidence of a visit to a politically suspect (i.e. left-wing) country, or a nation that Honduras regards as a 'client state of the former Soviet Union' (such as Syria), you are advised to get a new one.

If you fear your previous record may count against you, consider applying for a visa in advance. The staff at Honduran missions abroad may say you do not need a visa, but you should stress that you have heard of cases of people being turned away without one and try to insist.

Even if you have a 'clean' passport, you may still have to show sufficient funds for their proposed length of stay, typically $50 per day, plus a ticket out of the country. Many travellers simply plan to cut across to Nicaragua using local buses – there is no surface transport for which you can buy tickets in advance. The

Beware of your stamp collection

A Cuban stamp is not likely to help your case – one in my passport was enough to get me turned back from the El Amatillo frontier post. Curiously, shortly after he gave me my marching orders, one of the officials took me aside and explained that if I were to *fly* to the capital, Tegucigalpa, I would probably be allowed in. And so it proved; a mere seven-hour bus trip to San Salvador and a $100 flight later, I was admitted without fuss into Honduras. Another traveller told me later that the advantage of arriving by air is that the procedure required to deport you, involving finding seats on airlines and a couple of hours of form-filling, is much more of a performance. Turning someone away at a land frontier is simple.

Honduran authorities have come up with a bizarre solution: you may be told that you cannot enter Honduras unless you take up the opportunity of a **military escort** through the country, from the border with El Salvador to Nicaragua (or vice-versa). This is a less extravagant prospect than it sounds, involving a member of the Civil Guard being assigned to making sure you drive or take a bus through Honduras by the most direct route. You have to bear the expense, typically $100 plus the cost of the official's meals.

Assuming you avoid this inconvenience, you will face a more modest admission **fee** of around $2, in dollars or the local currency, lempira. No receipts are issued. Other charges may also be made – for baggage inspection, or customs checks carried out on Sundays or 'out of working hours'. There is plenty of scope for abuse.

Normally you will be allowed in for 30 days. You can attempt to **extend your stay** by increments of 30 days, up to a maximum of six months, at immigration offices (La Dirección General de Migración) in the following towns: Tegucigalpa, Comayagua, La Paz, Siguatepeque, Santa Rosa de Copán, San Pedro Sula, Tela and La Ceiba. The process usually involves less hassle if you apply to an office outside the capital. But if you stay more than 30 days, you will have to apply for an **exit visa**. These are obtainable only from the Ministry of Foreign Affairs in Tegucigalpa (Palacio de los Ministerios, Avenida Miguel Paz Barahona and Calle Los Dolores). There is, of course, a fee to pay – about $10. Outside the capital, go to one of the immigration offices listed above.

The duty-free allowance at **customs** is 200 cigarettes, 100 cigars or a generous 500g of tobacco, and two bottles of spirits. **Searches** on both entering and leaving Honduras can be rigorous. Be prepared to unpack all your bags and watch while every possession is minutely examined. If they find anything 'suspicious', be prepared for some in-depth questioning.

Any chance of a decent map?

You probably won't need one. The Pan-American Highway carves a distinct course across the flat foot of Honduras before swerving off into the hills at

Choluteca. The Nicaragua and El Salvador maps in this book should be adequate – you do not have to be a genius at navigation to work out the correct direction. But, if you want something more substantial than the one in this book, or your map of El Salvador or Nicaragua does not extend to cover the chunk of Honduras that the Highway ploughs through, ask at the frontier for the free map that the Ministerio de Cultura y Turismo (SECTUR) issues. Better in many ways, however, is the *Mapa Turística de Honduras* which is available from some fuel stations, and (in the cities) bookshops and hotels for around $3. The free map handed out by Avis has almost indecipherable maps of Honduras, Tegucigalpa and San Pedro Sula, and is near to useless.

That was then

The first visitors

Parts of Honduras were once settled by the Maya, but little is known about their exact movements. What is certain is that the ruins at Copán were built during the zenith of the Maya civilisation, between the sixth and tenth centuries. But Copán, like the other Maya cities in Central America, had long been abandoned by the time Christopher Columbus arrived, although a number of Indian settlements remained in other parts of the country.

The Conquest

Columbus came upon this part of Central America in 1502, on his last voyage to the New World. The territory was named Honduras, supposedly after Columbus himself had experience difficult seas. He is said to have exclaimed *'Gracias a Dios, somos fuera de estas honduras'* ('Thank God we are clear of these depths'), having sailed across the particularly deep waters off the north coast. The eastern cape, where Nicaragua meets Honduras, was subsequently called Gracias a Dios.

The Conquest of Honduras took place comparatively late. Spanish control was consolidated at the end of the 1530s. Since the colonists were already established in other parts of the region, the conquerors of Honduras arrived along several different routes. The first captains were sent into the territory in the early 1520s by Hernán Cortés, the conqueror of Mexico. Cristóbal de Olid was one of these, but he switched allegiance to Diego de Velázquez, governor of Cuba, before founding the first Spanish town of Triunfo de la Cruz on the north coast. Incensed by such disloyalty, Cortés sent Francisco de las Casas to deal with de Olid, which he did with brutal success. He then founded Trujillo, which became the country's first capital in 1825.

Only a decade later did Pedro de Alvarado (founder of San Salvador) arrive on the scene. He made forays into areas hitherto unexplored and founded the northern city of San Pedro Sula in 1536. Pedro de Alvarado returned to Spain the next year and the conquest of Honduras was continued by others. The northern areas were difficult to penetrate, so attention shifted southwards. In 1537 Comayagua was founded, replacing Trujillo as capital and becoming the political, religious and cultural centre of the country for over three centuries, until it was superseded by Tegucigalpa in 1880.

The foundation of Comayagua opened up areas – including those around Tegucigalpa – which were discovered to be rich in gold and silver. Prospective Spanish settlers began arriving from Guatemala, and tried to force the indigenous Indians to work for them. The Indians, led by Lenca Lempira, did not cooperate and numerous clashes followed. The impatient Spaniards put a treacherous end to Indian resistance by murdering Lempira and many of his 30,000 followers during a truce. The leader's name lives on in the national currency.

Gold and silver also attracted the attention of more unruly plunderers during the 17th and 18th centuries. Pirates from Europe based themselves strategically on the Bay Islands on the north coast of Honduras and attacked Spanish ships en route back to Europe. One of these pirates was the famous Welshman, Captain Henry Morgan. He managed to establish English authority over the Bay Islands during the 17th century. The Royal Navy held sway over these islands beyond Honduran independence, and controlled the Mosquito Coast which became a protectorate of the Crown. English settlers and Caribbean blacks made their homes on the Bay Islands, which retain many vestiges of this period. In 1859 the protectorate came to an end when the British signed a treaty with Honduras, surrendering control of the Mosquito Coast and the Bay Islands in return for recognition of territorial rights in British Honduras (now Belize). The departure of the British still rankles. A few eccentrics on the Bay Islands accuse Queen Victoria of selling out her loyal subjects.

Independence

In one of its brief forays out of obscurity, Honduras played an important part in the struggle for the region's independence from Spain. Indeed it was a Honduran, Francisco Morazán, who was one of the most famous figures in the Central American struggle to free itself. Although his dreams of a confederation came to nothing, Morazán is the country's national hero, and has hundreds of squares and streets named in his honour.

Honduras declared independence for the first time in 1821, and joined the United Provinces of Central America shortly afterwards. This fell apart by 1838, whereupon Honduras declared its independence once again. Self-government, however, brought the same problems as in the other member countries of the former federation: instability, growing disparity of wealth, rivalry between liberal and conservative factions, military dictatorship, and rebellion. The nation settled down into controlled chaos of the kind that was to characterise the next two centuries. Late in the 19th century there was an influx of Europeans who came to the New World to take advantage of the cheap peasant labour force and the low cost of land.

The Twentieth Century

The business ventures by incoming German and French settlers were negligible compared with the US fruit companies which turned Honduras into the

Banana Republic *par excellence*. The Americans brought improvements in the form of roads, railways and bridges, but these benefitted only the areas with plantations – hence the country's patchy transport network now.

Politically, Honduras wobbled through the 20th century. General Carías, president during the 1930s, was so paranoid that whenever he attended Mass machine guns were mounted inside the church. Following the election to the presidency in 1957 of the Liberal leader Villeda Morales, Honduras enjoyed six years of parliamentary democracy. People still regard this era with nostalgia. The government of Morales, like most before and after, was overthrown by the military, ending one of the few attempts to establish parliamentary democracy in Honduras. The country stagnated, politically and economically.

Neighbouring El Salvador was suffering even worse problems, and many Salvadorans sought better prospects in Honduras. The locals became increasingly resentful of what they saw as unrestricted immigration. The 'soccer war' of June 1969, triggered by Honduras beating El Salvador in a World Cup qualifying match, brought the tensions between the two countries to the surface.

In the 1980s, Honduras threw itself into the arms of Washington which proceeded to supply billions of dollars in aid in return for the nation's acquiescence as a base from which to launch Contra attacks into Nicaragua. Within the country, right-wing death squads were active. The Contra war against Nicaragua ended when free elections deposed the Sandinistas. In Honduras, presidential elections in 1989 resulted in victory for Rafael Leonardo Callejas, leader of the conservative National Party, over his Liberal rival Flores. He was ousted in 1993 by a Liberal, Carlos Roberto Reina, who passed on power to Carlos Flores Facussé in 1997.

Honduras has been spared the type of dictators inflicted on Nicaragua and Guatemala, but the people have endured similar oppression. Honduras has a poor human rights record, with leftists, trade unionists and journalists being long-standing victims of persecution, imprisonment and murder. Nevertheless, the nation was beginning to haul itself out of an economic morass when Hurricane Mitch struck in 1998, destroying thousands of lives and much of the nation's infrastructure.

This is now

When the current president took office, he promised to combat poverty and crime. Little did he know that the problems facing the Honduran people were about to get far worse. Living standards fell steadily during the 1990s, to the point where up to 80% of the population is on or below the poverty line, a situation greatly exacerbated by Hurricane Mitch. Other social problems include the increase in serious disease, an escalation in the number of street children, particularly around the capital, and a high crime rate, linked to the shipments of illegal drugs which pass through Honduras from Colombia.

As a result of the unstable political situation, and the dollars pumped in during the Contra war, the Honduran military has become extremely powerful. During 1999, there were rumours of a plot to overthrow the government, and as a result several high-ranking military officers were dismissed. A civilian defence minister was appointed, a move which proved extremely unpopular with the armed forces. Some observers fear that the original 'banana republic' is about to plunge into yet another crisis.

An afternoon in Honduras

When you finally get across the frontier, you deserve some good news. Here it is: the Honduran police have recently dismantled a criminal organisation that preyed on travellers near Goascorán on the Salvadoran border. The bad news: since Mitch, desperation on the part of many of the dispossessed, and opportunism on the part of organised crime faced with the most limited policing, means that anyone in any vehicle on any highway in Honduras is potentially at risk. In 1999, an international bus was hijacked and driven off the main road to a remote area. The passengers were robbed, and a woman was raped. These days, high-technology has come to the aid of armed criminals in the shape of mobile telephones that allow them to tail and target tourists. Kidnapping of foreigners is becoming more common.

All the more reason, then, to be relieved that you can 'do' Honduras in an afternoon – probably safely, if you stick to the non-tourist local bus and resolve not to stray from the main road. Another good reason why not: unmarked minefields still exist on both sides of the Honduras-Nicaragua border. An international mine-clearing effort headed by the Organization of American States (OAS) was making significant progress in clearing these areas, until the landslides and floods resulting from Hurricane Mitch scattered many of the remaining mines, rendering the border unsafe once again.

Wherever you are driving, carry your documents at all times since police spot-checks are not uncommon. Even soldiers may approach you in the street and demand to see your papers. Don't hand over your passport to anyone without first checking their credentials – stolen passports are big business in Honduras. All soldiers and policemen carry documents and should be prepared to demonstrate their authority.

On the Highway

All the main highways in Honduras are paved, but they comprise just one-ninth of the total road network, and many were devastated by Hurricane Mitch. Dozens of bridges were washed away. Most secondary roads are dirt tracks and in poor condition, particularly during the wet season when mountain roads become little more than mud rivers and may well be impassable. Waterways which are small streams most of the year become raging torrents, sometimes flooding bridges. **Buses** are mostly the standard beaten-up, run-down and over-crowded vehicles that look like Meccano projects gone wrong. For longer-distance trips, e.g. from the frontier at El Amatillo or the neighbouring town of Goascorán to Tegucigalpa, old Greyhound buses are pressed into service.

One of the more unusual practices to occur in Honduran buses is that of handing round a piece of paper on which the passengers are expected to write their names. This operation is an exercise in petty security – the list is handed into the police at roadside checkpoints. Do not **drive** after dark. Be prepared for large chunks of any road having been washed away. Attempts are being made to repair the road network with massive construction programmes involving American and Japanese funding. You are obliged to stop at police and military checkpoints which occur at frequent intervals along certain roads, particularly in frontier areas.

Each of the main highways has a number, which, in practice, is rarely used. The *least* important, in the national context, is the Pan-American Highway – CA1 – which enters Honduras from El Salvador at El Amatillo and leaves via El Espino on the Nicaraguan border. The most significant is the Northern Highway – CA5 – from Tegucigalpa to San Pedro Sula, via Comayagua and Siguatepeque, continuing north to Puerto Cortés. The Western Highway – CA4 – runs from San Pedro Sula to Nueva Ocotepeque via La Entrada and Santa Rosa de Copán, giving access to both Guatemalan and Salvadoran borders. The Southern Highway – CA5 – connects Tegucigalpa to the Pan-American Highway (at Jícaro Galán east of Nacaome), with some daunting curves in the mountains. If you decide to deviate to the capital, then the Eastern Highway – CA6 – links Tegucigalpa to Las Manos on the border with Nicaragua, via Danlí and El Paraíso.

City driving is not a pleasant experience. The streets, where they still exist, resemble the Somme in 1918. The vast craters have done nothing to curtail the ambition of local drivers, who are possibly the worst in Central America. Beware of the curious sequence used for traffic lights, which often confuses foreigners: red – green – red and amber – red.

Most **car rental** agencies have representation in both the capital (at the Hotel Honduras Maya) and airports of Tegucigalpa and San Pedro Sula.

Hitch-hiking
Given the poverty of Honduras, it is no surprise that local people frequently hitch rides. It should also be no surprise that 'rich' Westerners are expected to pay at least the equivalent of the bus fare, which is not going to amount to more than around 40 lempira ($3) even if you hitch all the way through.

The flyover option
There isn't one. The only domestic flights are those linking the capital, Tegucigalpa, with San Pedro Sula, La Ceiba and the Bay Islands. These are among the world's more dangerous airlines – so bad that the Americans have banned all Honduran airlines from flying to the USA. And you'll be waiting all your life for a train. The flyover option most travellers take is to hop across from San Salvador to San José, missing out the benighted nations of Honduras and Nicaragua.

Is Honduras a good place to start or finish a trip along the Pan-American Highway?
No.

A worthwhile diversion: Copán

Honduras' leading tourist draw is superb. The Mayan ruins of Copán compare in scale and magnificence with the other great Maya sites of Central America. The problem is that the ruins are far from accessible from the Pan-American Highway, but a journey across the country could be worthwhile. Unlike the more famous archaeological sites further north, Copán is relatively unspoilt by tourism. The site is well kept, and efforts have been made to preserve the beauty and tranquillity of the setting. If you do not have the ruins to yourself, you may at least feel as if you do.

Copán, the most southerly of the great Mayan cities, marks the peak of the Late Classic period of the Maya civilisation (AD500-800), although archaeological evidence shows that the Mayans settled on the site as early as 2000BC. It is thought that the ruins thus far excavated make up only a quarter of a site. The city may have covered the entire valley, and some believe it to have been the capital of the Mayan empire. Like other Mayan cities, Copán was abandoned long before the Spanish arrived, for reasons which remain uncertain.

A Spanish official reported in a letter to Philip II of Spain that he had discovered ruins in the area. But Copán was only rediscovered in the 19th century, smothered in jungle. A number of archaeologists investigated the site, and in the 1930s a major rebuilding programme began. Restoration and excavation work is continuing, so you can expect parts of the site to be out-of-bounds.

No other Mayan site has such a large number of stelae and altars decorated with faces and figures. But the great pyramids and the layout of the site leave the most lasting impression. The main path beyond the entrance to the site itself leads straight to the Great Plaza, but bear right and visit the western and eastern plazas first, since the approach to the Great Plaza is far more spectacular from the southern end. On the southern boundary of Copán is the Acropolis, a huge elevated complex containing temples and pyramids, the Tribuna de Espectadores (Spectators' Gallery) with fine carvings, and the Escalinata de los Jaguares (Jaguar Staircase) which separates the Eastern and Western Plazas.

In front of Temple 16, the tallest pyramid at Copán on the east side of the Western Plaza, is a famous altar showing the 16 kings of the Copán dynasty. Continuing round into the Eastern Plaza you can climb up the beautiful Temple 22 on the northern side, whose entrance is through the mouth of a two-headed serpent. Walking west along the top of this temple, you get a fine view of the Great Plaza which stretches out below.

Descending down the steps to the left, the first main structure to your right is the great Escalinata Jeroglífica (Hieroglyphic Staircase), which climbs a pyramid and is in many ways the most remarkable structure in Copán. Only some of the hieroglyphics covering the stone blocks have been decoded, but are thought to refer to astronomical and scientific subjects. Notice the birds and snakes decorating the sides as well as the mythical creatures up the steps. The 63 steps lead to a small temple at the top. The staircase, damaged by an earthquake at some time, was restored by the Carnegie Institute in the 1930s, but is now covered with a tarpaulin to protect it from the elements.

Just north is the Juego de Pelota (Ball Court), dating from the 8th century. This court is one of several at Copán, but is the only one which has been restored. It was used for a game played between two teams whose aim is thought to have been to keep a large rubber ball in play without using their hands. Archaeologists believe this game had some religious importance; judging from the gear that the players wore, it was also very dangerous. Copán museum contains scenes of the game being played.

Beyond the Central Court is the Great Plaza itself, a large grassy area where the tiers of seats provided room for 50,000 people – about the same as the National Stadium in Tegucigalpa. There are six richly carved stelae, and in the centre is a round stone which was probably a sacrificial altar; notice the channels for letting the blood drain away.

To get to Copán, you first have to reach the Honduran town of La Entrada (60km/37 miles away), or approach from the Guatemalan frontier at El Florido (13km/8 miles). If you intend just to nip across for the day you can spend a couple of dollars on a kind of 'day pass' at the border that lets you out of Guatemala and back again without all the usual rigmarole. There are frequent minibuses from La Entrada, infrequent ones from El Florido (I hitched). It is well worth staying at the village of Copán Ruinas (1km from the site), so you get the place to yourself at the end of one day and/or the start of the next. The most elegant and time-saving way to include Copán on your itinerary is to veer away from the Highway at Guatemala City, travelling to Chiquimula then onwards to El Florido. From Copán, you would then head east to Tegucigalpa and onward to Nicaragua, rejoining the Highway north of Estelí – and missing El Salvador completely.

What's different about Honduras?
Who are the Hondurans?
Nine out of ten of the local people are *mestizo* as a result of the high degree of intermarriage between the Spanish and Indians during the colonial period. Only a few per cent of Hondurans are of pure Indian descent, and they live mainly in western and northern Honduras. The group you are most likely to encounter are the Lencas, who live mostly in central and southwestern Honduras. Black people, originally from Africa, were first brought to the area from the West Indies as slaves soon after the arrival of the Spanish. At the turn of the century there was a new influx of blacks – including from Belize and the West Indies – who came to Honduras to work on the banana plantations. Due

to intermarrying, however, only about 2% are pure-blooded.

There is also a sizeable community of Garifuna – or Black Caribs – living in the northern coastal area. These are descendants of Carib Indians from South America and black slaves. In the late 18th century they were deported by the British from the Antilles to the Bay Islands, from where they spread to the mainland. Like the Garifuna along the Atlantic coast of Guatemala and Belize, the Honduran Garifuna retain a strong sense of community, and their traditions have survived to an extent found in few other parts of the country.

Other racial groups include the fair-skinned descendants of British pirates who live on the Bay Islands (the consequences of inter-breeding are apparent), and a tiny minority of Spaniards of pure Spanish descent. Honduras is also the adoptive home of thousands of Nicaraguan and Salvadoran refugees. With peace returning to Nicaragua, most of the Nicaraguans have returned, but many Salvadorans have established homes and lifestyles for themselves in Honduras, and look set to stay.

Hondureños tend to be less exuberant than their Central American neighbours. Tourists have become even more of a novelty in the country since Mitch. The Hondurans, like the people everywhere in the region, are gracious hosts and – with the notable exception of frontier officials – will almost always go out of their way to help you. Women can expect to attract attention from the men, but this rarely progresses beyond a comment or whistle.

What they eat
Honduras is not a gourmet's paradise, and a strong culinary tradition is hard to trace except among the Garifuna communities along the north coast. In most of the country, *Sopa de mondongo* (tripe soup) is common but is definitely an acquired taste. The other leading candidate for Honduras' national dish is the *pincho* (kebab); in a reasonable restaurant, a skewer full of beef and vegetables will set you back $2. To eat more cheaply, order tacos or enchiladas at an ordinary café – they cost about $0.50 each. Rice and beans, with assorted accompaniments, is the other staple.

For the despairing vegetarian there are a couple of vegetarian restaurants in Tegucigalpa. Fish is best eaten along the Caribbean coast. A visit to the north coast or Bay Islands also brings relief to those bored with the repertoire found in most Honduran restaurants. It is here that you will find the Garifuna communities which use a lot of coconut in their cooking, particularly in the preparation of fish and seafood. *Pan de coco* (coconut bread) is also a local speciality.

When the roads are in good enough repair, luscious fruit is shipped south from the banana and avocado plantations of northern Honduras.

What they drink
The four brands of local **beer** – Port Royal, Imperial, Nacional and Salvavidas – taste like most other characterless lagers, although Port Royal, brewed in San Pedro Sula and exported to the USA, has a little more flavour than the rest. A

bottle of beer in a bar costs $0.60, and since some bars serve *bocas* (the Central American equivalent of Spanish tapas), you can save on your meal bills too.

In Honduras the term *refresco* refers to almost any non-alcoholic drink: Coca Cola and the hideously sweet local fizzy concoctions, but also natural juices. Fresh fruit juices are cheaper than bottled drinks and sell for $0.20 each.

What they read, watch and listen to

The principal daily **newspapers** are *El Heraldo* and *La Tribuna* (both published in Tegucigalpa) and *El Tiempo* and *La Prensa* (published in San Pedro Sula). *El Heraldo* has close affiliation with the military, while *La Tribuna* has links with the Liberal Party; *El Tiempo* gives the most independent news coverage of national and international news. All these papers cost about $0.20 and include limited information on entertainment in Tegucigalpa and San Pedro Sula. There are six **television** channels and over 150 **radio** stations, almost all of them dreadful.

Festivals and holidays

January 1	New Year's Day
April	Holy Week
April 14	Americas' Day
May 1	Labour Day
June 29	San Pedro's Day (San Pedro Sula)
September 15	Independence Day
October 3	Francisco Morazán's birthday
October 12	Discovery of America Day
October 21	Army Day
December 25	Christmas Day

What they spend

The Lempira (abbreviated Lp) is divided into 100 centavos (c). For the original Banana Republic, inflation in Honduras is relatively low and exchange rates are surprisingly stable. The official rate has been fixed at US$1 = Lp2 for 70 years, but is used for only a few purposes such as pricing international air tickets and calculating the foreign debt of the country. There are amusing local names for some of the coins: 5c = conquinto, 10c = búfalo, 20c = daime (as in the American 'dime'; the coin is even the same size), and 50c = tostón.

It is rarely worth going to a bank to **change money**, but if you insist you may find one open 9am-3pm. The bureaucracy is monstrous, the rules are baffling (some banks will change only American Express traveller's cheques, while others deal only with Visa). Touts are a well-established part of the financial community, and most are also colourful local characters. Expect a premium against bank rates of around 10% for cash, 6% for travellers cheques. The black market dealers at the international airports and land frontiers are less generous, taking advantage of the fact that you are unlikely to know the prevailing black market rate.

Even if you run out of lempiras completely, traders in all but the most out-of-the-way places will accept US dollars and give a reasonable rate. The one occasion when you might wish to use a bank is to draw cash at an ATM (mostly in the big cities) or to procure some currency (lempiras only) on a credit card. This could easily take an hour or more.

Anything worth buying?

Not really. Prices in Honduras are among the lowest in Central America, but so is quality. There are a number of craft centres around the country, which produce wood carvings, blankets, straw hats and baskets, but they are a long way from the Pan-American Highway. Shops open from Monday to Friday, 9am-6pm (usually closing noon-2pm for lunch), and 8am-noon on Saturdays. Pulperías – general stores – keep longer hours.

Keeping in touch

The whole telecommunications network was devastated by Hurricane Mitch, so don't expect too much in the way of good connections either for voice or e-mail. **Internet** cafés have yet to make much impression on Honduras, with just a few starting up in Tegucigalpa and San Pedro Sula. A thorough search of Choluteca, the only town of any size on the Pan-American Highway, revealed not a single terminal in town. This will no doubt change soon, but at present the best options are across the border in Estelí, Nicaragua. **Telephone** numbers in Honduras have seven digits and there are no area codes. When the network is functioning, international calls can be dialled direct from private phones (access code 00), made from card-operated payphones or placed through the operator at offices of the state telecommunications company Hondutel. It has offices in all the main towns, but the further you are from the two biggest cities, the slower the service and the poorer the lines. Useful numbers include: long-distance operator – 191; international operator – 197; fire – 198; police – 199.

Telegrams may be sent from Hondutel offices, and the main towns usually offer a 24-hour service. The rate for telegrams to the UK is $0.30 per word, to the USA $0.20.

Air mail letters take about a week from Honduras to reach addresses in North America or Europe. Post offices are open from 7am-8pm Monday to Friday, 8am-noon on Saturdays. At larger post offices, *Poste Restante/Lista de Correos* has a separate window. The filing system used is arcane in the extreme: based as much upon the country of origin and/or the first name of the recipient as the last name. Therefore try to persuade the clerk to look under all possible combinations. If you are fortunate enough to find a piece of mail, you must buy a stamp worth about $0.10 at a different counter to retrieve it.

Set your watch back 50 years

The inelegant shambles at the border post resembles a Jurassic car park to which the aeons have been particularly cruel. Once you shake off the disintegrating

Tarmac and crumbling buildings, you can begin to enjoy the landscape – if you haven't been too spoilt by the scenic story so far. Were southern Honduras located in a more ordinary part of the world, then its casual beauty would place the country high on any list of desirable places to hike, view wildlife and dive. But with even more attractive alternatives in such close proximity, the dusty road through the flatlands of Honduras is less than inspiring.

The Highway descends slowly for around 12km (seven miles) to the plain, and continues for a further 30km (18 miles) to the first significant road junction – the town of **Jícaro Galán**. This has grown up solely because it happens to be where the Pan-American Highway meets the main road to the capital, Tegucigalpa. You may find yourself changing buses here. The only saving graces are (a) that buses are fairly frequent in all directions, and (b) that if you get stuck after the closedown in services at around 6pm, the Oasis Colonial Hotel is surprisingly tolerable.

From here, the road dives due south towards the Pacific, and almost dips a toe in the ocean – for the first close encounter since Mexico. But before that, the bus is likely to take you on a tour around the hot, listless town of **San Lorenzo**. By the time the circuit has finished, you will be even more glad that you do not happen to be Honduran. If you decide to stay, there are a couple of options – the Hotel Morazán and the Hotel Miramonte.

A wayward capital: Amapala

One reason to be cheerful about Honduras is located 40km (25 miles) south from here. If you take the bus from San Lorenzo to Coyolito, you will cross a bridge on to Isla Zacate Grande and arrive at the foot of a volcano. From here, a launch departs for Tigre Island, and the port of **Amapala**. Located in the Gulf of Fonseca, Amapala was – for a short time in 1876 – capital of Honduras. It also used to be the country's main Pacific seaport, but has now been superseded by the port of San Lorenzo further east. Amapala in particular and El Tigre in general are virtually dead, although a few disused hotels and houses recall the port's former glory. If you are travelling through the area, it is worth a detour just to appreciate the setting: on a clear day you can see Cosigüina volcano in Nicaragua, and Conchagua and San Miguel volcanoes in El Salvador.

The Gulf of Fonseca – known by the indigenous locals as Teca – was discovered in the 16th century by Andrés Niño who named it in honour of his patron, Juan Rodríguez de Fonseca. In 1578 another great explorer, Francis Drake, passed through and spent some time on El Tigre. Romantics like to believe that some of Drake's treasure remains buried near Sirena cave on Playa Grande. This is the best beach on El Tigre, but even so the swimming is not particularly good. It would be more interesting to hire a dugout and investigate the nearby lagoons and islands. Getting around on the island itself is done mostly on foot.

Accommodation in Amapala is limited. There are a few simple hospedajes and it is also possible to rent private houses along the beach.

Choluteca: the closest you get to a city

City boys and girls will be getting a bit tetchy by now, so Choluteca will come as something of an urban relief. Founded in 1535, Choluteca was one of the oldest colonial towns in Honduras. It slumps in the centre of a cattle-breeding area, 34km (21 miles) east of San Lorenzo and 60km (38 miles) west of El Espino on the Nicaraguan border.

The place suffered less than some from Hurricane Mitch, and the original 17th-century village church (now the Casa de la Cultura) is well preserved in bleached white paint, but most other buildings are in a bad state of repair. Nevertheless it is an interesting enough place to get a flavour of humdrum Honduran life. Choluteca is mildly famous for two things: bequeathing the last part of its name to the Gulf over which it presides (called Fonseca on the maps, Teca by the locals) and its white doves, called *zanates*, which roost in the trees every evening and make a terrific racket. As if in retribution against the noise endured the rest of the year, these doves are hunted voraciously between November and March. The local festival – in honour of the Virgin of the Conception – falls on December 8-16.

There are plenty of cheap, if tatty, **places to stay** – on the Pan-American Highway, this is the obvious venue to break your journey. The main street is Calle Vicente Williams, and most of the places are on or close to it. The best are the Hotel Catedral and the Santa Rosa, which have a selection of reasonably-priced rooms, from the most basic to those with private facilities. No hotel, however, whatever the class, can escape the problems which result from the lack of water towards the end of the dry season; you may find water in the taps (and the cistern) in the morning but not in the evening. This applies almost anywhere in southern and western Honduras.

Eating opportunities are mostly modest. The most ambitious option is La Jungla, a big barn of a place on the road leading east out of town. It promises, and delivers, *comida típica*.

For **moving on**, there are buses from the *terminal* to the frontier – or the town of San Marcos de Colón, just before it, from around 6am to 3pm. If you can't be bothered to walk to the bus station, a taxi anywhere in town costs $0.50 per person. You could also consider renting a taxi for the entire trip to the frontier, which is likely to cost around $20 for the whole vehicle. If there are three or four of you travelling together, this is an attractive option.

The two best **beaches** along this stretch of the Pacific Coast – at Cedeño and Ratón – are both accessible from Choluteca. There are hourly buses to Playa de Cedeño, 13km (8 miles) southwest of the town. This is a pleasant fishing community, and although facilities are few (there are a couple of shops and basic accommodation), hordes of people descend on the place at weekends and holidays. Northwest along the coast is Punta Ratón. At the southern end of the beach is a small reserve where, between August and November, sea turtles come to lay their eggs. There is no coastal road connecting Cedeño and Punta Ratón; you must therefore take the side road which branches west off the road from Choluteca.

A side trip to Tegucigalpa

In the early 1990s, there was a string of fatal plane crashes at the capital's airport, most of them attributable to excessive proximity to the mountains that ring the airport. The accidents presented something of a problem for the late, great radio presenter Brian Redhead. Unversed in the intricacies of Latin American pronunciation, he insisted in referring only to the 'Honduran capital'.

The five tricky syllables of Tegucigalpa comprise the original Indian term of 'silver hill'. The presence of precious metals was the original attraction for the Spanish, in the 16th century, to establish a small riverside encampment. Gold and silver mined in the surrounding area gradually brought wealth and importance to the town which replaced Comayagua as capital of Honduras in 1880. Today, Tegucigalpa is a run-down, sprawling city. The mountains which surround the city are one of the few reminders that there is fresh air to be breathed. The streets and squares of the centre are seething with heavy traffic, while poor suburbs are chasing back up the hillsides after the devastation of Mitch. Even as it tries to rebuild, Tegucigalpa has to cope with an ever-increasing population. A million people live in the capital, compared with only 150,000 in the early 1960s.

Tegucigalpa today is the archetypal Central American capital. It bears the hallmarks of a city hastily planned, or rather hastily built with no planning. There is little attraction in strolling along the banks of the diminutive and foul-smelling Choluteca river, but it is harsh to dismiss Tegucigalpa as an unattractive city. Though the capital retains little of its colonial splendour, the magnificent cathedral and a number of fine churches and mansions have survived the worst ravages of Mitch and the earthquakes which shake Honduras periodically. There may be few sights as such, but there is much enjoyment to be had by watching the locals in the squares in the heart of the city, particularly the Parque Central. This square is always full of activity and is big enough to provide a momentary respite from the appalling pollution which circulates around the narrow streets.

The atmosphere of Tegucigalpa is rather like that of a sleepy Spanish provincial city, and visitors remain something of a novelty. As the capital of a country where people have lost count of the political coups, Tegucigalpa has had its share of violence, but the city feels relaxed, and most areas are safe. It is also comfortable; however dirty the capital may be, at an altitude of 3,200 feet (975m) it does have a bearable climate. Although the temperatures can get hot during the day, the evenings are always cool. Ironically in view of all the flooding, with its hillside location and its ever-expanding population, Tegucigalpa has huge water-supply problems. Rationing is common, and water is often available only in the morning.

You can reach Tegucigalpa from almost anywhere in Honduras. From Choluteca, San Marcos de Colón and the Nicaraguan frontier, **Transportes Mi**

Esperanza runs to and from the foot of Avenida 6 in Comayagüela. The funniest and one of the most centrally located **hotels** in Tegucigalpa is Hotel MacArthur (tel 237-9839), in the Barrio Abajo, at Avenida Lempira 554. The hotel is a huge colonial mansion. Rooms cost $33 single/$38 double. The management is friendly and can arrange for laundry to be done.

One of the best **restaurants** in town is El Patio, on Calle Los Dolores between Avenidas Miguel Paz Barahona and Miguel de Cervantes, a couple of blocks west of the Parque Central. It calls itself the *restaurante típico de la capital*, and is certainly as typical as you'll get in the centre. It is easy to spot, thanks to the large neon sign and bull skulls with illuminated light bulbs for eyes. Inside, the food is plentiful and delicious; pinchos (kebabs) are a speciality. Even before you order you will be brought a piping hot dish of frijoles and tortillas. El Patio has a branch on the Boulevard Morazán. Most other 'good' restaurants tend to be pretentious and expensive. You may prefer to join the locals at one of the many cheap and cheerful places in town, such as the Cafetería El Jardín on Avenida Cristóbal Colón.

The best choice of **cafés and bars** is east of the main square. The Paradiso Café on Avenida Miguel Paz Barahona (next to the Shell garage near the church of San Francisco) is a café-cum-bookshop-cum-art gallery. It has a distinctly French air, and is a meeting place for local intellectuals. There is a good choice of drinks but not much food, although croissants are available; prices are higher than average. Plaza San Francisco is the best place for bars, one of which – the Mesón el Criollo – is open 24 hours.

To Nicaragua

If you plan a detour to the Nicaraguan city of León, make the decision before you leave Choluteca: the road splits at the city, with the alternative route keeping close to the coast while the Pan-American Highway heads into the hills. Five kilometres (three miles) out of town, you pass a United Nations-run 'city' of breezeblock and corrugated tin, which is where many of the people made homeless by Mitch have been housed.

Shortly afterwards, you begin one of the most exciting ascents in the whole Highway. Drivers miss out on it – or at least they *should* miss out, because to avert their eyes from the road itself is to court disaster. Large chunks of the road have been washed down the steep slope of the foothills. Sometimes there may be a warning in the shape of a sign saying *Media Via* ('half way'), otherwise only a pile of earth or scattering of branches announces that the Pan-American Highway has been temporarily replaced by a gaping void – at least on the downhill side. Just after kilometre marker 166, there is a memorial to 10 Costa Ricans whose bus went over the side. Passengers, meanwhile, get superb views across the coastal plain – which was mostly flooded by Mitch – and across the Bay of Fonseca to the islands and El Salvador.

It gets even better as you wind into the hills. The far southeast of Honduras is Wild West country, with scenery on an ambitious scale. To linger and enjoy it, there are a couple of places to stay: Monte Lorenzo (887 4819) at km172, and the Finca El Recreo, at km180, a fun ranch in a lovely setting.

Shortly before arriving at the Nicaraguan frontier, the road climbs to the town of San Marcos de Colón (population 20,000), from where there is a good view of the Gulf of Fonseca. The Hotel Esperanza is cheap, and friendly; the owner is from El Salvador, and the hotel is full of his compatriots.

Crossing points along the Nicaraguan frontier were liable to disruption throughout the 1980s. The border was heavily fortified, and travellers often had to fork out a bribe in order to be let across. The most used crossing was, and is, that at El Espino (the name refers to a town just on the Nicaraguan side that was severely depopulated during the Contra War). The crossing itself is one of the loveliest locations for any frontier post, and the light traffic means it is unspoilt – and fairly quick to get out.

The Honduran border is actually split: you have your baggage checked, and show your passport, to get 'pre-clearance' (a piece of paper with your name and passport number, near the bus drop-off point. Then you must walk about 500m to the Customs buildings for more formalities, and the chance to pay $2 to leave the country. This border is good for changing money, both dollars and miscellaneous Central American currencies.

Waging a Contra War

Honduras became a key base during the 1980s for opposition to the Sandinista regime in Nicaragua, and for attempts by the US government to unseat the Sandinistas.

The US State Department suspended economic and military aid to Nicaragua in 1979, causing the then-president, Anastasio Somoza, to flee the country. The Sandinistas took over, with Daniel Ortega as their leader, and, despite early promises, the new regime became increasingly anti-democratic. Television stations were seized, democratic elections were postponed, and the government turned increasingly towards Cuba and the Soviet bloc for economic and ideological support. Mounting concern about what was going on inside Nicaragua caused the Americans – while still pursuing an official policy of support for the Sandinista regime – to provide assistance to the various opposition groups forming outside Nicaragua, the Contras.

The CIA became involved in funding the Contra forces, to enable them to build up the scale of their operations. A base for insurgency was established in Honduras. When CIA funding was used up, the effectiveness of the Contras began to decline, and they appealed to other governments. America resumed support, and a network of companies and facilities supporting the opposition to the regime in Nicaragua was set up under the direction of Oliver North.

In November 1986, following several extensive enquiries in the United States, it was announced that the proceeds from the sale of arms to Iran were being diverted to the Contras at a time when the US military had been prohibited from providing aid to the Contras. Support for the Contras declined, and they began to return to their bases outside Nicaragua.

Nicaragua

HONDURAN FRONTIER - COSTA RICAN FRONTIER

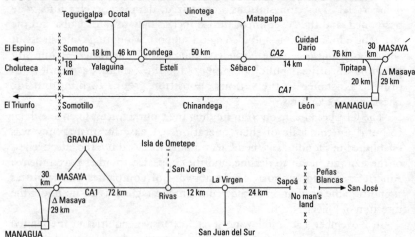

You said you wanted a revolution?

The people living on the Caribbean island of San Andrés, 500km east of Nicaragua, are philosophical. Life on one of the farthest-flung fragments of Colombia might not always be comfortable, but things could be worse: Nicaragua might have won its territorial claim to the island.

To be regarded as an even worse option than South America's pariah state, Colombia, is an unenviable position for any country to be in. How different the world, and in particular Nicaragua's neighbourhood, would have been if the canal through Central America had been dug some way north and west of Panama. There were very good reasons for so doing, and indeed it would have probably have been far less of a logistical undertaking than the Panama Canal proved. But a combination of shennanigans and seismology meant that Nicaragua was not destined to earn the small fortune that comes with being the link between two oceans – and the interference from Washington that involves. Central America's largest country got all the interference without any of the

286

benefits. At the back end of the 20th century, Nicaragua's people suffered for their beliefs – and even when those beliefs had been modified, it has taken an age for the shambles left by its role as proxy Cold War battleground to be cleared.

The Sandinista Revolution of 1979 was that great rarity – a change of government in a Latin American country that saw the will of the people triumph over a brutal and corrupt regime. But the success of the left-wing guerrillas was wilfully misinterpreted by Washington DC, and small-town USA, as signalling that the Communists were about to cross the Rio Grande and install Marxism-Leninism. The 'Contra war' of the 1980s, funded by the USA through devious means, drained the revolutionary reserves of cash and energy, while sanctions helped to trigger economic traumas more extreme than anywhere else in the world. The victory of a new government in 1990 did not bring the promised salvation, and the effects of Hurricane Mitch picked up the destructive baton dropped by the Contras.

Which helps explain why, even compared with Honduras, Nicaragua looks a right old mess once you get over the border. Many local people are living in hardship, with decrepit homes and an infrastructure that – in the case of some of the vehicles that keep the place moving – is literally held together with string. Yet the Revolution has left a legacy of social enhancements from health clinics to cultural institutes. And though Nicaragua was never a slice of Eastern Europe in Central America, as some would have you believe, there are still enough vivid murals on the streets to symbolise the power and popularity of Sandinismo – the force for political and social change inspired by Augusto Sandino.

'Nicaragua, a country blessed by nature', is the tourist institute's boast. A country devastated by nature, plundered by adventurers and completely shafted by politicians is closer to the mark. Nicaragua is light on cultural heritage, since acts of God and man from earthquakes to foreign invasion have brutally scarred much of its architecture; nevertheless the fine cities of Granada (just off the Highway) and León (a long way off it) remain two of the colonial gems of Central America. The country might be the largest in Central America (the size of England and Wales or the American state of Iowa) but it is by no means the most beautiful in the region, though it has a respectable collection of lakes, volcanoes, beaches and even a coral reef. Across on the east coast, the main town of Bluefields has more of an affinity with the islands of the Caribbean than with the starkly ugly capital city, Managua.

Like El Salvador, Nicaragua boasts a fine collection of volcanoes, among the few things in the country untouched by the war. The highest mountains are along the Honduran border. The central mountainous region is heavily forested and acts as a natural barrier between the Caribbean coast and western Nicaragua, dividing the country in half both physically and culturally. The eastern lowlands take up over one-third of Nicaragua but the impenetrability of the terrain means that less than a tenth of the population lives here.

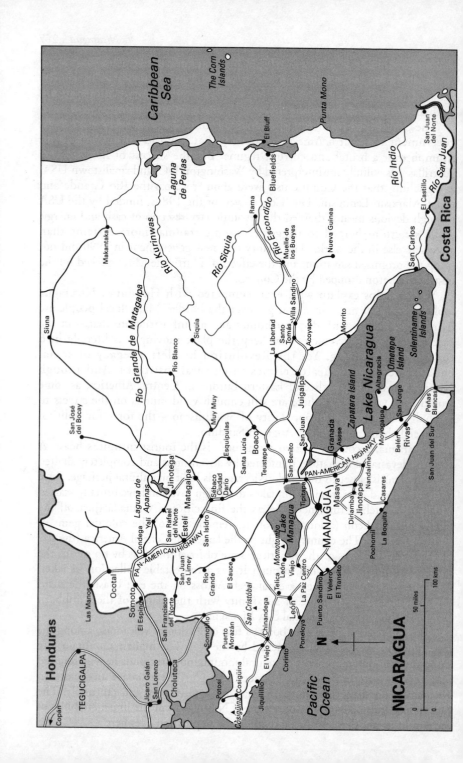

The Caribbean coast, nearly 500km (300 miles) long, is dotted with lagoons, swamps and some of Central America's most unspoilt beaches. Inland lies dense jungle and offshore are coral reefs, cays and islands. Western Nicaragua, through which the Highway cuts, is very different from the Atlantic coast, being dominated by the volcanoes strung along the Pacific coastline, and interspersed with lakes. Lake Nicaragua is the largest in Central America and has a unique marine life, and Managua is the only capital city in the world to be dotted with crater lakes. More than one visitor has commented that it is a shame the place has not been swallowed up completely, because Managua is a place of unparalleled ugliness and awfulness even by the undemanding standards of Central America. But, fortunately, ambiguity about the precise route carved by the Pan-American Highway through central Nicaragua means that you need never find out how bad the capital really is. What you will discover, though, is the remarkable stoicism of the people in the face of natural and man-made catastrophe.

At the frontier

The highest border post on the Pan-American Highway is between Honduras and Nicaragua. The line of the frontier itself has an arbitrary quality, and the ragged collection of official buildings looks hopelessly out of place in the fresh, cool highlands. The Pan-American Highway crosses at El Espino, though if you are travelling from Tegucigalpa you will cross at Las Manos, north of Ocotal. Strangely, the look of the frontier crossing points is remarkably similar, as are the formalities. Both resemble farms rather than international border posts, with pigs and chickens rootling around in the mud and dust. If you are planning to hitch-hike out – often the only option – then be especially nice to all the officials, since you may be relying on them later for a ride.

The arbitrary line on the map was the focus of plenty of attention during the 1980s. Guerrillas opposed to the Revolution based themselves inside Honduras, from where they launched raids into Nicaragua. The two countries were not actually at war, but you would be forgiven for thinking so, such was the extent of soldiers and military hardware on either side of the border. These days, the business of crossing the line is much easier – providing, as always, your papers are in order.

Red tape

Your passport must be valid for at least six months after the date of entry. Whether you enter by air or land you may be asked to show an onward or return air ticket. Travellers without a ticket can usually get in by showing sufficient funds to finance a stay, or producing an air ticket for a flight back home from another country.

Entry visas are required for visitors from the world's two most populous countries – China and India – plus 16 other nations, from Albania to Vietnam. British, US and almost all European nationals do not require tourist visas for a stay of up to 90 days. Everyone, though, must buy a **tourist card**, price $5, upon entry.

You can **extend your entry permit** at the Immigration Department (*Migración*) on Pista de la Resistencia, near the Israel Lewites bus terminal in Managua. This often proves problematic but if you succeed, processing should take a week or so. Being caught with an expired visa or entry permit is, theoretically, an offence punishable by prison.

At the border, having checked out of Honduras at the Migración window, you come first to a hut which marks the start of Nicaragua. An official will probably fill out the immigration form for you; you can safely ignore the sign reading hopefully 'One Dollar For Tip', but you may be asked where you intend to stay in the country; El Mesón in Estelí is as good a response as any.

Next, you reach a big cabin in the middle of the road where you pay the **frontier fee** of C24 'border tax' plus $5 for a tourist card. There are extra charges if you have the temerity to arrive on a Saturday, Sunday or public holiday. You can pay for all these in either dollars or córdobas, and the officials are usually happy to change money with you. **Customs** searches, if they take place at all, are usually perfunctory. You may officially take 200 cigarettes (or 500g tobacco) and three litres of alcoholic liquor into Nicaragua duty free. Prohibited articles include canned meats, dairy products, and military uniforms – leaving these out of your rucksack should not be too great a hardship. More awkward is the official requirement to have a prescription for all medicines in your possession, but this is rarely enforced. If you are carrying medication which you believe may raise interest, a letter from your doctor – ideally translated into Spanish – should help.

Finally, you reach another hut, where someone else will check that all your papers are in order before allowing you past the chain strung across the road.

Bringing in a car

If you have made it so far with a vehicle, you will be used to the long-drawn-out performance at each border, and entering Nicaragua is no exception. You can expect the full rigmarole of ownership, insurance and licence checks, with fees for each of these rigorous tasks and a likely fumigation for which you will also pay.

Any chance of a decent map?

Kevin Healey's Traveller's Reference Map of Nicaragua, published by ITMB in Vancouver and widely available in specialist shops in the UK and USA, does a creditable job of covering the whole country at a scale of 1:750,000, with a 1:50,000 map of Managua. Maps of other Nicaraguan cities are virtually non-existent. The Instituto Geográfico Nacional publishes topographical maps, but a permit is usually required to buy them. The IGN has its offices in a complex of government buildings east of the Israel Lewites bus station in Managua.

That was then

The first visitors

Little record of Nicaragua's past before Columbus survives – it has none of the large archaeological sites found in other Central American countries. The Indians who inhabited Nicaragua before the advent of the Spanish belonged to many different tribes. The two principal groups in the north and east were the Miskitos, ancestors of the Indians now living along the Caribbean coast, and the Sumos. Both were nomadic groups who sailed across from Colombia. The peoples in southern Nicaragua – mainly in the area between Lakes Managua and Nicaragua and the Pacific – lived in more permanent settlements. Other groups included the Lencas, found also in Honduras and El Salvador, who lived mainly in eastern areas; the Chorotegas, who came from Mexico; and the Chontales, thought to have been descendants of the Maya.

The Conquest

Christopher Columbus sighted Nicaragua in 1502, and was the first European to do so. Further exploration began 20 years later, when Pedrarias the Cruel, the notorious founder of the original settlement in Panama, sent Gil González Dávila off on an expedition. In 1523 the explorer landed on the Pacific coast. The country was then under the leadership of the Indian chief, Nicarao, from whom the name Nicaragua derives. The chief and his followers were converted swiftly to Christianity, and lavished gold on the Spanish conquistadores. The promise of gold encouraged further expeditions, and in 1524 Hernández de Córdoba landed and proceeded to conquer Nicaragua. But Córdoba's plan to set himself up as governor aroused the wrath of Pedrarias, who sent in an army to assert his own authority, and had Córdoba executed.

Nicaragua was eventually swallowed up into the administrative area under the command of the Governor-General based in Guatemala. Before his execution, Hernández de Córdoba had founded the country's first two towns, Granada and León, both in 1524. León was much the poorer, but was eventually chosen as capital because of its proximity to the Pacific coast.

The Spanish established a hold on western Nicaragua, and many Indians were killed off by disease. The conquistadores made no attempt to penetrate the wild and forested areas to the east, and the coastal bays provided shelter for pirates eager to plunder Spanish shipping in the Caribbean. During the 17th and 18th century a few British loggers also established themselves along the coast. This area – like much of the coast of Honduras – gradually came under the control of the British. In 1780 it was declared the British Protectorate of Mosquito (or Mosquitia), and a Miskito Indian – Jeremy I – was crowned king. Encouraged by this turn of events, Britain tried to extend its power by venturing inland, but Horatio Nelson's foray up the Río San Juan met with defeat – and Captain Nelson lost an eye in the process. The British maintained their hold on the east, however, and shipped in Jamaicans to settle along the coast. This area still has a strong identity of its own, and many people speak English.

Independence

Nicaragua gained full independence in 1838 in line with the other Central American nations. Internal troubles started soon afterwards, as rivalry brewed between the towns of Granada and León. While León was the official capital of

Nicaragua, a position supported by the Liberals, the Conservatives regarded Granada as the country's effective capital. (In modern terms, both groups were conservative.) This rivalry was exploited by an American called William Walker, one of the more bizarre and colourful characters in Nicaragua's history. Walker was a lawyer-turned-adventurer from Nashville who landed in Nicaragua in 1855 with a band of mercenaries in a bid to seize power. At the behest of a group of liberal fanatics – and with the tacit approval of the US government – he attacked and captured Granada. After a short period as Commander of the Armed Forces, Walker managed to get himself elected president of Nicaragua; one of his first acts was to suspend the laws against slavery. Co-operation among the other Central American states ended his term as ruler and resulted in Walker's expulsion from the country. But the American did not give up and mounted a couple more expeditions, both of which proved abortive. Eventually he was captured by the Royal Navy and handed over to the Honduran authorities, who tried and executed him in Trujillo in 1860.

Walker's adventures were symptomatic of growing US influence in the area. After 1856 there was a period of comparative tranquillity while Nicaragua was ruled by a series of Conservative presidents. A revolution in 1893, however, brought a Liberal called José Santo Zelaya to power. He instigated reforms, challenged the power of the church and of the landed élite.

The Twentieth Century

The USA grew increasingly concerned by Zelaya's activities and in 1909 it backed a Conservative revolution which forced the President to resign. This marked the beginning of serious American intervention, with Washington exercising more control by lending the new government money. US Marines had been sent to Nicaragua in 1909 as a show of force following the execution of two American mercenaries. They ended up staying on and off for over 20 years, principally to ensure that customs dues which had been offered as collateral for a US loan were collected, but the Marines also became involved in the country's internal affairs. The USA was also keen to have a hand in the development of a trans-isthmian canal, for which the original proposed site was Nicaragua. Eventually it was decided that the risk from seismic activity was too great; Panama was chosen instead, and duly had its heart cut out for the US-run Panama Canal Zone.

The degree of US involvement was resented increasingly within Nicaragua. In 1927, General Augusto César Sandino and other nationalists launched a guerrilla war against the US Marines which succeeded in getting the Americans withdrawn by President Roosevelt in 1933. But General Anastasio Somoza García had already been trained to head the National Guard which took over the Marines' security role. At the beginning of 1934, amid political jostling as the vacuum left by the USA was filled, Somoza invited Sandino to his home for talks. Driving back from the house, the nationalist leader was murdered by Somoza's National Guard. In 1935 Somoza deposed the Liberal president, Juan Batista Sacasa, and established a military régime with himself as president. He and his family ruled Nicaragua right up until 1979.

The Nicaraguan economy grew, but largely to the benefit of the Somozas and their friends. Virtually everything – from banks to communications networks – was owned or operated by them. Anastasio Somoza was assassinated in 1956, but was succeeded by his son who held power intermittently until 1967. Another son, Anastasio Somoza Debayle, took over the presidency, a position he held – with a short break – until 1979. These years were characterised by despotism, repression, corruption and greed. One of the worst examples was in 1972 when, after another devastating earthquake, much of the money sent from abroad as aid was pocketed by the Somozas; this largely explains the present ruinous condition of Managua.

The guerrilla movement survived the assassination of Sandino. In 1961, the Frente Sandinista de Liberación Nacional (FSLN) was formed as a guerrilla group to fight Somoza. The rebels took up Sandino's name and cause. Through the 60s and 70s they waged sporadic warfare against the Somozas. Their campaigns steadily gained in support and even *La Prensa*, a traditionally Conservative newspaper, printed editorials critical of the government. When its editor, Pedro Joaquín Chamorro, was murdered in 1978, even the wrath of right-wingers was aroused; previously they had paid little heed to the abuses of the Somoza regime. This event helped spark off the insurrection. In a final offensive in 1978-9, the Sandinistas ousted the last of the ruling Somozas. Anastasio Somoza (who was later assassinated in Paraguay) fled to Miami on 17 July 1979. Two days later the Sandinistas marched triumphantly into Managua.

Separated at birth?

Following the revolution, activists in a number of British cities set up support organisations to help the young régime. Some of these developed into official twinning arrangements. For example, the dusty Pacific port of Puerto Morazán became twinned with Bristol; Puerto Morazán got the better of this deal. The university city and former capital León linked up with Oxford, a much better match.

Volunteers from these British cities, and elsewhere in Europe, showed their solidarity with the Revolution by signing up to work bringing in the coffee harvest, repairing war damage, or helping with reafforestation. The footwear favoured by many of these foreign volunteers meant they were often described as *sandalistas*. These *brigadistas* or *internacionalistas* (as they were officially known) were welcomed as a sign of international solidarity and a means of enlarging contacts worldwide. Going on a brigade was never a soft option: the work was back-breaking. Participants were expected to eat rice, beans and tortillas three times a day and sleep in the company of rats. For this four-week 'holiday', you paid £1,100 – a lot more than a complete package tour could cost these days.

The Sandinista Regime

A junta consisting of leaders of the FSLN and their civilian allies was established in 1979. Real power during the 1980s, however, lay in the hands of the nine Sandinista *comandantes*. Daniel Ortega was a classic revolutionary who had suffered imprisonment and torture under the Somoza regime, and played a leading role in the overthrow of the dictatorship; as such he was the natural choice to head the junta.

The government launched a far-reaching programme providing for the nationalisation of industry and radical social and land reforms. Health centres were established all over the country, and literacy increased dramatically. The government was given little chance to develop social welfare, however, following the election to the US presidency of Ronald Reagan in 1980. Nicaragua's contact with Cuba, and its alleged dealings with the left-wing rebels in El Salvador, made it a target for American intervention. In 1981, the USA began a campaign to destabilise Nicaragua, heralding a decade of bloodshed and hardship. The campaign hinged on the creation of the 'Contra' guerrilla army, which began as little more than a motley crew of ex-National Guard members. The Contras were joined by other disaffected Nicaraguans, including Miskito Indians from the Atlantic coast – they were unhappy at the central government's clumsy attempts at imposing policies on what was an essentially autonomous region. The rebels received millions of dollars in aid from the USA during the 1980s, and the Sandinista government had little choice but to use much of the country's resources to finance the war effort.

In an effort to legitimise Sandinista rule, elections were held in November 1984. Although international observers declared the elections free and fair, the main opposition candidate withdrew shortly before the contest under US pressure. The Sandinistas won two-thirds of the vote, but the Reagan administration described the elections as a Soviet-style sham. In January 1985, Daniel Ortega began a six-year term as president. The war continued relentlessly. Throughout the 1980s, attempts by other Central American countries to establish a peace treaty foundered. In 1985 Reagan ordered a trade embargo. Aid to the Contras increased and the war intensified, with the rebels establishing bases within Nicaragua as well as in Honduras. Nicaragua became more reliant upon the Soviet Union. Serious peace talks began only in 1987, when the Arias Peace Plan called for the end of outside aid to the Contras, and the disbanding of the rebels in return for bringing forward the elections.

As relations between the West and the USSR improved at the end of the 1980s, Cold War-style political games lost their relevance and there was a gradual shift from the military to the political arena. In February 1988 Congress suspended military aid following the Iran-Contra scandal involving the diversion of arms sale funds to the Nicaraguan rebels. In August 1989 the Central American presidents signed the Tela peace agreement which was something of a diplomatic coup for the Sandinistas. It laid down provisions for the Contra camps in Honduras to be dismantled, and for the guerrillas to be repatriated or resettled in other countries.

The elections held in February 1990 were fought between the Sandinistas and the US-backed National Opposition Union (UNO), a hastily patched-together 14-party coalition ranging from communists to conservatives. Violeta, Pedro Joaquín Chamorro's widow, was chosen as leader of the party as the only one able to hold such a disparate group together. She had joined the Sandinista junta in 1979, but became disillusioned with the direction Ortega was taking and later aligned herself with the Contras. Emulating her husband, she became editor of *La Prensa* newspaper, the Sandinistas' fiercest critic.

Chamorro's connection with the Contras gave her scant credibility abroad. Furthermore, the UNO was prey to internal wrangling, was badly organised and united only in its opposition to the FSLN. The international press regarded a Sandinista victory as inevitable and the polls suggested the same. Ortega's election promise of *todo será mejor* ('everything will be better') could not, however, counter the effect of almost a decade of war. Chamorro's campaign promises of an end to US sanctions, an amnesty, and the abolition of conscription, sounded good to Nicaraguans sick of violence and economic mayhem. The elections produced a big win for Violeta, who won 55% of the vote, compared to Ortega's 39.5%. The elections were among the fairest ever seen in Central America. Amid general Sandinista discontent, Daniel Ortega handed over power in April 1990.

Post-Sandinista Nicaragua

Violeta Chamorro, whose childhood ambition was to be a secretary, became Central America's first female president. Her decision to retain Daniel Ortega's brother, Humberto, as head of the Sandinista military was welcomed by the FSLN but caused anger among those UNO deputies who were demanding a purge of the Sandinistas from both the army and the police. In the first seven months after Chamorro took office, the Central Bank devalued the currency 46

No more heroes?
Most Nicaraguan towns used to have their own Galería de Héroes y Mártires, dedicated to those who died during the Revolution. These 'museums' displayed photographs of the local men and women killed in the struggle, and occasionally had related exhibits – from blood-stained shirts to home-made tanks. Other museums were the converted childhood homes of heroes of the Revolution, such as Carlos Fonseca. The museums set up by the Sandinistas have largely been closed down, as have the monuments, memorials and murals created under the Ortega government. But in towns and cities with a pro-Sandanista population, there are still many murals which adorn walls to proclaim the success of the Revolution. Go now while slogans last.

times. Nevertheless, national reconciliation began. But her conciliatory approach led to factional splits within her party, which ceased to be a credible force until it re-invented itself in 1993 to embrace some FSLN members. This move caused the United States to suspend aid to Nicaragua.

Discontent and opposition grew: a pro-Sandinista group occupied Estelí in 1993. A spate of political kidnappings took place, and there was student violence in protest against the government's broken promises on education funding. In addition, demands increased for the return of land, which had been misappropriated by the Somozistas and retained by the Sandinistas, to its rightful owners.

In 1996, the candidate of the Liberal Alliance, Arnoldo Alemán, became president. He was previously the mayor of Managua, and an old Somoza crony. Openly anti-Sandinista, he willingly returned land to its former owners, which incurred protests by the FSLN. Unemployment increased, and allegations of scandal and corruption surrounded Alemán and his government. His unpopularity peaked in October 1998, when the northern part of the country was devastated by Hurricane Mitch; Alemán questioned the severity of the damage, and refused to declare a state of emergency. International aid poured in, but the relief organisations expressed concern that money intended for the victims of the hurricane would be creamed off by the government. Strong opposition has continued from the FSLN, but their own internal divisions have made them less effective than they might be.

Rewriting, or painting, history

When Daniel Ortega was deposed in 1990, aspects of life under Sandinista rule were quickly expunged. In May of that year, Arnaldo Alemán – then mayor of Managua – cut off the fuel supply to the eternal flame burning on the tomb of Carlos Fonseca, one of the architects of the Revolution. In June, Sandinista books were publicly burnt in León. Paint donated by the US government to 'beautify the capital' was used to destroy some of the more vivid Sandinista murals.

This is now

Despite the damage to the country's infrastructure inflicted by Hurricane Mitch, Nicaragua's economic situation is showing signs of improvement. One danger is that the economy has a narrow base, making it particularly vulnerable to fluctuations in the price of commodities such as oil or coffee. In 2000, increasingly many travellers were converging on Nicaragua because of high prices in Costa Rica, but that is still a long way from the tourism boom still being enjoyed by the southern neighbour. The best hope that the government can cling to is that interest in a canal through Nicaragua is renewed, which could come about if Panama proves unstable now that the Americans have bequeathed 'their' canal to the local people.

On the Highway

You may not immediately see any great difference between the Pan-American Highway in Honduras and the same road in Nicaragua: both are dismal excuses for international superhighways. But while Honduras has the excuse of Hurricane Mitch, in much of Nicaragua the reason is war damage exacerbated by a couple of decades of neglect.

The Pan-American Highway is the best of the lot, entirely paved for the 384km (240 miles) between the Honduran and Costa Rican borders. The curious thing is: no-one can tell me exactly where it goes. There is no argument that it enters Nicaragua at El Espino, and heads 220km south as CA-1 to the mangy town of Tipitapa, on the shore of Lake Managua. But here, the Panamericana loses the plot. Some maps show it heading due west into Managua and turning sharp left (south) to Jinotepe. Others mark it going south from Tipitapa to Masaya. Here, again, versions differ, with one continuing south and the other veering off for a little detour to Granada before rejoining the southbound track. All three pretenders are united by the time they meet at a ragged junction just north of Nandaime – where the reconciled road continues as CA-1 (if you look at the map) or CA-2 (if you check the signposts). No arguments, though, that this Highway exits for Costa Rica at Peñas Blancas. Having tried all three variants, I heartily recommend the Masaya-Granada version.

Even the Pan-American Highway is not immune from the damage caused during the rains, and there are pot-holes everywhere. The other trunk roads are those from Managua to Granada, León, and Rama, the latter being comparatively new. All are paved, whereas most branch roads, except those serving important towns, are dirt tracks. One piece of good news: *topes*, the speed bumps that inconvenience traffic all over Central America, are relatively rare in Nicaragua. Or maybe it's just that you can't tell they're there amid all the rest of the devastation.

If you think the roads are bad, you should see the vehicles that attempt to use them. From beaten-up American saloons in such poor nick that even a Cuban motorist would turn his nose up at them, to horses which are almost as antiquated as the carts they are obliged to drag behind them, Nicaragua's transport is a mess.

The **buses** are more crowded and less roadworthy than anywhere else in Central America, which – as you will appreciate by now – is quite an achievement. There are now some fast, air-conditioned minibuses running on the main routes to or from Managua, but they are the exception. Many buses are still unchanged from the day when they were taken out of service as school buses in North America, complete with octagonal 'Stop' sign (or, in the case of those from Quebec, 'Arret'). Some still have the original sign, in English, reading NO Standing Smoking Eating Drinking. All but the second command are routinely ignored. It is still the only place where I have seen passengers hanging on to the sides of a bus, dangling precariously from a window frame (from which the glass has long since vanished). Buses along the Pan-American Highway tend to be the best of a bad lot. When travelling off the Highway, be prepared for longer waits and the likelihood of a ride in a (poorly) converted truck. Buses, whether trucks or not, are often called *camionetas*, a term that also covers pick-up trucks piled high with people and their possessions. Most are operated by private companies, but the state travel organisation Enabin runs some services.

Another superlative about bus travel in Nicaragua is the inordinate good humour displayed by the occupants of what may loosely be described as 'public transport'. Extra passengers will usually be accommodated, come what may. Gringos are looked after much more than they deserve to be (they are, after all, using up valuable space). On the rare occasion when a seat becomes available, you will probably be offered it.

Great work of fiction?

Ambitiously, a German has compiled a *Nicaragua Timetable* listing details of bus, ship and air travel. You can obtain it for $8 from Mathias Hock Services, Grazer Weg 38, D60599 Frankfurt, Germany (tel +49 69 655 710).

If you are **driving**, beware of being on the road after dark since some vehicles have long since lost their headlights. You should also be aware of the unusual rules that surround a traffic accident. Traditionally, vehicles involved in accidents in Nicaragua are not moved (even to clear traffic) until a policeman gives approval. Any driver who does not comply may automatically be deemed legally liable for the accident. That is only the first of many difficulties: any driver who is party to an accident where injuries are sustained will be taken into custody, even if the driver is insured and appears not to have been at fault. You could stay in prison for weeks or months until a judicial decision is reached; the usual shortcut is for the injured party to sign a waiver relieving the driver of further liability, as the result of a cash settlement. For more information on rules of the road, in Spanish at least, you could consult cancilleria.gob.ni.

All in all, **hitch-hiking** is a better prospect than driving. Known locally as *el ride*, hitching became a way of life during the 1980s. As the number of roadworthy vehicles decreased, so the number of hitchers increased; most drivers who had room in their car or truck felt obliged to give a lift to anyone waiting by the road, particularly along the minor roads with poor transport services. Hitching is still arguably the best way to travel in Nicaragua. Not only is it more comfortable travelling in the back of a pick-up truck than in a bus, it is usually quicker and an excellent way to meet people. Since it is such an accepted way of getting around, some women travellers do not feel nervous about joining in.

Alone of the Central American nations, Nicaragua has long had a good **bicycle** rental organisation: Si Bicicletas, No Bombas (Bicycles not Bombs) in the capital rents out hunky all-terrain bikes for reasonable amounts, enabling you to see the country as many locals see it.

The flyover option

Not advisable, unless you are overflying the whole country and therefore not planning to travel on the local domestic airlines. During the war it was said that Sandinista soldiers would rather endure the unaptly named Bluefields Express to the coast – 16 hours of discomfort on bus and boat – than risk an hour's flight on Aeronica's clapped out fleet. The US authorities said in 2000 that 'flights make use of small, uncontrolled airstrips outside of Managua, with minimal safety equipment and little boarding security. In the last three years, there have been two incidents of hijacking of commuter flights departing from these airports.'

What's different about Nicaragua?

Horses and courses, for a start. The country has developed its own strategies for coping with adversities, and some idiosyncracies for urban living. Horse-drawn carts are a common form of transport in most Nicaraguan towns. (When the economy was at its lowest ebb, even beasts of burden were in short supply, and human power was used.) An interesting and relaxing horse-drawn ride would, in other countries, constitute a tourist attraction; here, it is a fact of economic life.

One advantage of letting the dray take the strain is that you don't have to figure out where you're going. Nicaraguan addresses are some of the strangest in the world. They are given with respect to certain landmarks (which may no longer exist) in two components. The first is distance, in *cuadras* (blocks) or *varas* (literally 'yards', but normally distances are so approximate that metres are no less meaningful). The second is direction, usually one of *norte* (north), *oeste* or *poniente* (west), *sur* (south), *este* or *oriente* (east), though these may be superseded in certain places by terms such as *al lago* ('towards the lake'). The only solution is to keep asking the locals.

Is Nicaragua a good place to start or finish a trip along the Pan-American Highway?

It would be eccentric to start or finish in Nicaragua, because the place you would need to fly to or from is Managua, the ugliest capital in the western world. All the good bits of Nicaragua keep a safe distance from Managua, and are predominately found north and south of the capital. So you would be likely to miss out on at least half the attractions of the country. But if you are that pressed for time, then fly into Managua's airport, ignore the city itself and head for Masaya, Granada and Lake Nicaragua, continuing south into Costa Rica and Panama.

Who are the Nicaraguans?

Three-quarters of Nicaraguans are mestizo, of mixed Spanish and Indian blood. Just 4% are pure Indian, and most of these indigenous people live along the Mosquito Coast in eastern Nicaragua. The main groups are the Sumos, Ramas and Miskitos, of which the Miskitos are the largest. It is said that the word Miskito derives from 'musket' after the guns that were given to the local Indians when the British first arrived in the area in the 17th century, but this may be romantic fabrication. Also concentrated along the Caribbean coast are the blacks, who make up 9% of the population. They are descended from people brought by the British from Jamaica and other Caribbean islands to colonise the area in the 18th century. There is also a small number of Garifuna, descendants of African slaves and Carib Indians. Many Nicaraguans along the Atlantic coast speak variants of English, but the steady influx of mestizos into the region over the years means that Spanish is spoken increasingly.

'Dour, unfriendly and antagonistic' is not the sort of description normally used in the context of Central Americans, but those terms have been used by foreigners to describe people in Nicaragua. Visitors who spend their time in Managua, one of the least user-friendly capitals in the world, might draw the same conclusions. Life in the city does no-one any favours, and as a result many of the citizens can appear on the surface to be in a perpetually bad mood. But drawing conclusions about a nation's people from the way that a few Managuans push and shove and are needlessly rude, is a mistake on a par with characterising all Americans as rude after a spell on the New York subway or dismissing the British as mindless thugs from the behaviour of a few soccer hooligans. The people of Nicaragua have endured almost complete economic collapse, and have more important things to do than worry about whether you're having a nice time. Having said that, however, most of the locals are as warm, friendly and hospitable as any in the region. In rural areas the people are often surprised and pleased to see foreigners – the sensation of an entire village falling quiet in order to stare at a couple of foreigners who have just got off the bus is awesome, but harmless. It is also a little unnerving at first to hear *Adiós* spoken in reply to your greeting of *Buenos días*, but this is an idiosyncracy of the Nicaraguan language and is not meant as an affront.

What they eat

The *comedores* offer a reliable and familiar plateful of rice, frijoles, anonymous lumps of meat, fried banana, etc. Cassava (*yuca*) and *chicharrón* (fried pork skins – not to everyone's liking), are also typical comedor fare. Mexican-style food is rare, though some small bars serve tacos and nacatamales – a local version of the tamales (stuffed corn cakes baked in banana skins) found elsewhere in Central America. More unusual dishes are rarely served in restaurants, but during your visit you should have at least one chance to try iguana (*garrobo*) and even armadillo if you're really lucky.

What they drink

Nicaragua boasts the best rum and beer in Central America. The most famous brand of rum is Flor de Caña, sold all over the region. It is *seco* (white) or *oro* (gold, sweeter than the seco). The high-quality five-year old version is hard to find. The local beers are Victoria and Toña. While the former is rather too malty, Toña is delicious, although not as strong as some other Central American beers. The price of a bottle is generally around $1, but can be twice as much in a Managuan restaurant.

Pepsi and Coca Cola are the most popular non-alcoholic drinks, but local, hideously sweet bottled drinks are also available under the brand name Rojitas. You should stick to the usual fruit juices and licuados. Among the local specialities are those which have corn as the main ingredient: the most common ones are *chicha* (fermented corn drink), *tiste* (cacao and corn) and *posol con leche* (corn and milk). Bottled water is not commonplace, but you sometimes see Ensa mineral water on sale.

Nicaragua is noted for its coffee, but the highest quality beans are exported, and you will almost always be offered instant. It is likely to be served extremely weak and very milky.

What they read, watch and listen to

The two leading **newspapers** in Nicaragua are *Barricada* and *La Prensa*. Both have strong political alignments, to the Sandinistas and the conservatives respectively. A third paper is the *Nuevo Diario*. It is less partisan, but nonetheless supports the leftist line. There are various local papers, including *El Centroamericano* (León) and *Sunrise*, a bilingual newspaper published in Bluefields.

Underground **radio** broadcasts played an important part in the Revolution when illicit stations such as Venceremos in León broadcast FSLN propaganda

Disclaiming political responsibility

An example of the complexity of Nicaragua's political personality was evident when the Chamorro regime came to power. One of the few home-grown programmes was *Extra Visión*, broadcast every evening in the prime-time slot at 9.30pm. It was a news programme made by an independent company sympathetic to the Sandinistas. The new government did not immediately replace it, but before and after the show a disclaimer flashed up on to the screen, reading: 'This space was sold by the previous administration. It does not reflect the feelings of the new administration.'

to counter the Somoza line, and various Sandinista-run stations operated during the 1980s. When La Voz, a pro-Sandinista radio station, became Radio Nicaragua and started supporting the Chamorro government in 1990, a group of the radio's employees broke away to set up their own Radio Ya, with equipment donated by the USSR. Miraculously, the equipment still works and the station is remarkably popular.

The state **television** channels broadcast imported material. US programmes predominate, although some Latin American and British material is broadcast too. Brazilian soap operas are popular, as are unfunny Mexican comedies.

How they enjoy themselves

Baseball was brought to Nicaragua by US marines in the 1920s, and enjoys a fanatical following. Children play it in the streets, using whatever equipment they can find – a book for a bat and a hat for a glove. **Basketball** and **volleyball** are other popular spectator sports, **soccer** less so. A certain amount of bullfighting still goes on, but the animal is not killed. As far as participation sports are concerned, fishing on Lake Nicaragua (where marine fish including sharks and tarpons are found) is the most popular. While swimming in Nicaragua's lakes is not recommended, there are some fine beaches along the coasts, particularly on the Caribbean.

Festivals and holidays

January 1	New Year
March/April	Holy Week
May 1	Labour Day
September 14	Anniversary of the Battle of San Jacinto
September 15	Independence Day
November 1	All Saints' Day
December 8	Immaculate Conception
December 25	Christmas Day

What they spend

The córdoba is now relatively robust, but there is still an active parallel market offering slightly better rates than the banks. Moneychangers are sometimes referred to as *coyotes* and are found mainly in Managua, León, Granada, Matagalpa and at the borders; but if you ask around in any town there is usually someone to change money with.

Anything worth buying?

Masaya is the town most famous for its craftsmen, who make beautiful hammocks among other things. Much of their work is on sale in the huge

Who wants to be a millionnaire?
Nicaragua began the 1990s with the unenviable record of having the weakest currency in the world. In November 1990, a momentous event took place in Nicaragua: the value of the Nicaraguan córdoba dropped to one-millionth of a dollar. With inflation running at 30,000% annually, it didn't hold that level for very long – the price of a newspaper could double from one day to the next. The treasury could not afford to print new banknotes, so new denominations are stamped in crudely over the old notes. New shorthands were invented: one million córdobas was referred to as *un peso*, while 100,000 córdobas became *un real*; the term had previously been used to describe 10 centavos.

In an effort to boost the standing of Nicaragua's currency, the new government introduced the córdoba oro on a par with the US dollar, with the slogan *córdoba oro – la moneda sólida*. This was soon rebutted with cries of *córdoba de sangre* and *córdoba de hambre*, blood and hunger being images familiar to most Nicaraguans. Much hardship and many erased zeros later, the córdoba is doing creditably well.

Roberto Huembes market in Managua (where you can also buy more practical things such as loo roll, toothbrushes, and mosquito coils), but the market in Masaya itself is better and cheaper for crafts. The stalls in Managua, however, have crafts from other, more remote, parts of the country, including soapstone carvings from San Juan de Limay (northeast of Estelí) and jewellery from the Atlantic coast.

Shops generally open 8am-noon and 2pm-5.30pm/6pm Monday to Friday. Most close at noon on Saturday and do not open at all on Sunday.

Keeping in touch

Telephone
The state telecommunications company is Telcor, hived off and officially known these days as Enitel, but no more efficient for all that. Most phone offices open 7am-10pm. Even in these digital days, it can take some time for international calls to be put through since lines are often busy, particularly at weekends and in the evening. From an office, the cost of a three-minute call to the UK is about $14.50, to the USA $12.50 – figures that have not changed in a decade. You may be better off buying a phone card, but first make sure that you can find a functioning card-operated public phone, marked Publitel. As a last resort, it is possible to make collect calls to both the USA and Europe.

Domestic phone calls are not significantly more reliable than international ones. All numbers are seven digits, of which the first three are a kind of area code – Estelí 713, Masaya 522, Granada 552; Managua has many prefixes. If you are dialling another number within the same area, just use the seven digits; for long-distance calls, precede them with a zero. A functioning payphone is relatively rare, so the network is supplemented in busy areas by enterprising traders selling calls from mobile phones; you would usually pay $1 for a quick call anywhere in the country. When dialling into Nicaragua from abroad, the country code is 505.

Internet access is intermittent, as a result of the poor telecommunications network. Cyber cafés have not yet become widespread, and those that exist tend to have long queues of forlorn-looking travellers. When you finally get on to a terminal, you may well find that accessing your mail provider is often beyond its capabilities.

Air **mail** from Managua to the UK and Europe takes two to four weeks, while post sent from outside the capital can easily take six weeks. To send a postcard to the UK costs about 60c, to the USA 40c. Post offices open 9am-5.30pm, Monday to Saturday. Postcards are annoyingly expensive and hard to find. **Poste Restante** mail from Europe takes about 10 days to reach Nicaragua. Take your passport when collecting mail since letters are not handed over unless you can prove your identity. Letters are held for a month, after which time they may or may not be returned to sender.

The outdoors – how great?

Nicaragua is the only country in Central America in which the protection of the environment is part of the constitution. During the 1980s, however, conservation was never a top priority, and in addition the Contra war did terrible damage to the forested areas of northern Nicaragua. There are many areas which need attention – from the pocket of dense forest in the Cosiguina peninsula northwest of León, to the jungle along the Caribbean coast. Among the animals found in Nicaragua are pumas, jaguar and monkeys, and there is also abundant birdlife.

The Masaya National Park, east of Managua, is the only reserve of any importance at present. Be careful when straying off the beaten track in the north of Nicaragua, because reverberations of the Contra War continue to be felt – land mines pose a danger to anyone venturing off the main roads.

A word of warning

Crime has increased considerably over the last few years. Be wary about walking alone through the streets of Managua after dark, since there is little street lighting. Even in other towns the locals advise people to be off the streets by 9.30pm. Be careful when travelling by bus: as well as people picking your pockets, watch out for people who snatch watches as you try to board. The city buses in Managua have an especially bad reputation.

The US State Department issued the following warning in March 2000: 'There are frequent accounts of robberies, kidnappings and extortion committed by armed criminal groups, particularly in remote areas in the northern/central departments of Nueva Segovia, Madriz, Jinotega, Matagalpa,

Estelí and Boaco. These actions are primarily directed at local residents. However, travel in these areas is discouraged.

'Boundary disputes involving the governments of Nicaragua, Honduras and Costa Rica persist, particularly in the Caribbean coastal waters adjoining these countries, and on the San Juan River along the Nicaragua-Costa Rica border. Passengers and crews of foreign fishing boats have been detained and/or fined and vessels impounded.'

The natural world offers plenty of hazards, too. Nicaragua is frequently hit by hurricanes. Edith and Fifi caused mass devastation in 1971 and 1974 respectively; in 1988 Hurricane Joan wreaked havoc in the Atlantic coast; and a decade later Mitch came to town, wrecking parts of the north of Nicaragua.

Contaminated water, and malaria, remain the two main health hazards for travellers. It is generally considered safe to drink the water in Managua (although it tends to be over-chlorinated), but you may decide not to try it anywhere else.

From the frontier to the capital

Enjoy the scenery along the Honduran border, because you are close to the highest point in the whole of Nicaragua (Pico Mogotón, 2,106m, which straddles the frontier, and it doesn't get much better than this.

If you have no vehicle, you are likely to have plenty of time to enjoy the scenery, because transport is scarce. You can either loiter around the frontier itself, or wander off down the road to enjoy rather more serene surroundings. Either way, all the traffic will be channelled past your waiting thumb. There are some collective taxis linking the frontier with Somoto, 18km (11 miles) east. These charge $1 for a 'seat', though that term should be interpreted loosely as seven customers are squeezed into a small Japanese saloon. (From the northern border at Las Manos, the same applies to Ocotal, 25km/16 miles south).

If all you do is change from a collective taxi to a bus at Somoto, you are unlikely to regard it as the highlight of your trip. A market town at the heart of a major agricultural region, its one claim to fame is a beautiful church. There are two basic hotels and one simple restaurant, should you need to stay overnight, but it will not be the most exciting night of your life.

Ocotal is a bit more interesting. Nuevo Segovia, the province over which it presides, was one of the first regions to be occupied by the Spanish who were attracted by its gold and silver mines, and gold is still mined in the area. Ocotal itself is a lovely town on a plateau – a sea of red-tiled roofs surrounded by hills. If you are interested in exploring a seldom-visited area there is one trip you can do which is strongly recommended. Twenty-five kilometres (16 miles) east of Ocotal, along a road which passes through the picturesque villages of Mozonte, San Fernando and Santa Clara, is Ciudad Antigua. This was the main town of the province of Segovia in colonial times, when the province occupied the whole of northern Nicaragua. The town was founded by the Spanish governor,

Eduardo Contreras. You can see the remains of a few colonial buildings in the village, and there is a pretty church.

The roads from both frontier points meet at Yalagüina, 58km (36 miles) north of Estelí – about an hour away, if you are lucky. Progress could be slowed by repairs following Hurricane Mitch – just south of Yalagüina, a temporary causeway is being replaced by a big new bridge. At Condega, you could branch off east (left) to Jinotega and Matagalpa. But if you have no pressing need to do so, keep straight on for one of the modest highlights of the Highway through Nicaragua.

Estelí: Sandino's last resort

Blink, and you could miss the three grubby signposts directing you to Estelí, the capital of the department of the same name. The Pan-American Highway bypasses the town, and if all you saw was the view from the road, you would conclude it was nothing but a dusty truckstop. In fact, Estelí is a small (population 20,000), comfortable (600m/2,000ft high) and radical town, where the memories of the Revolution have prevailed longer than elsewhere; it was badly damaged during the fighting during and after the Sandinistas' victory. It is popular among travellers, many of whom come here to learn Spanish – several language schools cater for them. Estelí is also the centre of Nicaragua's tobacco industry, and exports cigars.

The town is long and thin, stretching for about 3km from north to south, with the Pan-American Highway marking the eastern edge of town. The **Parque Central** is six blocks east of the Highway, and almost everything of interest is within a couple of blocks. The **bus station** is a long way south of the centre, with collective taxis running to and from the Parque Central for around $0.25.

There is a relatively wide choice of **places to stay**, many of which grew up during the 1980s when brigade workers began coming to the area. With the exception of the expensive Hotel Alameda (713 6292, $60 double), lodgings scattered along the Pan-American are pretty horrible; those in town are much better. Most travellers converge, with good reason, on El Mesón, one block north of the cathedral and Parque Central (tel 713 2655). It is a cheerful place, with a decent restaurant and small, poky rooms dotted around a courtyard of sorts. The staff are jolly and helpful, and a room costs $10 single/$15 double. There are other options on Avenida Bolívar, the main street, particularly towards the southern end near the hospital and bus station. The Hospedaje Chepito and the Hospedaje and Comedor Amaresquero are recommended. More expensive but nearer the Parque Central is Hotel Nicarao. Another hotel is the Marelia opposite the school south of the hospital.

The best place to **eat** is White House Pizzas, two blocks east of the Parque Central. On the walls are resistance movement posters from all over the world, and there are a few crafts on sale. Another interesting place, if it is still functioning, is the Comedor Popular La Soya, one of a chain of restaurants in Nicaragua which has been trying to promote the use of the soya bean. Wherever you choose, eat early since bars and restaurants close early, i.e. around 9pm.

The Parque Central is dominated by the 19th-century **cathedral**, and occupied by a fine bunch of hustlers who will heckle you but do no harm at all. They may also pose in front of the strident **murals** that decorate many of the available surfaces, and which show a more idealistic Nicaragua than the one you will encounter in the 21st century. In the centre is a monument to Nicaraguan mothers. A short distance south of the cathedral is – or more accurately, *was* – the Galería de Héroes y Mártires, which documented the town during the fighting. Among the exhibits were weapons used by the National Guard and the Sandinistas during the Revolution. The problem is that it was closed down under the Chamorro government and shows little sign of reopening.

Also in the Parque Central are some **prehistoric carved rocks** (petroglyphs) depicting humans, animals and birds. These were brought from **Las Pintadas**, an archaeological site eight kilometres (five miles) west of town; in the same vicinity, at the foot of Mount Quaibu, you can see idols and stone carvings. To the north are the ruins of an Indian village. Within walking distance of Estelí is a waterfall called the Salto de Extanzuela, about five kilometres (three miles) south of town. It is in a nice spot surrounded by trees; the waterfall and its deep pool are best seen during the wet season. To get there, walk along the highway south of town for about a kilometre and take a right turn down a dirt track which leads to the village of San Nicolás and beyond to the falls.

There is a bank on the southwest corner of the Parque Central; many of the traders in the market around the corner are happy to try to beat the exchange rates. The worst internet location in Nicaragua is on the northwest corner, where you will spend many dollars and unhappy hours trying to make a connection.

Moving on – a highland excursion

The obvious move is to get the hourly bus (6am-3pm) from the terminal towards Managua, but if time is on your side you could enjoy a fine loop to the east, through fascinating and unspoilt communities in cowboy territory. There are trucks and meagre traffic along the 90-minute journey into the hills and the village of **La Concordia**. In this village, horses seem to outnumber people. Arriving here is rather like walking into a saloon in a Western movie – everyone stops talking and watches your every step. There is no sense of hostility, but it is certainly an unusual experience.

Six kilometres east from here, a left turn takes you another kilometre to **San Rafael Norte**. As you approach, the first sight is the cemetery on the hillside and the church above it. The rest of the small town is strung along a muddy high street and a large Parque Central-cum-basketball pitch. The church, however, is stunning for a town of this size – it would not look out of place in an Italian city, with (fake) marble pillars, vivid murals and one of the few stained glass windows in Nicaragua. The men favour sitting around – on Sundays they gather outside to chat and gossip while their wives are inside attending the service. The only place to stay is the Pensión Vargas on the main street.

Next along the loop is **Jinotega**, 20km (12 miles) southeast, but unless you need to stop for the night you could happily pass straight through the departmental capital. Having risen above the clouds in places, you descend to a plateau almost 900 metres above sea level. A more beautiful setting for a town can hardly be imagined. Unfortunately Jinotega, the 'city of mists', is one of the least attractive and most run-down places in Nicaragua. Ramshackle houses are sprawled along muddy, pot-holed streets. The town's only attraction is its long and elegant church, with a now-headless statue of the revolutionary Carlos Fonseca opposite. The smartest place to stay is the Hotel Bolper (632 2966), which charges $16 double. On the first paved north-south road between the bus station and the city centre are the Hotel Brumas and the Pensión Patricia, neither of which is remotely enticing. Nevertheless, both are preferable to the Comedor Hozpedage (sic), close to the bus station, which should be regarded only as a last resort. For food, try the Restaurant El Oasis del Viajero or the Comedor Araica, both close to the bus station.

The main road to Matagalpa takes you high up into the hills, and provides spectacular views over the highlands. Along the way, you pass the entrance to **Selva Negra** forest, 10km (six miles) north of Matagalpa, between kilometre markers 139 and 140. The turn-off is on the right, by an old burnt-out tank of Somoza's.

Wild wood

Selva Negra ('black wood') and Santa María de Ostuma nearby contain large areas of virgin forest, although increased coffee production means that huge chunks of it have been cut down. The cultivation of coffee has also threatened the wildlife which ranges from big cats including pumas and ocelots, to sloths, wart hogs and spider monkeys. The birdlife, however, is among the most abundant found anywhere in Nicaragua, and includes hummingbirds, trogons, and emerald toucanets; some people have even claimed to have seen quetzals. The forest is full of trails, and walking here is a safer proposition than elsewhere in the northern highlands; there are no reported cases of mines being discovered. The best time to go birdwatching is at dawn or dusk. The Hotel de la Montaña Selva Negra (612 5713, selvanegra@tmx.com.ni), a couple of kilometres from the main road at kilometre 140, is an excellent retreat, perched 1,350m above speed level. A double room costs $40, with some bungalows available at $60.

Matagalpa lies in the highlands about 125km (80 miles) north of Managua. It is the capital of the department of the same name, one of the largest and most populous regions of the country. The town is home to 70,000 people. Although not particularly attractive itself, Matagalpa's setting amid hilly, coffee-growing country is lovely. In addition, being almost 700m (2,400ft) above sea level, the temperatures are generally cool and pleasant – but if you are heading for the lowlands of Nicaragua, don't get too used to the idea.

The town has few paved roads – the hills around Matagalpa are covered with a maze of muddy tracks disappearing into the distance. Simple wooden houses are scattered along these winding streets. The town was badly damaged during the Revolution, and reconstruction work has been limited.   This is a place to sample life in a highland town rather than to go sightseeing. The large, colonial-style cathedral, built in 1874 by the Jesuits, is unimaginative and stark inside, but has a story to it: in 1881, during an Indian uprising, it remained unscathed because the Indians had helped build it. Parque Darío is equally uninspiring. Parque Darío contains the ubiquitous monument to Rubén Darío – in the standard pose, hand under chin – and also one to the unknown guerrilla. The most interesting place to visit is Casa Carlos Fonseca, the home of one of the founder members of the Sandinista movement, and commander-in-chief of the FSLN forces during the Revolution; his bearded and bespectacled figure used to be stencilled on walls all over the country.

Just south of Matagalpa is the town's cemetery; you can't miss it as you depart for Sébaco. Most of the graves seem to be sliding down the hill. One is the tomb of Ben Linder, a 28-year old American aid worker who was murdered in 1987. The first American *cooperante* to be killed by the Contras, his death caused outrage in Nicaragua, and Daniel Ortega was one of the coffin-bearers at his funeral. His headstone is engraved with a unicycle in memory of the one on which Ben used to ride around Matagalpa. Matagalpa's local holiday is Día de La Merced, on 24 September.

Matagalpa's bus station is about five blocks west of Parque Darío. There are direct buses to the capital from Matagalpa until around 4pm. It is also possible to reach Managua by taking a bus east for 28km (18 miles) to the Pan-American Highway at Sébaco, and flagging down any southbound bus from there (but don't expect a seat).

Most of the **hospedajes** in Matagalpa are of a poor standard, and also have a habit of getting booked up. The best place is the Hospedaje Colonial on Parque Darío which has double rooms for $12. It has a lively little café in the back. A cheaper option is the Hospedaje María Rivera around the corner on the Calle Central. This is a dingy place with rooms at $3 per person. As a last resort, or if you are short of cash and wish to pay with a credit card, go to the Hotel Ideal (612 2483), a couple of blocks north and west of the cathedral. Rooms are categorised as A, B, C or D, with prices ranging from $40 down to $12 (though at this price the rooms are noisy, pokey and flea-ridden). The restaurant is usually empty, but the bar is lively in the evenings.

Matagalpa has a good supply of **comedores**, both along the main street, and around the market east of the cathedral. These are often busy, particularly in the evenings, and are good places to meet the locals. For a more sedate and secluded meal go to one of the more expensive restaurants. Among them is the Don Diego, which specialises in pizzas. Around the corner is the Lanchería

Marcia, which serves decent tacos, but is rather low-key. A more lively place is Los Pinchitos, off the main street a couple of blocks north of Parque Darío, which caters for dedicated meat-eaters. Nor is it cheap – a meal for two with beer costs about $20. Ice cream is popular in Matagalpa; the best place to eat it is the Sorbetería Copelia, on the corner of Parque Darío, which also sells surprisingly good hamburgers.

Men hanging around the market offer to **change dollars**, and there are various banks, including the Banco Nacional de Desarrollo just south of the rather fearsome Sandinista monument (which has now become little more than the town's urinal). The shop at the top of Calle Central sells a few crafts, ceramics and the odd hat; and in the Centro Popular de la Cultura just north of the cathedral you can buy Salvadoran and other souvenirs.

The **hills** around Matagalpa were the scene of much fighting between the Contras and the army during the 80s. However tempting it is to go tramping around the countryside, this should only be done with circumspection, preferably in the company of a local Nicaraguan. Mines scattered during the war are thought still to litter the highlands. Esquipulas, down a dirt road southeast of Matagalpa, would also be a good base for hikes, but the same advice applies here. Nevertheless, Espquipulas is in a lovely position, and is accessible by bus from both Matagalpa and Managua.

The road from Matagalpa rejoins the Pan-American Highway at kilometre post 105km, a place called Sébaco. Though it looks like little more than a big road junction, it is the centre of an orange-growing region. At kilometre post 91 on the Highway, a road heads east to Ciudad Darío. Nicaragua's best loved poet, Rubén Darío, was born here in 1867. The house where he was born is still standing and has been turned into a museum. The town's church is elegant with a tall steeple, unlike most of the rather squat churches elsewhere in Nicaragua. Apart from these features, Ciudad Darío is just another dusty small town.

Fifty-three kilometres (32 miles) south from here, just before the Panamericana reaches San Benito, you pass the site of the historic battle of San Jacinto. In 1856 the American adventurer William Walker fought Nicaraguan patriots. led by Andrés Castro. It was Walker's first defeat and signalled a decline in his fortunes which ended in his expulsion from the country. There is a monument to Andrés Castro on the eastern side of the Highway. At San Benito itself, the road bound for Rama turns off. This is not a recommended excursion.

Twelve miles (20km) northeast of the capital, off the Pan-American highway, is the small town of Tipitapa. Its location, on the banks of the Río Tipitapa which connects the Managua and Nicaragua lakes, sounds auspicious. Unfortunately its former role as a spa has ended, and the only possible attraction is the Guapote restaurant on the south side of town – and the fact that you can change buses here to Masaya, handily avoiding Managua. You will know when you reach Tipitapa because everything has to slow right down to start winding through the side streets, past some well-preserved Sandinista graffiti. The Parque Central is a mess, with a desultory *proyecto* under way.

A lowland excursion

From Estelí or Matagalpa, there is an option to divert west towards the Pacific and enjoy the crumbling grace of the former capital, León. North of Sébaco a road turns off to the south and eventually joins the Pacific Highway north of León, skirting the Maribios volcanic range which runs west of Lake Managua. Cross-country buses and trucks between San Isidro (north of Sébaco) and León use this route; the journey takes about three hours and costs $3. A diversion to León will add hours and 100km to your trip, but could be a real highlight.

One way to reduce the time and distance is to take a shortcut from Choluteca in Honduras, crossing the frontier at Guasaule. This will take you through **Chinandega**, a town that enjoyed some prosperity after cotton was introduced into the area, but was dealt a heavy blow when the ferry service across the Gulf of Fonseca to El Salvador was suspended. Just northwest of Chinandega, along the Potosí road, is **El Viejo**. This is a colonial village whose church is of some architectural interest, but is best known for its contents. Inside is a life-size statue of the Black Christ, called 'Christ of the Good Way', said to date from the 17th century. There is also a representation of the Immaculate Conception covered with jewels which were given in gratitude by pilgrims for miracles attributed to the Virgin Mary.

Off the Camino Real going southwest from Chinandega towards Corinto is **El Realejo**, the ruins of a colonial port. Only a few ruined buildings mark the site of what was once the most important fort in the area during Spanish rule. El Realejo can also be reached along an unpaved road which branches off the Léon road near Chichigalpa, 12km southeast of Chinandega

First capital: León

Nicaragua's first capital, and second-largest city, is 88km (55 miles) northwest of Managua. Unlike Managua, León has a strong sense of identity and a great historical past of which you can still see much evidence. It also has fearsome temperatures: León has the reputation for being the dustiest and hottest place in Nicaragua.

León was founded by Hernández de Córdoba in 1524, and was the second Spanish settlement in the country after Granada. The first site was actually at León Viejo, 20 miles (32km) east of the present city, but an earthquake in 1609 destroyed the city, and León was moved the following year to a new site near the Indian village of Subtiava; this village has now been swallowed up by the city. León's term as capital lasted for more than two centuries, ending in 1858. It acquired a reputation as the country's intellectual and cultural centre. Its architectural heritage is unrivalled and the reputation of its university is unsurpassed nationally.

Sadly, León has suffered over the years. It has never been safe from natural disasters, and the Cerro Negro and Momotombo volcanoes smoke menacingly in the distance. Volcanic ash deposited by past eruptions is still shaken off the rafters of old houses by the occasional earth tremor. Many of its elegant buildings, including over thirty churches, are crumbling. Earthquakes have hit the city periodically, and the city was the scene of some of the most savage fighting during the Revolution. León is one of the most politically alive towns anywhere, a characteristic which partly accounts for its present dilapidation. It played an active role in the rebellion leading up to the overthrow of Somoza, and much of the town was bombed by the air force, killing hundreds of people and damaging a large number of buildings. Many houses are riddled with bullet holes and almost every church bears scars of some kind. The streets are still paved with the cobbles which during the Revolution were torn up to build barricades. A more recent blow was the eruption of nearby Volcán Negro, which doused the city in ash and sand.

Despite the aura of neglect León is one of the jolliest places in Nicaragua. The streets are full of bustle, although the pace is more relaxed away from the centre. The low-slung, pastel-shaded houses exude an atmosphere akin to that of provincial Spain.

The best time to observe the spirit of León is during Holy Week or one of its other festivals; these are held on 20 June (commemorating the liberation of the town by the Sandinistas), 24 September and 1 November (All Saints' Day).

The **bus** station is on the northeastern outskirts of the town, about 20 minutes' walk (or a horse-drawn cab) from the Parque Central. Express buses to Managua's Israel Lewites terminal take about 90 minutes and cost around $5. Second-class buses take twice as long for half the price. Buses are supplemented by **collective taxis**, costing around $7. The telephone bureau and post office are on the Parque Central. Moneychangers hang around the market end of the cathedral, at the corner of 1 Calle Norte and Avenida 1 NE, which is where all the banks are located.

For a comfortable **place to stay**, go to the Hotel Europa (311 0016), which is two blocks north and five blocks east of the Parque Central, on 2 Calle Norte; the postal address, curiously, is 3 Calle Noreste, 4ta Avenida. Don't be put off by the fact that a railway line runs right past the hotel – the last train departed around 1995. A large double room costs $20 with fan, $25 with air-conditioning. The budget options are around the old railway station, east of the Parque Central. One of the better ones is the friendly, family-run Pensión Télica, four blocks north of the station.

No sex, please – we're Sandinistas

At the Hotel América (on the corner of Avenida Santiago Arguëllo and Calle 1 Sur, just a couple of blocks east of the cathedral), a sign above reception persisted long after the Ortega government had been thrown out: 'Prohibited – armed and uniformed soldiers accompanied by a woman; civilians accompanied by a female student in uniform – by order of the Sandinista police of León'.

The apparently wide range of **restaurants** in León is deceptive, since many of them are empty and uninviting most of the time. Sitting in a totally empty and unatmospheric restaurant is not much fun (and doesn't say much for the food), so you should take time to find a good place. One such is the Comedor La Merienda on 2 Calle Sur between Avenidas 1 and 2 Poniente. Although the service is slow and offhand, the food – from burritos to iguana – is excellent. Breakfasts are good, with two set menus, and there is tasty seafood at lunch and dinner. Considering the surroundings, prices are high, and a huge cartoon on the wall shows a diner about to be beaten up by a waiter, with the caption *La propina es voluntaria* – tips optional. For a more upmarket meal go to the Solmar seafood restaurant opposite the church of La Merced on 1 Calle Norte (between Avenida Central and 1 Poniente), although it too can be alarmingly empty on occasions. The Antojitos Solmar, on Avenida Central between 2 and 3 Calles Norte, has a steady trickle of customers but most are only there for the beer – the food served is lukewarm and uninviting. Finding bars and simple comedores is easier. The string of cafés on Avenida 1 Poniente, near the Parque Central, are popular with students; there is even a pool hall. The outdoor café at the northeast corner of the Parque Central is expensive but worthwhile if you want to enjoy ice cream at the closest Nicaragua has to a pavement café.

Any **exploration** has to begin at the Parque Central. The square used to be known as the Plaza de Armas, but was temporarily renamed Parque Jérez, after a 19th-century Liberal leader, by the Sandinistas. The collosal **cathedral** is the largest of its kind in Central America. Construction, which began in 1746, took 70 years to complete. Local legend says that the huge baroque design was never intended for León, and that plans for a much smaller church were mixed up with those for a new cathedral for the Peruvian capital of Lima. Few Nicaraguan historians support this enchanting theory, however. Most assert that the squat building, which has proved to be earthquake-resistant, must have been designed specifically for León. Indeed the cathedral has survived earthquakes and revolutions equally well, and the interior is virtually intact. Its prize possession is a shrine adorned with a white topaz given by Philip II of Spain, but this is usually kept under lock and key. There is also a fine statue of Christ carved in ivory, and statues of the Apostles – beneath one of these is the tomb of Rubén Darío, Nicaragua's most famous poet, guarded by a grieving lion, the symbol of León.

It is impossible to describe all the the city's **churches**, but some deserve singling out. Most of these, like the cathedral, are bold, baroque structures – the facades are striking with their high relief decoration and large, heavy columns; the interiors as a rule are less interesting. (Note that churches are usually closed for a couple of hours in the middle of the day, and some don't open until the afternoon.) Begin at the eastern end of Calle Central, at the church of El Calvario. It is most noted for its beautifully decorated ceiling. Northwest of here, on 2 Calle Norte, is La Recolección, which was built in the late 18th century. Its facade, with the carved vines entwined around the columns and other motifs of typical Indian influence, is probably the finest in León. A block south and west is La Merced. It is hard to get a good vantage point from which to properly admire this church but it too has an interesting facade. Its tower was damaged by an earthquake in 1885, but has been reconstructed.

Opposite La Merced is the Science Faculty of the **university** where there are some interesting murals, both inside and outside. On the nearby corner (1 Calle Norte and Avenida 1 Poniente) is **Casa Cuun**, the student's union; inside are portraits of Che Guevara and Sandino. The walls of the park across the street are also adorned with murals and graffiti. León's students played an important role in the Revolution, and those who died in the struggle are among those remembered in the **Galería de Héroes y Mártires** which is in the white house behind railings on the right just west of Casa Cuun. There is a map of the attack launched by the FSLN on León in 1979. One of the most rousing murals is on the northeastern corner of the main square. Here a memorial to the Insurrection is backed by a huge mural, giving a chronological account and vivid interpretation of life in Nicaragua since before Columbus until 1979, ending with a rather twee picture of children running off happily to fly a kite.

Three blocks west of the Parque Central on the corner of Avenida 4 Poniente is the **Rubén Darío Museum**. You can find out more about the only Nicaraguan poet to have had international influence. Some consider him the greatest poet that Latin America has produced, but the writer Paul Theroux wrote of him 'Every country has the writers she requires and deserves, which is why Nicaragua, in 200 years of literacy, has produced one writer – a mediocre poet'. The museum, contained in the house where Darío spent his childhood, is well laid-out and includes manuscripts and personal possessions. One of the more gruesome exhibits is a photograph of the poet on his deathbed. The museum is open 9am-noon and 2pm-5pm Tuesday to Saturday, and 9am-noon on Sunday. The house where he died is two blocks east of the church of La Recolección and is marked by a commemorative plaque. On the nearby corner is the church of San Francisco, whose most notable feature is an elaborate gold altarpiece.

Down the hill south of the Parque Central are the ruins of Somoza's **prison**, a grim reminder of life in Nicaragua before the Revolution. You can wander around the ruins and perhaps visit the cells where Somoza's political opponents were confined. If you continue south across the foul-smelling Río Chiquito you can walk up to the church of Guadalupe which is in a commanding position at the top of the hill – there is a fine view across León. At the end of the street behind the church is the huge cemetery.

The old Indian village of **Subtiava** survives to the west of the centre and is well worth the half-hour walk. The alignment of streets and amount of outdoor life in this area make it perfect for photography in the hour before sunset. The church of San Juan Bautista was built in 1530 long before León was moved to this site, making it the oldest church in León. It is among the finest churches in

Nicaragua; built of petrified wood, it has a fine facade and contains a most beautiful colonial altarpiece. The wooden figures inside are thought to have come from Guatemala. Unfortunately it is set in an area of wasteland, and has been clumsily patched up. Nearby is the recently-restored small town museum and the ruins of the Vera Cruz parish church.

El Fortín de Acosasco was a former stronghold of the National Guard and now lies in ruins on a hill three kilometres southwest of León. It was from this fort that León was bombed during the insurrection. You can peer into old prison cells and the so-called 'tunnel' where prisoners were thrown and left to die. On 7 July every year since the Revolution there has been a march to commemorate the taking of the fort by the Sandinistas. Visiting the fort at any other time is a moving but rather grim experience.   To get there, head south across the river from the cathedral, continue for just over a mile and then walk up the hill.

East of León

León Viejo was the original site of León, founded in 1524 – yet it was uncovered only in the 1960s. Until then it had been preserved under a layer of ash which covered the area following an eruption of Momotombo volcano which towers over the old town. Although it was this same volcano which caused the destruction of León Viejo, local legend has it that divine punishment lay behind the town's demise. God's wrath was reputedly aroused by a series of evil deeds committed by Pedrarias the Cruel, governor at the time. Hernández de Córdoba (León's founder) was one of his victims – he was beheaded in the square in front of the cathedral. Pedrarias' greatest wrath, however, was reserved for rebellious local Indians and anyone who supported them. Indians were torn apart by dogs in punishment for their resistance, and León's bishop, Antonio Valdivieso, who lived in the house behind the cathedral, was allegedly murdered by members of the Spanish governor's family, for speaking out in their defence. The old Camino Real (Royal Road) ran through the centre of the old city, and was lined with fine buildings. Only a few private houses, and the convent and church of La Merced survive. The church was built in 1528 and contains the tomb of Pedrarias the Cruel.

León Viejo can be reached down an unpaved road that turns off the Pacific Highway at La Paz Centro, 28km (17 miles) from León and 40 km (25 miles) northwest of Managua. La Paz Centro is accessible by any León-Managua bus using this road – i.e. not the old one which runs further south. There are infrequent buses, but otherwise take a taxi, or hitch the 10 miles (16km) to the site.

Fifteen kilometres (nine miles) beyond León Viejo, on the northern shores of Lake Managua, is **Momotombo Volcano**. It was originally over 1,600m (one mile) high, but a series of explosions literally blew the top off, and it now measures just 1,280m (4,500 feet). The volcano is no less impressive, however, and is visible from miles around. The last eruption was in 1965, and the volcano continues to spew out smoke and steam. A local legend claims that the priests who climbed the mountain in the early colonial period in order to bless it – such was the Spanish custom – never returned.

Momotombo is an arduous climb – the path is not always well-defined, the terrain is rough and gives way to scree near the top. In addition, the sulphurous fumes are strong at the summit, and lengthy exposure to them is not recommended. The views, however, are magnificent, and there is a path across the top which enables you to see into the crater. It is possible to climb to the top and down again in a day, but you need to start early and be fit.

The southern approach to Momotombo is best. This involves following the path past the geothermal electricity plant which has been built at the base of the southern slopes. It is in theory necessary to get permission to make the climb from the Instituto Nacional de Energía (INE) in Managua, which runs the plant; the office is on Pista de la Resistencia, just east of Plaza 19 de Julio. In practice, however, it seems that if you go straight to Momotombo you are unlikely to be asked to show a permit. On the other hand it is probably worth your while talking to someone at INE or at the plant itself, just to get advice on how best to tackle the climb.

Momotombo, like León Viejo, is reached via La Paz Centro. Buses run to Puerto Momotombo – where accommodation is available – which lies about 8km (5 miles) southwest of the geothermal plant. This stretch, along a dirt road, must be done on foot.

West of León

The Pacific Ocean is only 19km (12 miles) west of León, and the resort of **Poneloya** is a good place to escape to when the heat of the city gets too much. After the Revolution many of the rich families with homes here abandoned their mansions. Some returned following the fall of the Sandinistas, but Poneloya continues to crumble. Even at weekends the beach is seldom busy – Holy Week seems to be the only time when crowds descend. At other times the main activity is fishing, and the fishermen are usually happy to take you out with them. They sell some of their catch on the beach in the late afternoon, a boon for those with the energy and inclination for a barbecue. The broad grey-sand beach is unpolluted, but the waves are big and the current strong. The safest swimming is at the southern end of the beach, where you'll also find a few small comedores.

Bus 101 from León takes 45 minutes to reach Poneloya. The last bus back from Poneloya leaves at 4pm, the last from León at 5pm. Accommodation in Poneloya is scarce. Hotel Lacayo is right on the beach and is a good place from which to watch the sunset. Its restaurant serves quite good seafood. It is possible to camp on the beach, but the mosquitoes are voracious.

Twenty-three kilometres (15 miles) east of León, the road to Managua splits. The 'new' Pacific Highway runs southeast to Managua and is officially known as Nic. 28, as distinct from Nic. 12, the old road between the two cities, which runs some way south of the new road. The old road passes through more interesting countryside than the new one, especially close to Managua, and gives access to the Pacific coast, but it is a much rougher and slower road. Another benefit of the new, northerly road is access to the **Laguna de Xiloa**, a volcanic lake just beyond the northwest outskirts of Managua. Until the Revolution, access was restricted to members of Somoza's National Guard; now it is a popular resort for Managuans, especially on summer weekends. In contrast with the polluted volcanic lakes in Managua itself, Lake Xiloa is surprisingly clean and good for swimming. There are restaurants, campgrounds and facilities for watersports. You can rent boats or bicycles. Buses from the Carretera to Xiloa run only at the weekends, so it is deserted during the week; unless you have a car, you must walk, take a taxi or hitch.

Managua: a city in need of salvation

The best bypass in the world is the one that whisks the Pan-American Highway past Nicaragua's capital. There would be few contenders that could match Managua in the world's-ugliest-capital stakes.

The city's complete lack of charm is not a result of malevolent Spanish colonists or even town planners; rather, it is due to a succession of political and seismic misfortunes. The absence of colonial sights is no surprise considering that, until 1858, Managua was nothing more than a small fishing village. In that year it replaced León as the country's first capital. A more ill-advised site could hardly have been chosen; earthquakes have wreaked sporadic havoc on the city ever since. The first serious one occurred in 1931 and destroyed three-quarters of the city. The capital was restored only to be wrecked again in 1972, when a similar degree of destruction killed over 12,000 people. Hence Managua resembles a building site more than a modern capital, and an untidy, disorganised building site at that.

Much of the city centre was abandoned following the 1972 earthquake, and other buildings were destroyed in the 1979 Revolution. Rebuilding has been haphazard, making the city feel as though it is nothing more than a collection of suburbs and skyscrapers, interspersed by shacks and shanties. Managua has no heart, no focus and no sense of cohesion. City-dwellers elsewhere in the world might wish for more open space, but Managua is in the curious position of having far too much. Few other capital cities have cows grazing along what passes loosely for the main street. The city centre is an extraordinary mixture of modern government offices, revolutionary monuments, derelict buildings and cardboard shanties. Oh, and it gets furiously hot, as the capital is just 40m (130ft) above sea level. You should visit Nicaragua's capital only if you want to witness the sombre sight of a city dismembered by nature and man.

Get lost

Seeing a large-scale **map** of Managua for the first time is unnerving. The large blank areas look like *terra incognita*, and most individual streets are

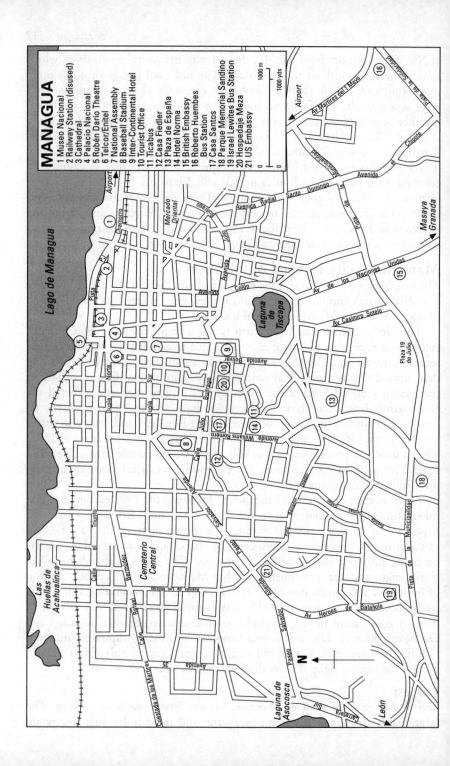

MANAGUA

1 Museo Nacional
2 Railway Station (disused)
3 Cathedral
4 Palacio Nacional
5 Rubén Darío Theatre
6 Telcor/Enitel
7 National Assembly
8 Baseball Stadium
9 Inter-Continental Hotel
10 Tourist Office
11 Ticabus
12 Casa Fiedler
13 Plaza de España
14 Hotel Norma
15 British Embassy
16 Roberto Huembes Bus Station
17 Casa Santos
18 Parque Memorial Sandino
19 Israel Lewites Bus Station
20 Hospedaje Meza
21 US Embassy

not shown, let alone street names. Few streets actually have signs, and few locals use names anyway. The problem has been compounded by the re-naming and re-re-naming of streets as power has switched from one regime to the next.

The really difficult concept to come to terms with, though, is the way that Managua refuses to comply with most of the known principles of human geography – it doesn't look, or feel, like a proper Latin American capital (though it certainly smells like one). Where you would expect the centre to be, at the Parque Central and adjacent cathedral, you find mainly overgrown rubble. Whoever approved relocating Nicaragua's capital to a place that stands (shakily) above a maze of geological fault lines, and built the centre directly over the most fragile, wasn't the sharpest quill in the inkwell. What's left of the old centre of Managua is concentrated around the city's main square, Plaza de la República – formerly Plaza de la Revolución.

The Parque Central is adjacent. Both squares are near the lakeshore and at the northern end of one of Managua's most important thoroughfares, Avenida Bolívar; this is a useful street, running southwest from the Plaza de la República to the Plaza de España.

After one bout of destruction too many, the city has had to find a new identity in the suburbs, and – in Nicaraguan fashion – has acquired a split personality. The centre initially moved south along Avenida Bolívar, and developed around the axis that runs between the Inter-Continental Hotel and the Plaza de España. It is best thought of as the 'old new' centre, and is three to four kilometres south of the lake. The Inter-Continental was one of the few buildings to survive the 1972 earthquake, and has become the city's most notable landmark – though the intended resemblance to a Mayan pyramid is hard to credit. The Plaza de España is one of the few squares in the city worth getting to know, because several banks and airline offices are here. The zone takes in the **Barrio Martha Quezada** ('Gringolandia', where most backpackers end up), a ten-block-square area where the small contingent of Westerners tends to congregate. The boundaries of this area are Calle Julio Buitrago and Avenida Williams Romero and Avenida Bolívar. Don't expect too vibrant an atmosphere; although it has the city's greatest concentration of places to go in the evenings, these bars and restaurants are fairly scattered. The streets are dimly-lit and the atmosphere is decidedly suburban. Nevertheless it is one of the few parts of Managua where walking is a feasible way to get around – elsewhere the distances are too long, or the ambience is too threatening, or both.

The 'new new' centre is developing in Altimira, strung out along the Avenida de las Naciones Unidas (also known as the Carretera a Masaya), a couple of kilometres southeast of here. The starting point is marked by the vast new metropolitan cathedral, and the new Metrocentro, and the area continues through an upmarket zone where many embassies (including the British mission) are located.

As in the rest of Nicaragua, addresses in Managua are given with reference to a particular building or landmark. Distance is specified in *cuadras* (blocks) or *varas* (yards). Direction is trickier, until you get a feel for the city: *al lago*, towards the lake, means north; *al sur* is south; *arriba* ('up') means east; *abajo* ('down') is west. Unless you possess a compass or an especially keen sense of direction, these directions mean little except near the lakeshore. To complicate matters, certain addresses make references to buildings destroyed in the last earthquake. Directions such as 'opposite where the Ecuadorean Embassy used to be' are of little use without the help of a local citizen.

Arrival and departure

Augusto César Sandino international **airport** is on the edge of Managua. If you arrive at night, get a taxi. To hire one from outside the airport costs at least $20 to addresses in Managua, but if you cross the road you should be able to pick up a cab for $10. Negotiate as competently as you can; taxi drivers at the arrivals hall in Managua realise, as at any international airport, there is a large number of foreigners who are tired, confused and have just acquired large amounts of a currency that they do not yet fully understand. The more enterprising drivers try to profit accordingly. City buses into Managua run from across the main road to the Oscar Benavides bus station, still close to the airport and too far east from anywhere interesting; from here you can get a bus heading west (118 goes to the Inter-Continental), or a taxi much more cheaply than from the airport.

Managua has several **bus** terminals on the fringes of the city, each serving a different area of the country. Since most terminals are adjacent to large markets there is plenty to keep you occupied if you have an hour or three to kill. The *panamericanista* who arrives down the Highway from Estelí will end up some distance from the city at the Plaza Mayoreo terminal, just south and west of the airport and adjacent to the Mercado Mayoreo. Anyone who plans to continue to Masaya, Granada and Rivas will depart from the Roberto Huembes Terminal on Pista de la Solidaridad, close to Avenida Mártires del 1 de Mayo. The terminal is also called Central or Eduardo Contreras, other names of the adjacent market.

If you have taken the Pacific coast detour via León, you will turn up at the Israel Lewites Terminal, buried in the southwest of the city just north of Pista de la Municipalidad (formerly Resistencia) at the junction with Avenida Héroes de Batahola, in the southwest of the city. By a quirk of route-planning, many of the city's buses pass by Israel Lewites.

Ticabus services run to and from the terminal in 'Gringolandia', two blocks east of the Casino Royale cinema (formerly Cine Dorado, the name which is still used). Ticabus has links to San Salvador, Tegucigalpa and San José; call 222 6094 for schedules and fares.

Getting around

Managua covers a huge area, so walking around is often impractical. Some experienced travellers visiting Managua for the first time scoff at the idea of taking taxis; within a day or two they become worn-out. This is not surprising in a city where a stroll between the main bus stations takes two or three hours. **Buses** are overcrowded and infrequent, but fast when they actually get going, since there is little to impede buses as they speed through the wasteland from one cluster of buildings to the next. The fare is around $0.15 (two córdobas early in 2000) for a journey anywhere in the city. Upon boarding you drop the coins into the slot by the driver, or pay his assistant. You should start moving back almost immediately in order to disembark where you want to. Unfortunately everyone has the same idea, so a massive scrum can develop at the backs of buses. To relieve the pressure on public transport, private **trucks** duplicate the bus routes – they charge slightly higher fares but are more frequent and less crowded.

The chaos and confusion of the bus service persuades many visitors to take **taxis** instead. These are easy to find, and not too expensive – a three-mile journey might cost $2 if you are the only passenger. Most taxis, though, work on a collective basis, distributing a number of passengers to a variety of destinations. The circuitous routes taken by colectivos enables you to see parts of the capital you might otherwise miss. It is common practice among cab drivers to try to rip off foreigners, which you can circumvent by fixing the fare in advance; stand your ground and be prepared to try two or three different drivers in order to get a reasonable price. When opening negotiations, try to look confident so that drivers assume you know what the fare should be.

The most radical **bicycle** rental shop in Central America is Si Bicicletas No Bombas ('Bicycles Not Bombs'), on the eastern side of the city, on Avenida Cristián Pérez, opposite the Cementario Oriental. You will need to leave a deposit of $100 in travellers' cheques or cash to take away one of the Taiwanese mountain bikes.

A room
A late arrival by air or bus could dump you a long way east of the city at the airport or nearby Plaza Mayoreo bus station – and temptingly close to the **Hotel Camino Real** (tel 263 1381, fax 263 1415, info@caminoreal.com.ni). A room at this place, which is largely frequented by flight crews from the more wealthy airlines, costs $200, single or double. A much better bet is just east, at the **Hotel Las Mercedes** (tel 263 1011, fax 263 1083, lm@munditel.com.ni), part of the Best Western chain, where a single/double room costs 'only' $75/$81.

In the 'old new' centre of town, the lumbering **Hotel Inter-Continental** on Avenida Bolívar (tel 228 3530, fax 228 3087, managua@interconti.com) costs $212 a night, single or double. It boasts a swimming pool which non-residents are sometimes allowed to use, and the restaurants are good.

The best place to look for cheap accommodation is in Gringolandia southwest of the Inter-Continental Hotel. The Casino Royale (formerly Cine Dorado) is often used as a landmark since the cheapest hospedajes are nearby, and the cinema is a reference point in their addresses. Among these, the **Hotel Norma** (one block south, one block east; tel 222 3498), and the **Casa de Huéspedes Santos** (one block north, one block east) are recommended. One block north and two-and-a-half blocks east of the cinema, the **Hospedaje Meza** (tel 222 2046) is cheap, clean and friendly. It is a safe place to leave bags while you travel around the country, and there is an excellent comedor on the nearby corner.

Of the more expensive places in this area, the **Casa Fiedler** (six blocks west of the cinema, street address 8 Calle Suroeste 1320; tel 266 6622) is the best. It is safe, clean and serves an excellent breakfast. A double room with fan costs $25, though the price increases steeply to $40 if you want air-conditioning and your own bathroom. If Casa Fiedler is full try the **Casa de Huéspedes Tres Laureles** in the next street (9 Calle Suroeste; tel 222 4440).

A meal

For good, fresh and cheap local food, the stalls in any of the city's **markets** are best, with the Oriental and Israel Lewites markets just ahead of the rest. Gringolandia has easily the best of Managua's modest selection of more formal restaurants. One of the most popular places is **Los Antojitos**, a high-class Mexican place opposite the Inter-Continental which is frequented by a mix of travellers, expats and wealthy Managuans. It has a large terrace which is sheltered by an enormous tree. There are more tables inside, and on the walls are some impressive pictures of Managua before the 1972 earthquake. The food is excellent; it is well worth splashing out on the plato típico, about $15. One block west is a Salvadoran restaurant called **El Cipitío** (tel 222 4929). The food is expensive but good, and it has a convivial atmosphere. The *plato Salvadoreño* includes pupusas (stuffed tortillas) and other Salvadoran specialities. Other places in the area include Tacos, a good bar for a snack and a beer before supper, and the Breakfast Place just north which, despite its name, stays open late into the evening.

The air-conditioned restaurants in the Inter-Continental hotel are worth visiting, if only as an escape from the sultry heat outside. The breakfast buffet is particularly recommended for those with hearty appetites since you can eat as much as you like for $5; the Sunday brunch deal is also good. A more congenial place to have a coffee or lunch is the **Libro-Café Amatl**, two blocks south and one block west of the Inter-Continental. Further south still, at the Plaza España, the **Plaza** restaurant was set up to introduce more varied cuisine. It was originally an Australian co-operative, but is now run by its Nicaraguan chefs. The vegetable curry is particularly recommended. North on Avenida Bolívar, between the Inter-Continental and Plaza de la República, there are a couple of cafés which are convenient for lunch or a drink if you are doing what approximates to 'sightseeing' during the day.

An exploration

A walk through central Managua can feel at times like trespassing on private grief. Nevertheless, start in **Avenida Bolívar**, in the vicinity of the Inter-Continental. This road was once lined with buildings but is now skirted either side by 'parks' (as the capital's wasteland is offically described) for much of its length. This 'main' street gives you a good idea how extensive was the damage done by the earthquake.

As you walk north, you pass on the right a heavily guarded area. Within this compound, on Pista Larreynaga, is the National Assembly. The tall white building next to it is the Bank of America; the most earthquake-proof building in Managua, it is a good landmark. On the opposite side of Avenida Bolívar is a huge **Sandinista monument** dedicated to the workers: an awesome figure brandishing a machine gun and a pick, with an inscription that reads *Solo los obreros y campesinos irán hasta el Fin* (Only the workers and the peasants will go to the End). The monument seems likely itself to become extinct soon. If you turn around and look south, you should be able to see the most sobering sight in Managua: the impressive black figure of **Sandino** which overlooks the city from the top of the hill behind the Inter-Continental. This huge silhouette was erected in April 1990 shortly before Ortega stepped down as president. It marks the spot where Sandino was murdered in 1934, and overlooks the Presidential House. A closer view of it can be had from the southern shore of Laguna de Tiscapa, southeast of Avenida Bolívar.

On the right beyond Parque Velásquez is **Plaza de la República**. This square is dominated by the Cathedral, which provides dramatic evidence of the devastation of the 1972 earthquake. Once the tallest building in the capital, it is now in ruins. The facade and side walls are intact though riddled with cracks. There is no roof, and weeds grow unchecked where once there were rows of pews. Some of the altars and statues are still in place. A staircase has survived and it is possible to go upstairs to look down into the interior of the church and out over the square.

Opposite the cathedral are a couple of cafés and a few street traders. Notice the pillboxes beneath the trees. On the south side of the square is the **Palacio Nacional**. This colonial building was named the Palace of the Heroes of the Revolution by the Sandinistas, and it still bears a plaque to that effect. The building was the scene of a key event in the Revolution. In 1978 Carlos Fonseca and a band of Sandinistas disguised as National Guardsmen led an assault on the palace, and forced Somoza's cabal to agree to the release of all political prisoners, airtime on the radio, and a national pay increase. Under the Sandinistas, construction work began to turn the palace into government offices; it now houses the Finance Ministry, but doubles as an art gallery. Inside are murals by the Mexican artist Arnold Belkin, which were commissioned by the Sandinistas and show an unusual combination of cubist and naturalistic styles. The palace is open 8am-4pm from Monday to Friday. You may be able to get on to the roof (up the stairs which lead off the left-hand courtyard) from where there is a splendid view.

In total contrast to the crumbling cathedral is the incongruous modern **theatre** in the Parque Central, just north of Plaza de la República. In the square is a statue of Rubén Darío, Nicaragua's most famous poet, after whom the theatre is named. Nearby is the tomb of Carlos Fonseca, one of the founders of the FSLN who was murdered by the National Guard in 1976; the flame over his tomb was extinguished in 1990 after the election. To the west of the theatre,

The theory of Revolution

The place to learn about the theory and practice of rebellion used to be the Museo de la Revolución, adjacent to the Roberto Huembes bus terminal in the city's southeast, off Pista de la Municipalidad. There is some talk that this revolutionary museum will re-open, which will give the capital back an important link with the recent past. It houses a fascinating collection of photographs – of Sandino and other revolutionary heroes – and, without resorting to political dogma, gives a good outline of the Sandinistas' rise to power and their links with other revolutionary groups in the region. Exhibits include torture instruments used by the Somoza regime and weapons used during the Revolution of 1978-9, from improvised tanks to armoured Ladas.

on the shores of the lake, is an ugly, Soviet-style grandstand formerly used during political parades and rallies. This is a quiet spot in which to have a drink and look out over the lake – hidden as you are behind this huge slab of concrete, it is hard to believe you're in a city.

Nicaragua's leading museum, the **Museo Nacional** is east of the main square, just north of the railway line at the start of Pista P J Chamorro. The museum is somewhat musty and neglected, and some would say dull. Nevertheless, it is worth a visit to see one of Nicaragua's few pre-Columbian collections. It includes ceramics and jewellery, some of which were found on Ometepe Island in Lake Nicaragua. Much of the collection was lost during the 1972 earthquake. The museum opens daily except Monday, 9am-noon and 2pm-5pm.

West of the Plaza de la República is Managua's one archaeological site, **Las Huellas de Acahualinca**. It has been described as 'Pompeii but twice as old'; it certainly ten times less interesting, and few locals have heard of the site, let alone visited it. Las Huellas are prehistoric footprints that have been preserved in lava near the shores of the lake. The footprints were discovered late in the 19th century and are said to have been left by humans and animals as they fled from a volcanic eruption; it was the ash from the eruption which preserved the footprints for so long. Deciding the age of the footprints has proved controversial: most archaeologists now agree that they are over 5,000 years old, with some claiming the age to be 50,000 years. The majority of the prints are deep and close together, supporting the theory that people were carrying boats and belongings in order to make their escape across the lake. Do not go with high expectations. The site, by a small lagoon, is hardly atmospheric, caught between the polluted lake and the railway track. There is a museum with a small collection of archaeological artifacts. To get to Acahualinca catch bus 112 from near the Telcor building. To walk there (follow Calle El Triunfo) takes a good half-hour from the Plaza de la República. The site, tucked away among huts, is not easy to find, so ask for directions when you get close. Opening hours are erratic, but if the site is closed, just hop over the fence. Almost due south of Las Huellas, on the other side of Calle El Triunfo is the Central Cemetery, where Pedro Joaquín Chamorro is buried.

A night out
The best cinema in Managua, with an imaginative programme of films, is the Cinemateca de Nicaragua on Avenida Bolívar, just south of the Palacio Nacional. The most intriguing place for a night out (if it is still open) is the Asociación Sandinista de Trabajadores de la Cultura (Sandinista Workers' Centre), near the baseball stadium at the northern end of Gringolandia. Live music, including reggae and jazz, is put on in the evenings. The atmosphere is one of a working man's club, which is exactly what it is. Most of Managua's commercial nightclubs are patronised by the wealthiest members of Nicaraguan society, and their offspring.

A shopping expedition
As in other Central American capitals, the markets provide the most entertaining shopping. Most travellers prefer **Mercado Roberto Huembes** (also known as Eduardo Contreras), on Pista de la Solidaridad. It is particularly lively on Saturday mornings. As well as stalls selling meat (including iguana) and fresh produce, this market is the best source of crafts in the capital. You can even buy English-language magazines, books, etc. and practical things such as loo rolls and mosquito coils. There are some excellent food stalls too and musicians and other street entertainers can sometimes be seen here.

For more serious shoppers, Managua has recently acquired some shiny new and air-conditioned *Centros Comerciales*, of which the original is the **Managua**, southeast of Pista de la Solidaridad and close to the Avenida de las Naciones Unidas/Carretera de Masaya. It contains a wide range of shops – the Sonorama record shop is a good source of local music. The current trendiest place to shop is the **Metrocentro**, on the southeast corner of the junction between Avenida de las Naciones Unidas (also known as the Carretera de Masaya) and the Pista de la Municipalidad, opposite the hideous new cathedral.

A limited selection of **books** on Nicaragua is available in the tourist office and in the Inter-Continental hotel. The Librería Vanguardia at the top of Calle José Martí, just east of Laguna de Tiscapa, is attached to the publishing house of the same name, and has a good selection of Nicaraguan poetry and literature, including books covering political, historical and feminist topics. Posters and postcards are on sale.

Keeping in touch
The main **post and telephone office** (Telcor/Enitel) is on Avenida Simón Bolívar, across the street from Plaza de la República. Hours vary according to which service you wish to use, but the office opens Monday to Friday and Saturday mornings. The telephone office opens 7am-10.30pm, the telegraph office 24 hours, and poste restante 8am-4pm. To pick up letters go to windows 14 and 15 – identification is essential.

The area to look for **internet** access is Altamira and, inevitably, Gringolandia, though do not expect the same speed and reliability of connection that you might get elsewhere in other Central American capitals.

A word of advice

Since the ending of the Sandinista regime, Managua has become a significantly more dangerous place. In April 2000, the US State Department issued the following warning: 'Armed and unarmed robberies occur on crowded buses and in open markets, particularly the large Mercado Oriental. Carjackings and gang activity are rising in Managua. Gang violence, including robberies, assaults and stabbings, is particularly prevalent in poorer neighbourhoods.' The areas in which you might feel uncomfortable are numerous, but in the course of your stay you are unlikely to find yourself straying in to them – except for the Mercado Oriental and its surrounding Barrio Jardin, just east of the old centre.

The **British Embassy** is reached by the first turning right when heading out of Managua from the Metrocentro shopping complex along the Avenida de las Naciones Unidas/Carretera a Masaya. The Embassy is the fourth house on the right (tel 278 0014/278 0034). The **US Embassy** is a long way south and west of the city, at Kilometre 4.5, Carretera Sur (tel 266 6010).

A day at the seaside

You will not be in Managua for long before the desire to get out and enjoy some fresh air seizes you. The two Pacific beaches closest to Managua are **Pochomil** and **Masachapa**, about 56km (35 miles) southwest of the capital. Pochomil is the more popular of the two, and has the most facilities. Despite the fact that the water at both is dirty and that there are sharks, these beaches are very busy at weekends and holidays. Buses for both beaches leave from Israel Lewites terminal. To escape the crowds, you could buy your way into **Montelimar**, a modern all-inclusive resort five kilometres (three miles) northwest of Masachapa. To reach it, you drive through huge sugar cane plantations which were once part of the Somoza estate. Anastasio Somoza had a villa here, and the views of the coast and the Pacific are magnificent. Near the town is a small cave decorated with a design of vertical lines, thought to have been influenced by the Mayan Indians. The luxury hotel includes tennis courts, a casino, golf course and airstrip, and looks like upmarket counterparts elsewhere. The difference is that this was a Sandinista project, which was completed only after they lost power.

Moving on

The fast track to the Costa Rican frontier leaves Managua along the Carretera Sur. Diriamba, 40km (25 miles) south of the capital, has a picturesque old church in the Parque Central, but is better known for its festivities held on 20 January in honour of San Sebastián. A dirt road leads south from Diriamba to the fishing village of Casares. A few miles west is La Boquita whose beach is visited by turtles every year between August and November. Five kilometres (three miles) south of Diriamba along the Pan-American is Jinotepe, the main town of Carazo department, whose parish church is modelled on León cathedral – at about one-tenth scale.

Much the best plan, though, is to head southeast from Managua through Masaya province. It is one of the most densely populated in the country and is an important agricultural region, especially for tobacco. More to the point, it contains some beautiful natural and man-made attractions. Just after kilometre 22 on the Carretera de Masaya, there is a turning to the **Masaya National Park**. The main attraction of this park is **Volcán Santiago**. The volcano is a magnificent sight, and the views from the top, particularly across Lake Managua to Momotombo Volcano, are even better. This 590m (1,950ft) mountain is shrouded in mystery and is the subject of ancient legends. In pre-Columbian times Indians threw women into Santiago's bubbling crater to appease the goddess of fire, Chaciutique; objects discovered in the lava flows in the area are thought to have been offerings made to the same goddess. The first European, a Spanish monk, climbed Santiago in 1529, and named it 'The Mouth of Hell'.

The early Spanish also erected a large cross at the top to ward off the devil which the Spanish believed had been attracted by the sacrificial rites practised by the Indians. Equally fanciful were the rumours that Santiago's crater was full of boiling gold – several expeditions climbed Santiago during the 16th century in search of this 'gold', which turned out to be nothing but molten stone.

The last big eruption was in 1772. As you approach the park you cross a huge lava flow which covers the volcano's northern slopes. There are actually two craters, Masaya and Santiago. The first is extinct, while the other, which collapsed in 1986, continues to rumble and belch sulphurous fumes. Santiago crater, almost a mile wide, is at its most active at dawn and dusk. The crater is coloured by chemical deposits, and a unique species of parrot nests on its sheer cliffs. During the Sandinista era, it also became something of a shrine, with a cross said to commemorate opponents of Somoza who were thrown into the volcano and, on the lavafield, the initials of revolutionary movements worldwide were picked out in stone. There are a couple of lookout points, and various trails – some along the rim of the crater, and one leading down to the Laguna de Masaya. Coyotes are sometimes spotted in the park, but more easily sighted are the flowers which include orchids and the yellow *sacuanjoche*, Nicaragua's national flower.

From the park gate it is a 6km (4 mile) walk south to the crater, though you may be able to hitch a lift. Alternatively, hire a taxi in Managua or Masaya – which is not too expensive if shared by a group of people. Visit as early in the morning as possible to see Santiago at its most active and to avoid the heat of the midday sun. The park is open from 7am to 3pm daily except Mondays. You should be able to leave bags at the entrance lodge if you are just visiting in transit between Managua and Masaya. You must pay an entrance fee to visit the crater, and another to visit the small museum which explains the geology, fauna, flora and history of the area. The restaurant attached to the museum is one of the best in the country and consequently expensive; take supplies of food and drink unless you plan a splurge.

From the park, it is another 8km (5 miles) southeast to Masaya, along a road with plenty of buses and other, hitchable, traffic. But at the 26-kilometre (from Managua) mark you might want to stop off at **Nindirí**, an Indian village with a small archaeological museum that contains an interesting collection of Indian artifacts discovered in the area, from stone sculptures and musical instruments to huge funerary urns. Nindirí's church, built in 1798, is also worth visiting, and there are a number of crafts workshops.

An all-embracing bus ride

A few days before Christmas 1999, something strange happened: I found a woman working on a bus in a role other than that of a vendor. She was a conductor working on the route between Tipitapa and Masaya, though the term 'manageress' would be more appropriate given her attention to detail. She organised every passenger, and their possessions, with great precision (some would say bossiness), and publicly denounced anyone who failed to proffer the correct change. Clearly, the years under the Sandinistas helped Nicaragua become more oriented towards sexual equality than other countries in the region.

The road to Masaya cuts across fields as flat as a tortilla. Halfway along the journey, the bus jolted to a halt in the middle of nowhere. The passengers at the front started to cheer. A wedding party climbed aboard, led by a page boy in a dazzling white bow tie and a mother looking quietly proud. The bride wore a fabulous white dress that had somehow eluded the grime of daily life in Nicaragua, and she looked not a day older than 17.

Masaya: the city of (bedraggled) flowers

The departmental capital is small (home to 30,000 people), amiable and beautiful, though it still bears many scars of the Revolution, particularly the Parque Central where some buildings are riddled with bullet holes. Masaya struggles to live up to its claim to be 'the city of flowers', since the town has the decayed feel common to many Nicaraguan settlements. But a sizeable and active Indian community lives in and around the town, and their crafts add colour to the market – one of the best in the country. The indigenous people also dominate Masaya's festivals.

If you arrive by bus, hop off just beyond the **Auto-Hotel Billy** (which is not bad for an overnight stay) on the approach road. You will be at the **old railway station**, a fine early 20th-century building in cream and brown, which has been converted into artisans' workshops and a craft school; you are welcome to wander around. Two blocks south and west take you to the **Parque San**

Jerónimo, which was wrecked in the Revolution; the battle for Masaya is commemorated by the statue of a stone-throwing Sandinista.

The Calle Real San Jerónimo leads south to the centre of Masaya, which is a curiously shaped square – or, rather, three contiguous squares: Parques el Centenario, Vega Matús and 17 Octubre. They form an L-shape around the 19th-century Church of the Ascensión, whose facade is notable for the Indian motifs. On the corner of Parque Centenario is a bust of Sandino, and on the opposite side of the church is a monument to Sandinista soldiers who died in the town on 17 October 1977.

Two blocks east of the Parque Central is the **Mercado Viejo**, the old market, protected within stout walls. These days it is a centre for crafts (and tourists). The brightly coloured mats, baskets, masks and tapestries – many with ancient Indian motifs – are all good buys. Another local product is the hammock, among the best to be found anywhere in Central America. At the hammock factory La Siesta – three blocks west and one block north of the Parque Central – you can buy direct from the manufacturer.

To commune with humanity, pick up one of the collective taxis that circulate through the town – or a horse-drawn cart – across town to the vast, rambling **market**. Bananas, beer, baskets and black market dealers confront you – and that's just in the car park outside. The locals come here to buy food, but many stalls sell crafts too. The market, a dozen blocks east of the Parque Central, is far more manageable than its counterparts in Managua, and is probably better.

To see the craftsmen and women at work, and to see an interesting part of town, visit **Monimbó**. This is the principal Indian district in Masaya and can be reached by walking along Calle San Sebastián which runs due south of the Parque Central. On the left about five blocks down is the church of San Sebastián; the fresco depicting the martyrdom of Sebastian has a strong Indian flavour. In 1978 the church was the scene of an appalling massacre by the National Guard, in which hundreds of people died. From here walk northwest along a road which takes you to the modest church of Magdalena. Many woodcarvers and leatherworkers work along Calle Central which is up to the left from the church. It is a broad, cobbled and often empty street, the quiet broken only by the sound of craftsmen's hammers.

If you aim northwest you will finish up overlooking Laguna de Masaya from the Malecón – literally 'pier', but in practice a promenade alongside the shimmering lake, with the volcano smouldering in the background. Towards dusk, it is a magical place to be, though the gaunt, grey frame of the baseball stadium does not add to the sense of communing with nature. From the promenade you cannot see the degree of pollution in the lake, and it is one of the best places in Central America to see the sunset. Even the locals, who have seen it hundreds of times before, congregate here to watch the sun go down.

On the walk back to town, look north to see Fort Coyotepe on the top of the hill in the distance. This fortress, also known as La Fortillera, was once used as a torture centre by the Somozas. It is on a hill to the right, about a mile west of Masaya and a short distance before a road branches north to Tipitapa. To visit it, take any bus along the main road and walk from the turn-off. The fort is now virtually deserted and has a rather eerie atmosphere, but there are fine views.

September, October and November are the months when the town's most important festivals take place. The main celebrations in honour of Masaya's patron saint, San Jerónimo, are held on 30 September. El Torovenado is the name given to the various processions which take place over the three months. El Torovenado del Malinche (usually held on a Sunday in November) is the most lively, with great activity in the streets. More traditional, however, is the Torovenado del Pueblo which usually falls on a Sunday at the end of October. There is often dancing on Sundays during October, when people wear traditional costumes and marimba bands play.

Buses to Masaya leave several times an hour from the Roberto Huembes terminal in Managua. Masaya's bus terminal is adjacent to the main market, 12 blocks east of the town centre, so unless you want to go straight to the market get off before the end of the line – the old railway station is a good place. Passengers on through buses between Managua and Granada must alight at the Shell garage on the highway and walk half an hour south to the centre or catch a local bus or horse and trap.

Most of the town's motley and unappealing selection of **bars and restaurants** are within a block of the Parque Central. It is much better to head out to the market and dine there at one of the dozens of comedores that are set up for the benefit of shoppers and traders. Then venture across the unkempt football field that serves as the town's bus terminal and find one of the buses that leave approximately half-hourly between 6am and 6pm for the 16km (10 mile) run to Nicaragua's grandest city.

If you possibly can, plan to stop halfway for a short, sharp hike.

Up hill and down crater
The **Laguna de Apoyo**, south of the main road from Masaya to Granada, is Nicaragua's largest crater lake – and a highly recommended excursion. There are two possible approaches to the lake. One road leading to the lake branches off the main road 7km (4 miles) before Granada, at the 37 kilometre mark. From here it is a 90-minute walk, pleasant but shadeless, to the village right above the lake; at the only T-junction you encounter, you should turn left. Trucks cover the route several times daily; hitching is likely to be most successful at the weekend.

Once at the village, a road leads off to the right. But it is another 5km (3 miles) down to the lake by road, so take the path instead. It starts opposite the shop on the corner and drops quickly down to the lakeshore. (Leave any bags you have at the shop since the path is steep, and slippery in places.) It should take about half-an-hour to reach the bottom. The views that open out in front of you as you descend are magnificent. Towards the bottom it becomes unclear which path to take, but as long as you continue downwards it doesn't really matter which you choose. The trees continue right down to the shores of the lake, so there is no beach as such – and, anyway, the water is cold, dark and uninviting.

For the best views of the lake go to the small village of Santa Catarina, on the main Rivas-Managua road southwest of the lake. From the main road walk a mile northeast to El Mirador, a lookout point behind the church. It offers a spectacular view of Granada, the lake and Mombacho volcano (1,224m), which last erupted in 1560. The site is busy at weekends, but at other times it is a quiet spot and a wonderful place to sit and read or have a picnic. A track off to the right leads down to the lakeshore, but you must return the same way. Santa Catarina is a lovely village and worth a visit in its own right.

First city: Granada

Contenders for primacy among Nicaragua's cities amount to just two. Supporters of León would make greater claims for their city's primacy, but no-one can dispute the singular feature of Granada: that it was the first city established by Europeans on the mainland of the Americas. Granada lies on the north-western shores of Lake Nicaragua, and this position makes it accessible by ship from the Caribbean along the San Juan river. This was the route used by Francisco Hernández de Córdoba, when he established the first Spanish settlement in Nicaragua in 1524. Even though it lies at a low, hot and humid level, the new community was named after the Andalucian mountain city which was his home.

Granada soon became the country's principal trading centre. A prosperous and peaceable existence was destined to end, however, as Granada came to the attention of English, French and Dutch pirates. Ruins of forts built to forestall attacks can still be seen along the banks of the Río San Juan and on islands in the lake. Further disaster came in 1856 when much of the town was burnt down by the American adventurer William Walker during his campaign to gain control of the country. In view of the town's suffering, it is surprising that any fine colonial buildings have survived. They are gradually being restored, and parts of the city are wonderfully atmospheric. Granada's collection of churches cannot be compared to that found in León, but the Parque Central is undoubtedly the most charming in Nicaragua. With trees, benches and cafés it is strongly reminiscent of Spain; and, unlike in Masaya, most of the buildings around the square are intact, including the striking cathedral. Granada was once the retreat of Somoza, and he spent a lot on the upkeep of the town. Granada has risen from post-Revolutionary slumber to become the tourist centre of Nicaragua. Despite its relative prosperity, it remains a relaxed and quiet place – and a good location to try to get under the skin of this complex country.

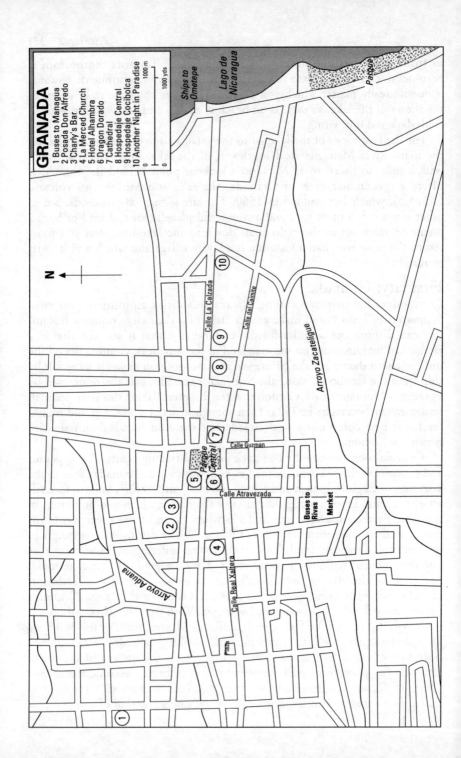

GRANADA

1 Buses to Managua
2 Posada Don Alfredo
3 Charly's Bar
4 La Merced Church
5 Hotel Alhambra
6 Dragon Dorado
7 Cathedral
8 Hospedaje Central
9 Hospedaje Cocibolca
10 Another Night in Paradise

Ships to Ometepe

Lago de Nicaragua

Parque

N

Calle La Calzada
Calle del Caimito
Arroyo Zacatelique

Calle Guzman
Parque Central
Calle Atravezada

Arroyo Aduana

Calle Real Xaltera

Buses to Rivas
Market

Plaza

Getting your bearings

Granada is a million times more manageable than Managua. The large **Parque Central** is really a square-and-a-half, with the extreme western edge marked by the main north-south axis, Calle La Atravesada. On the eastern side, the **cathedral** separates the square from the broad main street down to the lake, La Calzada. In the opposite direction, the Calle Real Xalteva extends from the south side of the square to the west. It crosses the Avenida Heróes y Martires about one kilometre west of the square. Here, the road for the south sets off, while the road to Masaya and Managua runs northwest.

Confusingly, all the east-west streets are prefixed Calle and most, but not all, of the north-south streets are Avenidas. And you will not be amazed by now that the street names are in a constant state of flux. The ones used here and shown on the map are those in force early in 2000.

Buses from the Roberto Huembes terminal in **Managua** take an hour or two to cover the 45km (28 miles), depending on traffic and the number of people trying to get on or off en route. They depart every 15 minutes or so from 5am to 6pm, and drop passengers at the fenced lot on the Avenida Heróes y Martires, three blocks north of the Calle Real; this is a long walk from the centre, so get a horse and cart. The usual fare is $1. An alternative is to take the smaller, faster and much more expensive Managua Express bus, which arrives at the south side of the Parque Central. Buses and trucks to and from other parts of Nicaragua terminate at street corners close to the market, three blocks south and three blocks west of the Parque Central. Services run direct to Masaya from the corner of Calle 3 Sur and 1 Avenida. Buses for **Nandaime** and **Rivas** run from the patch of wasteland on Avenida Central at Calle 5. Buses to and from Rivas are infrequent, so the best option is to take anything going south and change buses at Nandaime if necessary.

For **International services** south across the border to Costa Rica and Panama, Ticabus, Nicabus and Panaline offer early morning departures, but you must book in advance. If you wish, you can arrange to be picked up from Rivas instead, though this is probably not worth the extra uncertainty and expense compared with getting a bus from Rivas south to the border and another to San José.

An intriguing alternative is to switch to **Lake Nicaragua** for part of the journey; if you get one of the infrequent boats across from Granada to the Isla de Ometepe and onward from there to San Carlos. At the start of 2000, there were supposed to be departures to Ometepe on Mondays and Thursdays at 2pm, and on Saturdays at noon, but these are subject to delay and cancellation.

For city transport there is a fleet of stripy yellow and white buses, supplemented by horse-drawn carts; there is a rank for these on the north side of the market.

A room

There is a better choice of places to stay in Granada than anywhere else in Nicaragua. The undoubted favourite among backpackers is the **Hospedaje Central** (tel 552 5900), on the south side of La Calzada one block behind the cathedral. Besides offering cheap beds (a single room costs $5, a double $9), it

Life in the fast lane

What you first notice about the Hospedaje Central are the travellers' murals by Jill and Hugo. Next, you will catch sight of the owner, a middle aged American called Bill, who lives a reckless life. Each day he religiously takes eight kinds of medication for high blood pressure and a heart condition. Unfortunately, this is counteracted by 50 cigarettes and copious amounts of the hospedaje's free coffee. Bill remains enthusiastic: each day he strolls through his travellers' paradise, eyes goggling behind stained bi-focals, greeting his guests with the expected 'Good morning', followed by 'And did you have wild and kinky sex last night?'.

sells beer and trips out onto the lake. The restaurant serves large gringo burgers (the term means burgers for gringos, not of them). The breakfasts are American sized.

Just beyond the Hospedaje Central (heading to the lake) is the **Cocibolca** guest house, which charges $4 for a single room, $7 for a double. Next, there is the **Hospedaje El Italiano** (tel/fax 552 7047), which has a bar, cable television and air conditioning. The per-person charge is $15.

Further east towards the lake is the **Hotel Granada** (tel 552 2974, fax 552 4128) opposite the Guadalupe church; rooms in this characterless modern block cost $28 single/$39 double, and some travellers have reported that apparent acrimony between the proprietor and her husband (shades of Fawlty Towers?) can make life difficult for guests. A better bet is the elegant **Alhambra** (tel 552 4486, fax 552 2035, hotalam@tmx.com.ni) on the Parque Central, whose name harks back to the Moorish palace in Spanish Granada, and which has palatial air-conditioned rooms with private bathrooms and cable TV for $38 single/$46 double.

These places are long-established and look likely to stay around for a while, but they have been joined by some ambitious and attractive new venues. Just east of the Hotel Granada is **Another Night in Paradise** (tel 552 7113), where a room costs around $20 single, $30 double. Most welcome of all is the **Posada Don Alfredo** (or Alfredo's for short, tel/fax 552 4455, alfred_baganz@ hotmail.com), run by a German gentleman named Alfred. It is tucked a little out of the way one block north of the church of La Merced on Calle 14 de Septiembre. This old hacienda has a beautiful courtyard (hammocks are optional), huge rooms and boasts, not inaccurately, of serving the best breakfasts in Nicaragua, 7am-11.30am daily. A room for two, which may turn out to have four beds, is yours for $25 – with breakfast an extra $5 each.

The **Hotel Valencia** is more upmarket still. You can find it half a block from La Merced at Calle Real Xalteva 110 (tel/fax 552 4828, hotel-valencia@hotmail.com). It is clean and comfortable, with cable TV in each room, but the price of $40 double is on the high side for Granada – and the pet monkey may not be to everyone's taste.

A meal

The choice of restaurants has increased hugely in a decade. On the main crossroads (Calle La Atravesada/Calle Real Xalteva), there is the choice of the (mostly) Chinese **Dragon Dorado**, and the steak-and-beer **Los Bocaditos**. **Sergio's Mexican Tacos** is almost adjacent to the Hospedaje Central on La Calzada, just behind (east of) the cathedral. There are a couple of upmarket places along La Calzada, but for simple, good and entertainingly cheap food, fill up at **Asados Loty**, on the same block as the Hospedaje Cocibolca, i.e. one-and-a-half blocks behind the cathedral. Grilled meat can be washed down with plenty of cold beer.

A drink

The locals drink enthusiastically at **Charly's**. at the corner of Calle La Atravesada, just northwest of the Alhambra Hotel, while backpackers converge on the **Hospedaje Central**.

A drink

Down at the lake, and south of Plaza España along the shore, is a recreational park created during the Sandinista era by Inturismo, when the national tourism authority was doing a creditable impression of the Soviet Union's Intourist. It might sound ghastly but is actually great fun and very popular among the locals, above all on Sundays when they come to swim, picnic, stroll up and down the promenade – and swig plenty of beer. A favourite pastime on a Sunday afternoon is to drink the day away in one of the many bars, some of which have live music. The area is being upgraded with the help of an unlikely trilogy of European cities: Frankfurt in Germany, Dordrecht in Holland and Trnava in Slovakia.

An exploration

The obvious place to start is the neo-classical **cathedral** on the Parque Central. It contains a famous statue of the Virgin (made in Seville) and examples of colonial art, most of which were brought from Europe. It features a bizarre montage of the French pilgrimage centre of Lourdes. Adjacent is the **Casa de los Leones**, one of the oldest buildings in the Americas. The first structure here dates from 1550, though most of the building was erected around 1720. It is a handsome colonial mansion that has been turned into a cultural centre called the Fundacio de los Tres Mundos, which stages events and has an agreeable café.

The most interesting church in Granada is the church of **San Francisco**, a block north and east of the Parque Central. It was first built in 1585, making it one of the oldest churches in Nicaragua. A plaque on the outside recalls how it was set on fire by William Walker in 1856. It was restored a decade later and has a striking blue and white decorated facade. Inside is the chapel of María Auxiliadora, decorated with Indian needlework. Fray Bartolomé de las Casas, the so-called 'Apostle of the Indies', preached here in the 1530s.

Attached to the church is the huge old monastery which used to house a school, and has finally become a municipal museum after a decade of procrastination and several million Swedish kronur. The most interesting exhibits are those outside, the granite statues which were discovered on the islands of Zapatera and Omotepe in Lake Nicaragua. Most of them are idols depicted with human bodies and animal heads, and are thought to have been the work of Chorotega Indians. There is lots of background information (in Spanish), which would be particularly useful for anyone planning to visit the islands; there are also maps showing where the main archaeological sites are. The museum is open 8am-4pm, Monday to Friday, and has an excellent bookshop.

Halfway to the lake along La Calzada is the church of **Guadalupe**. It lacks atmosphere but has an interesting history – during Walker's campaign it was taken over and used as a base and hospital. At the eastern end of Calle La Calzada, near the shore, are **Plaza España** and the pier. The square contains a monument to Hernandéz de Córdoba; Somoza's name has been rubbed out on the plaque beneath it.

The **Colegio Centro-América**, on the shores of the lake, north of the railway line, is at first sight an ordinary high school. Its interest stems from the collection of pre-Columbian sculptures in the middle of the grounds. These artifacts were removed from the islands in Lake Nicaragua, and are dotted randomly around the courtyard outside the metalwork department. Like the statues in Granada's museum, the figures are half man, half beast. To reach the Colegio, walk three blocks north from the post office then bear right for about a mile.

Two blocks west of the Parque Central is the striking church of **La Merced**, built in the 1780s. It also suffered at the hands of Walker's mercenary troops. The exterior is blackened by smoke and lichen, while the interior is embellished by a figure of Jesus in a fetching red cloak. The **market** extends a couple of blocks south from here, with produce piled high and some expert pickpockets.

Keeping in touch

The **Post Office** and **Telcor/Enitel** is on the northeast corner of Parque Central. **Internet** options are multiplying, with cyber cafés dotted around the town. The most conveniently located is on the southeast corner of the Parque Central. There are **banks** on Calle Real Xalteva, and plenty of parallel market dealers at the northwest corner of the market.

Moving on

To reach the point at which all three contenders for Pan-American Highway become reunited, take any bus heading to or beyond Nandaime. From Granada, there are relatively few buses going through to Rivas, the next big town, so be prepared to hitch or wait for another bus at Nandaime, a dusty spot on the map where the main roads from Managua, Masaya and Granada converge. The town is blighted by its position at an important junction, but it boasts a beautiful parish church.

With a bit of luck you will drift over the next 46km (29 miles) in an hour or so, winding up at **Rivas**. It is the capital of the department which occupies the narrow strip of land between Lake Nicaragua and the Pacific. The town itself is three miles west of the lake, 108km (67 miles) south of Managua and 40km (25 miles) north of the Costa Rican border. The town is thought to have been built on the site of the village of Nicaraocoli. This was the home and capital of the Indian chief Nicarao, after whom the country is named. Rivas was also the scene of a famous battle in 1856 in which the Costa Rican patriot, Juan Santamaría, helped defeat William Walker and his band of mercenaries, sacrificing himself in the process.

The centre of Rivas lies about four blocks west of the Pan-American Highway. It has a pleasant Parque Central dominated by a huge Basilica. The dome contains a fascinating and hilarious fresco which depicts a sea battle in which the good ship *Communismo* is sinking.

The town's **bus station** is next to the market a few blocks north of the Parque Central, and has a rank for horse-drawn cabs here. There are a few cheap and basic **hospedajes** along the Pan-American Highway. One such is the Internacional which charges $12 for a double room and serves the weakest coffee in the western hemisphere. The Hospedaje Lidia, around the corner past the Texaco station, is cheaper and more comfortable. A room without a bath costs $6. By far the best place is the Hotel Cacique Nicarao (tel 453 3234, fax 453 3120), next to the cinema, which is clean and comfortable. A room costs about $35 single, $45 double. Out on the highway, north of the centre, a cheaper option is the Brisas del Mombacho.

At the Rinconcito Salvadoreño, a small open-air **restaurant** on the Parque Central, you can eat delicious, piping-hot pupusas (traditional Salvadoran stuffed tortillas). For a meal more typical of Nicaragua go to the unnamed comedor next to the Hospedaje Internacional, or one of the nearby outdoor street stalls. Rivas is better off for **bars**, the best of which are on the highway. These include the 'blue' bar (it has no name) on the left just north of the Texaco station. It's a lively place where a lot of serious drinking takes place, particularly at the weekend when people also dance to the strains of an ancient and distorted juke box.

An easy one-hour walk north of Rivas takes you to the small port of **San Jorge**, which has a pleasant colonial church. Ferries sail to Ometepe Island from here, and there are good views of Concepción and Maderas volcanoes from the pier. The water is unfortunately dirty and most unappealing. Near San Jorge is the village of **Buenos Aires**, which boasts one of the best-preserved colonial churches in the country. Finally, just northeast of Rivas is **Popoynapa**. Its church of Jesús del Rescate attracts many pilgrims during the Week of Sorrows which falls shortly before Easter.

By the Shell station south of Rivas is one of the very few **roundabouts** anywhere along the Pan-American Highway. At the centre is a not-unattractive fountain, which would be even more fetching if it were working. Try to sit on the left of your bus, heading south, for some stirring scenery on the next stretch, as two stately cones rise from the east.

The lake of miracles: Lago de Nicaragua

A huge blue eye on the map of the nation, the Lago de Nicaragua is the largest lake in Central America. It measures 148km (92 miles) at its broadest point, and boasts fish that have evolved specifically to live in it. Lake Nicaragua is the only freshwater lake in the world to contain sharks, sawfish and other fish which usually live only in salt water. One explanation for this is that the lake was once a bay on the Pacific which was cut off from the sea by a volcanic eruption; its salinity decreased only slowly, allowing the marine life trapped in it time to adapt to fresh water. In fact, many of the fish spend time in both salt and fresh water: they swim up the Río San Juan from the Caribbean to feed and, as they acclimatise to the salt-free water, swim further upstream until eventually they reach the lake.

There are over 300 islands in Lake Nicaragua, most of them uninhabited. Many of them are covered in lush vegetation which provides an excellent habitat for wildlife. Birdlife is particularly abundant, and cranes, bitterns, herons and egrets are often spotted. The best time to see them is in the early morning or late afternoon. Fish also thrive here and fishing is the main source of income for the people living in the villages around the lake. *Guapote* (rainbow bass) and *moharra* fish are caught in large numbers and end up in many of the local restaurants.

The islands are important historically, and there are a number of archaeological sites. Most of the ancient Indian artifacts discovered are now in the San Francisco museum in Granada and in other museums in Nicaragua and abroad. Some islands were sequestrated before the Revolution by rich Nicaraguans who built homes for themselves here – among them was Anastasio Somoza Debayle, the last of the Somoza dynasty to hold power.

Ferry services run to the larger islands from a few towns along the shores of the lake, but to reach the smaller islands you must charter a boat. Granada is a base from which to catch ferries and to hire boats on Lake Nicaragua, although there are also ferries from San Jorge on the lake's western shore near Rivas. Ferries from Granada run from the pier near Plaza España, but to hire boats go to Puerto Asese, 5km (3 miles) south of Granada. Boats can be rented by the hour. Rates are expensive, typically $15 per hour, although the cost decreases the longer you wish to stay out – four hours, for example, would cost around $50. If you want to go out under your own steam, rowing boats are available. There is no public transport to Puerto Asese – to walk there follow the road which runs across the headland south of the Inturismo park. Transport back from the port late in the day can be a problem, so don't arrange to get back from a trip too late; the road from the port has a reputation for robbers.

San Pablo Fortress, on one of the smaller islands in the northern part of the lake, was first constructed in the 18th century and was one of a series built to protect Granada from pirate attack. What you see today is a reconstruction completed in the 1970s, but some of the old cannons are still there, and there are good views.

Though it is the second largest island in the lake, **Isla Zapatera** is thinly populated. It is about 20km (12 miles) from Granada, and makes a good day trip – no accommodation is available. Ferries don't run to the island, so you must hire your own boat. There are a number of archaeological sites on the island, although most of the relics have been removed. The main ones are Punta de las Figuras, La Guinea, and Sonzapote. At Sonzapote you can see where statues once stood, as well as a number of royal tombs. Try and arrange to get a boat to the nearby **Isla del Muerto** ('Island of the Dead')where some of the greatest archaeological finds in Nicaragua – including petroglyphs and tombs – were discovered. You can still see some extraordinary pre-Columbian graffiti.

Most people, though, aim for **Isla Ometepe**, the largest island in the lake, and also the most dramatic. The volcanoes of Concepción (1,610m/5,313ft), the second highest in the country, and Las Maderas (1,345m/4,440ft), dominate the lake. The two main villages are Moyogalpa and Alta Gracia, both of which are in the northern half of the island at the foot of Concepción. The island is home to 20,000 people. Climbing the volcanoes is not recommended – they are both active, and being steep-sided makes scaling them exceedingly difficult. You can go on less ambitious hikes around the island. A 13km (8 mile) path links Alta Gracia with Moyogalpa across the northern slopes of Concepción, for example, and there are also trails along the coast.

Boats from Granada's pier depart at 2pm on Mondays and Thursdays and 12 noon on Saturdays, at least in theory, and take 4-5 hours. There are more frequent boats to Moyogalpa from San Jorge on the western shore, the journey from here taking about an hour. Base yourself at Moyogalpa, which has a better choice of accommodation. The best place to stay is the super-sumptuous Hotel Ometepelt (tel 459 4276, fax 459 4132), charging an impressive $200 per room, per night, while a more realistic option is the Cari Hotel (tel 459 4196, fax 4263) – $15 single, $30 double.

San Juan del Sur

Thirty kilometres (17 miles) south of Rivas is the small fishing village of San Juan del Sur, population 5,000. It is a lovely port, overlooking a beautiful sandy bay that sweeps around in a gentle arc, protected by a ring of stout hills. Of all the places in Nicaragua where you could swim, sunbathe and slacken the pace of travel, this has to be the most enticing.

Yet the people most attracted to San Juan del Sur have usually been foreigners. As mentioned, for a while in the 19th century it was an essential node on the journey from the east to the west coast of the USA. It became popular towards the end of the 20th century among foreign brigade workers who came here for a rest after their stints in the northern highlands. There is less of a rush to reach San Juan del Sur now than in the 1850s. The road to the port branches off the Pan-American Highway at La Virgen, a dusty halt 12km

The fast track across America

The **Río San Juan** is a splendid river, lined with thick jungle, and extends 200km (137 miles) between the Atlantic coast and the town of San Carlos, at the mouth of Lake Nicaragua. It is alive with birds: ibis and hummingbirds as well as waterbirds such as herons and egrets. But most of the people who made the trip were not in the least interested in wildlife; they were in search of Californian gold.

During the period of the British Protectorate, the port of San Juan del Norte was known as Greytown, and became immensely prosperous because of the Gold Rush. The fastest way from the East Coast of the USA to California was to sail down to San Juan del Norte, take a steamer up the Río San Juan and across Lake Nicaragua, from where stagecoaches ran overland to San Juan del Sur on the Pacific Coast – soon, a railway was built to accellerate the journey to the Pacific. Here, boats provided the last link in the chain of transport to San Francisco. From 1851-1871 over 150,000 people followed this route. Washington ended British control of San Juan del Norte in the 19th century by bombing the town; a few people continued to live there but they finally left after a Contra attack in the 1980s.

A plan to build a trans-isthmian canal between the Lake and the Pacific was rejected in the 19th century in favour of Panama. The decision, in retrospect, seems perverse. There are points in Nicaragua (notably just south of Rivas) where a river that flows into Lake Nicaragua and out to the Atlantic is only five km (three miles) away from one flowing to the Pacific.

The capacity of the Panama Canal is strictly limited, so recently there has been renewed interest in its potential, particularly from Japanese investors. Only 25km (15 miles) of new canal would need to be dug up (though deep water channels would have to be dredged along the Río San Juan and at points across the lake). Furthermore, this neck of land is low lying, so a sea level channel is feasible. Before Nicaragua is bisected by a canal large enough to carry the world's biggest ships, several problems must be addressed. They include how to minimise environmental damage and how to deal with the variation in tides: the Pacific coast has wide deviations, while the Caribbean has relatively small tides.

(7 miles) south of Rivas. There is one bus a day from and to Managua, and a few buses from Rivas, but hitching is easy – there is only one possible destination along the road from the Pan-American Highway.

The approach to the town is less than glorious: the outskirts have an air of neglect. But once you reach the seafront, you forgive the place everything for its sublime location (though if one of the rental quad bikes is out and about, the tranquility will be shattered). Amble along the beachside road to the north, and you will find the amazing fire-ravaged remains of what was once a handsome rail terminus, the last dry land that the California gold-diggers set foot upon before reaching San Francisco. A collection of shacks has been established in the ruins, but no doubt some investor is planning to refurbish the station and turn it into an upmarket hotel.

The present choice of **places to stay** is topped, in terms of location, by the Hotel Estrella (tel 458 2210), with balconies overlooking the Pacific, charging around $15 single/$20 double. But although the hotel is great to look at, it is in poor condition. The Casa Blanca hotel, one block north past a small craft market, may appeal rather more. Once you get away from the seafront, prices fall; at the Casa de Huéspedes Mercedes (tel 458 2564), just inland from the town market, beds are available for $5 or less.

The best **places to eat** are along the beach – cafés such as Marie's Bar and Restaurant serve the El Gringo breakfast of egg, bacon, cheese and fried potatoes for $2.50. Almost opposite, dangling over the beach, the Restaurant El Timón has excellent fish for lunch and supper. The food stalls in the market are good for snacks at breakfast or lunch.

The water in the bay is calm and safe for **swimming** and **surfing**, but it is cold and has become increasingly dirty in recent years. There is a cleaner beach a mile or so north of the village, but better still are Playa del Coco and Playa del Tamarindo, about 15km (9 miles) southeast near Ostional. A dirt road runs along the coast, or you could try to strike a deal with one of the local fishing boats.

Heading back to the Pan-American Highway, your entire field of vision seems to be filled by the volcanoes of Concepción and Las Maderas in Lake Nicaragua. To reach Costa Rica, turn right on the Highway for the last ten miles to the frontier at Peñas Blancas. People who prefer to make an informal entrance to Costa Rica could try continuing along past Ostional on the dirt road across the border to the settlement of La Cruz. But this would leave you in the tricky position of not having checked out of Nicaragua, nor into Costa Rica. So it is better to do things by the book, even though it is a lengthy process.

First, get along the Highway to Sapoá, the last town in Nicaragua. Here, you begin the process of checks to get out of the country, the ratio is three listless soldiers checking your papers, for each official who is actually doing anything sensible. In exchange for each small service, you can expect to pay $1. Costa Rica is actually four kilometres away from the first border check, and this buffer zone actually falls entirely within Nicaraguan territory. You will need to pay a couple of dollars for a ride on the no-man's land shuttle, which bumps across to a new building – still in Nicaragua. Here, you hand over your $2 fee (or more, if it happens to be a weekend) to leave the country, collect your exit stamp, pass yet another guard who checks that you have signed out correctly – and discover that the Costa Rican border is still another 10 minutes' walk away along a leafy and not-unattractive avenue. Even before you encounter the Costa Rican formalities, the whole performance is long-drawn-out and tiresome. Be patient.

Better still, get a ride with a local hero.

Boxer at the border

Walter and Stefan dropped me at the end of the road from San Juan del Sur, and whizzed off in their smart rental car towards Managua. So close to the Costa Rican border, yet so far to walk in the midday heat.

The wheezing and rumbling in the distance turned out to be issuing from a beaten-up Daewoo Tico, one of the worst cars ever produced by capitalism. But what was much more significant about the vehicle that swayed to an uneasy halt beside my waiting thumb on the Highway at La Virgen was the man at the wheel.

Donald Laguna sounds like a made-up name, the sort of moniker a journeyman boxer might adopt to boost his billing credibility. It had indeed appeared on plenty of pre-fight posters and post-fight medals. Yet it was, he promised, his real name.

In Nicaragua, Donald Laguna is a local hero. The peak of his sporting life as fighter was during the Eighties, when Nicaragua needed all the self-help it could get. He became, in the words he spelt out carefully with surprisingly delicate hands, 'Campeon de Boxeo Latino-Americano Peso Lijero Junior' – Latin America's junior featherweight boxing champion.

The story he told was of rags-to-not-quite-riches, of punching his way from a poor part of Managua to become Nicaragua's leading boxer. In the days when Nicaragua had to seek friends in strange places, he took part in contests in Moscow and East Berlin.

Drivers, of course, can tell hitchers any old nonsense they wish when they pick you up. But they cannot organise every official at every checkpoint on the Nicaraguan side of the border to wave through a rusting heap of Korean junk, smiling at, and saluting, the man behind the slightly dodgy wheel. Donald was clearly a legend in his own Daewoo.

Costa Rica

NICARAGUAN FRONTIER - PANAMANIAN FRONTIER

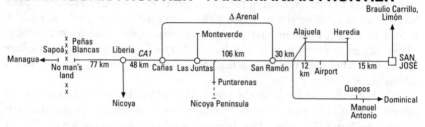

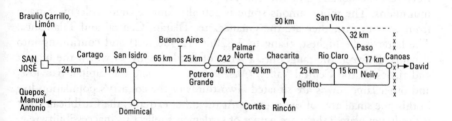

Twice the price and half as nice as paradise?

In the scrum of people that constitutes immigration controls on the Costa Rican side of the frontier, I got talking to a traveller heading in the opposite direction. "I can't wait to get into Nicaragua", he said. "Costa Rica is twice as expensive and half as interesting as the rest of Central America." Clearly he had not been to Honduras. Certainly, prices are high in Costa Rica, but only those with an aversion for jungle, exotic wildlife and idyllic beaches are likely to think it boring. Costa Rica is also one of the most peaceful nations in the world, no mean achievement in a region that has seen more than its fair share of conflict.

The 'rich coast' is the most prosperous country in Central America, and is arguably also the most attractive. Majestic natural beauty, from volcanoes to rainforest, is Costa Rica's main attraction. Trips into the wilds revolve around the country's large number of national parks which provide safe homes for a remarkable variety of fauna and flora: Costa Rica, smaller than the state of West Virginia, boasts four times as many species of bird as the whole of North

America. Between forays into the jungle, you can seek solace on some fine beaches on both the Atlantic and Pacific coasts. Perhaps surprisingly, it retains few vestiges of its colonial past, let alone its pre-Columbian beginnings. Indian culture has been eradicated in Costa Rica.

Perhaps because of the lack of ethnic variety – and thus of a potential source of strife – Costa Rica has survived and evolved for the past half-century without an army. Such a concept would be unheard of in the other Central American states, but Costa Rica has achieved a political stability that enhances its attractiveness to visitors. During the 1980s Costa Rica was the traditional place for journalists covering the struggles within Central America to take a break. It is held to be 'safe', and to have a certain familiarity for those from the West. Many villages in Costa Rica do not have a Parque Central so much as a village green; were the grass not so parched, you could imagine a game of cricket taking place.

Physically the country is small: only 120km (75 miles) wide at its narrowest point, 288km (180 miles) at its broadest. From northwest to southeast it stretches 440km (275 miles). The Atlantic and Pacific oceans wash over distinct terrains and cultures: the Atlantic side is low, humid and Caribbean in its nature, while the Pacific coast is rugged, cooler and thoroughly Hispanic. Between the oceans and the coastal plains, Costa Rica is dominated by mountains. The mountainous spine is actually four separate volcanic ranges: from west to east, they are the Guanacaste, Tilarán, Central and Talamanca. The latter is the highest, rising to 3,820m (12,500 feet) and continuing into Panama. Between the ranges lies a series of fertile basins, of which the biggest and richest is the Central Valley *(Meseta Central)* where the capital, San José, and other large towns are situated. Two-thirds of the country's population live in this one small area of the country. At the other extreme, the Caribbean coast is thinly populated: the place names of settlements reflect its inaccessibility (e.g. the village of Larga Distancia) and its British influences (Bristol and Liverpool are villages west of Limón).

Inevitably, Costa Rica's appeal has brought a few problems. Parts of the Pacific Coast have been colonised by foreigners, notably North Americans, and more migrants are sure to follow. Nevertheless, anyone who ventures away from the most popular national parks and beaches will find villages and people that are as relaxed, friendly and welcoming as anywhere in Central America. Life in Costa Rica may not have the edge that it does in Panama or Nicaragua, but to those on the Pan-American Highway this may come as a relief. You can contrast the poverty, character and colour of other countries in the region with the relative prosperity and peace of Costa Rica.

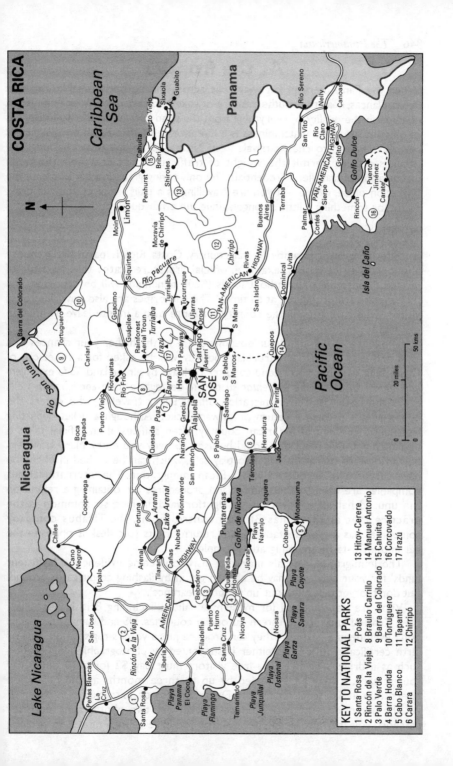

COSTA RICA

Lake Nicaragua

Nicaragua

Caribbean Sea

Panama

Pacific Ocean

Golfo de Nicoya

Golfo Dulce

Isla del Caño

N

KEY TO NATIONAL PARKS

1 Santa Rosa
2 Rincón de la Vieja
3 Palo Verde
4 Barra Honda
5 Cabo Blanco
6 Carara
7 Poás
8 Braulio Carrillo
9 Barra del Colorado
10 Tortuguero
11 Tapantí
12 Chirripó
13 Hitoy-Cerere
14 Manuel Antonio
15 Cahuita
16 Corcovado
17 Irazú

50 kms

20 miles

At the frontier

When the Pan-American Highway rolls across the border from Nicaragua at Peñas Blancas, near the southern shore of Lake Nicaragua, you notice an instant upgrade in the quality of everything from the road surface to the attentiveness of officials. The extra watchfulness is a nuisance: the Costa Rican border guards seem extra keen to check arrivals from Nicaragua, so delays can be long. The officials do not permit the weight of traffic to attenuate their thorough examination of travellers' credentials. The only saving grace is a bar opposite the Migración office, where – if you are travelling as a pair – one of you can drink coffee, or something a little stronger, while the other queues up.

Red tape

Despite being an apparently liberal country, Costa Rica is particularly choosy about who is let in. For example, official literature states that persons of unkempt appearance or without funds ($200 minimum) will be deported, and that 'gypsies are prohibited at all times'. The authorities are also unwilling to let visitors who have been in the country for more than a month leave without an exit visa.

The better order that your documents are in, the higher your chances of a swift and easy process. In particular, you may well be asked for a ticket out of Costa Rica, whether you intend to enter or leave by air or land. *Todo extranjero que ingrese al país, debe presentar su tiquete de regreso o de continuación viaje,* reads the notice at the immigration office: 'Every traveller who enters the country must present a return or onward ticket'. Although a ticket departing from another Central American country often suffices, if an official takes a dislike to you this regulation could be used to deny you entry. Many travellers buy an onward or return ticket to play safe, which can be cashed in once you have successfully negotiated Costa Rican immigration. The international bus companies are used to the routine, and procedures for obtaining a refund on the unused half of a ticket are straightforward. In fact, so common is the practice that at the Peñas Blancas control point, the Ticabus company sometimes has a representative selling return tickets (the desk is opposite the bar in the Costa Rican immigration complex).

The immigration officials may also insist on seeing evidence of 'sufficient funds' for your stay; you may be able to get in by flashing credit cards around. But don't forget that bit about 'unkempt appearance'.

Visas are not required for most nationalities, including British, Australian, New Zealand and most Western European countries. US and Canadian citizens don't even need a passport; they can produce just a voter's registration card or birth certificate, so long as either is supported by photographic identification such as a driver's licence. Visa-free visitors must pay $2 for a 30 or 90-day tourist card. It may be extended by up to three months at the Migración directorate in San José; ask for the Departamento de Extranjeros. In order to get the extension, you must produce a ticket out, two photographs and your passport; you may also need to show that you have enough money to prolong your stay, and be required to have a blood test for the Aids virus, HIV. Allow a few days for your new tourist card to be processed. An alternative is to get an exit visa (see below) which adds 30 days to your permitted stay. A better plan could well be to leave the country for at least three days, then come back in.

For visa applications or enquiries, contact the nearest Costa Rican Embassy. The addresses of the missions in the UK and USA are: Flat 1, 14 Lancaster Gate, London W2 3LH (tel 020 7723 1772), and 1825 Connecticut Avenue, NW, Suite 211, Washington DC 20009 (tel 202 234 2945). The US Embassy maintains a website containing plenty of useful information for Americans and other nationalities at usembassy.or.cr; this location can also be accessed through the Department of State's website at state.gov.

If you outstay the permitted length of your visit, you could find leaving Costa Rica can be almost as hard as getting in. You will need an **exit visa**, which states, among other things, that you have met your tax obligations under Costa Rican law. An exit visa costs about $5 and is valid for 30 days from the date of issue; it therefore constitutes an automatic extension to your visa or tourist card. If you have an air ticket out of Costa Rica you can ask a travel agent to get the visa for you. Otherwise, you must go to the Tribunales de Justicia in San José (Calle 17, Avenidas 6 and 8). Expect to queue for hours.

Frontier fees

In addition to the basic $2 charge (payable in dollars or colones), you may be charged for miscellaneous other items, including a donation to the Costa Rican Red Cross.

Customs

Baggage is often searched thoroughly, with the authorities particularly keen on tracking down drugs. Some travellers have reported that customs officials who have failed to find narcotics of the mind-changing variety have seized upon a relatively innocent medicine such as antibiotics or oral contraceptives.

Duty-free limits are three litres of alcholic liquor and '500 grams of manufactured tobacco', which corresponds to 400 cigarettes. You are also allowed 'two kilograms of sweets' and 'sporting weapons and up to 200 rounds of ammunition'.

Bringing in a car

Expect to pay a wide range of fees. All vehicles must be insured with the national insurance institute, INS. This is automatic in the case of hired cars, and must be arranged at the frontier if you bring in your own vehicle. A foreign driving licence is valid for three months.

Any chance of a decent map?

The Costa Rican tourist board (ICT) produces a free 1:1m map of the country, which is next to useless. An excellent alternative is the Insight Map of the country, price £4.99, which covers the country at 1:730,000, with a larger-scale map of the Meseta Central and a good city plan of San José.

More detailed maps are available at the ICT headquarters at Avenida 4, Calles 5 and 7 in San José. Topographical maps suitable for hikers are produced by the Instituto Geográfico Nacional (IGN) at the Ministry of Public Works on

Avenida 20 between Calles 9 and 11. Most maps are stocked by the good bookshops in the capital, or you can buy direct from the IGN. The office is open from 8.30am-3.30pm; to get there take the Barrio La Cruz bus from the Parque Central.

That was then

The first visitors

Before the Spanish conquest, the population of Indians in Costa Rica was smaller than that found in the other Central American countries, and there were no civilisations comparable with the Mayas. The people of Costa Rica kept a low profile during pre-Columbian times, but resisted the Spanish Conquest more fiercely than any other indigenous group in the region. Dotted around the country are *reservas indigenas* for various groups: the Matambú and Guataso in the north; the Barbilla-Dantas, Chirripó and Zapatón in the centre; and the Guaymí, Boruca and Talamanca in the south and east.

The Conquest

Columbus came upon Costa Rica on his fruitful voyage to the New World in 1502, landing on Isla Uvita – just off the coast at present-day Limón – on 18 September. He saw natives wearing gold jewellery and believed he had discovered a 'rich coast', hence the country's name. Attempts at colonisation began in 1506 under the Spanish conquistador Diego de Niceusa, but his efforts were thwarted by disease, which flourished on the low-lying Atlantic coast, and by hostility from the resident Carib Indians.

The first successful colonisation was made by Gil González de Avila from his base in newly-conquered Panama. He was able to explore the Pacific coast, where the terrain, climate, and natives were friendlier. He converted thousands of Indians to Catholicism, and procured a substantial haul of treasure, but the cost in human life was high: the Indian population was virtually obliterated, partly by genocide, but particularly by imported diseases to which the indigenous people had no resistance. The first successful settlers, however, were pioneers akin to those who settled North America and Australasia, unlike the typical Spanish conquistadores who merely plundered and exploited. The climate in the Central Valley suited them, but proved little temptation to others; much of the country remained unexplored.

Independence

The settlers mixed little with the few surviving Indians. Seeing themselves as self-sufficient sons of Spain, they supported continuing affiliation with the mother country, even to the extent of sending troops to Nicaragua to help crush a rebellion against Spain in 1811. This and other rebellions, however, placed the question of political allegiance on the agenda, and by the end of that decade opinion had swung towards self-rule. Costa Rica supported the declaration of independence made in Guatemala in 1821 and joined the United Provinces of Central America in 1823. When this federation collapsed in 1838, Costa Rica became – perhaps reluctantly – fully independent. It was a miserably poor country in comparison with its neighbours, though the development first of coffee and then of bananas as export crops increased its wealth and population. Power percolated into the hands of wealthy Spanish families, who selected Juan Rafael Mora – a successful coffee-grower – as President.

Mora was to face the first test of Costa Rica's independence. The American adventurer William Walker instigated an expeditionary force to take power in Central America, with a view to instituting slavery and building a canal linking the Atlantic with the Pacific. As described in the chapter on Nicaragua, Walker nearly succeeded. The turning point was in February 1856. Mora, leading a rather ragged army, forced Walker and his heavily-armed men back from the borders of Nicaragua. The single incident which the fighting focussed upon was the torching of Walker's Nicaraguan hide-out in Rivas, by Juan Santamaría, a 14-year-old drummer boy. He volunteered to set light to the building, driving the invaders out but perishing himself in the process. He is now the Costa Rican national hero.

President Mora earned little praise for his efforts. After a second skirmish with William Walker, he faced an election in 1859 which he won only through massive vote-rigging. He was deposed later that year, then staged an unsuccessful coup attempt in 1860, after which he was executed. Only posthumously did Mora receive credit for his fight for independence, and he is now commemorated in hundreds of street names.

The rich coffee-growers gradually loosened their grip on power, and a true democratic tradition began early. Free primary education was made mandatory in 1869, and the death penalty was abolished. The first in a noteworthy series of enlightened presidents was Bernardo Soto, who introduced free elections in 1889, at least for white males; the power of the rich was curtailed, and a tradition of social democracy began.

The Twentieth Century

It has been argued that only Nicaragua under the Sandinistas has matched the progressive social policies of Costa Rica. Today, the literacy rate in Costa Rica is said to be the second highest in the Americas, and average life expectancy is over 70 years. The path to freedom was not without its pitfalls, however. In 1917, defence minister Federico Tinoco staged a successful coup, and ruled for three years until deposed by liberal elements who oversaw a return to democracy. In 1940, the newly-elected Rafael Calderón Guardia instituted left-wing reforms in a curious alliance between the church and the communists. For all his philanthropic virtues, he was not averse to vote-rigging. A clause in Costa Rica's constitution forbids a president holding office for two successive four-year terms, but Calderón sought to overcome this by installing a puppet president, Teodoro Picado, who ruled from 1944. Many Costa Ricans became increasingly resentful at this manipulation, and when Calderón himself sought re-election in 1948, he was defeated. His government refused to accept the result, and a rebellion was organised by the fledgling social democratic National Liberation Party (PLN), under exiled intellectual Pepe Figueres.

After six weeks of bloodshed, a treaty was signed which installed Figueres as provisional president. Although an arch-conservative in his early years, with time he became more liberal in his approach; he was even an adviser to the Sandinistas before they came to power. In a curious mix of enlightened and repressive policies, he banned the communist party and the trades unions, implemented universal franchise, nationalised the banks and abolished the army; this last move was not entirely selfless and idealistic, since Figueres saw the army as a threat to his regime. Nevertheless, the move enabled money to be directed away from defence to health, education, and other needy areas. Figueres was known affectionately as 'Don Pepe'; when he died in 1990, his funeral was attended by prominent Central American leaders, many of whom acknowledged his contribution to democracy in the region.

For the second half of the 20th century, Costa Rica maintained democracy against considerable odds. Presidents from the PLN have alternated with those of the opposition coalition, which is by now an almost Peronist party, reliant upon support from business interests and the working class. It was this party that, in 1983, declared 'neutrality in perpetuity' for Costa Rica. From 1986-90 the president was Oscar Arias of the PLN, whose efforts to find a solution to the conflicts in Central America won him the 1987 Nobel Peace Prize – which he accepted on behalf of the whole country. The Costa Ricans promptly voted his party out of office at the first opportunity. With the prize money Arias initiated a Foundation for Peace and Democracy which is headed by his wife, Margarita Penón.

Arias' successor in 1990 was the leader of the right-wing opposition Social Christian Union Party (PUSC), Rafael Calderón Fournier, the son of Rafael Calderón Guardia. The poor, particularly those in the cities, welcomed him. But their high expectations were not met. His presidency was dominated by economic austerity, during which he reduced spending on education and public health, causing tensions that gradually spilled over into unrest as taxes rose, living standards fell and poverty increased. This culminated in a teachers' strike in the summer of 1995.

This is now

In political terms Costa Rica is stable; the challenge for any government is in balancing the need for economic change with the demands of social welfare. Miguel Angel Rodríguez became president in 1998, but austerity has continued and relations with the trade unions have been tense. The nation's overriding economic handicap is its huge foreign debt of $1.6 billion, over $500 for each man, woman and child. Maintaining the interest payments on this amount is a constant struggle in a developing economy, and has acted as a severe brake on growth, as does the penchant for printing paper money.

Costa Rica, however, has pioneered the practice of capitalising upon the growing concern for the health of the planet. It has used the threat of exploiting some of its virgin rainforest to negotiate 'debt for nature' agreements with some of its creditors, whereby a proportion of loans is converted to low-value bonds which are then used to fund environmental preservation projects.

On the Highway

If you have bumped and swerved across Nicaragua, you will be delighted with the enhanced quality of roads in Costa Rica. Driving feels familiar to those acquainted with motoring in the USA, with wide, well-surfaced highways, and good signposting, especially on the Pan-American Highway. Nevertheless, there are problems, as the tourism authorities readily admit. All too quickly, even top-category roads can deteriorate into dirt tracks which are impassable in the wet season. Rockslides are also a hazard, particularly after heavy rain. Many roads narrow from time to time to a single carriageway, with passing places. This is most common on dirt-track back roads, but can also happen in parts of the Pan-American Highway.

The ICT warns that special care needs to be taken on three stretches of the Interamericana, as it is locally known: between Barranca (the turn-off for Puntarenas) and San José, where there's heavy traffic on a narrow, curving road; between Cartago and San Isidro, because of landslides and heavy fog; and between Buenos Aires and Palmar, where 'falling rocks and landslides may totally obstruct the road'.

Changing course

Plans have been drawn up to re-route the Pan-American Highway for much of its length. It will follow the existing route from the Nicaraguan frontier to a point just east of Puntarenas; close by is a site mooted for a new international airport. From here it will run all the way along the Pacific coast to the town of Palmar Norte, where it rejoins the existing road. There is a road or track in place already for the entire length of the proposed route, but it is in dreadful condition for most of its course. When it is improved, many hours will be saved on the journey through Costa Rica since this route is much straighter and flatter, and avoids the tortuous Cerro de la Muerte ('hill of death') between Cartago and San Isidro. The new route would improve access to the Pacific coast, increasing tourism still further, and move Costa Rica's economic centre of gravity west. San José will no longer be on the main route, and could become something of a backwater.

Travelling by bus

All buses are privately run and there is no visible sign of co-operation between them. In cities, buses depart from several different places; in the capital there are a couple of dozen bus terminals. The authorities have been planning to condense these to just three for the last decade or two, but nothing much has happened.

Wherever you start your journey, a certain amount of advance planning is essential for long-distance runs; many services are heavily booked. For some shorter trips, advance reservation is impossible; instead, turn up at least 15 minutes before the official departure time. At busy times (e.g. Friday and Sunday afternoons and around public holidays) try to get there an hour ahead. If the bus is full before departure time, the driver may leave anyway.

The quality of vehicles is usually high, though you might not think so if you end up standing for the entire journey; bus companies are allowed to sell rather more tickets than there are seats available. Refreshment stops are made frequently.

Driving

For such a peaceable nation, Tico drivers can be positively devilish, and Costa Rica has the highest accident rate in Central America. City driving can be especially unnerving since the traffic positively roars along the broad avenues of San José. Furthermore, signposting is confusing in the capital and elsewhere; rather than direction signs for nearby places such as Alajuela, you might see a sign for Managua or Panamá.

Carreteras Nacionales are marked on maps (and some road signs) by a number in a shield; the Pan-American Highway is CN1 from the border with Nicaragua to San José, CN2 between the capital and the Panamanian frontier, though a separate numbering system also describes the Highway as C1 for its entire length. Secondary roads are *Carreteras Regionales*, indicated by the road number enclosed by a circle.

Tolls are charged on the modest network of freeways around San José, e.g. $1 for the road between Cartago and the capital, but these apply only between 6am and 8pm. **Parking** in San José is tricky. There are meters but supervised lots are safer. Expect to pay $3 for the first hour, $1 per hour thereafter, or $6 or $8 for an overnight stay. At night some sets of **traffic lights** are switched so that they flash – orange for the priority road, meaning proceed with care, and red for the secondary road, where drivers are obliged to stop before continuing. It is legal to turn right against a red light, which is disconcerting for those not used to this habit.

Rental vehicles carry special number plates, which benefit villains enormously: the plates indicate a driver's affluence and make the vehicle an obvious target for robbers. Rates start at about $50 per day for unlimited distance, plus $10-$15 for insurance. This buys you a small hatchback. A jeep-type vehicle costs around $75 a day. Some agencies also hire out camping equipment. The main international companies have offices at San José airport, or can be contacted at a range of locations, mostly on the west of the city centre.

San José is one of the few places in Central America where you can rent a **motorcycle**; contact Motocicletas La Castellana on Calle 8 between Avenidas 10 and 12 in the capital; tel 222 0055; fax 223 2759.

Hitch-hiking

In line with the relatively high standard of living in Costa Rica, hitching is easy and fun. You can expect fast lifts, in both senses. While you should always offer some cash, about the same as the bus fare, this will usually be declined.

Tours

Packaged tourism is well advanced in Costa Rica. Dozens of companies, mostly based in San José, offer tours ranging from a few hours to a week. The benefits include comfortable, air-conditioned buses which go direct to places of interest difficult to reach by public transport; meals and hotels arranged for you; and a local guide who can provide an insight into history, culture and nature.

There are several disadvantages: it is generally much cheaper to travel by public transport, the tours lack flexibility, and it is difficult to meet local people when you're surrounded by a busload of fellow tourists. Most of the companies and the tours they offer are much-of-a-muchness. Partly this is because rival operators work together, acting as agents for each other or combining tours. Always call the operators direct, since agents often add a fee (as well as getting commission from the tour company).

The flyover option

The terrain of Costa Rica means that surface transport is slow, though scenic. Flying can give equally rewarding views and save many hours, particularly if you choose the Pacific option from San José – a short hop to Quepos can save a long trip, much of which is doubling back. Furthermore, taking a domestic flight is unlikely to break your budget. Air fares are usually three or four times as much as the equivalent bus fare, but are still reasonable; one-way trips cost as little as $30. Tax of 10% can be avoided if you buy your ticket in the UK, USA, or another country which charges no tax on foreign air tickets.

Internal flights are operated by government-owned Sansa (tel 233 0397) and the private airline Travelair (tel 220 3054), using small propeller aircraft. It was a Sansa plane that crashed in San José at the tail end of 1999. Given the mountainous terrain, there are risks attached to flying (but these are lower than on the roads). Most flights radiate from the airports in the capital: either José Santamaría airport, the main international gateway, or the nearby domestic airfield of Tobias Bolaños, just north of the suburb of Pavas.

In addition, a number of **charter companies** operate within Costa Rica, and visitors intent on flying to the national parks may well be able to negotiate a trip on one of them; tour companies which run their own flight services do not always fill their seats, and sometimes sell tickets to independent travellers. To enquire about this possibility, you should try to contact the company itself.

What's different about Costa Rica?

Travellers flying in direct from North America or Europe sometimes express surprise at how 'civilised' Costa Rica seems – tattier than the developed world, but with most of the trappings of Western life. The streets are well-paved and clean, most of the people are well-fed, educated and sophisticated. You can also enjoy the luxuries of safe drinking water and hotels where the occupants outnumber the insects. It is perhaps a successful and sanitised prototype of how the whole region could be if a lasting peace is achieved.

Is Costa Rica a good place to start or finish a trip along the Pan-American Highway?

In terms of air links, yes. San José may have been struck off the British Airways route network in April 2000, but it still has excellent air links from abroad. From Europe, the only direct flights are on Martinair from Amsterdam; the apparently 'direct' Iberia flights from Madrid involve a change of planes in Miami. The fastest route from Europe is usually via Miami, with same-day connections from major cities. Furthermore the network of cheap domestic flights from San José makes other destinations easy to reach.

Who are the Costa Ricans?

Citizens of Costa Rica are known as Ticos (for men, or collectively) or Ticas (for women). The degree of homogeneity between them is much higher than other Central American nationalities. In the interior and on the Pacific coast almost everyone is of Spanish blood. There are fewer than 20,000 Indians left; many of them are fully integrated into Costa Rican society and indistinguishable from other Ticos, though a few scattered communities survive. One such group is the Guaymí, who spread across the Panamanian frontier earlier this century and who until 1990 were refused residents' status. The Talamanca Indians live in relative isolation in the valleys between the Talamanca mountains and the Caribbean coast, and other tribes, including the Cabécar and the Bribri, live in the Pacific region near the Panamanian border.

Only on the Caribbean coast is there a substantial ethnic variation, comprising the blacks (mostly descended from the slaves who worked in the West Indies, rather than from Caribs) and the Chinese who have a small but intensely economically-active community. An increasing minority comprises *pensionados*, retired people from North America who are given permission to settle if they can show that they are rich enough.

Travellers just passing through Costa Rica sometimes leave with the impression that the Ticos are less friendly than other Central Americans. But while the tourist industry has imbued some Costa Ricans with an air of disinterest, this is not a characteristic of the majority of the local people, particularly those away from the touristy spots.

Greetings differ somewhat in Costa Rica from the other countries in the region. In particular, the local way to shake hands among friends is to grip the other person's wrist or forearm, a gesture which feels quite uncomfortable at first; practise with a friend. Kissing is also common though, as elsewhere, it is not advisable to indulge in strident public displays of affection.

What they speak

In keeping with their close ties to Spain, the language spoken in most of Costa Rica is, like that in Colombia, the closest thing to pure Castilian in the New World. People involved in the tourist trade in most parts of the country are likely to speak some English, but your average Tico will look completely blank if you talk to him in anything but Spanish. On the Caribbean coast, the people's roots are Caribbean and Chinese rather than Indian and Hispanic; the language has more in common with the patois of the West Indies than with Spanish.

If you want to learn Spanish in Costa Rica, there are numerous institutes in San José which teach foreigners. But the Spanish courses in Guatemala are much cheaper.

What they eat

Costa Rica is different from its neighbours in many ways, but even here you can expect to be presented with a plateful of *pinto* – the Central American staple of rice and beans – for breakfast. *Casado* is similar to the *plato típico* found elsewhere, and consists of a plate piled high with rice, beans, stew and salad – a complete meal which is tasty, filling and nutritious. You pay extra for an egg on top (*casado especial*) or a solid lump of meat (*con bisteck*). One inconvenience in Costa Rica is an almost total absence of mid-range restaurants. A casado in a café might cost $1, while a steak in an upmarket restaurant could $10, with little in between. *Soda* is the term used for a simple café or restaurant, and this is the place you are most likely to find cheap, local food. Most restaurants are closed on Sunday evenings.

Ceviche, a bowl of raw fish marinated in lime juice with coriander and chilli, is found elsewhere in Central America. San José, however, has the greatest number of cevicherías of anywhere in the world. The rest of the food in the average Costa Rican restaurant is rarely outstanding, consisting of steak, chicken or Mexican dishes.

What they drink

Costa Rica is the only Central American country with a health warning on bottles: *tomar licor es nocivo para la salud* (drinking liquor is bad for your health). There have been proposals to restrict the sale of alcohol until after 6pm, rather than from 11am as is the case at present. Most places close around midnight, though some places in touristy areas stay open until 4am.

There are few surprises in the Costa Rican drinker's diet. Beer and rum take top places, with a bottle of beer or a shot of rum costing upwards of $1. Bavaria and Imperial are the local beers; the former is tastier and more expensive. Try to take advantage of the *hora feliz* (happy hour), which many bars offer from 5pm to 7pm each day. Alternatively, cut costs by getting beer from a supermarket for $0.50 a can, or rum for $4 a bottle. A dismal selection of Chilean and Californian wines cost from $4 a bottle in supermarkets, and from $10 in restaurants.

Among soft drinks, Pepsi is most popular followed by Squirt lemonade and Milory, which is either orange or pineapple flavoured and horribly sweet.

What they read, listen to and watch

There are three daily Spanish-language **newspapers** in Costa Rica. The top newspaper is *La Nación*, a right-of-centre tabloid. Its *Viva* supplement contains listings for events in the capital and elsewhere, plus a column with salacious gossip about the British royal family. *La República* is more staid, while *Al Día* is unashamedly sensationalist. In San José and nearby towns there is an evening newspaper – *La Prensa Libre* – with good listings. To see listings in English, buy the weekly *Tico Times*. Other English-language papers, such as the *Miami Herald*, *USA Today* and the *Financial Times* are widely available in the capital, but hard to find elsewhere.

Radio is good in San José, with lots of American/British and Latin music on the FM band: try 90.8, 96.7 or 100. Elsewhere, what you hear is what you get. None of the six Spanish-speaking **television** channels is likely to hold the visitor's attention for long, consisting mainly of risible soap operas and gory footage of accidents on the Pan-American Highway. Satellite TV from the USA is what sustains English-speaking expatriates in Costa Rica; many homes, hotels and restaurants have a dish, with CNN and (occasionally) BBC World on offer.

Festivals and holidays

January 1	New Year's Day (culmination of a week of festivities)
March 19	Feast of St Joseph, patron saint of San José
March/April	Holy week; public holidays on Maundy Thursday and Good Friday
April 11	Juan Santamaría day
May 1	Labour Day
May 15	Farmers' Day – the date of the farmers' patron saint, San Isidro. In Terra Blanca, residents stage a procession celebrating the driving away of a plague of locusts in 1877.
June 29	Saints Peter and Paul
July 25	Annexation of the province of Guanacaste
August 2	Day of the Virgin of Los Angeles, patron saint of Costa Rica
August 15	Assumption; Mother's Day in Costa Rica
September 15	Independence Day, the biggest event of the year.
October 15	Columbus Day
December 25	Christmas Day

How they enjoy themselves

Costa Rica, a country with only a small indigenous population, has had to nurture a 'folklore' scene, largely for the benefit of tourists who come in search of native traditions. The only place you are likely to see traditional dance and music is in the National Theatre in the capital.

The biggest moment in Costa Rica's **sporting** history remains their defeat of Scotland in their opening match in the 1990 World Cup finals. Even before that, **soccer** was the main spectator sport. In small villages the Parque Central often comprises a soccer pitch.

Bullfighting takes over at festival time. The bulls are not killed and are, instead, allowed to run riot.

What they spend

The colón, which is sometimes referred to as a 'peso'. Its depreciation against the US dollar is controlled, and amounts to about 25% each year, on a 'crawling peg' system that sees the rate change every week or so. The prevailing rate of exchange is displayed prominently in banks and published in newspapers, and matched closely by parallel market dealers. *La República* also lists the rates for the Guatemalan quetzal, the Honduran lempira and the Salvadoran colón, and quotes rates for the US dollar against major world currencies. You can therefore calculate cross rates for the pound to quetzales, the Deutschmark to lempiras and the Yen to colones, if this is the sort of activity which appeals to you.

The smallest denomination of notes and coins is a frequent casualty of the devaluation of the colón; try to familiarise yourself with those denominations that are legal tender, so you can foil attempts to pass dud notes and coins. This is tricky because coins of the same value vary in size – although the government has issued new, smaller coins, the old ones are still in circulation.

Because the local currency depreciates at frequent intervals, do not **change** too much in one go. There are three publicly owned banks and numerous private ones, but all give the same rate for dollars. The procedures for changing money at banks are long-winded, so expect to spend an hour or more waiting. Arrive as early as possible, preferably on the dot of 9am. Most banks charge 1% commission when exchanging travellers cheques. The upmarket hotels usually have exchange facilities; although the process is faster here, the exchange rate may not be as good as in the banks.

Many travellers change money on the parallel market simply to eliminate the time spent queuing. Touts offer a premium on the banks' rates for both travellers cheques and cash. The biggest concentration is outside the Hotel Plaza in central San José. Outside the capital, hotels and restaurants will change or accept foreign currency, although the rate is likely to be poor. But the moneychangers at frontiers are generally reliable, and can help out when you leave Costa Rica. Not only will they take a deteriorating currency off your hands, they can help circumvent the official rule that you can exchange only around $50-worth of colones back into dollars.

Visa and **MasterCard** are valid for cash advances at several banks. There are plenty of ATMs in San José and elsewhere where you can use credit or debit cards, which is handy because the process for drawing cash at a bank counter is painfully slow. It involves the bank writing out a cheque to you, which you have to wait in line to cash. For this performance they charge commission of 3%, on top of the fee that your card company levies. **American Express** is of limited use, although it enables you to buy dollar travellers' cheques (not cash) from the American Express office in San José (Tam Travel Agency, Calle 1, Avenidas Central and 1).

Banks are open 9am to 3pm, Monday-Friday. A few banks in San José have longer opening hours. These include the Banco Nacional de Costa Rica (Avenida 1 and Calle 7), which is open from 8am to 6pm, Monday-Friday.

Anything worth buying?

Some visitors visit Costa Rica simply to shop. Nicaraguans come over to buy consumer goods which are unavailable or expensive at home, while tourists in luxury hotels have a full range of souvenir shops. These phenomena conceal the fact that there is little that Costa Rica produces that many Westerners would want. San José boasts branches of Benetton, supermarkets and smart crafts shops. These come as a shock to those used to the colourful Indian markets of Guatemala or the small corner shops of Nicaragua.

Value added tax of 10% is applied to almost everything. When buying groceries, etc., note that the local term for a general store is *comisariato*; the terms *abastacador* and *pulpería* are also used. The local cigarettes cost around $1 for a pack of 20; Derby and Rex are the leading brands, with Viceroy for those who prefer a milder smoke. American cigarettes cost around $1.30. Imported tobacco and cigarette papers are sold at the main market in San José.

Keeping in touch

Internet access

Costa Rica is highly wired, with cyber cafés springing up all over the capital and in many smaller towns and resorts. The shock you may experience, though, is the relatively high cost of access; $5 for an hour is nothing exceptional. Radiográfica Costarricense, Racsa for short, deals with online services as well as telegrams, telexes and faxes. Its main office in San José at Calle 1, Avenida 5, is open 7am-10pm.

Mail

Like most other enterprises, the postal system in Costa Rica functions more efficiently than that of its neighbours. Letters to the USA or Europe often get through in less than a week. Stamps for airmail postcards to the UK cost around $0.40, to the US $0.35; letters cost a little more. Post offices generally open 7.30-11.30am, and 1.30-5.30pm. There is usually a choice of slots in post offices; for letters abroad use the box marked 'Exterior'.

If writing to someone in Costa Rica, you will find that most postal addresses are post office boxes (known as *apartados*). Nevertheless, letters posted to the actual building should still get there. Postal (or zip) codes are gradually finding their way into the Costa Rican address system.

For **poste restante**, the address of the main post office (Correo Central) in the capital is Calle 2, Avenidas 1 and 3, 1000 San José. There is a small charge for each piece, and you must show your passport when collecting. Letters are returned to sender about a month after delivery. Ask family and friends to resist sending parcels to you in Costa Rica: collecting them involves much bureaucracy, and the paying of fees which usually exceed the value of the contents.

Telephone

The country has seven-figure **telephone numbers**; there are no area codes, so dial all the numbers from wherever you are. Some out-of-the-way communities still have just a single number with an operator who puts calls through to the appropriate extension. The international prefix is 00. International calls can be made from ICE telephone offices (the acronym stands for Instituto Costarricense de Electricidad), and also from those of Radiográfica Costarricense.

ICE sells *tarjetas telefónicas*, and phone cards comprise the cheapest way to make calls abroad. The ease of connection may be good, but the price is high. A three-minute call to the USA costs $12 (possibly less to Florida), to Europe US$15. Many **payphones** are out of order, and most of those that are working take phonecards rather than the rapidly depreciating coinage. But if you find one of the old-style payphones, put a coin in the slide. If it is working, the coin will drop when your call is connected. In the country, public phones are often in the local grocer's shop. These are ordinary phones with a meter, so you just settle up at the end of the call.

Some local telephone offices are equipped with fax machines. You can fax a page of A4 to Florida for $3, to elsewhere in the USA for $4 or to the UK for $5.

Costa Rica is covered by two **phone books**, one covering the capital and its hinterland (*Metropolitana*), the other the rest of the country (*Provincias*). In the latter, towns are listed alphabetically. If your Spanish is up to it, you can call directory enquiries on 113. Other useful numbers: international operator 116; time (in Spanish) 112; fire 118; police 117.

The outdoors – how great?

No other country in Latin America has embarked upon such a vigorous programme of conservation, and few places in the world can boast such a fine range of flora and fauna. One-eighth of the country is designated as parkland or nature reserve, a figure which should increase as more 'debt-for-nature' swaps are negotiated. There are places where you can swim in crystalline waters egged on by chattering monkeys, stare into the still-bubbling heart of a volcano, or watch sea turtles, pelicans and macaws in their natural setting. For this, you will pay a fee of a few dollars.

Most national parks have camping facilities, but reserves and wildlife refuges rarely do. For a useful table of the facilities and attractions of all Costa Rica's protected areas, get the National Parks brochure from the tourist office in San José. Admission to each National Park is a flat $6.

White-water rafting is possible all over the place, but the main rivers used are the Chirripó, Reventazón, Sarapiquí, and Pacuare, of which the latter is probably the most impressive. Good background reading for anyone thinking of exploring the country's rivers is *Rivers of Costa Rica: a Canoeing, Kayaking and Rafting Guide* by Mayfield and Gatto (Menasha Ridge, Birmingham, USA). Those without the cash to splash on an organised trip may have to be content with splashing around in the surf off the Pacific coast.

In some of the more developed resorts there are facilities for **windsurfing** and **sport-fishing**. Opportunities for **diving** or **snorkelling** are better than the other Central American countries, though these take place a very long way from the Pan-American Highway: the Cahuita National Park, on the Atlantic coast, and the Isla del Coco, way out in the Pacific, are the best spots.

A word of warning

Despite being a peaceable nation, **crime** is a serious problem. Western concepts of 'civilisation' are more advanced in Costa Rica than elsewhere in the region. So too is the propensity of some of the locals to steal your possessions. Theft is a threat whether you are strolling around San José or camping in a national park. Travellers who have become accustomed to the scrupulous honesty of people in country areas of Central America are in for an unpleasant shock when the washing hung up outside a cabina disappears overnight.

San José likes to cultivate its image as a safe haven for tourists, but there appears to be quite a well-established network of robbers who prey on, above all, wealthy American visitors. Less well-off travellers should also be watchful; a particularly dangerous area is the northwestern quadrant, where many bus stations and budget hotels are located. Another western habit which has caught on in Costa Rica is using drugs, and users have fuelled the rise in petty crime.

Travellers may find the attentions of the **police** intimidating. Although Costa Rica has no army, it has a highly efficient and well-armed police force, which spends part of its time checking the credentials of tourists. All foreigners are supposed to carry identification at all times.

One risk which is higher in Costa Rica than elsewhere is that of attack from wildlife, notably **snakes**, because of the accessibility of the country's wilderness. Although your most likely confrontation with a creature is a monkey stealing your lunch, on a stroll through the rainforest you could encounter one of Costa Rica's several varieties of poisonous snakes, including the lethal *fer de lance*.

The way to San José

You detect a certain distrust of the neighbours in the north of Costa Rica. When the border formalities from Nicaragua are finally completed and you get going, a sign informs you that the way to San José is straight ahead, 295km away. Yet it will be a matter of only a few minutes before you are obliged to stop once more. Three kilometres (two miles) south of the checkpoint you reach a Puesto de Control Policial, where your papers will be checked. This

The *dry* canal zone?

Something that could transform the far north of Costa Rica is the country's very own 'canal'. For 30 years there have been discussions about an ocean-to-ocean link from Puerto Soley, tucked on the Pacific a few kilometres west of the Highway, across to Parismina, a sleepy village on the Caribbean coast, about halfway between the Nicaraguan border and the port of Limón.

How, you might wonder, do they intend to dig a canal for a distance of 250km (150 miles)? The short answer: they don't. What the plan involves is actually a railway line, a 'dry canal' The idea is that superfreighters too large for Panama will unload their containers on the Atlantic side, where a shuttle of fast trains will whisk the cargo across the country to the Pacific.

At a highly conservative estimate, the project would cost $2 billion and take five years to build. Whether the world's shipping lines would be at all impressed is another matter, and it seems unlikely in the extreme that any railway will ever be built.

The tragedy is that a *canal seco* of sorts existed until the 1990s. Two of Central America's most dramatic railway lines, from Limó on the Atlantic side and Puntarenas on the Pacific, converged on the fine station of San José, and would have provided an excellent transcontinental rail line had they not been allowed to slide into obsolescence.

process is repeated several times in the next 20km, which serves to liven up some plain terrain.

The expanses of savannah are typical of Guanacaste, a hot, dry province dominated by cattle ranches, wild and sparsely populated this far north. The rest of the country does not look, nor feel, like this; indeed, the province was a late addition to Costa Rica, and each July 25 the Annexation of the province of Guanacaste is celebrated. Folk traditions are strong in Guanacaste; Costa Rica's most identifiable national dances and music come from this region where many people are descended from the Chorotega Indians.

The final frontier control point is on the edge of Costa Rica's northernmost National Park, **Guanacaste**. The Pan-American Highway delineates the western edge of the park for 10km, then acts as the division between Guanacaste and Santa Rosa National Park.

If you drive straight through, you may feel slightly sacrilegious wondering whether this is as good as it gets. If you are expecting instant, big, butch rainforest, you will be seriously disappointed. In 'summer' (from December to March), the landscape here is plain in both senses, a flat, windswept expanse of whispering grasses filling the wide gaps between trees that are broad of beam but naked of cover. Only the distant cones first of Volcán Orosi, later of the

Rincón de la Vieja volcano, off to the left (east), provides relief. The time to come here is just after the start of the wet season in April or May, when the parks come alive with colour.

Santa Rosa National Park is the more important of the two. It takes up the whole of the Santa Elena peninsula that juts into the Pacific directly west of the Highway. The road that leads west to the park headquarters is about 45km (28 miles) south of the Nicaraguan frontier at Peñas Blancas. From the turn-off you can walk or hitch the 8km (5 miles) to the park headquarters in the village of Santa Rosa.

The chief 'sight' at Santa Rosa is a museum in the restored 19th-century ranch house known as La Casona. This was the site of the celebrated Battle of Santa Rosa against William Walker, who invaded from Nicaragua in 1856. The museum contains a motley collection of exhibits, including maps, old documents and rifles. Of more recent interest is the secret airstrip in the grounds of the park which was made famous by the Iran-Contra scandal; it was allegedly used to supply the rebels in Nicaragua with arms. There is a campground (with a few facilities) at Santa Rosa, and although there is a small restaurant in the village, you should bring some food supplies. A mosquito net is advisable too.

Protecting Papagayo?

Hiking through dry deciduous forest will make you feel many miles away from anything approaching mass tourism. But if all the plans for the Golfo de Papagayo go ahead, the beautiful arc of wilderness where the forest meets the Pacific in a fringe of mangrove will be replaced by all the trappings of a modern international resort area.

Papagayo, the name adopted for the whole project, is a venture in which the government has leased land to international investors. It is part of a plan to boost tourism in the northwest of Costa Rica, based around the newly expanded airport just south of Liberia.

Those in favour of the plan say that it will bring much-needed jobs and wealth to a far-flung corner of the country. Ranged against them are environmentalists who fear that deforestation and destruction of mangrove swamps will cause permanent damage – not least to the image of Costa Rica as an environmental example to the world.

It could be that the fate of the bay will be decided by holidaymakers – and the ecologists will be encouraged by the initial experience from the British holiday industry. In 1997, Airtours – then the second-biggest mass market holiday company – launched a brochure to the 'undiscovered' paradise of Costa Rica, using charter flights from Gatwick to Liberia's airport. The problem was: of the tens of thousands of holidays on offer, only a few hundred were booked. The programme was scrapped before a single charter flight took off.

The park consists of grasslands, savannah, and woodland, and also protects the largest area of tropical dry forest in Central America. Mangrove swamps are found in the coastal areas. The park is teeming with wildlife. Animals are pleasingly easy to see, particularly in the open areas where you are likely to encounter deer and coyote. Monkeys, peccaries and armadillo live in the forest.

There is a variety of trails, for easy and strenuous hikes; local *campesinos* who live within the park can act as guides. It is also possible to hire horses. From the village of Santa Rosa a dirt track leads 13km (8 miles) south to Playa Naranjo, about three hours' walk. The long, sandy beach on the Golfo de Papagayo is often deserted, and it is possible to camp. A couple of hours' walk northwest of Playa Naranjo is Playa Nancite which is one of the few surviving nesting sites of the Olive Ridley turtle; between August and October thousands of them come ashore to lay their eggs. Pacific Green and Leatherback turtles also frequent the beach. You can stay overnight in simple dormitories, or camp. If you walk from Playa Naranjo while the tide is high you will have to swim across a deep river mouth; this can be waded across at low tide.

Liberia, the provincial capital of Guanacaste is a steamy cattle town, but it is not an unpleasant place to rest up. Lying just east of the Pan-American Highway, Liberia is an important junction for those heading south to the Nicoya Peninsula. Liberia is also the jumping-off point for visits to the Rincón de la Vieja National Park, northeast of the town.

All that most people see, though, is a dusty set of traffic signals (the first since Managua) at a junction that rejoices in the name 'four gas stations corner'. One was knocked down recently, and now there are three, but the name endures. The junction also boasts a Papa John's pizzeria and a Burger King, the Hotel-Restaurant El Bramadero and the Hotel Boyeres (with a 24-hour bar). A couple more attractive places to stay: 1km south, the Hacienda La Pacifica at Corobici Bridge, and the Hotel Capazuri, 5km south. There are also some options in a town centre which is as attractive as the Highway detritus is unattractive.

If you are planning to stop off here, there are six or seven buses a day to San José, between 7am and 8pm, and some departures that head down the Pan-American Highway but turn off for Puntarenas.

A diversion to **Rincón de la Vieja** could provide your first introduction to a 'proper' national park, about 26km (16 miles) up an exceedingly rough road northeast of Liberia. It is centred around Rincón de la Vieja volcano (1,895m/6,216 feet) which dominates the area, although the summit is often shrouded in cloud. You can climb to the top, but this should only be undertaken with a good map and a compass, or with a guide. There are geysers, hot springs and mudpots known as Pilas de Barro, at the base of the southern slopes. These can be reached along trails, but be careful where you tread because the ground is not completely solid.

The surrounding park consists mostly of dry tropical forest where you sometimes see sloths and monkeys, although Rincón is most famous for its population of coatimundi. Seek advice on trails from the park rangers; they can also organise tours and horses.

There is no public transport to the park, and if you don't have your own car you must get a taxi from Liberia unless you manage to get a lift with one of the park rangers who visit Liberia fairly frequently. You should be able to camp, and there is a youth hostel – Albergue de Montaña – in the ranch known as the Hacienda Guachipelín.

A tempting detour: the Nicoya peninsula

The tongue of land drooping down from the Pan-American Highway is not the highest, wildest, or most scenic area of Costa Rica, but its splendid isolation makes it attractive to many travellers. The west coast of the peninsula is lined with beautiful beaches. The best known is Ostional, where thousands of green turtles lay their eggs between May and October, and which has been declared a wildlife reserve. Others, mostly within easy reach of Santa Cruz, include Junquillal, Nosara, Garza, Sámara, Carrillo, Nacascolo and Playa del Coco; the last two are particularly recommended. Some are served by public transport, while others can be reached only by driving, hitching or walking.

The two main towns on the peninsula are Santa Cruz and Nicoya, each competing for the title of most 'folkloric' place in Costa Rica. Santa Cruz is currently the folklore capital of the country, famous for its colourful fiestas, food, and dances, including the Punto Guanacasteco. Santa Cruz is 40km (25 miles) south of the Pan-American Highway at Liberia, along highway 21. A few miles east of Santa Cruz is the charming village of Guaitil which is well-known for its ceramics; these show the influence of the potters' Chorotega ancestors. Nicoya is another 16km (10 miles) further southeast of Santa Cruz and Guaitil, and is accessible from both. The town has a quaint 17th-century church, and a few other examples of Spanish colonial architecture.

From the southern part of the peninsula you can complete the loop with a boat to the port of Puntarenas, across the Gulf of Nicoya, from Playa Naranjo. But before you do so, make the diversion truly worthwhile at the place you can take revenge on the rigours of the road: **Montezuma**. A small, peaceful village near the foot of the peninsula, Montezuma has a few hotels, some good internet connections, and a reputation for being idyllic. It is within easy reach of some fine beaches and the Cabo Blanco Reserve. Most travellers find it easy to spend a few days or weeks relaxing here. Playa Grande, half an hour's walk north of Montezuma, is the best beach for bathing. There is also a huge waterfall, a 15-minute walk up the Montezuma River from the village, which is another good place to swim; it is a lovely spot, and the walk along the creek is pleasant too.

Of the places to stay in Montezuma, Lucy's and Jenny's are both recommended. You would do better, however, to stay on the beaches north or south of the village, all within walking distance. There are cabins, or you can camp, but beware of marauding monkeys. The best local source of information is Chico's Bar, next door to the Montezuma Hotel.

Some tricky lanes lead from Montezuma to the Paquera ferry, from where you can head across to Los Plantanos dock in Puntarenas.

An even better detour: Arenal

If you continue along the Pan-American Highway southeast from Liberia, you reach Cañas in 46km (29 miles), a place not worth a stop – but well worth changing buses at, to leave the Highway and discover one of the finest regions of Costa Rica.

At Cañas, a road branches off to **Tilarán**, a pleasant town in the hills 20km (12 miles) to the east, and five kilometres (three miles) from the shore of Arenal lake. Buses run every hour during the day from Cañas to Tilarán. The modern church is spectacular, and the walk up to the crucifix on the hill is worth doing (in the Parque Central, turn your back to the church and go forward to the corner on your left; now the crucifix can be seen at 11 o'clock). Cabañas Naralit (tel 695 5393) is the most expensive place to stay (single $30, double $45), but it is clean and new. (The strange name is Tilarán spelt backwards.) The Hotel Guadelupe, two blocks downhill from the square, starting at the corner adjacent to El Sueño's restaurant (tel 695 5943) is spotless, new, has cable TV and table tennis, and is half the price of the Naralit. Cabañas El Sueño in the square, and Tilarán around the corner from the bus station are both friendly and clean. The former is a bit more expensive, with singles at $10 and doubles for $15. Restaurant Chino, one block back from the square on the same side as the Hotel Tilerán is cheap and gives big portions.

Lake Arenal is a long (30km), narrow (5km at its widest) fissure that has been expanded by man. The waters of the original lake used to flow down to the Atlantic, but dams built for a hydroelectric plant – the largest in Central America – have diverted the waters so that they now irrigate the Pacific coastal area. The reservoir is popular among local tourists who come here at the weekend to fish and go boating.

The journey around the lake from Tilarán to Arenal follows a rickety road broken up by rivers flowing into the lake. Traffic crosses these on the narrow bridges made of old telegraph poles and railway tracks. If you are travelling by bus, don't look over the side; the impression you get, that the vehicle is a couple of inches away from tumbling down a ravine, is entirely correct. If you make the journey by night, you may be lucky enough to see blazes of pyrotechnics above the volcano, followed by the streaks of red lava flowing down the sides. On a clear night, the moonlight reflecting from the lake completes the scene.

The small town of Arenal offers the possibility of fishing, water-skiing or windsurfing. If you prefer to rest, it is a good place to relax with glorious views of the lake and volcano – and a neat little botanical garden. The Hotel Pequeña Helvicia is Swiss owned, Swiss-clean and has a pool, costing $30 single, $40 double. Cabañas Rodríguez is simple, clean and friendly, costing $8 single, $12 double.

The journey east along the lakeshore continues to Tabacón, near the eastern end of the lake, where there is a thermal pool fed by waters from Arenal volcano. It has been turned into something of a playground for the Ray-Ban wearing classes weekending from San José. In return for $10 or so, you can cavort in a warm and slightly smelly swimming pool, whizz down a waterslide, and enjoy a drink or two without leaving the water. Alternatively, if all you want to do is enjoy the feel of water heated from the centre of the earth, then you can get cheaper access on the other side of the road.

Bubbling Over

The last time the perfect cone of **Arenal volcano** (1,633m/5,356 feet) flexed its seismic muscles with a serious eruption was in 1968. As well as the volcano emitting poisonous gases and huge amounts of lava and ash, the whole of the surrounding area spontaneously combusted and was ravaged by fire. Arenal has not erupted since, but remains active, continually spewing out smoke, fire, and white-hot rock. Explosions occur every few hours and make climbing the volcano extremely dangerous. The activity of the volcano can be as dramatic as a firework display, and as such it is best admired from a distance, and at night.

You can view the Arenal volcano from many points in the vicinity, but the best place to stay is in the overgrown village of **Fortuna**, 8km (5 miles) east of the summit. It is a rather ragged collection of souvenir stores, cafés and lodges, but the distant view of Arenal lifts the tone. The best place to stay in terms of comfort is Las Cabañitas (tel 479 9400), with well-furnished cabins and a swimming pool, but it is inconveniently far from Fortuna itself and room rates are high at $40 single/$50 double. El Bosque, in town, is clean, friendly and cheap ($8 single, $12 double)

The best way to **see the volcano** is on a pre-arranged tour from Fortuna. These tend to depart early evening, and usually include a soak in the thermal baths afterwards. Unfortunately, the activity of the volcano is obscured by mist and clouds about half the time but it can still be heard rumbling in the background. For whitewater rafting, Desafío Tours (479 9464) is recommended. You can also arrange trips into various places, including Nicaragua with Jocar Tours (479 9147) or Paraíso Tropical (479 9222). Beware of touts offering trips in the street.

To complete the loop, continue south through forested hills typical of Alajuela province, and plough through the San Carlos plains, a rich agricultural area, to reach the town of **Quesada**, still 96km (60 miles) from San José. Confusingly it is officially known as Ciudad Quesada, and colloquially known by the name of the region, San Carlos.

There are plenty of hotels in Quesada, the best being El Central on the Parque Central but, unless you miss the last bus out, there is little reason to stay in Quesada. There are hourly buses during the day from here onwards to San José.

And a third choice: Monteverde and its Cloud Forest
This detour could be a definite highlight of your trip. Situated in the Cordillera de Tilarán, on a green mountain plateau nearly a mile above sea level, **Monteverde** is a private reserve founded by Quakers in 1951. The Quakers came here from Alabama after Costa Rica decided to get rid of its army in 1948 – a move which suited the Quakers' ideals (although the motive behind the Costa Rican government's decision was not entirely fired by pacifism). The incomers bought land, built homes, and developed a dairy farm. The community runs a thriving cheese factory, which visitors can tour.

When the Quakers set up their community, they left a large area of virgin rainforest untouched, and Monteverde has become one of the last ecologically intact pieces of cloud forest in the country. Hardwood trees dominate the forest, while vines, lianas and spectacular ferns all compete for space under the canopy. Monteverde is a birdwatcher's approximation to paradise: while the number of visitors has scared away most of the animals (including jaguar, ocelot, monkeys, and anteaters), the birds remain relatively easy to spot – exotic birds are as common in Monteverde as sparrows are in Britain. Monteverde is one of the last nesting areas of the quetzal, but this endangered bird is elusive; they are best seen between January and May. Monteverde is also one of the best places in the country to see hummingbirds, toucans, and parakeets.

The place to head for is **Santa Elena**, which you can most easily reach from Las Juntas, a short way off the Highway 25km (16 miles) southeast of Cañas. From Las Juntas, you will probably need to hitch unless you have your own transport. The alternative way to Santa Elena is on a 40km (25 mile) dirt track which branches north off the Pan-American Highway at the point it crosses the Río Lagarto. This road is unpaved, full of ruts and very steep. The bus takes at least two hours to cover the distance, but this gives you plenty of time to enjoy the views. There is one bus a day to Santa Elena from Puntarenas, and another from San José. Hitching is unreliable. You could also try to get here from Lake Arenal, at least during the dry season, from Tilarán via the enchanting village of Nubes. When you finally reach Santa Elena, it is a further 45-minute walk east to the park.

Check out the website monteverdenfo.com before you arrive for maps and details of bus schedules. Monteverde is not a place to be visited in a single day, and **hotels** have sprung up to keep pace with the increased tourist interest. Most of these are moderately expensive, and can get booked up during the dry season.

Anyone who is satisfied by anything but high-class luxury should stay in one of the two hospedajes in Santa Elena, both of which are clean, friendly, excellent value and highly recommended. **Pension Santa Elena**, just below the bank (tel 645 5051, fax 645 6060, mundonet@sol.rasca.co.cr), used to be the youth hostel, and remains the travellers' refuge. The kitchen is open for use, and beers are available. Jacques Bertaud has livened the place up and employs travellers to help run the place. Sharing a dorm $5, single $7, double $12. The **Hospedaje Colibri** ('hummingbird') just below Pension Santa Elena at the end of the small lane is quieter. Look out for the squirrels in the trees opposite and if you are lucky, a toucan. Single rooms are $6, doubles $9.

An interesting alternative is the Mirador Lodge (tel 645 6554, fax 645 5087, e-mail miradorq@sol.racsa.co.cr), about half an hour away by jeep. Although this place looks a bit jerry-built (with a roof of corrugated iron, a dining room and a few cabins), the location cannot be faulted. The rate is $25 per person, including breakfast, with dinner at an additional $5.

The following are alternatives to the smart international restaurants found at the hotels around Monteverde: Good Italian of all types is available at the restaurant of the **Heliconia Hotel** ($10 per head). **Johnny's Pizza** 15 minutes walk toward Monteverde from Santa Elena makes faultless pizza. The two restaurants at the centre of town, **Daiquiri** and **Morphos**, are relatively inexpensive. Morphos is a bit cheaper and has pretty cloud-forest murals. The bakery next door is not bad for takeaway pastries and hot chocolate.

The Monteverde administrative centre issues a free map of the park in return for the entrance fee of $6. Trails through the forest are well-marked, perhaps rather too much so for the true rainforest fan who prefers a more adventurous experience. The visitors' centre also has information on the wildlife, and there are naturalists who can serve as guides for walking or riding tours. You should familiarise yourself here with the harmful creatures at large in the park. These include the fer-de-lance snake, chiggers (which burrow through the skin into your feet, and stay there until some extreme persuasion is applied), and the poisonous golden toad; specimens of some of them can be seen pickled in jars. Good protection and care are essential. It can get cool so take a jumper, and you need raingear at any time of year. If you don't have your own protective footwear, it is possible to hire wellies.

There is a variety of trails in both the Monteverde and the Santa Elena reserves. The word on the street is that there are more animals at Monteverde. Most trails are well marked (perhaps rather too much so for the true rainforest fan) and will make an enjoyable morning or afternoon walk. The birds are most busy at dawn and early afternoon so this is the best time for true twitchers.

The administrative centres at the entrances sell drinks and maps. Entrance is $6 (no student discounts). Guides are available at the visitors' centres or in town. It can get cool so take a jumper and you need raingear at any time of the year. Wellies can be hired at Pension Santa Elena.

SkyTreks and SkyTrips are trips which should be seen as something of an alternative to just walking along the trails for two reasons: firstly, you will find yourself in a large group of people whose chattering is likely to scare away all other wildlife; and secondly, the very nature of the trips is filled with such adrenaline-filled excitement that the low "rhubarbs" are elevated to "oohs" and "aahs" and "yahoos" carrying across the canopy top.

In fact, both types of tours are fun and the excellent guidance of the biologists provide an incisive perspective on the ecology at both ground and canopy levels. SkyTrips involve walking along narrow rope bridges. SkyTreks include these bridges and whizzing along cables while strapped up like a Christmas turkey in a climbing harness but, unlike a real turkey, those participating will come close to experiencing the thrill of flying through the tree tops. Check out the Monteverde web site for a slide show.

SkyTreks cost $35 for adults, $28 for students. SkyTrips cost $22. Both trips last three hours and can be booked at Pension Santa Elena. The walk up to where the Treks and Trips begin is quite pleasant if fairly steep. Ask for directions beforehand and follow the signs along the way. The monstrous orange building on the right indicates your arrival after about 80 minutes. The alternative is the pre-booked bus, leaving half an hour before the time of the trips, from just above the bank ($1 both ways).

When you decide to leave, the easy way out is to retrace your steps back down to the Pan-American Highway. The interesting way out is to head through the hills, valleys and rivers from Santa Elena to Fortuna – the village that serves the Arenal volcano. There are three perfectly good ways to do this: (1) take the jeep, boat, jeep route for $25 to the settlement of Río Chiquito, cross lake Arenal, then get a mini-bus to Fortuna; (2) take the same route but with some horse riding at the middle section; (3) take the bus to Tilarán and then go around the lake to Fortuna (eight hours, $4).

• There is also a fourth option, which is likely to be the most rewarding. Take a jeep to Mirador (about half an hour up one of the worst roads in Costa Rica), ride a horse to Castillo, take the boat across lake and then a jeep to Fortuna ($60 group, $70 with just guide). Lionel of the Mirador is a recommended guide. The path you follow is an ancient one that used to form an important link between the Atlantic and Pacific coasts. It involves descending a muddy and treacherous track and crossing a fast-flowing river three times. From September to December the river can become so high that you have to turn back. Even during the dry season, all precious equipment must be wrapped in waterproof bags prior to departure. A cool nerve and adventurous spirit are essential. Departure is normally at 8am. Ask for a horse to suit your capabilities.

Nearly back on track: Puntarenas
Whether you sail across from the Nicoya Peninsula, or just take the 14km (9 mile) detour from the Pan-American Highway, **Puntarenas** is worth visiting. It

Equine adventure

Sabine Hein, a wandering German architect and photographer (sabinehein@yahoo.com), describes the first time she made the trip.

'Jorgé, my guide for the day, strode in with bandy legs and a moustachioed, weathered face, carrying a large machete and ready to take another witless tourist on an adventure. We went outside and I was introduced to my horse, José. By Western standards he was small, but looked knowledgeable and well kept. We mounted and began the three-hour horse ride. It took two hours to reach the first river crossing; along the way we had to round up some stray cattle and cut our way around a fallen tree. The air warmed as the altitude fell. The horses deftly threaded their way through the quagmires of mud and boulders that formed the path.

'When we arrived at the first river crossing, I turned to see Jorgé's steed gradually disappear below the gushing current: hooves, knees, belly ... then, finally, he started coming out again and arrived at the other side, and beckoned me across. I do not remember that first crossing, or the second – only that I did it, was relieved and proud and that my feet were soaking. The third crossing was not so bad.

'After the crossings the path followed the valley towards the lake. After two hours in complete wilderness, the odd farm emerged. To the left-hand side the slope was covered in an impenetrable bank of dense forest. In contrast, the slope to the right had begun to be cleared, ready for the plump cattle and horses which occupy this fertile stretch. But for the private reserves like Monteverde, all of this countryside would be similarly stripped.

'The path swung out of the valley onto a stone track that traces the south side of the lake towards Castillo. The horses picked up pace. The lake looked beautiful to the left. Ten minutes before reaching Castillo we turned a corner and there was the Arenal volcano, with steam rolling off the side.

'At Castillo, I boarded the launch and was sped across the lake. We passed some swooping cormorants that failed to keep up and I was lucky to spot an enormous and iridescent kingfisher. On the other side there was a small wait for the minibus during which time the dodgy Rojas brothers tried to tempt me with various excursions at cut-rate prices – now I had sadly arrived back to the real world.'

is perched on a narrow spit of land 128km (80 miles) west of San José, and is the capital of the province of the same name.

Until the railway between San José and the Caribbean coast was built at the end of the 19th century and allowed Puerto Limón to prosper, Puntarenas was the country's main port. It is no longer a commercial port and is a seedy, but fascinating place: lively, particularly in the evenings, with plenty of cheap bars (if that is how you get your thrills).

Model prison

One of the islands just offshore from Puntarenas is Isla San Lucas, which until recently was an island prison where in-mates lived in a virtually self-sufficient community. It was firmly on the tourist circuit, with the prisoners selling crafts to the visitors, taking people on tours, etc, with only perfunctory security. The authorities were unwilling to accept this curious kind of anarchy, and closed down San Lucas as the 1990s ended.

If you arrive by **boat** from the Nicoya Peninsula, there are five or so sailings a day from both Paquera and Playa Naranjo, costing $5 for the 90-minute journey. From the Highway, you need to branch off at Barranca, from which there are frequent buses.

Of the many **hotels**, none is outstanding, though the Tioga (tel 661 0271) in Barrio Carmen has good service and a swimming pool included in the nightly rate of $40 single, $50 double. The Porto Bello next door has similar prices, and is friendlier and therefore recommended. The Hotel Cayuga (tel 661 0344), on Avenida Central has seen better days, but is fairly clean and cheap at $15 single, $21 double. For something a lot cheaper, aim for the Hotel Cabezas (tel 661 1045), on Avenida 1, between Calles 2 and 4. It is possible to camp on the beach, but theft is a problem and you should not leave your tent unattended.

Food is unlikely to be the highlight of your stay, and you will struggle to do better than the unappealing fare served at the numerous Chinese restaurants in town. The restaurants on the sea-front are overpriced.

Puntarenas is on the same latitude as San José, but the journey east to the capital is far from straightforward. The main route takes you back on to the Pan-American Highway at Barranca, and heads up to the hills and the west end of the *autopista* leading into San José. Just north of the Highway after the motorway begins is **Sarchí** which was once a charming place, but is now a tourist trap. It is renowned for its 'ox cart' art, which was begun by local artists about a century ago, but has now been thoroughly exploited. The village is full of houses painted in a similar style to the carts and is totally over the top.

A second option leaves the Pan-American Highway at Macacona and edges south to San Mateo, where it joins the route coming in from Quepos and the Pacific Coast to the capital.

· The third route is the one to take if you want to anticipate the big 21st century development on the Pan-American Highway. It will swerve south at Barranca, and follow the line of the road that brushes against the Pacific for 25km (15 miles). At this juncture, the San José bypass continues south, while if

Strange lines on a strange map
As a province, Puntarenas is the largest and the most oddly shaped in all of
Costa Rica. It stretches along most of the length of the Pacific coast from
the Nicoya Gulf in the northwest to the Panamanian frontier. At its
midpoint around Dominical, it is only a mile wide. The furthest point
from Puntarenas, is the tip of a peninsula shared with Panama – and is
more distant from the provincial capital than is the Nicaraguan capital,
Managua.

you are heading for the capital then you turn left.

Whichever way you choose, you reach **Alajuela**, capital of the province, and
rather less ambitious than Puntarenas. A town of about 30,000, Alajuela is
seldom thought of as anything but the nearest place to the international airport,
which is five kilometres (three miles) to the south. If you have an early flight
you may decide to stay at one of the hotels near the bus station, but otherwise
there is little reason to stay overnight. There are two moderately interesting
churches, and a market (best on Saturdays), but the main point of interest in
Alajuela is the Juan Santamaría Museum. Housed in an old jail north of the
Parque Central (Avenida 2, Calles Central and 2), the museum highlights the
life of the boy – a native of Alajuela and Costa Rica's national hero because of
his role in the defeat of William Walker in 1856. It also includes exhibits
relating to the history and culture of the town, ranging from old weapons to
locally-produced crafts.

Another 12km (seven miles) east takes you to **Heredia**, yet another
provincial capital, which almost merges with the western outskirts of San José.
Heredia province is the heartland of Costa Rica's coffee plantations, and has a
population of 30,000. Founded in the 18th century, Heredia is a friendly town
with shady streets and Spanish-style houses, and a few pleasant parks. But there
are few sights other than its attractive colonial church built in 1796, and the
small fortress nearby.

Of greater interest are the villages in the surrounding area, many of which
have attractive churches. Barva de Heredia is a pre-Spanish settlement a couple
of miles north of the provincial capital. It is the oldest town in the Central
Valley, and ambitious restoration projects are underway to try to recreate the
old colonial atmosphere. A couple of miles north, in San Pedro de Barva, is a
Coffee Museum, housed in a 19th-century ranch house.

Buses to both places leave from Avenida 1, Calles 1 and 3 in Heredia. There is a
constant stream of buses to Heredia from San José which leave from Calle 1,
Avenidas 7 and 9. Services operate every few minutes between 5.30am and
10pm. There are some decent hotels in both Heredia and Barva de Heredia, but
you would do better to stay in the village of San José de la Montaña. It is in the

mountains, a short distance north of Barva de Heredia, and there are a number of hotels with spectacular views over the valley. There are buses every hour from near the Mercado Central in Heredia.

San José: American Beauty?

Costa Rica's capital has a good try at emulating Miami or Manhattan, with high-rises and wide avenues to match cities in the USA. One big difference, you might conclude, is that San José's streets are cleaner and clearer of debris, both inanimate and animate. Another is that the setting of San José is far more dramatic than most American cities, with glimpses from the city's streets revealing views of majestic mountains. Downtown, however, fast food has taken over from Latin chic as the dominating influence. Costa Rica's tallest building, the Central Bank, towers over a city centre devoted largely to purveying fried chicken and hamburgers. It may come as a relief to find somewhere firmly on the beaten track. If you need to fix up visas, phone home, or catch up with world events, San José is the place to be. Nevertheless, there are interesting nooks and odd crannies where you can remind yourself that you are, indeed, in Central America. And buried between the skyscrapers, San José possesses one of the finest collections of pre-Columbian gold in Latin America.

Getting your bearings

Most of the city is strung out along the main thoroughfare, the Avenida Central, the local representation of the Pan-American Highway. The Autopista General Cañas sweeps in from the northwest, and turns into Calle 42 along the eastern edge of La Sabana park. It then turns sharp left (east) and cuts straight through the middle of town, initially with the alias Paseo Colón. In the centre of town, it is colloquially known as the Boulevar. Avenidas above it are odd-numbered; those below it have even numbers. The most notable is Avenida 2, which in the centre of town is effectively San José's High Street. Calles run north-south, spreading out from Calle Central with even numbers to the west, odd numbers to the east. The heart of the city is a block of about five avenidas by ten calles. The Parque Central is enclosed by Calles Central and 2, and Avenidas 2 and 4. Most of the important buildings are north and east of this square. Indeed, the Plaza de la Cultura – bounded by Avenidas Central and 2, and Calles 3 and 5 – is more of a commercial and cultural centre. Most government buildings are in the east. To the west is the market, plus budget hotels and most of the capital's many bus terminals. Note that Avenida Central and Calle Central are sometimes called Avenida 0 and Calle 0 respectively.

Despite the apparent logic of the grid pattern, addresses are of limited use when you come to asking the locals for directions. In true Central American style, the average *Josefino* bothers little about street names and numbers, preferring to use prominent buildings as landmarks, even structures which are no longer there. One of the capital's districts is called Coca Cola because a soft drink bottling plant used to be there.

A good map is given away by the tourist office below the Plaza de la Cultura, and is sold in bookshops for $1.

Arrival and Departure

Juan Santamaría, the international **airport**, is 25km (15 miles) west of the city centre. There is a bureau de change inside the arrivals hall, but its opening hours are not tailored to the needs of arriving passengers. If it is shut, there will be plenty of men with wads of notes and calculators waiting outside the doors of the arrival hall.

If your destination is not San José but a town in the west or northwest of Costa Rica, note that buses from the capital to these areas pass the airport. Although there is no official stop on the road outside, it is often possible to flag a bus down; ask airport staff to point you to the right road. Buses pass the airport about 15 minutes after leaving San José, so you should be able to compute from the times given in tourist offfice publications.

Buses for the city centre depart from a stop behind the car hire offices, across the road from the terminal exit. The fare into town is $0.50, and the journey time is around half an hour. The bus runs to the terminal on Avenida 2 between Calles 10 and 12, on the western edge of the city centre. Services run from 5am to midnight in both directions. For early morning **departures** from San José, most travellers are obliged to catch the 5am bus from the city terminal. Arrive at least ten minutes early, since the first bus of the day fills up quickly with other travellers and airport workers. A departure tax of $10 (payable in colones) is charged as you enter the airport. This tax is not devoted to lining the pockets of airport bureaucrats (as is often the case elsewhere in Central America). In Costa Rica the fee includes contributions to the Red Cross, the National Museum, the police and the health service. To deter Costa Ricans from travelling abroad, locals have to pay more. The duty-free shop is a rip-off, as is the cafe in the departure 'lounge'. San José's airport is prone to fog, which can seriously disrupt service. A replacement airport at Orotina, 58km (35 miles) west of the capital, was planned to open in the year 2000, but there is no sign of anything having been done.

The **domestic airport** used to be handily located almost downtown, but it has now moved out to Tobias Bolaños airfield, 15km (9 miles) west. Any bus to Pavas will take you close.

Virtually every street corner in San José seems to be a **bus** terminal for some town or other; there are at least twenty different stopping points. Most are concentrated in the northwest quadrant of town (surrounded by Avenidas Central and 7, Calles 4 and 20), a rough area which you may prefer not to visit after dark. The two which you are most likely to use are fairly visible: the one from Liberia, which is on the corner of Avenida 1 and Calle 14; and the Tracopa terminal for buses to Golfito, the Panamanian border and the rest of the southeast, two blocks further north, on the diagonal that protrudes from the junction of Calle 14 and Avenida 5. The whole area is known as 'Coca Cola', but there is also a distinct location on Calle 16 between Avenidas 1 and 3, that is officially the Coca Cola terminal and has a large number of buses to destinations around the country.

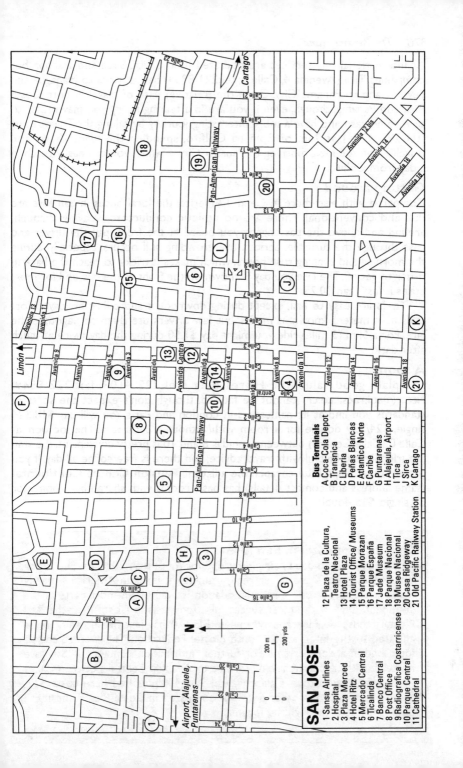

International bus services are operated by the Tica, Sirca and Tracopa bus companies. Tica (Avenida 4, Calle 9; tel 221 8954) has services to Managua and beyond, and to Panama City. Given the (relative) ease of travel in both Costa Rica and Panama, though, even if you are in a tearing hurry you may prefer to save some cash and have a more interesting journey by taking the Tracopa bus (tel 221 4214) at 7am or 3pm to Golfito, spending the night there, and travelling on the next morning to Panama City – which you can easily reach in a day from Golfito.

Getting around

Compared with elsewhere in Central America, the local buses in San José are dull and conventional. There are no athletic conductors weaving through, around and above the passengers; you board at the front, pay the driver and pass through the turnstile. Serious overcrowding still occurs, especially during the morning and evening rush hours, which makes it tricky to reach the back in order to get off. The fare you pay is shown on the front of the bus, and for most buses is less than $0.25.

Taxis are easy to hail, except during downpours and public holidays. Most taxis have meters, known as *marias*. but few drivers use them so negotiate the fare. For a 5km (3 mile) ride you might pay $1.50 during the day, twice as much after dark.

A room

For plain good value, the **Hotel Ritz** (tel 222 4103, fax 222 8849, ritzcr@sol.racsa.co.cr) cannot be faulted, though don't expect the sorts of standards you find at its namesakes in London and Paris. You will pay $18/$24 single, $24/$29 double for a room with/without a bathroom. The location, at Calle 0 (Calle Central) between Avenidas 8 and 10 is pretty convenient, the staff are friendly and helpful with travel advice, and there is free coffee all day. If you prefer something a little cheaper, the adjacent **Pension Centro Continental** (same address and contact details) has basic rooms with shared bathrooms for $8 single, $15 double.

Only living hostel in San José

Youth hostels have been going in Europe for more than 70 years, but during this lifetime they have never really caught on in Latin America – partly because cheap, accessible accommodation is available in most parts of the continent. One of the most successful attempts is in Costa Rica; the Red Costarricense de Albergues Juveniles (RECAJ) has just five hostels, and is affiliated to the International Youth Hostel Federation. The average charge for a bed in a dorm is $12. For further information contact the San José hostel; it is the Albergue Juvenil Toruma on Avenida Central, between Calles 29 and 31 in Barrio La California (tel 224 4085). A bed here costs $12, about average for the other dozen or so hostels in Costa Rica. You can call book any hostel through the Toruma.

Going up a notch, the **Hotel Plaza** (Avenida Central between Calles 1 and 3; tel 222 5535) is right in the centre of town, charging $35 single, $50 double. Its late check-out time, 3pm, could be useful if you are catching an evening flight.

If you are on a low budget, try the interesting **Casa Ridgeway** on Calle 15 at Avenida 6b (tel 233 6168), sponsored by US Citizens in Costa Rica for Peace. It is part of the Quaker-run Friends' Peace Center and charges around $7 per night for those 'who want access to peace activities'. The **Pensión Ticalinda** (Avenida 2, between Calles 7 and 9; tel 233 0528) is a well-known travellers' haunt, and is centrally located. Recently it has become tattier and less friendly, and the area has become more risky. It is cheap, at around $7 per person, but don't expect much comfort or privacy.

A meal

McDonalds and Archie's Fried Chicken overlook the Plaza de la Cultura, US fast food outlets have made the same inroads in San José that they have in other Central American capitals. But there are plenty of local options. For breakfast or lunch try the **Soda Central** on Avenida 1 between Calles 3 and 5, close to some low-budget hotels; it serves an excellent casado. For lunch or dinner, you can't beat the engaging **Restaurant Pollo Campesino**, in an unlikely location on the corner of Avenida 2 and Calle 7. You will probably see a long queue snaking out of the door, but most of these people will be ordering the main dish, excellent chicken roasted over coffeewood embers, to take away. Inside, the waiting staff are helpful and friendly, and you can dine very well for a few dollars, in a congenial atmosphere.

For a quick, cheap lunch head for the **Mercado Central** on Avenida Central between Calles 6 and 8, which contains countless ceviche bars. Vegetarians will gravitate towards **Vishnu's** on Avenida 1 between Calles 1 and 3. To start or finish your evening go to the **Soda Palace** on the north side of the Parque Central. This is a large and bustling café which has good *bocas* (tapas), a mixed and colourful clientele, and is a popular meeting place for local musicians.

The best area for **bars** is along Calle 2 south of the Parque Central, though recently it has become a lot more edgy. On Friday night there appears to be a competition among the locals as to how many empty beer bottles you can amass on your table. Two recommended ones are the Bar Restaurant (sic) on the corner of Avenida 10, and the Familiar on the corner of Avenida 14; the latter serves ceviche. Further west, on the corner of Avenida 8 and Calle 16, is the Bar Santa Lucía which has a predominantly young clientele. For a more civilised and also more expensive drink go to the Shakespeare Bar which is in the basement of the Sala Garbo Theatre on Calle 28, a block south of Paseo Colón. This is the nearest thing to Covent Garden you will find in San José. It has more character than most places in the city.

For a splurge, head a couple of kilometres north to the *centro comerciale* known as **El Pueblo**, reached with a bit of a tangle from the northern end of Calle 3 or 5. It has several bars and restaurants, of which the best is La Cocina de Leña, with superb meats and good service. . The Turrialba steak is particularly recommended. Even with plenty to drink, the bill is unlikely to be more than $25 per person.

An exploration

For a good view of the city, go to the eighth floor of the Banco de Costa Rica on Avenida Central, Calles 4 and 6 (near the Mercado Central). From many places in San José you get glimpses of the imposing scenery beyond, but the view of the mountains from the capital is considerably better than that of the city from the mountains. San José was founded comparatively late, in 1737, and succeeded Cartago as capital of the country only in 1823. Historical buildings have been largely swamped by modern architecture, and there are few buildings of interest. You can see the most worthwhile things in a morning, but allow extra time if you stop off at any of the museums. These are probably the capital's main cultural attraction; information on these is given separately, below.

A good place to start a tour is the **Parque Central**. It is dominated by the rather plain **Metropolitan Cathedral**, which looks more like a Victorian railway station than a place of worship. There are some attractive murals above the altar, though fluorescent lights in the shape of the moon and stars add an edge of tackiness. The square itself is generally lively, and musicians sometimes play in the large concrete bandstand; there are orchestral performances on Sunday mornings.

Walking along Avenida 2, you come to the **Teatro Nacional** on your left. The late 19th-century theatre is one of the most impressive buildings in Central America. It is a fine structure of classic design, built in marble and mahogany, with lashings of gilt; the auditorium is ornate but surprisingly small. For performances the seating is uncomfortable, and daytime visits are more rewarding if you want to take in the charm of the place. It is open for visitors from 9am to 6pm, Monday-Friday, for a fee of around $1; note that the cheapest tickets for a performance cost about the same. Guides are on hand to show you around and answer questions, but most speak only Spanish. The theatre's final attraction is the opulent café on the left as you go in. It caters largely for foreigners, and prices are consequently high, but the surroundings make it worthwhile. You do not need to have a ticket (for either a visit or a performance) to visit the café. The theatre is closed completely on Sundays and Mondays.

Just north of the theatre is the **Plaza de la Cultura**, with a motley collection of people and stalls. Under the Plaza, stretching almost to the vaults of the neighbouring Central Bank, are three floors of exhibition space housing subterranean museums. Each is sponsored by the Central Bank. The museums are open daily except Sunday and Monday from 10am to 5pm. Security is tight; all bags, cameras, etc, must be checked in.

The **Museo de Oro Precolombino** is easily the most interesting of the three. It boasts a remarkable collection of gold – mined, refined, and crafted by the pre-Columbian native Indians. At first there appears to be little more than an impressive array of earrings, but further investigation reveals amazing artistry and skill in moulding the gold. The processes are explained in Spanish. Those particularly interested in pre-Columbian American culture will notice the distinct synthesis between Andean and Mesoamerican cultures. This collection of over 1,600 pieces of gold is unique in Central America, so make the most of it.

The admission fee of $5 also gets you in to the **Museo Numismática**, a small and dreary money museum, of interest mainly to students of finance who wish to trace the depreciation of Costa Rican currency from solid gold escudos (the precursor of the colón) to the present-day high denomination notes.

Heading from the Plaza de la Cultura north up Calle 5, you come to **Parque Morazán**, with a statue of Simón Bolívar. A short distance to the east is **Parque España**, a quiet, shady square, and one of the most pleasant in the city. Artists bring their work here to sell on Sundays. A number of interesting buildings overlook the square. On the eastern side is the old **National Liquor Factory** (Fábrica Nacional de Licores), which is one of the oldest commercial buildings in San José and was founded by President Mora in 1856. On the north side of the square is the **Casa Amarilla** (Yellow House) which is home to the Foreign Ministry. The other building of interest is the **Edificio Metálico** which was made from parts shipped from France, and is now a school. On the north side of the square, on Avenida 7, is the **Jade Museum**, one of the highlights of the capital; see below for more details.

Avenida 3 takes you east of Parque España to the **Parque Nacional**. The main feature of this square is a group of bronze statues – made in the studios of Rodin in France – depicting the five Central American republics driving out William Walker. To the north is the **Biblioteca Nacional**, and to the west the **Presidential Palace**. The **Legislative Assembly** (Palacio Nacional) is on the south side of the Parque Nacional; you can go inside when the parliament is in session. Just east of the Parque Nacional is the old **Atlantic railway station**, now a museum of sorts, with a big old locomotive outside.

Continuing south past the Legislative Assembly, you reach the **Museo Nacional** overlooking the Plaza de la Democracía. This is the country's top museum, housed in an imposing building on Calle 17 between Avenidas Central and 2. Formerly the Bellavista Fortress, it was the army headquarters until the forces' disbandment in 1948; you can still see bullet holes in the turrets, dating from the uprising that year. The museum contains a huge archaeological and historical collection, including pre-Columbian jade and gold. There is also a section devoted to natural history, art and furniture. The museum opens 8.30am-5pm Tuesday to Saturday, 9am-5pm on Sundays, and is closed on Mondays. Admission is $3, though students get in free.

The other possible contender for 'best museum in Costa Rica' is the **Museo de Jade**. a well-laid-out collection of pre-Columbian jade. Other archaeological finds, including gold and pottery, are on display. The museum is housed on the 11th floor of the Instituto Nacional de Seguros on Avenida 7 and Calle 9. It is open 8am-5pm, daily except Monday, admission $3.

A rather grisly option is the **Criminology Museum**, housed in the Supreme Court Building on Calle 21, between Avenidas 6 and 8. The museum includes an interesting if macabre collection of objects. Among them is a hand chopped off by a jealous wife using a machete, a cranium split by an axe, the organs (preserved in alcohol) of people who had poisoned themselves, and the lungs and livers of those who have died of lung cancer or cirrhosis of the liver. The museum was last known to open for just six hours a week, 1pm-3pm on Monday, Wednesday and Friday.

A night out

The best, or at least safest, nightlife to be found in San José tends to be in the commercial complexes. At El Pueblo there are a couple of bars with music, which are much more entertaining than the tacky discos in the city centre. Admission is usually free, but beers are twice the going rate. If all you want to do is enjoy a glass of rum and a few tapas, stick to the cheap and less glitzy bars.

San José has a livelier classical music scene than elsewhere in Central America. There are regular concerts at the National Theatre, including several performances designed to bring serious music to a wider audience. **Una Hora de Música** is a series of Sunday lunchtime chamber concerts in the National Theatre which are broadcast throughout the country. Concerts are also staged at the National in the evenings, and at other venues including the Plaza del Sol.

The National Theatre is also the place to go for the best theatrical entertainment; the box office is in the small building adjacent to the theatre in the Plaza de la Cultura. Prices begin at around $2 and increase to about $10 for good seats at a top-class show. For information on other theatres, and cinemas, see the listings in the *Tico Times* or the national dailies.

A shopping expedition

The shops and pavement hawkers on Avenida Central purvey a spectacular amount of tat. The Mercado Central (between Avenidas Central and 1, Calles 6 and 8) sells tacky souvenirs, but you can also get hammocks and there are some interesting herbalists' stalls. One place to avoid buying is the Plaza de la Cultura, where hawkers sell shoddy goods ranging from jewellery to cocaine of dubious purity. The speciality is Guatemalan trinkets which are sold at massive mark-ups. The Sol Maya store, on Paseo Colón between Calles 16 and 20 (opposite the San Juan de Dios Hospital), is better value and sells crafts from all over Central America. The best source of newspapers and magazines in English is the Candy Shop at the side of the Grand Hotel facing the Plaza de la Cultura.

If you are homesick for food rather than words, the Magnolia store on Avenida Central between Calle Central and Calle 1 sells British and American specialities, such as Twining's tea, Campbell's soup, and Spam. Possibly the best selection of 21st century in Central America is at Elektra, in the basement of the Centro Colón, on Paseo Colón between Calles 38 and 40.

A Christmas story

Perhaps the most gratifying element of my most recent trip through Central America was the optimism of the people, which was reflected in cities like San Salvador and Panama City by a more relaxed feeling. But sometimes, after a few years away from a place, you can discern an extra edge. San Jose seemed several degrees riskier since my last visit in 1996, and to prove the point I was badly mugged on Christmas morning.

It happened like this. At 5.30am on 25 December 1999, I set off from the Ritz to the bus terminal for the southeast. A hazy light had already established itself. I searched in vain for a taxi, though. Anxious to get to the terminal quickly and try to book a seat out of town on the 7am bus, I cut through the empty backstreets in the west of town. On Avenida 6, I was enjoying the rare calm of San José on Christmas morning, unaware of the footsteps behind me until they broke into a run. As you will know if you has ever been the victim of a mugging, a split-second before contact you know what is going to happen next. An arm snapped around my throat and tugged my head backwards. I didn't see the other arm, but feared it carried a knife.

That I could issue nothing more than a choked cry of alarm was irrelevant: even if I could have yelled, there was no-one around to respond. With a speed clarity that is difficult to credit in retrospect, I spent the next second running through the immediate consequences of the attack. I would certainly lose my wallet, and watch, and possibly my passport too. Assuming I was not badly hurt, I would spend at least the next three days trying to get a new passport – the British Embassy would be closed because of Christmas. And, I thought, what rotten luck to be mugged on my birthday.

Having sped down that little line of thought, I swerved back to the present – and the realisation that the villain had momentarily loosened his grip on my neck. I didn't have to be much of a contortionist to wriggle free and run like fury round the corner and for the three blocks to Avenida Central (my 'flight' instinct is much better developed than the 'fight' urge), with cash and even spectacles intact.

By 'badly mugged', I mean he was a useless mugger.

A word of advice

When the American Embassy starts warning about attacks on its own staff in San José, you know it's time to start worrying. 'Two US Embassy employees have been carjacked by armed assailants in the past year', says the State Department, which continues 'Crime is increasing, and tourists as well as the local populace are frequent victims. While most crimes are non-violent, including pickpocketing and house and car break-ins, criminals have shown a greater willingness in recent years to use violence. Local law enforcement agencies have limited capabilities. American women have been victims of sexual assaults at beach resorts on both coasts and in San Jose in recent years. There have been several attempted sexual assaults, including one rape, by taxi drivers.'.

Keeping in touch

A message
The best places to look for **internet** facilities are, strangely, in the *centros comerciales* on the outskirts, rather than the city centre itself. The San Pedro area, where the University of Costa Rica is located, also has a number of options.

A letter
The main **Post Office** is a fine building, guarded by stone lions, on Calle 2 between Avenidas 1 and 3. The section where poste restante mail can be picked up is on the left as you face the building; go in the door marked Certificados.

An emergency
Ambulance (Cruz Roja): 221 5818; **Fire**: 118; **Police**: 117. The main **hospital** is San Juan de Dios on Avenida Central between Calle 14 and 16 (tel 222 0166). The **British Embassy** is on the 11th floor of the Centro Comercial Colón, Paseo Colón between Calles 38 and 40; tel 221 5566. Open 8am to noon and 1pm to 4pm, Monday-Friday; outside these hours, an emergency contact number is posted on the door of the embassy and is given out on the recorded message service. The US Embassy is in the western suburb of Pavas (tel 220 3050). For emergencies arising outside normal business hours, Americans may call 220 3127 and ask for the duty officer.

A Day Trip to the Treetops
Braulio Carillo national park, in the mountains northeast of San José, has fast-flowing rivers, dramatic canyons and some of the finest rainforest in the world. The first thing that is unusual about it is that the Guápiles Highway from San José to Puerto Limón crosses right through the middle of it. Stranger still, just on the far side of the park, a chairlift has been installed that will whisk you through the rainforest at the level of the canopy.

The **Rainforest Aerial Tram** is an experience unlike any other, made possible by a visionary naturalist named Donald Perry from the USA, a ski-lift from Italy, and the Sandinista armed forces from Nicaragua. Mr Perry came up with a relatively uninvasive way for tourists to explore the rainforest, gliding 30m (100 feet) above ground level in what are basically cages that allow you to look down and wonder at the flora and fauna – which includes ocelots, tapirs, sloths and raccoons. He bought the hardware, and hired the Sandinistas to use one of their Soviet helicopters to help install it without damaging the terrain.

There is much more to the place than an eco-theme-park ride. A series of exhibits in huts explains the creation of the tram, and the singular nature of rainforest. Man's various attempts to eradicate it are outlined, together with the creatures than depend on it. You should take all this in before heading off for a ride with one of the local guides, who will point out the highlights from neanderthal epiphytes to dozing sloths.

To make the day trip on your own, take any bus heading along the Guápiles Highway, for example to Guápiles itself or Limón, and alight at the well-signposted turning. From here, it is a half-hour walk to the tram headquarters (you have a good chance of hitching a ride).

Admission is a steep $55, which you can't really argue with – there is no similar attraction with which you can compare the Rainforest Aerial Tram. For only around $10 you can sign up for one of the various organised tours from San José; the organisers benefit from cheaper group rates to keep the total cost of a package down.

Across the Divide

Until now, the attractions have all lain somewhere off the Highway. Now, though, the Panamericana comes into its own, soaring into rugged mountain scenery as it sets about crossing the Continental Divide.

This is the imaginary line that is defined by the way that water flows. A raindrop that falls to the east will benefit, eventually, the Atlantic; a drop to the west ends up in the Pacific. For most of its length, the Pan-American Highway keeps well to the west of the Divide, clinging close to the Pacific. Somewhere in the Central Valley, the Highway wanders over to the Atlantic side, and over the stretch east from San José is where the road has to claw its way back to the Pacific. The authorities warn about the dangers of this stretch of the road, which reaches more than two miles above sea level.

Most people make the journey across the mountains in one swoop, but through force of circumstance – the bus was fully booked, even for standing passengers – I hitched instead, having first taken a $0.50 bus ride on the 24km (15 mile) trip to **Cartago**.

This provincial capital does not have the air of a town that was founded in 1563, nor of one that was capital of Costa Rica until 1823. It is hard to believe that it was ever the country's most important cultural centre. Most of the finest buildings have been destroyed by earthquakes, and many of the Spanish-style houses which have survived are in a bad state of repair. Even the trains travelling between San José and Puerto Limón no longer pass through Cartago (indeed, they no longer pass through anywhere, but some mourn for the days when the expected time of arrival of trains was written on a blackboard at the station).

The highlight of the Parque Central, and perhaps of Cartago, is La Parroquia, the ruin on the eastern side of the square. This is the site of the first parish church which was founded in 1575. Rebuilt a number of times during the colonial era, the church was virtually destroyed by an earthquake in 1841. Years later reconstruction in stone began, but before it was completed another tremor in 1910 reduced the church to the condition in which you see it today.

The area enclosed within the ruined shell has been turned into a garden where the locals come to sit, children to play, and artists to paint.

Seven blocks east of the Parque Central is the 18th-century Basilica of the Virgen de Los ángeles, the patron saint of Costa Rica. Rebuilt in the early 20th century in an ornate Byzantine style, this is a church of rather confused design. The church was allegedly built after the image of the black Virgen de Los Angeles, known as La Negrita, appeared repeatedly on a rock in the spot where the church now stands. This very rock (so it is said) can be seen in the crypt, and there is a small statue of the black virgin above the main altar. Pilgrims come all year round to give praise, but the most important day of the year is August 2, when La Negrita is taken on a procession through the streets.

Altitude slickness

Bienvenidos a la carretera mas alto en el país, reads a sign on this stretch of the Panamericana. You are invited to visit a café called the Soda Everest. And a settlement along the road is named Siberia. Get the picture? People and vehicles function significantly less well at this height, so take great care if you are driving. The local bus drivers are good at handling the roads (those who are not, do not survive).

The Highway swerves around Cartago and starts climbing swiftly, twisting through gaunt mountains. At the turn-off for Santa María Dota, 30 miles (48km) southeast of San José, is one of the few possibilities to connect with the Pacific. There is a dirt track from Santa María to Quepos on the Pacific coast, but allow all day for such a journey.

The higher you climb along the Highway, the more evidence of habitation dwindles – and the more the surroundings resemble the Scottish Highlands, with the same sparse vegetation stretched thinly across rugged hills, and stirring vistas that melt into the mist. If you have the choice, stop at the Mirador Quetzales at kilometre 70. You won't see any of these rare birds, but you will enjoy some fine views – quite possibly of the clouds gathering in the valley below you. There are, surprisingly, some places to stay along the way: at km 77, the Casa Refugia de Ojo de Agua, and later at the Hotel Mambito, the place that welcomes you 'to the highest highway in the land'.

Near the summit, on the San José side, is a roadhouse called **Arbolito** where most buses pause. You can sample life in the clouds, and buy some of the delicious apples grown in the area. The café serves tortillas with local cheese or hamburgers, and a sweet herbal tea. The road follows the crest of the Talamanca mountains and reaches a peak when it goes over the top of **Cerro de la Muerte**, the 'Mountain of Death'. At this point, road users are over two miles high, at 3,491m (12,926 feet) to be exact. Actually, you might feel a tiny sense of disappointment with the summit itself. The mountain has sprouted a forest of transmitter aerials, which bring considerable benefit to the local people but blight the skyscape.

One thing you will definitely feel is a few jolts. Sometimes the road here freezes, and the Tarmac is badly cracked and badly patched. By kilometre marker 95, it's all over, and the hotel/restaurant complex at La Georgina doesn't even have much of a view. There is a scenic reprise at kilometre 119, where the Vista del Valle boasts a souvenir shop, and further along at the Mirador La Torre – close to where a huge rock looms over the Highway.

San Isidro is the first large town you reach after San José, lying 136km (85 miles) and three hours southeast of the capital; its full name is San Isidro de El General. It is a useful starting place for trips to the Chirripó National Park and down to the Pacific coast, but little else. After the glorious journey, San Isidro is an unglorified bus station with a café attached.

Heading south from San Isidro along the Pan-American Highway the scenery once more becomes attractive. Particularly beautiful is the valley of the Río Grande de Térraba, where the highway suddenly turns west towards Palmar. Those carrying on to San Vito can cross on the new bridge. If you are heading for Panama, this is the shortest route – but it is it not recommended in the wet season from May to November.

Little Italy

San Vito was founded in the 1950s by Italian immigrants. The chances of finding decent *pasta al pesto* is higher here than in elsewhere on Costa Rica, and nearby there are other attractions, too. Being situated among lush forested mountains, it is deliciously cool and has fine views and pleasant surroundings. From San Vito you can visit the Wilson Botanical Gardens, six kilometres (four miles) south on the Neily road. Trails in the surrounding forest reserve can bring you into close proximity to some wonderful birds. There are a couple of hotels in San Vito itself, but for greater tranquility go to the Botanical Gardens where you can stay quite cheaply in communal rooms; bring your own food.

If your destination is Panama, you could continue east through the villages of Lourdes and Sabalito to the Panamanian town of Río Sereno and onwards through the hills to La Concepción. Alternatively, there are buses twice a day south to Neily, where you rejoin the Pan-American Highway.

At the end of the 'dog-leg' performed by the Pan-American Highway is **Palmar**, split into two by the road into Palmar Norte and Palmar Sur. Here the highway makes another hairpin bend before heading down towards the Panamanian border. Should you need to stay overnight in this dusty (in the wet season, muddy) three-by-three-block, there is little choice but the Hotel Osa. The other important thing about Palmar is that this is where anyone taking the Pacific coastal option to its concluson will rejoin the Highway.

The Southern Pacific route

The toughest choice you will have to make on the entire journey is whether to traverse the highest point on the route, and enjoy some stunning mountain scenery along the way, or opt for the coastal experience – drifting along a lazy road by the seashore. The answer will probably depend on how much of a hurry you are in: the mountain route will get you to Palmar in about five hours flat out. The Pacific route would take at least double that, but the whole point of it is to stop for some days along the coast. Either way, you should have a superb journey on your way to the Panamanian border. But if you are planning to take the coastal route from San José, you need to start off by going back the way you came.

West of San José's main airport, the road to the coast bends south, and begins to twist through the hills. Beyond the small town of Orotina a road turns off for Puntarenas; when plans to divert the Pan-American highway are complete, this will become the main route through Costa Rica. Head due south from here along a dirt track and you can visit the Carara Biological Reserve. The wildlife, including monkeys and macaws, is hard to spot, but there are a few trails and it is a good place to break a journey.

The main road continues on a wide arc, first touching the coast at Tarcoles, about 85km (53 miles) from San José. As you cross the bridge over the Río Grande de Tárcoles, keep a look out for the flamingoes and alligators which can sometimes be seen on the banks. South and east of here there are several fine beaches, although they get crowded at weekends because of their proximity to San José. The main ones are Herradura and Jacó. Herradura beach, a mile from the highway, is the smaller and quieter of the two, and the sea is also safer for swimming. There are a few cabinas, and facilities for camping. Jacó beach is more developed (with accommodation to suit all pockets) and dirtier. The black sand beach is 8km (5 miles) long, and the waves can get big enough for surfing. Beware of rip tides.

To escape the crowds, continue south towards the scruffy settlement of Parrita. Playa Palma, just north of the town, is one of the nicest beaches in this area. Beyond Parrita the road southeast to Quepos passes through palm plantations, crossing numerous muddy streams on precarious bridges.

Quepos

Look at the map, and you will see that Quepos is only 50km (30 miles) due south of San José – but 160km away by road. Its official name is Puerto Quepos, a port built by United Brands to handle the export of bananas grown in plantations along this stretch of coast. Bananas were superseded by palm oil, and latterly by tourism. It is a most beguiling place, with stilted houses scattered just offshore, mangrove swamps, and a lovely seafront best admired at sunset. The setting, with mountains providing a backdrop, is as close to perfect as makes no difference.

The **bus** station's setting is less than perfect, being in the middle of a muddy piece of wasteground north of the seafront. There are three buses a day from San José to Quepos, continuing to Manuel Antonio National Park. Services leave the Coca Cola terminal in the capital three times a day (at 6am, noon and 6pm).

The journey takes just over three hours to Quepos, 20 minutes more to Manuel Antonio. The fare is $5. Alternatively take the most cost-effective flight in Costa Rica: Sansa has two services to and from San José every day except Sunday, taking just 20 minutes and costing only $20. The airport is just north of the town but the Sansa office is in a shop just east of the town centre on the road to Manuel Antonio, close to the post office.

Buses down the coast to Dominical depart at 5am and 1.30pm, taking 90 minutes to Dominical and continuing to San Isidro on the Pan-American highway; this is ideal for Panama-bound travellers.

A room

The accommodation in Quepos is far from first rate apart from the Hotel Sirena (tel 777 0528), which is small, new, just outside of town and has everything you would expect for around $15 single/$25 double. Other hotels worth trying out are Melissa and Malinche, next to each other at the centre of town, towards the sea from the bus station: They are OK but a bit pricey and some rooms lack windows: single $10, double $18, with another $10 for air conditioning.

In the opposite direction, toward the football pitch there is Hotel Villas Mar y Sol which has seen better days since its French manageress decided to spend more time pampering her enormous (but harmless) dog rather than mending shelves: It does, however, have private bathrooms, hot water, laundry facilities and so on: Single and double rooms are both $20, with another $5 for air conditioning.

Cabinas Hellen (tel 777 0504), 100m towards the sea from the football pitch on the same road as Iguana Tours: friendly, family-run, clean and quiet with effective fans – recommended. Single $14, double $18. The cheapest place is Doña Luisa next to the football pitch, which is fairly basic: Singles and doubles are $8.

A meal and a drink

Due to the burgeoning tourism that has been attracted to the park, restaurants in town tend to serve poorly cooked Western dishes (especially Italian), and charge too much. One exception to this is the small locals' restaurant just up from the bus station on the opposite side of the street: look for the barstools outside the large open window. The dishes are generously served and reasonably priced and they also tend to show Western films on the TV at night. On the seafront there is the Café Milagro that serves excellent if expensive coffee and snacks and Cuban cigars. Next door you should find McQuepos, which will be doling out the burgers if a certain American fast food chain has not sued.

There are a few bars around and plenty of them are full of jolly North Americans to chat to. Those searching for adventure can try out the local disco that fills with the local girls squeezed into pink boob tubes, plastic stilettos and silver leggings. Their male counterparts mimic the bygone fashions of the North American homeboy with baggy shorts, netted baseball vests and plenty of gold jewellery.

A word of advice

At the far corner of the football pitch is Iguana Tours. The staff are helpful and the prices are competitive. Services offered include internet access, guides to the park and sport fishing. The only other internet café is opposite hotel Melissa; both charge $8 per hour. If you find that one of the banks only accepts national Visa, go to the other which accepts Visa and cards on the Cirrus network. The post office overlooks the football pitch. To learn Spanish, try COSI in Manuel Antonio Hotel (tel 253 9272, fax 253 2117: $350 per week with accommodation).

Manuel Antonio is Costa Rica's smallest national park. It is also one of the country's most delightful, and is the main reason people come to the area. It is 8km (5 miles) southeast of Quepos, along a twisting road that starts just outside Iguana Tours.

There are buses from Quepos at 5.45am, 7.15am and then about every half-hour until around 5pm, after which you will have to take a taxi ($5) or hitch. If you prefer, you can walk to the Park in less than 90 minutes, with the first stretch away from the main road. Before Iguana Tours turn right, away from the football pitch. Continue for 250m until the road splits into three, then take the track to the right. This track meets the road after about 1.5km (a mile). The road itself is not going to win any Corniche of the Year prizes. It winds up, down and around the ragged coastline in a fairly uninspired manner until meeting the Playa Espadilla at Manuel Antonio. Beside the road lies a procession of hotels and restaurants whose gaudy placards offer everything to satisfy the hearts desire of any tourist – from 'Foaming Jacuzzis' to 'Poolside Pizza'.

One kilometre before the park, the road drops down to Manuel Antonio village's delightful beach, Playa Espadilla, where the spray catches bright rainbows of light in an amphitheatre of tropical vegetation. To reach the park, continue to the end of the beach. The park entrance is across that waist-deep stream at the end of the beach; porters will ferry tourists across for a dollar each. As with all Costa Rican parks, entrance costs $6. The gates open 7am-4pm, and some travellers report the anti-social practice of early birds arriving before seven and jumping over the gates to avoid payment.

The park is a fine combination of beach and jungle, with cliffs providing good views over the Pacific. The white sandy beaches are among the best in the country. Manuel Antonio is a gem of a park, but as the most popular and accessible area of rainforest in Costa Rica it is usually crowded, and there seems to be an endless procession of minibuses loaded with tourists on a whistlestop tour of the great outdoors. If the sunrise chirp of parrots and the buzz of cicadas is more appealing than the whirr of video cameras, arrive at dawn or shortly afterwards.

A complete tour of the park at a comfortable pace takes about four hours. This does not include lazing around on the beautiful beaches or a bit of snorkelling. (It is safe to bathe in some places and dangerous in others; the map at the gates gives clear information about which is which.) Most of the trails are easy to follow, and there are stretches where you feel as if you are very much in the wilds. In the wet season some of the tracks can be difficult. Guides are available; these are not necessary for finding your way around, but may help you spot the wildlife. Parts of the park are blocked off for regeneration. From the entrance hut follow the path, turn right for half-hour loop around Punta Catedral. Playa Manuel Antonio is where most people congregate, a crescent-shaped beach where monkeys descend at noon in the hope of swiping bathers' picnics. A little way inland the track leads through dense forest to another beach, known as Puerto Escondido. From here you can follow a track uphill which leads to a mirador. The trail leads eventually to Playa Playita; the undergrowth gets thick, so you may not make it all the way.

The animals you are most likely to see include monkeys, sloths, agouti (brown rodents the size of a piglet), and iguana; Manuel Antonio is one of the few surviving habitats of the squirrel monkey. If you see none of these you can expect to see thousands of fluorescent orange Halloween crabs. The beaches are lovely, but crowded at the weekend. It is best to swim actually in the park because Playa Espadilla (the main beach near the bus stop and hotels) has dangerous rip tides.

There are plenty of hotels, but most of these are fairly expensive. The best value is the Manuel Antonio Hotel (777 7237), with Sicomono (777 0777) providing an eco-option. cheapest is the Youth Hostel Costa Linda (tel 777 0304), some way back from the road, but signposted. It is also possible to camp, although not inside the park.

The road along the coast from Quepos is fine and fast during the dry season, slow and miserable in the wet. The village of **Dominical** is 42km (26 miles) southeast. Surfers rave about the main beach at Dominical, but it can be dangerous for swimmers. The beaches further south are better for swimming. Just a couple of miles away is the rocky Punta Dominical, and further south are Matapalo, Barú and Uvita. If you want to rejoin the Pan-American Highway early, there is a good paved road which takes you through beautiful hill country. Landslides cause occasional problems. But the new bridge at Uvita should allow you to get through to Palmar without too many problems, so long as you are either driving or hitching.

Anyone hitching the stretch of the Panamericana will quickly be aware how thin the traffic has become – one vehicle in each direction every five minutes constitutes a rush-hour. Long-distance buses on the Highway act as local services, stopping every few minutes to pick up shoppers and schoolchildren, and take ages; at least there is plenty of good scenery to admire. Landslides often slow traffic down, particularly during the wet season. The line of the

Panamericana is paralleled by the Ferrocarril del Sur that linked Palmar with Golfito and the Panamanian border. The settlements here have names derived from kilometre markers on the old railway.

Just past El 40, at the village of Villa Briceño, there is a turn to the south signposted for the **Esquinas Rainforest Lodge**, a splendid Austrian-sponsored community tourism venture. The distance shown is four kilometres, but six or seven is more accurate. The lodge comprises a scattering of thatched cabins set among the hills midway between the Highway and the sea. A series of trails leads into the rainforest, though these can be hard to follow. There is a fine swimming pool set in the middle of the grounds, plus a dining hall/library which is a splendid place to relax after a hard day in the rainforest (the self-service bar helps too). As an early entry in the visitors' book notes, 'the project was conceived with love and optimism'.

All this does not come cheap: I paid $75 per night for a blissful (and mosquito-free) cabin, and three excellent meals. You can find out more at regenwald.au, or e-mail esquinas@sol.racsa.co.cr, or call 293 0780 for the San José office, or 382 5798 for the lodge.

There is, on the map at least, a road from Esquinas leading down to the last 'proper' town in Costa Rica, **Golfito**. At most times of the year, though, you will need to take the Highway to Río Claro, from where Golfito is 22km (14 miles). Golfito is in a beautiful position overlooking the Golfo Dulce and the Osa Peninsula. The town lies at the foot of a cliff and is surrounded by forested hills. Golfito is hot and humid, yet it is one of the most atmospheric towns in Costa Rica and has the sort of hotels and restaurants that foreign travellers appreciate.

Until recently Golfito was occupied by the United Fruit Company. The North Americans moved here in the 1930s to develop new banana plantations following the decline – through disease and strikes – of those in the Limón region. Golfito became the company's headquarters in Costa Rica. United Fruit moved out in 1985 following a drop in sales, a number of acrimonious strikes, and rising production costs. African palm plantations have replaced the banana plantations, but many Golfiteños remain unemployed or have left in search of work elsewhere.

As a result of the American involvement, Golfito consists of two distinctive parts. The so-called Zona Americana is in the northern part of the town; the atmosphere is tranquil, and you can see the fine wooden houses where the plantation administrators once lived. These are in great contrast with the buildings in the Pueblo Civil or old town further south, where many houses have been abandoned and are boarded up. This end of Golfito has the atmosphere more usually associated with ports, and has a number of seedy-looking, men-only bars. Nevertheless, the old town has the hotels and restaurants, and is the liveliest part of Golfito.

There is little to do around Golfito, yet it is a great place to spend some time. Don't miss the abandoned railway station with its collection of rusty old carriages; the old track is overgrown and runs alongside the main street.

Tracopa **buses** to Golfito from San José take seven or eight hours. They terminate at the Tracopa office on the edge of the Zona Americana, stopping outside the Hotel Delfina in the Pueblo Civil a few minutes earlier. There are buses onwards to Neily, and sometimes to the Panamanian frontier at Paso Canoas. Buses and four-wheel-drive taxis ferry people along the coastal road between the Pueblo Civil and the Zona Americana. The **airport** is close to the Zona Americana. There are non-stop flights to and from San José at least daily.

Opposite the main bus stop is the **Hotel Delfina** (tel 775 0047) which occupies a grand old building near the waterfront. Clean rooms (with the odd cockroach) cost $20 for a double. Further north is the Hotel Golfito (tel 775 0043), which is a bit gloomier and a bit cheaper. Golfito has a disproportionate number of restaurants, most of them concentrated near the seafront in the Pueblo Civil. Breakfast is best at Luís Brune's, a quasi-American place opposite the Texaco garage on the seafront, but cheapest in the market, a ten-minute walk up the coast.

From Golfito, there are flights and ferries across to the **Osa Peninsula**, a large, inaccessible thumb that juts out into the Pacific Ocean west of Golfito. It is best known for the **Corcovado National Park**, an important and isolated area of virgin rainforest which occupies one third of the peninsula. Corcovado became a protected area in response to the serious damage resulting from the effects of logging, gold prospecting, and an increased number of settlers. Despite campaigns to force out the gold prospectors, they continue to pan for gold on the fringes of the park.

The park contains a wide variety of habitats, from swamp to forest, as well as miles of empty beaches. Corcovado may be best known for its relatively undisturbed rainforest, but it is also considered to be one of the most complete ecosystems in the world, being totally different geographically from the rest of Costa Rica. A huge range of wildlife lives here, including many reptiles, tapir, jaguar, ocelot, and monkeys; among the finest birds seen here are the rare harpy eagle, toucans and scarlet macaws; there are also many exotic butterflies. Magnificent trees towering up to 60m (200 feet) form the tallest canopy in Central America.

Corcovado is hot and humid at any time of year and is best visited during the dry season, particularly January to April. The insects are voracious and a mosquito net is essential. Accommodation is primitive. Access to the park is via Puerto Jiménez. From here there are buses to La Palma (taking about an hour), from where you can walk in three or four hours to Los Patos, on the northeastern edge of the park. (Trucks acting as taxis also run between Puerto Jiménez and La Palma.) The Sirena research station on the west coast of the peninsula is another four or five hours from Los Patos. Cheap lodging is

available here, and would be a good place to spend your first night. It is possible
to rent horses here too.

A possible hike from Sirena is north along the coast to Llorona where
there is another shelter. From Llorona you can go on walks along trails inland,
or walk further north to the edge of the park at San Pedrillo, from where it is
possible to get a boat to Isla del Caño which lies 17km (11 miles) off the
coast. This is the largest uninhabited island in the world. The island is part of
the park and boasts abundant marine life and an important area of coral; you
may spot whales, sharks, tuna, and dolphins from the boat. On the island
itself is an Indian cemetery where some important archaeological artifacts
have been unearthed.

There is little else worth stopping for in southeastern Costa Rica, although
those heading south to Panama may wish to break their journey. There are
hotels in Neily, 18km (11 miles) northwest of the border; buses and collective
taxis from here to the border are frequent and take 20 minutes. Checking out of
Costa Rica is likely to take longer than checking in to Panama.

Jurassic Park

Stephen Spielberg's film was shot mainly in Hawaii, but the supposed
location of the dinosaur theme park was the Isla del Coco, a volcanic island
lying about 320km (200 miles) southwest of the Osa Peninsula, and is
covered in dense and humid tropical rainforest. It is a national park, and
permits and tours should be arranged in San José; there is no regular boat
service. The waters around the island are rich in fish and other marine life,
and are great for diving. The island was once used as a base by pirates, and
hunting for lost treasure is a popular pastime; over 400 expeditions have
searched in vain. While there is lush vegetation on the island, there are few
animals (or dinosaurs). Birds, on the other hand, are abundant.

Panama

COSTA RICAN FRONTIER - DARIÉN GAP

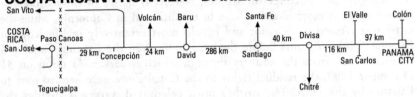

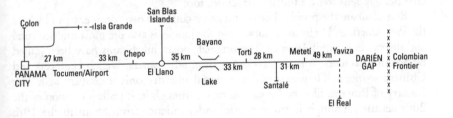

The young country

A shriek slices through the dusk. It cuts through the cacophony of hoots and grunts, squeaks and squawks. As if responding to a command, two creatures – as extrovert as they are invisible – try to out-rasp each other. One emulates a chainsaw, the other a dentist's drill, their efforts reinforced by reverberations from distant hills. And beneath all this is the thrum of a hidden river deep in the valley – the resonant bass line in the symphony of the night.

The best ensemble in life is the orchestra of nightfall in the jungle, and nowhere is the rainforest so intensely, infectiously vocal as the Darién. The Gap between the Americas is nature's last resort, the one place where the Highway engineers have admitted defeat – at least for the time being. Getting there, it has to be said, is less than half the fun. Indeed, hauling your possessions, yourself and your spirit through the tough terrain is one of the more physically punishing things you can attempt.

Happily, you can have a fine and fulfilling time without going so deep into Panama. The country at the end of the map, the crooked bookend of Latin America, has so much to offer that an excursion into the the fuzzy part at the end is a highly optional extra. Most of what you might want to experience without switching into expedition mode is within easy reach of the Highway. There is much more besides off the well-beaten track, but leave that for later. First, you should understand – and enjoy – a much-misunderstood country.

Panama welds together the two disparate halves of the Americas, and in turn its name is welded to several other terms. Panama Red, for example, a particularly sought-after and powerful type of cannabis; and the Panama Hat, the headgear of choice for the tropics. Neither is native to the nation: the former is much more likely to have been cultivated in California, while the latter was created in Ecuador and is sold most extensively in Mexico, not Panama. Until 12 hours before the year 2000, even the Panama Canal was semi-detached from the country through which it carves. At noon on 31 December 1999, the residual rights to the Canal Zone were handed over to Panama by the USA. The world's most celebrated waterway divides the Americas yet unites the greatest oceans. This 65km (40 mile) man-made channel happens to be a tourist attraction, too.

Best of all are the people. The country that connects two continents, and where the Pan-American Highway dissolves into the jungle, is also the most multicultural and diverse in Central America. The original Indian inhabitants have been joined by Spanish invaders, African slaves, American adventurers, French engineers and Chinese workers. They acquired a national identity only a century ago. The country of Panama, like the Canal that carves through it, is really a creation of the 20th century. Though it enjoyed brief independence from Spain in the 19th century, it merged with Colombia. The separation, in 1903, was at the behest of Washington. The Americans wanted control over the 'Big Ditch' that they planned to dig, and later established the Panama Canal Zone as a US colony. Had the Canal been built elsewhere – and, as you will discover, it was a close-run thing – Panama might well still be nothing but a far-flung province of Colombia.

As the land bridge suspended precariously between South and Central America, Panama is significantly out of step with the rest of the region. For a start, you will have to adjust your watch as you cross the border from Costa Rica. From Nuevo Laredo on the Texas border to the frontier with Panama, local time sticks tenaciously to GMT minus six. East of that point, it leaps ahead by an hour, handily placing it on the same zone as two other cities to which it aspires – Miami and New York. The most southerly and easterly country in Central America is an enigma in many other ways. Panama is relatively small, the size of Scotland or South Carolina. The population, a mix of Hispanics, blacks and native Indians, is amplified by a miscellany of fortune seekers and their descendants. Many came to build, or to run, the Canal, the nation's icon that has boosted Panama's influence upon world development way beyond the impact that its two million people would suggest.

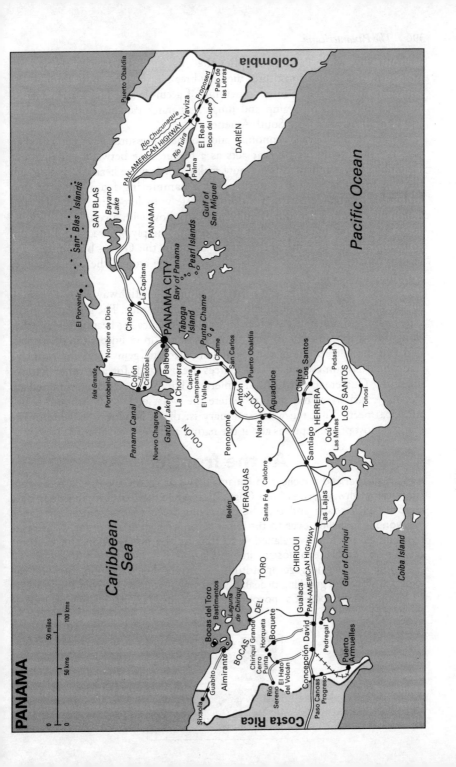

Ironically, while Panama supplies the missing link between the world's greatest oceans, it also constitutes the only break in the land route through the Americas, making the country something of a cul-de-sac. The Darién Gap, a hundred-mile strip of swamp and jungle, separates Panama from Colombia, and Central America from South America.

So far, technological, economic and political pressures have conspired to preserve the fragile jungle that acts as a buffer zone between Panama and Colombia. Environmentalists are now making their voice heard, too, although the rainforest is taking something of a hammering from the way that Colombia's narco-terrorists are doing battle with left-wing guerrillas and Colombia's army. When things quieten down, those with a couple of weeks to spare, a couple of hundred dollars and a copious supply of insect repellent, can contemplate the adventurous journey through the Gap – but, unless the security situation improves rapidly, choose to edge around the poisoned limb stretching into Colombia.

Yet even if you venture no further along the Highway than Tocumen airport, just east of the capital, you can claim rich rewards. The highlands in the west rival the mountains elsewhere in Central America for beauty. The beaches along the Caribbean coast are among the finest and most unspoilt in the region. Old Panama City is one of the region's architectural gems. And the country's traditional costumes, music and dances are a match for any other nation, including Guatemala, in Central America. The *Sun* newspaper summed up Panama concisely as the country 'where the worst of both North and South America meet'. That ten-word summary is, thank goodness, as wide of the mark as most preconceptions about the nation at the end of the road.

At the frontier

Almost all overland travellers to Panama arrive at Paso Canoas where the Pan-American Highway arrives from Costa Rica. While the Costa Rican side is fairly chaotic, with roads and travellers arriving from several directions, once everyone is funnelled over to the Panamanian side, a certain order is restored. Formalities are mostly relaxed – so long as the immigration and customs officials do not take too close an interest in you.

If your clothing, luggage or attitude do attract their attention, then you can expect a slow and gruelling ordeal. (By the way, if you return from Panama City to Miami, you can expect a thorough inspection by US Customs officials looking for drugs.)

MUSEO DEL CANAL
INTEROCEANICO
DE PANAMA

ENTRADA
Niño   Adulto   Martes a Domingo
                    9:30 a.m. a 5:30 p.m.
                    Tels: 211-1649/1650
                         211-1994/1995

Dodging the formalities – option one

If you like the idea of missing out on the whole process, opt for the border crossing between San Vito in Costa Rica and Río Sereno where there are no proper frontier controls. Few people make the journey, but those who don't miss out on some spectacular scenery. One reason this part of the Chiriquí highlands remains off-the-beaten-track is the fact that the road across the border from Costa Rica to Río Sereno is not shown on all maps.

You can reach San Vito on a bus from the point well inside Costa Rica where the Pan-American Highway suddenly veers sharp right to head *west*, rather than its normal eastbound trajectory. At this junction, close to Potrero Grande, there will be a fair amount of traffic going east, so you can hitch-hike without much difficulty; get used to it, because there is no public transport beyond San Vito to Río Sereno, a distance of 20km (12 miles); try your luck hitching. There is a guard post of sorts midway between San Vito and Río Sereno, at the start of an extremely rough road which continues until Río Sereno. From here there are hourly buses to David. The journey through the mountains, which takes you above the clouds in places, is staggering. There is no immigration check at the frontier or in Río Sereno. Instead, go to the police station in David or, if you are heading straight to Panama City, to the immigration department there, to regularise your position. Failure to do so will make it very difficult to get out of Panama, except by the same route back to Costa Rica. When you call in, make your story sound as innocent as possible in case officials are suspicious of your motives for choosing such a backward route.

Dodging the formalities – option two

North of Chiriquí lies the province of Bocas del Toro. The province consists of a long slice of the mainland plus a bay dotted with islands, many of them coral. The area is distinctly West Indian. On the islands, a Caribbean patois based on English is spoken by most people. Separated from the south by the Talamanca mountains, Bocas del Toro was for a long time virtually cut off. These days it is connected with the city of David, which means there is a new surface route from Costa Rica. If your travels have taken you across to the Atlantic coast at Puerto Limón, you will be just 50km (30 miles) from the Panamanian border. A bus will take you to Bribri, and a bus, pick-up or hitched lift on from there to Sixaola will plant you on the frontier. There are controls, but formalities tend to be more relaxed than on the Pan-American Highway.

From Guabito, the Panamanian side of the frontier, there is a road of sorts to Almirante, a scruffy and smelly place where you will not want to dwell. There are ferries (journey time 90 minutes) across to Bocas del Toro, the island town that gives its name to the whole province – and a place that is pleasant and surprisingly tranquil. Though smaller and poorer than in the days when the banana industry was at its peak, it has an old-fashioned, rather sleepy atmosphere. The gracious turn-of-the-century houses are surprisingly well kept, and there has been no profusion of the ugly characterless buildings which blight other Panamanian towns. Another boat trip takes around five hours to the mainland town of Chiriquí Grande, on the shore of the bay southeast of Bocas. From here, a new road has been completed to the Highway just east of David. Alternatively, there are cheap and fairly frequent flights to the capital.

Nada es fácil, 'nothing is easy', serves as a good motif to any journey in Latin America. The last-but-one time I entered Panama overland, dusk was rolling in with the urgency of Pacific breakers. The *jefe* had clearly endured a bad day at the tatty office whose one nod towards technology was a malfunctioning typewriter. His humour had not been improved by consuming an impressive amount of rum. All in all, he was best avoided this sultry evening in March.

March was, though, exactly what I had been obliged to do by the three rifle-toting soldiers under his command. They had picked me out as I emerged from the jungle into the threadbare clearing on the Caribbean coast known as Puerto Obaldía. I had intended to quench my thirst and scrape off the accumulated sweat and insects before making a dignified voluntary surrender to the authorities. This was not an option, since the jefe was keen to make a quick decision about the suitability of this week's gringo for admission to his fine country, by assessing all the available documentary evidence.

The trouble was: by now, it was almost dark. The technology did not extend to electricity, let alone a lightbulb. The only temper that counted was rising as fast as the light was sinking. So before we could even begin, I had to rummage through my pack to find a torch. By its flickering light, the jefe perused first my passport, then a much-fingered list, then the passport again. As only a Latin American official can do, he managed to shake his head, suck in through his teeth, frown and smirk simultaneously. This is neither a pretty nor an optimistic sight.

El problema was that nowhere on his list of 'nationalities that do not require a visa' did 'United Kingdom of Great Britain and Northern Ireland' appear. That was that, he slurred. I was on the next bus out, and could try my luck at the Peruvian consulate in Medellín, Colombia. The trouble was, there is no bus from, to, or within Puerto Obaldía.

Trying, in the dark, to read a blurred and faded list of approved nationalities upside down is not an easy business. Focussing more precisely than the jefe, I could tell that 'Gran Bretaña' did not appear; nor did the standard Latin default nationality of Inglés, which plenty of Scots and Welsh people have been forced to adopt for the purposes of bureaucracy. Failure was not an attractive option. The jungle had been tough enough in daylight, with a guide who had disappeared into the shadows when the riflemen turned up. To be sent back in the dark would be to consign me to, at best, a night of bruises and bites. And at worst ... you don't need a hyperactive imagination to conjure up the possibilities when you are caught between the devilish Colombian paramilitaries and the deep blue Caribbean sea.

At last, there it was: Reino Unido, showing that UK citizens would be allowed in with no formality beyond the transfer of a few sweaty dollars. Except: at whatever military academy he attended, there was no class in expressions of national identity, no instruction that 'United Kingdom of Great Britain and Northern Ireland' was the same as 'Reino Unido'. Thank goodness for the European Union: sandwiched between the Greek and French translations, in six-point type (one-third smaller than this), is the representation in Spanish.

If small-scale diplomacy can be compared to a football match, that was the equivalent of my going one-up just before the half-time whistle. My opponent's interval refreshments consisted of a gulp or two more of vicious-smelling fluid, and a cigarette that threatened to ignite it. After the break, he went on the offensive by ordering a minute inspection of all my possessions, strewn out across the dusty floor of his office. Fortunately, the torch beam had waned enough for his men not to be able to find (a) the spare batteries and (b) the copious notebooks that could suggest a motive less pure than simple tourism.

'*Nada*' was the conclusion for this routine, though the scattering of my uncollected possessions looked nothing like nothing to me. Victory of a kind was mine, though it was followed by some inflated and non-negotiable 'fees' and the ignominy of shovelling my originally-clean-but-by-now filthy clothes back into the rucksack by the light of a sliver of moon and the last feeble microvolts of battery life.

Red Tape

People from the European Union, or the USA or Canada, do not need visas for tourist trips. There are two requirements that may be insisted upon; the more likely is that you are in possession of an **onward or return ticket**. The circumstances in which you might not are fairly limited, because most sensible travellers intending to fly out will have bought a ticket in advance (not least to dodge the 10% Panamanian tax on international air travel). The main reason is that you intend to leave overland informally, e.g. back the way you came using local buses or onwards through Darién or through the San Blas Islands. You can circumvent difficult questioning by having a long-distance bus ticket that shows you returning to Costa Rica, but you will have considerable trouble subsequently trying to get a refund. Or, buy well in advance a *full-fare* air ticket from Panama City to a nearby destination, which might well be San José. Don't leave it open – make a definite booking which you can later change without charge and get a full refund.

If you decide to take a chance, then make sure you have a good story ready – or, better still, a handsome wad of **cash dollars or travellers' cheques**. This is, in any event, a good idea, because you should be able to show that you can support yourself during your stay.

Frontier fees

Anyone arriving on foot or on an international bus service will be pleased and surprised to learn that Panama makes no charge for visitors. The authorities make up for it when you come to leave by air, levying a departure tax of $20.

Bringing in a car

If you've made it this far with your vehicle and sanity intact, then you will be dismayed to learn that Panama can be, depending on apparently fluid rules and the mood of the officials, either dead simple or murderously difficult about importing a vehicle. You may be stung for just a single dollar for fumigation of your vehicle, and allowed in for 30 days without further formality. Or you could find yourself limited to a stay of just three days, and paying miscellaneous taxes amounting to $20 – and then having to visit an office in the city of David or the capital during working hours to arrange an extension.

And another thing: the level of car crime is such that any modern car, whether occupied or not, is a potential target for thieves.

Any chance of a decent map?
Yes, but the big problem is that you'll need to track down a hard-to-find address in Panama City before you can buy one. The Instituto Geográfico Nacional Tommy Guardia (IGNTG) is on Vía Simón Bolívar, in the university district of the capital, but few cab drivers know exactly where. It is open 8.30am-4pm Monday to Friday, and sells some superb maps including a natty relief map of the whole country. But if you are heading for Darién, be warned that they are short on detail.

That was then

The first visitors
Panama is a land of solutions: currently, to the 'how do we get shipping from the Atlantic to the Pacific without sailing around Cape Horn? conundrum; originally, to the 'how do we populate South America?' problem. The indigenous peoples of Bolivia, Brazil and elsewhere in the continent can trace their genes to the people who found a way across the Darién Gap perhaps 20,000 years ago. Some of them strayed no further than Panama, and up to 60 separate tribal groups were occupying present Panamanian territory when the Spanish arrived. Of these, the significant survivors are the Kuna, Chocó and Guaymí communities. The relative inaccessibility of their homelands has enabled them to keep their cultures relatively robust.

The Conquest
For once, Columbus was pipped at the coast. A Spanish explorer called Rodrigo de Bastidas was the first European to encounter Panama. He arrived in 1501. His crew included a junior seaman named Vasco Núñez de Balboa. Christopher Columbus visited the isthmus a year later during his fourth and final voyage. The discoverer is commemorated in the names of the contiguous towns of Cristóbal and Colón on the Atlantic coast. His visit was not nearly so significant as that of Vasco Núñez de Balboa who returned – as a stowaway – eight years later in the second wave of Spanish colonists. A series of calamities befell the leaders of this expedition, and Balboa rose through the ranks to command the survivors. They found little resistance among the many native Indian groups in the area, and the terrain did not impede the progress from the Atlantic through to the Pacific.

In 1513, following a march of 27 days, Balboa made his way across the mountains of Darién, and became the first European to reach the Pacific. (The poet Keats makes a glaring historical error by giving credit for first seeing the

Pacific to placing 'stout Cortés' on a peak in Darién.) Yet Balboa did not live to found Panama's first settlement. He incurred the wrath of Pedro Arias Dávila, more commonly known as Pedrarias the Cruel, the notorious governor in control of much of the isthmus at the time. Balboa was found guilty of treason and beheaded, leaving the way clear for Pedrarias to establish Panama's first capital on the Pacific.

The discovery that the Pacific coast was only a couple of days' march from the Atlantic made Panama an excellent base for further exploration. The fact that it is the narrowest country in the Americas sealed its economic fate. Missions could be launched both north and south from either coast, although it was the Pacific side that most attracted the Spanish. A trade route was established between the oceans on a trail used for centuries by Indians; the route, the so-called Camino Real, is now part-submerged by the artificial lake created for the Canal. It emerged on the Atlantic side at Portobelo, some way east of the present Canal mouth. Initially all Spanish trade from the Pacific passed through Panama, which became for a time the primary focus of Spain's operations in Latin America. Being regarded as little more than a short-cut has caused Panama problems ever since.

Getting rich quick

Panama has always been seen as a place to make money fast, or at least get access to some wealth. In 1671 a Welsh pirate called Captain Henry Morgan, whose name is still celebrated on a bottle of rum, attacked the Atlantic coast, made his way across the isthmus and destroyed Panama. As well as making a great deal of money, Morgan also helped the British aim of loosening Spanish control of the main trade route between the Pacific and Europe. Panama City was rebuilt a few miles to the west of what is now known as Panamá Viejo.

An official British invasion took place in 1739 under Admiral Vernon, who captured Portobelo. The Spanish abandoned their trade through Panama. As settlements spread south along the Pacific coast of South America, the sea route around Cape Horn became the main one used by merchant ships. The loss of Spanish interest in Panama and the trans-isthmian route created a power vacuum. Independence was declared in 1821. Shortly afterwards, rather than join the Central American Confederation of Nations, Panama opted to join what was known as Gran Colombia. This federation, which had been created in 1819, consisted of Venezuela, Colombia, Peru, Ecuador and Bolivia; it was the brainchild of Simón Bolívar, who dreamed of a great Latin American nation. Although Gran Colombia broke up a decade later, Panama remained attached to Colombia.

Gold fever

The route around the Cape was followed by people settling the west coast of the USA. In 1849, however, the Californian Gold Rush meant that a huge number of prospectors were desperate to reach the west coast as quickly as possible. Many died on their journey through the disease-infested isthmus, but the migration spurred the building of a railway across Panama, thus linking the Atlantic with the Pacific. Although railway technology was only twenty years old, a bold track was laid across the isthmus and proved immensely successful when it opened in 1855. Migrants from the eastern USA sailed down to Panama, took a train for a couple of hours – paying the outrageous fare of $25 – and boarded other vessels to sail up the west coast. (The line still exists, slightly re-routed by the Canal, though passenger services were suspended in December 1989, following the US invasion.)

For a time Panama enjoyed great wealth from this line. Sovereignty, though, was still in the hands of Colombia, a tricky state of affairs given the difficulty of controlling Panama across a strip of inaccessible jungle and swamp. Panama's fortunes took a downturn from 1869 when the first trans-continental railway opened in the USA. It was during this period, however, that the prospect of a canal across Central America became a serious proposition.

A man, a plan, a disaster

Much discussion took place as to the most suitable route to be taken by a trans-isthmian canal. The two leading candidates were Panama and Nicaragua, and the latter seemed to have the edge initially. Shipping could navigate the existing Río San Juan upstream to Lake Nicaragua, and then cross the lake to a point only 20 miles (32km) from the Pacific. After a staggering amount of mischevious spin-doctoring on the part of Panamanian lobbyists, the Nicaraguan option was eventually dismissed as being too prone to seismic activity, and Panama became the favoured route. The French engineer who had built the Suez Canal, Ferdinand de Lesseps, was signed up as the man most likely to succeed. When he arrived in Panama in 1881, it was believed that the Canal was as good as built. Lesseps' experience, however, had been with a sea-level canal, and he believed he could build a similar channel in Panama without using locks.

After 11 years of building, during which 22,000 workers died, the French company in charge of the project went bankrupt. It negotiated the sale to the USA of the 20 miles of work-in-progress along the Chagres river, but this plan was overruled by the Colombian parliament.

A man, a better plan, a canal

The Americans had long realised the strategic importance of the isthmus, and encouraged the Panamanians to declare independence. They did so in 1903, and after a little unfriendly persuasion on the part of the USA, Colombia had little choice but to acquiesce. Two weeks later the Americans signed an agreement with the fledgling state to build a canal and to appropriate the land on either side. With no effective government in place, the treaty was signed by a French engineer acting as Panama's ambassador to the USA.

Led by George Washington Goethals, the American engineers set about finishing the project – but with two important modifications. Rather than sending in thousands more labourers to their likely deaths, the strip of land across the isthmus was effectively rid of disease. Furthermore, Lesseps' ambitious plan to build a sea-level canal was abandoned in favour of locks near each coast. The Panama Canal, described by Theodore Roosevelt as one of the great works of the world, was opened to shipping in 1914.

Having built the Canal, the Americans were reluctant to yield any control over it. The five-mile band of land on either side was US property, another country – the Panama Canal Zone – which sliced the heart from Panama. Administration of the Zone from Washington meant effective US control over the rest of Panama. Even though the capital and the majority of Panamanians were outside the Zone, the Americans maintained that Panama had protectorate status. Some observers claim that these manoeuvrings set the tone for US intervention in Central America for the remainder of the 20th century.

Reclaiming the Zone

At first the Panamanians seemed content to live as they traditionally had, taking a slice of the trade passing through the isthmus. The USA gave away little, however, and eventually pressure from poverty-stricken Panamanians resulted in a loosening of political and economic ties between the USA and Panama. In 1939, the protectorate status was dropped, but economic dependence continued.

During the 20th century Panama saw a string of mostly highly dubious leaders. Occasional bursts of democracy have always been suppressed by a succession of military coups. The most tenacious legitimate politician was Arnulfo Arias Madrid, who got himself elected as president on no fewer than three occasions. The last success, in 1968, was short-lived. Ten days after the election, Omar Torrijos seized power in an army-backed coup. He instigated a range of social programmes, and established links with liberation movements in Nicaragua and El Salvador as well as Castro's Cuba. Breaking the US economic blockade, Panama supplied Cuba with everything from beer to computers. Yet he also successfully negotiated with President Jimmy Carter in 1977 for the handover of the Canal and closure of US bases. The Americans agreed to give up its control of the Zone at noon on 31 December 1999.

Torrijos subsequently began moves towards civilian government, which he intended should be led by the party he had formed – the Partido Revolucionario Democrático (PRD). But he died in an air crash in Coclé province in 1981, an incident which some attribute to CIA sabotage. He is warmly remembered by most Panamanians for having bequeathed upon the country a greater sense of national identity. His successor, Eric Devalle, tried bravely but naïvely to diminish the influence of the army. Effective control was wrested by General Manuel Noriega, though Devalle remained for the time being as President in title only.

General Noriega was a despot ruthless even by Central American standards. He used his power as the country's leader to amass a personal fortune and condoned barbaric treatment of those who opposed him. He continued the tradition of his predecessors in engendering a sense of weariness born of oppression, of social and economic desperation, and of the consequent lawlessness.

Supposedly free elections were held in May 1989, and Noriega claimed a substantial victory for his Coalición para la Liberación Nacional (COLINA) over the Alianza Democrática de Oposición Civilista (ADOC). This flew in the face of all available evidence, which suggested that the alliance led by his opponent – Guillermo Endara – had won two-thirds of the vote. By December, Noriega had proclaimed himself head of state, and it was this move that provoked an invasion by US forces. They encountered little real resistance among the corrupt and inefficient Panamanian military. Around 4,000 died in the fighting, and 15,000 Panamanians became homeless.

After Noriega had surrendered and was hauled off for trial in Florida, the Americans installed Guillermo Endara – the candidate who had lost out in a rigged election – as president. In a move intended to reflect the presumed share of votes in the flawed election, his alliance was granted two-thirds of the seats in the country's parliament. Their 'prize' was a foreign debt of $1.6 billion, or $1,000 owed by every Panamanian adult; most of Panama's population earn less than this in a year. Apart from solving the debt crisis, Endara's ambitious plans included constitutional reforms to remove power from the military by disbanding the army, Costa Rica-style.

His ambitions were rudely interrupted by the 1994 elections, which brought together an interesting selection of candidates. The outsider was the Panamanian salsa star, Rubén Blades of the Papa Egoró (loosely translating as 'Mother Earth') party. In second place was Mireyra Moscoso, the widow of Arnulfo Arias and leader of the Arnulfista party that was named for him. The winner was Ernesto Pérez Balladeres of the PRD. He endeavoured to re-apply the Torrijos doctrine of a strong state but free economic policies with some success, but his regime was tainted by revelations of connections with the Cali cocaine cartel. Given the record of presidential impropriety, this can hardly have come as much of a surprise to the electorate.

Problem presidents

Panama took almost all of the 20th century to get the hang of electing a sound, durable and uncorrupt *presidente*. But in the meantime, the electorate had several laughs at their leaders' expense.

Manuel Noriega was universally known as 'pineapple-face' because of what might be termed a problem complexion. Building on the drug-running activities which he had established in the military, Noriega accrued a personal fortune. He also incurred the wrath of the USA, which described him as a corrupt, debauched thug, and a narco-terrorist. On the principle that anyone so detested by the Americans must have some good qualities, Noriega earned a surprising degree of public acclaim. Supporters called him El Man, and depicted the US campaign against him as an affront to Panamanian nationalism.

When President George Bush launched 'Operation Just Cause' in 1989, with an invasion force of 27,000 troops, Noriega took refuge in the Vatican mission in Panama City, but surrendered eventually to AC/DC and Bruce Springsteen: rock music had been played at him solidly for days. He was taken to Miami, where he became prisoner 41586. While Noriega got used to the comforts of a cell in Florida, the citizens of Panama City were left to come to terms with the devastation caused by the invasion – and to start making fun of their new leader.

Guillermo Endara was unable to establish any real authority, not least because of his rather comical image. He weighed 17 stone, and when he came to power the extra-marital affairs of his 23-year-old wife were discussed at great length in the Panamanian press. Accusations were also made of his involvement in laundering Colombian drug money.

This is now
The last year of US involvement saw possibly the hardest-fought election in the country's troubled history. In 1999, the two leading candidates each had an intense personal motive for success. Mireyra Moscoso wanted to take the US 'surrender' and lead Panama into the 21st century as the nation's first-ever woman president. Her rival was Martin Torrijos, son of the man who had negotiated the handover. Moscoso's promise of more help for the poor won the day, by 45% to 38%.

Anyone who has made the journey all the way through Central America will gasp at the sight of Panama City, a mighty Manhattan compared with the feeble attempts at building a world city in places like Guatemala City and Managua. But the gleaming glass and steel skyscrapers do not reflect the abject poverty in which thousands of Panamanians still live. Their endeavours to climb from the bottom of the economic ladder are affecting the rest of the country, with settlers pushing east into the Darién in the hope of carving a living out of the jungle – all too often, literally.

No other president has to deal with an economy perched on three slippery sources of foreign exchange: banana exports, drug trafficking and Canal revenues. The first two are in decline, for different reasons, while traffic through the Canal is showing a slight fall. Salvation is likely to come from the increased world price of oil, which changes the economics of shipping operations in favour of the Canal on certain journeys. If it becomes sufficiently advantageous, though, there will be increased speculation about the possible construction of a new, bigger canal through Nicaragua; if this were to happen, the Panamanian economy would be devastated.

On the Highway
Panama's main street is numbered C-1, and locally known as the Carretera *Inter*americana – which is ironic, since Panama is the one country covered by the book which does not have the Highway leaving from two separate borders. But at least, for most of its length, the Pan-American Highway will give you a comfortable ride.

Some people say that a good reflection of the economic health of a developing country is the condition of its buses. Given the precarious economic state of Panama, you might expect buses in an appalling state of repair. In fact, in the western half of Panama the opposite is true. Fast, comfortable and air-conditioned buses and minibuses serve a large number of destinations. A 50km (30 mile) run that would be an endurance test in Costa Rica or a variation on hell in Nicaragua becomes a pleasant and civilised trip in Panama.

Even the standard overcrowded Central American city bus is far less crowded in Panama than its counterparts elsewhere. And while fares are slightly higher than in most countries, they are actually better value because of the much higher comfort level. The seven-hour run from David to Panama City in air-conditioned comfort costs around $20, while a short hop works out at around $1 for 20km (12 miles).

The trip between David and Panama City is the premier route. There are buses approximately every hour each way from 7am to 7pm, plus additional overnight journeys. These buses serve intermediate points such as Aguadulce and Santiago, though joining en route is difficult at busy times.

Driving
It has been said that the Panamanians run their cars like they run their country, i.e. with scant respect for others or for authority. Only the brave drive after dark, particularly in the cities. Traffic signals take an age to change, so many drivers ignore them at night. The risk of being robbed is minimised by not stopping at red lights, but this increases the danger of collision.

Both inside and outside the Canal Area, many road signs were clearly intended for the US forces: signs are in English and show miles per hour.

Slow down for the roadside *Sección de Transit* posts, where guards like to take a good look at you. Along the Pan-American Highway road distances are given frequently.

All the main multi-national **car rental** companies are represented in Panama. Hertz, National, Budget and others have counters at the international airport.

Hitch-hiking
Almost wherever you are in Panama, the hitch-hiking is excellent. There is a large and friendly population of motorists, well-disposed to foreign visitors. The only places you are likely to have problems in hitching are in the environs of Panama City, where there are plenty of taxis which will assume (probably correctly) that you can afford to pay for them; on the Trans-Istmica, where everyone will wonder why you're not aboard one of the buses that rumble past every few minutes; and on the minor roads of Darién and Kuna Yala, through sheer lack of traffic.

The flyover option
There are lots of domestic flights in Panama, and they are relatively cheap. This is good news, whether you are just looking for a fast-track option to

speed you from the second city, David, to the capital in time to catch your flight home, or wishing to explore Darién or the San Blas Islands. The national network is based on the old US Air Force base of Albrook Field on the fringes of Panama City, officially Aeropuerto Marcos Gelabert. To book a flight, go direct to one of the airlines' offices rather than dealing through an agent; there have been cases of agencies telling travellers they are booked on flights which are already full.

The main domestic airline is Aeroperlas, whose name is a contraction (more or less) of Aerolineas Pacifico Atlantico. You can book on 315 7500 or via aeroperlas.com. The airline, has frequent flights from Albrook to Bahía Piña, Bocas del Toro, Colón, Contadora, Changuinola, Chitré, David, El Real (the airport for Yaviza in Darién, Garachiné, Jaqué, La Palma, Sambú and Santiago. Aerotaxi/Ansa (315 0275 or 0276 or 0299) is the specialist for San Blas, with daily services to most of the islands (and connecting services between them). Mapiex Aero (315 0888) has a limited number of flights to Bocas del Toro, Changuinola, and David. The planes used on many routes are so small that you, as well as your luggage, will be weighed, and charged extra if you are above average for either.

What's different about Panama?

It's an hour ahead of the rest of the region. Panama is the only Central American country to follow Eastern Standard Time, i.e. it is five hours, rather than six, behind GMT throughout the year. This makes good sense for so easterly a country – if it stayed in sync with Costa Rica and the rest of Central America, the sun would rise each day before 5am and set before 6pm. Try to avoid following the example of some travellers who have missed museum opening hours or, more seriously, flights through failing to put watches forward by one hour when entering Panama from the west.

Climate

Temperatures are high throughout the year, with little chance of escaping the heat due to Panama's relatively low elevation. Humidity is highest immediately before the wet season, which runs from March to December. April, say some, is a particularly bad month for crime.

You might think that Panama is the one Central American country where there is little difference in climate between the Atlantic and Pacific coasts, since only 80km (50 miles) separates them in places. However, rainfall in Colón is a soggy 3.5m (130 inches) each year, about twice that in Panama City on the Pacific side. Most of the rain falls in short, heavy showers.

Is Panama a good place to start or finish a trip along the Pan-American Highway?

Yes. Not only because of the many attractions of the place, but because of the superb links to the rest of the Americas. Panama City is easily the most accessible destination in Central America. Never mind that one Panamanian airline, Air Panama International, was grounded following allegations of smuggling cocaine to the USA: the main national airline, Copa, is one of Central America's better carriers, being closely aligned with Continental Airlines. Between them, they offer daily services to and from New York (Newark) and Houston, which are the main gateways for visitors from the UK.

American Airlines has flights from Chicago and Dallas, and is one of several airlines flying to and from Miami. There are half a dozen flights a day each way between Panama City and Miami, the city described as Panama's 'Valley of the Fallen' because of its popularity with exiles escaping corruption charges.

Within Latin America, there are flights at least daily to all the capital cities in this book. There are also links on several airlines to Bogotá, Barranquilla, Medellín and Cartagena in Colombia; Guayaquil and Quito (Ecuador); Lima (Peru); La Paz (Bolivia); Asunción (Paraguay); Buenos Aires (Argentina); Rio and Manaus (Brazil) and Santiago de Chile.

From Europe, the most direct route between the UK and Panama is via Bogotá in Colombia or a Caribbean city such as Havana, but transferring at a US airport will probably be cheaper. A round-trip from London to Panama City in low season should cost less than £500, even with all the taxes involved.

Who are the Panamanians?

The usual ethnic mingling did not take place so markedly in Panama, partly because the surviving Indian groups are geographically isolated. Numerically, most Panamanians are poor Hispanics, with a substantial mestizo community. The next largest group, making up some 20% of the total, comprises poor blacks, descendants of slaves from the British West Indies brought in to work on the railway and Canal. They maintain English as their first language and have their biggest concentration along the Atlantic coast, particularly around Colón. There are also several isolated communities of blacks in the Darién Gap.

Some Indians survived the ravages of successive invasions and disease, but they make up only about 5% of the population. The most numerous groups are the Cuna people of the semi-autonomous San Blas Territory, the Chocó people of Darién, and the Guaymí people of the western Panamanian provinces of Bocas del Toro and Chiriquí. Languages and cultures have survived surprisingly successfully. Further information on these indigenous peoples is included in the relevant geographical sections.

Particularly in Panama City and its environs, you will see some Asian Indians and Chinese. These people tend to be wealthier than most, although many merchants lost everything in the looting that followed the American invasion. There is a small proportion of very rich, mainly Hispanic Panamanians, who live in the posh suburbs of the capital under the protection of armed guards. People who live within the Canal Area are significantly better off than those outside. The 'Zonians', so-called because of their former status as citizens of the US-controlled Zone, are resented by some Panamanians.

The friendliness of the Panamanians is one of the joys of the country – while you can't expect everyone in Panama City or Colón to show instant pleasure that you have deigned to visit their country, elsewhere the relaxed and open nature of the local people is remarkable. This is particularly true in rural areas, where the Panamanians' light-heartedness is contagious and a constant source of entertainment. It is heart-warming to discover that people in one of the more corrupt societies in Central America can be so trusting of strangers. Many Panamanians will go out of their way to ensure your safe passage through the country; you can expect to be warned repeatedly about the number of thieves on the streets, and against venturing into a dangerous area.

What they eat

Panama City offers more varieties of fast food than the average American suburb, but there are plenty of good local restaurants serving regional specialities, both inside and outside the capital. The national dish is *sancocho*, a dubious-looking soup-cum-stew with meat, chicken and vegetables, which is served with rice. Also popular, and a good deal tastier is *ceviche*, marinated raw fish as found elsewhere in Central America. Other interesting dishes include *carimañola* (mashed cassava wrapped around spicy minced beef and fried); *ropa vieja* ('old clothes', consisting of shredded beef, green pepper and spices, usually served with rice and plantain); *arroz con coco y titi* (rice with coconut and small dried shrimp); and *buñuelos de viento* (fritters served with syrup). Unfortunately, these dishes are rarely served in restaurants. The ubiquitous rice and beans, together with Mexican dishes, from tamales to tacos, are more common. Cassava (*yuca*) crops up on menus in Panama more frequently than in any other Central American country. It comes fried in cubes, boiled, or fried in slices. It is a delicious accompaniment, having more flavour and texture than potato. Fried slices of plantain are common, and are usually called *tajadas*.

Unlike most Central American countries where chicken and beef are the only meats worth eating, in Panama pork (*lechón*) is also popular and can be surprisingly good. Seafood is good too, and Panama City has a healthy supply of fish restaurants. Indeed the capital is one of the world's best cities in which to eat out – the rich racial mix of its population is reflected in the variety of restaurants. Many restaurants are run by Chinese, but most offer both Chinese and locally-inspired food. For lunch look for *menus ejecutivos*, which are cheap set meals.

Delicious fresh fruit is as common as anywhere in Central America, although there is a fad for fruit imported from the USA. This is expensive, costing as much as a dollar for an apple. For the same amount you can buy perhaps a dozen locally-grown oranges.

What they drink

Hardened Central American travellers will be used to the choice of beer or rum. Beer is known as lager Alemaña. The most popular brands are Balboa, Atlas, Soberana, Panamá, and Lowenbrau. The latter is brewed locally, and is weaker but tastier than the others. There is little to distinguish between the brews, and you may opt for the one with the best advertising campaign: Balboa is held up as the beer *por hombres*, and the slogan for another brand is *Si no hay Panamá, no hay cerveza* – If there's no Panamá, there's no beer. For obscure historical reasons, beer is sold by the half Imperial pint (10 fluid ounces). Wine is more common than elsewhere and is also less expensive – the most common is Chilean Concha y Toro.

Like the rest of Central America, Panama is excellent soft drink territory. Particularly recommended is coconut milk, sold for 25c by street traders who wheel around supermarket trolleys loaded with a barrel of the stuff; a coconut perched on top indicates the trade. Other non-alcoholic drinks include the usual range of fresh fruit juices and bottled fizzy drinks. The coffee is of generally bad quality. Even in a cattle area like the Azuero peninsula where milk churns line the sides of the roads, evaporated milk is almost always used in coffee.

What they read, watch and listen to

Spanish-language newspapers include *Crítica Libre*, *La Prensa*, *Panamá América*, *La Estrella de Panamá* and *La República*. *La Prensa's* coverage of events is probably the best, and its *Revista* section is a good source of information on theatre, cinema and exhibition programmes in the capital. The most offensive paper is *El Policio*, a kind of Panamanian *Sunday Sport* in which sex, violence and grotesque reports of medical cases predominate. *El Siglo* is another sensationalist paper. For a good read at the weekend buy *El Panamá América Dominical*. This Sunday edition has a syndicated US problem page, here entitled *Querida Abby*, plus horoscopes by someone calling herself Frances Drake, and English soccer results.

You are more likely to spend an evening in your hotel room in front of the box than anywhere else in the region. This isn't because there's nothing worth going out for – it's because even the cheapest room may have a **television** which picks up a wide range of channels. See the daily newspapers for listings, but I bet you spend your time flipping between BBC World and CNN. Local commercial channels usually have a dominant theme – for example, Channel 2 covers sport, and Channel 11 is a predominantly educational station. English-language radio disappeared when the American Forces Network shut down, but there are plenty of stations playing British and American music.

What you should read

Getting to Know the General (Penguin, 1984) is Graham Greene's touching account of his friendship with President Omar Torrijos, and it paints a good picture of life and intrigue in Panama and the rest of Central America. A very different image is projected by P. J. O'Rourke, who devotes a chapter of *Holidays in Hell* (Picador, 1988) to a country he describes as 'a put-up job, sleazed into existence by Teddy Roosevelt so he'd have somewhere to put the Big Ditch'.

Given the degree of US involvement in Panama, it is understandable that much of the literature should be American. The most recent and complete tome on the country is *Divorcing the Dictator* by Frederick Kempe (Putnam, 1990). For the definitive story of the Canal, told with clarity, intelligence and engagement read *The Path Between the Seas* by David McCullough (Touchstone, 1977) – this account is widely available in Panama, though usually above its cover price of $16.99. The best work of recent fiction is John Le Carré's *The Tailor of Panama*.

How they enjoy themselves

For many visitors to Panama, it is only when they have satiated their curiosity to see the Canal, that they wonder if the country has any other worthwhile features. It most certainly has.

Unlike the other Central American nations, Panama has no pre-Columbian ruins. This is because the Indians in Panama used only perishable materials, such as timber and leaves, in their buildings. Artifacts, however, have survived, primarily pottery, stone-carvings and gold. Although many objects have found their way into foreign museums, you can see a small collection in the Museo

Festivals and holidays

Panama has more public holidays than its neighbours; these are shown below in bold. Note that much of the country closes down in Holy Week, and again in the first week of November. In addition to the national holidays, every town and village has its own festivals. Panama City stages its carnival each February.

1 January	New Year's Day
February/March	Mardi Gras festival, notably in Panama City and Las Tablas
March/April	Good Friday
July	Boat races, Taboga Island
15 August	Foundation of Panama City (holiday only in the capital)
September	Agricultural fair, Bocas del Toro
11 October	Anniversary of the 1968 Revolution
1 November	National Anthem Day
2 November	All Souls' Day
3 November	Independence from Colombia Day
4 November	National Flag Day
5 November	Independence Day (Colón only)
10 November	First Call of Independence
28 November	Independence from Spain
8 December	Immaculate Conception/Mothers' Day
25 December	Christmas Day

Nacional del Hombre Panameño in Panama City – when it finally re-opens, perhaps some time in 2003. Other provincial museums, such as the Museo de Herrera in Chitré and the Museo de Historia y Arte in David, have their own small collections.

Relics of the colonial era are much easier to find. Two of the finest examples are the old part of the capital, and Panamá Viejo (a short distance east of Panama City). In addition, there are some impressive old fortresses on the Atlantic coast around Colón, foremost among which is Portobelo. Some of the most interesting colonial towns are in the Azuero Peninsula west of Panama City. This area not only boasts a number of fine colonial churches, but is also famous for its traditions – the festivals in this part of the country are renowned for the costumes and dances. Dancing is a popular pastime throughout Panama – even the smallest village has a hall, usually referred to as *jardín*, where dances are held. The music played is akin to salsa.

What they spend

The Balboa is a sad little currency, because it is perhaps the only one in the world with no paper component. The Panamanian currency is tied to the American greenback so tightly that there are no notes for the Balboa; indeed, the country's constitution prohibits the circulation of any paper currency other than the US dollar. Adopting the courtesy title of the Balboa (written B/.), the dollar circulates freely and in poor condition, since most of the notes have been carried around in sweaty back pockets for years. The coins in circulation are a mixture of Panamanian 25c, 10c, 5c and 1c pieces, together with their US counterparts of quarters, dimes, nickels and pennies. The Panamanian and US versions are the same size, although the engraving differs. There is also a large 50c coin in Panama known as a peso (its US equivalent is uncommon). You can take in or out as much foreign or Panamanian currency as you like, but plainly the country's coins are of limited interest elsewhere.

Panama's adherence to parity with the US dollar is of considerable benefit to the traveller. The problems of convertibility which afflict every other currency in Central America, from the Costa Rican colón to the Guatemalan quetzal, are unknown in Panama. Furthermore, it is easy to obtain US dollars in exchange for travellers cheques, or on a credit card, which can be most useful for travels elsewhere in the region. To draw cash on a Visa card, go to any branch of Chase Manhattan Bank – the procedure is quick and easy. Banks open 8am to 1.30pm, Monday-Friday. Bureaux de change keep longer hours, but are rarely prepared to cash travellers' cheques without levying a heavy fee.

In the capital many hotels – apart from the most basic pensiones – accept payment by travellers cheque or credit card, but this cannot be taken for granted in more rural areas.

Unofficial dealers

There is a substantial market for other Central American currencies practised quite openly and legitimately in the banks and bureaux de change of Panama City. By comparing rates it should be possible to stock up with Costa Rica colones, Nicaraguan córdobas, etc, with little risk that you'll be swindled. Bear in mind the high crime levels in Panama City, and never carry much cash around with you.

Travelling budget

Prices are similar to those in Costa Rica, which means well above the average for Central America and Mexico. The difference is that your cash buys much better value: a $20 hotel room in Panama City is likely to be a more pleasant prospect than one in San José.

Once you get into the Darién or the San Blas islands, your spending is likely to decline because of the absence of anything much to buy. But if you decide to cross into Colombia – having first established that it is safe to do so – then you will need plentiful cash dollars to pay for guides, accommodation and supplies.

Anything worth buying?

There is a certain reassurance to shopping in Panama, at least as far as US citizens are concerned. The names of stores, like 7-Eleven, are familiar, and 24-hour supermarkets are not uncommon. The range of goods on offer also has a comfortable sameness and cheapness. A radio can be had for $9, a video cassette recorder for $20; the latter might be useful in certain circumstances, but not while travelling around Central America. If you are serious about buying electronic equipment, and unconcerned about your personal safety, visit the Free Zone in Colón where goods are imported and re-exported duty-free. I did my Christmas shopping there.

More enjoyable shopping can be done elsewhere. The most interesting souvenirs and presents are Panama hats or the traditional crafts of the indigenous Indians. Hats are sold in shops and markets in many Panamanian towns, and can be had for around $10 – more if you are looking for the highest quality. The most famous Indian craft is the *mola* made by the Cuna women of the San Blas islands. Mola is the name given to colourful reverse appliqué which is used to decorate their blouses. Molas are best bought on the islands, but they are also sold on the mainland, mostly in Panama City. They can be bought in shops and also from stalls – virtually the only place you find stalls designed to attract tourists are in the Canal Area.

Aborrotería is a common term used to refer to a corner shop.

Keeping in touch

Telephone

One legacy of American control is a highly efficient telecommunications network run by the INTEL organisation. The whole country has automatic dialling and there are no area codes. Rates between towns are reasonably cheap. In some areas, long-distance calls from payphones (which look like the standard US payphone) require the call to be intercepted by an operator. He or she, who may speak in English if pushed, explains how much to insert in 5c, 10c and 25c coins, up to a maximum of $2.10. After the first three minutes the operator will ask for further payment. Local calls from a payphone cost 5c for three minutes. To make the call, put in the money, dial the number. When the receiver is picked up at the other end the money will go through with a clink. Ten seconds before cutting you off, it will beep at you to insert more coins. Some shops have phones for public use, and charge 10c per local call. Gradually, though, modern payphones that take phone cards are being introduced. All manner of shops sell cards, from $5 up.

International calls can be made from payphones, but it may be easier to go to an INTEL office. A three-minute call (station-to-station) to the USA costs $7, to the UK $10, plus a tax of $1 per call. The person-to-person supplement is 30%. Rates for calls to the USA and Central America are reduced from 7pm to 7am, but those to Europe are not. Two directories cover the whole country – one for the capital and the Canal Area, the other for the Provincias, i.e. everywhere else. The blue section of the book is the Yellow Pages in English. *Useful Numbers*: correct time – 105; directory inquiries – 102; international operator – 106; USA direct dial – 109; national operator – 101;

Mail
The proliferation of courier company offices in Panama City is an indication of the lack of confidence in the Panamanian postal system. Any despatch which looks as though it might contain anything of value is likely to disappear. Postcards are relatively safe, therefore, and take about a week to reach addresses in North America or Europe. To send a postcard costs 35c to Europe, 25c to the USA and 40c to Australia. If your cards are ready to post, the clerk in the post office will often cancel the stamps in front of you. Post offices are open 7am-5.45pm Monday to Friday, 7am-4.45pm on Saturdays.

Internet
Panama City is better wired than any of the other capitals, but once you are out of the city it is tricky to find a connection – mainly because, with so few travellers visiting, there is simply not the demand for internet cafés. So they are thin on the ground, and expensive because of the lack of competition – $5 per hour is not unknown. So get out of the café and into the country.

The outdoors – how great?
In contrast to its neighbour to the north, Costa Rica, Panama has few national parks, and those there are are badly organised. The two most worth visiting are Barra Colorado island in the Canal, which is run by the Smithsonian Institute, and the Bastimentos Marine Park in Bocas del Toro province. There is good hiking – and even horse riding – to be done in the Chiriquí highlands north of David, but if you enjoy immersing yourself in the wilds the best place to do this is the Darién Gap, an area not for the faint-hearted.

Those who enjoy being outside but prefer to avoid jungle and swamp can repair to one of the country's beaches. There is a good selection on both the Atlantic and Pacific coasts, although the most accessible are those washed by the Gulf of Panama, west of the capital. These are also the most developed and are crowded at weekends. For more secluded and less spoilt beaches head north to Bocas del Toro province and the San Blas Islands. Along the same coast, but less remote are the beaches along the Caribbean east of Colón. The added attraction of the northern coast is the coral reef which provides opportunities for snorkelling, and diving, although the facilities for the latter are not always available. The most developed resorts also offer other watersports, from windsurfing to waterskiing.

Staying safe

'Human nature appears to have broken down entirely in Colón, where violent attacks in busy streets in broad daylight are increasingly common.' That was what I reported in 1991; thankfully, both the city at the northern end of the Canal in particular and the nation in general have become much safer in the last decade. Stories of earrings being ripped from earlobes in broad daylight, and of spectacles being stolen from the noses of short-sighted visitors have declined significantly.

The Foreign Office advice in April 2000 was appropriate: 'Beware of pickpockets on buses and at bus stations. Be alert for muggers in downtown areas, the old town (Casco Viejo) in Panama City and in the old Panama City ruins (Panamá Viejo). Occasional holdups occur in restaurants elsewhere. There have been recent muggings on the Panama to Colón road at the Madden Dam, where tourists often stop to take photographs.'

Another threat is posed by the highway robbers who periodically hold up buses on the Pan-American and Trans-Isthmian highways. Express buses are popular targets, especially those which run at night. Attacks of this nature do not happen every day, but nevertheless you are advised to travel during daylight wherever possible. Among those responsible for hold-ups in the past have been guerrillas of the Movimiento 20 del Diciembre (the day of the US invasion), more commonly referred to as M-20.

Whatever the precautions you take, there is still an unhealthy possibility that you will be robbed, above all in the cities. Travellers are particularly vulnerable when carrying large amounts of luggage, so treat yourself to more taxis than you might otherwise – even in Panama City they are surprisingly cheap. If you are travelling around the country before returning to the capital, leave as much as possible in one of the more secure hotels.

Plenty of private individuals carry handguns. Some enterprises in Panama City bear signs reading 'Do not enter this business with arms – sorry about the inconvenience'. The tourist board has successfully lobbied for tourist police, who mostly ride mountain bikes around the Casco Viejo in Panama City, and out at Panamá Viejo. During the course of researching this book, the only theft that any of us incurred was in Panama City while chatting to the tourist police. Neither they nor us noticed the villain stealing a book.

British visitors, staying longer than a month, are asked to register at the British Embassy in Panama City (tel 269 0866).

Health warning

In spring 2000, the authorities reported an epidemic of the pulmonary viral infection hantavirus, which is spread by rats, in the central provinces of Herrara and Los Santos. Several people died, and 'sanitary controls' were implemented which included spot checks on travellers. In addition, the number of cases of dengue fever was increasing rapidly.

Drugs

The tourist handout *Aquí Panamá* proclaims that 'Panama, thanks to its geographical position, has become a distribution centre for goods of the most prestigious firms'. These enterprises include the cocaine cartels of Colombia. Hoardings sponsored by the Municipality of Panama City and the shoe company Reebok implore *El jóven no consume drogas.* Yet the young in Panama certainly consume drugs with a vengeance. The crime scene in Colón reflects the extent of the drug scene.

Safe houses?

Elsewhere in the world you might choose your accommodation on criteria such as whether or not it has a bathroom, freedom from insects, internet access, or an en-suite jacuzzi. In Panama, however, the first criterion is security: thieves have no compunction about stealing from hotel rooms. Places recommended in this book are normally secure.

Such tourist trade as there was fell drastically after the American invasion, so rates in fancier hotels are low. Do not hesitate to ask for a further reduction at the front desk; hoteliers in Panama are often prepared to negotiate. One more warning: if you are down to your last few dollars, beware of the 10% tax that is sometimes added to quoted rates.

From the frontier to the capital

The Pan-American Highway east from the Costa Rican border at Paso Canoas runs 592km (370 miles) to Panama City. The road is in good condition and traverses some beautiful country. As you hurtle along the Pan-American, many of the townscapes seem uninspiring and unattractive. The heart of these towns or villages, however, almost always lies off the main road, so first impressions are often wrong.

Panama begins where Costa Rica ends, amid extravagant volcanic terrain. If you arrive from Costa Rica on foot, you will probably be hustled on to a local bus going as far as David, 53km (37 miles) east of Paso Canoas. Should you really want to head straight for Panama City, you can take one of these and change at David for the hourly service to the capital – but look first to see if one of the handful of direct buses is at the frontiers.

Appropriately named Western visitors delight in being photographed in front of signs announcing the nation's second city, **David**. Pronounced Da-*veed*, it is an atmospheric introduction to provincial Panama – Wild West gone to seed. It is also a good base for trips into the majestic mountains. An hour uphill from David nestles Boquete, a cool, quiet, once-elegant resort which offers gentle strolls around town and rugged hikes to volcanic summits.

At **Concepción**, 15 miles (24km) west of David, another road heads off north into the highlands. Nineteen miles (30km) along it, and almost two hours by bus from David, is Hato del Volcán, usually referred to simply as **Volcán**. The village itself is unremarkable, though it is surprisingly developed and has plenty of eateries (including two pizzerias), and even a couple of car hire places. The locals rent out horses too.

From Volcán a good road leads to Volcán National Park where quetzals are sometimes spotted, and to the northeast a road leads through the Chiriquí Viejo valley to **Cerro Punta**, a village over 6,600 feet (2,000m) above sea level. This is a good base from which to explore the area and to walk, although there is less accommodation than in Volcán; try the Pensión Eterna Primavera. One of the best walks from Cerro Punta follows a trail down to Boquete: while doing this from Boquete would mean walking almost entirely uphill, from Cerro Punta it is an excellent and pleasurable hike – allow about seven hours. The track is clearly marked for the most part, but take plenty of food, tough footwear and a map; do not go alone.

Buses from David serve both Volcán and Cerro Punta, and leave hourly. All buses go via Concepción ($1 and half an hour from David) which is also served by minibuses every 10 minutes. Through buses usually pause for at least 15 minutes in the Parque Central before heading up into the highlands. There are also buses to Cerro Punta originating from Volcán.

The City of David

The third largest city in Panama after the capital and Colón. David, population 50,000, is the capital of Chiriquí province. It is the first large city as you enter Panama from Costa Rica, and is the main jumping-off point for the Chiriquí highlands. Modern developments have masked much of its colonial past, and even the Parque Central (also known as Parque Cervantes) lacks the atmosphere of most Panamanian squares – the church is also one of the country's least inspiring. The Museo de Historia y de Arte, however, is in a fine building and contains a varied collection of archaeological and ethnographical displays. The museum is on Avenida 8 Este and Calle Aristides Romero, and opens 8am-5pm, Tuesday to Saturday. David's local festival is held on 19 March.

The **bus station** in David is on the eastern edge of town. It boasts something few other stations have – a left-luggage office, located at the middle of the station. Buses (marked Frontera) leave David every 15 minutes or so from 6am to 5pm for the Costa Rican frontier at El Progreso/Paso Canoas, 33 miles (53km) west. You can **fly** onwards to Panama City – or take a side trip to the Bocas del Toro – from the diminutive airport 5km (3 miles) out of town.

The Pan-American bypasses David to the north. Within the city, calles run

The hill station

Twenty-four miles (38km) north of David is **Boquete**. The long, straight road from David climbs slowly and steadily, before a sudden descent into Boquete, nestling among forested mountains. The town itself can hardly be described as attractive, but the setting is perfect, and the climate cool – bring a jumper for the evenings. Like El Valle in Coclé province, Boquete is a place Panamanians like to escape to. It is often described as a resort, but is hardly thronging with visitors.

The countryside around Boquete is inviting to the keen walker. There are a few trails – to make the most of these you should get a topographical map of the area from the IGN in Panama City – plus mountain streams and waterfalls which are good for swimming. Tourist brochures claim there are jaguar and puma in the area, adding that these creatures are 'excellent game for hunting' – no wonder Panama's national parks lack a sense of mission. During the main tourist season you can sometimes hire horses.

It is possible to hike up Volcán de Chiriquí, which towers over Boquete and provides magnificent views. To walk up the extinct Volcán Barú, the highest peak in the country at 3,474m, is less easy. There is a road right to the top, but only four-wheel drive vehicles can cope with the final stretch. The total distance to be covered is around 12 miles (20km), and it is a long, hard climb. To find the right road, walk a few hundred yards north from the Parque Central in Boquete, past the mock policeman and San Juan Bautista church. On the left is a street with INTEL and post offices – follow this as it winds up into the hills. A few buses serve the small communities on the slopes – and there is occasionally hitchable traffic – so you may not have to walk the entire way. It is pleasant to walk up this road even if you don't intend going all the way up – there are wonderful views and many Indians live on the slopes and work on the coffee and orange plantations.

Buses to Boquete from David leave every half hour and take about an hour. The town is divided into Bajo Boquete and Alto Boquete – the former consists of a few houses scattered along the road before you descend into Boquete proper. The journey back to David is downhill all the way and takes just 40 minutes. The last bus down leaves at 6.45pm. Cyclists can take bikes on the bus uphill, and freewheel back down to David. On a clear day the views of the Pacific and miscellaneous small volcanoes are splendid.

Boquete's few **hotels** are expensive. The flashiest place in town is the Panamonte Hotel (tel: 720-1327)which boasts Greta Garbo and Richard Nixon as former guests. Less smart but still fairly expensive is the Hotel Fundadores (tel: 720-1298), opposite the Texaco station on the approach to Boquete. There are also a couple of pensiones, including the Virginia (tel: 720-1260) and the Marilos (tel: 720-1380), and it is possible to camp.

Most **restaurants** and comedores are on the Parque Central, and offer simple fare. Refresquería El Tunel serves a hearty breakfast.

east-west; Calle Central, which actually runs a block south of the Parque Central, is the dividing line – above it, streets are Calle A Norte, Calle B Norte etc, while below it the letter is suffixed Sur. Avenidas go north-south and are numbered with reference to Avenida Central which is three blocks west of the main square. To complicate matters, the principal avenidas have names as well as numbers – Avenida 2 Este is known as Avenida Cincuentenario, 3 Este as Bolívar, and 4 Este most confusingly of all as 3 de Noviembre. In this section only numbers are used.

The best-value **hotel** in David is the Iris in the Parque Central, which is comfortable and clean and worth the $20 a double room costs. Cheaper places are found on Avenida 5 Este, which runs a block east of the main square. Less convenient and noisy are the hotels on the Pan-American Highway.

For **breakfast** try the Marisol on Avenida 4 Este at Calle Central. None of the restaurants and cafés around the Parque Central is particularly inviting and some, like the 24-hour Cantina Parque on Calle A Norte between the main square and Avenida 5 Este, are obviously men-only. Try a good steak house, Los Churrascos, a block from the Parque Central at Calle A Norte and Avenida 3 Este. The cheapest meals can be had around the bus station and in the market, which is at the northern end of Avenida 3 Este.

The **tourist office** is on Avenida 4 Este between the main square and Calle Central. The entrance is adjacent to the shop on the corner of the square – go upstairs and the office is on the right at the end of the corridor. Citibank is on the northwest corner of Parque Central.

The Highway is not exactly riveting on the long haul into Panama City, with most places of interest being north or south of the main road. **Santiago**, an old town with a population of about 30,000, lies on the Pan-American Highway about 40km (25 miles) west of Divisa. It is the capital of Veraguas province, a grain-growing area which is exceedingly hot in summer. North of Santiago on the road to Santa Fé, is San Francisco, which has a fine colonial church. Another town with a fine church is La Mesa, just south of the Highway west of Santiago. Continuing west you pass the turning for **Las Lajas**. The town itself is of little interest, but within walking or taxi distance are some pleasant beaches. Las Lajas is in **Chiriquí** province which is arguably the most attractive in the country, and the most popular inland holiday region for Panamanians.

Chiriquí is an Indian word meaning Valley of the Moon. The province consists largely of coastal plain, but inland are the dramatic highlands of the *Cordillera Central*, which includes a number of volcanoes. The province is agriculturally prosperous; cattle-rearing is widespread in the lowlands, and fruit and vegetable plantations thrive on the rich volcanic soil. The province has been described as the 'Switzerland of Central America'. Those who have been to Honduras, which also claims the appellation of 'little Switzerland of Central America, may be forgiven for wondering whether they are actually touring Central America or the Alps. The Panamanian province probably lays better claim to the title owing to the Swiss chalet-style architecture found in the region. This stems from the large foreign community in the Chiriquí highlands, many of whom are Swiss, German and Slovenian. Such immigration is a comparatively recent development – during the Conquest, the Spanish chose to settle in the lowlands, and only at the start of the 20th century did people begin to make their homes up in the hills. As a result, pockets of indigenous people have survived in Chiriquí. These are the Guaymí Indians, who are more extrovert than most of the indigenous peoples of Central America. The women are highly visible in their long, brightly-coloured dresses, while the men wear western-style clothes. You are most likely to see the Guaymí if you venture up into the mountains.

The local sport, seldom played these days, is *balsería*, a banal but brutal team game which involves nothing more complex than hurling a boomerang-shaped piece of balsa wood at the opponents' shins.

An equally interesting detour is to head south from the Pan-American Highway towards the **Azuero peninsula**. Take the turn to Ocú, a small town about 30 minutes south of the Pan-American, and continue on through the villages of Las Minas and Pesé to La Arena and onwards to Chitré. The journey takes you through stunning hill country, and is one of the most enjoyable trips in Panama. These small rural communities have no facilities for visitors, but the people are extraordinarily friendly and it is not difficult to find someone to put you up in Pesé or Las Minas.

The Azuero Peninsula is a coffee-growing and cattle-rearing region divided into the Herrera and Los Santos provinces. It is a magical area with beautiful vistas and rural images which seem to have been taken straight out of a Western movie. Panamanian traditions, such as they are, are strongest in these central lowlands; much folklore and many crafts – including the Panama hat – originated hereabouts. Several towns on the peninsula retain interesting vestiges of their colonial past, and the local festivals are among the most colourful in the country: at Chitré (February), Los Santos (April), Las Tablas (Lent) and Ocú (January). The eastern side of the peninsula is the most accessible, and at the southern end are some fine unspoilt beaches.

Unlike other slow, quiet towns on the peninsula, **Chitré** – the capital of Herrera province – is a bustling place. It may not have the charm of Los Santos, but it is a lively and friendly town. From a traveller's point of view, Chitré has the best facilities on the peninsula. Most buses serving the area originate from here.

The church is not spectacular – the interior, with its mahogany ceiling and altarpiece, feels rather oppressive. It does, however, reflect the prosperity of Chitré, illustrated elsewhere by the number of shops, hotels and airline offices. Chitré's one formal attraction is the Museo de Herrera, housed in a distinctive blue house on the corner of Parque La Bandera. It is open 8.30am-noon and 1pm-4pm Tuesday to Saturday, and 9am-noon on Sundays. Downstairs there are archaeological exhibits, including some wonderful ceramics and a replica of the grave of an Indian tribal leader, while upstairs the focus is on ethnography – this is a good place to spend an hour finding out about the traditional costumes and crafts of Herrera. The museum's many photographs of the town's main festival, held each October 19, highlight the traditional Danza de los Diabólicos.

The town's market is on the south side of the Parque Central. Here and on other streets people sell Panama hats – expect to pay $15-$20 for one of the finer ones. For more fragile excess baggage walk to the village of La Arena, a short distance north of Chitré, where some of the locals make plain but interesting pottery.

Hotel Rex (tel. 996-6660) on the Parque Central charges $20-$24 and takes credit cards. For a cheaper option try the Pensión Central in Avenida Herrera (tel: 996-0059), on the right as you walk east from the church. It is shabby and has double rooms for $10.

Just south of Chitré, almost contiguous to it, is **Los Santos**. Two more different places would be hard to find. Los Santos is an enchanting, sleepy town, with a population of around 15,000. Horses and bicycles seem to outnumber the cars, and the local buses are extraordinarily old-fashioned. Los Santos is not somewhere to visit if you enjoy boundless activity – but in this lies its appeal. No other town gives so sweet a taste of life in rural Panama.

The Parque Central is dominated by the church of Augustinas and Anastasias, an impressive 18th-century structure which is surprisingly large for so small a town. The interior is made entirely of wood, and contains some interesting carving. Many of the statues date from the 18th-century, and there is some silverware from the same period. To the left of the main altar is the seated figure of St Peter – his arms move (but not of their own volition). Behind him is a wooden eagle, made during the colonial period, which has a chest that opens. Above the main church door hangs a huge and rather ragged paper flower that plays an important role during the town's annual festival in April. Following a procession through the streets everyone gathers outside the church, where a string attached to this huge flower is pulled releasing doves hidden among its petals.

Lodgings are scarce in Los Santos. Virtually the only option is the large Hotel La Villa (tel: 996-9321 or 996-4845) which has a swimming pool and charges $29 for a double room. Midway between Chitré and Los Santos is the Hotel Hong Kong, but it is an uninspiring place. For budget rooms, stay in Chitré instead.

Similarly, *comedores* are rare, and you will probably have to be content with the local bars. Try either Bar La Cita (a slightly rough-looking place) or the more sedate, blue-painted refresquería-cum-bookshop opposite. Both are southeast of the Parque Central on Avenida 10 de Noviembre.

Los Santos is not the capital of the province which bears its name. This honour is held by the town of **Las Tablas**, 15 miles (27km) southeast. Beyond Las Tablas a rough road winds down to Pedasí at the tip of the peninsula. This pleasant colonial town is another highlight of the Azuero peninsula. It is served by irregular colectivos from Las Tablas. Pedasí boasts a fine beach which is almost always deserted, and there is a small bird sanctuary nearby; both are about 30 minutes walk from the centre. There is one pensión in Pedasí; accommodation is also available at Las Tablas, but this is not such a pleasant town.

To return to Chitré along a different route, follow the inland road via Tonosí, but be warned that the road is abysmal and public transport virtually non-existent. If you don't want to venture as far as Pedasí, there are plenty of beaches east of Chitré and Los Santos. Wherever you choose to swim, beware of swimming too far out because of the risk of sharks.

Back on the Highway, **Natá** is a small, historic town 18km (11 miles) west of Penonomé, and much more interesting than most places actually on the main road. It has a celebrated church built in 1522, and other fine buildings dating from the Spanish era. The Church of Santiago Apostol is claimed to be the oldest in Latin America still used for worship. Notice the Indian faces that have been given to the statues of Christian saints. In the small garden in front of the church is a stone wheel which was found in hills nearby and dates from pre-Columbian times.

Penonomé, population 35,000, is the capital of Coclé province and is not a beautiful town. Penonomé was founded in pre-Columbian times, but a volcanic eruption destroyed this settlement – archaeological relics can be seen in the Museo Conte. There are a few hotels, including affordable ones near the Parque Central, and a good natural swimming pool in the river just north of town.

After Penonomé, the road loops down to run along the coast. There are miles of beaches along this stretch, most of them easily accessible from the Highway. Being within easy reach of Panama City, they are popular, and the accommodation tends to be expensive. The first you reach is Santa Clara, about two hours from Panama City, which has the best sand. Consequently, there are plenty of hotels, and most of them are expensive. Among the cheapest are Cabañas Las Sirenas (tel: 232-5841) and Cabañas Vista Bella (tel: 232-5848); Hospedaje Las Sirenas is reasonable.

The next along, Río Mar, has good surfing. **San Carlos**, 97km (59 miles) west of Panama City, is the main town along this stretch of coast as well as a beach resort. But better prospects can be found beyond it, at Playa Coronado (the most developed), Nueva Gorgona (good surfing) and, at the end of a long spit of land that curls around towards Taboga island, Punta Chame.

The volcano that swallowed a town

In the hills of Coclé province, 27km (15 miles) north of San Carlos, is the small and remarkable town of El Valle – located in the huge crater of an extinct volcano, over 800m (2,500) feet above sea level. Its cool climate and medicinal spas make it a popular resort during the summer; it is especially crowded on Sundays when the market takes place. The mountain scenery and rainforest around El Valle is impressive. The area is renowned for the golden frogs (found also in the Cerro Campana National Park), and trees with virtually square trunks. There is also scope for hiking in the surrounding hills, and La India Dormida (The Sleeping Indian) is a popular mountain to climb.

Buses to El Valle run every hour or so from San Carlos. El Valle is worth staying in simply to escape the heat of the lowlands, and it is a good base for day trips to the coast. Cheap accommodation is available at a couple of pensiones; try Cabañas de Potosí (tel: 983-6181).

At Arraján, the last town before you reach the capital, there is a 20km (12 mile) stretch of freeway through rolling hills punctuated with ranks of prefabricated houses. Most buses take the old Pan-American in the hope of picking up extra passengers. The two highways re-unite before the Bridge of the Americas, which leaps across the entrance to the Canal.

Walking the Canal

If you are not burdened by too much luggage, do your utmost to persuade the bus driver to drop you off at the western side of the Puente de las Américas, a graceful structure built in 1962. If you manage to cross through the four-lane, fast-moving traffic, you will find yourself at a look-out point which gives superb views of the Canal, stretching north into the mist rising from the jungle.

Now start walking. This is not going to be an entirely pleasant experience, but it is one that will reward the effort. Steel yourself for a multiple assault on your ears (from the noise of trucks and buses growling and rumbling across the bridge); your nose (from the fumes they emit); and your nerves, as you feel increasingly trapped between the tidal wave of traffic and the mesh fencing which is all that stands between you and a 100m (330ft) plunge into the Pacific. One local whispered that its purpose was to stop homicides, not suicides.

The original name of the bridge that links the Americas was Thatcher Ferry Bridge (no connection with the former British Prime Minister), after the shuttle boat service that used to operate across the divide. Now, the elegant steel arch provides the perfect framing for the Canal. From the very centre, you can observe the choreography of the tiny tugs, ungainly freighters and prim cruise ships as they jostle for position to make the journey between oceans.

When you reach the Panama City side, your problems are only just beginning. You are on the wrong side of the freeway, and even if you manage to dodge the juggernauts and make it to the other (southern) side, there is virtually no chance of persuading anything to stop. Instead, slide down the slip road to a suburban street where, sooner or later, a taxi will arrive and hustle you into the cauldron of humanity that is Panama City.

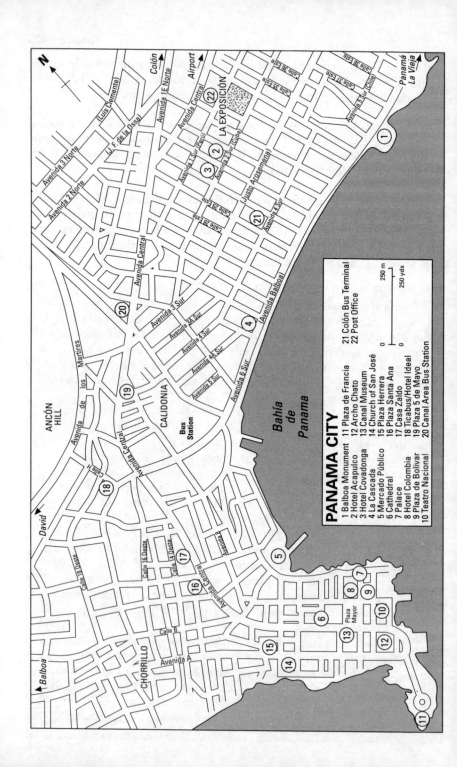

PANAMA CITY

1 Balboa Monument
2 Hotel Acapulco
3 Hotel Covadonga
4 La Cascada
5 Mercado Público
6 Cathedral
7 Palace
8 Hotel Colombia
9 Plaza de Bolivar
10 Teatro Nacional
11 Plaza de Francia
12 Archo Chato
13 Canal Museum
14 Church of San José
15 Plaza Herrera
16 Plaza Santa Ana
17 Casa Zaldo
18 Ticabus/Hotel Ideal
19 Plaza 5 de Mayo
20 Canal Area Bus Station
21 Colón Bus Terminal
22 Post Office

Panama – the ultimate city of the Americas

A silent, moustachioed figure gazes out from a balcony of the Hotel Colonial, gazing down on a plaza that has seen a million better days. Across the broad arc of the bay around which Panama City curls so exquisitely, multi-billion-dollar deals are being sealed behind the smoked glass of a mini-Manhattan skyscraper.

The only Central American capital on the Pacific, Panama City is fast, exuberant and contrary. It has everything from extravagant modern architecture to some of the region's worst slums, and from exceptional colonial churches to shopping streets exuding crass commercialism. In the old city centre you can be just yards away from barracks destroyed in the 1989 invasion, yet protected by an atmosphere of gentler decay.It is uniquely cosmopolitan, lying at one mouth of the Canal which links the world's greatest oceans; the mixture of races in Panama City is almost unequalled.

The original Panama City was founded in 1519 a few miles east of the modern capital, as a storage place for gold being shipped from Peru to Spain. Panamá Viejo, as it is now known, became a starting point for expeditions to South America. The town prospered, and for over a century treasure flowed along the Camino Real across the isthmus. The lure of gold was the city's downfall; the swashbuckling Welsh pirate, Henry Morgan, attacked and burned the city in 1671. It is said that he needed 200 mules to carry off the booty. The ruins of Panamá Viejo can still be seen, though suburbia is rapidly encroaching upon them.

Two years after Morgan's attack, the survivors founded Panama City on its present site. The setting is admirable, backed by hills and overlooking the Pacific; it is the only Central American capital on an ocean. The charms of the old quarter are a surprise to most visitors, but some people find the capital a stifling place – it is hot, there are few open spaces, and overcrowding is a serious problem. Nevertheless, wandering through the streets during the day is not an unpleasant experience. Indeed it is hard to picture the invasion of US troops in December 1989, launched to capture General Noriega. The citizens remember the attack and the thousands who died only too clearly, however. The worst hit area was El Chorrillo, the poorest district in Panama City. It has now been bulldozed, leaving areas of wasteland reminiscent of those found in Managua.

City essentials

Getting your bearings

The layout of the capital is most easily understood if you consider the far end first. The main road into Panama City from the northeast passes straggling clusters of poor housing that are the hallmark of most Third World suburbs. It becomes the Vía España, the capital's main street, lined with banks, shopping centres and smart hotels. Further west, the road becomes Avenida Central.

This continues south past the affluent area of Bella Vista, and then right into the heart of the old city; this is known as Casco Viejo to distinguish it from Panamá Viejo, the original settlement. It passes two important squares on the way – Plaza 5 de Mayo and Plaza Santa Ana – and is the city's principal shopping street. Another busy street is Avenida de los Mártires (formerly 4 de Julio and sometimes called Avenida Tivoli), which lies west of Avenida Central and connects Panama City to the Canal Area.

Five blocks east of Avenida Central, Avenida Balboa runs along the seafront. Avenida Balboa runs northeast into Vía Paitilla from which roads branch into Punta Paitilla at the other end of Panama Bay from Casco Viejo. Paitilla is another flashy residential area with tower blocks that are something of an eyesore.

The best **map** of the city is available from the Instituto Geográfico Nacional Tommy Guardia (IGNTG) on Vía Simón Bolívar, in the university district. It is open 8.30am-4pm Monday to Friday. The IGN is worth visiting to get all kinds of maps. The **tourist office**, out of town at the Atlapa Convention Center, gives out a plan of the city which is fairly reliable and includes maps of David and Colón. If you can't be bothered to go there, you could try the **tourist booth** in the middle of Avenida Central; if it isn't open. or doesn't have a map, you can nip in and buy one at Casa Zaldo, on Avenida Central just north of Plaza Santa Ana.

No map of Panama City corresponds 100% to reality, largely because street names are constantly being changed. Since the locals continue to use the old names, you are best off asking around as much as possible. In the middle part of the city, some avenidas have numbers as well as names:

Avenida 1 Norte – José Espinar

Avenida 2 Norte – J.F. de la Ossa

Avenida 3 Norte – Luís F. Clement

Avenida 1 Sur – Perú

Avenida 2 Sur – Cuba

Avenida 3 Sur – Justo Arosemena

Avenida 4 Sur – Méjico

Avenida 5 Sur – Chile

Avenida 6 Sur – Balboa

North of Calle 45 things begin to go badly wrong. Numbered avenues take on entirely new names, with Avenida 4 Sur becoming Nicanor de Obarrio and Avenida 6 Sur turning into Vía Brasil. To confuse matters further, some streets in the old quarter are being named rather than numbered, furthermore with different names on either side of Avenida Central. These have not caught on with the local people, but are used on street signs, adding to the chaos.

Arrival and departure

Omar Torrijos international **airport** is at Tocumen, 27km (17 miles) out on the Highway east of the capital. It is one of the most modern in the region and boasts something the others don't – a 24-hour left-luggage office. The tourist information desk, however, is seldom staffed. You will be steered towards a cab, costing around $20, for the half-hour run into town. A much cheaper alternative is to get the bus. About 200m from the airport, along the main highway, is a stop where buses to the centre of town pass every 15 or 20 minutes. These buses (marked Tocumen/El Chorrillo) take about an hour to reach the centre. Unless you have other, more specific plans, Plaza 5 de Mayo is a good place to get off. Panama City's **domestic airport** is the old US base at Albrook Field, officially known as Marcos Gelabert, just north of the city and a $3 cab ride away.

Bus passengers who have come straight through from Costa Rica or Nicaragua are dropped at the Ticabus terminal office on 17 Calle Oeste 15-55, beneath the Hotel Ideal. Buses from here to Managua via San José leave at 7am on Monday, Wednesday and Friday, and services only as far as San José depart at 11am on Monday, Tuesday, Thursday and Saturday. Journey times are 14 hours to San José and 24 hours to Managua, without allowing for delays at border posts.

Buses to the Canal Area, including Balboa, Paraíso and Miraflores, leave from the Canal Area bus station. This is behind Plaza 5 de Mayo on Avenida Central at Calle 24 Oeste, adjacent to Parque 9 de Enero.

Buses west along the Pan-American Highway to David are operated by Transportes Panama-David and depart from Calle 17 Este and Avenida Balboa; this is adjacent to, but fenced off from, the main Avenida B bus terminal. For the express overnight service, book a ticket in advance if possible.

Getting around

Small **buses** (known as chivas, meaning goats) run along all the major streets. Pay the fare of 10c or 20c when you exit. The city buses, as in most capitals, are not known for their security, so be watchful. Officially licensed **taxis** have yellow number plates with red characters, and have their numbers painted on the front doors. In theory taxis charge by the zone, which should mean that the fare from one point in the city to another is fixed. For example, one person making a short journey within a single zone should pay 75c while five people crossing all five zones pay $3. Many taxi drivers disregard the official tariffs, and charge foreigners about 50% more than the fare should be. Always establish the fare in advance, but don't expect to gain much from haggling.

If you want to go on an extended trip out of town, agree on an hourly rate – e.g. $10 for the first hour, $5 for each subsequent hour. For long-distance journeys there are set tariffs, which are high (e.g. $20 for 30 miles).

Colonic irritation

The Panama Railway was originally part of the fastest route from the East to the West Coast of the USA. Travellers willingly paid $25 for a two-hour journey from Colón to Panama City, since it saved several weeks of sailing around Cape Horn. Before passenger trains stopped running in the aftermath of the 1989 invasion, the fare had fallen to $2. The 90-minute journey provided the best view of the Canal for those not travelling by ship. Before December 1989 there were departures four times a day, and for a time after that it seemed likely that the line would be reactivated. But the line fell into disrepair, the rolling stock rusted for lack of rolling, and the station at each end of the line has now been converted into a souvenir stand.

A room

A large chunk of this book was written in room 449 of the **Hotel Covadonga**, which costs $20 single/$30 double. Like most of the places in that area, it is excellent value with good, friendly staff. Best of all, it has a swimming pool on the roof, open 24 hours.

Of the alternatives, the **Hotel California** (Via España and Calle 43, tel 263 7844) is at the lower end of the expensive market, with double rooms, providing hot water and a TV, for $28, triple for $33. The proprietor has a good reputation and is concerned for his guests' welfare. On the ground floor is a café which is pleasant and well-frequented. More central is the **Acapulco** (Calle 30 Este between Avenidas 1 and 2 Sur, 225 3832) where a double room with bathroom, air-conditioning and TV costs $26. The Benidorm restaurant, which forms part of the building, is disappointing. If the Acapulco is full or too pricey, a few blocks east is **Pensión América** (Avenida 3 Sur and Calle 33, tel 225 1140) with double rooms for $16.50, singles for $14.30. Also nearby is **Pensión Colón** (Avenida 1 Sur and Calle 30, tel 225 5888), but rooms tend to be noisy.

The best place to stay for its position is the **Hotel Colonial** (tel 222 9311) on Plaza de Bolívar, in the old quarter. Do not expect luxury for your $11 (double) or $8 (single), but the surroundings are magnificent; ask for a room overlooking the square. Along the same lines is, or rather was, the **Hotel Central** (tel 262 8044) in the Plaza Mayor. A couple of years ago rooms were going at $8 for a double, but a ritzy refurbishment means you are unlikely to get much change out of $100 these days.

If proximity to the Ticabus terminal is important, stay at the **Hotel Ideal** (Calle 17 Este; tel 262 2400) which merges imperceptibly with the bus station. This huge complex includes a swimming pool, cafeteria, shops, laundry and barbers. A double room costs $20, with reductions for Ticabus passengers. The tight security reflects the nature of the neighbourhood – at night the doors are heavily padlocked, not only at the entrance but also between reception and bedrooms.

A meal

Apart from the plethora of fast food joints that afflict most Central American capitals, the restaurants in Panama City reflect the cosmopolitan nature of the capital.

For undiluted Panamanian excess go to the wonderfully extravagant – but strangely inexpensive – **La Cascada** on the seafront at Avenida 6 Sur (Cuba) and Calle 25. It is an open-air seafood restaurant with wacky décor. Ornamental fish compete for space in a labyrinth of tanks which are crossed by quaint little bridges. The 15-page menu is a daunting prospect, but only part of it is devoted to the meals on offer – the rest is self-congratulatory but amusing waffle. Servings are huge; however tempting the starters and side dishes may be, do not order any if you want any hope of finishing your meal. The ambience and experience is certainly more memorable than the meal, but nevertheless La Cascada is lively and not to be missed. Its sister restaurant is **La Casa de las Costillitas**, specialising in ribs and steak, on Calle Argentina at Avenida 1B.

Heading further away from the centre you hit an area known as El Cangrejo which has a good selection of restaurants, most of them expensive. The establishments on Vía Argentina are typical of the district: **El Trapiche**, which serves Panamanian food, is one of the more interesting. For a more affordable meal go to **Cubares** (tel 264 8905), a Cuban restaurant on the corner of Calle 52 and Vía España. It is dimly-lit, and the dance floor and TV screens appear to be the main attractions. Nevertheless the music is good and the food a great deal better than you would get in a restaurant in Cuba. Try a mojito (a cocktail of rum, mint and lime) during the happy hour from 5pm-7pm. For ice cream which is as good as the excellent stuff made in Cuba, go to **La Inmaculada** parlour on Avenida 3 Sur between Calles 37 and 38.

The cafeteria in the **Hotel Ideal** at Calle 17 Este (tel 262 2400) is one of the cheapest places in town, and is a good place to eat at any time of day. Expect to pay $8-$10 for a whole meal. Other cheap and cheerful places include the Angelica María Café in the Plaza Mayor where you can get a hearty breakfast of refrescos, coffee, fried cassava, eggs and steak. Alternatively go to the **Mercado Público** on Avenida Alfaro – levels of sanitation may leave a little to be desired but meals are cheap.

If you feel hungry at odd hours, the **Hotel Soloy** (Avenida 1 Sur and Calle 30) has an all-night coffee shop with a 'midnight special' menu. The same hotel has a 'panoramic' bar on the top floor, but the view from inside is obscured by condensation from the air-conditioning; slip outside for a much better view of the city. Nearby is an absolutely typical Panamanian bar, a fairly seedy pick-up joint but entertaining for an early evening beer and ceviche or late-night rum: it is **Le Petit Montmartre**, on Calle 26 Oeste close to Avenida Central. Women are not allowed in the **Salón Tocumen**, an even more dubious dive along the street at Avenida Central and Calle 24.

The best short walk in Panama

The body of Panama City may now be slumped across a vast area, but the soul is still alive and well and living in the **Casco Viejo**, or the old town, which occupies the spur of land at the southern end of the bay. The mix of colonial Spanish and 19th-century French influences is reminiscent of New Orleans, with splashes of Havana and Cartagena thrown in. The cobbled streets and shady squares are lined by white-washed houses with wrought-iron balconies and fine colonial churches. It houses the most important government offices, and cultural buildings. Yet much of it is a complete slum, with crumbling structures and an air of neglect.

Some restoration work has been carried out, recognising that this area is the capital's main tourist attraction, and no doubt in a few years it will be replenished to something like its former glories. Perhaps even some of the wealthy people who used to live here but moved away to the smart suburbs will return if the inner-city regeneration continues. The old quarter is one of the outstanding architectural sights of Central America, and is in stark contrast to the concrete blocks which characterise the rest of the capital.

Begin your exploration on Avenida Alfaro (also known as Avenida Norte), a street bustling with activity as fishermen try to sell their catches. Vultures circle around the fishing boats competing for scraps or lurk menacingly around the rubbish dumps. The **Mercado Público** is a two-storey affair with fish and meat on sale downstairs, fruit and vegetables upstairs; around the market are plenty of cheap places to eat or drink. For something more civilised, continue east, and at the junction, turn right, head up the hill and bear left. You should arrive at the new and sophisticated Café Morales.

Further along Avenida Alfaro you can begin to get a taste of the fine colonial houses typical of Casco Viejo. Between 6 and 5 Calles is the presidential palace; it is usually referred to as the **Palacio de las Garzas**, or Palace of Herons, after a couple of herons that stalk around the courtyard. This fine building was once the residence of the Spanish Governors during the colonial period, and is the official home of the Panamanian presidents. The palace, which shows Moorish influences, was begun in 1673, although alterations and restoration disguise its age. You may not be able to get very close to the palace if the president is in residence. If you are diverted around the 'exclusion zone', go inland (south) on Calle 8 to see the poverty so close to the presidential palace, and turn left (east) along Avenida B.

Beyond the palace, turn right down Calle 4 which leads to the lovely Plaza de Bolívar. In the centre is a rather camp **statue of Simón Bolívar**, 'Libertador' of Latin America. He overlooks a magnificent mansion which became the Hotel Colonial, but is now being upgraded as the ultra-luxurious **Hotel Colombia**, which will be *the* place to stay when it finally opens. Opposite is the 18th-century church of **San Francisco**, whose open tower reveals a fine stone staircase. Inside, a superb mosaic hovers above the altar.

Alongside the church is the **Teatro Nacional**. The theatre, completed in 1907 and restored in 1974, was designed by Ruggieri who also designed La Scala in Milan. Shakespeare and Wagner are among the notable busts arrayed outside. If it is open – not always the case during the day – you should take a look at the murals in the main hall and at the glittering auditorium. Performances are sporadic, most of them featuring the country's Symphony Orchestra. Attached to the theatre is the **National Palace**, also designed by Ruggieri.

Walking between the church and theatre – towards the sea – and veering to the right you join the Avenida Central. On the left is the shell of a building which was once an army sports hall. It is a good place to take photographs and look at the view of the old sea wall. A little further, steps lead up to the **Paseo de las Bóvedas** – Promenade of the Dungeons. This walkway runs along the top of the sea wall and gives a magnificent all-round view of the bay, from the Bridge of the Americas across the Canal round to Punta Paitilla. Underneath, the old dungeons have been converted into art galleries and an upmarket restaurant. At the end is an obelisk topped by the **cock of freedom**, a symbol of France. Resembling Cleopatra's Needle in London, the structure was erected in honour of Ferdinand de Lesseps and his French engineers, who failed in their attempt to build a canal. In 1920 the square enclosed by the sea wall was named Plaza de Francia, also in recognition of the role played by the French. It is a shady and often deserted square, dominated by the Palace of Justice. Nearby is an arcade where a series of plaques record the history of the construction of the Canal – you can see where sections of the text have been rewritten. There are busts of Lesseps and other important figures connected with the project, and also a monument to a Cuban scientist, Carlos Finlay, whose discovery that yellow fever is transmitted by mosquitoes was essential to sanitizing the jungle prior to the successful attempt to dig the Canal.

Walking down Callejón A, along the left side of the French Embassy you come to the church of **Santo Domingo**, on Calle 3. This ruined church is notable for its broad *Arco Chato* or flat arch. Built entirely of bricks with no internal support, the arch has remained intact for over 300 years. Its survival is said to have played a vital part in the debate over whether the trans-isthmian canal should be built in Panama or earthquake-ridden Nicaragua. In a restored chapel next door is the Museum of Colonial Religious Art, which opens 9am-4pm, Monday to Saturday.

Taking a right turn, you rejoin Avenida Central which takes you to the heart of the colonial city – the **Plaza Mayor**, also known as Plaza Catedral or Plaza Independencia. The Cathedral was begun in 1688 and took over a century to complete. The bells and some brickwork were taken from the cathedral in Panamá Viejo. Its two towers, inlaid with mother-of-pearl, are highly distinctive, while the interior is unexceptional. On the south side of the square is the so-called **Cabildo**, the former headquarters of first the French and then the US canal company. It now houses the excellent **Canal Museum**.

Next door is the Italianate **Palacio Municipal**, where a Panama's Act of Independence was signed in 1903. On the second floor is the Museo de Historia de Panamá, which is open Monday to Friday, 9am-3.30pm. This is an

The ditch and the dirt

Assuming you plan to head out to the Canal, you should do yourself the favour of getting acquainted with the story of its construction at the Museo del Canal Interoceanico (tel 211 1649 or 211 1650, sinfo.net/pcmuseum). European visitors may be pleased to learn that it exists thanks to the EU, which paid for its conversion from the Post Office.

The constructors, and curators, have done a superb job. In a series of displays that traces the story of selecting a route, via 'El Gold Rush' and a set of Nicaraguan stamps showing a smouldering volcano that was cited as evidence of seismic uncertainty, to the register of votes in the US Senate for the transfer of the Canal in 1978. There are some fascinating photographs of the Canal's construction, and the detritus of digging the Big Ditch.

The museum opens 9.30am-5.30pm, daily except Monday, admission $2.

excellent museum with a fascinating array of maps, showing everything from Casco Viejo in the 17th century to the routes taken by explorers and pirates through Central America. The Archbishop's Palace and the old (and still, barely, functioning) Hotel Central are the other notable buildings in the square.

Northwest of Plaza Mayor, at the corner of Avenida A and Calle 8, is the 17th-century church of **San José**. It contains the gold altar which was saved from the ravages of Henry Morgan and his men in Panamá La Vieja. If the main door is shut, go round to the side and ring the bell. North along Avenida Central is the restored church of **La Merced**, and further up is Plaza Santa Ana. This is a small but bustling square with a mildly attractive 17th-century church, and is a popular venue for political debate. It is said to be the heart of Panamanian democracy, such as it is, and is the nearest thing you'll get to Speakers Corner in Central America. The square is more distinguishable, however, by its resident population of drunks, beggars and shoeshiners.

Museum pieces

Panama City has a better concentration of museums than any of its rival Central American capitals. Some of the city's stock has already been mentioned, but several more deserve a visit. The **Museo Nacional del Hombre Panameño** on Plaza 5 de Mayo is housed in the old neo-classical railway station opposite the International Hotel. This is a fine anthropological and archeological museum which gives an insight into Panama's pre-Columbian history and its ethnic groups. One off-beat exhibit is the Popemobile that was used during John Paul II's visit to Panama in 1983. The museum was closed for refurbishment during the first half of 2000, but with luck should be finished by the time you get there.

The **Museo Afro-Antillano** resides in a former church on the corner of Justo Arosemena and Calle 24, and tells the story of the West Indian community who came to Panama to work on the Canal, and have established strong roots here. It shows where the workers came from (20,000 from Barbados alone), and contains relics from the days of digging. You may be intrigued by the way that West African cultural links were preserved, and that a West Indian named Sidney A Young was the founder of the *Panama Tribune*.

A bit of a strange one is the **Museo de Ciencias Naturales** on Avenida 2 Sur (Cuba) between Calles 29 and 30. This natural history museum is small but interesting. It opens 9am-3.30pm Tuesday to Saturday, 1pm-4.30pm on Sunday. Among the exhibits is a bizarre tableau of a stuffed tiger apparently mounting a stuffed deer, and a relief map showing the convoluted geology of Panama.

One final oddity is located in a nondescript villa on the corner of Avenida Cuba and Calle 34. **The Museo Casa del Banco Nacional** invites visitors to admire the place where the nation's finances were first organised. It makes the fiscal history of a country that lacks its own currency remarkably interesting.

Suburban values

Thanks largely to the attentions of the Americans, the western fringes of Panama City are worth exploring. High on the hill to the west of the old quarter is **Ancón**. The name is a Spanish word meaning 'cove', and dates back to the colonial period when the Spanish used the top of the hill as a lookout post to warn of potential pirate attack. During the 19th century Ancón lost military importance, but it was considered a healthy spot by the French who built a hospital here – the forerunner of the present Gorgas Hospital for Tropical Diseases, named after the man who eradicated the worst diseases from the Canal Zone. When the Americans gained control of the Canal Zone, Ancón was incorporated into the canal's defence and communication system.

To walk up the hill, approach from Avenida de los Mártires and proceed up Quarry Heights. There are a couple of observation points offering fine views both of the city, and of the Canal and Balboa to the west. To get back down to Avenida de los Mártires continue on a circular route down Gorgas Road.

North of Ancón, lurking behind the shanty suburb of Curundu, is Panama City's very own piece of 'rainforest paradise'. the "Parque National Metropolitano is a small but beautiful hill where, miraculously, a lot of natural forest has survived. There are well-laid trails around the park, and excellent views – not least of the planes landing at Albrook airport. To reach the park, you have little choice but to take a taxi.

Balboa is the main port on the Pacific. Now that most of the Americans have departed, it bears less similarity to a characterless, purpose-built US suburb. An unsuitably grand staircase leads up to the so-called Balboa Heights on which is perched the Panama Canal Commission administration building. At the foot of the steps is a **monument** to Major-General George Washington Goethals, the canal's chief engineer, describing him as a 'master-builder...engineer of genius...man of vision'. It was 'dedicated by his fellow Americans', and is of white marble with three studs, each suggesting a set of locks. Go inside the administration building to see the superb **murals**=depicting the construction of the Canal. The entrance is around the back and opening hours are 7.15am-4.15pm daily. Downstairs is one of the most dismal cafeterias in Panama. At the foot of the hill is the train station which, sadly, has been converted into a McDonald's and a Blockbuster Video.

Until 1999, a good vantage point from which to watch the Canal traffic was the "Balboa Yacht Club", beautifully located beneath the Puente de las Américas. Unfortunately, the club was destroyed by fire. If and when a replacement is built, you will be able to reach it by following the road which turns off the Estadio de Jamaica, the main road through Balboa, by the YMCA – i.e. before Balboa Heights.

Buses to Balboa leave from the Canal Area bus station on Avenida Central at Calle 24 Oeste in Panama City; alternatively pick one up along Avenida de los Mártires, or pay around $3 for a cab.

Firecrackers and a damp squib

A Central American country disappeared one lunchtime in 1999. Until noon on 31 December, the Panama Canal Zone had functioned as a nation independent of the state of Panama which it so casually bisected. So you would imagine that Panama's Millennium party on New Year's Eve would be the greatest on the planet. On paper. Panama, remember, had achieved its independence only at the start of the 20th century, promptly to have it snatched away when the Americans carved the heart out of the country to take possession of the Canal. Thanks to the negotiating skills of Omar Torrijos, the transfer of the Canal to the Panamanians was successfully negotiated in 1978.

Twenty-one years later, the man who gave away the Canal turned up – along with miscellaneous other politicians from all over the Americas. Except that former US president Jimmy Carter and the other past and present heads of state were a fortnight early. The dignitaries said they wouldn't come if they had to turn up on 31 December, because they all wanted to be at home for the Millennium – most cited family ties, though this excuse doubtless disguised a fear of political instability fuelled by alcohol and Millennium Bug problems. Even the 'real' event failed to materialise. A huge digital clock outside the Canal Administration Building counted down the seconds until noon on New Year's Eve, but in the end the ceremony was staged one day early because of fears of violence.

Even so, the handover was correctly seen as a momentous achievement for a nation that, only 10 years earlier, had been invaded by the USA in order to topple General Noriega. Panama's president, Mireya Moscoso, was clearly happy in a sober sort of way.

A game

For spectators the best sporting venues are in Panama City. Foremost among these is the Hipódromo Presidente Ramón which is in the suburb of Río Abajo not far from the airport. Races are held on Thursdays, Saturdays and Sundays. Baseball is also popular, and the main stadium is the Estadio Justo de Arosemena near Balboa. Ask at the tourist office or look in the papers for information on fixtures and other sporting events.

A shopping expedition

Going shopping in Panama City is something of an endurance test. Avenida Central, the main commercial street, is at the best of times low-intensity chaos, where you must fight your way through a sea of shoppers and hawkers. The main attraction is the nation's finest store: Gran Morrison – and yes, it does sell the music of the great Van Morrison.

> ## Van the Gran
> Upon my return from Panama at the start of 2000, I told the writer and broadcaster Danny Baker about Gran Morrison. Listeners to his Virgin Radio programme promptly came up with a long list of places which *nearly* share the name of a celebrity. Among the highlights: Luton, it is claimed, boasts a travel agency called Tom's Cruises. An Italian restaurant in the James Herriot country of North Yorkshire glories in the title All Pizzas Great or Small. Perhaps it gets its mozzarella from the fromagerie known as Cheeses of Nazareth.

Between Plaza Santa Ana and the seafront is a lane known as Salsipuedes or 'Get out if you can' – an apt name for one of the city's most chaotic shopping streets. It is also Panama City's Chinatown, hence the preponderance of Chinese restaurants which are the best in town. Although entertaining during the day, this area is best avoided after dark. The northern reaches of Avenida Central are given over to more upmarket shopping centres – one such is the Plaza New York at Calle 50. The existence of a shop called Saks should not excite you too much – this is no Fifth Avenue.

The best **bookshop** is in the university area on Avenida M.E. Batista in La Cresta district north of Vía España. For books about Panama, go to Casa Zaldo, a department store on Avenida Central, on the left north of Plaza Santa Ana.

A word of advice

The main **tourist office** is at the Atlapa Convention Center, on Vía Israel, in the San Francisco area north of Punta Paitilla (tel 226 7000/4002). The office is hard to find, being located on the first floor of the huge conference centre opposite the Marriott Hotel. Look opposite the Gents' toilet. It is open 8.30am-3.30pm, Monday to Friday. To get there catch any bus along Avenida 6 Sur which is bound for Panamá La Vieja. There is also a small office planted right in the middle of the Avenida Central, but it keeps erratic opening hours.

Certain areas have a particularly bad reputation. Among these are the Calidonia district, northwest of Plaza 5 de Mayo. More dangerous, however, is what remains of El Chorrillo, west of the old town, where there is extreme deprivation. This district is not recommended at any time – people have been stabbed in the street in broad daylight.

The long wheelbase of the law

The tourist police in Panama City are hilarious. They roam around on mountain bikes looking for people to help. I got the bus out to Panamá La Viejo to look around the ruins before a flight. Two tourist policemen followed my every step around the site at a discreet distance, stopped all the rush-hour traffic to let me cross the road to the King's Bridge. Then, when I was ready to go to the airport, they forced a taxi to stop and take me there (via the new and unused Corredor Sur toll route) for $10.

Keeping in touch

A message

All the internet cafés are concentrated in the upmarket side of town, and advertise their presence with highly visible neon signs. Most are well-equipped with fast servers and terminals. Prices are on the high side, typically $4 per hour, but competition is forcing rates down. The best-equipped is Stratos, on Via Argentina, opposite El Trapiche restaurant. It opens 10am-10pm from Tuesday to Saturday, 2-10pm on Sundays.

A stamp

You are five years too late to visit the fine old **post office** in the Plaza Mayor of the old city – it has become the Canal Museum. The handiest office is now the one on the south side of Avenida Central between Calles 34 and 35; there is a philatelic office next door. Offices open 7am-5.45pm Monday to Friday, and 7am-4.45pm on Saturday. If you are collecting a parcel, go to Encomiendos Postales Transístmicos on Avenida Bolívar (behind the Sears' shop).

A call

INTEL has its HQ, and an impressive number of telephone booths, on Avenida 2 Sur (Samuel Lewis), near the corner of Vía España. As well as making international phone calls, you can send a fax abroad for $5 per page. The office is open 7.30am-9.45pm. For INTEL information phone 263 7077.

An emergency

The main Santo Tomás **hospital** is near the seafront opposite the Balboa monument (tel 225 1436 or 227-4122). If you're ill and someone else is paying go to the HCA Centro Médico in Paitilla (tel 263 6060). There are a number of late-night **pharmacies** – the Arrocha chain has several branches which are open 24 hours, including one on Vía España. To call the **police**, dial 104.

The **UK Embassy** is at Torre Swiss Bank, 4th floor, Calle 53, Urbanización Orbarrio, Zona 1 (tel 269 0866 or 1178). It opens 8am-noon, Monday to Friday. The **US Consulate** is at Edificio San Diego on Avenida 6 Sur and Calle 40. The consulate is in a big office building a couple of blocks from the embassy. The building is unmarked, but the black and white tiles on the external wall make it easy to spot. It opens 8am-12.30pm Monday to Friday. In an emergency phone 227 1777.

Two day trips

Panamá La Vieja

The ruins of the old capital, destroyed by Henry Morgan and his fellow pirates in 1671, are seven kilometres (four miles) northeast of Panama City. They have been engulfed by suburbs and many have become little more than playgrounds for the local children. Some of the buildings have been identified from an early

17th-century map, while the function of others remains a mystery. A more modern annotated map of the old city is published by the tourist board, and you should be able to pick one up at the site for $3. Note that some maps, and people, refer to the area as Panamá Viejo.

The ruins appear suddenly just beyond an Esso service station, so ask to get off the bus here. Among the first buildings you see are a 17th-century fort and a couple of convents. The first of these is the **Convent de la Merced**, where Francisco Pizarro and his crew took Communion before setting out on their final expedition to Peru. These ruins are less manicured than those in the heart of Panamá La Vieja, and are perhaps more atmospheric as a result. In the main square, little of the cathedral, completed in 1626, has survived, although the tower still stands in a remarkable state of preservation. It dominates the plaza and the other ruins, which include the remains of the Town Hall, destroyed by an earthquake in 1612.

Near the river is the so-called **House of the Genoese** in which slaves were sold; you can see the stone where slaves were shown before bidding began. To the north, overlooking the sea, is the **Convent of San José**, which escaped being destroyed because of its distance from the centre. Its gold, Baroque altar was saved from the clutches of Henry Morgan by the priests (or nuns) who painted it black or covered it in mud, according to which legend you believe. It is now in the church of San José in Panama City. From the church it is a short walk to the **Puente del Rey** (King's Bridge); this was built in 1620 and linked the city to the road across the isthmus along which gold was transported by mule to Nombre de Dios and Portobelo.

To get to Panamá La Vieja take any bus marked *PMA Viejo*, e.g. bus I or 2 from Avenida 6 Sur or Vía España. Robberies sometimes take place within the ruins, so keep an eye out for dodgy characters. With luck, the tourist police may be idling around.

Taboga Island

The 'island of flowers' lies just 20km (12 miles) off the coast of Panama City. What was once a base for pirates is now a fishing village, albeit one which is largely dependent on tourism. There are some good beaches but these are busy at weekends (when watersports take over), and the water isn't terribly clean. Nevertheless, the lush, tropical vegetation is beautiful, and the island has managed to retain some of its tranquillity – there are few cars, and the evenings are cool. It also boasts an ancient church, said to be the second oldest in the Western Hemisphere. The best time to see the island is on 16 July, when there are celebrations in honour of the Virgen del Carmen, the patron saint of the island. An image of the virgin is placed in a dugout filled with flowers which sails around the island followed by a motley collection of boats loaded with worshippers.

The hour's journey out to Taboga from Balboa is worth doing in its own right just to experience going along the Canal a short distance and under the Puente de las Américas. Boats depart from Pier 18 at 8.30am and 4pm on Monday, Tuesday, Thursday and Friday, and additionally at 10am, 11.30am and 3pm on Saturday and Sunday. Ferries return from Taboga at 10am and 5.30pm during the week, with an increased service at weekends. These times seem to change constantly, so you may wish to check beforehand with the tourist office.

Pier (*muelle*) 18 is just off the main road through Balboa – look for the sign on the left saying *Bienvenidos al Puerto de Balboa*. On the island, there are just a couple of hotels, Hotel Chu being the cheaper of the two, with rooms costing $25-$35. It has a pleasant terrace with good views.

Twilight in the Zone

When the Americans finished building the Panama Canal in 1914, they wanted to protect the investment – after all, it was the greatest sum of money that the US Treasury had ever spent on anything. So Washington cordoned off a five-mile strip either side of the waterway between the Atlantic and the Pacific as the Canal Zone. Since then it has effectively been owned and operated by the US as a colony of Washington.

A belt of land on either side of the Canal acts as a buffer between the waterway and reality, reality in this case being the merciless tropical jungle. Towns have been built to cater for the needs of the expatriate engineers and servicemen. Balboa, at the Pacific end, is their home town. It looks like Coral Gables or Orange County, transplanted to the tropics from small town USA. Drugstores, road signs in English, and gum-chewing adolescents sporting dental braces, are the prevalent sights.

For the ultimate canal holiday, visit the Panama Canal Area. Sighting a ship appearing suddenly in the middle of the Central American jungle is guaranteed to make the most blasé traveller exclaim. The Canal is not just an astonishing piece of engineering, it is also a source of joy for statisticians: since it opened on 15 August 1914 it has carried 700,000 vessels. American taxpayers have sunk $3.5 billion into the Canal, of which only two-thirds has been recovered in tolls. Each ship pays around US$30,000 for a 'quality transit service', as the administration terms it. Fees are calculated according to the vessel's displacement, and the least spent was by a swimmer in 1928 who paid 36c to cover the length of the Canal. On a typical day 33 ships use the Canal, earning the administration a million dollars. The money is used to pay for maintenance, which costs $2 million per week, pilot fees (every ship is guided through by four pilots) and the huge cost of maintaining security. Unlike the Suez Canal, ships can travel in both directions, and do so continuously. On average each vessel spends ten hours waiting and ten hours sailing through the Canal.

The mechanics of the Canal are relatively straightforward, and have changed remarkably little since 1914. The operation hinges upon regular and predictable rainfall into the vast artificial lakes of Miraflores and Gatún. This water is used to replenish the locks which lift ships over the Continental Divide. The lock chambers were far larger than any which had previously been made, measuring

1000 by 100 feet. The original gates are still in place, and are in fine condition; despite their weight they can be opened manually in half an hour should the motors fail. Ships are guided through the locks by six 'mules', small railway locomotives made by Mitsubishi of Japan which resemble something out of *Gulliver's Travels* as they struggle to manoeuver the ships towering above them.

On the scale of world shipping, however, the ships using the Canal are small. The Canal was designed to take shipping far larger than any in existence in 1914, and it is still capable of carrying 95% of the world's vessels. Unfortunately, the 5% of ships too large for the Canal carry a huge proportion of the world's freight. Panama is understandably concerned that a proposed new canal through Nicaragua would wreck its own operation. One possible solution might be to enhance the canal's accessibility for visitors. Tourist boats sail along the Canal only very rarely. Taking the bus along the Trans-Isthmian highway is a poor substitute since seldom does the road permit glimpses of the Canal, except during the descent into Colón. The best way to admire the 'Big Ditch' is to visit one of the three sets of locks, where you can watch the mechanics of the raising and lowering of ships.

The **Canal Area** (formerly Canal Zone) is the term used to describe the territory either side of the Canal which has always been under the control of the United States. When the USA bought the rights to the Canal, it also bought the rights to a Canal Zone. It has a population of about 40,000, most of whom are involved in the operation of the Canal.

Until 1 October 1979 there were eight countries in Central America, not seven. The Panama Canal Zone was a fully fledged country, cutting Panama proper in two, owned and operated by the US government. The Carter administration set about decolonising its slice of the isthmus, and on that date

The day before the handover, I wandered around the Canal Zone, which felt like a party venue the morning after. The bitterness the servicemen felt about abandoning what they regard as American property was obvious from the graffiti they've left behind: 'It's all yours, suckers', was one of the more polite examples painted on a wall of a former American barracks. But among the diplomatic community, there was the feeling that the current state of affairs could not continue into the 21st century, and that it was handed over with dignity on both sides – though the departing Americans were clearly concerned about the hands into which 'their' Canal was passing. I talked to one Western diplomat who said he felt the Canal would work just fine for the next few years, not least because the Panamanians had 21 years of notice to get ready for control. But he warned that if Panama's future leaders 'start skimming off some of the revenue' and slackening off on the immensely complicated maintenance that is needed to keep it going, there could well be problems down the line.

the Zone and its government were formally dissolved. Control of the Canal passed to the Panama Canal Commission, which is actually a US government agency. A more significant change took place in 1990. Prior to that year, the USA had a majority of the nine seats on the board, and the Administrator was an American; in 1990 the positions were reversed.

The Canal Area was finally handed over to the Panamanians on New Year's Eve 1999. Its former status as a piece of US territory is still much in evidence. Even the signposts are in English, and the speed limits in miles per hour. Yet the Panama Canal has not been a wholly beneficial exercise for the USA. Damage caused by the Canal to the American trade balance is incalculable, since the Panama Canal's primary trade route is between the Far East and the US East Coast; it has cut the cost of importing Japanese cars, Korean CD players and Taiwanese calculators, much to the detriment of American industry and US reserves.

The Trans-Isthmian Highway is a terrifying road, dominated by high-speed trucks carrying containers from one ocean to the other. Express buses between Panama City and Colón also storm down the highway and are not ideal for admiring the scenery. Sit on the left for the journey north to catch what glimpses you can of the Canal, but don't neglect the landscape to the east, which is more interesting along most of the route.

As well as the Trans-Isthmian Highway there is a road which roughly follows the line of the railway as far as Gamboa. Buses along this route leave from the Canal Area bus station in Panama City. Some buses, including those to Chilibre, take either route – those following the main highway are marked *Transístmica*.

Your best chance of going the length of the Canal is as a linehandler on a yacht – yachts are allowed to go through the Canal on certain days, and owners require a statutory minimum of four linehandlers. The best place to make contacts is at the Yacht Club in Cristóbal, adjacent to Colón. You don't have to have experience, and persistence is generally rewarded.

Buses from the Canal Area terminal go through Balboa and follow the road which runs parallel to the railway as far as Albrook airfield (the domestic airport). Railway buffs and photographers may be interested by the rusting locomotives and wagons bearing the faded message *Comercio Mondial en Marcha* ('World Commerce on the Move).

The **Miraflores Locks** are the first locks beyond Balboa, and mark the first stage of a ship's climb up the Canal. Miraflores is the most popular place for watching the Canal, and there is an observation deck which is an excellent vantage point from which to watch the ships go through the locks – the sight of these huge vessels rising as water surges into the locks is terrific. The best place to begin the tour is with the English-language audio-visual presentation, based around a big model of the Canal, which explains the history and workings of the channel. The observation deck has a modest display of photographs of the Canal, including one of the locks empty of water – during the dry season the locks are emptied for an overhaul. The capacity of each is 20 million gallons.

The Visitor Center at Miraflores Locks opens 9am-5pm daily. Traffic is at its busiest between 9am and 10am, and after 3pm. If you turn up around noon, then you may find there is nothing much going on. To Miraflores take any bus from the Canal Area bus station or Balboa which is bound for Miraflores or points further along that road – such as Paraíso, Gamboa or Pedro Miguel. The journey takes about 20 minutes. Make it clear that you want to go to the locks since it is not obvious where you need to get off – in fact the bus stop is right outside another former US military camp. If you are in Balboa and don't wish to wait for the bus there are plenty of taxis which are only too happy to take you to Miraflores for $10 or so.

The next set of locks is only a short distance beyond Miraflores Lake at **Pedro Miguel**, where the Canal is hoisted to 17 metres (55 feet) above sea level. You can get physically closer to the Canal here, and the skill and courage of its builders are yet more visible. North of Pedro Miguel Locks is the Gaillard Cut, formerly known as the Culebra Cut. It was the constant landslides in this stretch which were the main cause for the failure of the initial French attempt at building the Canal. Buses running from Panama City to Chilibre follow the line of the Canal this far; you can board at Miraflores or Pedro Miguel.

Further north on the right hand side, just past the turn-off for Paraíso, is the cemetery where hundreds of victims of the French attempt at building the Canal are buried. Close by is the US cemetery, a corner of a foreign field that is forever American – the Canal settlement allows for the cemetery to stay within US administration.

The road steers away from the Canal here and heads towards the Trans-Isthmian Highway. Nearby is the turn-off to Gamboa and the Botanical Garden which is part of the Parque Soberanía and one of the largest of its kind in the world.

The Canal rips straight through the middle of the tropical rainforest that drapes itself over Panama's Continental Divide – and former US defence buildings are being pressed into service to give unique access to the jungle. An old early-warning radar station that towers above the trees has been converted into an observation post for the amazing wildlife, with hotel rooms built in 45 metres (150 feet) above the forest floor. And the old US Country Club and Golf Course is now being opened to everyone (or, at least, those with cash to spare), as a rainforest lodge.

Beyond the Gaillard Cut ships enter **Gatún Lake**, but people travelling by bus must wait until the bus nears Colón before they can catch a glimpse of the world's largest man-made lake. Gatún Lake has served as a reservoir for the Canal since the building of the Gatún Dam, about 13km (8 miles) south of

Colón. The water in the reservoir is supposed to ensure that the water level in the Canal can be maintained. One of the reasons research is going on into the possibility of building a new canal is that the present one has shown signs of drying up. Destruction of Panama's forest has caused soil erosion with the result that Gatún Lake is gradually filling up with silt. On a number of occasions large vessels have been unable to use the Canal for this reason.

The lake is dotted with islands – formerly hilltops – between which the Canal follows a zigzagging course for some 37km (23 miles). Barra Colorado island was formed during the building of the channel, and many animals sought refuge there when the area was flooded. It is now a reserve and there are lots of trails through the rainforest. Trips must be arranged through the Smithsonian Tropical Research Institute in Ancón (opposite the Legislative Palace). It opens for short periods during the week, so call 252 5539 in advance. The terrain on the island is rough in places so take stout footwear. Ticks can also be a menace so make sure you are well protected.

At the northern end of the lake are the **Gatún Locks**, a series of three locks enabling ships to descend 28m (90 feet) to the level of the Atlantic. Access to this site is from Colón, a distance of 11km (7 miles). You can pick up a bus from the terminal in Colón; on the way back, you may be able to hitch a lift. The Gatun site has a very different feel to the other, more accessible locks – it has the feeling of being a strictly working area, though visitors can gain admittance to a public area.

The Canal Area of Colón, where ships are marshalled before the trip through the locks, is known as Cristóbal, and is only a mile or so (1.5km) from the centre of the city. Cristóbal is Panama's main Atlantic port.

Work your way through the Canal

Cristóbal has its own Yacht Club, and since the demise of the Balboa club in a fire it is the best place to look for linehandling work. Each yacht, however small, has to have four linehandlers on board. Previous experience is not essential, though it will help your case if you have crewed on a yacht before. Turn up when the office opens (9am-5pm, Monday to Friday; 9am-noon, Saturdays) and register your interest by pinning, with the staff's permission, a card on the noticeboard by the adjacent laundry building. You will either need to leave a hotel contact number, or be prepared to return repeatedly to the club. Either way, you will probably need to stay in Colón.

Colón – a city in need of a future

Once upon a time, Colón was a blight on the Zone's landscape. Panama's second largest city, with a population of 80,000, has a long-standing notoriety for rampant crime, with guidebooks warning that robbery in broad daylight is a feature of everyday life. The tourist literature states ambivalently: 'This port city has an atmosphere of its own'. Parts of the city at the Atlantic end of the Canal look like the set for some particularly grisly post-apocalypse movie, while the rest of the city is gradually being spruced up to its former neo-colonial glory.

One part of town that is neither neo-colonial nor glorious is the gruesome, high-security Duty-Free Zone, the *Zona Libre* which allows goods to be imported and re-exported free of duty. (Every hoarding on the Trans-Isthmian Highway seems devoted to promoting it.) Wheelers and dealers from all over the Americas converge to buy and sell cheap tat and expensive technology, all of which helps contribute a multicultural buzz to the place. As a port town, there is a constant flow of sailors passing through – most of the bars and nightclubs in Colón cater to this clientele, as do a certain number of female residents of the city.

Colón was founded in 1852, when construction of the railway across the isthmus began. It was known in those days as Aspinwall, after one of the founders of the railway. Towards the end of the 19th century, during negotiations for the secession of Panama from Colombia, rivalry between Colombian right and left-wingers exploded and led to Colón being set on fire on a number of occasions. The damage was so serious that the town had to be rebuilt.

Its situation at the Atlantic mouth of the Canal should have brought Colón great prosperity. But the town declined steadily during the 20th century, with rising unemployment and some of the worst slums on the continent. Plenty of overcrowded tenements still survice, and even away from the slum areas, the city is fairly grubby. But a visit to Colón is easy to recommend, though it is ideally tackled as a day-trip from Panama City – make it evident that you are carrying nothing of value, and you will probably be untroubled. Wear a T-shirt and shorts with a few dollars tucked into a back pocket, and you cease to be worth robbing.

Express **buses** leave when full – usually every five, ten or fifteen minutes – from the Colón bus station in central Panama City, at Calle 29 and Avenida Perú, just south of the Avenida Central and close to the Hotel Covadonga. Services run from 5am to 8 or 9pm; the fare is $2.50 and the journey takes 90 minutes when traffic is flowing freely, two hours at busy times and as little as 75 minutes when the new freeway across the Isthmus is built.

There are also lots of 'local' buses that cost half as much but take more than twice as long to cover the ground. . The bus terminal in Colón is a splendidly busy place at Calle 13 and Avenida Bolívar.

Those who are curious to get a glimpse of Colón without actually staying there can do so by taking the bus. Buses arriving from the south must do a huge loop through the city in order to reach the terminal. This means that you can see about as much as you need to without even stepping onto the pavement. Once at the bus station, if you don't like the feel of the place you can hop on to the next bus out. But to do so would be a terrible waste.

Aeroperlas has 14 flights to Colón each day from Albrook airport in Panama City; a one-way ticket costs around $30. The flights are scheduled for the benefit of commuters, and leave in two blocks: nine between 7am and 9.45am, the remaining five between 3.55pm and 5.40pm. In Panama City, call 315 7500; in Colón, 210 9500.

A room

Until construction of the Radisson hotel is completed west of the Zona Libre, the best place in town, from all points of view, is the **New Washington Hotel** (tel 411 7188 or 441 8120, fax 441 7397), at the top of the town on Calle Segunda. Built at the turn of the century, it fell into disrepair but has now been overhauled. The 124 rooms have bathrooms, TV and air-conditioning. There is a pool, a casino, 'Pharoah's Night Club' and fine views out to sea. What is described as 'Restaurant National Foods' serves better breakfast, lunch and dinner than you might think. For all this, you pay around $80 single, $100 double.

An excellent lower-budget alternative is the **Hotel Internacional de Colón**, a modern place on the corner of Avenida Bolivar and Calle 11 (tel 445 2930, fax 441 8879). Rooms are air-conditioned and have TV, yet the price is a modest $20 single/$28 double. For a little more character, try the Art Deco **Hotel Restaurant Plaza** on Avenida Central just south of Calle 7. Note that the Avenida is officially the Paseo del Centenario, but no-one ever calls it that.

A meal and a drink

There are plenty of places in town, but the food and drink at the Cristóbal Yacht Club is especially recommended both for its quality and the location: on a verandah looking out onto a forest of yacht masts with the Caribbean as a backdrop. You may feel more comfortable paying $1 each way for a cab rather than walking through a brief piece of wasteground separating Colón from Cristóbal.

Alternatively, try the Restaurant Aries on Avenida Bolívar just north of the old radio station, or the Jo Café Restaurant on Avenida Bolívar just south of the bus station.

An exploration

Friendly, engaging and gentle on the eye: that sums up Colón, apart from the extraordinary buses that look like devils and sound like Hell. Start at the northern end of the Avenida Central, the city's main street, which is densely populated with busts and statues. Top of the list, and the street, is Christ the Redeemer. As you move down the broad, attractive avenue, where mothers dote on their infants, you encounter Christopher Columbus – clutching an Indian girl under his right arm, he is described as the Immortal Discoverer of the New World. The statue was given by Eugenia, Empress of France, in 1866. Next, the inevitable Ferdinand de Lesseps celebrates the originator of the Canal. Of the buildings worth singling out, the cathedral, on Plaza 5 de Noviembre, is the one most worth seeing. You can reach it by heading a block west from the Avenida Central.

A shopping expedition

This will possibly be the highlight of your stay, because there are so many dimensions to it. At the old railway station, there is a Mercado de Artensanias, selling molas and pottery. Two blocks east and one north, you reach the city's market, with shops like Almacen Super Ganga in the vicinity for anything you can't find among the market stalls. But the most intriguing location is the Zona Libre, the 'Shopping Centre of the Americas", as it describes itself. It consists of a 360-hectare chunk of Colón that has been fenced off and filled with warehouses. Its chief business is re-export goods, but casual visitors are allowed in – you must show a passport to be able to do so. Touts (or guards, as they call themselves) will pester you to let them take you to certain stores; they are on commission. Goods cannot be taken out of the zone and can only be picked up at the airport if you do not have them sent back home. The entrance to the Zona Libre is on Calle 13 a couple of blocks east of Avenida Central. It opens 8am-5pm from Monday to Friday.

A message

The only **internet** location in town is on Calle 14 just west of Avenida Central, on the second floor of Almacen Jessica. It opens 9am-8pm from Monday to Saturday, 9am to 2pm on Sundays.

A word of warning

'If you walk in its (Colón's) streets, even in the middle of the day, expect to get mugged. It really is that bad ... walking in this city is very dangerous'. That is one guidebook's conclusion. Another warns: 'We have received repeated warnings of robbery in Colón, often within five minutes of arrival ... One traveller recommends having a few dollars handy, so that muggers are less likely to strip you for more.'

There is a lot of poverty and crime in Colón, but the traveller is not so guaranteed to come to grief as those warnings might suggest. As everywhere in Panama, the vast majority of people are trustworthy and concerned about your welfare. Perhaps I was lucky in the days I spent there, but on a list of dangerous cities – Barcelona, Georgetown Guyana and San José spring to mind – Colón failed to register.

Looking for treasure

Branch off to Portobelo, once the Clapham Junction of the Americas, where all the Spanish treasure was loaded. The old customs house remains, together with some charming early colonial dwellings, dotted randomly around a vast and slightly shabby sweep of lawns.

The small town of Portobelo lies 48km (30 miles) northeast of Colón. It is thought to have been named as such by Columbus himself, who came here in 1502. This old Spanish port and garrison was built following the destruction of the defences at Nombre de Dios, east of Portobelo. It marked the end of the Camino Real, the road from the other side of the isthmus along which Peruvian gold and other goods were transported before their despatch to Spain. As such, Portobelo became a thriving place and an important Spanish garrison for over two centuries. The heavy defences recall the threat of pirates who were attracted by the galleons loaded with treasure. Drake's Cove nearby is said to be the burial place of Sir Francis Drake who died at sea off Portobelo. Divers apparently still look for his leaden coffin.

Some of the locals have seized on the connection – there is a chicken and seafood restaurant called El Mirador de Drake just outside the town. Portobelo feels like the end of the road (it almost is), albeit a most spectacular one that cuts through jungle-covered hills and brushes occasionally against the Caribbean. Inactivity is the hallmark of Portobelo, and yet it is a charming place to visit. The main attraction are the ruined fortresses which, unlike the remains of Panamá Viejo, give a very good idea of what Portobelo was originally like. You can walk along the battlements and cannon are still in place. The huge old customs house, where the gold and other treasure was stored, has also survived, but is heavily restored.

Near the customs house is the 18th-century Cathedral of Jésus Nazareno. Alongside it is a ruined church which chickens have the run of. The more modern structure is a broad, handsome building. To the left of the altar is a statue of the Black Christ. This icon is said to have been saved from a sinking Spanish ship during the 17th century. Many a miracle has been attributed to it – indeed it is credited with shielding the town from cholera epidemics, and legend has it that when anyone tries to remove it from the church the seas become agitated. The seas apparently know when October comes around since they do not react when the statue is paraded through the streets every year on 21 October. This is an important festival, and people flock from all over the country to attend – some of them make the final approach to the church on their knees. Folk music, which some people have likened to the rhythms of New Orleans, is played in the street and people dance all night.

Many people go into Colón simply in order to leave straight away on a bus bound for Portobelo. This is not necessary, however, since the road to Portobelo branches off the Trans-Isthmian Highway at Sabanitas, about 30 minutes south of Colón. If you approach from Panama City, get off at Sabanitas and join a bus bound for Portobelo from Colón. Departures are erratic and if you get fed up of waiting there are plenty of taxis in Sabanitas, which will take you there for about $20; the journey takes about 70 minutes by bus (50 by taxi). The road passes a number of beaches. The one with most facilities is Playa Langosta, midway between Sabanitas and Portobelo. It is a pleasant, crescent-shaped bay, and has a Turicentro, with accommodation and other facilities.

Off the coast 16km (10 miles) further east from Portobelo is **Isla Grande**, a small island with a permanent population of 300, most of whom are descended from Africans. There are some lovely beaches and a coral reef offshore which is good for snorkelling. An image of Christ has been carved on the reef by one of the locals. Onshore there is a 100-foot steel lighthouse which was built by the French in 1893, which gives fine views over the whole island. If you enjoy a good festival, time your visit to coincide with the annual fiestas – on June 24 (St John the Apostle) and July 16 (Virgen del Carmen). At any other time of year, take plenty of books.

You can reach Isla Grande by bus, continuing east of Portobelo along the dirt road across the Tonosí river to La Guaira, from where there are plenty of boats shuttling back and forth (though you will need to negotiate a fare). From the moment you walk ashore, there are plenty of places to stay; at the lower end of the scale are the Cabañas Super Jackson, at the upper end a waterfront hotel/restaurant complex run by a Frenchman named Jacques-Yves.

East to Darién

'We are recommending people not to go to Darién at the moment because of trouble near the Colombian frontier' – Panama Tourist Board

That was the official view about the last leg of the Pan-American Highway at the tail end of 1999. Every other Central American country has the benefit of roads running through from one frontier to another, along the spine provided by the Pan-American Highway. In Panama, however, the roads peter out east of the Canal, upon encountering the Darién Gap. Penetrating this band of jungle, and other isolated areas of Panama, involves travelling by sea or air, and occasionally on foot. But it begins with a single bus to the end of the line.

The first piece of bad news that greeted me was that all the buses to Darién depart from an obscure, hard to reach bus station a couple of miles outside the centre, accessible only by taxi. The Darién run starts from the place that is clearly the poor relation of the Panamanian bus terminal family. Never mind, I thought as I approached the terminus, at least it is full of smart, new, air-conditioned minibuses.

Inevitably, there was no sign of mine. A couple of dozen prospective passengers saw the official departure time of 5.15am come and go. After half-an-hour, during which the most exciting thing to happen was a certain flickering as the sun decided whether or not to show its face, the wheeziest, clunkiest heap of steel ever to leave the Blue Bird works heaved itself around the corner and settled awkwardly in the appointed bay. This was to be our home for the next eight hours. Or would it be ten?

The vehicle posed one important question. How, precisely, was the driver of the Darién bus supposed to see the road that steadily deteriorates east of Panama? A standard Blue Bird schoolbus had become a mobile mural, blazing a lurid trail along the Pan-American Highway. D A R I E N was spelt out in mauve and two-tone blue along the top half of the front window. Above it, an elaborate image of Panama's Casco Vieja depicted a series of buildings that bring the sights of the city to people who have never ventured to the capital. Stylised beauty queens lay prone across the engine, while on the nearside a female warrior took on a dragon amid the stormy peaks of Darién. Beyond this Biblical battle, the skies cleared to bequeath the land with calm. And just so the curve above the passengers' windows was not left blank, an eagle dragged a shaft of colour the full length of the bus.

The question would, for the time being, go unanswered. The bus crew melted into the crowd, and the 'queue' itself began to lose interest and disperse in search of stretched legs or weak coffee. Before the last crew member disappeared I asked when we might be off. 'Six, I think, but I can't find the driver'. Meanwhile I was bombarded by sales pitches for a boxful of apples, while a man with 100 pairs of sunglasses attached to a board the size of a door was marketing shade in the pre-dawn gloom.

I realised things were going badly when other passengers started asking me what time the bus might be going. At last – well, to be precise, at 6.15am – the driver was spotted waddling towards the bus. Magically, all the passengers converged and clambered aboard expectantly. But the driver identified a problem with the rear nearside wheel and decided to change it. This bode ill for two reasons: first, it was a touch worrying to have a problem before departure to the end of the road; second, that there was no longer a spare wheel, which could be a big problem on a dirt road many miles from help.

By now the crowd had doubled, because all the people who had sensibly chosen an extra hour in bed and to travel on the 6.15am departure had all shown up. There was no sign of 'their' bus, so not unreasonably they chose to travel on the 5.15. At seven on the dot, the driver climbed aboard and theatrically pressed the starter.

Nothing happened. Indeed, nothing happened for the next hour until a rewiring job had been completed beneath the garish bonnet. Finally, he issued a triumphant yelp as the diesel's mighty yawn deafened the ensemble. The bus bulged with its two-and-a-bit load of passengers, and rode off into a rainbow that blazed above the Panama dawn. At the first set of traffic lights, the bus engine gave one final sneeze and died.

Buses for Darién depart from Curundu bus terminal, 3km north of the city centre and accessible only by taxi (the area is risky to walk through). There are departures, in theory at least, at 5.15am, 6.15am, 8.15am and 10.15am, with a fare of $1.50 to Chepo, $9 to Meretí and $14 to Yaviza. During the wet season, buses may run only as far as Meretí; from here, you can usually get a ride in a pick-up truck.

There are flights from Albrook to El Real (from which Yaviza is accessible by boat) at 8.45am on Mondays, Wednesdays, Fridays and Saturdays, on Aeroperlas (315 7500) for a fare of $40 each way.

The first significant settlement once you shake of the suburbs of Panama City is **Tocumen**, location for the international airport and a fair-sized place in its own right. This is the last place on the Pan-American Highway with a range of places to stay. **Chepo**, a lively town with a predominantly black population, is 60km (37 miles) east of the capital. The Highway is now well-surfaced and fast from here to **El Llano**. East of this scruffy settlement the Pan-American Highway is unpaved, and sections of it are tricky during the wet season. The road crosses Lake Bayano, and at the frontier of Darién province there is a small settlement of **Cañazas**. The Pan-American turns south here towards Santa Fe, and on the map its course is marked *Alineamiento Aproximado*. Everything is approximate around here. **Meretí** is the last town through which the Panamericana actually passes. You will be stopped here for police checks, during which you can expect to be closely questioned about your motives. If you need to stay overnight, the Hotel Felicidad and its restaurant will provide, though they may not generate the happiness promised in the name.

If you wish to stop off at La Palma (or take a flight from there back to Panama City), one way to do it is to take the road southwest from here to Puerto Quimba, though hitchable traffic is thin on the (bumpy) ground.

Yaviza itself is thought to be the site of a shipyard built by Balboa. Today it is jumbled collection of thatched and corrugated iron buildings dotted among open sewers, and gives the impression that nothing so adventurous as a ship could ever be built there. Yaviza marks the southernmost point of the Pan-American Highway and lies 240km (150 miles) east of Panama City. There is one hotel, the Tres Americas, which does not abuse its monopoly position too badly: it charges about $15 a night.

From Yaviza there are boats (on an ad hoc basis) to **El Real**, a commercial centre of Darién. Cargo boats leave for here from the Muelle Fiscal in the capital (next to the Mercado Público near the old city) on a fairly regular basis, and take passengers. The sea journey is tough, taking anything from 20 to 40 hours. The main port of the province, it was a way-station for gold mined in the area and held for shipment to Panama City. The port was sacked by pirates in 1680, and over the next three centuries suffered further attacks from pirates and Indian rebels. Although inaccessible by road, El Real is probably the best starting point for any venture into the Darién. There are cabins, and it is also possible to camp – stay near the Mercadero, where boats gather, a couple of miles out of town.

The Darién Gap – the end of the road

Few travellers venture this far east, because at present there is no safe way through the hundred miles of swamp and jungle separating Yaviza from the first signs of a road in Colombia. At one stage in the late 1980s and early 1990s, trans-Darién trips were now almost routine (and prices charged by locals correspondingly inflated), but violence between Colombian paramilitaries, rebels and drug-traffickers mean that bridging the gap is off-limits at present. When it eventually becomes feasible once more, it will still be far from safe. Preparation and planning are essential.

The province of Darién is wild and mostly impenetrable. Large parts of it are unexplored, a blank space on the map of Central America. The Darién Gap, 160km (100 miles) of jungle and swamp separating Panama and Colombia, is the one stretch of land between Alaska and Tierra del Fuego that has prevented the completion of the Highway. Unfavourable terrain is not the only obstacle; foot-and-mouth disease is widespread among cattle in Colombia and the rest of South America, and Panamanian farmers fear that a land link could spread it. Even though travel in Darién is possible only by boat, aircraft or on foot, the jungle is gradually disappearing. Loggers are felling an increasing number of trees, and settlers arriving from exhausted lands elsewhere in Panama have begun looking for cultivable land in Darién.

Despite these new arrivals, the province has fewer inhabitants now than when Balboa strode through it. Most of the people in the area are Indians from the Chocó region of Colombia. They mainly divide into two tribal groups, the Emberá and Wounaan. There are also several communities of blacks who are descended from slaves brought by the Spanish, and some Kuna Indians (though the latter live predominantly on the San Blas islands).

The immigrants who moved to Darién two centuries after the Conquest from the Chocó constitute a fascinating ethnic group. Emulating man's earliest activities they are hunter-gatherers. Although guns are now used by most Emberá and Wounaan, those in more isolated areas still use only bows and arrows. Their houses, known as *tambos*, are raised off the ground; the conical, thatched roofs make them highly distinctive. Most Emberá and Wounaan live along the river banks, but have only recently begun to establish communities in the Western sense – the first real village was created only in 1968 as a result of Panamanian government action.

Many of the people of Chocó prefer to live in their traditional isolation, and their customs have changed little: the men still wear loincloths and the women wear the traditional brightly-coloured wrap-around skirts. As with the Kuna, Emberá and Wounaan women maintain traditions more effectively than the men. Their languages are spoken mainly by the women, although many of the younger women are also familiar with Spanish. Western influence has inevitably brought other changes. The introduction of plastic means that there is no need to make pottery, and the number of baskets produced has diminished. Money was previously an unknown concept, but Emberá and Wounaan men now go off to work in towns and Colombian smugglers bring in whisky, cigarettes and clothes, upon which earnings are spent. Yet despite the incursions of the 20th century, the Emberá and Wounaan continue to believe in spirits and the powers of the shaman to cure the sick and cast spells. They are friendly, but tend to keep a respectful distance. You should reciprocate this when meeting them.

Warning

Writing in April 2000, the Foreign Office said 'Do not try to travel to Colombia by transitting the Darien. The border area is unsafe and political and criminal violence in Colombia often spills over into Panama. Two Europeans were kidnapped and killed on the border in March 1997.' I investigated the possibility of crossing the Gap through the overland route in both 1998 and 1999, and on each occasion every source warned that this would be foolhardy in the extreme.

When and if the danger dissipates, the trip across the Darién Gap will still constitute a monumental challenge. As Balboa discovered, the local Indians have numerous trails through the Darién; today these are used by Western travellers and Colombian smugglers. Certain stretches can be covered only by boat, so you must rely upon the willingness of the locals for transport. Co-operation is usually forthcoming, but may involve waiting for a day or two.

The trek should be considered only during the dry season between December and March; at other times, rivers become torrents and the terrain is waterlogged. By the end of the dry season the rivers are often too low for boats, so it is best to go mid-season. With so many variables it is impossible to predict how long the journey through the Gap will take. People have been known to do it in five days, but most travellers take at least two weeks. Similarly, it is difficult to predict how much the trip will cost. As more visitors make the trip, some of the locals along the route are beginning to exploit their monopoly position to charge travellers high fees for boat journeys. You should expect to pay out over $300 in addition to any equipment you need. The boat trips and guides incur the main expenses; the cost of food and accommodation is minimal. Going overland is certainly not the cheapest way to reach Colombia; to save money, go by air.

The prospect of a week or two spent trudging through thick jungle, and travelling by boat along meandering waterways lined with impenetrable vegetation and across swampland, does not appeal to everyone. If you are tempted, make sure you choose good company. It is possible to hire a guide for the whole or part of the way, but make sure he is thoroughly trustworthy – the Darién Gap has a reputation for bandits.

A large amount of organisation and equipment is essential before setting out for the Darién. Good footwear and long, tough trousers are vital; while most things can be obtained in Panama City, you would do well to come prepared with reliable shoes and heavy-duty clothing. Protection is the key since wildlife is profuse. Leeches, ticks and mosquitoes carrying malaria and other diseases are out to get you. Take copious quantities of insect repellent and a mosquito net, and of course an adequate supply of anti-malaria tablets (though the strains around here have acquired immunity to most prophylactics).

You may be able to stay with the locals in some villages, but you need to be prepared to camp or sling up a hammock; whatever option you choose, you must always approach the village chief first. Take plenty of food (canned and dried), although you should be able to arrange meals in most of the villages. Be particularly careful about what you eat since the Darién Gap is not a convenient place in which to fall ill. Take plenty of plastic bags to keep your belongings dry when travelling by boat. A torch is also essential, even though the main villages now have electricity.

The book that covers trekking across the Gap in most detail is Bradt Publications' *Backpacking in Mexico and Central America*. The best maps are available from the Instituto Geográfico Tommy Guardia in Panama City, though the main one – named La Palma at 1:250,000, is worryingly blank. Finally, don't forget to sort out the necessary visas, return tickets, etc.

The Route

More people cross the Darién Gap from Panama to Colombia than vice-versa. If, instead, you intend to travel east-west, much of the following information still applies but the itinerary is reversed.

The first place to head for is Boca de Cupe, the last settlement of any size before you reach Colombia – it is here that you must get your Panamanian exit stamp. You should be able to stay in someone's house overnight without too much difficulty. From Yaviza, the trail to Boca de Cupe takes you through the villages of Pinogana, Unión de Chocó, Yape and Capeti, and involves crossing a couple of rivers. It is a comparatively easy walk, particularly the last stretch. You may be able to get a boat for part of the way, e.g. to Boca de Cupe from Pinogana. Some people do this stretch in a day, but it would be better to do it in two stages, staying with a family at Unión de Chocó, for example. A guide from here to Boca de Cupe costs about $50. If you start from El Real, it is possible to go to Boca de Cupe by motorised dugout – ask around at the Mercadero. Boats going direct to Boca de Cupe do not leave that frequently, so if you don't want to charter one specially, be prepared either to wait around for a few days or to do the journey in stages. If you do the trip in one go, it should take about four hours.

From Boca de Cupe you must go by boat to Púcuro, a Kuna village and the next overnight stop. The boat journey should take four to six hours, but again be prepared to wait a few days to find a boat willing to take you. Once in Púcuro, the village chief should let you stay in the meeting hall; if not, camp or find somewhere to hang your hammock.

From Púcuro, head 18km (11 miles) south to Paya. This journey must usually be done on foot, though at the start of the dry season the water levels are sometimes high enough for boats to cover the stretch. Even on foot, the distance can be covered in about eight hours. The trail is in good condition and the terrain not particularly difficult (especially when compared to what awaits you beyond Paya), but you may still consider hiring a guide in Púcuro; for this you must pay about $30. If you can afford to take your time, there are good places to camp by some of the rivers. This path is heavily used by the local Indians.

Paya was for centuries the capital of the Kuna empire. In its heyday it was the centre of Kuna learning, and Indians came from all over the territory to learn about magic, medicine, etc. from the most illustrious shamen. Paya has declined steadily since the 19th century and is much smaller than it was. Like the San Blas islands where most Kuna live, Paya is a good place to buy mola, made by the Kuna women. The police are happy to provide floor space for hikers and do not usually require payment; you may also be able to stay in a private home or in the meeting house. Whatever the case, you must first ask permission from the chief. There are usually missionaries of some kind in Paya, and they may put you up.

The final Panamanian border check is in Paya – if you are entering Panama from Colombia it is here that they will dip any leather you have into antiseptic, to stop any risk of spreading foot-and-mouth disease. Searches on the way in to Panama tend to be thorough.

From Paya, your next destination is the Palo de las Letras where a cement block at the top of the mountain marks the Colombian border. This is the hardest stretch of the whole trek, and you are advised to hire a guide in Paya to take you over the mountains and down to Cristales on the Cacarica River on the other side. The trail is narrow and overgrown for much of the way, and the stretch down to Cristales is particularly difficult, and involves crossing a number of rivers. It is an easy area in which to get lost – without a guide you must take a machete and a compass. A guide from Paya to Cristales (with one night camping out) costs at least $100. Rather than staying in Cristales itself, if you continue for 30 minutes you reach a ranger station of the Katios National Park where you can stay overnight. The park consists of a huge area of tropical forest containing a magnificent bird population. There are also ranger stations at Travesía (sometimes called La Loma) and Sautatá on the Río Atrato; both have accommodation and are the best places from which to visit the park. It is possible to hire mules.

Cristales lies at the end of the overland trail through the Darién Gap – from here you must continue by boat. The Río Cacarica leads to the Río Atrato which marks the southern edge of the Darién. It is this oppressive swamp that makes construction of the Pan-American Highway along this stretch so difficult. You may find you can get a lift in a boat direct to Turbo, a hot and dusty Colombian port on the Caribbean with a couple of hotels. If you don't get a lift with a local in a dugout or a banana boat, you may find someone from the park headquarters is going to Turbo to pick up supplies.

Otherwise, the journey must be done in stages. The first stage takes you along the Cacarica river to Bijao, a cattle and lumber town which is usually full of smugglers; the boat ride takes 90 minutes and costs about $40. There is a Colombian guard post here, where your papers are usually checked. From here it is possible to go by boat straight to Turbo. You are more likely, however, to get a boat just to Cacarica, or beyond to Travesía (also known as Puente América), on the banks of the Río Atrato – motorised dugouts run from Bijao along this stretch of river; expect to pay about $40 to Travesía, a journey of about three hours. From Travesía it is easy to get transport to Turbo – there are express boats which take about two hours to do the journey; since you must cross the open, have your waterproofs handy.

Turbo is a grim port on the very edge of Colombia and legality, occupied largely by smugglers. The best thing about it is that buses run direct to Medellín and Cartagena, so long as the roads are not closed by guerrilla activity. If this happens, you can fly to Medellín. Some people manage to get their Colombian entry stamp in Turbo, although most must go to the immigration authorities in Apartado, about 32km (20 miles) towards Medellín.

An alternative

If you are not keen on the idea of covering the whole Darién route, you could go on a boat trip for part of the way, and then return. From El Real, for example, you could go as far as Púcuro without having to do any hiking. In La Palma, capital of Darién province, it is possible to hire canoes (usually motorised) for trips up the Tuira, Tupisa and Chukunaque rivers. This gives you a chance to visit Chocó villages, such as Mogue, and to sample an environment which most Westerners find alien but richly rewarding – a description that could apply to the whole of Central America.

The marine bypass: the San Blas connection

This archipelago stretches for some 320km (200 miles) along the Caribbean coast between Colón and the border with Colombia. It consists of 365 islands close to the shore, many of which are tiny and uninhabited. Some just have a few houses, others whole villages. Most boast fine white sand and beautifully clear waters with coral reefs. There is ample scope for diving, but this is an expensive pastime – snorkelling is cheaper, and swimming is free. The most interesting aspect of the San Blas, however, is the Kuna people.

The Kuna Indians

The islands and part of the mainland, which make up the semi-autonomous San Blas Territory, are inhabited primarily by the Kuna (or Cuna), who have dominated this region for centuries. At one time the Kuna claimed the whole of the southern isthmus and part of coastal Colombia as their territory, but when the Spanish tried to enslave them they fled to the mountains of eastern Panama and the San Blas islands. The Kuna are a fiercely independent people and have indulged in considerable inbreeding; they boast the world's highest incidence of albinos, described as 'children of the moon'. It is a matriarchal society – property is handed down from mother to daughter – and the highest deity is the Earth Mother.

The Kuna acquired a degree of self-determination after declaring independence in 1925. They vote nationally, but do not pay taxes. Although the majority of Kuna live on the islands, most of their food is grown on the mainland simply due to a lack of cultivable land offshore. Coconuts are the accepted currency, and as a result coconut palms are prized possessions and are keenly guarded; land, however, is owned communally. The Kuna Indians trade heavily with the Colombians, principally in fishing and coconuts.

Many Kuna men work on the mainland, wear Western clothes, and speak Spanish and even a little English. Nevertheless, on the island many of the ancient customs have survived, especially among the women who speak only the Kuna language and remain strongly traditional in the way they dress. They wear sarong-style skirts, headscarves, and colourful blouses decorated with the reverse appliqué known as *mola*. This refined style of patchwork is done by hand following traditional designs, and is much admired by aficionados of primitive art. It was invented when missionaries discouraged the custom of body painting in favour of clothes. Black and red are the predominant colours, and are used symbolically – black for evil, red for the sun. The women also wear an array of earrings and noserings, together with strings of coloured beads around their arms and ankles. The Kuna call themselves the 'golden people", and the amount of gold jewellery worn by a wife indicates her husband's wealth.

The Kuna are good business people – as well as being keen to persuade you to buy molas (also found in Colón and Panama City), they make you pay for taking photographs – take lots of small change.

The most reliable way to get to the islands is by air: Aerotaxi/Ansi has regular flights from Albrook airport in Panama City to Ailigandí, Cartí, El Porvenir and Puerto Obaldia (on the mainland near the Colombian frontier). A much more fun way to travel, though, is one of the cargo boats that ply between Colón and Puerto Obaldia. Island-hopping in this manner costs very little, and on each island there is always somewhere to stay. It is essential to be polite, to seek out the head man in each community, and to wait for him to nominate where you should spend the night.

Where 'proper' **accommodation** is available, it is generally expensive (e.g. over $100 a double). There are hotels on El Porvenir, Ustupo, Nalunega, Ailigandí and Wichub Walla islands.

Welcome to Colombia

If you thought Panama was wild, wait until you reach its troubled neighbour. The cities of Cartagena, Medellín and Bogotá are beautiful, if flawed, and you will need to increase your sensitivity to the prospect of theft or attack. Nonetheless, Colombia remains the most undervalued tourist destination in the world. South America's most seductive nation satiates all your travel desires, but only after making you suffer. Narco-traffickers, Marxist guerrillas and trigger-happy soldiers coalesce into a nightmare of violence. 'The hills are alive with the sound of bandidos,' is the approximate summary offered by the locals. But you can experience the considerable pleasure of walking into the country from Panama.

The easy way to walk a very mild version of the Darién Gap is to fly from Panama City, or take a boat from Colón, to Puerto Obaldia. From here, pay a guide around $20 to lead you over the long, difficult trail across the hills – taking around six hours, more if you have a lot of baggage. You arrive first at La Miel, a tiny village, which is where your guide may leave you. From here it is a quick haul uphill to the tablet announcing you are entering the Republic of Colombia. You descend to Sapzurro, the first place of any significance in Colombia, from where you can take a boat around to Capurganá. But it is more satisfying to clamber for a couple more hours over steep hills, until you can look down upon the sublime sight of a Caribbean seaside resort.

A wild scream stops you dead. It turns out to be the afternoon flight from Medellín making the usual approach to Capurganá. At the end of the steep and difficult descent, you notice the airport bus is a donkey and wagon. In one of the most peaceful and beautiful locations that has the good fortune to be washed by the gentle Caribbean Sea, there is little need for transport. This is Capurganá, the last resort outpost of the most mixed-up country in the world.

Everything about the place is soft. The warm air envelops you with comforting caresses that ease away the cold sweat of fear. The streets of Capurganá are paved with sand. And the people who inhabit the town at the end of the world are welcoming and jolly. The beach is a sandy trampoline billowing out to meet the Caribbean then retreating playfully from the preposterously blue sea. All the colours seem to have been artificially enhanced in order to look good for the holiday brochures. But the tourist hordes have yet to materialise.

A fair crowd gathers at the only functioning restaurant in town, which sprawls out on a pier striped in deck-chair pastels. The confidence of your swagger towards a table is only momentarily dented by the sight of a fence made from the flattened fuselage of a Cessna that clearly didn't make the turn in time on the implausibly tight approach to the tiny airport, whose runway is about the size of a supermarket car park and in rather worse condition. Whatever you want, Capurganá will deliver. So long, that is, as what you want is red snapper grilled to imperfection but rescued by a Polar beer, salad and the surroundings.

Gabriel García Márquez describes his home country as 'One of the least secure and most disordered countries in the world.' Yet I dare you not to be entranced by the sheer beauty of Colombia and smitten with the eloquence and vibrancy of the people. Also, it's fun – and affordable. Life in Colombia might be cheap, but so is the cost of living. As you watch the unwittingly picturesque ferry that serves as the local bus drift off along the coast, content yourself with the knowledge that few people will ever experience the sultry side of life at this particular point seven degrees north of the Equator, where the umbilical of Panama ends and Colombia begins.

From Capurganá, you could fly to **Medellín** several times a day for around $50, or spend just a few dollars on a boat across the bay to the benighted port of **Turbo**. From here, there are sporadic buses to Medellín, when the conflict is not too intense. Before making definite onward travel plans, you should note that the Foreign Office warns 'Violence and kidnapping are serious problems in urban Colombia. In rural areas there is a risk of being caught up in guerrilla or paramilitary attacks, or opportunistic kidnapping. The border area with Panama is especially high risk, as are other areas outside government control. Visitors should not stray away from major urban areas or from established tourist routes and should be aware that even these can become dangerous, usually without warning. It is often safer to travel by air than to risk a road journey. Road travel after dark is extremely dangerous.'

Road travel of any kind is impossible beyond the end of the Highway in Yaviza, Panama. One day, perhaps in this century, the forces of commerce will triumph over environmental and political considerations, and a road will be driven through to Colombia. Until then, anyone who makes it this far realises that the Pan-American Highway is more than the world's mightiest road – it is also the longest cul-de-sac on the planet.

The End

Exchange Rates Table

EXCHANGE RATES: Mexico and Central America versus the pound, dollar and Euro

These exchange rates are as published by the Financial Times on 5 May 2000, subject to rounding. They can be expected to change significantly during the lifetime of this book, but give an idea about the likely cross-rates between currencies

Code: £ = pound sterling
US$/PB = US dollar/Panamanian Balboa
Mex P = Mexican Peso
Gua Q = Guatemalan Quetzal
Salv C = Salvadoran Colón
Hond L = Honduran Lempira
Nic C = Nicaraguan Córdoba
CR C = Costa Rican Colón

	£	US$/PB	Euro	Mex P	Gua Q	Salv C	Hond L	Nic C	CR C
£1 buys	1	1.55	1.70	14.57	11.90	13.60	23.40	19.10	470
1 US$/PB buys	0.65	1	1.10	9.40	7.75	8.80	14.75	12.50	305
1 Euro buys	0.59	0.90	1	8.50	7	8	13.25	11.25	275
1 Mex P buys	0.07	0.11	0.12	1	0.82	0.94	1.57	1.33	32
1 Gua Q buys	0.08	0.13	0.14	1.22	1	1.14	1.90	1.60	40
1 Salv C buys	0.07	0.11	0.12	1.06	0.88	1	1.65	1.45	35
1 Hond L buys	0.04	0.07	0.08	0.64	0.53	0.60	1	0.85	20
1 Nic C buys	0.05	0.08	0.09	0.75	0.62	0.70	1.18	1	22
100 CR C buys	0.21	0.33	0.37	3.14	2.58	2.93	4.83	4.11	100

Index

Vacation Work publish:

	Paperback	Hardback
The Directory of Summer Jobs Abroad	£9.99	£14.95
The Directory of Summer Jobs in Britain	£9.99	£14.95
Supplement to Summer Jobs in Britain and Abroad *published in May*	£6.00	–
Work Your Way Around the World	£12.95	–
The Good Cook's Guide to Working Worldwide	£11.95	–
Taking a Gap Year	£11.95	–
Working in Tourism – The UK, Europe & Beyond	£11.95	–
Kibbutz Volunteer	£10.99	–
Working on Cruise Ships	£9.99	–
Teaching English Abroad	£11.95	–
The Au Pair & Nanny's Guide to Working Abroad	£10.99	–
Working in Ski Resorts – Europe & North America	£10.99	–
Working with Animals – The UK, Europe & Worldwide	£11.95	–
Accounting Jobs Worldwide	£11.95	–
Working with the Environment	£11.95	–
Health Professionals Abroad	£11.95	–
The Directory of Jobs & Careers Abroad	£11.95	£16.95
The International Directory of Voluntary Work	£10.99	£15.95
The Directory of Work & Study in Developing Countries	£9.99	£14.99
Live & Work in Saudi & the Gulf	£10.99	–
Live & Work in Japan	£10.99	–
Live & Work in Russia & Eastern Europe	£10.99	–
Live & Work in France	£10.99	–
Live & Work in Australia & New Zealand	£10.99	–
Live & Work in the USA & Canada	£10.99	–
Live & Work in Germany	£10.99	–
Live & Work in Belgium, The Netherlands & Luxembourg	£10.99	–
Live & Work in Spain & Portugal	£10.99	–
Live & Work in Italy	£10.99	–
Live & Work in Scandinavia	£10.99	–
Panamericana: On the Road through Mexico and Central America	£12.95	–
Travellers Survival Kit: Mauritius, Seychelles & Réunion	£10.99	–
Travellers Survival Kit: Madagascar, Mayotte & Comoros	£10.99	–
Travellers Survival Kit: Sri Lanka	£10.99	–
Travellers Survival Kit: Mozambique	£10.99	–
Travellers Survival Kit: Cuba	£10.99	–
Travellers Survival Kit: Lebanon	£10.99	–
Travellers Survival Kit: South Africa	£10.99	–
Travellers Survival Kit: India	£10.99	–
Travellers Survival Kit: Russia & the Republics	£9.95	–
Travellers Survival Kit: Western Europe	£8.95	–
Travellers Survival Kit: Eastern Europe	£9.95	–
Travellers Survival Kit: South America	£15.95	–
Travellers Survival Kit: USA & Canada	£10.99	–
Travellers Survival Kit: Australia & New Zealand	£11.95	–

Distributors of:

	Paperback	Hardback
Summer Jobs USA	£12.95	–
Internships (On-the-Job Training Opportunities in the USA)	£16.95	–
Sports Scholarships in the USA	£16.95	–
Scholarships for Study in the USA & Canada	£14.95	–
Colleges & Universities in the USA	£15.95	–
Green Volunteers	£10.99	–

Vacation Work Publications, 9 Park End Street, Oxford OX1 1HJ
Tel 01865–241978   Fax 01865–790885

Visit us online for more information on our unrivalled range of titles for work,
travel and adventure, readers' feedback and regular updates:

www.vacationwork.co.uk